EAST ANGLIAN ARCHAEOLOGY

Iron Age Fortification Beside the River Lark: Excavations at Mildenhall, Suffolk

by Tim Havard, Mary Alexander and Ray Holt

with contributions from
M.J. Allen, S. Anderson, P.L. Armitage,
A. Breen, M. Brudenell, S. Cobain, A. Crawford,
J. Geber, L. Higbee, N. Holbrook, R. Ixer,
E.R. McSloy, G. Monteil, A. Mudd, F. Roe,
R. Scaife, D. Smith, J. Sommerville, N. Suttie and
T.P. Young

principal illustrations by
Jonathan Bennett with contributions from
Daniel Bashford, Lorna Gray, Lucy Martin,
Aleksandra Osinska and Robert Read

photographs by
Tim Havard, Gay Gilmour, Ray Holt,
Andy Pascoe and Alex Webster

East Anglian Archaeology
Report No.169, 2019

Cotswold Archaeology

EAST ANGLIAN ARCHAEOLOGY
REPORT NO.169

Published by
Cotswold Archaeology
Building 11
Kemble Enterprise Park
Cirencester
Gloucestershire GL7 6BQ
www.cotswoldarchaeology.co.uk

in conjunction with
ALGAO East
www.algao.org.uk/england

Editor: Edward Martin
Managing Editor: Jenny Glazebrook

Editorial Board:
James Albone, Historic Environment, Norfolk County Council
Abby Antrobus, Archaeological Service, Suffolk County Council
Brian Ayers, University of East Anglia
Stewart Bryant, Archaeological Consultant
Will Fletcher, Historic England
Kasia Gdaniec, Historic Environment, Cambridgeshire County Council
Andrew Hutcheson, Community and Environment, Norfolk County Council
Maria Medlycott, Historic Environment, Essex County Council
Zoe Outram, Historic England Science Advisor
Debbie Priddy, Historic England
Adrian Tindall, Archaeological Consultant
Simon Wood, Historic Environment, Hertfordshire County Council

Set in Times New Roman by Jenny Glazebrook using Corel Ventura™
Printed by Henry Ling Limited, The Dorset Press

Mapping in figures 1.1, 1.2, 1.4, 5.10, 6.1, 6.2 is reproduced from the Ordnance Survey on
behalf of the controller of Her Majesty's Stationery Office, © Crown copyright and database
rights 2019 Ordnance Survey 0100031673

Published with the aid of funding from J Sainsbury plc

East Anglian Archaeology was established in 1975 by the Scole Committee for Archaeology in
East Anglia. The scope of the series expanded in 2002 to include all six eastern counties.
Responsibility for publication rests with the editorial board in partnership with the Association
of Local Government Archaeological Officers, East of England (ALGAO East).

For details of *East Anglian Archaeology*, see last page

Cover illustration
Iron Age weaving comb probably made from a horse metapodial. *Image by Lucy Martin*

Contents

List of Figures

List of Tables

Contributors

Mary Alexander
Cotswold Archaeology (Post-Excavation Manager)

Michael J. Allen
Allen Environmental Archaeology (sediment, land snails and pollen)

Sue Anderson
Spoilheap Archaeology (post-Roman pottery)

Philip L. Armitage
Brixham Heritage Museum (fish bone)

Anthony Breen
Independent (Archive and Documentary Research)

Matt Brudenell
ABCeramic Specialists (prehistoric pottery)

Sarah Cobain
Cotswold Archaeology (radiocarbon analysis, plant macrofossils and charcoal)

Angus Crawford
formerly Cotswold Archaeology (coins)

Jonny Geber
(formerly Cotswold Archaeology) University of Edinburgh, (human and animal bone)

Tim Havard
Cotswold Archaeology (Senior Project Officer)

Frances Healey
University of Cardiff (radiocarbon advisor)

Lorraine Higbee
Wessex Archaeology (animal bone)

Neil Holbrook
Cotswold Archaeology (Chief Executive)

Ray Holt
formerly Cotswold Archaeology (Project Officer)

Rob Ixer
University of Leicester (thin-section analysis)

E.R. McSloy
Cotswold Archaeology (metal, stone, glass beads, Roman pottery, fired clay, worked bone and antler)

Gwladys Monteil
University of Nottingham (samian pottery)

Andrew Mudd
Cotswold Archaeology (Post-Excavation Manager)

Fiona Roe
Independent (worked stone)

Rob Scaife
University of Southampton (pollen)

David Smith
University of Birmingham (insects)

Jacky Sommerville
Cotswold Archaeology (flint)

Neil Suttie
University of Liverpool (archaeomagnetic dating)

Tim P. Young
GeoArch (metallurgy)

Acknowledgements

None of the work undertaken and reported upon here would have been possible without the financial support of J Sainsbury plc through their consultants Henry Riley LLP, for whom particular thanks go to Mike Hays, Senior Associate, for his close involvement in the project and his support throughout, and to Mike Cowle, Associate. The fieldwork proceeded smoothly, and in a safe environment, thanks to the co-operation and support of the principal site contractors, and our thanks go to Lee Crame, Project Manager, and Scott Larner, Site Manager, of Longcross Construction. Our appreciation also goes to Dr Jess Tipper, County Archaeologist, Suffolk County Council, for monitoring and advice during fieldwork, and for comments on the assessment report.

The fieldwork was managed for Cotswold Archaeology (CA) by Simon Cox and Richard Young. The excavation was directed by Tim Havard and Ray Holt, and thanks are owed to all the excavation team, but in particular to project supervisors Andy Pascoe and Alex Wilkinson. Sylvia Warman, formerly of Cotswold Archaeology, provided on-site sampling advice, and Richard Payne of ARCA visited the site to aid interpretation of sediment deposition and to advise on sediment sampling. The post-excavation programme was managed by Mary Alexander. Tim Havard and Ray Holt undertook the site analysis and reporting, which was carried through into the publication stage by Tim Havard. Individual authors are acknowledged in the report. The mammal and bird bone report by Lorraine Higbee uses the quantification and analysis undertaken by Jonny Geber. Finds and soils processing and quantification was undertaken to a high standard by CA staff. X-rays and metalwork cleaning were undertaken by Karen Barker of the Antiquities Conservation Service. Radiocarbon dating was provided by Scottish Universities Environmental Research Centre (SUERC), East Kilbride, Scotland. Petrotech Ltd undertook the thin-section preparation. We also thank Frances Healy, whose expertise and advice was vital in determining the value of Bayesian analysis for the relative dating of the site sequence. Figures and finds illustrations were undertaken by Jon Bennett, Dan Bashford and Aleksandra Osinska of Cotswold Archaeology, with some additional pottery illustration by Robert Read Graphic Services.

Abbreviations

ABG	associated bone group (animal bone)
ADS	Archaeology Data Service
AMS	Accelerator Mass Spectrometry
AOD	Above Ordnance Datum
ARCA	Specialist geoarchaeological contractor based at Winchester University
BGS	British Geological Survey
BM	British Museum
BP	before present (set at 1950)
BTM	Historic Environment Record code for Barton Mills
CA	Cotswold Archaeology
EVE	Estimated Vessel Equivalent
FAS	fuel ash slags
FHS	flake hammerscale
HER	Historic Environment Record
IfA	Institute of field Archaeologists (now Chartered Institute for Archaeologists)
LLP	Limited Liability Partnership
MNE	minimum number of elements (animal bone)
MNI	minimum number of individuals (bone)
MNL	Historic Environment Record code for Mildenhall parish
MPRG	Medieval Pottery Research Group
MSW	mean sherd weight
MWE	meat weight estimate
MWS	mandible wear stages (animal bone)
NGR	National Grid Reference
NISP	number of identified specimens present (animal bone)
PCRG	Prehistoric Ceramics Research Group
SCCAS	Suffolk County Council Archaeological Service
SHC	smithing hearth cake
SHS	spheroidal hammerscale
SUERC	Scottish Universities Environmental Research Centre

Summary

Excavations by Cotswold Archaeology on the site of a new supermarket at Mildenhall produced evidence for nearly continuous human activity from the Late Bronze Age to the medieval period. A Late Bronze Age waterhole backfilled with domestic refuse was excavated on the higher ground above the floodplain of the River Lark. The Middle Iron Age was a period of intense activity on the site, of which the most notable features were the pair of massive ditches which defined the eastern part of an enclosure, possibly a defensive feature built to dominate the crossing point of the River Lark. A third ditch of comparable size may date to the Middle or Late Iron Age. Numerous pits were found in the interior of the enclosure, and a pair of very large post-settings were located between the paired ditches. A possible focus for settlement beyond the west of the excavated area was suggested by the greater density of pits towards this side. The ditches fell out of use before the Roman period when a farmstead occupied the higher ground. In this period the flood plain was utilised with a series of field ditches, although the area was prone to flooding in the later Roman period. Activity on the site continued throughout the Saxon period, and spanned the early, middle and later periods. Activities associated with farming took place on the higher ground; use of the flood plain was limited by the wet environment. The evidence suggests there was a process of deliberate land reclamation on the floodplain during the medieval period, after which the area was divided into fields. On the higher ground, a large ditch running north to south may have been dug to demarcate the medieval town boundary, but this association is uncertain. Features excavated from this period represented activities undertaken on the periphery of settlement, including crop-processing, animal husbandry, and iron-working. A well-preserved kiln base may have been used for the production of lime, using chalk quarried from the edge of the higher ground. There was a rapid decline in the use of the area from the 14th century onwards and it was farmland until the modern development took place.

There was good preservation of environmental evidence from all periods of activity, and the sizeable assemblages of animal bone and crop waste allowed comparisons to be made in farming practices over time. The assemblage of decorated Middle Iron Age pottery from the site is the largest found in the region to date.

Résumé

Des fouilles entreprises par Cotswold Archaeology sur le site d'un nouveau supermarché à Mildenhall ont apporté la preuve d'une activité humaine pratiquement continue depuis l'âge du bronze tardif jusqu'à la période médiévale. Une mare de l'âge du bronze tardif, remplie d'ordures ménagères, a été fouillée sur le terrain dominant la plaine inondée de la rivière Lark. Le site connut une période d'activité intense pendant l'âge du fer moyen. Celle-ci se caractérisait principalement par la présence de deux grands fossés délimitant la partie est d'une enceinte qui pourrait être un dispositif défensif construit pour dominer le point de franchissement de la rivière Lark. Un troisième fossé semble dater de l'âge du fer moyen ou tardif. On a découvert un nombre important de fosses dans l'enceinte et deux très grands emplacements pour des poteaux ont été localisés entre les deux fossés. La présence éventuelle d'une implantation à l'ouest de la zone fouillée est suggérée par la plus forte densité de fosses de ce côté. Les fossés cessèrent d'être utilisés avant la période romaine lors de l'occupation par une ferme du terrain en hauteur. Pendant cette période, la plaine inondée était exploitée et présentait un ensemble de fossés de terre, bien que la zone fût sujette à des inondations à la période romaine tardive. L'activité continua sur le site pendant toute la période saxonne, depuis son commencement jusqu'à sa fin. Le terrain en hauteur accueillit des activités liées à l'agriculture, l'exploitation de la plaine inondée étant limitée par l'environnement humide. Il existe des traces qui laissent à penser que la plaine inondée fut récupérée de façon délibérée pendant la période médiévale. La zone fut ensuite divisée en champs. Sur le terrain en hauteur, un grand fossé fut creusé du nord vers le sud pour marquer la limite de la ville médiévale. Il ne s'agit toutefois que d'une simple hypothèse. Les objets découverts au cours des fouilles correspondant à cette période renvoient à des activités menées à la périphérie de l'implantation. Parmi celles-ci, on trouve les cultures, l'élevage et le travail du fer. Un four bien conservé a peut-être été utilisé pour la production de chaux obtenue à partir de craie extraite de la bordure du terrain en hauteur. À partir du quatorzième siècle, on assista à une rapide diminution de l'exploitation de la zone qui demeura une terre agricole jusqu'à la période du développement moderne.

Il existe des traces bien préservées de l'environnement pour toutes les périodes d'activité et les ensembles considérables de déchets agricoles et d'ossements d'animaux mis à jour ont permis d'établir des comparaisons avec les pratiques agricoles au fil du temps. L'ensemble des poteries décorées de l'âge du fer moyen extraites du site constitue à ce jour la plus grande découverte de la région.

(Traduction: Didier Don)

Zusammenfassung

Cotswold Archaeology führte am Ort eines neuen Supermarkts in Mildenhall Ausgrabungen durch, die Belege für eine fast durchgängige menschliche Aktivität von der späten Bronzezeit bis zum Mittelalter zutage förderten. Auf dem Gelände oberhalb der Niederung des Flusses Lark wurde ein Wasserloch aus der späten Bronzezeit ausgegraben, das mit Hausabfällen verfüllt war. Die mittlere Eisenzeit sah eine Phase intensiver Aktivität an dieser Stätte, zu deren auffälligsten Merkmalen ein massiver Doppelgraben im Osten einer Einhegung zählte, die vermutlich erbaut wurde, um die Furt über den Fluss Lark zu kontrollieren. Ein dritter Graben von vergleichbarer Größe stammt wahrscheinlich aus der mittleren oder jüngeren Eisenzeit. Im Inneren der Einhegung fanden sich zahlreiche Gruben, zudem wurde ein Paar besonders großer Pfostenstellungen zwischen dem Doppelgraben ausgemacht. Westlich der Ausgrabungsstätte war die Grubendichte höher, was darauf hindeutet, dass hier vermutlich der Siedlungsschwerpunkt lag. Die Nutzung der Gräben kam noch vor der Römerzeit, als sich auf dem höheren Gelände ein Gehöft befand, zum Erliegen. In dieser Periode war die Niederung von einer Reihe von Feldgräben durchzogen, obwohl das Gebiet gegen Ende der Römerzeit für Überschwemmungen anfällig war. Die Aktivitäten an der Stätte hielten über den gesamten Zeitraum der angelsächsischen Periode an. Die Landwirtschaft fand in höherer Lage statt, da die Niederung aufgrund der Durchfeuchtung der Landschaft nur in begrenztem Umfang genutzt werden konnte. Es gibt Hinweise darauf, dass im Mittelalter eine bewusste Landgewinnung im Flusstal stattfand und das Gebiet danach in Felder unterteilt wurde. Auf dem höheren Gelände verlief in nordsüdlicher Richtung ein großer Graben, der womöglich als mittelalterliche Stadtbegrenzung ausgehoben wurde, allerdings ist diese Auslegung nicht verbürgt. Die Ausgrabungsbefunde aus jener Zeit zeigen Aktivitäten, die am Rand der Siedlung stattfanden, etwa die Ernteaufbereitung, Nutztierhaltung und Eisenverarbeitung. Ein gut erhaltenes Ofenfundament könnte der Kalkherstellung gedient haben, bei der Kalkstein zum Einsatz kam, der am Rand des erhöhten Geländes abgebaut wurde. Ab dem 14. Jahrhundert wurde das Gebiet zunehmend weniger genutzt; bis zu seiner Erschließung in der Neuzeit diente es nur noch landwirtschaftlichen Zwecken.

Zu allen Aktivitätsphasen gab es gut erhaltene umweltarchäologische Befunde, wobei das umfangreiche Fundmaterial an Tierknochen und Ernteabfällen einen Vergleich der landwirtschaftlichen Praktiken im Zeitverlauf ermöglichte. Der von der Ausgrabungsstätte stammende Komplex verzierter Tongefäße aus der mittleren Eisenzeit ist der größte, der bislang in der Region gefunden wurde.

(Übersetzung: Gerlinde Krug)

Chapter 1. Introduction

I. Introduction

Archaeological evaluation, followed by a programme of excavation, was carried out by Cotswold Archaeology (CA) on land at Recreation Way, Mildenhall, Suffolk, (centred on NGR: TL 7132 7447; Figs 1.1 and 1.2). The fieldwork followed an archaeological desk-based assessment (DBA) for the site (Jordan 2009). The evaluation was undertaken in 2009 (Brett 2009; Suffolk HER MNL 622), and the excavation was carried out between February and November, 2010. The programme of archaeological works was undertaken for Henry Riley LLP, on behalf of J Sainsbury Ltd, as a required condition of planning consent for the construction of a new supermarket, car park and other associated works. Due to the fluid nature of the construction programme, regular site 'look ahead' meetings were held in consultation with the client and Dr Jess Tipper during the fieldwork stage, to determine the extent of further archaeological works and methodologies.

Much of the fieldwork took place within the construction compound while other preparatory ground works were in progress (see Chapter 1.V for methodology), and for safety reasons there were limited opportunities for the public to view the excavations while in progress. However, an education day for local schools was organised, with opportunities for children to learn about the excavations and view some of the finds (Fig. 1.3).

II. Location, geology and topography

The site covered an area of approximately 4.3ha to the east of Mildenhall town centre, on the northern side of the valley of the River Lark. It was bounded by Recreation Way to the north, Jubilee Way to the west, the municipal swimming pool and the Jubilee Centre to the east, and playing fields to the south (Fig. 1.2).

Immediately prior to the excavation, the northern part of the site was occupied by the Mildenhall Social Club building (a two-storey 20th-century structure) with an associated bowling green and car park. The existing ground level sloped gently downwards from approximately 12.5m AOD at the northern extent of the site, to around 7.5m AOD adjacent to the Jubilee Centre. The southern part of the site comprised an extensive grassed area, previously used as sports pitches, which was situated on the former floodplain of the River Lark, immediately to the south of the Jubilee Centre and the Council Office. This part of the site sloped downwards from north to south, from approximately 7.3m AOD to 5.9m AOD, although this slope was largely the result of modern landscaping (Fig. 1.4). The current course of the River Lark, raised 2m above the surrounding ground level, is the result of canalisation in the 18th century.

The underlying solid geology of the area, as recorded by the British Geological Survey (BGS 2014), is Zig Zag chalk formation of the Cretaceous Period. This forms part of a small chalk plateau representing the southern limit of chalkland at the fen edges which is free draining, unlike the adjacent peat and alluvial soils of the fen (Suffolk Landscape 2014). Peat deposits dating from the Quaternary Period were recorded in the southern part of the site, and principally in the floodplain area (Fig.1.5). These formed part of the 'deep peat, or mixtures of peat and sandy deposits' characteristic of valley meadows and fens found along the valley of the River Lark, particularly at Mildenhall and further upstream (Suffolk Landscape 2014). The excavation revealed solid chalk bedrock throughout the northern part of the site, with a pronounced downwards slope of about 2m at its southern extent in Area 2. The edge of the chalk was also identified throughout the northern half of Area 3, on a broad east/west alignment. Alluvially-derived silts and clays partially overlay the southern extent of the chalk in Areas 2 and 3, with peat-like deposits present at the southern extent of Area 3.

III. Archaeological background

Previous work
The archaeological potential of the site was researched by a desk-based assessment (Jordan 2009) as a preliminary stage of archaeological investigation, and was followed by the excavation of a series of evaluation trenches (Brett 2009). Details of the desk-based assessment and evaluation are included in this section. Prior to these investigations, no other archaeological work had been undertaken within the site.

Prehistoric periods
Excavations at Bridge House Dairies, 400m to the south-west of the site and south of the River Lark, by Archaeological Solutions in 2009 (Woolhouse 2010), revealed prehistoric remains dating from the Early Neolithic period to the Late Iron Age. A sparse scatter of Early Neolithic struck flints represented the earliest identified activity on the site. A single small pit contained parts of two Late Neolithic Grooved Ware vessels, and a human skull fragment, which had been deliberately placed on the base of the pit. Two other pits contained Early Bronze Age beaker pottery. The main phase of activity, dated to the Middle and Late Iron Age, was a long-lived system of paddocks separated by trackways located on a raised promontory in the floodplain of the River Lark. Close proximity to contemporary settlement was suggested by the dense clusters of refuse pits within the eastern part of the excavated area. The settlement appeared to have been abandoned by the time of the Roman conquest.

Mesolithic, Neolithic and Bronze Age worked flints were recovered by fieldwalking in the vicinity of the site at Recreation Way (MNL 127), and Palaeolithic deposits are known from antiquarian observations to the north-east (MNL 004, MNL 314). A Late Iron Age buckle fastener

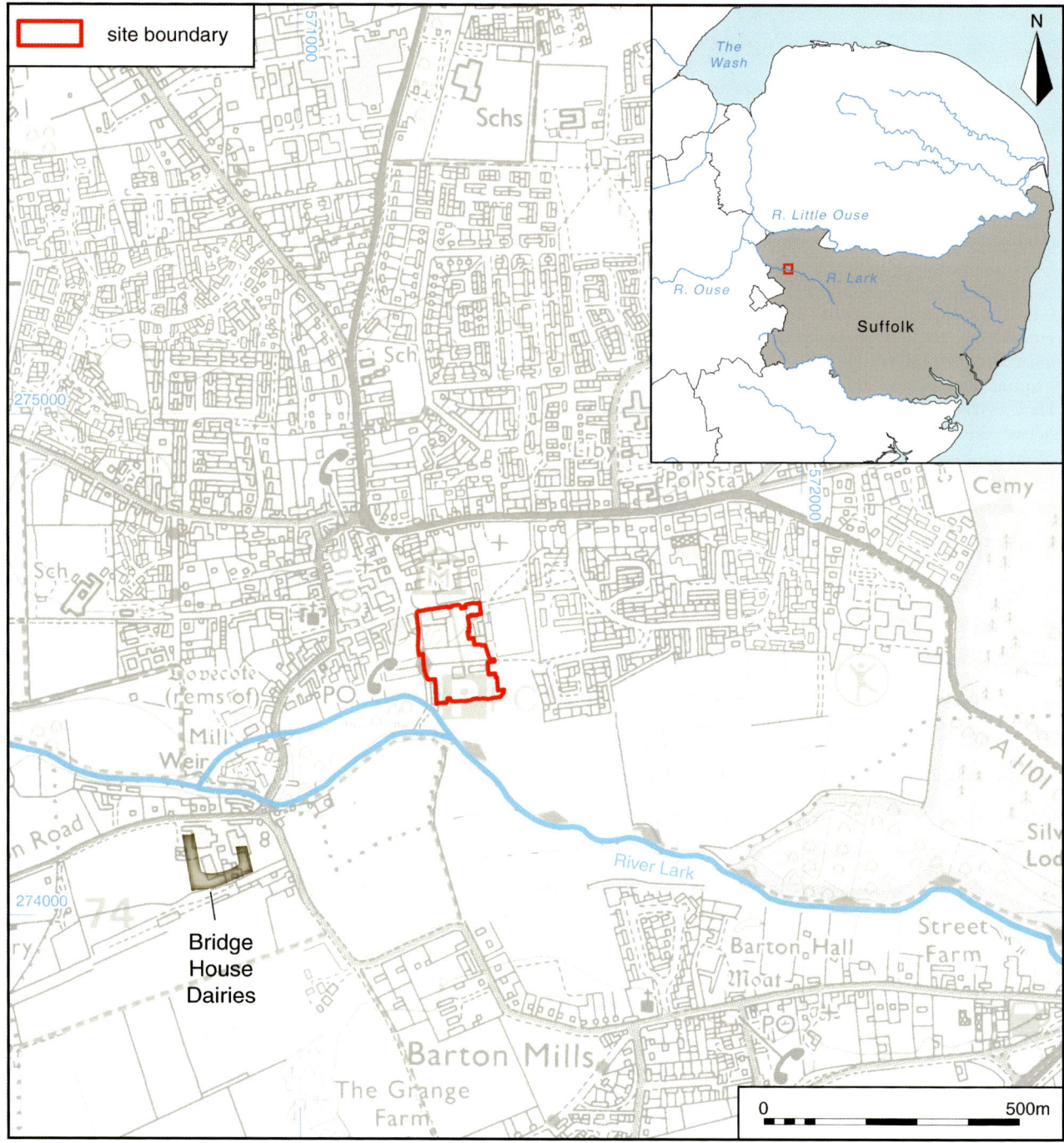

Figure 1.1 Site location

was found immediately to the south of the site by a metal detectorist (MNL 166, Fig. 6.2).

Roman

Mildenhall is renowned for the Mildenhall treasure, a hoard of Late Roman silverware, which was supposedly found approximately 2.5km to the west of the town centre, at West Row on the fen edge. Evidence of Roman activity closer to the site is largely known through metal detecting and fieldwalking. Finds recovered include metalwork and Roman coins. Additionally, a cremation burial and copper brooch were recorded to the south of the site, at Barton Mills (BTM 001, BTM 029, Fig. 6.2).

Saxon

The place-name *Mildenhall* is pre-conquest in origin (see Chapter 1.IV below), suggesting Saxon antecedents to the medieval settlement. Some Saxon finds have been recorded in the vicinity of the site including an inhumation which was uncovered in 1906, in the town centre, 250m to the west of the site; a single Saxon spearhead recorded 500m to the west of the site MNL 061; a small quantity of Saxon pottery recorded 600m to the east of the site (MNL 127) and a brooch which was recovered 800m to the south of the site (BTM 015).

Medieval and later

The medieval centre of Mildenhall lay to the north-west of the site, where the medieval church and market cross are

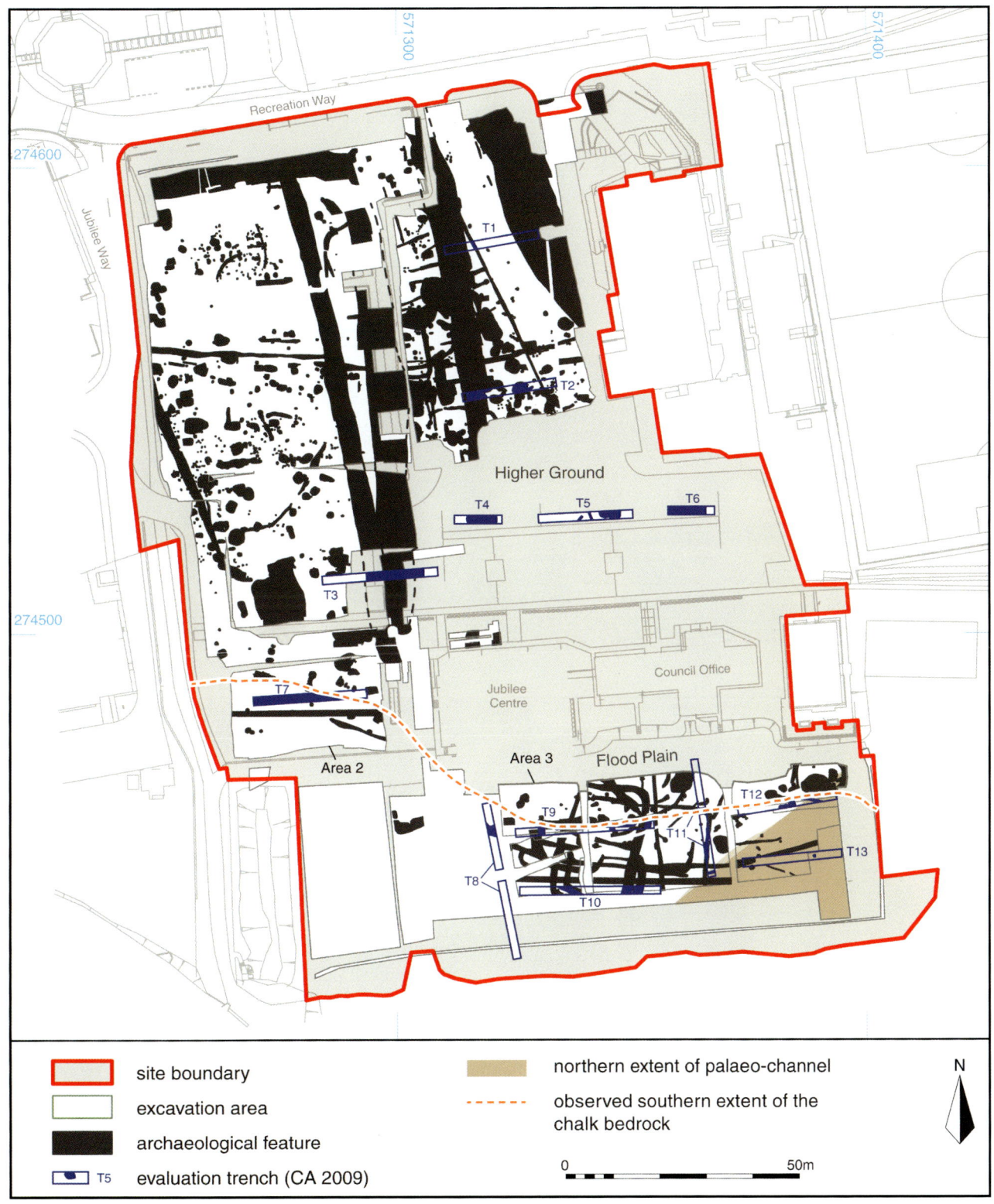

Figure 1.2 All-feature plan

located. Nineteenth-century cartographic evidence suggests that the site was agricultural land on the outskirts of the town, and as such remained undeveloped until the 20th century.

Borehole and window sampling

In 2007, boreholes were sunk into the northern and central areas of the site for geotechnical and geoenvironmental information, augmented by window samples (STATS 2007). These recorded a variable thickness of made ground, extending from 1.8m below ground level (BGL) in the northern area to 2.45m BGL in the central area of the site, thus indicating that these areas had been heavily landscaped, probably during the course of redevelopment in the 1960s.

Figure 1.3 School visit

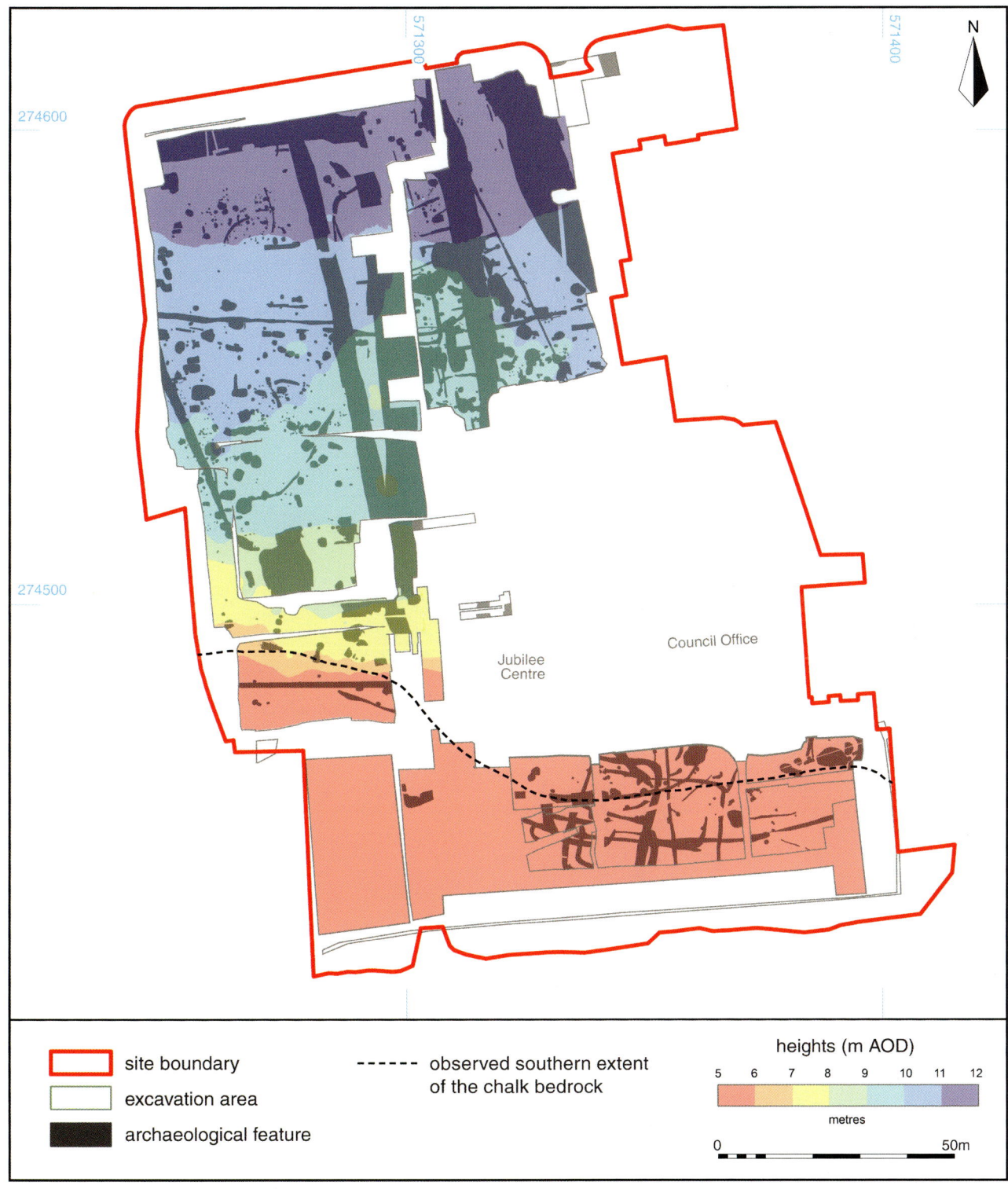

Previous archaeological investigation of the Recreation Way site

An archaeological evaluation of the site (Brett 2009) comprised the excavation of thirteen trenches (Fig.1.2). This identified archaeological features and deposits across the site which ranged from prehistoric to modern in date. Worked flint was recovered from alluvial deposits identified in trenches located towards the southern extent of site. Iron Age pottery was recovered from ditches and features which, although interpreted during the evaluation as quarry-pits, were shown upon excavation to represent

the upper fills of the three large defensive ditches. The evaluation also identified a number of Roman ditches, pits and a gully in the higher ground to the north, and an alluvial layer of the same date in the southern, lower part of the site. Trenches in the southern part of the site also revealed a pit containing a single sherd of pottery possibly dated to the 5th to 8th centuries AD, together with possible peat deposits of likely medieval date. A column sample through these deposits was found to contain high levels of hemp pollen.

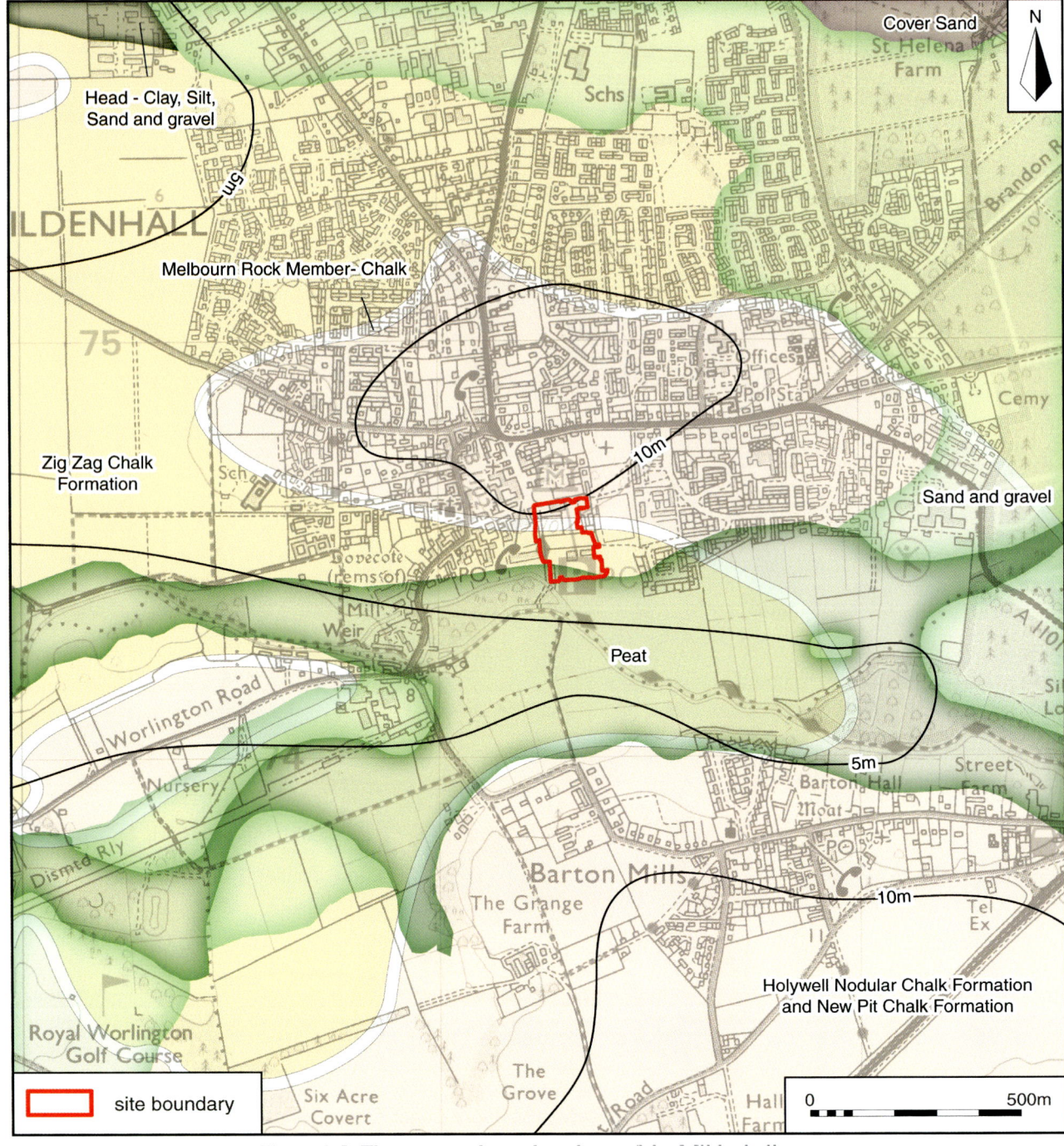

Figure 1.5 The topography and geology of the Mildenhall area

IV. Historical background
by Anthony Breen

The earliest written reference to Mildenhall is in the charter of Edward the Confessor granting the lands in *Mildenhale* as 'his mother possessed them' to the abbey of Bury St Edmunds in about 1043 (Hart 1966). Other than between 1070 and 1189 when the manor returned to the crown, Mildenhall remained in possession of the abbey up to the time of its dissolution in 1539. During this time, the wealth and prosperity of the manor increased, providing revenues of cash and agricultural surplus to the abbey. In such a period of prosperity, the settlement at Mildenhall developed into a small town, with a church, weekly market and annual fair. The urban centre, referred to as High

Town in the late medieval period, was bounded to the south by the River Lark, which provided the location for watermills and fisheries. By 1286, there were two watermills and a windmill in Mildenhall, (Hervey 1925). Mildenhall's riverside location was fundamental to the development of the town. Until the 17th century it was the furthest navigable point of the River Lark (Bailey 1989, 153–4) and any goods coming from, or being transported to, the coast would require off-loading or loading here at the riverside. By 1377, Mildenhall was the fourth largest town in the county, and seventy-sixth in the country, but in the late 14th century its fortunes began to wane (Middleton-Stewart 2011). The abandonment of some tenements on the fringes of the High Town area, which began in this period, was accelerated by a devastating fire

Figure 1.6 Site of the former Mildenhall Social Club and bowling green, looking south-east

in the 16th century, and many properties were not subsequently rebuilt. Following the Dissolution, the manor first passed to the crown. The crown appears to have leased the manor to a succession of different tenants, until in 1746 the manor and estates passed to William Bunbury (Copinger 1909). The estates remained with the Bunbury family until the lands were sold at auction in July 1933 (HD1180/57).

By the 19th century, Mildenhall was the largest of Suffolk's historic parishes, with a total area of over 15,990 acres. However, until the 18th century over 8,450 acres were uninhabitable fens and marshland, and another 1,250 acres on the eastern side of the parish were open warren. The lands forming the remaining area of the parish were subdivided between the four hamlets of Holywell, Beck Row, West Row and High Town. High Town, a name still used on road signs, included the site of the parish church and market, and the site at Recreation Way is situated within this area. A significant change in the landscape of the parish occurred at the start of the 19th century, when large areas of former common and open fields were enclosed as a result of an Act of Parliament passed in 1807. Documents produced for the enclosure of the parish contain information relevant to the history of this site, and are discussed in Chapter 3 below.

V. Methodology and recording

Fieldwork methodology
Following the archaeological evaluation and borehole survey (Brett 2009, Gearey 2010), parts of the development area were subject to further evaluation,

watching brief or excavation; the appropriate mitigation strategy being based on the results of the foregoing archaeological investigations, and on the impact of the development on underlying deposits (Brett and Young 2010 and Cox 2010). For the majority of the land within the new development, the mitigation strategy was for open-area excavation, with the required depth determined by the formation levels for the carpark and new buildings (Figs 1.6 and 1.7). The evaluations, excavations and watching briefs were undertaken sequentially, but not necessarily contiguously, in a series of numbered areas in order to co-ordinate with the sequence of groundworks required for the new development. This resulted in some problems in recording, and although every attempt was made to trace the continuation of features from one area to the next, site conditions, including varying levels of truncation and the presence of service runs, conspired to prevent this in some cases. To simplify references to areas of the site, all archaeological investigations in the northern part of the site where the solid chalk natural substrate was encountered have been included within one area, and are referred to throughout the report as the 'higher ground'. Areas 2 and 3, which are separated from the main area of excavation and are distinguished from the higher ground by their topography and the character of the archaeological deposits, retain their Area designations.

The fieldwork was undertaken in accordance with recognised professional standards, including the *Standard and Guidance for Archaeological Excavation* (IfA 2008 and Gurney 2003). Investigation within the evaluation and excavation areas commenced with the removal of topsoil and subsoil by mechanical excavator with a toothless grading bucket, under archaeological supervision, down to the first significant archaeological deposits. For those areas necessitating a watching brief, an archaeologist was present during intrusive groundworks.

The archaeological features thus exposed were hand-excavated to the bottom of the archaeological stratigraphy where practicable, the only exception to this being a well whose base could not be reached even by machine excavation. Deposits relating to funerary/ritual activity (*e.g.* burials) and domestic/industrial activity (*e.g.* pits, postholes, hearths, floor surfaces/floor make-up deposits) were investigated by the removal of 100% of the deposit. Features relating to agricultural and other activities were subject to the following strategy: a 50% minimum of all pit fills was excavated (unless they fell into the category above) along with a 10% minimum of fills from linear features, augmented by machine excavation where necessary. Slots excavated across linear features were a minimum of 1m in width, whereas those excavated through the large enclosure ditches were stepped and widened by mechanical excavator to permit safe access to the base of the ditch. Some large homogeneous deposits, including the peat in Area 3, were removed by mechanical excavator under close archaeological supervision. Any proposed variation to this strategy was subject to discussion with Dr Jess Tipper of SCCAS.

Recording and sampling

All features were planned and recorded in accordance with *CA Technical Manual 1* (CA 2007). Each context was recorded on a pro-forma context sheet by written and measured description; principal deposits were recorded by drawn plans (Scale 1:20 or 1:50 as appropriate), and sections (Scale 1:10 or 1:20 as appropriate). Photographs (monochrome print and digital) were taken as required. All finds and samples were bagged separately, and related to the context record.

Deposits were assessed for their environmental potential and sampled appropriately in accordance with *CA Technical Manual 2* (CA 2003) and advice from Cotswold Archaeology's Environmental Officer, including site visits. Bulk samples of forty litres were taken for environmental and artefact recovery; chosen contexts that were smaller than forty litres in total were 100% sampled. A series of column samples were taken for geoarchaeological assessment (Fig. 5.10), with assistance and advice by Richard Payne (ARCA), who carried out on-site examination of some depositional sequences.

All artefacts recovered from the excavation were retained in accordance with *CA Technical Manual 3* (CA 1995), with the exception of those deposits discussed below. The evaluation results from the floodplain area, and the machine stripping of Area 2, showed that a number of the widespread peat and alluvial deposits were extremely rich in large, and often complete, animal bones (cattle, horse, deer etc.). A series of spatially separated bulk samples were taken for finds recovery. Sample size was forty litres, with a minimum of ten litres for the thinnest deposits. Animal bone encountered during the machining of the peat between the baulks in Area 3 and during hand cleaning the alluvial deposits in Area 2 was not retained.

Post-excavation work

Post-excavation work was undertaken following standard guidance (English Heritage 1991; 2006), which recommends that projects are assessed for their potential to achieve the project aims following the completion of the fieldwork phase. Features were assigned to periods based on a stratigraphic sequence established through single context excavation. These periods were then dated, largely on the basis of the artefactual record, but in some instances features were assigned to a period from their morphology and their location relative to other better stratified or dated deposits.

Havard and Holt (2010) summarised the potential of the archaeological data, established updated aims and objectives for the project, and determined that the results of the project should be published as a monograph.

VI. Aims and structure of the report

This report presents the results of analysis of the excavated data, together with a synthesis of the available evidence. The results of this synthesis are interpreted and discussed according to their significance within local, regional and national frameworks. Although the site covers a considerable time-depth, the evidence varies in its nature and content through time. This report aims to contribute to the understanding of the character and patterns of settlement in the Mildenhall region in the Iron Age, Roman, Saxon and early medieval periods, and makes a smaller, but nonetheless significant contribution to patterns of activity in the Late Bronze Age, and the specialist analysis of data has been undertaken with this specific aim in view. It was deemed inappropriate to undertake detailed analysis of the historical records of Mildenhall in late medieval and post-medieval times, as the evidence from Recreation Way makes no meaningful contribution to the understanding of this period. Analysis of historical records was principally undertaken to provide an historic reference point for evidence of activity and land-use of the site in the earlier medieval period, and for the contraction of activity apparent in the evidence of the 14th to 16th centuries.

The report follows a traditional format. This introductory chapter is followed by an interpretation of the sequence of excavated features, which are discussed by period in Chapter 2. Chapter 3 comprises a summary of the historical sources that are pertinent to the understanding of the development of the site in the medieval period. Chapter 4 presents summaries of the analyses undertaken on the artefacts, and Chapter 5 presents summaries of the analysis of the zoological and environmental evidence. Chapter 6 draws together all the evidence from the preceding chapters in a period-based discussion, and places the site in its wider context. The detailed analysis undertaken for this publication is available via the internet in the form of archive reports and datasets, and will be hosted on the Cotswold Archaeology website and/or will be available from the Archaeology Data Service (ADS) http://archaeologydataservice.ac.uk.

VII. Dating and phasing

Dating evidence in the form of pottery was abundant, with a total of 5,416 sherds with dates ranging from the Late Bronze Age (*c.* 1,000–800 BC) to the 21st century. In addition, broad prehistoric dating was provided by some worked flint, and further dating evidence was provided by one Iron Age and two Roman coins, some of the more diagnostic pieces of metalwork, and worked bone. The dating from artefacts was augmented by a programme of radiocarbon dating, and samples were also taken for archaeomagnetic dating from burnt deposits within a hearth. The possibility of refining dating sequences in the Iron Age by Bayesian statistical analysis was assessed, but the inherent problems in the calibration curve for dates of this period, coupled with insufficient material from suitable contexts, meant that this option was not pursued. It is evident from this exercise that more informed sampling strategies directed specifically towards the requirements of Bayesian analysis should be incorporated into the design stage of future projects. What also became apparent during the course of the post-excavation analysis was that there was a paucity of dateable material of any kind from many of the key features, including the three large Iron Age ditches.

The definition of periods within the archaeological sequence rested on a firm chronological basis provided by detailed analysis of the stratigraphic sequence, and the form, character and spatial relationships of deposits and cut features. This, taken with the evidence discussed above, provided the basis of the dating arguments presented at the beginning of each period summary within Chapter 2, and for the interpretations of the archaeology discussed therein. The problems of refining the dating of pottery and other artefacts characteristic of certain periods are discussed within the specialist artefact reports, and will not be rehearsed here. General to all but the earliest period, however, was the problem of residuality. Further problems were created by the levels of truncation across the site, which varied to such an extent that the true ground-surface level could not be ascertained for much of the pre-modern period of activity, and for many features evidence of final phases of disuse and infilling was not present. The phasing scheme has been constructed using the best possible interpretation of the available evidence, but such caveats must be borne in mind.

The site sequence has been divided into nine basic periods:

Period 1: Earlier prehistoric and the palaeochannel, Late Mesolithic/Early Neolithic: *c.* 6500–3000BC
Period 2: Late Bronze Age: *c.* 1000–800 BC
Period 3: Middle Iron Age: *c.* 350/300–50 BC
Period 4: Late Iron Age: *c.* 50 BC– AD 50
Period 5: Roman: *c.* AD 70–400
Period 6: Saxon: *c.* 6th–11th centuries
Period 7: Medieval: *c.* later 11th–16th centuries
Period 8: Post-medieval: *c.* 16th–19th centuries
Period 9: Modern: *c.* 20th–21st centuries

Periods 1–7 are discussed in detail, Period 8 is summarised and Period 9 is not discussed within this report, other than in terms of the impact of modern activities on the survival of underlying deposits.

For simplicity's sake the term Saxon rather than Anglo-Saxon is used throughout.

All radiocarbon dates in the text are quoted at a calibrated date of 95.4% probability, with the laboratory reference, and the radiocarbon age (BP).

Figure 1.7 Area of carpark under excavation, looking north-west

9

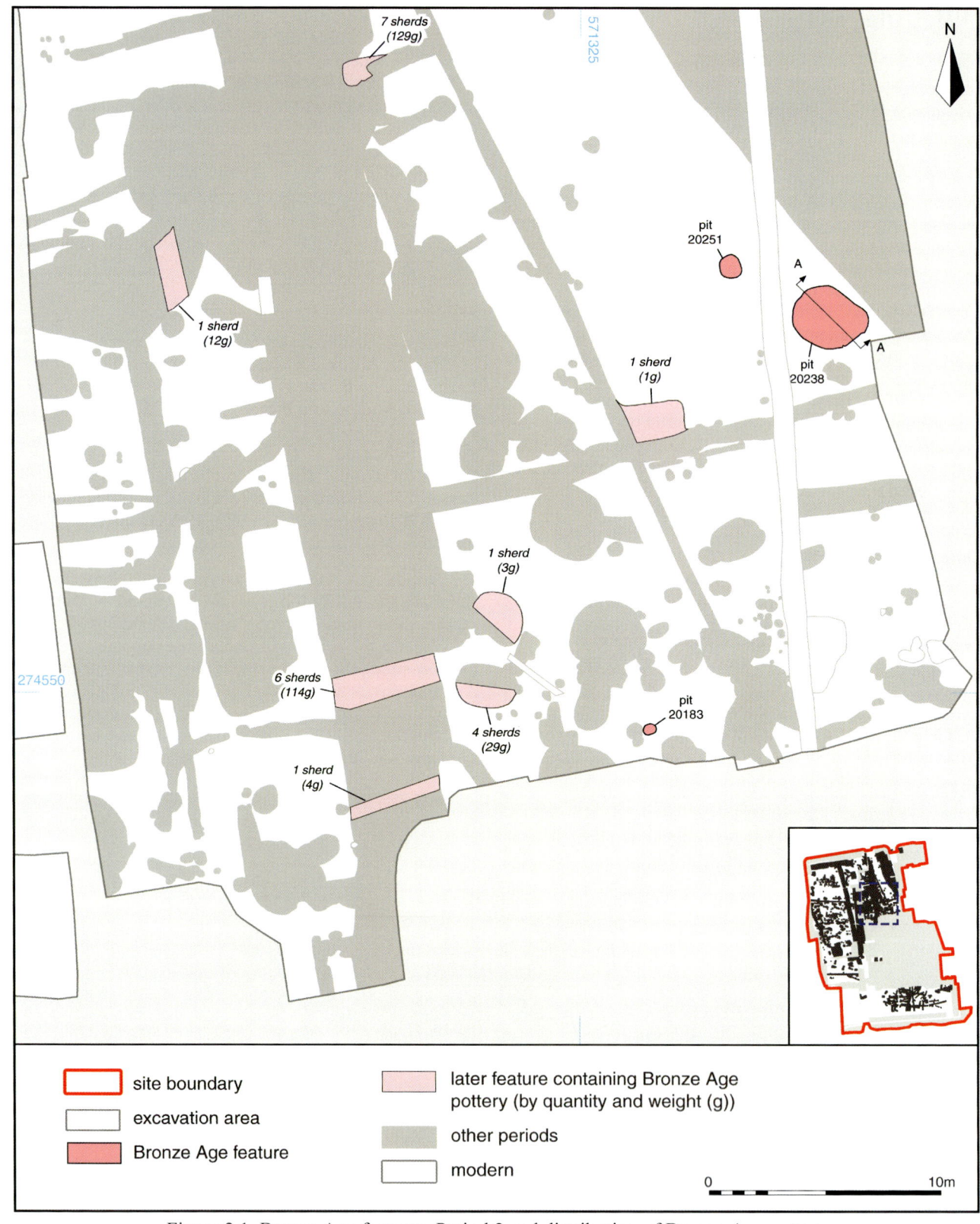

7 sherds (129g)

571325

pit 20251

A

pit 20238

1 sherd (12g)

1 sherd (1g)

1 sherd (3g)

274550

6 sherds (114g)

pit 20183

4 sherds (29g)

1 sherd (4g)

N

site boundary	later feature containing Bronze Age pottery (by quantity and weight (g))
excavation area	other periods
Bronze Age feature	modern

0   10m

Figure 2.1 Bronze Age features, Period 2 and distribution of Bronze Age pottery

Chapter 2. Period Narratives

I. Period 1: Earlier prehistoric periods and palaeochannel, Late Mesolithic/Early Neolithic: *c*. 6500 BC–3000 BC

A total of 289 worked flint flakes, and 500 unworked burnt pieces of flint, were recovered from the site. The abraded condition of the worked pieces, and the range of patination found within a single context, suggested re-deposition. The flint derived predominantly from primary chalk sources, although secondary sources such as river gravels were also utilised (see Chapter 4.IV for further discussion). Much of the flint recovered displayed characteristics typical of Bronze Age working, although tools of Mesolithic and Neolithic style were also present.

The earliest conventional dating evidence recovered from the floodplain area on site indicated activity from the Late Bronze Age to Early Iron Age periods, although prehistoric activity was suggested by approximately twenty-six flint flakes recovered from deposits which stratigraphically preceded the earliest datable features. In addition, fifteen residual flint flakes were recovered in later features in Area 3.

The deposits of a former water-course crossed the south-eastern corner of Area 3, on a north-east/south-west alignment (Fig. 1.2). The extent of the palaeochannel was plotted from sandy alluvial deposits which were interpreted as infilling the palaeochannel. A section through the palaeochannel was excavated mechanically and, although safety considerations and the rapid ingress of water prevented excavation of a complete section, it was shown to be at least 1.8m deep, and at least 17m wide. A monolith sample, taken through the uppermost channel deposits, and subject to geoarchaeological analysis (Chapter 5.VII), suggested a sequence of fine sands deposited during a phase of faster-flowing water, which were then sealed by darker sandy humic silts deposited when water flow decreased and vegetation growth within the channel increased. Waterlogged seeds recovered from two of the layers deposited in slower-flowing water were submitted for radiocarbon dating. Seeds from layer 3612 returned two dates of 805–555 cal BC (SUERC-48045; 2562±30BP), and 132–332 cal AD (SUERC-48044; 1789±30BP). Sedge seed, recovered from layer 3593 above, produced a radiocarbon date of 931–821 cal BC (SUERC-50899; 2739±26BP), suggesting that the seed dated to the Roman period in context 3612 is intrusive. A trench hand-dug through the uppermost deposits on the northern edge of the palaeochannel produced nine flint flakes, including two bladelets and a blade, typical of the Late Mesolithic/Early Neolithic period. The condition of these flakes was variable, with some appearing to be fresh whilst others were rolled. A single small sherd of Late Bronze Age pottery was recovered from deposit 3123, on the interface between the edge of the chalk bedrock and the palaeochannel. Whilst some of the flint within the upper fills may have been residual, it seems reasonable to assume that the channel was open during the Late Mesolithic/Early Neolithic period, and dried up during the

Late Bronze Age or early Iron Age. Other activity, contemporary with that suggested by flint recovered from the palaeochannel, was indicated by burnt, unworked flint recovered from weathered natural chalk on the edge of the floodplain, and several fresh flakes recovered from an alluvially-derived deposit on the edge of the chalk bedrock. Both deposits were stratigraphically earlier than the Roman activity identified in Area 3. The quantity, and rolled condition, of many of the flakes recovered from Area 3 suggests periodic low-level activity during the Late Mesolithic/Early Neolithic period. As the palaeochannel dried up, alluvial deposits accumulated across Area 3, increasing in depth towards the south. These deposits presumably derived from the flooding of the River Lark, which may well have meandered closer to the southern edge of the site before it was canalised. The present course of the river is the consequence of 18th-century canalisation (Chapter 3). A radiocarbon date of 196–44 cal BC (SUERC-48049; 2093±30BP) was obtained from a horse maxilla from alluvial deposit 3663 in the western part of Area 3, and other small fragments of animal bone were present in the alluvium, but were all sealed by alluvial deposits of Roman or later date. Some signs of activity were indicated by a posthole, a pit and a possible remnant buried soil found above a sequence of undated alluvial deposits, and a small number of pits cut into the top of palaeochannel fills in the eastern part of Area 3. All were undated, but sealed by Roman deposits. Residual Middle Iron Age pottery recovered from several later contexts in Area 3 may derive from this activity, although these features could equally be Roman.

In Area 2, two small undated pits, 2031 and 2042, were cut into the edge of the natural chalk in Area 2, but were sealed by alluvial deposits of Roman date, as were three undated chalky alluvial deposits.

II. Period 2: Late Bronze Age: *c*. 1000–800 BC

Late Bronze Age activity centred on a large pit, 20238, a smaller pit, 20251 and a tree-throw hollow 20183, all of which were located towards the south-eastern extent of the higher ground (Fig. 2.1). A number of residual sherds of Late Bronze Age pottery recovered from later features were mostly recorded within 25m of pit 20238. Five residual sherds recovered from features in the eastern part of Area 3 suggest further activity of this period within the lower part of the site. The Late Bronze Age pottery belongs to the Plainware phase of the Post-Deverel Rimbury ceramic tradition, conventionally dated *c*. 1100–800 BC. Pottery from the large pit, 20238, suggests a date between *c*. 1000–800 BC, (see Brudenell, Chapter 4.VII), and this dating is broadly supported by two radiocarbon dates from fills of the pit 1003–844 BC (SUERC-48048; 2779±30BP) and 895–798 BC (SUERC-48047; 2669±30BP).

Pit 20238 (Fig. 2.2) lay immediately to the west of the later Ditch 6. The pit was roughly circular in plan, with steeply sloped sides and a flat base. Some irregularity in

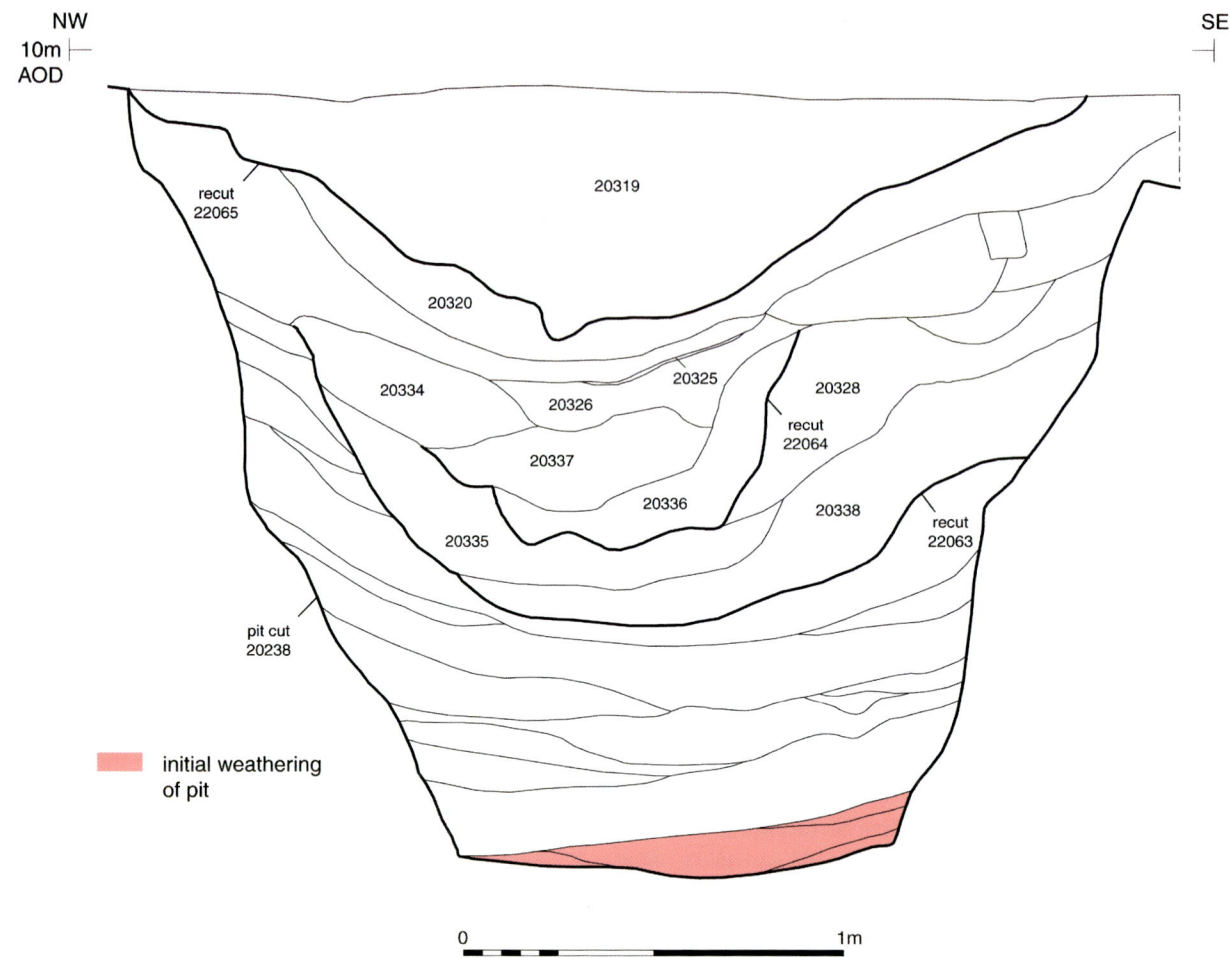

NW
10m
AOD

SE

recut
22065

20319

20320

20334

20326

20325

20328

recut
22064

20337

20336

20338

recut
22063

20335

pit cut
20238

initial weathering
of pit

0   1m

Figure 2.2 Late Bronze Age pit 20238

the sides was caused by the collapse of pockets of sand within the natural chalk substrate through which the pit had been cut. It measured between 2.5m and 2.9m in diameter and just over 2m in depth. The earliest fills, from which little artefactual material was recovered, were characterised by sand and chalk-rich deposits indicating weathering, and possible collapse of the exposed pit sides. This was sealed by a prolonged sequence of fills derived from weathering and silting and small scale episodes of refuse disposal representing periodic cleaning out and re-use of the pit, possibly for storage, although this remains conjectural. The small quantities of pottery, animal bone and worked flint recovered from these fills may represent accidental inclusions.

Following a major re-cut as 22063, the presence of a larger quantity of animal bone, pottery and fired clay fragments suggests deliberate use of the pit for refuse disposal. Re-fitting sherds identified between contexts, together with the fragmentation and abrasion of the pottery, is indicative of secondary disposal of material from refuse heaps or middens. However, the recovery of the complete profile of a fragmented coarseware vessel, together with the shoulder, lower walls and the base of a second vessel from fill 20335, suggested greater care of deposition than was the case with the majority of pottery

recovered from the re-cut pit. A radiocarbon date of 1003–844 BC (SUERC-48048; 2779±30BP) was obtained from a fragment of human skull from these fills. A second, smaller re-cut 22064 was followed by further accumulation of domestic waste, including pottery, 0.8kg of animal bone, small quantities of worked flint and daub and other undiagnostic fired-clay fragments. A radiocarbon date of 895–798 BC (SUERC-48047; 2669±30BP) was obtained from charred seeds from fill 20336, which was sealed by further fills continuing small-scale refuse disposal and soil formation within the pit. The high chalk content of the uppermost fill, 20320, suggested that some eventual capping of the pit had taken place. The pit was re-cut for a third time as 22065, before falling out of use.

The animal bone recovered from the pit fills was dominated by cattle bone, with at least three other domestic taxa represented. The remains of at least two sheep, with horse, roe deer, pig and dog also present in the assemblage, the composition of which suggested the deposition of waste material into the pit.

Plant macrofossil remains recovered from this feature were abundant, and consisted principally of barley, spelt wheat and emmer/spelt wheat grains. The composition of this assemblage was consistent with the processing of grain on a small scale, prior to cooking. As with the animal bone, it appears that this material was derived from the deposition of waste material in the pit.

Other features dated to the Late Bronze Age were few (Fig 2.1). Close to pit 20238 a single pit, 20251, was circular in plan, and measured 0.96m in diameter and 0.42m in depth, with vertical sides and a flat base. A tree-throw hollow, 20183, located towards the south-eastern corner of the higher ground, contained two small sherds of Late Bronze Age pottery, together with pieces of worked flint, fragments of fired clay and animal bone.

III. Periods 3 and 4: Middle and Late Iron Age

Period 3: Middle Iron Age c. 350/300–50 BC

Only eight sherds of pottery of probable Early Iron Age date were recovered from the site. There is some ambiguity in dating between Late Bronze Age and Early Iron Age pottery as noted in Chapter 4.VII, but an Early Iron Age date was indicated by some diagnostic elements of these sherds (Brudenell, Chapter 4.VII). Four residual sherds were recovered in three later features, which were located within 15m of each other, towards the south-western extent of the higher ground. Neither a source for the Early Iron Age pottery, nor a focus for on-site activity of this period was apparent from sherd distribution.

By contrast, the Middle Iron Age was a period of intense activity on the site (Fig. 2.3), of which the most notable feature was the pair of massive ditches (1 and 5) which defined the eastern part of Enclosure C. Another equally substantial ditch on the eastern edge of the excavated area may also have been constructed during this period, although it remains undated, and is discussed as a feature of the later Iron Age (see Ditch 6, Period 4). Numerous pits survived in truncated form, both within the enclosed area and to the east of it. These features were dated by a large assemblage of Middle Iron Age pottery which was dominated by handmade wares of local origin (Brudenell, Chapter 4.VII). The dating of a number of features was confirmed by the radiocarbon dates discussed below. Although there were numerous postholes within the enclosed area, and to the east, none contained dating evidence which pre-dated the Roman period. Although it is probable that some of these postholes belong to this period, no substantial constructions could be identified. A possible focus for settlement beyond the west of the excavated area is suggested by the greater density of pits towards this side.

Evidence of activity from this period was largely confined to the higher ground. The accumulation of alluvial layers pre-dating the Roman period in the lower parts of Areas 2 and 3 indicated that conditions in these areas were not favourable for any significant use throughout the Iron Age period.

A possible precursor of the innermost enclosure ditch, Ditch 39 (Figs 2.3 and 2.4), was identified in two sections towards the centre of the higher ground. While its full extent was not traced, it ran for at least 16m on a broadly similar alignment to Ditch 1, and may have extended a further 20m to the south, where a humic soil was recorded beneath Ditch 1. It measured at least 2.8m wide, and 0.85m deep, with a flat base and a steep western side, the eastern side having been removed by Ditch 1. The dark, grey-black humic fill suggested that the ditch had been open for a long period of time, although no dating evidence was recovered from the fill. A monolith sample taken through fill 15579 produced a small amount of burnt cereal processing waste, which had been tipped into the base of the open ditch. The purpose of this ditch remains unclear; it may have represented an earlier phase of the enclosure defined by Ditches 1 and 5, although it appeared much smaller in size than either of the later ditches. Ditch 39 fell out of use when it was deliberately backfilled with re-deposited natural chalk, which was probably upcast during the construction of Ditch 1.

The northern and eastern sides of Enclosure C were defined by two large ditches, Ditch 1 and Ditch 5 (Fig. 2.3). An area of at least 100m by 35m was enclosed, and there was no evidence for the western side of the enclosure within the site. The inner ditch (Ditch 1) terminated approximately 15m from the edge of the higher ground, suggesting that the floodplain of the River Lark may have served as a natural boundary. It could not be established which of the two large ditches was constructed first, although it appears probable that Ditch 5 may have fallen out of use before Ditch 1. No extant traces of any banks associated with either ditch survived.

The innermost ditch, Ditch 1 (Figs 2.4–2.7), ran for approximately 100m on a north/south alignment, before turning through 90 degrees and continuing to the west for at least another 35m. Three sections excavated across its full width showed that the ditch measured between 7.2m and 7.8m in width, and between 3.2m and 3.6m in depth, with a generally V-shaped profile. A notch in the base of the ditch, which was particularly pronounced in cut 17260 (Fig. 2.6), probably served as a defensive feature.

The presence of a bank on the interior, western side of the ditch could be inferred from the absence of any Middle Iron Age features within 10m of the ditch (Fig 2.3). The ditch was initially infilled by several deposits of loose chalk which were probably derived from the erosion of the newly constructed bank, although not all of these deposits appear to have been tipped in from the interior side. The ditch was left open to weathering and a series of silt-rich deposits infilled its base. These deposits were interspersed with chalkier deposits which had eroded from the ditch sides (Fig. 2.7). Two small sherds of Middle Iron Age pottery, and some animal bone, were recovered from fills approximately 0.6m above the base of the ditch. Above these deposits, the sequence differed between each of the excavated sections along its north-south axis. In a section approximately 20m to the south, the ditch had been deliberately infilled from the exterior, eastern side to within 0.4m of the top of the surviving ditch, with re-deposited natural chalk and light, white-grey re-deposited ditch silts, which are thought to derive from Ditch 5 and the partial slighting of its bank. The other two sections across the full width of the ditch showed that it had been deliberately infilled, probably with bank material from the interior western side of the ditch (Fig. 2.6).

The ditch was subsequently re-cut, following the deliberate infilling. This resulted in a shallower ditch, between 1.3m and 1.8m in depth, and two of the sections across the full width of the ditch showed that the re-cut had moved the ditch approximately 2m to the west. The ditch was then left open to infill naturally, as evidenced by the small quantities of Middle Iron Age pottery which were recovered from contexts 17217 and 17327 (Fig. 2.6).

An excavated section through Ditch 1 (Fig. 2.7), along its east-west axis, showed that this stretch of the ditch had

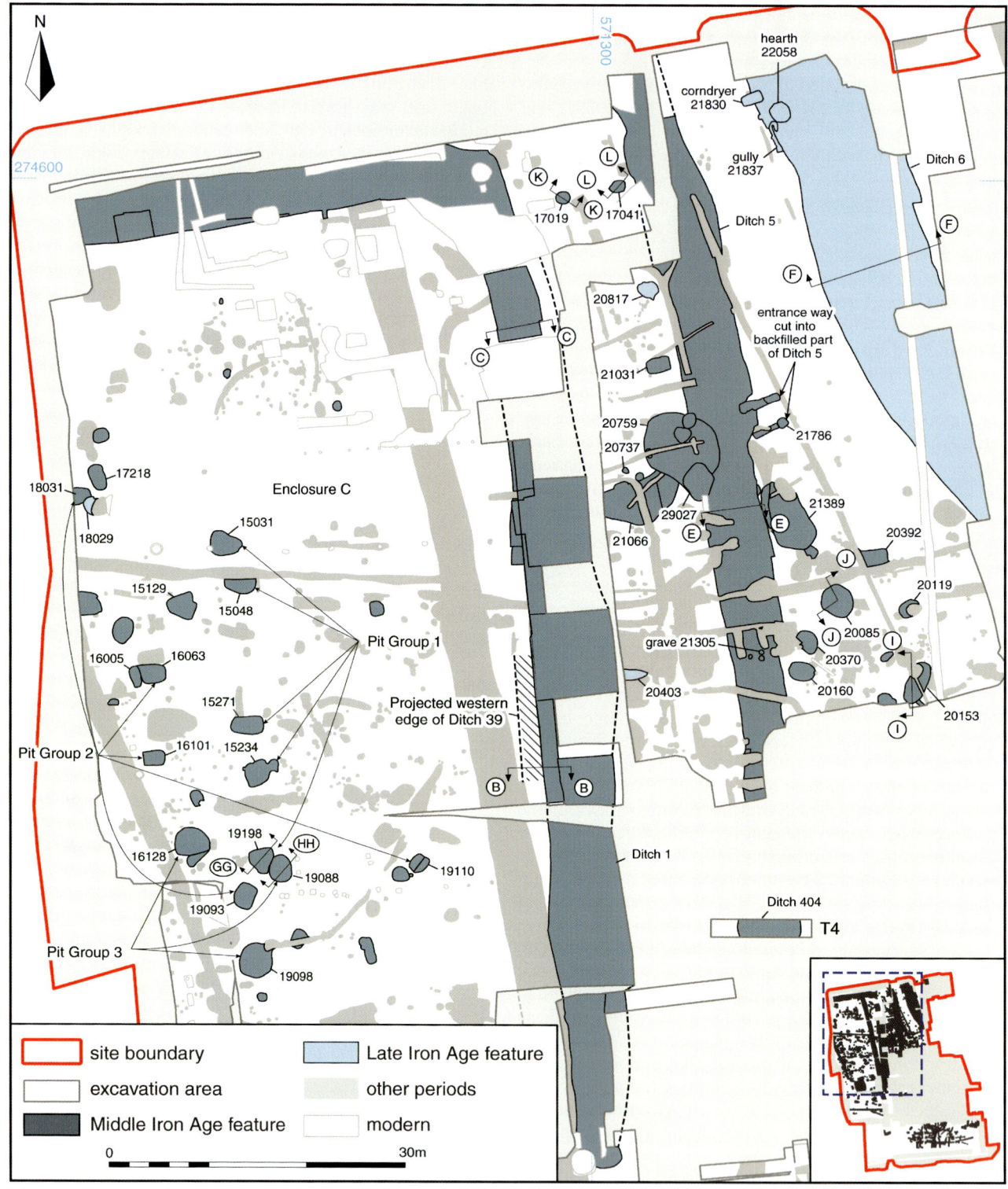

Figure 2.3 Middle Iron Age Period 3 and Late Iron Age Period 4

been fully backfilled with bank material from the interior, southern side of the enclosure. Geoarchaeological analysis of a monolith sample showed that the topsoil between the layers of chalk represented re-deposited material rather than *in situ* soil development between episodes of backfilling (see Allen, Chapter 5.VII). There was no evidence to suggest that this backfilling was not contemporary with that seen in the north/south-aligned section of the ditch. However, the absence of the re-cut

evident in other parts of Ditch 1 suggested that the ditch remained backfilled here.

Ditch 5 (Figs 2.3 and 2.8) lay approximately 11m to the east of Ditch 1, and ran on a parallel north/south alignment before turning slightly to the west at the north end of the site, presumably to follow the same course as Ditch 1. The southern extent of Ditch 5 was not established, although ditch 404 in Evaluation Trench 4 (Fig. 2.3), indicated a likely continuation to the south of the excavated area. The ditch could not be traced in Area 3,

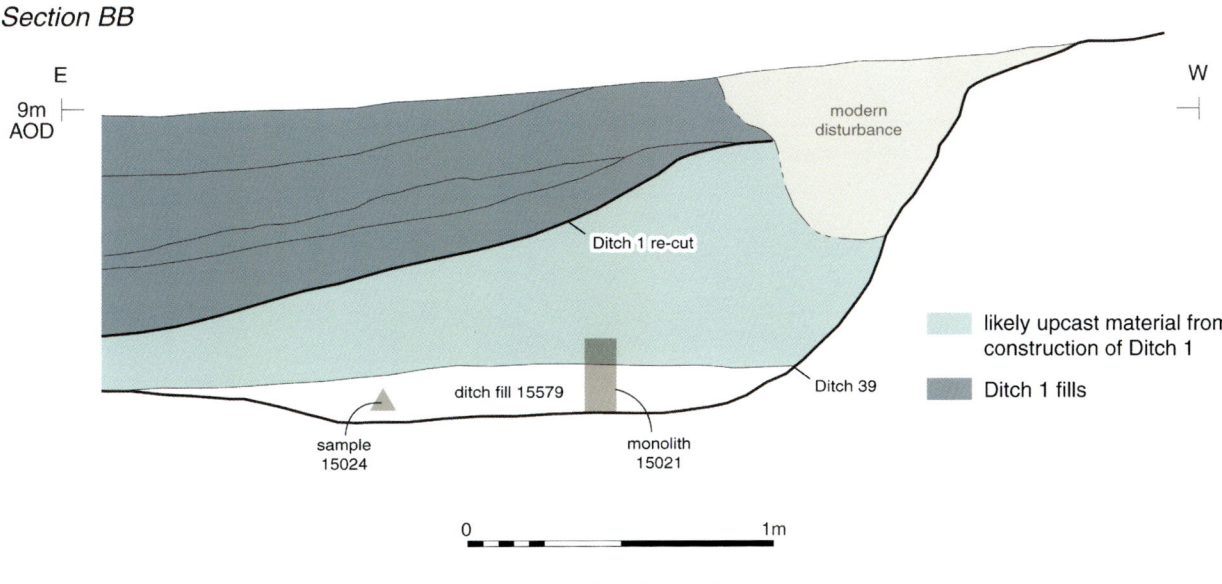

Figure 2.4 Ditch 39

Figure 2.5 Ditch 1, looking south-east

and is assumed to terminate somewhere beneath the existing buildings. Three sections excavated across the full width of the ditch showed that the ditch measured between 4.4m and 6.2m in width and between 2.3m and 2.9m in depth, becoming slightly narrower towards the southern extent of the excavated area. The three sections had broadly similar V-shaped profiles, with gradients of between 45° and 60°. A pronounced notch, similar to that in Ditch 1, which was present in the northernmost section, was not seen in the two sections to the south, where the

ditch had a flat base. As with Ditch 1, no extant traces of any bank survived, although the ditch fills suggest that this may have been on the interior western side.

The basal fills of the ditch generally comprised light-grey silt and chalk deposits which were derived from the weathering of the exposed ditch sides and localised episodes of slippage from the bank to the west, although apparently not on the scale that occurred soon after the construction of Ditch 1. The initial period of weathering and silting infilled the base of the ditch to varying depths

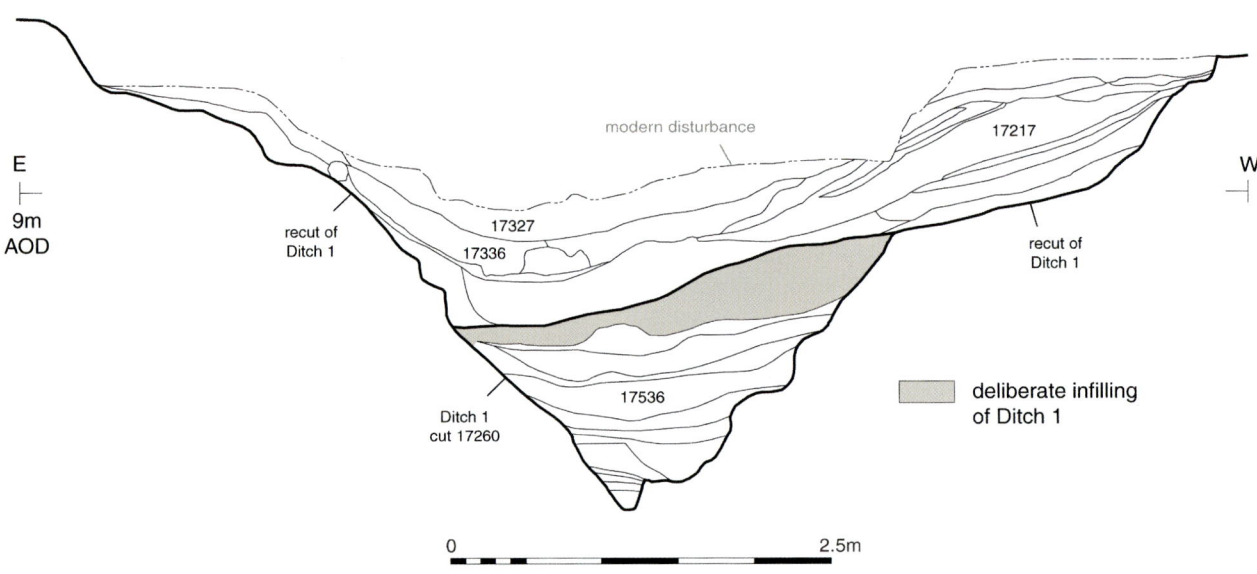

Section CC

E
9m
AOD

W

modern disturbance

17217

recut of
Ditch 1

17327

17336

recut of
Ditch 1

Ditch 1
cut 17260

17536

deliberate infilling
of Ditch 1

0   2.5m

Figure 2.6 Ditch 1, cut 17260

Figure 2.7 Ditch 1, looking north-west (scales 2m and 1m)

of between 0.4m and 0.9m, from which small quantities of Middle Iron Age pottery were recovered. A localised re-cut was identified in one section. Grave 21305 (Figs 2.3 and 2.28), containing skeleton 21386, had been cut into these basal fills from approximately 0.6m above the base of the ditch. Although contained within a cut, the skeleton was far from complete, and only the skull and two vertebrae survived. A radiocarbon date of 341–49 BC (SUERC-48057; 2115±30BP) obtained from the skull confirmed the assumptions of a Middle Iron Age date from pottery from the backfill. The grave was overlaid by weathering and silting deposits, from which more sherds of Middle Iron Age pottery were recovered.

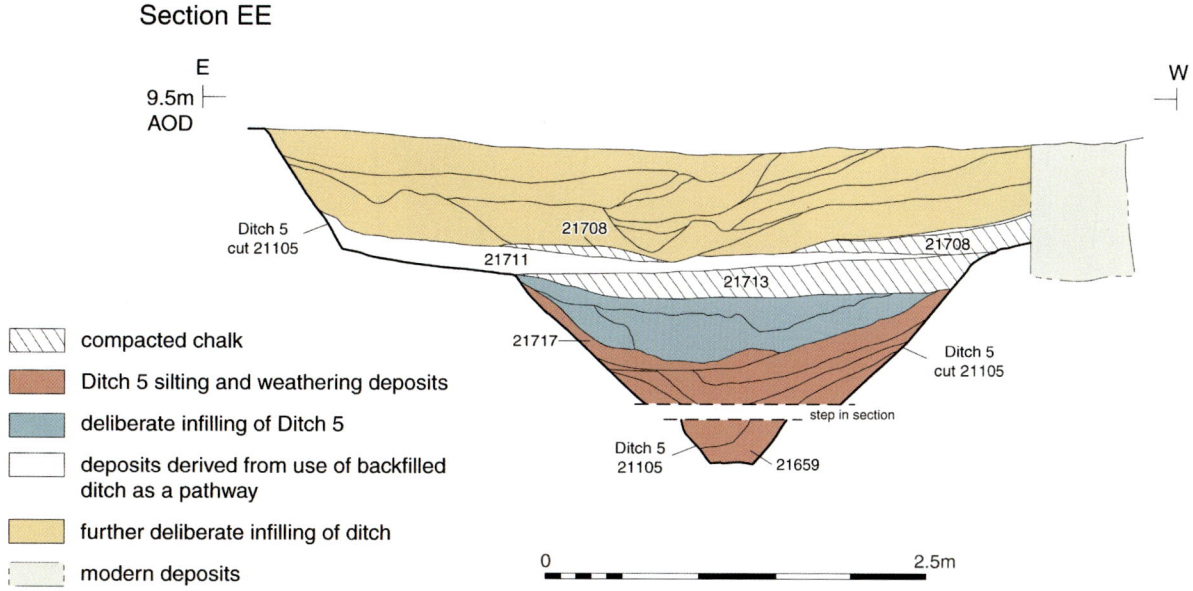

Section EE

E
9.5m
AOD

W

Ditch 5
cut 21105

21708

21708

21711

21713

compacted chalk

Ditch 5 silting and weathering deposits

deliberate infilling of Ditch 5

deposits derived from use of backfilled
ditch as a pathway

further deliberate infilling of ditch

modern deposits

21717

Ditch 5
cut 21105

step in section

Ditch 5
21105

21659

0   2.5m

Figure 2.8 Ditch 5, cut 21105

At some later stage, the ditch was backfilled, probably with material from the bank to the west (Fig. 2.8), comprising a mixture of loose chalk rubble, chalk-rich deposits and re-deposited topsoil from which two sherds of Middle Iron Age pottery were recovered.

Ditch 5 may have ceased to function as a defensive ditch following the slighting of its banks. Along the length of the ditch, the depth of backfill reached almost to the top of the surviving natural chalk, and the central section was sealed by a compacted chalk deposit 21713 (Fig. 2.8), which had been deliberately laid to create a level surface. This top of this deposit coincided with the bottom of a cut which widened the ditch by approximately 1m on its eastern, exterior, side but which was not present in the other two sections. A dark-brown silty layer 21711, which appeared to have accumulated over layer 21713, filled the cut on the eastern side of the ditch, and was sealed by another compacted chalk levelling deposit 21708 (Fig. 2.8). A similar sequence of compacted chalk levelling deposits and intervening dark silty layers, of approximately 0.4m depth, was also present in the northern full section at a depth of between 0.8m and 1m from the surviving top of the natural chalk. The sequence represented a series of re-laid surfaces, which suggested this part of the ditch was in long-term use as a pathway. This sequence was sealed in turn by further backfilling to the top of the surviving natural chalk. While the small quantity of Middle Iron Age pottery recovered could be considered residual, no other dating evidence was recovered to suggest a later date for the backfilling. The upper profile of the ditch, and any evidence for its survival into the Roman period, had been removed by modern truncation, which appeared to have been particularly severe in the northern part of the site.

An entrance-way, approximately 1.8m wide and defined by two parallel lines of elongated/oval pits and postholes, lay immediately to the east of Ditch 5 (Fig. 2.3). The postholes and pits generally had near-vertical sides and flat bases, and were between 0.5m and 0.92m deep. Some pits were of a more elongated oval shape,

presumably to facilitate the tilting of posts into their settings. At least one of the posts appeared to have been re-set, and one pit was cut into the second phase of backfill within the ditch. Although the pottery recovered from the packing fills of some of the postholes was exclusively Middle Iron Age in date, it is possible that this material may be residual, and that the entranceway may belong to the Late Iron Age or even later, as it was aligned at a right angle to Ditch 4 of Period 6.

No evidence, either in terms of stratigraphic relationships or datable artefactual material, was identified to offer a chronology of the construction of Ditches 1 and 5. Sufficient space existed between the ditches to allow for the construction of Ditch 5 and its bank while Ditch 1 remained open, and *vice versa*. If it is assumed that the banks of both ditches were slighted at the same time, it could be postulated that Ditch 1 had been open for a slightly longer period, as a greater depth of weathering and silting deposits had accumulated in the base of this ditch compared to that of Ditch 5. The greater size of Ditch 1 suggests a correspondingly greater defensive importance.

Several factors indicate that Ditch 5 was the first to fall out of use. A second episode of backfilling, which infilled the ditch to the top of surviving natural deposits, suggests its disuse in Period 3. Very little, if any, artefactual material post-dating the Iron Age was recovered from the upper fills of Ditch 5, while Roman material was recovered from the upper fills of Ditch 1. Two Period 3 features, pits 20737 and 21031 were located between Ditches 1 and 5 where the bank previously stood, and pits dated to Period 3 were cut into the top of Ditch 5. By contrast, no features pre-dating Period 5 were cut into the top of Ditch 1. The potential of Bayesian statistical analysis to refine the sequence of enclosure ditches was investigated, although the shortcomings of the calibration curve for this period, together with a lack of suitable material for dating key elements of the sequence, indicated that this analysis would not provide a meaningful outcome.

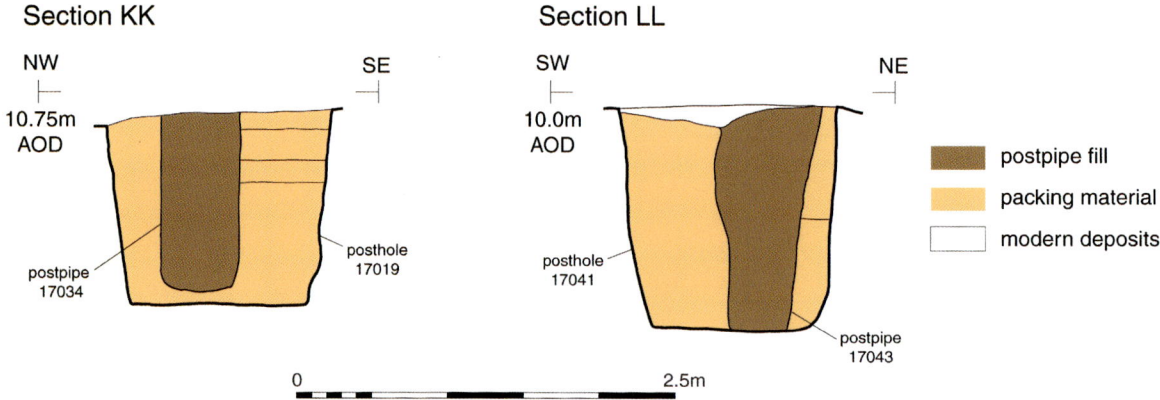

Figure 2.9 Postpits 17019 and 17041

Two massive postpits were cut into the natural chalk towards the northern extent of the higher ground area (Fig. 2.3). Postpit 17019 (Fig. 2.9) was circular in plan, measured 1.49m in diameter and 1.34m in depth, and had vertical sides and a flat base. It contained re-deposited chalk tightly packed around postpipe 17034, whose diameter of 0.52m indicated a substantial post. The vertical profile of the postpipe indicated that the post was left to rot *in situ*. Any attempt to remove such a large post would very probably have been detectable in the profile of the postpipe. The decay of the post in question dated to the later Roman period; fifteen sherds of 1st to 4th-century pottery were recovered from the postpipe, and a radiocarbon date of 340–535 AD (SUERC-48065; 1635± BP) was obtained from charred barley retrieved from the same deposit.

Postpit 17041 (Fig. 2.9), also circular in plan, measured 1.52m in diameter and 1.5m in depth, with vertical sides and a flat base. It contained chalk packed around a postpipe, 17043, whose diameter of 0.6m also indicated a large post. This displayed a similar vertical profile as that of postpipe 17034, and appeared similarly to have rotted *in situ*. Five sherds of 1st to 4th-century Roman pottery, and three sherds of Iron Age pottery, were recovered from the postpit.

The pottery and radiocarbon dates obtained from the postpits indicated a Roman date for the disuse of the postpits, but no evidence was recovered to date their construction. Both posts measured over 0.5m in diameter and, assuming a ratio of 1:3 for the depth of the postpit and size of the post, in excess of 4m in height. The two postpits formed an entrance just over 4m in width, and located between Ditches 1 and 5. It is possible that their construction in this location may be associated with the re-modelling and infilling of Ditch 5 outlined above, although their exact function is not fully understood. With no evidence for any attempt at burning or removal, posts of such size would have taken a considerable time to decay, and therefore a construction date earlier than the pottery and radiocarbon date from the postpits has to be assumed. The erection of these posts in the Roman period would seem unlikely, as the Roman corn-dryer could not have been constructed while the western post remained standing, and it is not apparent why the outskirts of a small Roman farmstead would have required such a monumental construction.

Period 3 features on the interior of Enclosure C (Fig. 2.3) almost exclusively comprised refuse pits, and no structural features of this period were recorded. A number of the postholes not dated to later periods may represent insubstantial structures such as out-buildings and fences, but without dating evidence, or recognisable patterning of Iron Age types of construction, such as round houses, it must be assumed that substantial buildings lay elsewhere. The likely proximity of settlement within the enclosure was suggested by the presence of small-scale dumps of chalk, presumably to mask odour, within several of the refuse pits. A degree of zoning of the location of the pits was also apparent, with a detectable increase towards the west, indicating a possible location of the main settlement. The absence of pits within 12m of the north/south-aligned part of Ditch 1, or within 18m of the east/west-aligned part of the same ditch (Fig. 2.3), may indicate the presence of a bank on the interior of the enclosure. Although the pits were diverse in shape and size, a number shared similar characteristics, and these are discussed as Pit Groups 1–3. All the pits were ultimately filled with material indicative of domestic waste. In very occasional instances, there were indications of the primary purpose of the pit. In this case, the analysis of artefact distribution did not help to identify zones of activity. The absence of gullies or smaller ditches suggested that there was no internal substantial sub-division of the enclosure, although the row of pits comprising Pit Group 1 suggested the alignment of a boundary, of which no other trace survived.

Pit Group 1 (Fig. 2.3) comprised five large pits forming an approximate north/south alignment broadly parallel with the western side of Ditch 1. The pits were sub-oval or sub-rectangular in plan, measured an average of 3.1m in length, 2.2m in width and 0.75m in depth and had steep, almost vertical sides and flat bases. The pits may have originally had a storage function, although the composition of the basal fills did not provide convincing evidence for this. Small quantities of indeterminate cereal grains were recovered from the first fill, 15032, of pit 15031, and a radiocarbon date of 353–56 cal BC (SUERC-48070; 2140±30BP) was obtained from carbonised grains recovered from the first fill, 15281, of pit 15234, although the large quantity of carbonised grain normally associated with grain-storage pits was absent. The assemblage of plant remains recovered from these pits was indicative of the disposal of cereal processing

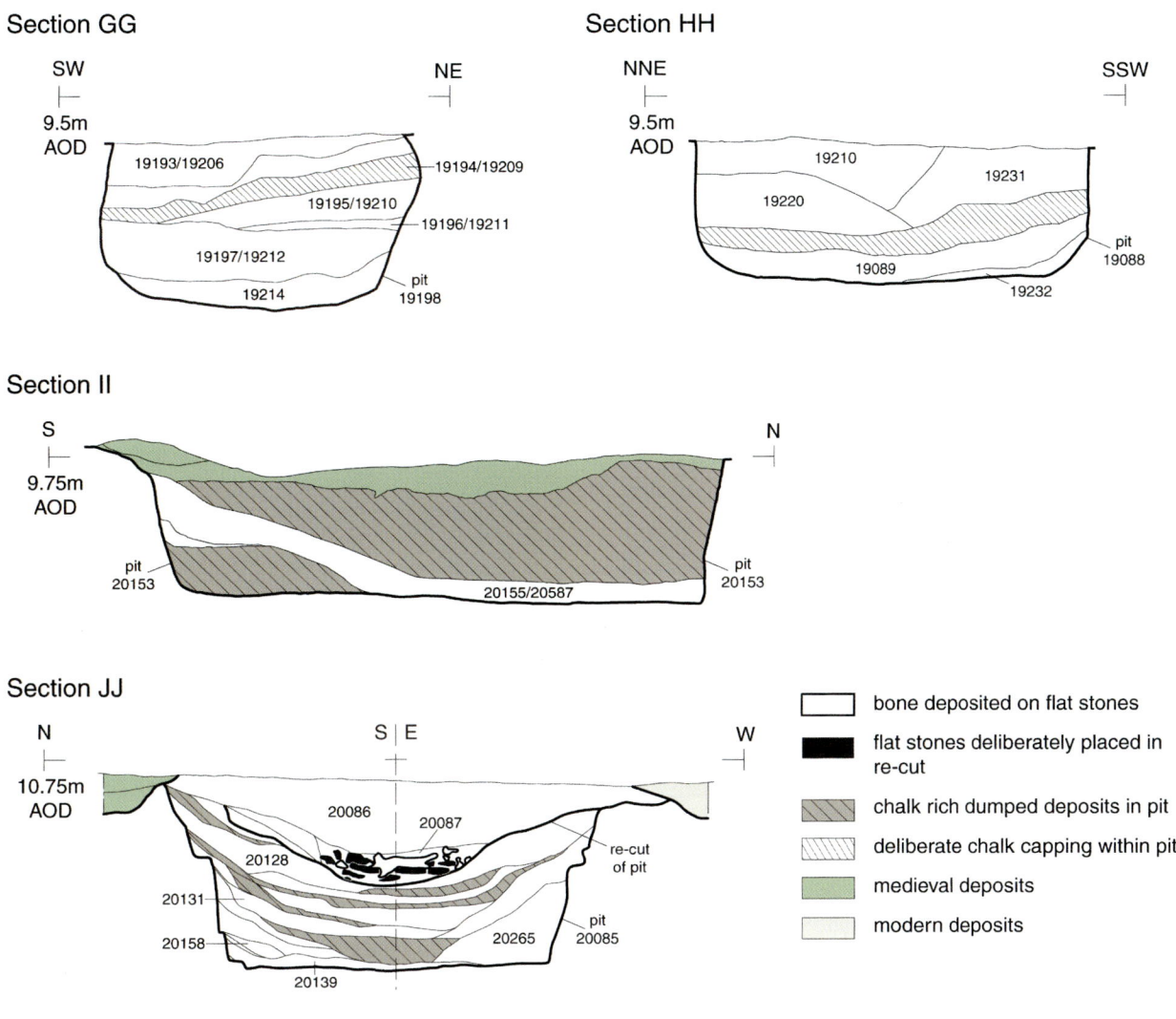

Section GG

SW NE
9.5m
AOD

19193/19206   19194/19209
19195/19210
19196/19211
19197/19212
19214   pit
19198

Section HH

NNE   SSW
9.5m
AOD

19210
19231
19220
19089   pit
19088
19232

Section II

S   N
9.75m
AOD

pit
20153
20155/20587
pit
20153

Section JJ

N   S | E   W
10.75m
AOD

20086
20087
20128   re-cut
of pit
20131
20158   pit
20265   20085
20139

0   2.5m

bone deposited on flat stones

flat stones deliberately placed in
re-cut

chalk rich dumped deposits in pit

deliberate chalk capping within pit

medieval deposits

modern deposits

Figure 2.10 Middle Iron Age pits

waste. The artefactual evidence recovered showed that the pits had largely become infilled through the dumping of domestic refuse. Quantities of Middle Iron Age pottery and animal bone were recovered from all pits within this group; over 1.2kg of Middle Iron Age pottery was recovered from the fills of pit 19198 (Figs 2.3 and 2.10), and over 7kg of animal bone from the fills of pit 15234. A bone weaving-comb (Figure 4.16, no. 4), a possible iron knife-blade or broad-bladed tool, (Figure 4.2, no. 14) and a copper-alloy strap-fitting (Figure 4.1, no. 1) were all recovered from the fills of pit 19198. Chalk-rich deposits had been tipped into all of the pits, and the lower fills of pits 19088 and 19198 were capped with chalk, presumably to mask odour emanating from the pit. The regularity of the alignment of Pit Group 1, 19m to the west of Ditch 1, suggests a degree of zoning within the enclosure (Fig. 2.3). Pit 19198 had been cut through pit 19088, of Group 3, before the latter had been completely filled up. Pit 15271 was fully backfilled with chalk when the pits fell out of use, although the others were all left open to infill naturally.

Pit Group 2 (Fig. 2.3) comprised pits of a rectangular shape, although these did not display the distinct spatial distribution of Pit Groups 1 and 3. Their size varied between 1.5m and 2.4m in length, between 0.7m and 1.7m in width and between 0.2m and 0.56m in depth, and they had steep sides and flat bases. As with Pit Group 1, the recovery of small amounts of wheat and oat grains from the basal fill of pit 19093 suggested that while these may have originally been used for storage, the fills relate to secondary use for the disposal of domestic refuse and gradual infilling with soil. Varying quantities of Middle Iron Age pottery and animal bone were recovered from each pit within this group. The finds from pit 16063 were particularly noteworthy; 1.2kg of pottery, over 14kg of animal bone, and a complete triangular loomweight were recovered from fill 16065. Two other loomweight fragments were recovered from the fill below (Fig. 4.15, nos 1–3). A complete disc-shaped spindlewhorl was discarded in the base of pit 16101 (Fig. 4.6 no. 2). Pit 19110 contained a layer of chalk backfill deeper than other chalk capping deposits seen within Pit Groups 1 and 3.

Pit Group 3 (Fig. 2.3) comprised three large, circular pits located towards the south-western extent of the area enclosed by Enclosure C. These measured between 2m and 3.5m in diameter, and between 0.4m and 0.88m in

Figure 2.11 Pit 20085, looking south-east (scale 1m)

depth, and had steep sides and flat bases. The first fill, 19232, of pit 19088 (Fig. 2.10), was rich in charcoal and contained emmer /spelt and barley grains, which provided evidence of its original use as a storage pit. This pit, and the other two pits within the group, were re-used for domestic refuse disposal, which included several sherds of Middle Iron Age pottery and quantities of animal bone. This included 1.3kg of animal bone from the upper fill of pit 19088, together with an iron fragment of a woodworker's gouge (Fig. 4.2, no. 12). Several thin deposits of chalk, presumably to mask odour, were dumped into the pits. Pit 16128 was fully backfilled with re-deposited chalk, as was pit 15271 of Pit Group 1, although there was no contemporary activity (such as the construction of buildings) identified in the vicinity to suggest why such a levelling process occurred.

Several other Period 3 refuse pits were located within Enclosure C. These pits generally had steep sides and flat bases, but displayed little regularity in terms of size, depth or shape in plan. Pit 15129 was the only Period 3 pit to have retained traces of a clay lining which, although heavily disturbed, was indicative of an original use as a storage pit. Oat, barley and wheat grains retrieved from an environmental sample taken from this pit may relate to its primary function as a storage pit, or to waste discarded during cereal processing. In addition, two mould fragments and three crucible fragments, indicative of the casting of copper alloys, had been deposited in the pit (Fig. 4.3, and Fig. 4.4, nos 1a and 1b). The pit was partially capped with chalk.

The pits located outside Enclosure C were principally confined to the south-eastern quarter of the higher ground, and there was a notable absence of these features in the northern half of the area, although the construction of Ditch 6 of Period 4 may have removed this evidence. Such pits varied in size, but had similar profiles and fill sequences to the majority of pits inside Enclosure C, and probably also served initially for storage purposes before being re-utilised as refuse pits. Like those within the enclosure, several of the pits outside showed signs of having been periodically capped with chalk.

Pit 20085 (Figs 2.3, 2.10 and 2.11), one of the largest of these pits, measured 3.1m in diameter and 1.35m in depth, and was initially used as a refuse pit which was frequently capped with small-scale dumps of chalk, again probably to mask odour. The pit was re-cut within its original footprint before it had become fully infilled, and subsequent fills were markedly different in character. Larger chalk lumps were prevalent within the fills, together with a much larger quantity of animal bone, mostly of cow and sheep/goat. A fragment of a possible bone weaving-tablet was recovered from fill 20086 (Fig. 4.16, no. 5). Several pieces of animal bone placed on flat stones in the centre of the pit appear to be a deliberate act of deposition. Following this, the pit was left open to infill naturally.

Pit 20153 (Figs 2.3 and 2.10), outside Enclosure C, was notable in being distinctly sub-rectangular in plan, with rounded corners and aligned north-east/south-west along its longest axis. It measured 4m in length, 2m in width and almost 1m in depth, and had been partially infilled with clean chalk soon after construction, on its south-western edge. A dark, charcoal-rich deposit, 20155/20587, which contained cereal processing waste, had been dumped into the pit over the chalk and covered the whole of the base of the pit, but this deposit was deeper towards the south-west, having been tipped into the pit from this direction. Six sherds of Middle Iron Age pottery, approximately 0.5kg of animal bone, and small quantities of daub were recovered from this fill, which also contained patches of grey ash suggesting successive rakings from a domestic hearth. Radiocarbon dates of 371–198 cal BC (SUERC-48056; 2209 ± 30BP) and 205–49 cal BC (SUERC-48055; 2115±30BP) were obtained from charcoal and animal bone respectively. Both were recovered from this deposit, which was sealed by the dumped chalk which fully infilled the pit.

Pits 20759, 21066 and 21389 (Fig. 2.3) were atypical of the Period 3 pits. They were large and shallow with the irregular plan typical of quarry pits. They appeared to be targeted on the chalk-rich backfills within Ditch 5, remnant bank deposits adjacent to the ditch, and the natural chalk substrate. Pit 21389 was located at the eastern extent of Ditch 5, and cut through several of the fills relating to the deliberate infilling of the ditch. It was sub-rectangular in plan, and measured 7.5m in length, 3.75m in width and 1.05m in depth, and had steep sides and a flat base. It had been infilled by many successive small-scale dumps of domestic refuse and chalk, from which moderate quantities of Middle Iron Age pottery, animal bone and unworked burnt flint were recovered, as well as a fragment of a bone toggle. Small amounts of Roman and Early Saxon pottery, found in the uppermost fill of this pit, indicate that it survived as a hollow for some considerable time after its initial use.

Eight metres to the west of pit 21389, pit 21066 had been cut into the natural chalk immediately adjacent to the western edge of Ditch 5. This pit was irregularly shaped in plan, and measured approximately 7.3m in length, a maximum of 3.8m in width, but only 0.45m in depth. It was left open to silt up naturally, and contained only small amounts of artefactual material. It was cut on its north-eastern edge by a larger extraction pit, 20759, which also cut into the backfill deposits within Ditch 5. This pit was sub-circular in plan, and measured approximately 7.5m in diameter, but only 0.45m in depth, and had gently-sloped sides and a generally flat base. It contained a series of white-grey silty fills, derived from weathering of the exposed pit sides, and small quantities of Middle Iron Age pottery and animal bone. The effect of this quarrying activity was the formation of a hollow or terrace feature, which was aligned east/west across Ditch 5, which then turned through ninety degrees to run on an approximate north/south alignment to the east of the ditch. The silty fills of pits 21066 and 20759 were sealed by a deep accumulation of largely homogenous topsoil deposits, which appeared to have been extensively re-worked. This hollow was still visible in the Roman period, and probably beyond. A Roman burial, 21080, was cut into the dark soils, and several other pieces of disarticulated human bone were recovered from this area. A second Roman burial, and a medieval burial, lay immediately to the north of the hollow.

Period 4: Late Iron Age c. 50 BC–AD 50
Available evidence indicates a decline in activity and a shift in focus away from the site during the Late Iron Age (Fig. 2.3). A massive ditch, Ditch 6, was located on the eastern edge of the higher ground, and it can be speculated that it enclosed some activity of this period beyond the site, as there was a marked paucity of features of this period within the area of the excavation. As in Period 3, conditions did not appear to have been suitable for exploitation of the lower, floodplain area.

The handmade pottery fabrics recognised as Late Iron Age types from the site generally date from anywhere between the mid to late 1st century BC and the mid-1st century AD, and were therefore probably in use at the same time as Middle Iron Age pottery types. It has been noted that the distinctive characteristics of Late Iron Age pottery, notably the distinctive wheel-made wares and other 'Beligicized' ceramic influences, were adopted in a slow and piecemeal fashion in most parts of Suffolk (see Brudenell, Chapter 4.VII for further discussion). In the assemblage from Recreation Way, as elsewhere, the handmade potting traditions of the Middle Iron Age persisted, making problematic the identification of Late Iron Age features from ceramic evidence alone. The majority of Late Iron Age pottery recovered was residual in later features, with only thirteen sherds recovered from Period 4 features. The ceramic evidence supports the assumption that the main focus of settlement had shifted away from the excavated area by c. 50 BC.

Ditch 6 (Figs 2.3, 2.12 and 2.13) lay along the north-eastern extent of the higher ground, on an approximate north-west/south-east alignment, and converged towards Ditch 5 at the northern limit of the site. Its western edge suggested the beginnings of a curve towards the east at its southern extent. It was substantially larger than either Ditches 1 or 5 of Period 3, and measured 11.3m wide and 4m deep with steeply-sloped sides and a flat base. The original extent of the ditch may have been greater, as it had been truncated by modern activity to the east of site. Only one section could be excavated across its full width, and a modern pipe trench prevented full exposure of its eastern side and base in section (Fig. 2.12). A second section, excavated across the western 7m of the ditch to a depth of 1m, was located 11m to the north of this. A large feature identified in Evaluation Trench 6 (Fig. 1.2) and interpreted at the time as a quarry pit, measured at least 8m wide and at least 1.75m deep and it has subsequently been reinterpreted as the southern continuation of this ditch.

Loose chalk, probably derived from construction, lay in the base of the ditch, and was sealed by a thin, grey silty layer. This was sealed on its western edge by several chalk-rich deposits deriving from a small-scale collapse of either a bank or the ditch sides. Following this, the ditch was left open for a prolonged period of time and a series of chalky silty deposits accumulated and infilled the ditch to a depth of approximately 3.5m (Fig. 2.13). There was no convincing evidence for any deliberate infilling or re-cutting of the ditch during this period, although any such signs of this may have been obscured on the eastern side of the section by the soil buffer left around the modern pipe trench.

The recovered dating evidence indicated that the ditch was open during the Late Iron Age. A radiocarbon date of 352–55 BC (SUERC–48064; 2137±30BP) was obtained from a fragment of neonate skull 22028 which had been placed in a chalk silt deposit, approximately 1m from the base of the ditch. A dog burial, 22027, contained within a later silty deposit, approximately 1.6m from the base of the ditch, was radiocarbon dated to 101 cal BC to AD 60 cal (SUERC-48060; 2017±30BP) (Fig. 2.12). Small quantities of Late Iron Age pottery were also recovered from fills 21992 and 22002.

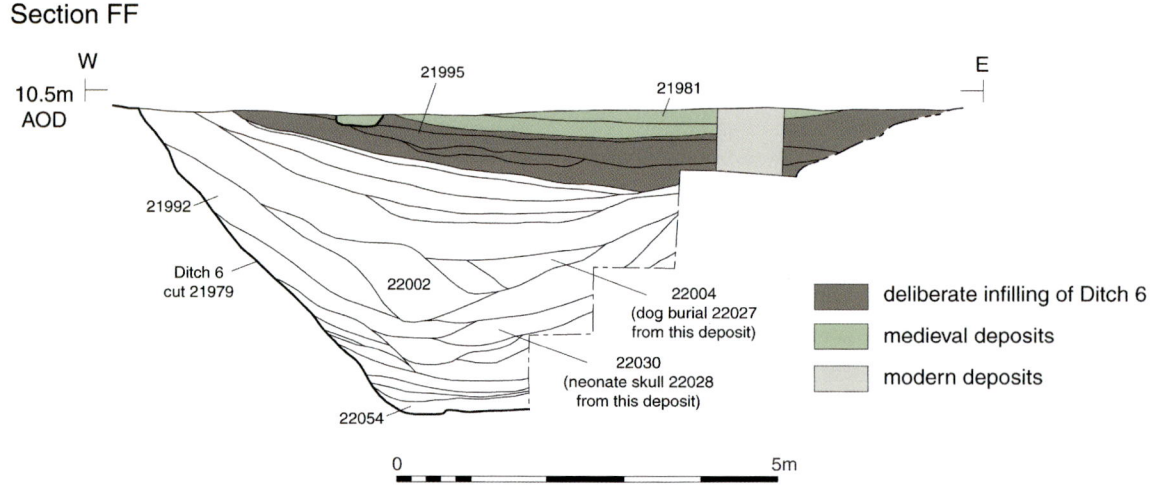

Section FF

W
21995
21981
E

10.5m
AOD

21992

Ditch 6
cut 21979

22002

22004
(dog burial 22027
from this deposit)

22030
(neonate skull 22028
from this deposit)

22054

▓ deliberate infilling of Ditch 6

▓ medieval deposits

☐ modern deposits

0   5m

Figure 2.12 Ditch 6

The ditch had infilled to such an extent during this period that it measured only 1m deep and approximately 9m wide. At this point it was almost fully infilled with re-deposited chalk. Dating evidence for this occurrence was sparse, and comprised eight sherds of 1st century AD pottery from deposit 20014, which was recorded in the northern, incomplete section across the ditch.

The base of a corn-drying oven, 21830, was cut into the western edge of Ditch 6, at the northern extent of the higher ground (Figs 2.3 and 2.14). It was sub-rectangular in plan, had steep sides and a base which sloped gently downwards from west to east, and measured 2.15m long, 1.1m wide and a maximum of 0.45m deep. This feature was lined with a layer of clay, which was approximately 0.08m thick, and sealed by a silty charcoal-rich deposit from which no artefactual material was recovered. Four postholes located in close proximity were probably associated with the corn dryer. The plant remains recovered from an environmental sample taken from the drying oven were representative of cereal processing waste, although the small quantities recovered suggest that it had been cleaned out after its final use. The date of the oven is uncertain, but given its proximity to the hearth described below they may have been contemporary.

A hearth, 22058 (Figs 2.3 and 2.15), lay immediately to the east of the drying oven, and was cut into the upper fills of Ditch 6, presumably to take advantage of the shelter available in the open ditch. Despite its proximity to

Figure 2.13 Ditch 6, oblique view, looking north-west (scale 2m)

Figure 2.14 Corn dryer 21830, looking east (scale 1m)

Figure 2.15 Hearth 22058, showing deposits 22042 (in foreground) and 22041, looking south (scale 1m)

the drying oven, no stratigraphic relationship existed between the two features. The hearth was sub-circular in plan, and measured between 1.8m and 2m in diameter, and was initially constructed from clay, which had been fired hard through use, and which was retained by pebbles arranged around its edge. The hearth had been re-laid on at least three occasions. Each layer was identified by a fired clay surface and localised charcoal lenses, which had been partially raked out downslope to the east, into the open ditch. Archaeomagnetic dating undertaken on deposit 22041 of the third re-laying of the hearth, covers three possible age ranges for the date of firing at a 95% confidence interval: an Iron Age date between 450–70 BC, a Saxon date of 550–810 AD, and a post-medieval date of 1610–1730 AD. The post-medieval date is discounted on archaeological grounds (Chapter 5.II). Above this, the hearth was re-built when its level was raised slightly by the deposition of an unfired clay layer 22039, within which a single potin coin, probably issued 50–45 BC, was embedded. Gully 21837, immediately to the south-west of the hearth and parallel to the western extent of Ditch 6, may have served as a windbreak for the hearth. The Iron Age archaeomagnetic date-range of 450–70 BC does not sit comfortably either with the stratigraphic sequence of ditch fills and the dating evidence from Ditch 6, or from the hearth itself, given that the coin shows wear and is likely to be a residual item. The hearth may conceivably be a later feature, belonging to Period 6, and by association, this date may also apply to the drying oven 21830 described above.

Only three pits could be dated with any certainty to Period 4. Pit 20817 located immediately to the west of Ditch 5, was sub-circular in plan with vertical sides and a flat base, and measured approximately 1.8m in diameter. It contained three clay-silt fills, from which a small quantity of Late Iron Age pottery and a moderate quantity of animal bone was recovered. Pit 18029, at the western extent of the site, was likely to have originally been sub-circular in plan, but its eastern extent was truncated by a later pit. It measured approximately 1.16m in diameter, and had steep sides and a flat base. It had been partially infilled with chalk before being re-used for refuse disposal, and three sherds of Late Iron Age pottery, and over 1kg of animal bone, were recovered from its fill. Eight sherds of Late Iron Age pottery were retrieved from pit 20403, just east of Ditch 1, which was identified in section only, in an area of intercutting Roman and Saxon pits (Fig. 2.3). The possibility that these sherds represent residual material in a later feature should not be discounted.

Ditch 5 was likely to have still been visible in relief during Period 4, as a small quantity of Late Iron Age pottery and a Late Iron Age Colchester-style brooch (Fig. 4.1, no. 6) were recovered from the backfill layers in the ditch which sealed Period 3 weathering and silting layers.

IV. Period 5: Roman *c.* AD 70–400

Both the higher ground and the floodplain were exploited in the Roman period (Fig. 2.16), although these areas were largely agricultural in nature, with little evidence to suggest the close proximity of the settlement of Middle and Late Iron Age date. Areas 2 and 3 on the lower floodplain were utilised for the first time, when several stock enclosures were constructed on the alluvial margins on the edge of the chalk bedrock, although this area was still prone to alluvial inundation.

The Roman pottery assemblage suggests that activity on the site spanned the Roman period from *c.* 70 AD to 400 AD (Chapter 4.VIII). The high percentage of re-deposited Roman pottery reflects the levels of disturbance resulting from later activity across the site. The coarsewares which dominate the assemblage persist throughout this period, and were not helpful in providing a framework for site chronology in cases where stratigraphic relationships could not be confirmed. Greater refinement in dating was achieved where the feature assemblages contained other fabrics. Grogged wares from the mid/later 1st century AD were present in some features, most notably in the fills of Iron Age Ditch 1, while Greywares in forms influenced by Dorset Black-Burnished wares, together with some Gaulish samian imports, indicated activity centred on the 2nd century AD and continuing into the first half of the 3rd century. Later Roman activity could be identified by a higher incidence of traded finewares, and by the presence of recognisable late vessel forms, particularly jars from Harrold, north Bedfordshire, the Hadham oxidised wares, and those from the Lower Nene Valley, which included 4th-century vessel forms, and an uncommon form of platter probably datable to the second half of the 4th century. There was little in the Roman pottery assemblage to indicate higher status; the low samian component and scarcity of amphora and specialist wares was consistent with a lower-status rural community. There was a slight increase in the incidence of finewares in later Roman contexts, including those of 4th-century date, although this is considered to reflect the wider patterns of pottery supply at this time, rather than any change in status.

Analysis of animal bone indicates that the pastoral economy during Period 5 was based primarily on sheep farming, as had been the case during Periods 3 and 4.

The floodplain

There is evidence for the Roman-period exploitation of the marginal area between the edge of the chalk bedrock and the floodplain. Two distinct phases of activity were indicated by the dating evidence recovered from Area 3: the first phase had a date-range of *c.* AD 70 to *c.* AD 150, and comprised a ditch and three pits, whilst the second, later, phase dated to the late 3rd and 4th centuries and consisted of a series of agricultural enclosures. Two alluvial deposits containing a small quantity of late 3rd to 4th-century pottery lay at the southern extent of the chalk bedrock in Area 2.

The evidence for Early Roman activity was limited to Ditch 7 and a few pits, and was focused on the central northern part of Area 3, on the edge of the chalk bedrock. There was no evidence of exploitation of the wetter ground to the south in the later Roman period.

Some form of activity pre-dating the ditch, but probably broadly contemporary with it, is indicated by two small, undated pits, cut into a remnant of a buried soil and sealed by a dump of chalk, 3995 (Fig. 2.16). This may have been laid to create a firm surface to the north of the ditch. Two other pits cut by Ditch 7 contained single sherds of late 1st to 2nd-century Roman pottery in their sandy silt fills. Pit 3998, identified in section only, was 0.14m deep, whereas pit 5102 was sub-oval in plan, had gently sloped sides and a concave base 0.22m deep.

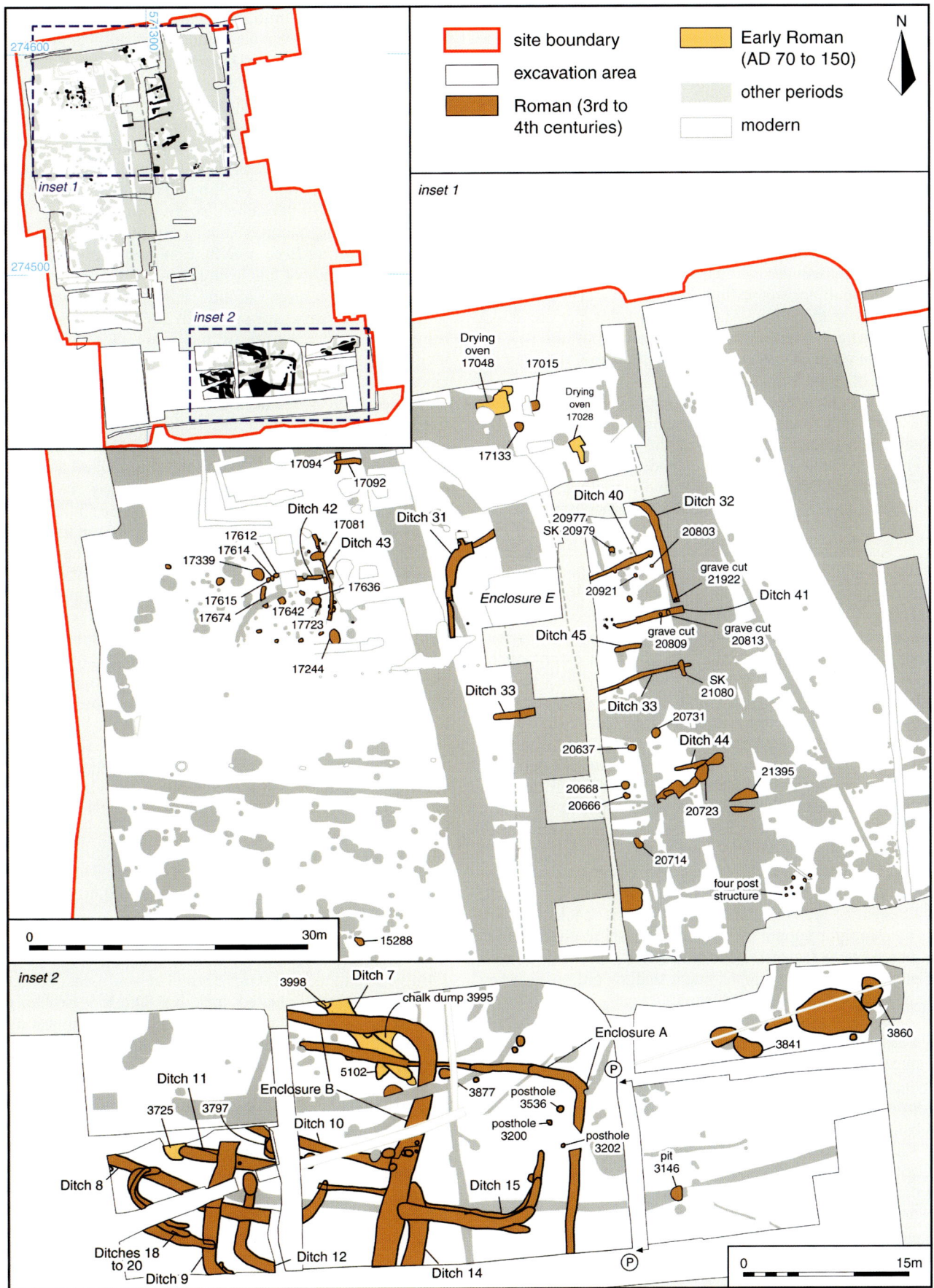

Figure 2.16 Roman Period 5

25

Ditch 7 ran on a north-west/south-east alignment, and terminated to the south-east, approximately 2m away from the edge of the natural chalk bedrock. Its northern terminus lay beyond the area of excavation. It measured between 1.8m and 2.1m wide, and a maximum of 0.75m deep, becoming deeper as it extended north, and had steeply-sloped irregular sides and an uneven base, which narrowed towards its terminus. The ditch was left to silt-up naturally, with no evidence of any re-cutting or maintenance. Some upcast chalk had washed back into the fill of the ditch, from which a total of fifteen sherds of late 1st to early 2nd-century pottery was recovered. Pottery of similar date was recovered from two small pits cut into the top of the ditch, suggesting that the ditch also fell out of use during this time. Another pit of this period, 3725, containing a single sherd of 2nd-century pottery, was cut into the edge of the chalk bedrock towards the western extent of Area 3.

After Ditch 7 fell out of use, there was no identifiable use of Area 3 until the construction of Enclosure A. A sequence of activity followed the construction of this enclosure with at least one episode of serious flooding. The pottery evidence suggests that activity spanned the late 3rd to 4th centuries, but the sequence could not be dated with any precision within that timeframe.

Enclosure A (Fig. 2.16) occupied the central part of Area 3 and, assuming that Ditch 12 formed its south-west corner, enclosed an area of approximately 30m by 20m. The northern and eastern arms of the ditch measured between 0.45m and 0.9m wide, and sloped down to a maximum of 0.41m deep at the southern extent of the enclosure. Ditch 12, cut into alluvial clay, was slightly larger, measuring between 0.8 and 1.05m wide, and 0.4m deep. All three exposed sides of the enclosure were re-cut frequently, and thus appeared to be prone to rapid silting. The western terminus of the enclosure was located on a high point of the chalk bedrock within Area 3, and the ditch had been cut to drain to the east and then the south, towards the alluvial sands and clays. A large amount of animal bone tipped into the northern enclosure ditch suggested use as a local refuse dump. Given its location on the alluvial margins at the edge of the chalk bedrock, Enclosure A was probably a stock enclosure, an interpretation supported by the paucity of internal features which could reasonably be associated with it; two small postholes, 3200 and 3202, and a shallow pit, 3877, being the only such features recorded.

In the north-eastern corner of Area 3, a series of pits were dug for chalk extraction. A large irregularly shaped pit, 3860, which measured approximately 6m by 4m, together with several smaller oval pits, had all been cut to a similar depth, around 0.3m, into the edge of the chalk bedrock. Following extraction, the pits silted up naturally with small amounts of waste, including several sherds of pottery of late 3rd to 4th-century date, which had been dumped into the open pits and was then sealed by fine-grained alluvial silty clays.

The north-western part of Area 3, which was excavated to just below the formation level required for construction, did not expose a full sequence of deposits. In this area the earliest excavated deposits comprised several dumped layers which had been steeply tipped off the edge of the chalk bedrock. This may conceivably have represented an attempt at land reclamation associated with the north-western corner of Enclosure A, although this could not be proved stratigraphically. Two pits and a short length of ditch, which were identified only in section, were cut into these dumped layers, but this does not appear to have been a long-lived or successful attempt at reclamation, as these deposits were later sealed by alluvially-derived silty clay resulting from an episode of flooding. Several other localised dumped deposits, also representing possible attempts at land reclamation, were identified in other parts of Area 3, and were sealed by alluvial deposits of the same date. Evidence suggests that frequent flooding occurred during this period (Fig. 2.21), possibly resulting from a change in course of the River Lark. The ditches of Enclosure A were sealed by thick deposits, average depth around 0.35m, of fine-grained, grey, silty clay which contained frequent chalk flecking. Similar alluvial deposits of the same date were also identified at the base of the chalk slope in Area 2. Geoarchaeological analysis of these deposits suggested their formation in a wet, low-lying environment fed by overbank flooding, with the depth of these deposits attesting to this occurring over a prolonged period of time. These deposits extended beyond the southern edge of the natural chalk in Area 3, and even sealed the chalk extraction pits in the north-east corner of Area 3. Alluvial deposits also sealed a scatter of pits, cut into both chalk and the edge of the alluvial margins, which had been used for small-scale refuse disposal, including animal bone and pottery. A small quantity of discarded cereal processing waste was recovered from a sample from pit 3146.

The alluvial margins in Area 3 were exploited again when flooding had receded. Ditch 8 (Fig. 2.16) was cut through the alluvial silts and clays, and measured a maximum of 1.15m wide and up to 0.5m in depth. It ran on a similar alignment to that of Enclosure A, but curved sharply to the north-east at its eastern extent, and terminated within the alluvial clays. Ditch 8 rapidly fell out of use, having silted up without any identifiable attempts at maintenance, and in one location appeared to have been deliberately infilled. Ditch 11, 2.5m to the north and on a similar alignment, had also been partially infilled. Both ditches may have been infilled in preparation for the construction of the ditch for Enclosure B, which cut across them.

Enclosure B (Fig. 2.16) was defined by ditches, both wider and deeper than those of Enclosure A, being up to 2.4m wide and at least 0.6m deep. The south-east corner lay beyond the excavated area but Ditch 9 probably formed the south-west corner of the enclosure, suggesting internal dimensions of approximately 25m by 15m. The medieval Ditch 43 (Chapter 2.VI) follows the alignment of the missing north-west side of the enclosure, and may have removed evidence of an earlier ditch. The northern extent of the enclosure was cut through natural chalk; the southern parts of the enclosure ditches suffered from waterlogging where they had been cut through alluvial layers. At least two phases of re-cutting of the main enclosure ditches were identified, and Ditch 14 appears to have been an attempt to drain this side of the enclosure. Moderate quantities of 3rd to 4th-century pottery and over 2kg of animal bone, mostly cow but some horse, were recovered from the fills of Enclosure B, including Ditches 9 and 14. As with the earlier enclosure, Enclosure B was probably used as a stock enclosure, which was later sub-divided by the construction of Ditch 10. Ditch 15 was added to the eastern side of the enclosure, and possibly also served to control movement of stock; posthole 3536 may relate to this function. Ditch 15 suffered the same waterlogging problems as the enclosure, and was re-cut on at least two occasions. A similar curving feature, defined by Ditches 18, 19 and 20 at the south-western extent of the enclosure, was also re-cut twice, following the effects of alluviation. A small quantity of cereal processing waste was discarded in Ditch 20.

Few features could reasonably be associated with the use of Enclosure B. Two sherds of 3rd to 4th-century pottery and a small quantity of animal bone were recovered from the silty fills of an oval pit inside the enclosure. Pit 3797 (Fig. 2.16), located towards the western side of the enclosure, contained a single sherd of late 2nd to 4th-century pottery, and was cut by Ditch 10.

The enclosure ditches, despite suffering from waterlogging and rapid silting, may have remained visible, although not in use, into the Early Saxon period (Chapter 2.V below).

The higher ground
It would appear that the area of higher ground was largely subject to agricultural exploitation during the Roman period. The number of features that can be ascribed to this period is small: two drying ovens, an agricultural enclosure, limited evidence for land division, a chalk extraction pit and a few other pits and postholes were identified. The nature of these features, and the four inhumation burials dated to this period, suggest a peripheral status for the excavated area. The small number of refuse pits (when compared to Period 3) may imply that the core settlement was no longer in such close proximity as during the Middle Iron Age. An average number of four pottery sherds per feature is notably small (see McSloy, Chapter 4.VIII), although the quantity of pottery found residually in later features implies that Roman material would have been found in greater quantities had the features of this period had not been subject to such high levels of truncation. The presence of residual Roman pottery in later features in the southern part of the higher ground is an indication that the spread of Roman activity was probably wider than the surviving features suggest. Despite the limited quantity of Roman pottery recovered, a distinct phase of 1st to 2nd-century activity could be identified, although this was confined to the central-northern extent of the site. Further refinement of chronology for Period 5 was hindered by the predominance of coarsewares. Ditch 1 was still open in the Roman period. The ditch was deliberately infilled towards its southern extent, when chalk and topsoil deposits, probably derived from surviving remnants of a bank, were pushed into the open ditch at some time in the mid to late 1st century AD. Small amounts of Roman pottery recovered from the upper fills of the same ditch, further to the north, indicated that here the ditch remained open well into the 2nd century AD.

Activity in the 1st and 2nd centuries was largely confined to a small area at the north end of the higher ground (Fig. 2.16), where two drying ovens were located in close proximity to each other. The western oven, 17048, was possibly T-shaped in plan, and had been cut into the upper fills of the corner of Ditch 1. A truncated rectangular east/west-aligned flue led to the truncated remains of a drying floor at its eastern end. A thin, charcoal-rich deposit, 17343, which contained cereal

processing waste at the eastern end of the flue, may have derived from the initial use of the oven, which appears to have collapsed soon after its initial use. The oven collapsed on at least two further occasions, with the debris from each collapse not being fully removed prior to each rebuilding. The recovery of over fifty sherds of late 1st to 2nd-century pottery, together with a quantity of animal bone recovered from these deposits, suggested that either limited refuse disposal occurred between rebuilds, or that such material was actually used in the construction. With the exception of deposit 17343, no fuel or processing residue was encountered. A stakehole, 17046, immediately to the east, probably formed part of its superstructure. The remains of a human foetus of approximately 31 weeks found within oven fill 17085 may have been re-deposited remains, possibly deriving from the upper fills of Ditch 1.

A second drying oven, 17028 (Figs 2.16 and 2.17), lay approximately 7m to the south-west of 17048. This had a rectangular flue, measuring 1.5m long, 0.65m wide and 0.45m deep, which led to a firing pit measuring 1.5m square and 0.5m deep. Both the flue and pit were lined with a compacted mixture of clay and chalk. A dark, sandy silt deposit, 17027, in the base of the square pit, contained cereal processing waste and a single fragment of animal bone, but no other finds. The oven was demolished, partially infilled with a mixture of chalk and demolition material, and then rebuilt on the same footprint as before. The rebuilt oven had a crushed chalk base, and a thin clay lining. The oven was partially infilled and then rebuilt again. Two small sherds of Roman pottery were recovered from deposits associated with this second rebuilding. With the exception of 17027, no deposits relating to fuel or processing residue were encountered.

Both drying ovens fell into disuse in the late 1st to 2nd century AD. Pottery of this date, together with a moderate quantity of animal bone, was recovered from silty clay deposits which had accumulated in the hollow left after the final collapse of 17048. Three sherds of pottery of the same date were recovered from the fill of a small pit cut through the last phase of use of 17028.

A shallow, sub-rectangular and flat bottomed pit, 17015, located to the south-east of 17048, may have represented another drying oven, although its western extent had suffered from extensive modern truncation.

Pit 17133 was located in close proximity to drying oven 17048, was circular in plan and measured 0.9m in diameter and 0.77m in depth. It had steep, slightly undercut sides typical of a storage pit, but had been used as a refuse pit before being backfilled with a mixture of chalk and clay. A small quantity of late 1st to 2nd-century pottery and animal bone was recovered.

Elements of a sub-rectangular ditched enclosure, Enclosure E (Fig. 2.16), were identified in the northern central part of the higher ground. It was formed by Ditches 31, 32 and 33, whose narrow width and discontinuous alignments were partly a result of modern truncation, and the narrow unexcavated baulks left between areas of excavation. No evidence of any re-cutting or maintenance of the enclosure ditches was observed. An area of approximately 22m by 18m was enclosed, with the western third of the enclosure lying to the west of Iron Age Ditch 1. The extent of modern truncation meant that it could not be established whether Ditch 1 in this area had been fully infilled when the enclosure was established. A

Figure 2.17 Drying oven 17028, fully excavated, looking south (scales 2m and 1m)

small amount of Roman pottery was recovered from the fills of the Enclosure E ditches, including one sherd of 2nd to early 3rd-century date, and several sherds of 2nd to 4th-century date. A probable entrance, defined by Ditches 41 and 45, lay at the south-eastern corner of the enclosure. The difficulty of recognising features cut into the upper fills of Ditch 5 in this area suggests that the entrance may have originally been more fully defined than was recognised during excavation.

The enclosure was probably used for stock management although few contemporary features were present on its interior. It was sub-divided by Ditch 40, which left a gap of just under 1m between the two parts of the enclosure. Two small undated postholes, 20803 and 20921, located immediately to the south of the ditch, possibly held a hurdle to control the movement of livestock between the two halves of the enclosure.

The location of a group of five undated stakeholes, which formed a rough circle approximately 0.9m in diameter, immediately adjacent to the western terminus of Ditch 41, suggested a likely association with Enclosure E. Four burials, identified in close proximity to each other towards the south-east corner of the enclosure, are discussed below.

Ditch 44, located 10.5m to the south of, and parallel to, the southern extent of Enclosure A was partially cut into the western side of the backfilled Ditch 5, and belonged to the same pattern of land use.

Further evidence for land division on the dry ground during Period 5 was limited to the north-west corner of the site, although similar features to the south of this may have been removed by modern truncation. Ditch 43 (Fig. 2.16) formed part of this cluster of features. The ditch ran on approximate north/south alignment for 10m, and began to curve gently to the west at its southern extent, where it was truncated by modern landscaping. It measured an average of 0.23m wide and 0.06m deep, and contained a single small sherd of Roman pottery. In several places the ditch had been cut through earlier postholes, one of which also contained a single sherd of Roman pottery, and the ditch appeared to replace an earlier fenceline. The line of posts was re-established when five postholes were cut into the top of the silty fills, one of which contained abundant slag droplets derived from ironworking (see Chapter 4.III). Four postholes (17643, 17607, 17482 and 17581) formed a semi-circular alignment at the southern end of Ditch 43, and suggested a possible southern continuation of the fenceline replaced by the later ditch. It is also possible that these postholes formed the southern arc of a roundhouse, although no such northern part could be identified. A large postpit, 17642, and two small postholes, 17636 and 17723, formed a short alignment to the west of, and parallel to, Ditch 43. Postpit 17244, 1m from the southern end of Ditch 43, was oval in plan with steep sides and a flat base, and measured 1.67m by 1.09 and 0.7m in depth. It contained chalk packing around a postpipe 0.5m in diameter. Four sherds of late 3rd to 4th-century AD pottery were recovered from the packing fills, together with one sherd of undiagnostic Roman pottery from the postpipe fills. Its location suggests an association with Ditch 43, although it was much more substantial than any other postholes in proximity.

Ditch 42 was constructed perpendicular to the west of Ditch 43, leaving a narrow gap of 0.4m between the two ditches. It was slightly wider and deeper, with silty fills which contained a single sherd of Roman pottery and abundant slag 'droplets' (Chapter 4.III). Although its western extent was removed by modern truncation, it was continued as a boundary, initially to the west and then turning to the south, by three postholes and a short length of curvilinear gully. The three postholes, 17612, 17614 and 17615 were of substantial size, measuring an average of 0.5m diameter and 0.45m in depth, and all contained displaced stone packing. The gully, 17674, was shallower, and contained a single sherd of Roman pottery.

Ditches 42 and 43, even considering the extent of modern truncation which had occurred to the south, did not define a major land division. The small size of the partially enclosed parcels of land was more characteristic of stock enclosures or possibly small agricultural structures.

A number of pits were distributed across the northern third of the higher ground, but with no readily identifiable pattern. Limited refuse disposal in several of these pits suggested that Period 5 settlement was likely to have been located to the north of the site. A large pit, 17339 (Fig. 2.16), lay adjacent to Ditch 42, and measured 1.4m long, 1.15m wide and 0.3m in depth. Two sherds of Roman pottery, 0.5kg of animal bone, and several large lumps of chalk, attested to the likely use of the pit for refuse disposal. A sub-rectangular pit, 17081, cut through the northern half of Ditch 43, and contained a small quantity of animal bone, a single sherd of 4th-century AD, or later, pottery, and a fragment of an iron knife-blade.

Four postholes defined a structure measuring 0.75m square at the south-eastern extent of the higher ground. The postholes were of fairly uniform size, measuring approximately 0.3m in diameter and 0.15m in depth, with steep sides. A single small sherd of 3rd to 4th-century AD pottery was recovered from the single fill of 20342 (not illustrated). Another four postholes, three of which formed an approximate north-east/south-west alignment, lay immediately to the east of this structure. The similar sizes of these postholes suggest a degree of spatial association.

To the south of Enclosure E were a number of pits used for refuse disposal. A large quantity of Roman pottery was recovered from the first fill of pit 20668, which was then deliberately backfilled with a mixture of chalk and re-deposited topsoil. Three pits of similar form, 20666, 20637 and 20731, located in close proximity to 20668, all contained small quantities of Roman pottery. Pit 20637 had a charcoal-rich basal fill, which contained a small amount of cereal processing residue. A large refuse pit, 21395, cut into the top of Ditch 5, contained a moderate quantity of late 3rd to 4th-century AD pottery, and over 0.7kg of animal bone.

Three intercutting pits, probably for chalk extraction, lay to the south of Ditch 44, and had been left open to infill naturally, with only small quantities of Roman pottery and animal bone recovered. The most eastern pit was cut by a refuse pit 20723 (Fig. 2.16). This was oval in plan, with steep sides and measured 1.8m along its longest axis and 0.6m deep. It contained a large quantity of early to mid-2nd-century Roman pottery, and in excess of 1.5kg of animal bone. One outlying pit, 15288, lay 25m to the west of the nearest other excavated feature of this period. It was oval in plan, with steep irregular sides and a flat base, and had two sandy, silt fills which contained a single small sherd of Roman pottery. Its apparent isolation may have largely been due to the effects of modern landscaping in

this part of the higher ground, which may have destroyed all but the deepest features.

Five burials of Period 5 were recorded on the area of dry ground, all located within 15m of each other and with a particular focus on the south-eastern corner of Enclosure E. An almost complete skeleton, 21080 (Fig. 2.28), of an adult male, was cut through the south-eastern corner of Enclosure E, and into the underlying upper fills of Ditch 5. A radiocarbon date of 81–234 AD (SUERC-48059; 1856±30BP) was obtained from the scapula. Nails recovered from the head, centre and foot area indicated the probable presence of a coffin. A single sherd of Saxon pottery recovered from the backfill sealing the burial, was considered to be intrusive, given the location of the burial on the edge of the hollow immediately to the south of Enclosure E.

Grave 21922 (Fig. 2.16) was located 5m to the north of skeleton 21080 on the same north/south alignment, and was also cut through the eastern side of Enclosure E into the underlying fills of Ditch 5. The burial (skeleton 21921) was of an older adult male, aged at least 45. The probable presence of a coffin was indicated by the recovery of ten nails from the grave fill, although their position was not recorded.

Grave 20813 contained the skeleton, 20812 (Fig. 2.28), of a younger child of 5-6 years old, and was cut into Ditch 41 of Enclosure E 2.5m to the south west of grave 21922. Unlike the two adult burials described above, grave 20813 was aligned approximately east/west. It was cut by grave slot 20809, which contained a disturbed partial neonate burial which was radiocarbon dated to 86–311 AD (SUERC-48066; 1830±30BP). The bone from this burial was not recognised as human during excavation, and was therefore not planned *in situ*. A single coffin nail was found in the fill.

Pit 20977 (Fig. 2.16), in the northern half of the enclosure, contained incomplete neonatal remains 20979. Disarticulated human bone was also recovered from the various deposits which had accumulated in the hollow to the south of the enclosure, although the exact dating of these remains was unclear, as the soil deposits which had accumulated in this hollow appeared to have been extensively re-worked in later periods.

V. Period 6: Saxon: *c.* 6th–11th centuries

Activity on the site continued throughout the Saxon period, and spanned the early, middle and later periods. The evidence for Saxon occupation of the higher ground comprised boundary ditches, a ditched enclosure, two probable drying ovens and a number of short gullies, in addition to other pits and postholes (Fig. 2.18). The eastern part of the site was associated with the densest activity. Although the north-western quarter of the site suffered less truncation than the area immediately to the south, there was a noticeable lack of features here. A number of pits and a short section of ditch were dug on the edge of the chalk escarpment and into Roman alluvial deposits on the floodplain (Fig. 2.19), but in contrast to the preceding Roman period there appear to have been no concerted attempts to enclose or drain this area, which continued to be flooded. Animal bone waste was found in large quantities in the alluvial deposits in Area 2 (Fig. 2.20).

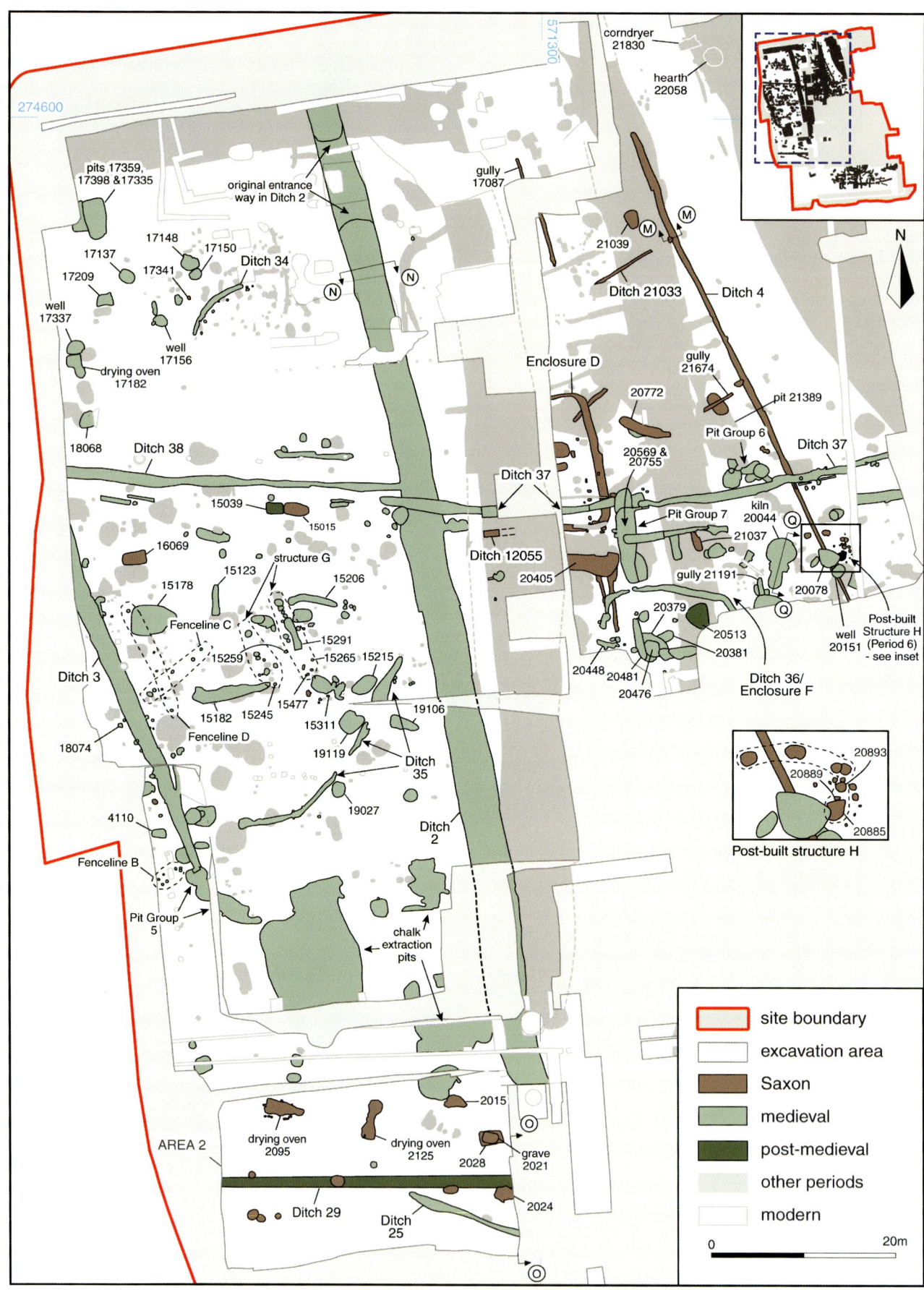

Figure 2.18 Saxon Period 6 and medieval Period 7, higher ground and Area 2

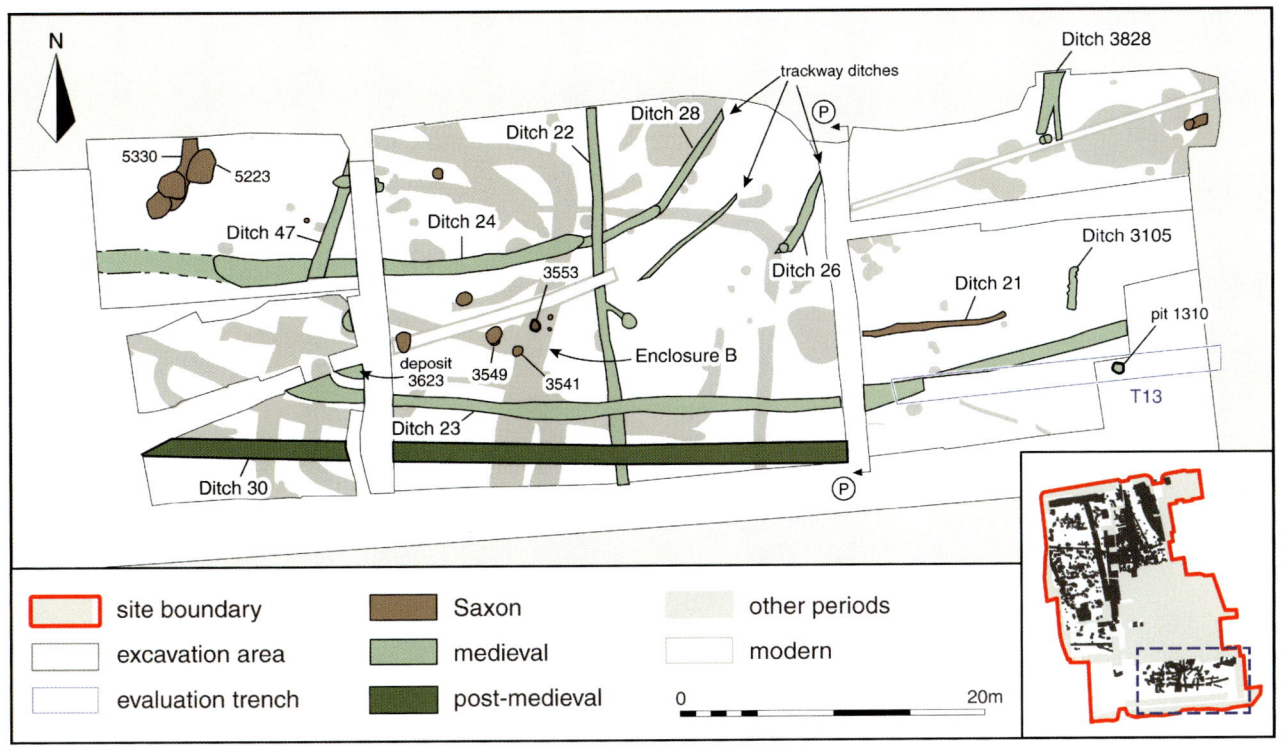

Figure 2.19 Saxon Period 6 and medieval Period 7, Area 3

Early Saxon pottery was present in a range of fabrics, including grass-tempered, sandy, calcareous and granitic-tempered sherds. Organic-tempered fabrics dominated, but there were also fairly high proportions of fine and medium sandy fabrics. Contemporary sites in Essex and Suffolk suggest that granitic-tempered pottery was probably in use during the 6th century, and organic-tempered pottery from the mid 6th century onwards. Approximately 45% of the Early Saxon pottery from this site is found in contexts assigned to the later periods, and is considered to derive from manure scatters (Chapter 4.IX), although some pits on the floodplain edge may actually be early in date.

Activity of Middle Saxon date was identified by the presence of Ipswich Ware in slightly larger quantities than the earlier Saxon material. Again, levels of residuality were high, with over 50% of Middle Saxon pottery found in later features, indicating either manuring, or the truncation of Middle Saxon features by later activity. The bulk of the Period 6 pottery recovered was of Late Saxon date, and was dominated by Thetford Ware and local variants in proportions similar to those of other local Late Saxon settlements.

The animal bone assemblage shows a distinct shift to a cattle-dominated pastoral economy in Period 6, compared to that of Periods 3 to 5.

The floodplain

Saxon activity on the floodplain was altogether less intensive than that seen during Period 5, and amounted to a single ditch and a number of pits, of which some may belong to the Early Saxon period (Fig. 2.19).

The location of a cluster of features containing late Roman or Early Saxon pottery, cut into the eastern extent of Enclosure B where it intersected with Ditch 10, suggested that Roman earthworks may still have been visible in the Saxon period. It is unlikely, however, that the enclosure was still in use, as it had extensively silted up. Two small pits, 3541 and 3553, contained small quantities of late 3rd to 4th-century or later pot. An adjacent pit, 3549, contained one sherd of 5th to 7th-century Saxon pottery. All three pits, once dug, had been left open to infill naturally. Two stakeholes, 3546 and 3548, containing the remnants of burnt stakes, were cut through the upper fill of the enclosure ditch, immediately to the east of 3553.

Ditch 21 was cut into the alluvial silts that were deposited during the later phase of Period 4 flooding (Fig. 2.21). Occupying an isolated position towards the east side of the area, its function was unclear. It ran on an east/west alignment in the eastern part of Area 3 (Fig. 2.19), measured a maximum of 0.5m wide and 0.35m deep, and contained a single sherd of Late Saxon pottery. It was left to silt up, with no sign of it having been maintained or re-cut. The ditch probably terminated under the baulk left between the eastern and central parts of Area 3, indicating a maximum length of 12.5m.

Three layers of calcareous/chalky gravel deposits, 2086, 2039 and 2096 (Fig. 2.20), had accumulated at the base of the chalk bedrock slope in Area 2, and contained massive quantities of animal bone. Approximately 19kg of animal bone, including 12kg of bovine material, was recovered from these deposits, which were of probable Late Saxon date. However, the quantity of residual Mid-Saxon and Roman pottery present in all three layers suggested that the deposition process had begun somewhat earlier. The later phase of these deposits was contemporary with the use of Enclosure D on the higher ground, and the disposal of large quantities of animal bone in pit 20405. Although these features lay almost 80m to the north, this activity may be related.

With the exception of the cluster of features described above, there was little coherent patterning evident within

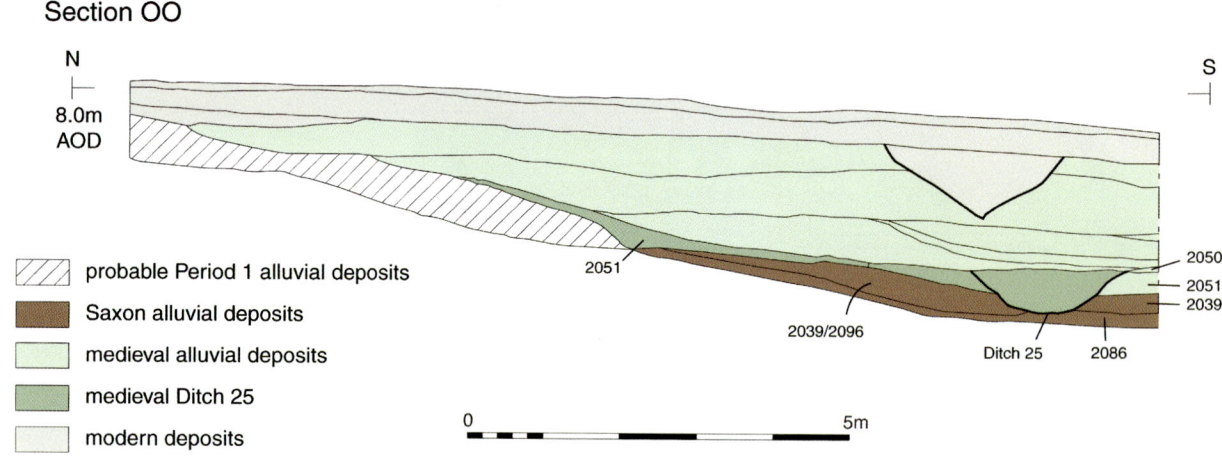

Section OO

probable Period 1 alluvial deposits

Saxon alluvial deposits

medieval alluvial deposits

medieval Ditch 25

modern deposits

2051

2050
2051
2039

2039/2096

Ditch 25   2086

0   5m

Figure 2.20 Area 2 deposit sequence

the distribution of discrete pits of Period 6 in the floodplain area. Pit 5223 (Fig. 2.19), in the north-western part of Area 3, contained a small amount animal bone and a single sherd of Late Saxon pottery, and was cut through an earlier short gully 5330, which also contained animal bone and a small amount of Mid-Saxon pottery. Seven irregular pits of Saxon date in Area 2 (Fig. 2.18) were cut through Roman alluvial layers and calcareous gravels of the edge of the chalk bedrock. One of these, pit 2024, contained a pair of iron shears and a part of a smithing-hearth cake. Five undated pits in the eastern part of Area 3 had been cut through earlier Roman alluvial deposits, were sealed by alluvial layers of medieval date, and were therefore interpreted as Saxon.

The higher ground
The only feature on the higher ground to contain exclusively Early Saxon pottery was pit 2015 (Fig. 2.18), which was located towards the southern extent of the chalk bedrock in Area 2. It contained a single small sherd (3g) of 5th to 7th-century pottery. Two other features that possibly date to this period were corn dryer 21830 and hearth 22058, discussed in Chapter 2.III, above (Figs 2.14 and 2.15). These features were cut into the slumped backfills of Ditch 6. Analysis of the spatial distribution of Early

Saxon pottery suggests a possible concentration towards the central area of the higher ground. The small quantities of pottery in question, in most cases a single sherd, limit any further inference regarding the possible focus of Early Saxon activity on the higher ground.

Ditch 4 (Figs 2.18 and 2.22) largely defined the eastern limit of activity during the Mid Saxon period. It measured at least 56m in length, and ran from its north-western terminus to beyond the excavation limit of the higher ground and had also been identified in Evaluation Trench 5. It measured up to 1m in width and 0.68m in depth, and had a steep V-shaped profile with a flat base. Several sections excavated through the deeper northern part of the ditch showed its likely use as a palisade, with chalk rubble packed around a central vertical slot. The southern half of the ditch was re-modelled in the 8th or 9th century, when it was partially infilled with chalk, and posts were re-erected in several locations. A single sherd of 8th to 9th-century pottery recovered from the uppermost silty fills suggested a possible date for the abandonment or infilling of the ditch.

Elements of land division, and a small paddock, lay to the west of Ditch 4 (Fig. 2.18). Gully 17087 lay 12m to the west of the northern part of Ditch 4 on a parallel alignment, and ran for approximately 12.5m, terminating

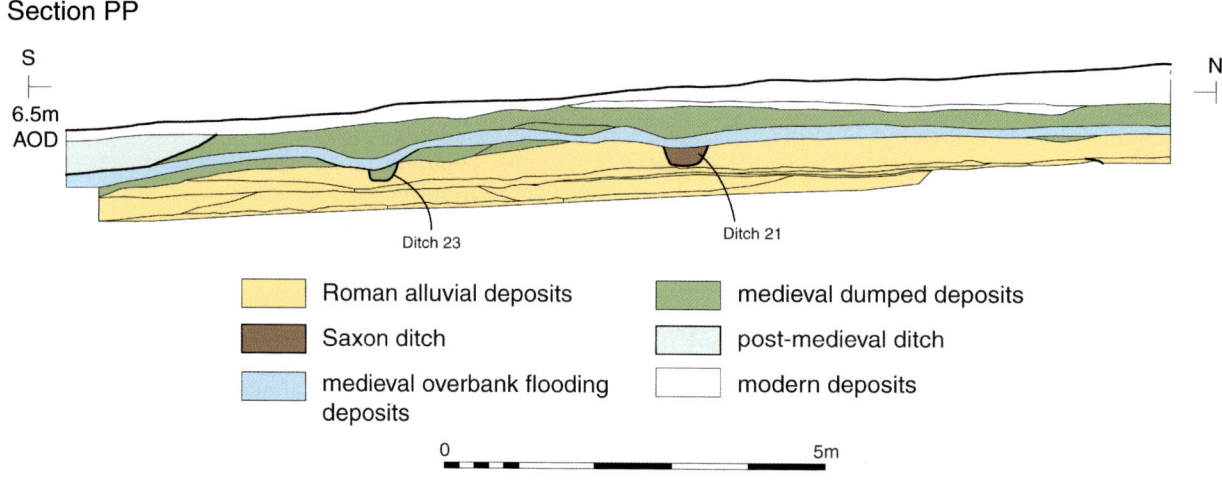

Section PP

6.5m
AOD

Ditch 23

Ditch 21

Roman alluvial deposits

Saxon ditch

medieval overbank flooding deposits

medieval dumped deposits

post-medieval ditch

modern deposits

0   5m

Figure 2.21 Area 3 deposit sequence

Figure 2.22 Ditch 4, looking north (scale 0.4m)

just to the north of the Roman Ditch 40, although it is unlikely that the latter was still visible at this time having fully silted up. Ditch 21033 lay to the south and at a right angle to gully 17087, and may have described the southern edge of a small paddock measuring approximately 16m long by 13m wide. A possible entrance, just over 2m wide, in the south-east corner of the paddock lay between the eastern extent of Ditch 21033 and a posthole, 20005 (not illustrated), immediately to the west of Ditch 4. Both gully 17087 and Ditch 21033 were undated, although a shallow gully, 21674 (Fig. 2.18), which lay approximately 18m to the south and appeared to belong to the same pattern of land management, was cut into the uppermost fills of pit 21389, which contained two sherds of Early Saxon pottery.

The northern terminus of Ditch 4, and indeed that of gully 17087, did not respect any other features of Period 6, or earlier periods. It must be assumed, therefore, that such features either lay beyond the excavated area or were removed by later activity.

Enclosure D (Fig. 2.18), located towards the centre of the higher ground, was defined by a rectilinear ditch which measured an average of 0.95m in width and 0.39m in depth. Although the full extent was not defined, an area of at least 14m by 4m was enclosed. A possible continuation of the enclosure was identified as Ditch 12055, but it is probable that the remainder of the enclosure could not be identified where it had cut through the upper chalky fills of Ditch 1, and it may also have been destroyed by the later construction of Ditch 2 in Period 7. The enclosure had been partially re-cut on its southern edge, and the lack of uniformity of the recorded profiles of other excavated sections suggested that piecemeal

maintenance had been undertaken on the rest of the ditch. Two stakeholes and a posthole immediately adjacent to the southern side of the enclosure, and a posthole cut into the enclosure ditch, further defined the enclosure. The silty ditch fills contained over 0.5kg of animal bone of mixed species, two small sherds of 10th to 11th-century pottery, and several residual sherds of Period 4 pottery, which were derived from earlier features cut by the enclosure.

An upturned cow skull placed on the base of the south-east corner of the enclosure ditch may be a deliberate deposit (Fig. 2.23). A row of six small undated postholes ran for approximately 9m just inside the eastern extent of Enclosure D on a parallel alignment. It is possible that this represents the surviving remnant of a structure. Two undated pits lay inside the enclosure. From surviving evidence, it is difficult to identify the purpose of the enclosure, which could have surrounded a domestic building or have been used for stock control. Its use may relate to pit 20405 described below.

Large pit 20405 (Fig. 2.18), to the south of Enclosure D, contained a very large quantity of animal bone, probably including the bones of a bull. Although the dating of the majority of pottery recovered suggested a slightly earlier 8th to 9th-century date, this feature may have been associated with the enclosure. The pit was an irregular, elongated oval in plan, measuring at least 5.5m in length (its full extent lying beyond the excavated area) and at least 2.3m in width, and 2.1m in depth at its westernmost excavated extent, becoming narrower and shallower towards its eastern edge. The original function of this feature was unclear; the steeply-sloped sides and narrow base displayed in its western section were more

Figure 2.23 Upturned cow skull in ditch of Enclosure D (scale 1m)

characteristic of a defensive feature than a pit excavated simply for refuse disposal or chalk extraction. If indeed it was utilised for chalk extraction, then the shallower eastern end would have provided ease of access.

Pit 20405 may have first been open in Period 5, although a single sherd of late 3rd to 4th-century pottery from its lowest fill, together with the small quantities of Roman pottery residual in later fills, may have derived from the fills of features cut by 20405. Following its initial construction, the pit was left open, and up to 0.5m of silty and chalk weathering fills accumulated in its base. A large amount of refuse, the majority of it animal bone but also including pottery and fired clay, was dumped into the open pit in the 8th and 9th centuries. The majority of the animal bone recovered was bovine, and included several skulls, one of which was deliberately placed upside down in the pit in a similar manner to that in the eastern side of Enclosure D. The pit was partially sealed with a thin deposit of chalk, and fell out of use for a period of time in which another 0.4m of silty chalk weathering fills accumulated. Refuse disposal, including the deposition of large quantities of animal bone, resumed again in the 8th and 9th centuries, and fully infilled the pit. A total of over 10kg of animal bone was disposed of in this second phase, the majority of it again bovine, but with a slightly higher proportion of sheep/goat recovered than before. A single sherd of 10th–11th century Thetford Ware, deposited during the second phase of refuse disposal, suggested that the pit was still open into the Late Saxon period, although this was the sole sherd of this date recovered.

A shallow elongated pit, 20772 (Fig. 2.18), located 3m to the east of Enclosure D, contained 1kg of animal bone,

the majority of it bovine, almost 2kg of fired clay and a small quantity of 8th to 9th-century pottery.

A drying oven, and two other features that may have served the same function, lay at the top of the chalk slope in Area 2 (Fig. 2.18). Drying oven 2095 had a rectangular flue, approximately 0.7m wide and becoming deeper from east to west, which led to a square pit almost 1.2m deep. The cut did not appear to have been lined. A line of postholes on the south side of the pit formed a windbreak, while two postholes on the northern side and one on the western side, on the edge of the construction cut, probably formed part of the superstructure. There was no scorching of the surrounding natural chalk, but two charcoal-rich silty deposits and a thin chalk spread in the deepest part of the square pit probably derived from use of the feature. No deposits lining the cut were identified. The superstructure of the feature either collapsed, or was demolished, into the cut. The resulting fill, 2091, contained over 24kg of daub, the majority bearing wattle and stake impressions. The daub fragments showed signs of having been exposed to a consistently high heat, although they did not display the evidence of vitrification that would be expected of exposure to an intense heat. Radiocarbon dates of 680–874 AD (SUERC-48050; 1245±30BP) and 721–943 AD (SUERC-48050; 1193±30BP) were obtained from a charred rye grain and field maple charcoal respectively, which were recovered from fill 2091. Following the collapse of the drying oven, the pit was backfilled with a mixture of chalk and clay. A possible robber pit was targeted on the eastern end of the backfilled pit.

A second possible drying oven, 2125, was located 7m to the east at the top of the natural chalk slope. It was aligned north-east/south-west, with a sub-rectangular flue

34

which became deeper towards the north-east and led to a larger deeper circular pit. The circular pit measured approximately 0.9m in diameter with a maximum of 0.85m in depth. It had possibly been lined with silty chalk, although the evidence for this was not conclusive, before being infilled with loose chalk. No other deposits derived from use of this feature were identified. There was no burnt material associated with the pit, and it is possible that it may not have been actually used.

A steep-sided rectangular pit, 2028 (Fig. 2.18), on the eastern side of Area 2, contained fills suggestive of a drying oven, although no there was no sign of any associated flue. The pit measured 2.5m in length, 1.5m in width and 0.7m in depth, and had a flat base. Intermittent remains of a clay lining in the base of the pit were sealed by silty charcoal-rich fill 2035 up to 0.13m deep at its eastern extent. The pit was possibly re-lined with light brown clay, which sealed 2035, and contained 8.7kg of daub fragments, many of which bore stake and wattle impressions. A second charcoal-rich silt layer, 2027, appeared to have accumulated in the pit after it was re-lined. The three contexts described above all displayed the regular profiles of deposits which had accumulated through use of the feature, rather than material which had simply been tipped into the open pit. The final fill, 2020, up to 0.5m depth of clean yellow clay, filled the pit to the level of the surviving natural chalk. However, the clay deposit was very clean and homogenous for a dumped levelling deposit, and could plausibly represent a substantial rebuilding of the feature. A grave cut into this deposit hampered further interpretation.

Both 2095 and 2125 contained significant quantities of cereal processing waste and charcoal, predominantly of alder or hazel, while no sample was recovered from 2028. Similar waste deposits, albeit on a smaller scale, were recovered from several pits located within 10m of the drying ovens on the edge of the higher ground.

Grave 2021 (Figs 2.18 and 2.28), was cut through deposit 2020, and contained the extended inhumation, 2019, of an adolescent female aged between 17 and 18. The location of the grave may have been deliberate. Although on a slightly different alignment, it was fully contained within the original pit. The backfill of the grave contained a single small sherd of residual pottery of probable Roman date.

Although oven 2095 was the only one of the three to produce definitive evidence of a Period 6 date, the similarity in location and function of features 2028 and 2021 indicates that they were probably contemporary with 2095. A chalk extraction pit, 2015, located close to 2028 and 2125, contained a small quantity of animal bone and pottery of Early Saxon date.

With the exception of these features located on the upper edge of the chalk slope, the western half of the higher ground was largely devoid of Period 6 features. Modern truncation may partly account for this, although earlier shallow features survived in the north-western area. The fills of pit 17341 (Fig. 2.18) and postholes 17634 and 17119 (not illustrated) all contained single sherds of Late Saxon pottery, and were the only evidence for Saxon activity in the north-western part of the higher ground, and their distribution did not form any discernible pattern. Two large rectangular pits, 15015 and 16069 (Fig. 2.18) further south, contained small quantities of 10th to 11th-century pottery and animal bone.

Elements of a post-built structure H lay in the south-east corner of the higher ground. A cluster of small and large postholes, representing two phases of construction, appear to define the north-east corner of a building, which may have been open to the west. Any southern half of the structure had been cut away by several Period 7 pits. The earlier phase of nine small postholes comprised an ill-defined structure enclosing an area of at least 2.1m by 1.2m. The easternmost three postholes and the westernmost two postholes measured an average of 0.1m in diameter, and 0.1m in depth, with vertical sides and a pointed base. The middle four postholes were slightly larger, measuring between 0.2m and 0.3m in diameter and 0.15m and 0.24m in depth, and had steep sides with a flat base. It could not be determined whether two postholes, 20889 and 20893, represented an internal part of this structure, or were in fact part of the later post-built structure. The fill of stakehole 20883 contained a single sherd of, presumably residual, Middle Iron Age pottery.

The original structure was replaced by a slightly larger structure extending to the north. The new structure was more substantial, and was defined by larger postholes measuring an average of 0.6m in diameter and 0.5m in depth, with steep or vertical sides and flat bases enclosing a larger area of at least 3.6m by 2.3m. As with the earlier structure, the southern half appeared to have been removed by later features. No packing materials survived within the postholes, although posthole 20885 contained a single small sherd of Late Saxon pottery. Dating evidence to support the phasing of these two structures was not conclusive, consisting of a single sherd of pottery. However, if these features are indeed of Late Saxon date, then their location to the east of Ditch 4 is consistent with the ditch falling out of use by the Late Saxon period.

Several other Period 6 pits were located in the eastern half of the higher ground although their distribution did not form any recognisable pattern. A small amount of 5th to 7th-century pottery recovered from the upper fill of a large Period 3 pit, 21389 (Fig. 2.3), suggested that it was still visible as a feature in the landscape in the Early Saxon period. Pits 21039 and 21037 (Fig. 2.18) were both cut into the upper fills of Ditch 5, and contained a small quantity of Late Saxon pottery and animal bone.

Ditch 1 may still have been visible as a hollow in the landscape in the early part of Period 6, although the provenance of a single Early Saxon sherd recovered from the upper fills of the ditch was uncertain.

VI. Period 7 Medieval: *c.* later 11th–16th centuries

Period 7 saw more intensive and organised activity than was seen during the preceding Saxon period (Figs. 2.18 and 2.19). On the floodplain, a process of deliberate land reclamation occurred, and was followed by elements of a later field system. On the higher ground, medieval activity comprised a major boundary ditch, a smaller ditch aligned parallel to this, a probable kiln, several agricultural enclosures formed by shallow ditches, a large number of pits, and an area of chalk extraction.

The dating evidence recovered suggests that activity continued from the later Saxon period through to the medieval period, with a large proportion of the pottery assemblage comprising material of later 11th to 13th-century date, with only a few diagnostic sherds of 14th-century date. This apparent decline in use of pottery from the 14th century onwards reflects a more general decline in settlement activity in this period. Only a small number of features dated to the 15th or 16th centuries were identified.

The higher ground

Towards the north end of the site it was apparent that Ditch 6 was still visible as a feature in the landscape in Period 6 where the backfilling of the ditch in Period 4 had subsided leaving a hollow. Topsoil, which formed over the ditch fills and hearth 22058 in the northern extent of the ditch, contained six sherds of 12th-century pottery and animal bone, whilst a similar topsoil accumulation excavated to the south of this contained twelve sherds of 13th to 14th-century pottery. There was some difficulty in constructing a chronology for the activity recorded on the higher ground. The small amount of dating evidence available from Ditches 2 and 3 indicates that these were in use by the 13th century, but it is not clear at what date they were originally established. It is possible that some of the features with 11th to 12th, or 11th to 13th-century dating may pre-date this land division. These include a kiln and several intercutting pits on the east side of the site, and in the north-west, a curvilinear ditch and associated postholes, a well and several other discrete pits.

A major boundary, Ditch 2, lay on a north-north-west/ south-south-east alignment, running almost parallel to the Middle Saxon Ditch 4. It was cut into the natural chalk, and measured an average of 4m in width and 1.6m in depth. It had steeply-sloped sides and a flat base (Figs 2.24 and 2.25). The south end of the ditch appeared to narrow towards the limit of excavation in Area 2, and may have terminated a few metres beyond it.

Section NN

Figure 2.24 Ditch 2, cut 17295

The ditch was initially constructed with an entrance-way 7.8m wide (Fig. 2.18), defined by two termini located towards its northern extent. Following the initial construction, the ditch was left open, probably for a short period, during which time silting and weathering deposits accumulated in the base of the ditch. The entrance through the northern part of the ditch was closed off by the construction of a short length of ditch to join together the two termini. A single sherd of 12th to 14th-century pottery from the fill of the re-modelling cut was the only piece of dating evidence recovered to indicate a likely date for the construction of the ditch. There was no *in situ* survival of any bank associated with Ditch 2, although the profile of chalk-rich backfill deposits indicated its probable location to the west of the ditch (Fig. 2.25).

Figure 2.25 Ditch 2, looking south (scale 2m)

The ditch was not in use for a long period of time before being backfilled, probably in the 13th century. Chalk-rich backfill deposits lay only 0.2m from the base of the ditch, and no signs of re-cuts or maintenance were apparent. A small amount of topsoil, containing 12th to 13th-century pottery, was dumped into the ditch from the eastern side. Several chalk-rich deposits tipping into the ditch from the western side, probably derived from demolition of the bank associated with the ditch. The pottery recovered from the backfill deposits included sherds of 13th-century date together with some residual 10th to 11th-century and earlier pottery.

Ditch 3 (Fig. 2.18) lay approximately 30m to the west of Ditch 2 on a broadly parallel alignment to the Saxon Ditch 4. The southern terminus, located towards the south-western extent of the higher ground, appeared to curve slightly to the east, although it was truncated by later pits of Period 7. The profile, V-shaped to the north, became steeper-sided and flatter-based towards the south, where the ditch became narrower and shallower. The variability suggested piecemeal construction or localised re-cutting. The sandy-silt fills of the ditch contained 11th to 13th-century pottery, together with sherds of Roman and prehistoric pottery, which probably derived from earlier features cut by Ditch 3.

Four postholes (not illustrated) were cut into upper fills of Ditch 3, with approximately six more located immediately adjacent to either side of the ditch. Eleven small sherds of 12th to 14th-century pottery contained within the fills of the postholes suggested that they were contemporary with, and further defined, the boundary formed by Ditch 3. Six small, undated postholes formed fenceline D (Fig. 2.18), which was 12m in length and ran on a parallel alignment 3m to the east of Ditch 3. Five postholes were cut into the fills of the eastern terminus of the ditch, but their distribution did not form any readily identifiable pattern.

The dating evidence recovered was too ambiguous to determine any chronology of construction and use between Ditches 2 and 3, although the latter certainly appeared to have been maintained and used for a longer period of time. The construction of such a major, though short-lived, boundary as Ditch 2 did not act as delineation for contemporary 13th-century activity. Features dating from the 12th century through to the 14th century were present on both sides of the ditch. Both ditches had fallen out of use by the 14th century, at the latest.

A cluster of features denoting activity in the early medieval period was found to the east of Ditch 2 towards the south of the excavated area. The most notable feature, kiln 20044 (Figs 2.18, 2.26 and 2.27), was key-shaped in plan, and located towards the south-eastern extent of the higher ground. The whole feature measured 5.8m in length, and 3.2m at its widest point, and was cut into the chalk to a depth of 1.3m.

The kiln chamber consisted of a large circular pit approximately 3.15m in diameter and 1.2m in depth. It had steep sides, which were stepped in two places, and a flat base. The first step was flat, measured 0.25m in width, and was cut into the natural chalk approximately 0.45m from the base of the pit. A second step, also flat and 0.25m wide, was cut into the side of the pit, 0.95m from its base. The first lining, 21016, of the pit was constructed from a white-grey sandy silt and densely packed chalk, which was placed directly on the lowest step. It was contem-porary with the flue block, 21015, which was constructed from crushed chalk and chalky cement-like material placed in the gap between the rake-out pit and the circular pit which formed a flue 0.4m in diameter.

The kiln was re-lined with another compacted chalk deposit, 20219, which filled in the earlier step in the side of the pit, and survived to the height of the upper step (Fig. 2.27). It also raised the height of the flue-block by at least 0.45m, and showed scorch marks on its outer surface. The kiln was re-modelled for a second time with the addition of another compacted chalk lining, 20220 and 20270, which was constructed to the height of the upper step in the side of the pit, displayed scorching on its outer surface and contained two sherds of 12th-century pottery. The circular pit was fully cleaned out after it was utilised for the final time, and was backfilled to the top of the surviving natural substrate with loose chalk rubble.

The rake-out pit, or stoking channel, an elongated oval in plan, measured 3m in length, a maximum of 2m in width and 1.3m in depth. It is possible that this feature may have been roofed to form a tunnel. Two deposits of material raked out from the kiln lay in the base of the channel. The earlier of these deposits, 20047, had largely been cleaned out, and survived only at the southern end of the channel, and in the flue-hole leading into the circular pit. Dating evidence retrieved from this deposit consisted of a single small sherd (1g) of 10th to 11th-century pottery, charcoal which was radiocarbon-dated to 1033–1204 AD (SUERC-48067; 910±30BP), and charred barley seeds which were radiocarbon-dated to 1445–1633 AD (SUERC-48068; 377±30BP). Given the concordance between the pottery and the charcoal dating, it must be assumed that the charred barley is an intrusive material that entered the feature following its abandonment. A small chalk collapse at the southern edge of the channel, possibly from its superstructure, sealed 20047 and was then in turn sealed by a second rake-out deposit, 20071 with a similar charcoal content to 20047, containing three small residual sherds of Roman pottery and a small quantity of animal bone. The generally uniform depth of this deposit, around 0.08m, was formed when the pit was cleaned out for a final time. Following this, the pit became redundant and was backfilled with re-deposited chalk to the top of the surviving natural substrate. The material used to backfill the pit contained two sherds of Roman pottery. A shallow gully, 21191, located to the south-west of kiln 20044, may have acted as a windbreak, or as drainage.

The exact purpose of the kiln was not clear; no waste deposits of lime were identified in the surrounding features, although a lime kiln is the most probable interpretation, given its internal surviving structure (discussed in Chapter 6.IV). The charcoal recovered from environmental samples from the kiln was dominated by alder/hazel with a small proportion of oak present. Considering the similarity of the recovered charcoal to that of cereal processing waste seen elsewhere, one other possible, though tentative, use of the kiln was for cereal processing, although none of the medieval pits in the vicinity contained any processing residue. Well 20151 (Fig. 2.18), which lay approximately 5m to the east, may have been associated with the kiln as it contained twelve sherds of 12th to 13th-century pottery, a date broadly consistent with the earlier of the two radiocarbon dates obtained from the kiln.

Figure 2.26 Kiln 20044 with lining 20219, looking south-west (scales 2m and 1m)

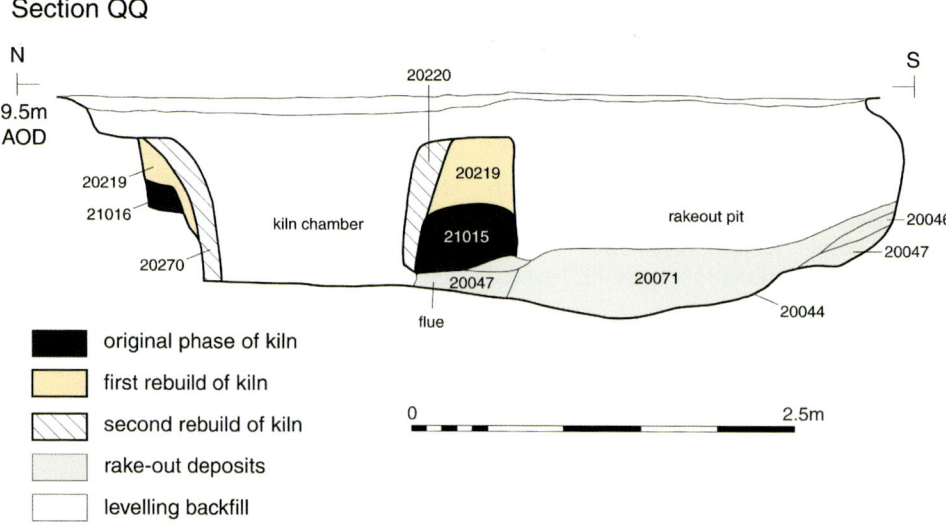

Figure 2.27 Kiln 20044

An area of seven intercutting circular and sub-circular pits (*Pit Group 6*, Fig. 2.18) lay 7m to the north of the kiln. The largest of these measured 2m in width, 1m in depth, and had steep sides, although other pits within this group were smaller and shallower. Four small sherds of 11th to 14th-century pottery, and a small quantity of animal bone, were contained within the silty pit-fills.

Pit Group 7 comprised an area of intercutting pits, all on the same north/south alignment and located approximately 15m to the west of the kiln. Two pits were sub-rectangular in plan with steep sides and flat bases, although other pits were more irregular in profile and plan. The largest pit, 20569, measured approximately 7m in length and 2m wide and had been extensively used for refuse disposal, containing over 2kg of 12th to 13th-century pottery, 1.4kg of animal bone and 0.4kg of oyster shell. Other pits contained smaller, although still substantial, quantities of the same material. The pits all contained silty-clay fills formed through refuse disposal and soil formation, with no evidence for any deliberate backfilling or levelling. Their relative proximity to kiln 20044 suggests that they may have originally been dug as quarry pits to provide chalk with which to construct the kiln linings.

A complex area of intercutting medieval pits lay inside Enclosure F, but probably pre-dated its construction and use (Fig. 2.18). These pits, which were dated to the 12th–14th century appear to have been used for refuse disposal, in particular one of the latest in the sequence, pit 20476 which was sub-circular in plan, with steep sides and a flat base. It contained a large quantity of 12th to 13th-century pottery and animal bone, and was backfilled with chalk to the top of the surviving natural. It was cut by gully 20481 which may have been part of the later enclosure.

Ditch 36, which formed the northern half of Enclosure F was partially segmented and sinuous in nature. It had a single sandy-silt fill which contained three sherds of 12th to 13th-century pottery and a small quantity of animal bone. An area of at least 18m in width was enclosed, although the full extent of the enclosure lay beyond the excavated area (Fig. 2.18). Several postholes and two short lengths of gully, 20448 and 20481, appeared to relate to a sub-division or possible entrance way broadly contemporary with the construction of the rest of the enclosure. Several small postholes within the enclosure did not form any readily identifiable pattern, but possibly formed internal features related to stock management.

To the west of Ditch 2 within the area bounded by Ditch 3, modern truncation had affected the survival of features. A focus of early medieval activity was located in the north-west part of the higher ground, but the apparent concentration of features there, and a dearth of evidence of activity immediately to the south, may partly reflect the differential levels of modern truncation in this part of the site.

Ditch 34 (Fig. 2.18) was curvilinear in plan, and a shallow 0.1m in depth. It had evidence of at least one posthole cut into its base and a single sandy-silt fill which contained a small quantity of 11th to 13th-century pottery. Eight small postholes ran along the eastern side of Ditch 34, and together with the ditch these may represent the truncated remains of a small stock enclosure, or alternatively a screening wall for some kind of craft or activity. Although there are no features surviving to the east, small deposits of slag and hammerscale were found in Ditch 2 to the east, and in the backfill of some features to the west (*i.e.* well 17156, drying oven 17182).

A number of features survived to the north and west of Ditch 34 (Fig. 2.18). The drying oven 17182, located near the west edge of the excavation, comprised a sub-rectangular flue, 1.5m in length by 1m in width, which led to a square pit to the north, measuring 1.6m by 1.5m. It had been lined on at least two occasions with a compacted sandy chalk, although no associated superstructure survived. The second phase of lining contained a single small sherd of 11th to 12th-century pottery. The pit, which resulted from the later demolition or robbing of the feature, had infilled naturally with a mixture of silty chalk and sand, and contained a single small sherd of 10th to 11th-century pottery.

A few metres to the west of Ditch 34 was well 17156, 1.4m in diameter. Hand excavation to a depth of 1.1m, followed by mechanical excavation to over 4m in depth, failed to find its base. The earliest hand-excavated fills, 17227 and 17228, derived from collapse of the sides of the well, and contained a single large sherd of 11th-century pottery. These deposits were sealed by topsoil-rich fills formed when the well was used for refuse disposal in the 12th century. A later well, 17337, may have been dug as a replacement at this time. Analysis of environmental samples taken from well 17156 indicated the presence of cess waste (Chapter 5.VIII).

Pit 17148 was sub-circular in plan, with steep sides and an uneven base, and measured 1.7m in diameter and a maximum of 0.46m in depth. It had a single dark-brown sandy-silt fill, which contained five small sherds of 11th to 12th-century pottery and a small quantity of animal bone and fired clay. This pit was one of a group of similarly-sized pits in the area, including 17137, 17150, and 18068. Pit 17209 contained sandy-silt fills and a single sherd of slightly later, 13th to 14th-century pottery.

Towards the south of the area between Ditches 2 and 3, Ditch 35 enclosed an area of short gullies, pits and postholes. Its north-east terminus lay 3m to the west of Ditch 2, and it is possible that the two ditches were not contemporary, in view of the likely size of the bank associated with Ditch 2 on its western side. Ditch 35 was not of a particularly uniform width (0.15m to 0.3m) or depth (0.1m to 0.5m), and contained silty fills which had accumulated in the 12th and 13th centuries with no evidence of deliberate backfilling. Three stakeholes cut into the centre of the southernmost segment further defined the boundary formed by Ditch 35. The location and change in alignment of the ditch could not readily be explained by contemporary features in the vicinity, although the ditch does appear to effectively divide the chalk extraction pits from the activity to the north.

Fenceline B, at the southern end of Ditch 3, consisted of a double alignment of postholes, set 0.5m apart, at a right angle to the western side of Ditch 3. The postholes were all between 0.25m and 0.3m in diameter, and no deeper than 0.12m. A modern disturbance in the centre of the fenceline likely removed more postholes.

Two parallel post and pit alignments, located centrally between Ditches 2 and 3, formed a stock management feature or a possible structure (G). Each alignment measured approximately 9m in length, and was defined by postholes and pits, at intervals of approximately 4m, dated by a small amount of 12th to 13th-century pottery in the postholes of the eastern alignment. Several pits and postholes (15245, 15259, 15265 and 15477) in the immediate vicinity contained small quantities of carbonised cereal remains suggesting the possibility that cereals may have been stored or processed in the structure. Ditch 15182, fenceline C, and other postholes in the area suggest that insubstantial structural remains possibly extended from structure G to the west.

Two other irregular lengths of ditch, 15123 and 15206, contained Period 7 pottery but did not form any coherent pattern.

A group of twelve pits, Pit Group 5, clustered together towards the southern extent of Ditch 3 were utilised for refuse disposal in the 12th and 13th centuries. These were sub-circular or oval in plan, between 1.6m and 1.9m in length, 0.6m and 1.4m in width, up to 0.9m in depth and all had flat bases. Small-scale refuse disposal, including animal bone and pottery, (for instance thirty-one sherds of 12th-century pottery from the fill of pit 4110), took place while soil was forming in the open pits. The boundary defined by Ditch 3 had probably become redundant as several of the pits were cut through the ditch.

Chalk extraction took place to the south of Ditch 3. The areas of extraction were characterised by shallow intercutting amorphous pits, which contained dark silty-clay fills. The concentration of these pits, towards the southern extent of the dry ground in an area of few other medieval features, may have been the product of deliberate zoning of activities during this period. Their re-use for refuse disposal in the 12th to 14th centuries was attested by approximately ninety sherds of medieval pottery and over 1kg of animal bone recovered. Of particular interest was a fragment of a bone comb with four surviving iron rivets, which was recovered from pit fill 19000.

Several other pits were also present in the southern half of the higher ground. Four large, irregular pits (19106, 19119, 15215 and 15311), located in close proximity either side of Ditch 35, were potentially earlier than Ditch 35 as they contained small quantities of 11th to 12th-century pottery and animal bone. Pit 15215 contained a fragment of crucible in Stamford Ware, with external sooting, but no metalworking residues. Large pit 15178, further west by Ditch 3, had steep sides and a flat base. It had infilled gradually through a combination of weathering, refuse disposal and soil formation, and contained in excess of thirty sherds of 13th to 14th-century pottery and 0.7kg of animal bone.

The pattern of land division of the dry-ground area was re-defined in the 13th or 14th century by an east/west-aligned boundary defined by Ditches 37 and 38. There was little activity to the north of this new boundary that was demonstrably later than the 13th century.

Ditch 37 lay on an east/west alignment in the south-eastern part of the higher ground, and continued to the west of the backfilled Ditch 2, which it had been cut through. It had an irregular profile measuring between 0.1m and 0.2m in width, and between 0.1m and 0.37m in depth. Only one re-cut was identified in the sections excavated, suggesting a lack of maintenance undertaken on the ditch. It became infilled gradually, with a sandy-silt deposit which contained pottery of 13th-century date.

Ditch 38 represented a western continuation of the boundary defined by Ditch 37. Its eastern terminus could not be identified in the backfill of Ditch 2, although it did not continue to the east. It was of similar size and width to

Ditch 37 and displayed the same irregularity in profile. No artefactual material was contained in its sandy silt fills.

Elements of a trackway were defined by several short lengths of ditch aligned parallel to the south of Ditches 37 and 38. Several postholes close to the southern edge of Ditch 37 may represent a fenceline. The limited dating evidence retrieved further suggests that the boundary defined by Ditches 37 and 38 was in use during the 13th and 14th centuries.

Medieval activity which post-dated the 14th century was limited to the north-west corner of the higher ground (Fig. 2.18). Two similar sized sub-rectangular pits, 17359 and 17398, both had vertical sides and flat bases, and measured around 1.7m in length, 0.8m in width and 0.75m in depth. Both had fills, which appeared to have formed through a combination of refuse disposal and soil formation and which contained 15th to 16th-century pottery, moderate amounts of animal bone and a small quantity of fired-clay fragments. They had both been infilled to the top of the surviving natural chalk before they were cut by pit 17335. This was very similar in form and size to the two earlier pits, but measured 1.15m in depth. It became infilled by the same process, and contained thirteen sherds of 15th to 16th-century pottery, 0.6kg of animal bone and a small quantity of fired clay. The regularity and similarity of form of the three pits suggests a common purpose, although any use of the pits beyond refuse disposal was not reflected in the artefactual material retrieved. Well 17337, located 11m to the south of the three pits, contained fifteen sherds of 13th to 16th-century pottery in its uppermost exposed fill, suggesting that it may have remained open into the later medieval period.

The floodplain

The floodplain area was subject to some localised land reclamation at this time, and a field system was established (Fig. 2.19). Alluvial deposits sealing medieval features suggested that the area continued to suffer the same flooding problems that had occurred during Periods 5 and 6. In keeping with the higher ground, the majority of the dating evidence recovered was later 11th to 14th-century in date, with a distinct decline in activity evident after the 14th century.

A trackway leading to the floodplain was defined by three narrow, shallow ditches on a north-east/south-west alignment, which cut through alluvial deposits at the northern end of Area 3. These appear to be the earliest recorded features following the period of alluvial inundation. The silty-clay fills which accumulated in the ditches contained small quantities of residual Roman pottery, and Ditch 26 contained a 4th-century *nummus*. A later ditch, Ditch 24, extended Ditch 28 in a westerly direction.

An attempt was made to extend the drier ground formed by the southern edge of the natural chalk in parts of Area 3, which appeared to post-date the trackway. Chalk and sand-rich deposits were dumped on the edge of the chalk, although the majority of such deposits, where identified in section, were on a small scale. The profile of one such deposit, 3623 (Fig. 2.19), indicated an attempt to form a rudimentary bank to combat water ingress. The dating evidence recovered from the dumped deposits gave a broad 11th to 14th-century date for this activity.

These measures were at least partially successful in reclaiming land as a system of ditches, no doubt serving both for drainage and to divide the land into fields, was dug into these deposits. Ditch 22 ran on a north/south alignment for at least 25m, had steeply sloped sides with a flat base, and measured an average of 0.55m in 0.44m in depth. It had a single, silty fill, and did not appear to have been maintained. Ditch 23 lay on an east/west alignment in the southern half of Area 3, and cut Ditch 22. It measured an average of 1.4m in width and 0.23m in depth, and had a shallow, uneven profile. Two other north/south-aligned ditches, 3105 and 3828, in the eastern part of Area 3, may be remnants of the same field system.

The lower part of the field system became inundated by episodes of overbank flooding in the 12th and 13th centuries, and Ditch 23, the southern half of Ditch 22, and Ditch 3105 became infilled by dark-brown humic silt (Fig. 2.21). Geoarchaeological analysis of these deposits indicated their likely formation in a wet low-lying floodplain environment, with areas of standing water fed by overbank flooding (Chapter 5.VII). Similar deposits also sealed earlier dumped deposits in the western part of Area 3.

The field system may have been re-aligned further upslope, probably in response to rising water levels, when Ditch 24 (Fig. 2.19) was constructed along the southern edge of the natural chalk. The eastern terminus of the ditch was cut through Ditch 28, and ran for 30m on an east/west alignment beyond the western extent of Area 3. It had moderately sloped sides and a concave base, and measured an average of 1.5m in width and approximately 0.5m in depth. It contained thirty-eight sherds of 13th-century pottery and a large amount of fired clay fragments derived from dumping of waste from some form of industrial processing. Ditch 47, cut through the material dumped into Ditch 24, may be a sub-division of the re-located field system.

Further dumping of material occurred in the north-western part of Area 3 during the 13th and 14th centuries. This sealed Ditches 24 and 47, and was probably undertaken in response to rising water levels, although the particularly pronounced edge of the natural chalk may have offered a convenient location for the tipping of refuse. A dark, blackened deposit, containing charcoal and fired clay, probably derived from the same source as the material tipped into Ditch 24.

The area at the base of the chalk slope in Area 2 also saw alluvial deposition from flooding during Period 7 (Fig. 2.20). A sandy floodplain alluvium, 2051, extended approximately half-way up the chalk slope, and contained a single sherd of 11th to 12th-century pottery. It was sealed by a dark, grey-black, fine-grained humic silt, 2050, whose character suggested deposition by slow-moving bodies of water. Environmental samples recovered from these two deposits contained discarded cereal remains and chaff, which had probably been processed on higher, drier ground, with processing waste subsequently disposed of in the marginal wetland area.

A brief period of drier conditions in Area 2 followed this. Ditch 25 (Figs 2.18 and 2.20) was cut through deposit 2050, and its location and alignment were suggestive of a boundary running along the lower edge of the chalk slope. A small posthole, located 4.5m to the north-west, may have continued the boundary formed by the ditch. Several

other small pits, which were devoid of artefactual material, were also cut through 2050.

Ditch 25 and the pits cut through 2050 were sealed by further alluvial deposits in the mid-12th to 13th century (Fig. 2.20). An undated pit was cut through this, and was sealed by further alluvial clay silts which contained two sherds of 15th to 16th-century pottery.

VII. Period 8: Post-medieval: *c*. 16th–19th centuries

Activities that could readily be attributed to Period 8 were limited, particularly compared to those identified in Period 7. A total of thirty-two sherds were grouped as late medieval or post-medieval in date, a third of which were glazed red earthenwares. Patterns of distribution suggest that the majority of these arrived on the site as a result of night-soil disposal. Only a few features could be ascribed to this period. It is difficult to assess the amount of post-medieval information lost to modern truncation, although the paucity of post-medieval features identified on site, suggests that any Period 8 activity was not on a particularly large scale.

Two ditches, approximately correlating with the boundaries shown on 19th and 20th-century mapping, ran on parallel east/west alignments in Areas 2 and 3 (Figs 2.18 and 2.19). Ditch 29 was cut through a dumped deposit of Period 8 and alluvial deposits which had accumulated at the edge of the chalk bedrock during Period 7. The ditch measured approximately 2.2m in width, with steep sides, and had a single, sandy-silt fill which contained two sherds of 16th to 18th-century date. No signs of ditch maintenance were visible.

Ditch 30 was cut through dumped deposits of Period 7. It was very similar in profile and size to Ditch 29, and did not appear to have been subject to any maintenance.

Ditches 29 and 30 correspond to a pair of parallel, east/west-aligned boundaries which were first depicted on Young's Map of Mildenhall of 1834 (EF 505/1/82), and were still shown on the 1970 Ordnance Survey map (Old-Maps 2014). Three isolated pits containing post-medieval pottery were located on the dry ground. Pit 15039, was sub-rectangular in plan, and measured 1.9m in length, 1.2m in width and 0.6m in depth. It contained two sherds of 16th to 18th-century pottery and several sherds of Period 7 pottery. Pit 16122, visible in section only (not shown), contained two chalky silt fills. The latter of these, 16124 contained a single sherd of 16th to 18th-century pottery, together with several residual Period 3 and Period 7 sherds which were derived from the earlier features through which the pit had been cut. A wide, shallow, circular pit, 20513, was cut into the upper fills of Ditch 5 at its southern extent. It was filled by three chalk-rich sandy-silt fills, the second of which, 20515, contained two sherds of 17th to 19th-century pottery plus twelve sherds of residual Period 3 pottery probably derived from the upper fills of Ditch 5.

The paucity of features on site, and the small amount of artefactual evidence retrieved from this period, indicated that the site principally comprised open fields during this time. This interpretation corresponds to the 19th-century cartographic depictions of the site.

VIII. Grave catalogue
by Tim Havard and Jonny Geber

The grave catalogue is arranged by period. Animal bone recovered from grave fills has been omitted from this report, as there was no evidence to suggest any deliberate deposition within graves. A full osteological catalogue of the human remains can be found in Appendix 1.

Period 3: Iron Age

Skeleton no. 21386, (Fig. 2.28)
Grave: grave 21305 cut into basal fills of Ditch 5. Grave fills 21306, 21310.
Burial: position not known; 10% complete (may represent a decapitated skull, although no perimortem trauma was evident).
Human bone: early middle adult male, aged 26–35 years; stature indeterminable.
Skeletal pathology: none.
Dental pathology: caries, calculus or hardened plaque, and slight dental attrition.
Grave fill finds: 7 sherds of Middle Iron Age pottery, 7 pieces of worked flint, including 3 chips, 3 flakes, 1 burnt.
Dating evidence: 341–49 cal. BC (95.4% probability; SUERC-48057).
Isotope values: $\delta\,^{13}C = -20.5$; $\delta\,^{13}N = 10.5$ (SUERC-48057).

Period 4: Late Iron Age

Skeleton no. 22028
Grave: none; buried within Iron Age Ditch 6, identified in section only, with no associated fills.
Burial: Supine; 75% complete.
Human bone: neonate, 39–41 weeks in utero; sex and stature indeterminable.
Skeletal pathology: none.
Dental pathology: none.
Grave fill finds: n/a.
Dating evidence: 352–55 cal. BC (95.4% probability; SUERC-48064).
Isotope values: $\delta\,^{13}C = -20.5$; $\delta\,^{13}N = 10.5$ (SUERC-48064).

Period 5: Roman

Skeleton no. 20808
Grave: buried within grave 20809 cut into Period 5 Ditch 41 (Enclosure E). Grave fill 20807.
Burial: position not known; 40% complete. Only recognised as human remains post-excavation.
Human bone: neonate, 36–38 weeks in utero; sex and stature indeterminable.
Skeletal pathology: none.
Dental pathology: none.
Grave fill finds: Pottery 30 sherds, 8 residual prehistoric sherds, 2 Roman sherds and 20 small intrusive post-Roman sherds. Glass: 1 fragment, fired clay: 92 undiagnostic fragments.
Dating evidence: cal. AD 86–311 (95.4% probability; SUERC-48066).
Isotope values: $\delta\,^{13}C = -19.1$; $\delta\,^{13}N = 12.0$ (SUERC-48066).

Skeleton no. 20812, (Fig. 2.28)
Grave: buried within east/west orientated grave 20813 cut into Ditch 41 (Enclosure E). Single nail, not *in situ*, within grave fill 20811.
Burial: extended, arms slightly flexed, with hands resting on hips; 80% complete.
Human bone: young child, aged 5–6 years; sex and stature indeterminable.
Skeletal pathology: none.
Dental pathology: none.
Grave fill finds: 4 sherds of 4th-century AD Late Roman pottery
Dating evidence: pottery recovered from grave fill, stratigraphically later than Roman Ditch 41 and earlier than Roman burial 20808.

Skeleton no. 21080, (Fig. 2.28)
Grave: no identifiable grave cut, has been placed into the hollow left by a quarry pit cut into western edge of Ditch 5. Sealed by 21081 and 21092. Several *in situ* nails recovered from around skeleton.
Burial: supine with left arm extended and right arm slightly flexed, with the hand on the right hip; 80% complete.
Human bone: early middle adult male, aged 26–35 years; stature: 170.86 ± 3.94cm (Trotter and Gleser 1958); 168.32 ± 3.85cm (Sjøvold 1990).

Skeletal pathology: joint degeneration and abnormal bone growth due to ageing, and the normal wear and tear of life were observed in the mid to lower spine. The right tibia displayed evidence of a fracture at the point of articulation with the ankle. This trauma led to an altered walking posture, producing a ripple effect of abnormal bone growth in the pelvis and ankle, together with surface polishing from bone on bone friction, also observed in the ankle. A further fracture was seen in the left wrist.
Dental pathology: caries, calculus, chronic abscesses, tooth loss, and moderate dental attrition.
Grave fill finds: n/a.
Dating evidence: cal. AD 81–234 (95.4% probability; SUERC-48059). Roman pottery recovered.

Skeleton no. 21921
Grave: a grave cut is assumed (21922) although not identified. Burial recognised during watching brief undertaken on mechanical excavation of remaining fills of Ditch 5. Coffin nails recovered from vicinity of burial.
Burial: position not known; 75% complete.
Human bone: older adult male aged = 46 years; stature: 171.90cm (Trotter and Gleser 1958); 169.25 ± 3.85cm (Sjøvold 1990).
Skeletal pathology: age-related joint degeneration was present in the lower spine. Both the right and left tibia and left fibula showed signs of infection, possibly as the result of trauma. The bone structure was inflamed on the left, and thickened on the right. The right femur displayed evidence of a benign tumour
Dental pathology: caries, inflammation of the gums and tooth loss.
Grave fill finds: n/a.
Dating evidence: cal. AD 86–242 (95.4% probability; SUERC-48058).
Isotope values: $\delta\,^{13}C = -19.7$; $\delta\,^{13}N = 10.2$ (SUERC-48058).

Skeleton no. 20979
Grave: buried within pit 20977. Fills 20978, 20979.
Burial: disarticulated; 20% complete. Only recognised as human remains during post-excavation.
Human bone: neonate, 37–38 weeks in utero; sex and stature indeterminable.
Skeletal pathology: none.
Dental pathology: none.
Grave fill finds: none.
Dating evidence: interpreted as being of Period 5 date, given proximity to two other neonate/infant Period 5 graves.

Period 6: Saxon

Skeleton no. 2019, (Fig. 2.28)
Grave: buried within grave cut 2021 through upper fill of Period 6 drying oven 2028, contained grave fill 2018.
Burial: supine, extended, left arm flexed with hand resting on left hip, right arm bent with forearm resting on lower abdomen; 75% complete.
Human bone: adolescent female, aged 17–18 years; stature indeterminable.
Skeletal pathology: uncommon occurrence in a female of the fusion of the coccyx to the sacrum. The bones of the right hand display evidence of a healed infection, resulting in lesions that may indicate tuberculosis.
Dental pathology: calculus and slight dental attrition.
Grave fill finds: one residual sherd of Roman pottery.
Dating evidence: interpreted as Period 6, as it is cut into a probable infilled drying oven of similar form to one in close proximity which was dated to Period 6.

Undated

Skeleton no. 22070
Grave: only recognised as human remains in post-excavation. Number assigned to distinguish an individual recovered from an extensively re-worked soil formed in the hollow to the south of Enclosure E. This contained 12th-century pottery and a large amount of residual material so dating is unclear.
Burial: disarticulated; 80% complete.
Human bone: adolescent aged 12–14 years; sex and stature indeterminable.
Skeletal pathology: none.
Dental pathology: none.
Grave fill finds: n/a.
Dating evidence: none. See above.

Skeleton no. 22071
Grave: only recognised as human remains in post-excavation. Number assigned to distinguish an individual recovered from an extensively

re-worked soil formed in the hollow to the south of Enclosure E. This contained 12th-century pottery and a large amount of residual material, so dating is unclear.
Burial: disarticulated; 10% complete.
Human bone: late middle adult male, aged 36–45 years; stature indeterminable.
Skeletal pathology: slight degeneration of the left hip joint (10×8mm).
Dental pathology: none.
Dating evidence: none. See above

Skeleton no. 22072
Grave: only recognised as human remains in post-excavation. Number assigned to distinguish an individual recovered from an extensively re-worked soil formed in the hollow to the south of Enclosure E. This contained 12th-century pottery and a large amount of residual material so dating is unclear.
Burial: disarticulated; 50% complete.
Human bone: early middle adult male, aged 26–35 years; stature 171.59 ± 4.57cm (Trotter and Gleser 1958); 168.60 ± 4.94cm (Sjøvold 1990).
Skeletal pathology: slight curvature of the spine.
Dental pathology: caries, calculus, chronic abscesses and slight dental attrition.
Dating evidence: none. See above.

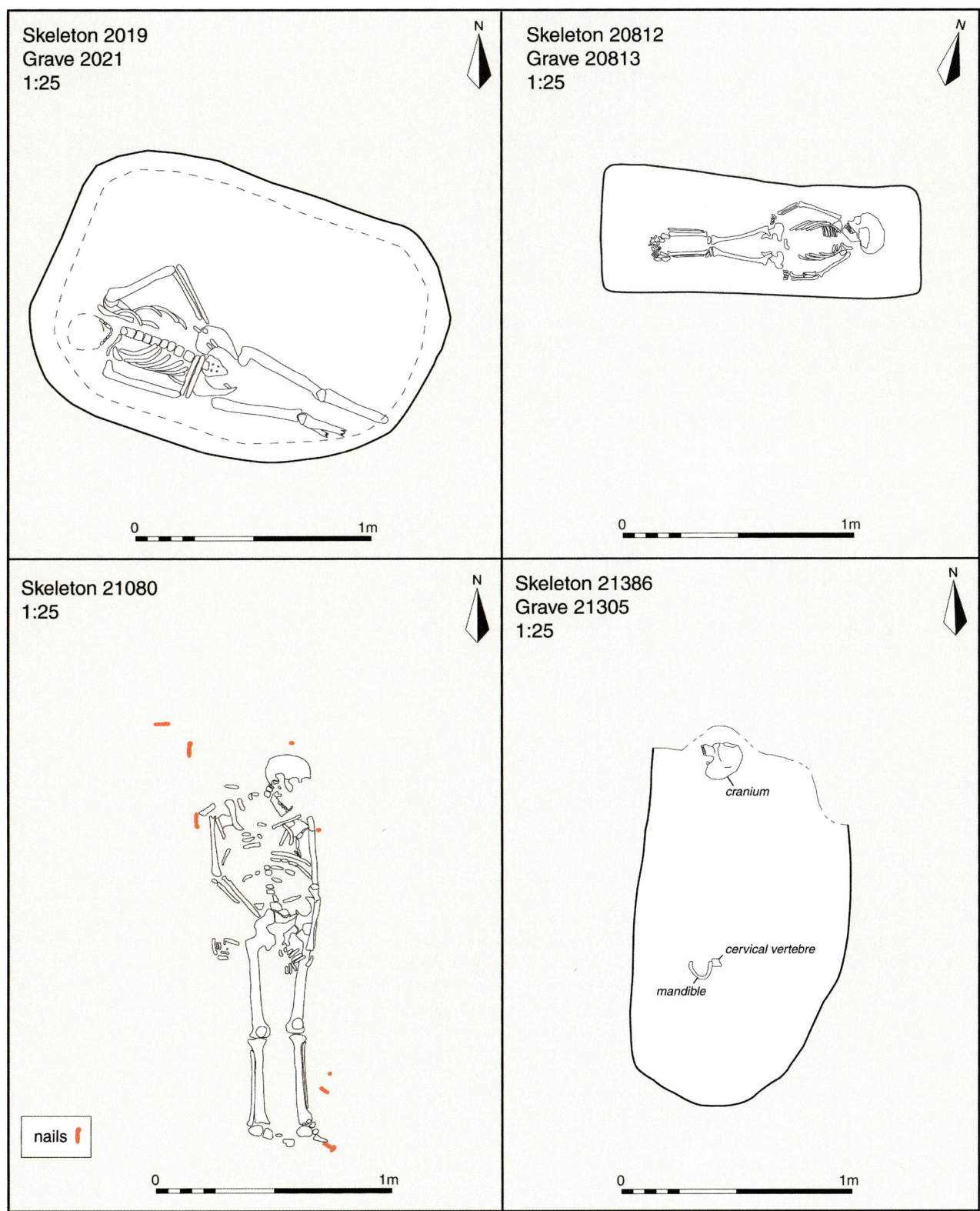

Figure 2.28 Illustrated burials

43

Chapter 3. Documentary Evidence
by Anthony Breen

I. Summary

The urban centre of Mildenhall, and the site of its medieval church and market, is known as High Town. This name has been in use since the late medieval period. The area includes Mill Street, leading to the site of Mildenhall's medieval water-mills and bridge over the River Lark. The water supply to the mills was channelled through a ditch and leet that formed the southern boundary of the properties situated in Mill Street and the present St Andrews Street, known in medieval records as Calkhill Street or by variants of that name. The medieval name for this street indicates quarrying for chalk and may relate to the quarry pits uncovered during excavation of the site (Chapter 2.VI). The leet was fed by the natural flow of the river and through the retention of water in the meadow system known as East Fens. Medieval property boundaries were established within the meadows by digging ditches at a right angle to the leet and running northwards to the medieval streets.

II. Documentary evidence relating to the site

This site is at the south-eastern corner of the medieval and later urban area. In 1834, the main area of the site was known as 'Home Close', while the area to the east was then known as East Field (EF 505/1/82 and 1374/27). Earlier in 1611, the area to the east was known as East Fenns (E18/454/14). By 1611, nearly all of the East Fen and adjoining lands were the property of Sir Henry North, lord of the manor of Mildenhall. The lands were consolidated into the hands of the North family in the late 16th and early 17th century. The south-western corner of this site adjoins the mill leet to the west, and the adjoining meadows and lands to the north are described in part of a deed dated 20 March 1583 (HD1749/2/16), which was identified during the research for this report. The deed mentions a number of former tenements that had been destroyed by fire. These tenements are listed in the Field Books of 1574 (E18/454/5-7). The date of the fire is uncertain. A date of 1507 is offered in some published sources, (Cromwell 1818; Anon. 1829; White 1874) but appears to be an error. The alternative date of 1567 given (Kirby 1735), is questionable, as some of the 'burnt' tenements mentioned in 1574 are described as devastated by fire in the Latin text of two earlier deeds (E18/452/16/4 (dated 1561) and E18/452/121/7 (dated 1564). Though the date of the fire is uncertain, the result was that the tenements immediately to the north of the Recreation Way site, and facing Calkhill Street to the west, were never rebuilt.

References to the Baille or Bayle in 15th and early 16th century sources suggest a former town ditch, a suggestion now partly supported by archaeological excavation ('Bayle' deed 1455 E18/452/16/1, rental 1483 E18/454/2 and rental 1501 E18/400/1/3, 'Baylepet' rental 1539 E18/454/4, deeds 'Baylestrete' (1541) and E18/452/16/2, (1572) E18/452/6/6-7).

The raise in the value of the manor of Mildenhall from £40 in 1065, to £130 by 1323, must be due in part to the development of its urban core. The town's prosperity lasted until the late 14th century, and then suffered a decline that led to the abandonment of some tenements on the fringes of the High Town area (Bailey 2007).

III. The Abbey of Bury St Edmunds

The earliest written reference to Mildenhall is in the charter of Edward the Confessor granting the lands in *Mildenhale,* as 'his mother possessed them', to the abbey of Bury St Edmunds in about 1043 (Hart 1966). It was then lent or leased to Stigand, the bishop of Winchester and later archbishop of Canterbury, 'On his disgrace and fall in 1070, his property, including Mildenhall, passed to the King' (Gransden 2007, 26). At the time of the Domesday Book *c.* 1086, the manor, including its mill and fisheries, was valued at £70 having been previously valued at £40 under Edward the Confessor *c.* 1065 (Rumble 1986). The manor remained with the crown until 1189, when Abbot Samson purchased it from Richard I, at a time when the king needed funds for the crusades and to off-set against his considerable debts. The king demanded £100 – a huge sum at the time, and one that reflected the wealth of the manor. The sum was raised 'with great difficulty' by the abbot and the convent, a circumstance that subsequently led to some debate between the abbot and the convent as to whom should enjoy its income (Gransden 2007, 27). Less than 10 years after the abbey purchased the manor, Richard 1 changed his seal in another expedient to raise money, and the abbey was one of many who were obliged to obtain and pay for a charter to renew the grant.

The church of St Mary of Mildenhall had also passed to the king in 1070 and had subsequently been granted to Battle abbey. As another valuable asset, the church was the subject of a number of claims and counterclaims until the abbot of St Edmunds was able to regain the church of Mildenhall at the end of the 12th century in exchange for an annual pension paid to Battle. The church was subsequently rated at 40 marks, and as one of the three most valuable of the convent's churches. This strengthening of the abbey's finances was considered to be one of the abbot's greatest achievements.

Testimony to the riches of Mildenhall in this period, is the lengthy and costly battle that the abbey underwent to defend its title to the manor in the king's court. In 1251 Richard de Clare laid claim to Mildenhall through a grant that he traced back to William the Conqueror; the suit was finally settled in 1259. In the assessment of the abbey's estates in 1291, the revenue from the manor was given at £99 14s 10½d a year, a higher amount than any other manor held by the abbey (Gransden 1964). The income from the mill alone was recorded at £16 9s 3¼d in accounts of 1247–1250. It was the single most valuable

Figure 3.1 Extract from pre-enclosure map of 1812 (scale approximately 1:5000)

manor in Suffolk 'comprising an enormous arable demesne of 1,200 acres, which in 1323 sent more than £130 in cash to the coffers of the cellarer of Bury St Edmunds abbey, in addition to large quantities of grain, livestock and other produce of equivalent value' (Bailey 2007). Income was also derived from rabbit farming, and the manor of Mildenhall was in possession of a number of warrens located on the edge of the Breckland (Gransden 2007, 260).

'Mildenhall, on the River Lark, was one the abbey's manors with a watermill and fishery (fisheries often existed as part of the complex of canals, sluices and weirs built to control a mill's supply of water power)' (Gransden 2007, 261). By 1286, there were two watermills and a windmill in Mildenhall, (Hervey 1925). Several other mills and a fishery were at Icklingham, an outlying vill of the manor of Mildenhall, which possessed a number of valuable natural resources, and which served to further enrich the income of the manor.

IV. The mills

The water supply was fed to the mills through a channel described in late medieval records as 'the lord's water ditch' or 'the several waters of the manor of Mildenhall leading from Berton to the water mill of Mildenhall'. This ditch formed the southern boundary of the properties to the west of this site.

The mills, described in later records 'as two water mills for corn under one roof", were continually repaired, and at times rebuilt (HD527/1). 'The huge mill at Mildenhall increased its revenue from £14 per annum to over £17 between the early 1400s and the 1460s, despite the town's steady economic decline' (Bailey 2007). The profits of the mill were secured by the abbot's right to mulcture whereby 'Within the same Town and Manor there hath been a custom time out of mind that all the Inhabitants Freeholders and Copyholders ought to doe their suit and mulcture to the mills by bringing all the Corn and grain (which they should spend in meal to be ground at those mills and not elsewhere ...)'. This manorial right was upheld by a judgement in the court of the Duchy of Lancaster in 1578, and as late as 1748 the lord of the manor was continuing to press his rights in respect of the mill (E18/452/37).

To assist the passage of the Lark Navigation Act of 1699 through Parliament, an agreement was made with Thomas Hanmer, lord of the manor of Mildenhall, to indemnify him as to loss of water to his mills at Mildenhall on condition 'that the said Thomas Hanmer shall & will not oppose the passing of the said bill' (E2/17/1 (18)). The meadow lands to the east of this site remained in use to hold and retain excess waters with the river engineered so that in 'great inundation will flow into East Fenn & can have as other passage or course than through mill meadows mill & outshotts into the river' (E18/452/37).

The northern channel of the Lark is illustrated on the Mildenhall Enclosure Map of 1812 (Fig. 3.1), held at the Bury St Edmunds Record Office. A site inspection during the preparation of the Desk-Based Assessment (Jordan 2009) suggested that this channel is possibly artificial, which has subsequently been confirmed (Dr Jess Tipper pers. comm.). The Lark was canalised in the early 18th century, and this artificial channel was probably constructed around this date. The southern channel of the

Lark may also have been constructed at this time, in order to serve as a leat for the mill to the west of the site.

V. The market

In 1220 the abbey gained a formal grant of charter to hold a market and annual fair at Mildenhall. A reference to land 'some time of Willelmus Mercator' (William the merchant) in a charter of Abbot Samson suggests that a mercantile interest was present in the 12th century (Davis 1954). Further evidence of economic activity is evident in the 1286 itinerary of the abbey's estates (Hervey 1925). Amongst the tenants in Mildenhall there are Henricus Le Mescon, Robertus Tinctor (dyer), Johannes Piscator (fisherman), Nicholaus Sutor (shoe-maker), Willelmus Mercator, Benedictus Le Couper, Benedictus Molendarius (miller) and Matildis le Vineter amongst others. 'By 1377, Mildenhall was the fourth largest town in the county and seventy-sixth in the country, but gradually its fortunes waned' (Bailey 2007, 281–2). In the 1381 Poll Tax returns for Mildenhall, 31 per cent of the adult population was engaged primarily in crafts and 51 per cent were labourers, significantly higher proportions than in rural communities (Bailey 2007). Surname evidence; Taillour, Lister (dyer), Webster, Fuller, Skarlet (the name of a type of cloth) and Turnay from 1381 suggests that a large number were employed in the manufacture of cloth. A number of mercers, clothiers and dyers can be identified in late medieval wills, deeds and in the rentals of 1501 (Breen 2008). Various tanners with premises in Mill Street can be identified from the same sources. Seven brewers are mentioned in the Poll Tax of 1381, and six taverns are named in 1501. An indication of decline is shown by the receipts of stallage, the payments for market stalls, which fell from around 13s 8d during the last two decades of the fourteenth century, to just 4s 5d by 1411. 'Consequently in 1413, royal assent was acquired to switch the market day from Tuesday to Friday, and to change the fair from 1 August to 29 September' (Bailey 2007, 266). A fresh charter was granted to the abbey in 1415, to hold the weekly markets on Fridays, and the market continues to operate under this charter.

Though the itinerary of 1286 lists some 242 tenants, only 90 were tenants of the abbey, the remainder being sub-tenants. Amongst the abbey's tenants, William 'Guamehil' (sic Tuamehil) held 46 acres of arable land and 22 acres of meadow, which was subdivided between 12 sub-tenants. His lands formed the sub-manor of Wamhill or Twamhill. Other sub-manors, Aspals and Carrils, were formed in the 14th century. Further lands and tenement were later granted to support other religious institutions, such as the small college of Michaelhouse, Cambridge, founded in 1324. This college was merged with Trinity College in 1546 (Trevelyan 1943). Amongst the other religious institutions were the nine parish guilds, and the two chantries (see Middleton-Stewart 2011).

Of the church itself, the earliest period of stonework within the chancel is possibly of 12th century date, with further work carried out c. 1220–1240, and in 1309–1344. The arcades, clerestory and roof of the nave date to the period 1410–1420, and the tower to 1446–1450.

Bailey (2007, 281–2) offers the following account of the late-medieval development and decline of Mildenhall:

The fortunes of Mildenhall were mixed. It enjoyed a period of prosperity in the later fourteenth century. ... Yet in the early fifteenth century its market began to decline, land values fell rapidly, its cloth production lost momentum, and by the middle of the century its economy was exhibiting clear signs of recession, although there were still enough individuals in Mildenhall with sufficient wealth to fund the construction of a stunning new church tower and nave roof. By the early sixteenth century many houses were abandoned and decaying, especially around Mill Street and East End.

VI. The Recreation Way site in 1583

In the field books of 1574 (E18/454/5–7), in a section described as on 'The east side of Calking Street', the tenements of John Allen, Trinity College, Thomas Baghott and Simon Clarke are all described as 'burnt'. As early as 1561, William Aleyn had sold to Simon Clarke 'one empty piece of land ... late built with one tenement and now devastated by fire lying in a way called Calkenstrete namely between the messuage called the Chaunterye on the south and the land of Thomas Backhott gentleman in part ... on the north of which ... the east head of the same abuts on ... Calkenstrete' (E18/452/16/4).

All these tenements are mentioned in the Latin text of deed dated 20 March 1583 either as part of the property conveyed or as an adjoining property mentioned in an abuttal. In deed of 1583 two properties formerly owned by John Allen had not been rebuilt, another messuage or dwelling house then in the 'tenure of Thomas Bakhott junior' had been rebuilt as a 'Newberne'. The 'Newberne' abutted to the east on land 'late Robert Thurstons called 'Hangmans Acre' which is described in the field books of 1574 as 'one parcel of land with a lime kilne'. Other parts of the property conveyed in 1583 included 'three pightles of pasture or marsh land lying in the Estfennes'. Nicholas Baggott had sold these lands to Roger, Lord North on 2 August 1581 (HD1749/2/16).

The properties of an earlier Nicholas Baggot or Bagot in 'High Town' are described in the rental of 1501 (Breen 2008, 68–9). Amongst which is 'one messuage with a croft adjoining ... the west head abuts on Calkehillstrete and the other on the land of the manor called Hangmanesacre now in the tenure of the said Nicholas'. He also held numerous pieces of meadow within the area of East Fens (Est Fennes) which included 'meadow late Thomas Harras called Kelle Medew', an earlier spelling of kiln.

Another property mentioned in the deed of 1583 is described as 'formerly William Gamlyn situated ...in ... Calkehyll Street namely between the tenement of Trinity College formerly belonging to the college of St Michael, Cambridge ... south'. This property had been sold to John Allen in 1546 following the death of William Gamlyn. It had been owned by Robert Costyn in 1540 (E18/452/6). In 1582 Rose Costen, the widow of another Robert Costen 'lymeburner' sold her 'dower rights in a third part of land called Lymkell' to Sir Roger North (E18/452/20A/8). Earlier in 1569 Robert Costen, the 'lyme burner' had sold his meadow 'formerly called Auncells now called Lymekells' to a Jasper Sharpe of Bury St Edmunds (E18/452/16/5) and he in his turn sold the property on to Thomas Poley of Mildenhall in 1573 (E18/452/14/14).

The documentary evidence for this period shows the area slow to recover from the effects of fire with the site of several former messuages (dwellings) remaining empty.

Figure 3.2 Extract from Young's map of 1834 (scale approximately 1:5000)

Behind the street frontage and in the immediate area of the site, former meadows, and possibly the site of the town's former gallows or gibbet had become the site of limekilns.

VII. The evidence of enclosure maps

There are various copies of the Mildenhall enclosure act, maps and award. In the Bunbury collection there is a hand-written copy of the act and related papers (E18/410/1). The related papers are a valuation of the tithes. There is a copy of the 1812 award in this collection (E18/410/2). There is a copy of the map and award bound in a single volume in the Mildenhall District Council collection. There are difficulties in using this copy of the map. The map was drawn on parchment and then folded to fit into the end of the award book (EF505/1/81). The folds are now so rigid it is very difficult to get this map to lie flat. A further copy of the map can be found in the Quarter Session Records (Q/RI 30B) and this map is rolled. In the Quarter Session Records there is a separate map showing those areas of the parish that were to be the subject of the enclosure (Q/RI 30A). An extract of this map is shown on Figure 3.1.

The enclosure maps do not show the entire parish, and instead depict the lands that were then enclosed, together with all the areas of old enclosure outside of the fen lands. These old enclosures were edged in green on the enclosure map (Q/RI 30B). In the borders of the enclosure map there is a schedule that lists the allotment of lands. This schedule is arranged in an alphabetical sequence according to the name of the owner. The lists are further subdivided according to the owners' entitlement to the allotment of lands. As an example, Sir Thomas Charles

Bunbury received allotments in lieu of his rights to the tithes as lay rector, the right of soil as lord of the manor and for his right of common also a manorial privilege. Others were allotted lands in proportion to their copyhold or freehold interests. A schedule of 'old inclosures, warrens and other lands within the said Parish not discharged from tithes' was written down in the 1812 award (Q/RI 24 page 221).

There is no complete list of all the owners and occupiers of the old enclosures. Their names and full details of their landholdings are not given in surviving schedules of lands shown on the enclosure map, and there is no schedule at all of the lands shown on the pre-enclosure map (Q/RI 30A). The Quarter Session copy of the award is in a separate volume (Q/RI 24). This volume includes enclosure awards for other parishes and the section relating to Mildenhall is set out between pages 107–233. Marginal glosses written against the text act a guide to the relevant sections of the award. The Enclosure Act was passed in 1807, and copies of the Act can be found in printed sources and apart from its short title, the reference to the Act is 47 Geo III c. 139.

On the enclosure map, the northern area of this site is shown as an old enclosure and is numbered 51 (Fig. 3.1). The southern area of this site is also shown as an old enclosure and is numbered 50. These numbers do not appear in the schedule entered in the edges of the map nor do they appear in the schedule of lands entered in the award. As these parcels are not depicted on the 1859 tithe map, it suggests that the payment of tithes in relation to these lands was settled at the time of the enclosure of the parish, or possibly at an earlier date. Outside the immediate area of this study, another old enclosure to the north-east of this site is labelled on the enclosure map as 'Lime Kiln Yard'. The curve of the southern boundary of Lime Kiln Yard is shown on Figure 3.1, but this piece is not labelled on the pre-enclosure map (ref. Q/RI 30A). On the map, the area to the east of this site to the south of the road, now known as Kingsway but then known as the Bury Road, is not marked as old enclosures and was subject to the enclosure of the parish. The pieces numbered 81 and 82 are described in the schedule written in the edges of the map as allotments to Charles Dyson of lands in 'East Fen Field', as freehold. In the schedule in the award, the executors of Charles Dyson are listed as the owners of the pieces numbered 53 and 54, corresponding to the fields 165 and 166 on the 1859 tithe map. These too are described as being in East Fen. The piece numbered 84 was also an allotment in East Fen Field, in this instance to Sir Thomas Bunbury in exchange for an old 'inclosure'.

VIII. William Young's map of Mildenhall parish 1834

An extract of William Young's 1834 map of Mildenhall parish is shown in Figure 3.2. The original reference for this map is EF505/1/82. A separate schedule of this map is in the solicitors' collection (1374/27). On the map the main area of this site is numbered 68 and is described in the schedule as 'Home Close'. Although no field boundaries are shown on the map, the field was then in the several occupations of Edward Curling, who held 2 acres 1 rood 6 perches, George Wilde, who held 2 acres 3 roods and 16 perches, and William Doughty, who held 3 aces 1 rood 17 perches. They were the tenants of Sir Henry E Bunbury. The total acreage was 8 acres 1 rood and 39 perches. The tenure of this property is not given in the reference book, but as the owner was Sir Henry E Bunbury, and the land was part of the estate until 1933, it should be assumed that the lands was then part of the demesne and held by his tenants. The meadows to the south adjoining the river are not individually numbered on this map.

Chapter 4. Artefact Reports

I. Coins
by Angus Crawford

The three coins listed below date to the Late Iron Age and Roman periods. The fourth coin recovered from the site was an unstratified 1938 threepenny piece.

Iron Age

1   Copper-alloy *potin*. Uninscribed Cantii. Class II. *Obv.* shows much stylised bust with central pellet; *Rev.* stylised bull of straight lines, with large central pellet. VA 135 (Van Arsdell 1989, 88 fig. 135–1); BM Types 715–20 (Hobbs 1996, 17). Hobbs suggests a mid to late first-century BC date range for such coins, while Van Arsdell is more precise, indicating an issue period of 50–45 BC. Period 4 hearth 22058, layer 22039 (soil sample find).

Roman

2   Copper-alloy *follis/nummus*. Diocletian. *Rev.* GENIOPOPVLIROMANI B/Γ across fields and TR (Trier) in exergue. Obverse is worn and mostly illegible *c*. AD 294–305. *Unstratified.*

3   Copper-alloy *nummus*. House of Constantine. *Rev.* GLORIA EXERCITUS (2 standards). Details uncertain. *c*. AD 330–35. Area 3, Period 7 Ditch 26, fill 3755.

II. Metal finds
by E.R. McSloy

A total of 132 metal objects were recorded. Tables 4.1 and 4.2 provide a summary of the assemblage according to material/functional category (adapted from Crummy 1983, 5–6), and by stratigraphic period.

A large proportion of the recovered metalwork consists of nails (55), or fragmentary and unclassifiable items. A total of twenty nails were recorded from inhumation burials of Roman date (20809, 20813, 21080 and 21922). Graves 20809 and 20813 contained only single nails, and these cannot with certainty be seen as evidence for a nailed coffin. Graves 21080 and 21922 produced seven and ten nails respectively. Six of those derived from 21080 were complete, measurable in the range 63–78mm, and of 'standard' flat-headed variety, typologically classified as Manning's 1B (1985). No trace of a wooden coffin was observed in the ground, although mineral-preserved wood was present with at least one nail from 21080. The positions of the nails from 21922 were not recorded; those in grave 21080 were located at the head, centre and foot area, and could indicate the presence of a nailed lid, with the main construction of the coffin utilising wooden joints.

The catalogue presented below lists items datable by form, or otherwise of intrinsic interest. Objects are listed by date and according to their functional category. The Iron Age group is the largest, though this remains restricted in its range and contains no items permitting close dating. Nos 1–3 (Fig. 4.1) are examples of ring-fittings, the function of which cannot be identified with certainty, although these could derive from sword belt/baldrics. A notable feature is the bifurcated section, which is not often noted with comparable objects, and which might represent a regional distinction. No. 4 ('shield clip') (Fig. 4.1) may similarly have derived from a warrior's accoutrements, though use with buckets or tankards are also possibilities.

The only brooches in the assemblage (nos 6–7, Fig. 4.1) relate to the Late Iron Age/early Roman 'transitional' period, at their earliest dating, and possibly one or two decades before AD 43. Roman brooches are wholly absent, and the scarcity of metalwork certainly dating to this period suggests that any activity relating to this period is likely to be peripheral to areas of habitation.

Functional	CuA	Fe	Pb
fasteners and fittings		57	
household	1		
metalworking		1	
personal adornment/dress	6	6	
tools		15	
transport		1	
unknown/scrap	6	32	2
weaponry	2		
weaponry/uncertain	1		
weights and measures			2

CuA = copper alloy, Fe = iron, pb = lead

Table 4.1 Metal finds summary by functional category

Functional	<>	1	2	3	4	5	6	7	9
fasteners and fittings	2	1	1	1	1	31		19	1
household						1			
metalworking									1
personal adornment/dress				2		2	2	2	4
tools				3	1	4	2	4	1
transport								1	
unknown/scrap	1			12		2	3	13	9
weaponry				1		1			
weaponry/uncertain								1	
weights and measures									2

Table 4.2 Metal finds summary by period

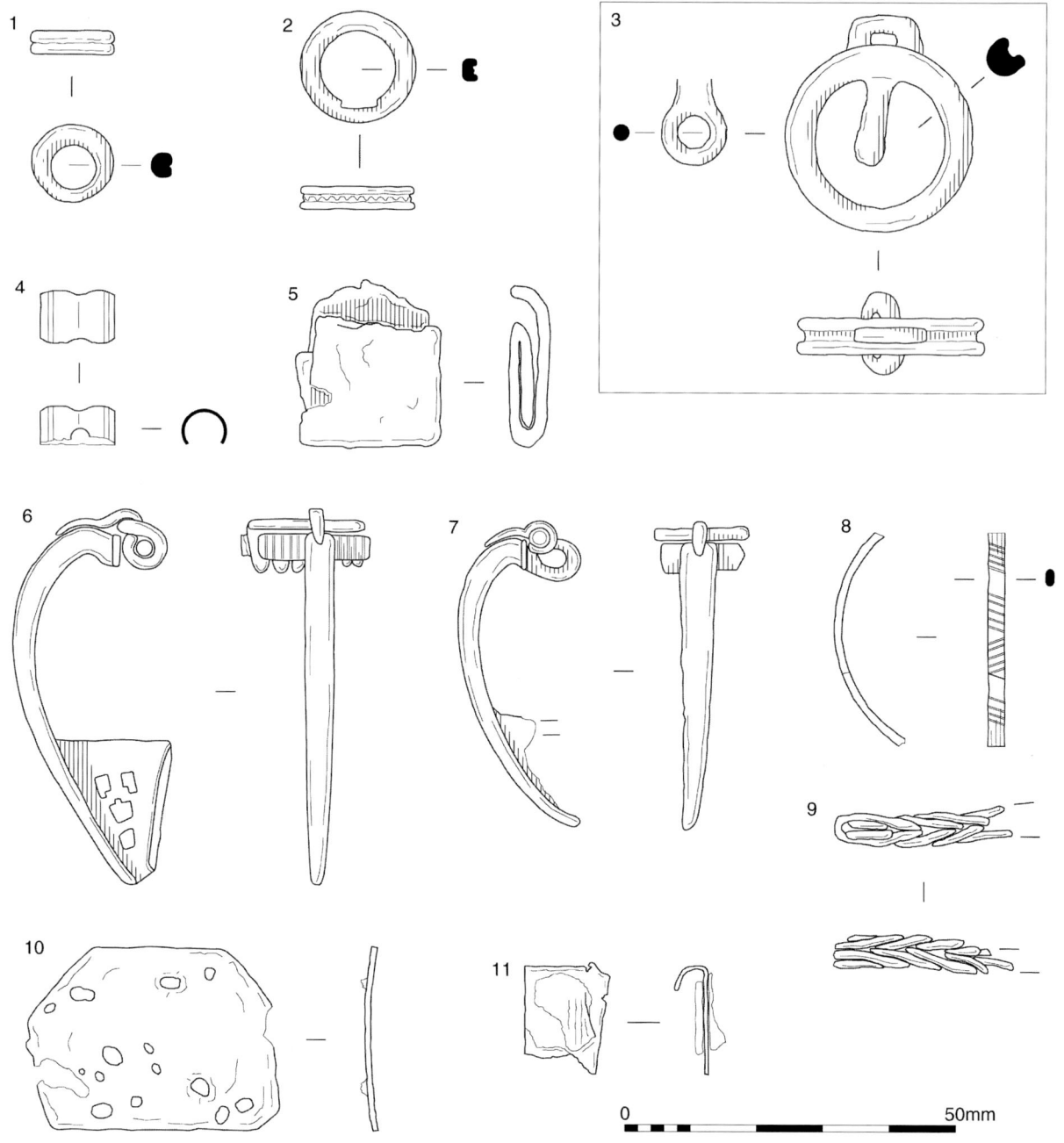

Figure 4.1 Copper alloy objects (scale 1:1) nos 1–11

Catalogue of objects of copper alloy
(Fig. 4.1)

Iron Age

Fasteners and fittings

1   Small cast ring. Asymmetric form, the hoop thickening in section from 3mm x 2mm to 4.5mm x 4mm. Bifid in section. A similar small asymmetric ring is illustrated from Glastonbury Lake Village (Bulleid and Gray 1911, plate XLIV, no. E195), and a bifid example comes from Camerton, Somerset (Jackson 1990, 48, no. 142), where possible use as strap terminal is suggested. Ext. diam. 14–15mm; int. diam. 12mm. Period 3; pit 19198 (fill 19210).

2   Small cast ring. Exterior of hoop recessed, and with band of cabled decoration. The latter is a feature of decorative metalwork of the Late Iron Age and early Roman periods. This example is similar to strap fasteners found with a sword dating to the 1st centuries BC/AD from Coleford, Gloucestershire (Webster 1990, 294–5). There is a

squared rebate set into the inner hoop, suggesting attachment in some way. Ext. diam. 19mm; int. diam. 14mm; thickness 4.5mm. Area 3; Period 6; gully 5330 (fill 5229).

3   Cast ring with internal hoop mounted at 90°, and opposite this an external, open rectangular projection. The main body of the ring is sub-rectangular in section, with a deep central groove. There are no close parallels for this example, though a Middle/Late Iron Age date is suggested by pottery in association. An elaborately decorated scabbard suspension ring from Mill Hill, Deal also features the rectangular projection and internal hoop, though this is cast 'flat' to the surface of the ring (Stead 1995, 87, no. 5). Ext. diam. 30mm; int. diam. 21mm; thickness 6mm. Period 3; pit 15234 (fill 15276).

4   Small, semi-tubular mount of waisted form, and with lateral grooves to each segment. There is damage to one longer edge. Such items are sometimes referred to as shield-clips, based partly on associations from the warrior burial from Mill Hill, Deal (Stead 1995). Dating is consistently of the Middle and later Iron Age, and a large number are known from Cadbury Castle, Dorset (O'Connor *et al.* 2000, fig.

117). Length 12.5mm; width 7.5mm. Area 3; Period 5; posthole 3536 (fill 3537).

Indeterminate/scrap

5   Folded strip fragment. The fragment occurred with pottery and a bone object of Iron Age date. Similar sheet fragments, folded as scrap for re-use, were plentiful finds at Danebury (Jope 1991, 333), and an Iron Age date is probable. Thickness 1mm; width 20mm. Period 3; pit 21031 (fill 21032).

Late Iron Age/Early Roman and Roman

Personal adornment and dress

6   Brooch. Pin missing, but otherwise complete. This is a Mackreth's C2b 'Standard British' Colchester, the 'b' denoting the squared-hole decoration to the catchplate (Mackreth 2011, 37–8). The bow of no. 6 is rounded in section, and plain. Decoration is limited to the catchplate, with its four irregularly-squared perforations and ribbed decoration to the wings. It is noteworthy in having an axial bar apparently formed from a rod with sheet metal 'sleeve', which may represent a later repair. The main dating associations given by Mackreth are pre-Flavian, and some examples are certainly pre-conquest (ibid. 28). Length 60mm; width 21mm. Period 4; Ditch 5 (fill 20994).

7   Brooch. Fragmentary, lacking much its spring/pin and catchplate. Sufficient of the latter remains for this to be identified as a second example of Mackreth's type C2b (2011, 37–8). The bow is rounded in section, and there is no decoration either to this, or the short wings. No. 7 is a residual find (from a medieval feature). Length 48mm; surviving width 15mm. Period 7; Pit Group 7, pit 20866 (fill 20867).

8   Joining fragments from a bracelet of Late Roman strip form, with repeated diagonal groove decoration (Crummy 1983, 41–42). Width 3.5mm; thickness 1mm. Area 3; Period 5; pit 3146 (soil sample find from fill 3145).

Indeterminate/'household'

9   Four short lengths of chain, of double loop-in-loop type. This technique appears to have been a Roman innovation, utilised primarily with jewellery (Johns 1996, 195–6), either as suspension or the linking of paired brooches. Length of longest section 28mm. Period 3; pit 15129 (fill 15131).

10 Sub-rectangular, and cut from thin sheet. There are at least four punched, rounded circular perforations around the edge, and two which are rectangular in shape and seemingly struck from the opposite face. Numerous riveted sheet fragments occur from Romano-British sites, and at least some would have functioned as patch repairs for metal vessels. Length 38mm; width 29mm; thickness 0.6mm. Area 3; Period 5; pit 3787 (fill 3788), beneath Enclosure A ditch (not shown).

Post-Roman

Personal adornment and dress

11 Buckle-plate fragment? From thin strip partly enclosing a strip made from folded sheet. Medieval? Width 12mm; surviving length 18mm. Area 2; Period 6; alluvium layer 2039.

Ironwork
(Fig. 4.2)

Iron Age tools

12 Woodworker's gouge. Solid, round-sectioned shaft, with possible stub from central tang. Small, tanged gouges of Iron Age date are known from Danebury, Hants (Cunliffe and Poole 1991, fig. 713 nos 2.246 and 2.247), and from a mid-1st century context from Hod Hill, Dorset (Manning 1985, 25, B48). The gouge is illustrated next to antler object no. 16 (Chapter 4.XI) which comes from the same deposit, and is probably part of the same tool. Surviving length 76mm; shaft diameter 15mm. Period 3; pit 19088 (fill 19089).

13 Metalworker's punch. Short, tapering shaft which is round-sectioned or sub-rectangular close to point. Flattened head from use. Comparable punches of Iron Age to mid-1st century date occur from Danebury (Cunliffe and Poole 1991, fig. 7.15 nos 2.256–7), and Hod Hill (Manning 1985, 11, A29). Length 74mm; shaft diameter 22–5mm. Area 3; Unphased deposit 3908.

14 Fragment of broad-bladed tool. The end of the short 'tang' appears burred, possibly due to striking. Surviving length 75mm; width 40mm; thickness 4mm. Period 3; pit 19198 (fill 19210).

Indeterminate

15 Hook. With terminal loop for suspension. Multiple uses might be imagined for this hook. A similar, Iron Age, example is known from Danebury (Cunliffe 1984, 368, fig. 7.24, no. 2.189). Length 63mm; width 30mm. Period 3; Ditch 5; (fill 20607).

Roman

16 Knife. Insufficient of this object survives to be sure of its original shape. The tang is at the same level as the blade back. The angle created between the tang and back suggests a down-turned blade, which is a feature of Manning's types 7–9 (1985, 111–114). Knives of this type appear to be mainly earlier Roman in date, and this example may be a residual object. Surviving length 71mm; width 22mm. Period 5; pit 17081 (fill 17074).

Medieval/post-medieval

Craft tools

17 Leather-worker's awl. Square sectioned, with rounded point. Numerous medieval examples of the same form are recorded by Goodall (1980, fig. 42). Length 104mm; thickness at centre 8mm. Period 7 pit 19027 (fill 19028).

18 Shears fragment. Only the looped spring and portion of the round-sectioned arms are present. Late Saxon dating is suggested by associated pottery. Surviving length 70mm; width at spring 21mm. Period 6; Area 2; pit 2024 (fill 2025).

Transport

19 Buckle. Simple rectangular frame, with pin and part of sheet metal 'roller' *in situ*. Numerous medieval examples of similar form are known, many of which are tinned (Egan and Pritchard 1991, fig. 60; Goodall 1980, fig. 128). There is a suggestion (*ibid.* 172) that buckles of this form were designed for use with the horse harness, the roller allowing freer movement and reducing chafing. Length 43mm; width 35mm. Area 12; Period 9 gully 12063 (fill 12062).

20 Horseshoe. A portion of one arm is absent, Rectangular nail holes (4 to surviving complete arm). Probably of Clark's Type 4 'standard late medieval', and probably 14th century or later (Clark 1995, 96–7). Length 114mm; width 120mm. Period 7 pit 17359 (fill 17386).

Fastenings and Fittings

21 Padlock key? Strip-like body, with flattened and up-turned bit, which is damaged and of indeterminate form. The terminal is missing, although this was probably bent under. Surviving length 150mm; width at centre 15mm. Period 7; pit 4110 (fill 4109).

Lead/lead alloy
(not illustrated)

Roman

Household

22 Pewter(?). Distorted, thickened rim and body fragment. From vessel of indeterminate form. Probably later Roman Surviving length 45mm. Evaluation Trench 11; Period 9; alluvium 1104.

Post Roman

Household

23 Lead. Approximately conical weight, with central perforation 9–8mm diam. Crudely-finished (hammered?) surfaces. Length 15mm; diam. 16–10mm; weight 21g. Evaluation Trench 12; Period 9; gully 12063 (fill 12062).

24 Weight from rolled strip of lead. Central perforation 7–5mm diam. Length 12mm; ext. diam. 18–13mm; weight 25g; Period 9; pit 15039 (fill 15036).

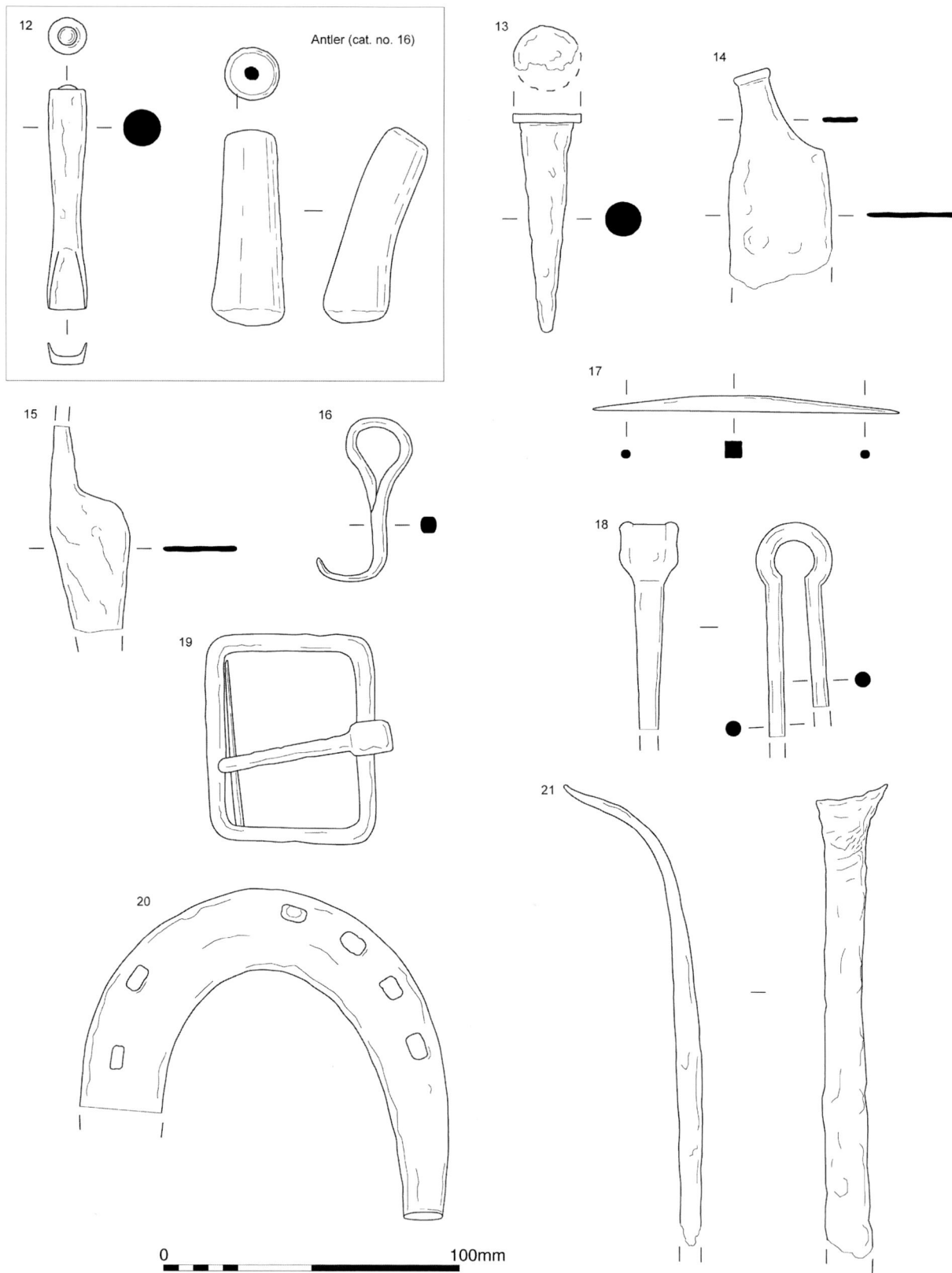

Figure 4.2 Fe objects (scale 1:2) nos 12–21 (no. 12 shown with bone and antler no. 16)

52

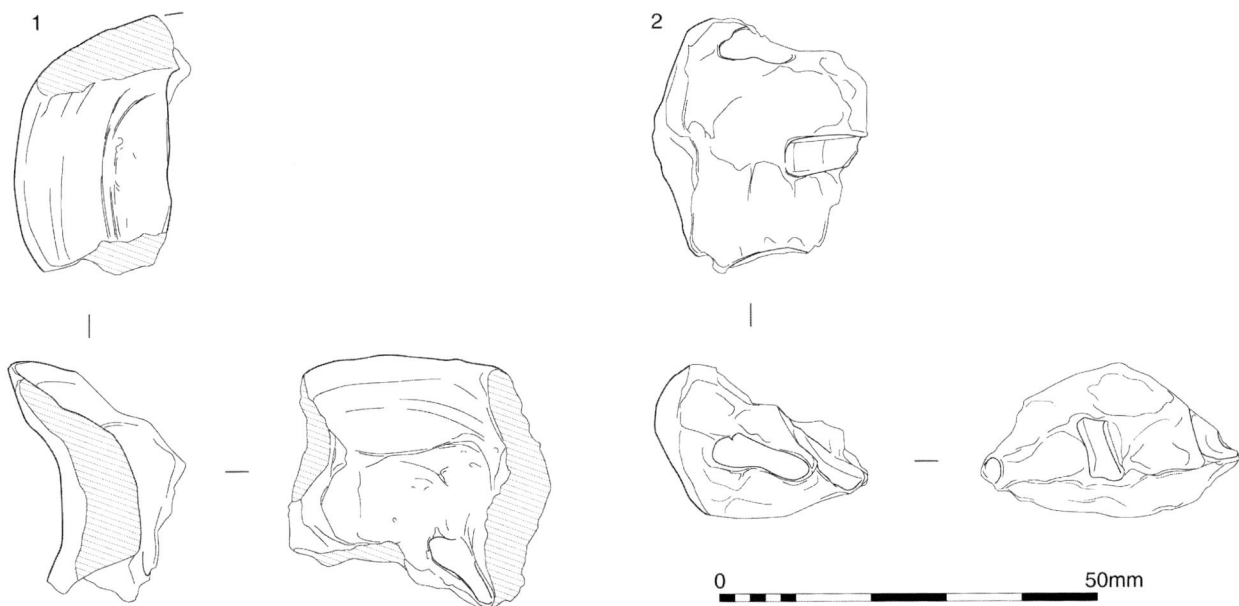

Figure 4.3 Clay mould fragments (scale 1:1) nos 1–2

III. Archaeometallurgical residues
by T.P. Young with a contribution by R. Ixer

Introduction
An assemblage comprising archaeometallurgical residues of mixed type was recorded, with material derived from 107 deposits and relating to deposits dating across the full stratigraphic age range. A comprehensive catalogue of material recorded, a significant proportion among which was derived from bulk soil samples, is contained in the archive.

Methodology
All materials were examined visually with a low-powered binocular microscope where required. The materials were not subjected to any high-magnification optical inspection, nor to any form of instrumental analysis.

Assemblage range
Evidence for the casting of copper alloys was recorded as a small number of ceramic crucible and mould fragments (below).

Evidence for ironworking occurs as a much larger quantity of macroscopic residues (slags) and micro-residues. The latter which were widely distributed among the magnetic residues, included flake hammerscale (FHS), spheroidal hammerscale (SHS) and slag flats (typically representing materials lost outside the forge hearth), together with various slag and clinker droplets (probably mostly particles formed within the hearth).

Identifiable macroscopic iron-working residues were mainly complete or broken examples of smithing hearth cakes (SHCs). These items are listed in Table 4.3. The weights of the cakes, where determinable, are all within the typical range of cakes produced during the end-user working of iron (blacksmithing) during their respective periods. Most of the small fragments of indeterminate iron slag are probably also fragments of SHCs (although too small to be identifiable as such).

Period	Area	Context	Piece weight (g)	Original weight (g)	Completeness	Remarks
4	20	20014	66		fragment	
5	3	5131	160	320	c. 50%	charcoal
6	2	2025	112		3 pieces crust	
6	2	2086	378	400	>95%	
6	3	5224	702	702	100%	
6	20	20294	31		fragment	charcoal, smooth top
6	20	21041	104		broken fragment	coarse dense
7	2	2011	130	260	c. 50%?	
7	2	2050	192		block (burr?)	
7	4	4112	122		fragment	
7	20	20198	288		6 pieces	
7	20	20609	162	220	c. 75%	exploding
9	3	3002	122	122	100%	

Table 4.3 Identifiable smithing hearth cake (SHC) fragments, ordered by period and context

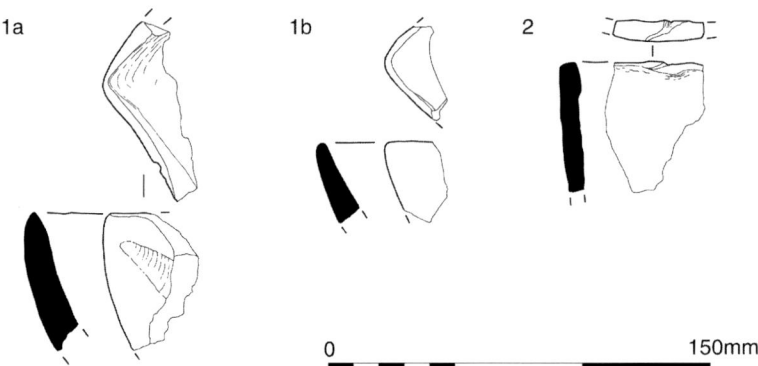

Figure 4.4 Crucible fragments (scale 1:3) nos 1a 1b, and 2

The assemblage includes a variety of less diagnostic materials, mainly lining slags (slags derived from the melting of the hearth/furnace wall) and fuel ash slags (FAS). The lining slags will be from metallurgical hearths or furnaces, but are not in this instance diagnostic of process or material. The fuel ash slags are not necessarily metallurgical in origin, and may originate in suitable conditions in structures such as drying ovens.

Discussion by period
Very limited evidence for metallurgical activity prior to Period 3 was recognised. The 'trace'-level evidence for ironworking associated with Period 2 ditch 5136 and pit 20238 are at odds with the dating of the deposits and very probably are the result of later disturbance. Similarly low level evidence occurred from a single Period 3 deposit (pit 16063) and this can probably be regarded as intrusive.

Period 3: Casting of copper-alloys
Evidence for the handling and casting of copper alloy occurs as mould fragments and crucibles recorded from the fills of two Period 3 (Middle Iron Age) pits, 15129 and 21786.

Mould fragments
(Fig. 4.3)
Two mould fragments were identified from pit 15129. The nature of the object(s) cast is unclear.

1 Mould fragment. Flared pouring gate in hard sandy fabric. Weight 12g. Period 3 pit 15129 (fill 15131)
2 Mould fragment in hard sandy fabric preserving three partial impressions of curved components. The central impression survives best and appears to form a disc *c.* 16mm in diameter and 4mm thick. Weight 13g. Period 3 pit 15129 (fill 15132)

Crucibles
(Fig. 4.4)
Fragments from two crucibles were identified (below), both moderately large (>60mm tall) vessels, and probably of 'triangular' or 'pyramidal' form. They appear to have been lightly used, if at all. Crucible 1 shows evidence of failure on one side – possibly having been placed immediately in front of the air blast. This example showed copper oxide droplets (representing corroded metal droplets) on both inner and outer surfaces. The crucible fabrics were subject to thin-section analysis (below), the results indicating use of quartz as the principal temper and that the fabrics were not significantly different from those characterising the pottery. The fabrics are not untypical of

prehistoric crucibles, where the emphasis is on the insulating, rather than the refractory, properties of the ceramic. At Danebury the 'triangular' crucibles replaced the handled forms in ceramic phase 4/5 and survived until at least ceramic phase 7 (Cunliffe 1984, 441), so are essentially Middle Iron Age. Similar forms of crucible in the latest Iron Age and later tend to be in much more refractory fabric.

A planar sheet of ceramic from Period 3 pit 21786 (fill 21794) resembles the crucible material in many ways. This sheet may have functioned as a 'heating tray' or just possibly a crucible lid – but is too incomplete to interpret fully.

1 Triangular form crucible. 15mm thick at base and 10mm at rounded rim; outside with dark dimpled slag locally; inside similar but smaller dimples and with abundant corroded Cu alloy droplets (only one on outside), raised areas just show clear reddish glaze. Clear glaze extends onto one lateral surface to 40mm below rim. Rim line appear as deformed and possibly twisted. Quartz and plant-tempered. Three sherds (72g.). Period 3 pit 15129 (fill 15132)
2 Crucible of uncertain form. *c.* 5mm thick, curved edge, one face shows increased vitrification and reddening to the outside, the other face is less vitrified, has a smoothed, lightly striated surface, but has a layer of black glass and sand adhering to the surface. Quartz sand tempered. One sherd (13g.). Period 3 pit 21786 (fill 21794)

Thin-section analysis of crucible fragments
by R. Ixer
Crucibles 1 and 2 were included as part of a wider thin-section analysis programme. Methodologies are as detailed for the main, pottery analysis (Chapter 4.VII). The aim of analysis was to characterise the crucible fabrics, permitting comparisons with Middle Iron Age pottery types and if possible determine local or other origins. Full macroscopic/ microscopic and petrographic descriptions are contained in the archive and the reporting is presented here only in summary. Descriptions for the Mildenhall fabric series and the petrographic fabrics are provided in Chapter 4.VII.

Crucible 1
(Period 3 pit fill 15132): Natural quartz sand-plant tempered ceramic.

Manufacture
This ceramic may be natural quartz sand-organic material tempered. The non-plastics are bimodal in their size distribution and the coarser fraction has a quite tight size range. There is enough burned-out plant matter to suggest it was deliberately added to the clay.

Provenance of the raw materials
There is little that can be positively said about the raw materials of this pot. The inorganic non-plastics are probably local in origin.

Remarks
Crucible 1 has a slightly different petrographic fabric with more equant-shaped, organic matter (some may not be grass), a higher concentration of fine-grained clasts and displays little petrographic fabric. The fabric of

this pot differs from most of the pottery sherds as the clay fraction has abundant, fine-grained quartz grains.

Crucible 2
(Period 3 pit fill 21794): sand tempered ceramic.

Manufacture
This ceramic may be natural quartz sand tempered. The non-plastics are bimodal in their size distribution and the coarser fraction has a quite tight size range suggesting tempering.

Provenance of the raw materials
Rare chalk clasts suggest that at least some of the raw materials (probably the clay rather than the temper) are local.

Remarks
The fabric of this pot is quite similar to many of the Iron Age pots but there is no organic component to the temper. Were it not for the over-firing, in thin section this could be mistaken for pottery Fabric Q1.

Summary
Crucible 2 appears to be very similar to the pottery fabric Ba (Q1). Crucible 1 was closest to pottery fabric Bb though it displays fewer similarities, and may have incorporated different plant matter. In common with the pottery the results of the thin-section analysis cannot with certainty determine origin, although there are indications from the inorganic non-plastics that both crucibles were made locally.

Period 4 (ironworking)
Limited evidence for iron smithing was recorded from six deposits. In most instances such activity was at 'trace' level, consisting of small quantities of micro residues (flake or spheroidal hammerscale). A fragmentary smithing hearth cake (SHC) was recorded from undated root disturbed ground (fill 20014).

Period 5 (ironworking)
Evidence for metallurgical activity was more abundant from Roman-phased deposits, noted from 17 deposits from both the higher ground and the floodplain. Included was material from eight deposits relating to the extensively sampled drying ovens 17048/17067. Most material from these features and from the period overall comprises small quantities of flake (FHS) or spheroidal hammerscale (SHS) or of ironworking slag and is suggestive of iron smithing. One feature, Ditch 42, fill 17520 produced abundant slag 'droplets' (or possible SHA) and Area 3 layer 5131, a portion of a smithing hearth cake. Most of the residues probably represent activities undertaken with a charcoal fuel however material tentatively identified as clinker (Area 3 deposit 3111 and deposit 17520) may suggest limited use of coal.

Period 6 (ironworking)
Fifteen deposits from both the higher ground and the floodplain produced evidence for ironworking (mostly smithing). Included were five mainly fragmentary smithing hearth cakes (Table 4.3). The remainder comprises mainly ironworking slag, probable (clay) hearth lining fragments and, rarely, quantities of flake hammerscale (pit 16069). Clinker identified from pit 21672 indicates some use of coal as fuel.

Period 7 (ironworking)
The Period 7 (medieval) phase produced the most widespread evidence for metallurgical activity, identified from forty-seven separate deposits across the site and including Areas 2 and 3. In common with the evidence from preceding phases that from Period 7 is mostly at trace level, provided by small quantities of microscopic residues, slags or lining. A total of five smithing hearth cakes were recorded (Table 4.3). Evidence for the use of coal as fuel was recorded as clinker or 'clinkery slag' from tree-throw feature 19060 (fill 19000), pit 19027 (fill 19028) and kiln 20044 (fill 20045).

Summary discussion
The assemblage as a whole suggests a persistent low level of metallurgical activity. Evidence for the casting of copper alloy objects is restricted to the Iron Age, and the limited occurrence of these materials might indicate an occasional activity rather than a persistent one. The local casting of copper alloy fittings and horse-gear is also a relatively common feature of Iron Age settlements – perhaps facilitated by travelling craftsmen.

There appears to be limited evidence for ironworking before the Late Iron Age (Period 4). Low-intensity iron smithing activity evidenced by smithing hearth cakes and modest incidence of micro-residues characterises this and the subsequent periods (Periods 5–7). It is most consistent with blacksmithing and the small community-scale activities associated with the repair and fabrication of tools and implements. The volumes of residue recovered suggest that the activities, or at least the main locations for waste disposal, were outside the excavated areas. Most of the residues encountered probably represent activities undertaken with a charcoal fuel; however the presence of clinker particles from among the Roman and later groups indicates the use of coal as fuel at times as well.

IV. Worked flint and chert
by Jacky Sommerville

Quantification
A total of 289 worked lithic items (11 of which were burnt), and 500 unmodified burnt pieces, were recovered from excavation (Table 4.4).

Raw material and composition
Most of the assemblage was made of good quality mid to dark-grey flint. Cortex was mostly (60%) chalky, suggesting the use of primary chalk sources, probably including flint from Grimes Graves, 13 miles away in Norfolk. This is the largest known Neolithic mine complex in Britain, and was exploited during the Later Neolithic and Early Bronze Age periods (Edmonds 1995, 117). However, 16% of the cortex was abraded, indicating that secondary sources (*i.e.* river gravels) were also used. Twenty-four items (8%) were of flint featuring earlier patination, which provided evidence for the reuse of old pieces of flint, a common Bronze Age trait (Edmonds 1995, 175–176). Sample sizes from Recreation Way were too small to demonstrate a difference in flint procurement across the Mesolithic, Neolithic and Bronze Age periods.

The condition of the flint assemblage suggests that a proportion of the lithics were disturbed after deposition: 32% were broken, 39% featured edge damage and 34% exhibited a degree of rolling. A third of the assemblage featured some cortication. Flints from the same contexts could be expected to exhibit similar cortication, having encountered the same post-deposition conditions. However, many contexts contained flints with varied cortication, suggesting that these may have been re-deposited.

Technology

Primary technology

Cores

Multi-platform flake cores were recovered from tree-throw fill 15070, Period 5 pit 20354, fill 20353 (cut by later features, not shown on plan), and Period 3 pit 20759, fill 21003. Deposit 21003 also produced a single-platform flake core, as did Period 7 Ditch 3105, fill 3104 in Area 3. A dual-platform flake core was recovered from Late Bronze Age pit 20238, fill 20336 (Fig. 2.2). The core from fill 15070 was not extensively worked, and the single platform core was made on a thermal (frost-shattered) blank, suggesting a probable Bronze Age dates for these items.

Medieval kiln 20044, fill 20045, produced a fragment of a small flake and a blade/bladelet core, and Saxon alluvium layer 2086 produced a single-platform, pyramidal blade core. Core rejuvenation flakes were recorded from fill 15045 of Period 3 pit 15048, Period 5 pit 3841, fill 3839, and the medieval spread, feature 3989. Blade technology and core rejuvenation were characteristic features of the Mesolithic and Early Neolithic periods (Edmonds 1995, 191).

Roman silt deposit 21092 produced a later Neolithic discoidal core, with centripetal (towards the centre) flake removals on both faces (Edmonds 1995, 82).

Unworked	
(Burnt	500)
Primary Technology	
Cores	9
Core fragment	1
Core rejuvenation flake	3
Flakes	200
Blades	14
Bladelets (blades =12mm wide)	7
Chips (flakes or shatter =10 mm long)	31
Shatter	1
Secondary Technology	
Arrowhead (leaf shaped)	1
Burin	1
Combined tool: scraper/notch	1
Microlith	1
Notch	1
Pick	1
Retouched blade	1
Retouched flake	8
Retouched miscellaneous	1
Scraper (end)	2
Scraper (irregular, concave)	2
Scraper (side)	1
Truncated flakes	2
Total	**789**

Table 4.4 The worked and burnt flint assemblage

Débitage

Of the 220 recovered items of *débitage* where reduction stage was established, eight (4%) were primary, 110 (50%) were secondary and 102 (46%) were tertiary. The lack of primary pieces suggests that initial flint working occurred off site, when raw material was imported and worked further (Inizan *et al.* 1992, 13). The presence of 31 chips (=10mm), along with the cores and rejuvenation flakes, also confirms that some knapping occurred on site. All but three of the chips were residual and so cannot indicate areas of knapping.

The recovery of 14 blades and seven bladelets is further evidence of Mesolithic and/or Early Neolithic activity. Seven of these were in Mesolithic, Neolithic or Bronze Age deposits, and the other 14 were residual, from undated deposits or otherwise unstratified.

One Levallois-type flake was recovered from fill 15045 of the Period 3 pit 15048. This reduction strategy featured during the Later Neolithic period (Edmonds 1995, 82).

Secondary technology

Scrapers

The end scraper recovered from Period 5 silting layer 5222 was made on a thick, broken flake, and featured steep, rather large removals along the distal ventral edge. The end scraper from medieval pit fill 19203 featured a small amount of irregular, crude retouch on the distal dorsal edge. Period 5 Enclosure A ditch fill 3878 produced a side-scraper made on a thermal flint. The left dorsal edge has abrupt to semi-abrupt retouch, and the right dorsal edge has a small area of steep retouch. Irregular concave scrapers were recovered from Period 6 pit 20405, fill 20406, and Period 5 pit 21639, fill 21640 (cut by later feature, not shown). That from deposit 20406 displayed crude, steep retouch on the distal/left dorsal edge. The scraper from deposit 21640 was made on a reused, patinated flake, and exhibited slightly irregular, semi-abrupt retouch along one edge.

Although the five scrapers are all residual finds, all feature somewhat irregular and/or crude retouch, and one is made on a thermal blank. These features are typical of Bronze Age flint working.

Arrowhead

A fragment of a broken leaf-shaped arrowhead (Fig. 4.5, no. 1), of Early Neolithic date, was recovered from Period 5 silting layer 3147.

Microlith

A microlith (Fig. 4.5, no. 2) was recorded in Period 2 Bronze Age silting layer 3231. Narrow blade microliths mostly belong to the Later Mesolithic period (Butler 2005, 96).

Combined tool

A combined end-and-side scraper and notched piece (Fig. 4.5, no.3) was recovered from Period 3 pit fill 20588.

Pick

A pick (Fig. 4.5, no. 4) was recorded in Period 7 pit 20078, fill 20080.

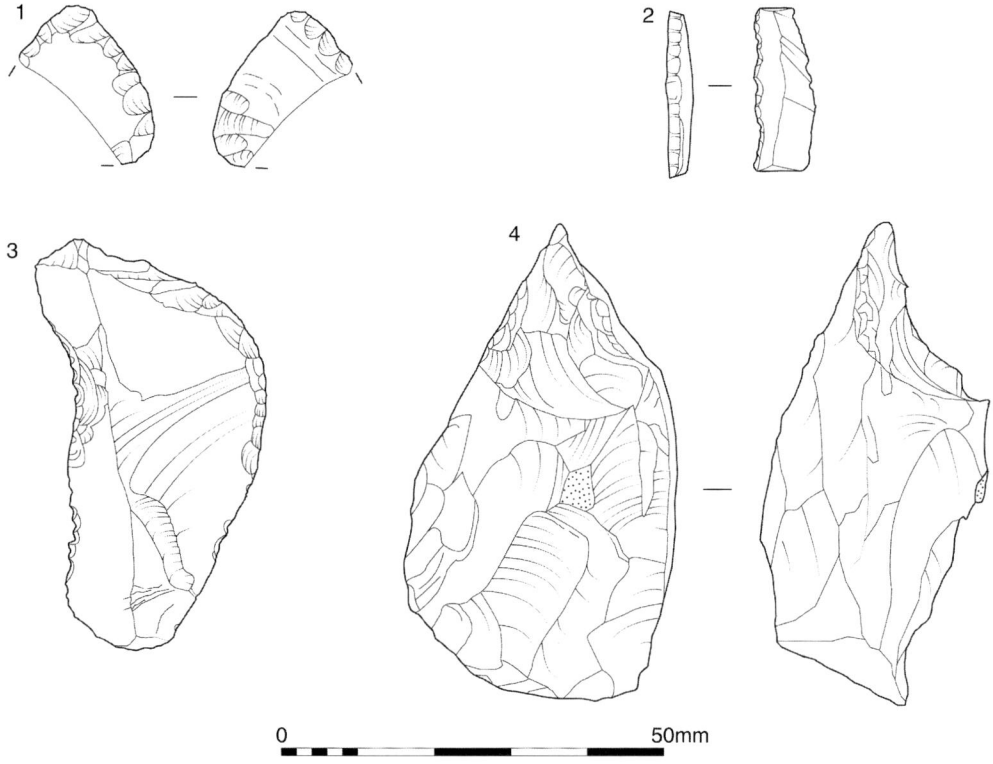

Figure 4.5 Flint (scale 1:1) nos 1–4

Burin

Period 5 layer 3562 produced a burin. The burin spall had been removed from a prominent arris on the dorsal face, to produce a sharp corner. Burins were used throughout the prehistoric period for bone and antler working (Butler 2005, 51).

Truncated flakes

Mesolithic truncated flakes (Butler 2005, 109), made on distal segments, were recovered from palaeochannel fill 3612, and fill 21246 of Ditch 5, of Period 3.

Stratified groups

The majority of contexts produced only one or two flint items, and few datable artefacts were recorded. However, two features contained *in situ* lithic material.

Seventeen items of worked flint, and 15 pieces of burnt, unworked flint were recovered from Period 2 Late Bronze Age pit 20238 (fills 20320, 20325, 20326, 20336, 20337, 21320, 21397 and 21664). The worked items include 13 flakes, three chips and one dual-platform, burnt flake core. This appears to represent a stratified group, as all of the flints were un-patinated and in fresh condition. One flake, with a heavily battered dorsal face, may have been detached from a hammerstone.

Deposit 20182, the sole fill of pit 20183 and dated by pottery to the Late Bronze Age, contains three flakes in fresh condition, which are likely to be *in situ*.

Conclusions

Much of the flint has typically Bronze Age characteristics, and includes crude, irregular tools and the reuse of older flint. Mesolithic tools were also present, *i.e.* the microlith, truncated pieces and bladelets. The Early Neolithic was represented by the leaf-shaped arrowhead, and the Later Neolithic by the discoidal core and Levallois-type flake. The blade cores, blades and core rejuvenation flakes date to the Mesolithic or Early Neolithic periods. The assemblage contains lithics from throughout the prehistoric period, and 73% of the worked flints were redeposited in features dated to the Iron Age or later.

Illustrated catalogue
(Fig. 4.5)

1 Broken leaf-shaped arrowhead fragment, heavily patinated. Type 4A (Green 1980, 72–94). It was made on a flake and featured fine, semi-invasive retouch around the whole of the remaining dorsal edges, and on portions of the ventral edges. Residual in Period 5 deposit 3147.

2 Straight-backed bladelet microlith (Jacobi 1978). Typically for this type, it displays fine, abrupt, blunting retouch (backing) along one edge (the right dorsal). Residual in Period 2 Bronze Age deposit 3231.

3 Combined end-and-side scraper and notched piece. It features steep retouch on the distal end of the dorsal face and semi-abrupt retouch on the distal portion of the right dorsal edge; the notch had been formed by retouch on the distal portion of left dorsal edge. Residual in Period 3 pit fill 20588 (fill of 20153).

4 Pick, made on a core. It displayed some battering and one end had been reworked into a triangular point. Residual in Period 7 pit fill 20080 (fill of 20078).

V. Worked stone and unworked/burnt stone
by Fiona Roe and E.R. McSloy

Introduction

The worked stone was examined, using a x10 hand lens where necessary to determine the different lithic materials. A full catalogue of the worked material, recording quantities (fragment count and weight) is included in the archive. The unworked, burnt stone was recorded at more basic level quantified by weight only and has not been retained.

Context	Feature	Class	Material	Description	Weight (g)
3172		quern	Millstone Grit	1 fragment, trace of worn surface	148
3528	3529	quern	Millstone Grit	1 fragment from rotary quern, part of rim, possible secondary use for whetting; 101 x 86 x 38mm	282
3916	3914	quern	Millstone Grit	3 fragments, burnt and weathered	95
5175	5176	millstone?	Niedermendig	1 block + small fragment, weathered but part of flat, worn surface survives, possible millstone fragment; 155 x 78 x 84mm	1222
17247	17248	quern	Millstone Grit	1 small fragment from rotary quern with one flat worn surface, burnt	84
20721	20723	quern	Millstone Grit	1 fragment, probably part of rotary quern, weathered, possible worn surface	267
20806	20983	quern	Niedermendig	8+ small fragments	13
21004	21005	quern	Niedermendig	2 small fragments, weathered	4

Table 4.5 Quern/millstone fragments from Roman-phased deposits

The assemblage includes objects from sixty-nine separate deposits, some of which are represented as multiple fragments. A small number of the objects are drawn and/or individually described, with most of the fragmentary items listed (Tables 4.5–4.8).

Stone sources
Niedermendig lava from the Mayen quarries in the Rhineland was recorded from forty-five contexts, mostly as small fragments lacking recordable features. Niedermendig lava was used extensively throughout the Roman period and again from the early and later medieval periods. The extensive use of this grinding material is clear and the pattern of its use seen at Mildenhall is repeated across East Anglia and further afield. The comparatively lightweight properties of this material and ease of transportation by boat doubtless led to such widespread use.

Millstone Grit, which occurs in the assemblage as six fragments, also seems to have arrived in East Anglia in some quantity, though probably mainly during the Roman period and this could have come most of the way by boat,

using available rivers and quite possibly an east coast sea route via the River Humber. Further quern/millstone materials comprise two fragments of greensand which is most likely to be Spilsby Sandstone.

Kimmeridge shale from Dorset occurs as a single find from an Iron Age deposit. Grey or black slate from medieval deposits may be imported, although might also be found in glacial deposits.

Assemblage composition by period

Period 3: Iron Age
A total of four objects were recorded from Period 3. With the exception of bracelet fragment no. 4 (not illustrated), all came from pits. Bracelet fragment no. 4 is the furthest travelled, originating from Kimmeridge, Dorset. Similar bracelets are abundant from Roman sites but were also widely distributed during the Iron Age. Most known Iron Age finds of shale bracelets are from southern England and this example is further from the source area than might be expected, although small fragments such as this must often have missed inclusion in the record. The single small

Context	Feature	Object type	Stone	Description	Weight (g)
2086	-	millstone	Niedermendig	1 large fragment from millstone, flat, worn grinding surface, rim trimmed with vertical grooves; 144 x 66 x 106mm	1474
2039	-	quern, rotary	Niedermendig	1 fragment from rotary quern, worn very thin, grinding surface now mainly worn smooth, other surface roughly pecked; 243 x 165mm, th 17–20mm	883
2039	-	quern	Niedermendig	1 fragment from rotary quern, worn thin, weathered but traces of wear on grinding surface and pecking on upper surface; 87 x 65 x 30mm	226
2039	-	quern	Niedermendig	2 fragments from rotary quern, worn grinding surface, pecked upper surface; 122 x 66 x 26mm and 78 x 72 x 30mm	507
2039	-	quern, rotary	Niedermendig	2 fragments from rotary quern, worn very thin, surface roughly pecked	521
15014	15015	quern	Niedermendig	3 small fragments	12
20406	20405	quern	Niedermendig	8+ fragments	109
20406	20405	quern	Niedermendig	4 small fragments, weathered	24
20580	20405	quern	Niedermendig	3 fragments, weathered	115
20582	20405	quern	Niedermendig	2+ fragments, weathered	31
20623	20405	quern	Niedermendig	3 small fragments	29
20729	20727	quern	Niedermendig	14+ small fragments, weathered	26
20729	20727	quern	Niedermendig	30+ fragments, weathered	259
20924	20405	quern	Niedermendig	2 fragments, weathered	146
21125	21127	quern	Niedermendig	14+ small fragments	15

Table 4.6 Quern/millstone fragments from Saxon-phased deposits

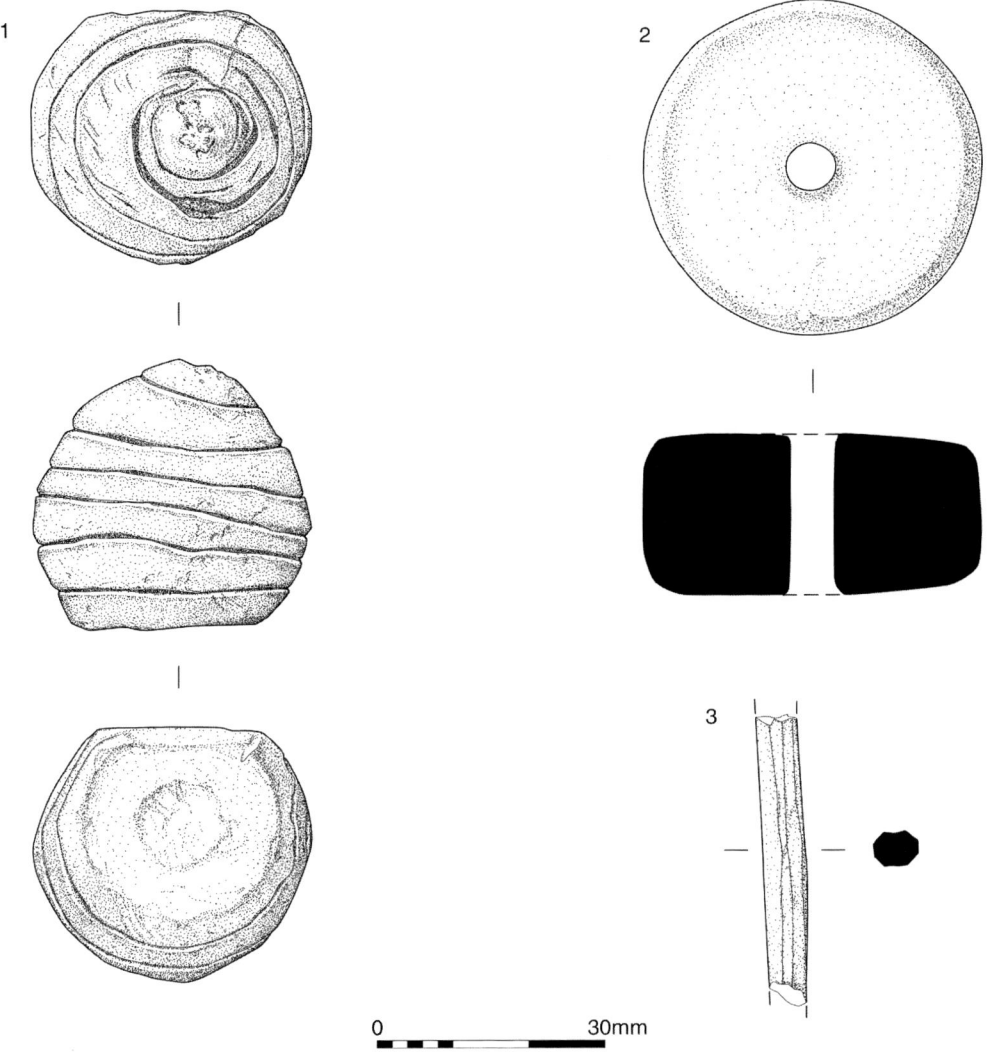

Figure 4.6 Stone (scale 1:1) nos 1–3

fragment of quern from pit 15129 was made from Spilsby sandstone. It is not possible to judge whether it came from a saddle or rotary quern, but it is known that numerous beehive querns were made from this variety of greensand (Ingle 1993–4, 30). The chalk weight no. 2 is probably local in origin. Similar, commonly crudely-made objects of chalk are known from Iron Age sites (Bayley 1985), and are variously interpreted as spindlewhorls or weights. Some may have functioned as weights for use with vertical, warp-weighted looms, although triangular-form weights more often associated with such a use are known from the site.

1   (Fig. 4.6, no. 2). Complete, disc-shaped spindlewhorl from fine grained grey sandstone, slightly calcareous. Central, straight, bored perforation. Diam. 45mm, th. 19.5mm; weight 64g. Period 3 pit 16101.

2   (Not ill.). Complete, discoid/roughly biconical chalk weight. Some wear from suspension in part of perforation. Diam. 69mm, th. 26mm; weight 127g. Period 3 pit 19215.

3   (Not ill.). Quern fragment. Spilsby sandstone. One flat worn surface, burnt; 70 x 54 x 57mm. Period 3 pit 15129.

4   (Not ill.). Kimmeridge shale bracelet fragment. Plain annular form with D-shaped section. 39 x 10 x 12.5mm. Period 3 Ditch 21105 (Ditch 5).

Period 5: Roman
(Table 4.5)
A total of eight objects of stone (2115g) was recorded from Roman phased deposits. All comprise quern (or millstone) fragments. The most commonly represented is Millstone Grit, most likely originating from Derbyshire or the Pennines and in common use in the Roman period (Roe 1996, 192). The five fragments recovered were too fragmentary for identification but might include both rotary querns and millstones.

Fragments of Niedermendig lava makes up the remainder of the Roman group. A probable millstone fragment from Area 3 Ditch 7 was identified based on its greater thicknesses (84mm). Its presence in a location not far from the River Lark raises the possibility of a Roman mill at the site, a possible precursor to the mill recorded from Mildenhall at the time of the Domesday Survey. Lava millstones are known from other Roman sites, not all of which have made their way into the literature, but one such millstone approximately 250mm in diameter was recorded at Westhawk Farm, Ashford, Kent (Roe 2008, 188). The remaining small fragments of lava recorded from the Roman-phased deposits are more typical of this material which disintegrates readily with time.

Context	Feature	Object type	Stone	Description	Weight (g)
2051		quern or millstone	Millstone Grit	1 block, weathered and stained by peat, one flat possibly worn surface, could be from rotary quern or millstone; 135 x 82 x 72mm	1385
2044		quern	Niedermendig	15+ small fragments	
3103		quern	Niedermendig	2+ small fragments	8
3625		quern	Niedermendig	1 fragment, weathered, trace of flat pecked surface	390
3022		quern	Niedermendig	1 fragment, smooth area on one surface	143
5198		quern	Niedermendig	20+ fragments, weathered	212
4088	4087	quern	Niedermendig	1 fragment, very weathered	104
4109	4110	quern	Niedermendig	5 small fragments	23
4083	4083	rod	slate, black	1 small rod with faceted sides, unknown purpose; 37.5 x 5 x 5mm	2
15126	15120	quern	Niedermendig	10+ fragments	148
15177	15178	quern	Niedermendig	3+ very small fragments	1
15180	15181	quern	Niedermendig	1 fragment	47
15184	15182	quern	Niedermendig	6 fragments, weathered	210
15419	15415	quern	Niedermendig	1 fragment, weathered	27
15418		quern	Niedermendig	1 fragment, weathered	170
15417		quern	Niedermendig	14+ small fragments	116
16030	16032	quern	greensand, possibly Spilsby	1 fragment probable rotary quern, small area of smoothly worn surface; 112 x 81 x 75mm	682
16004	16003	quern	Niedermendig	3 small fragments, weathered	41
16098	16095	quern	Niedermendig	11+ small fragments	44
19014	19015+ 19087	quern	Niedermendig	5+ fragments, weathered	148
20140	20138	quern	Niedermendig	3+ small fragments	37
20152	20151	quern	Niedermendig	5+ small fragments	24
20220	20044	quern	Niedermendig	2 small fragments, weathered	26
20425	20429	quern	Niedermendig	30+ small fragments	222
20867	20866	quern	Niedermendig	12 fragments, weathered	136
20991	20995	quern	Niedermendig	2 fragments, weathered	131
21003	21005	quern	Niedermendig	4+ fragments, weathered	227
21003	21005	quern	Niedermendig	4+ fragments, weathered	22
21003	21005	quern	Niedermendig	4 small fragments, weathered	9
21950	21944	quern	Niedermendig	5 small fragments	18
21950	21944	quern	Niedermendig	7+ small fragments	44
21061	21060	quern	Niedermendig	2 large fragments from rotary quern or possibly millstone, weathered, smaller fragment has flat, possibly worn surface	1430
21061	21060	quern	Niedermendig	1 fragment, weathered	39
21062	21060	quern	Niedermendig	1 fragment, weathered	38
21062	21060	quern	Niedermendig	1 fragment, weathered	371

Table 4.7 Quern/millstone fragments from medieval-phased deposits

				Period				
Unstrat.	2	3	4	5	6	7	9	
699	20514	668	269	2468	828	6816	177	

Table 4.8 Burnt stone summary weight (g) by period

Period 6: Anglo-Saxon
(Table 4.6)
The Period 6 worked stone consists entirely of Niedermendig lava fragments, recorded from ten deposits in Areas 2, and from features on the dry ground. Nearly all of it is in the familiar form of small fragments, however, there are three larger pieces from alluvium contexts on Area 2, where it was associated with pottery dating to the

9th to 11th centuries. All were worn thin; and it has not been possible to determine which of these fragments might originally have belonged to millstones. The recorded presence of a mill here in 1086 suggests that lava millstones might well have been in use as well as rotary querns. It can be suggested that the lava might have been delivered by sea to King's Lynn, as from there it should have been a relatively easy boat journey along the River Ouse and then the River Lark to Mildenhall.

Period 7: Medieval
(Table 4.7)
The medieval stone objects are more varied in character, although the largest collection of Niedermendig lava derives from this period. The majority comprises groups of small fragments which were recorded from 30

medieval-phased deposits, mainly in the area of the site less close to the river. Quern/millstone fragments from of non-Niedermendig type material are limited to single instances of millstone grit (Area 2 peat layer 2051), which is probably a residual Roman piece and of Spilsby Sandstone (Ditch 3). The latter is not necessarily redeposited from an earlier period, since querns from Lincoln demonstrate that Spilsby Sandstone apparently continued in use through the Saxon and Medieval periods and possibly later (Roe 1996).

The function of the facetted black slate object no. 5 is uncertain, though a stylus or a mason's tool for marking out are possibilities. An unworked fragment in a similar dark grey slate, a stone type which is not local to the area, was also recorded (pit 18020) and may be further evidence for the working of this material.

5 (Fig. 4.6, no. 3). Facetted (eight-sided) rod fragment from black slate. 37.5 x 5 x 5mm. Period 7 pit 4083.

Other (post-medieval and undated)
Further fragments (forty-three) of Niedermendig lava were recorded from four post-medieval/modern-phased deposits. All are likely to be re-deposited.

In addition there are two objects from unphased deposits (nos 6–7). Unstratified object no. 6 was smoothly hollowed on both main surfaces, probably from use as a mortar. Its dating is uncertain, however Iron Age date seems most likely. A nearly complete chalk gaming piece (no. 7) is tentatively dated to the medieval period. Chalk counters of approximately similar, domed, form (though undecorated) are known from Anglo-Scandinavian deposits at Coppergate, York (Mainman and Rogers 2000, 2566 and figs 1261, 1263). Further examples, some with crudely incised decoration, are also known from a late 12th-century building at Castle Acre, Norfolk (Coad and Streeton 1982, 260–63).

6 (Not ill.). Cobble of quartzitic sandstone with worn hollows on both main surfaces. 187 x 124 x 68mm; weight 2257g. Unstratified.

7 (Fig. 4.6, no. 1). Gaming piece(?) of chalk. Domed/beehive form with flat/concave base. Crudely-executed scored concentric rings/ spiral decoration to sides. Diam 36mm, height 34mm; weight 54g. Unstratified.

Burnt stone
(Table 4.8)
A substantial quantity of burnt stone (32.4kg) was recorded from the excavations. A significant proportion (20.5kg or 63%) was derived from Late Bronze Age phased deposits, principally the fills of Period 2 recut 22063 of pit 20238. The large bulk of material from this feature comprised pebble-sized or larger rounded clasts of quartzite or quartzitic sandstone. This uniformity suggests that material was deliberately collected, probably from riverine deposits, for a specific use. The most likely use for such material is as 'pot boilers'/heating stones for culinary/domestic use. Quantities of burnt stone from Period 3 (Iron Age) and subsequent periods are comparatively small. The mixed utilisation of quartzite pebbles as well as some tabular sandstone and limestone is less suggestive of deliberate selection and the burnt stone from Periods 3–4 may have related to a range domestic or industrial processes.

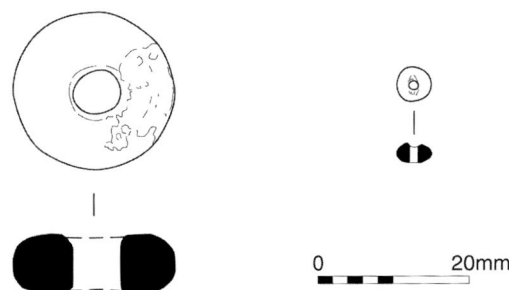

Figure 4.7 Glass objects (scale 1:1) nos 1–2

VI. Glass beads
by E.R. McSloy

Illustrated catalogue
(Fig. 4.7)

1 Plain annular bead. The surfaces were decayed and the obscured by a white crust almost certainly the result of calcareous burial conditions. Where a portion of this crust had fallen away, the colour of the bead can be seen to be a translucent yellow brown/amber colour. According to Guido's scheme this example fits best with her Group 6 (undecorated annular beads) and sub class v. (small translucent 'amber'). It is however unusually large for this grouping with most examples measuring under 15mm in diameter (Guido 1978, 65–8). The use of yellow/amber-coloured glasses appears to be largely confined to the 1st centuries BC/AD. The examples recorded by Guido occur mainly from the south or southeast (*ibid.* 68). Ext. Diam. 23mm; thickness 6mm. Period 3; pit 16005 (fill 16006).

2 Dark green translucent glass bead. Bi-convex in section. Pottery associated with this bead dated to the 12th to 13th centuries. Medieval glass beads appear to be uncommon, though those among the few published examples share similarities of size and colour with this example (Egan and Pritchard 1991). Diameter 5mm; thickness 3mm. Period 7; posthole 18074 (fill 18073).

VII. Later Prehistoric pottery
by Matt Brudenell with a contribution by R. Ixer

Introduction
The excavations yielded 1759 sherds of hand-recovered later Prehistoric pottery (26854g), with a further 380 sherds/crumbs deriving from soil samples (484g). The two major components of the assemblage were handmade Middle Iron Age-type wares (*c.* 350/300–50 BC/50 AD), which dominated the assemblage, and Late Bronze Age Post-Deverel Rimbury Plainwares (*c.* 1100–800 BC). Also present were a few Early Iron Age sherds (*c.* 600–350/300 BC), and a small group of both hand and wheel-made Late Iron Age-type ceramics, which most probably dated from the early to mid-1st century AD (Table 4.9).

This report provides a quantified characterisation of the hand-recovered pottery by ceramic phase period. The highly fragmented material recovered from the soil samples is quantified in Table 4.11, but is not otherwise discussed.

Methodology
All the pottery has been fully recorded following the recommendations laid out by the Prehistoric Ceramics Research Group (PCRG 2009). After a full inspection of the assemblage, fabric groups were allocated on the basis of dominant inclusion types, their density and modal size.

Ceramic phase/type	Date range	No/Wt (g) sherds	% by Wt (g)	MNV	EVE
Late Bronze Age	*c.* 1100–800 BC	377/4093	15.2	43	3.3
Early Iron Age	*c.* 600–350/300 BC	8/219	0.8	2	0.8
Middle Iron Age	*c.* 350/300–50 BC/**50 AD[?]**	1308/21690	80.8	243	22.5
Late Iron Age	*c.* 50 BC–50 AD	66/852	3.2	11	0.7

MNV = minimum number of vessels calculated as the total number of different rims and bases identified. EVE = estimated vessel equivalent

Table 4.9 Prehistoric pottery frequencies

Sherds were counted, weighed (to the nearest whole gram) and assigned to a fabric group. Sherds broken in excavation were counted as single entities. Sherd type was recorded, along with technology (wheel-made or handmade), evidence for surface treatment, decoration, and the presence of soot and/or residues. Rim and base-forms were described using a codified system recorded in the catalogue, and were assigned vessel numbers. Where possible, rim and base diameters were measured, and surviving percentages noted. In cases where a sherd or groups of refitting sherds retained portions of the rim and shoulder, the vessel was also categorised by form. The Late Bronze Age and Early Iron Age vessels were classified using a form-series devised by the author (Brudenell 2011b; 2012), and the class scheme created by John Barrett (1980), while Middle Iron Age-type forms were codified using the series developed by J.D. Hill (Hill and Horne 2003, 174; Hill and Braddock 2006, 155–156). All pottery was subject to sherd size analysis. Sherds less than 4cm in diameter were classified as 'small'; sherds measuring 4–8cm were classified as 'medium', and sherds over 8cm in diameter were classified as 'large'. A programme of refitting was also conducted, and sherd joins were noted within, and between, contexts. The quantified data is presented on an Excel data sheet held in the site archive.

Condition and residuality

The hand-recovered assemblage was in good condition. The mean sherd weight was relatively high at 15.3g, and only 53% of sherds were classified as small (43% medium; 4% large). Thoroughly abraded fragments were scarce, and few of the shell and calcareous inclusions had leached from sherd surfaces. Residues also survived intact on many fragments, with a total of 117 sherds (2673g; 7% by sherd count) retaining traces of soot and/or carbonised food crusts.

Levels of residuality, however, were high, reflecting the long sequence of occupation at the site (Table 4.10). In total, a maximum of 657 sherds (10589g) were classified as residual, representing 37% of the prehistoric pottery assemblage by sherd count, or 39% by weight. In the case of the Early Iron Age material, all of the pottery was residual, with no context phased to this period. Interestingly, the condition of the residual pottery was indistinguishable to that from period contexts, with mean sherd weights and sherd size frequencies displaying no major differences. This suggests that material disturbed from earlier contexts was not being extensively reworked, and may not have been exposed for long periods, or shifted far from its original context of deposition.

The Mildenhall fabric series

Most of the clays and tempering agents used in the production of the site's prehistoric pottery could have been obtained from the immediate locality. Flint and chalk were readily available from the site's own sub-soils, while sands and suitable potting clays could have been extracted from the terrace gravels and alluvial deposits flanking the adjacent River Lark. The origin of the shelly fabrics is harder to identify, though some presumably derived from fossiliferous Jurassic clays whose nearest outcrops lay *c.* 12–14km west of Mildenhall, around the eastern fen-edge. This region may also provide the source for two sherds with limestone inclusions (fabric QL1, possibly from the Wicken area), and the single sherd with glauconitic pellets (fabric GL1, possibly from the Cambridgeshire Greensand belt). The other distinctive, and potentially non-local, fabric is Q6, which is remarkably similar to a series of Early-Middle Iron Age fabrics recorded around Ipswich at the Whitehouse Industrial Estate (Suffolk HER: IPS247) and Morland Road (Brudenell 2011c; Suffolk HER: IPS617).

Fabric series
(Table 4.11)

Quartz sand fabrics
Q1: Moderate to common sub-angular quartz sand. Fabric is hard, compact, and abrasive to touch when un-burnished. Matrix may contain rare to sparse fragments of crushed and partially burnt flint (up to 3mm in diameter); rare flecks of mica; rare voids from burnt-out vegetable matter; very rare calcareous grits (up to 2mm in size), and/or very rare sub-rounded quartz grains (up to 2mm in size).
Q2: Sparse to common fine quartz sand. Fabric is hard, compact and better-sorted than Q1. Texture is less abrasive, and the matrix trends do not contain other inclusions, except rare to very rare mica.
Q3: Sparse to common fine quartz sand, and sparse to common mica. Fabric is hard, compact and well-sorted; sparkling slightly when turned in the light.
Q4: Moderate to common sub-angular quartz sand and sparse linear voids from burnt-out vegetable matter clearly visible on sherds surfaces. Fabric is hard, and often abrasive to touch when un-burnished. Matrix may contain a range of other rare or very rare inclusion similar to Q1.
Q5: Sparse to common quartz and sparse fine to medium voids (up to 1.5mm), possibly from dissolved calcareous inclusions. Fabric may be related to QCH1 or QCH2.
Q6: Sparse to moderate quartz sand, and moderate sub-rounded quartz grains (up to 2.5mm in diameter).
Q: Generic category for sherd with quartz sand too small to assign to type.

Quartz sand and organic-tempered fabrics
QVE1: Sparse to moderate quartz sand and sparse to moderate linear voids from burnt-out vegetable matter visible throughout the clay matrix. Related to Q4, the fabric is often hard and abrasive to touch when un-burnished.
QVE2: Sparse to moderate quartz sand and moderate to common linear voids from burnt-out vegetable matter visible throughout the clay matrix.
QVE3: Sparse to moderate quartz sand, moderate linear voids from burnt-out vegetable matter, and moderate mica. Surface sparkles slightly when turned in the light.

Period	Late Bronze (No/Wt)	Early Iron Age (No/Wt)	Middle Iron Age (No/Wt)	Late Iron Age (No/Wt)	Total
2	342/3713	-	-	-	342/3713
3	r22/314	r4/33	720/11963	i1/5	747/12315
4	r1/5	-	r?30/480	13/180	44/665
5	r6/15	r2/84	r261/4317	r26/309	295/4725
6	-	-	r37/456	r2/10	39/466
7	r5/45	r1/16	r185/3311	r14/172	205/3544
8	-	-	-	-	-
9	r1/1	r1/86	r58/935	3/33	63/1055
Unassigned	-	-	17/228	7/143	24/371
Total	**377/4093**	**8/219**	**1308/21690**	**66/852**	**1759/26854**

r = residual sherds in later contexts. i = intrusive sherds in earlier contexts. r? = Middle Iron Age-type sherds from Period 4 contexts potentially contemporary with 'true' Late Iron Age-type wares (see discussion below)

Table 4.10 Prehistoric pottery by period

Fabric Type	Fabric Group	No	Wt (g)	% of assemblage by Wt
F	Flint	35 (35)	60 (81)	0.2
F1	Flint	147	1708	6.4
F2	Flint	85	1140	4.2
F3	Flint	21	244	0.9
F4	Flint	41	140	0.5
FQ1	Flint and sand	2	46	0.2
FQ2	Flint and sand	24	682	2.5
FQ3	Flint and sand	15	215	0.8
FQ4	Flint and sand	4	17	0.1
G1	Grog	6	150	0.6
G2	Grog	3	10	<0.1
G3	Grog	8	84	0.3
GL1	Glauconite	1	5	<0.1
Q	Sand	4 (341)	5 (396)	<0.1
Q1	Sand	787	13020	48.5
Q2	Sand	133	1626	6.1
Q3	Sand	140	1864	6.9
Q4	Sand	128	2688	10.0
Q5	Sand	11	153	0.6
Q6	Sand	2	31	0.1
QCH1	Sand and calcareous	11	203	0.8
QCH2	Sand and calcareous	17	235	0.9
QL1	Sand and calcareous	2	31	0.1
QI1	Quartzite	5	33	0.1
QVE1	Sand and vegetable matter	46 (2)	1065 (5)	4.0
QVE2	Sand and vegetable matter	26	479	1.8
QVE3	Sand and vegetable matter	7	152	0.6
QVE4	Sand and vegetable matter	4	168	0.6
S1	Shell	7	230	0.9
S2	Shell	18 (2)	151 (2)	0.6
S3	Shell	2	34	0.1
S4	Shell	13	149	0.6
S5	Shell	4	36	0.1
Total		**1759**	**26854**	**100.1**

Table 4.11 Quantification of prehistoric pottery fabrics. Figures in brackets refer to pottery from soil samples

QVE4: Rare to sparse fine quartz sand and moderate linear voids from burnt-out vegetable matter. Fabric has a soft silky texture, though no grog is visible.

Quartz sand and calcareous inclusion fabrics
QCH1: Moderate to common quartz sand and sparse to moderate calcareous flecking (mainly under 1mm in size). Fabric is generally hard and compact.
QCH2: Sparse to common quartz sand and sparse fine to medium chalk inclusions (mainly 1–2mm in size with occasional larger fragments).
QL1: Moderate quartz sand and sparse to common fine or medium limestone inclusions (up to 2mm in size).

Glauconitic fabrics
GL1: Common to abundant sand-sized glauconite (?) pellets.

Crushed burnt flint and quartz sand fabrics
FQ1: Moderate to common medium to very coarse burnt flint (2–4mm) in a sandy clay matrix. Fabric is hard and abrasive to touch.
FQ2: Moderate to common medium to coarse burnt flint (2–3mm in size) in a dense sandy clay matrix. Fabric is hard and abrasive to touch.
FQ3: Sparse to common fine to medium burnt flint (1–2mm in size) in a dense sandy clay matrix.
FQ4: Sparse to moderate fine burnt flint (mainly <1mm in size) in a dense sandy clay matrix.

F1: Sparse to common medium to very coarse burnt flint (2–4mm). Matrix contains very rare to sparse quartz sand.
F2: Moderate to common medium to coarse burnt flint (2–3mm). Matrix contains very rare to sparse quartz sand.
F3: Sparse to common fine to medium burnt flint (1–2mm). Matrix contains very rare to sparse quartz sand.
F4: Sparse to common fine burnt flint (mainly <1mm). Matrix contains very rare to sparse quartz, sparse sand.
F: Generic category for sherds with flint inclusions too small to assign to a numbered fabric group.

Quartzite fabrics
QI1: Sparse to common fine to medium angular quartzite (up to 2mm) in a sandy clay matrix. Some sherds may contain rare to sparse flecks of mica.

Shell fabrics
S1: Common medium to very coarse shell (1–5mm in size). A compact fabric, poorly sorted.
S2: Moderate to common medium to coarse shell (1–3mm in size), poorly sorted.
S3: Abundant medium shell (1–2mm in size), poorly sorted.
S4: Sparse to common fine shell or shell flecking (mainly <1mm, with rare larger inclusions). Matrix occasionally contains a background of quartz sand.
S5: Rare to spare medium shell (1–2mm) and rare to moderate calcareous flecks (mainly <1mm). Matrix occasionally contains a background of quartz sand.
S: Generic category for sherds with shell inclusions too small to assign to a numbered fabric group.

Grog fabrics
G1: Sparse to moderate medium grog (mainly 1–2mm with rare larger inclusions) in a sandy clay matrix. Fabric sometimes has calcareous flecks or voids (up to 2mm) possibly from dissolved calcareous inclusions.
G2: Sparse to moderate fine grog (mainly <1mm in size). Fabric is compact with a silky texture.
G3: Moderate to common quartz sand and fine grog (mainly <1mm in size). The fabric is generally hard, compact and well-sorted. Matrix occasionally contains flecks of mica.

Thin-section analysis
by R. Ixer

Eight pottery sherd samples were provided for petrographical examination. Initially, the exposed surfaces, cut surface and thin-section of the ten samples were investigated using a x20 hand lens and the rock-colour chart of the Geological Society of America (GSA 1995), and GEO Sedimentary Grain Card, to determine colour and geological fabric. A standard thin-section was prepared from each of the samples. Each section was investigated using transmitted light petrography, in plane-polarised and crossed-polarised light, using x6.3 and x12.5 objectives with x12.5 eye pieces, giving overall magnifications of x80 and x155.

The selected samples comprised sherds taken from La Tène-decorated vessels in quartz sand-tempered fabrics (Q1, Q2, Q3 and Q4), and two 'control' samples from undecorated quartz sand-tempered fabrics (Q1). Analysis sought to determine whether the group was coherent in terms of its fabric, and if the group was wholly, or in part, of non-local origin.

Detailed petrographical characterisation of the samples is contained in the archive. The report presented here is limited to the discussion of manufacture and the geographical provenance of the raw materials. Where possible, the origin of the raw materials used in the manufacture of the pot was geographically sourced, and divided into local (less than 10km), regional (50km) or exotic categories, with reference to the findspot.

Results

Quartz or chert-tempered. Fabric A
Thin-section petrography (on a single example) supports macroscopic Fabric Group Q3 as a distinct fabric group. Sherd 6 (LT decorated vessel sherd from Period 5 pit 20714, fill 20715) is from a very well made, quartz/chert-tempered pot, probably made from local raw materials. It is clearly different in manufacture from all the other samples, as the non-plastic components appear crushed. The grain-size of the temper is fine sand, or less (<187–187μm in size), and this is far finer than any other of the investigated ceramics. The pot has a higher preparation index, as defined by Ixer and Lunt (1991), than the other ceramics. This is consistent with macroscopic Fabric Q3, in being distinctive and separate from the other sherds.

Fabric B
None of these pots/ceramics shows signs of crushed, inorganic non-plastics. Petrographically, they represent a continuum, including the addition of natural quartz sand ± plant material to clean and/or fine sandy clays. Quartz sand tempering is present, or probably present, in all of the pots. The petrographical evidence for plant-tempering is less clear, although Class Bb is probably plant-tempered.

Sand-tempered Ba
Thin-section petrography of samples 5 (Period 3 pit 15234, fill 15276); 7 (Period 5 pit fill 20715) and 8 (Period 3 pit 20759, fill 21258) supports the identification of macroscopic Fabric Group Q1 as a fabric group. However, it should be noted that most could be plant-poor QVE1. This is a fairly coherent, sand-tempered fabric group. All the ceramics are natural, sand-tempered fabrics, with rounded to sub-rounded, medium to coarse sands (375–750μm in size), and most carry rare organic matter, often as single, large linear clasts. The amount of plant matter varies; it is absent in Sample 8, and very rare in nos 5 and 7, and in no ceramic is there sufficient plant matter to suggest its use as tempering. This petrographic group equates quite well with Fabric Q1, although in thin-section the grains are seen to be more sub-rounded than sub-angular. The chert is both burned and unburned, and is integral to the quartz sand rather than as an

intentionally added, crushed temper. Minor amounts of rounded micrite, possibly chalk, are present in Sample 5. Although Sample 8 is a clear member of Ba, it has some differences from the other members of this group and may have a different geographical origin. The evidence for this is slight, however.

Plant tempered in sandy clays or Plant/Sand-tempered Bb
Thin-section petrography of Samples 1 (Period 9 subsoil 20002); 2 (Period 3 pit fill 20159); 3 (Period 3 pit fill 20265) and 4 (Period 9 pit fill 20588) is less supportive of macroscopic Fabric Groups Q4 and Q2, and rather supports the macroscopic Fabric Groups QVE1 and QV2. However, the numbers of thin-section samples is restricted, and the boundaries within the macroscopic groups are unknown. Thin-section petrography should not take precedence over the macroscopic conclusions if based on larger numbers of samples.

This is a non-coherent group that may encompass two or more sub-groups. It is difficult to determine whether the non-plastics show a bimodal or unimodal size distribution. If it is bimodal, then the pots are plant-medium sand-tempered in a fine clay (non-plastics <187µm in diameter), but if unimodal, then the pots are plant-tempered in a medium-grained sandy clay (250–375, but up to 500µm in diameter). Where it is possible to determine the plant matter, it appears to be grass and is therefore an intentional temper. Sherds 1, 20002, and 4, 20588, have a finer-grained ('cleaner') main paste component than Sherds 2 and 3. Sherd 4 is locally poorly-mixed, with thin, fine sand(y) clay laminae, devoid of plant matter or larger non-plastic clasts, suggesting that the main clay used was a fine sandy clay. If so, this sherd is plant-fine to medium sand (187–275µm diameter), tempered in a very fine-grained sandy clay.

Sherds 2, 20159, and 3, 20265, possibly display a unimodal size distribution, and so would be plant-tempered in medium-grained sandy clays. However, if the rare 'autogrog' that is present represents the main paste, then the pots are medium sand/plant-tempered in a very fine sandy clay, like sherd 4. Sherd 1 appears to be plant-tempered in a fine-medium grained sandy clay, but may be plant-medium sand tempered in a very fine sandy clay.

Manufacture: tempering
Sample 6 (Period 5 pit 20714, fill 20715) is tempered with crushed quartz and chert, and is different from the others. This is a very carefully-made pot. All the other ceramics appear to be tempered with an uncrushed, natural, quartz-dominated sand, accompanied by plant material in Samples 1–4. The natural sand has a tight size-range, and may have been size-graded intentionally. Carbonate, including micrite (possibly chalk), and bone clasts, are rare, and have not been intentionally added.

Origin of the raw materials
The main inorganic non-plastic is monocrystalline quartz, and this is accompanied by minor amounts of feldspar, including both plagioclase and potassium feldspar groups alongside quartz-rich rock clasts dominated by chert and meta-sandstone, plus trace-amounts of acid igneous and low-grade metamorphic rocks. All these components are common within Eastern England glacial till/boulder clay, and are ultimately derived from sandstones. In addition, there is little that is diagnostic about the clay, as there is little evidence for chalk within it (that might suggest a local origin), and the identifiable components of the clay fraction, namely quartz, white mica and heavy minerals (zircon and tourmaline), are to be expected in most English secondary clays.

Hence, despite the sherds and crucibles having a variety of pastes/main clays, no ceramics can be precisely provenanced with certainty. However, none can be clearly seen to be exotic with reference to their find spot, and all the sherds could be manufactured from local (less than 20km) materials.

Conclusions
All the ceramics could be of local, and certainly regional, manufacture. With the exception of Sample 6 (Period 5 pit 20714, pit fill 20715), they are natural quartz sand ± plant tempered within a restricted set of recipes. There are no fundamental petrographical differences between the decorated and undecorated sherds. There is no evidence for pots being imported from non-local areas characterised by having very different raw materials. But as there are few petrographical indications of raw materials from different sources, it is not possible to determine whether the sherds include pots from different local areas (with essentially the same raw materials) or if they were all made in the same place using naturally unhomogeneous ingredients. Mineralogical differences, namely the presence/absence of zircon and tourmaline in the clay fraction, and variation in the composition and amount of the sparse igneous and metamorphic rock clasts in the sand temper, only hint at different local sources as they may just as easily reflect a natural variation in any single local clay and sand source.

The thin-section petrography strongly supports the macroscopically-defined Fabrics Q1 and Q3, but is less supportive of Q2 and Q4. It may be that there is a continuum between these last two fabrics and fabric QVE1 and QVE2 (these would have been preferred microscopically).

The Late Bronze Age pottery
An assemblage, comprising 377 sherds (4093g) of Late Bronze Age Plainware pottery, was recovered from the excavations, displaying a mean sherd weight (MSW) of 10.9g (68% small sherds; 28% medium; 3% large). The pottery was recovered from a total of thirty-seven contexts from a range of features. The only large assemblage derived from contexts associated with the filling and reworking of pit 20238 (associated re-cuts with pottery: 20325 and 22063–5), which yielded a combined total of 335 sherds weighing 3655g. None of the other features yielded more than seven sherds apiece, with most containing just one or two fragments. The vast majority of these were residual in Period 3–9 contexts (see Table 4.10, thirty-five sherds, 380g), and other than the material associated with aforementioned pit 20238 (and associated re-cuts), the only other non-residual pottery derived from pits 20251 (three sherds, 26g) 20980 (one sherd, 9g), and posthole 20183 (two sherds, 3g).

Fabrics and forms
Fifteen Late Bronze Age fabrics types were distinguished in the assemblage, each assignable to one of seven principal groups (Table 4.12). By weight, 99% of the

Fabric Type	Fabric Group	No/Wt sherds	% (by Wt)	No/Wt sherds burnished	% of fabric burnished (by Wt)	MNV	MNV burnished
F	Flint	35/60	1.5	-	-	2	-
F1	Flint	147/1708	41.7	6/44	2.6	15	1
F2	Flint	83/1114	27.2	7/49	4.4	11	1
F3	Flint	21/244	6	10/205	84.0	-	5
F4	Flint	41/140	3.4	36/119	85.0	7	-
FQ1	Flint and sand	2/46	1.1	-	-	-	-
FQ2	Flint and sand	23/596	14.6	-	-	3	-
FQ3	Flint and sand	13/123	3.0	-	-	2	-
FQ4	Flint and sand	2/12	0.3	2/12	100.0	1	1
GL1	Glauconite	1/5	0.1	1/5	100.0	-	-
Q3	Sand	1/3	0.1	1/3	100.0	-	-
QCH2	Sand and calc.	2/6	0.1	-	-	-	-
QI1	Quartzite	4/17	0.4	1/7	41.2	1	-
S2	Shell	1/15	0.4	1/15	100	1	1
S4	Shell	1/4	0.1	-	-	-	-
Total		**377/4093**	**100.0**	**65/459**	**11.2**	**43**	**9**

MNV = minimum number of vessels, calculated as the total number of different rims and bases

Table 4.12 Late Bronze Age fabric frequencies and the relationship to burnishing and vessel counts

pottery was tempered with burnt flint, or a combination of flint and sand, prominent amongst which were fabric types F1 and F2, accounting for 69% of the assemblage alone. The dominance of burnt-flint fabrics is typical of Late Bronze Age Post-Deverel Rimbury (PDR) assemblages in Suffolk and parts of Eastern England (Brudenell 2012); the grade and density of the inclusions varying along the spectrum of coarse to fine, and sparse to common, linked largely to the quality of the ware and vessel size. In general, fabrics F1–2 and FQ1–2 can be classified as 'coarse' fabrics (85% of the assemblage by weight); F3 and FQ3 as 'intermediate' (9%), and F4 and FQ4 as 'fine' (4%). The remaining 1% of pottery in the assemblage was shared amongst minor fabric groups containing sand, shell, sand-and-calcareous inclusions, quartzite and glauconite.

Based on the total number of different rims and bases identified, the assemblage represents a minimum of forty-three vessels with an Estimated Vessel Equivalent (EVE) of 3.3. This figure includes twenty-eight separate rims (five of which were measurable), fourteen bases (five with pinched-out feet; four with heavy gritting on the underside) and one complete vessel profile. Jars, bowls and cups were all identified, although in total only eight vessels were sufficiently intact to allow attribution of form (twenty-seven sherds, 428g). Following Barrett's (1980) classification, four of these may be described as Class I coarseware jars: a weakly-shouldered jar with fingertip decoration around the girth (Form G; Fig, 4.8, no. 3); a high-shouldered jar with in-sloped neck and short, upright rim (Form F; Fig. 4.8, no. 2); a barrel-shaped jar with short, upright rim (Form D; Fig. 4.8, no. 6), and a neck-less jar with convex walls (Form B; Fig. 4.8, no. 1). The bowls included a burnished Class IV vessel with a round shoulder and short upright neck (Form K; Fig. 4.8, no. 5), and the complete profile of a deep Class III coarseware bowl of bipartite profile (Form M; Fig. 4.8, no. 7). In both form and size, the latter is very similar to the bowl published from Beeston Regis, Norfolk which contained a

hoard of Ewart Park-type socketed axes closely dated to between c. 1020–800 BC (Lawson 1980, 218, fig. 1). The two Class V cup-forms in the assemblage included a round-bodied vessel with an everted, tapered rim (Form T), and a cup with slightly convex walls (Form S; Fig. 4.8, no. 4).

Surface treatment and decoration
Burnishing was relatively common, with sixty-five sherds treated (459g), representing 17% of the assemblage by count (11.2% by weight). Although sherds in a variety of fabrics were burnished, only the fine and intermediate flint-gritted wares were regularly treated – i.e. fabric types F3 and F4. Decoration was absent from the burnished finewares, but was found on a total of eight un-burnished sherds (105g) from a maximum of five vessels. Forms of application were confined to finger-tipping and scoring. Fingertip-impressions were present on fragments of two separate neck-cordons (five sherds, 57g, e.g. Fig. 4.8, no. 8), a single rim-top (one sherd, 12g), and the shoulder of a coarseware jar (one sherd, 33g, discussed above). Scoring was identified on one body sherd (3g).

Deposition
The only significant group of non-residual Late Bronze Age pottery derived from contexts associated with the filling and reworking of pit 20238. By both sherd count and weight, this yielded 89% of the pottery in the Late Bronze Age assemblage as a whole, or 98% of the non-residual material from Period 2 contexts. The pottery, which included fragments of a minimum of thirty-eight different vessels, was primarily recovered from the sequence of re-cuts in the upper profile of pit 20238 (contexts 22063–5). The fills from these re-cuts yielded ceramics in varying states of fragmentation and abrasion, the character of the material suggesting that the pottery derived from one or more surface refuse-heaps/midden-dumps; contexts in which an assortment of spent materials accumulated (Brudenell and Cooper 2008). This material

Fabric Type	Fabric Group	No/Wt sherds	% (by Wt)	No/Wt sherds burnished	% of fabric burnished (by Wt)	MNV	MNV burnished
F2	Flint	2/26	11.9	1/16	61.5	-	-
FQ2	Flint and sand	1/86	39.3	1/86	100.0	1	1
FQ3	Flint and sand	2/92	42.0	2/92	100.0	1	1
FQ4	Flint and sand	2/5	2.3	-	-	-	-
Q1	Sand	1/10	4.6	-	-	-	-
Total		**8/219**	**100.1**	**4/194**	**88.6**	**2**	**2**

MNV = minimum number of vessels, calculated as the total number of different rims and bases

Table 4.13 Early Iron Age fabric frequencies and the relationship to burnishing and vessel counts

had been mixed and reworked, with refitting sherds identified between contexts 20319–20 and 20336–8. However, there were indications that some elements of this assemblage were compiled and deposited with greater care, as context 20335 contained the complete profile of a broken coarseware bowl, and the shoulder, lower walls and base of a second coarseware vessel.

The Early Iron Age pottery
Only eight sherds (219g) of probable Early Iron Age pottery were identified in the assemblage, all of which were residual (Tables 4.9 and 4.10). The pottery was in sand (5% by weight), flint (12%), and flint and sand-tempered fabrics (84%), similar to those of the Late Bronze Age assemblage (Table 4.13). There was therefore some ambiguity in dating, as has been noted elsewhere (Martin 1999, 74) though the flint in the pottery assigned to Early Iron Age at this site tended to be crushed to a more uniform size and did not regularly penetrate the sherd surfaces. Of key importance, however, were a series of diagnostic sherds, the most significant of which was a pedestal base recovered from pit 20513 (Fig. 4.8, no. 10). These base-forms were modelled on continental prototypes of the 6th century BC and later (Hodson 1962, 142; Barrett 1978, 286–287), and are a type-fossil of the Early Iron Age in this region. Other diagnostic sherds included an angular shoulder sherd from silting layer 3147, and a shoulder-sherd with linear stab-marks from pit 18015.

The Middle Iron Age-type pottery
The excavations yielded 1308 sherds (21690g) of handmade Middle Iron Age-type pottery displaying a high MSW of 16.6g (49% small sherds; 47% medium; 4% large). Based on the total number of different rims and bases identified, this represents a minimum of 243 vessels with an EVE of 22.5 (151 different rims; 88 different bases; 4 complete vessel profiles). The pottery is referred to as Middle Iron Age-*type* in this report because the currency of these handmade wares persisted until at least the mid-1st century BC, and beyond, in most parts of Suffolk and northern East Anglia. In other words, the currency of the region's ceramic traditions in the later 1st millennium BC do not map neatly onto conventional period divisions.

The term Middle Iron Age-type ware is therefore used to denote handmade ceramics that belong to this long-lived and largely conservative potting tradition, whose main *floruit* was between *c.* 350–50 BC in Suffolk.

Material of this type was found in 260 contexts, which were recorded from a wide range of features. In total, just under half these Middle Iron Age-type sherds were residual (571 sherds, 9499g, see Table 4.10). With the exception of six pits (Period 7 pits 19119, 21005 and 21663, and two modern pits), all the features with residual pottery yielded fewer than ten Middle Iron Age-type sherds. The six pits contained between eleven and forty-seven sherds apiece, with large groups (>500g) derived from 19119 and 21005.

The non-residual sherds (720 sherds, 11963g) derived from sixty-eight Period 3 features, of which fifty-eight were pits. Given the caveats about ceramic dating and periodisation cited above, is possible that material classed as 'residual' from Period 4 contexts may actually be of Late Iron Age origin, given the extended currency of these handmade wares (marked 'r?' in Table 4.10). The issue of residuality was difficult to resolve in many instances, although as the assemblage in question comprised only thirty sherds (480g) from two features, this has limited implications for the broader phasing of the site, or for the characterisation and discussion of this material.

Fabrics, forms and vessel sizes
The assemblage was characterised by sherds in dense sandy fabrics, with only a small percentage of shelly wares and sherds with other distinctive inclusions (quartzite and other calcareous inclusions). Although twenty Middle Iron Age fabric-types were ultimately distinguished, 87% of the pottery by weight had quartz sand as the principle ingredient, with a further 9% containing a mix of sand and burnt-out vegetable matter (Table 4.14). Thin-section petrography was conducted on a sample of eight Middle Iron Age-type sandy wares in fabrics Q1 (samples 5, 7 and 8), Q2 (samples 1 and 4), Q3 (sample 6) and Q4 (samples 2 and 3). The results support the macroscopic definition of fabric types Q3 and Q1 (defined petrographically as fabric A and Ba respectively), but indicate that Q2 and Q4 form a non-coherent group of sand and plant-tempered wares (defined petrographically as fabric Bb), probably in continuum with fabrics QVE1 and QVE2. The implication is that pots were being made within a restricted series of fabric recipes, with only subtle variations observed in the balance of ingredients (sand or sand and vegetable matter). Although there are hints from the mineralogical fraction of the clay that different local sources may have been exploited, these may simply reflect natural variations in the character of a single clay and sand source.

Fabric Type	Fabric Group	No/Wt sherds	% (by Wt)	No/Wt sherds burnished	% of fabric burnished (by Wt)	MNV	MNV burnished
Q	Sand	4/5	<0.1	-	-	1	-
Q1	Sand	757/12635	58.3	354/6285	49.7	133	53
Q2	Sand	120/1550	7.1	98/1265	81.6	23	21
Q3	Sand	134/1805	8.3	111/1424	78.9	23	19
Q4	Sand	128/2688	12.4	63/1131	42.1	27	10
Q5	Sand	11/153	0.7	8/128	83.7	4	4
Q6	Sand	2/31	0.1	-	-	-	-
QCH1	Sand and calc.	11/203	0.9	6/167	82.3	2	1
QCH2	Sand and calc.	15/229	1.1	12/200	87.3	4	2
QL1	Sand and calc.	2/31	0.1	-	-	-	-
QI1	Quartzite	1/16	0.1	1/16	100.0	-	-
QVE1	Sand and veg.	46/1065	4.9	27/642	60.3	5	4
QVE2	Sand and veg.	26/479	2.2	9/190	39.7	8	3
QVE3	Sand and veg.	7/152	0.7	-	-	1	-
QVE4	Sand and veg.	4/168	0.8	3/154	91.7	1	1
S1	Shell	6/152	0.7	3/72	47.4	1	-
S2	Shell	17/136	0.6	4/53	39.0	5	2
S3	Shell	2/34	0.2	3/29	85.3	1	-
S4	Shell	11/122	0.6	-	-	2	1
S5	Shell	4/36	0.2	2/14	38.9	2	1
Total		**1308/21690**	**100.0**	**704/11770**	**54.3**	**243**	**122**

MNV = minimum number of vessels, calculated as the total number of different rims and bases

Table 4.14 Middle Iron Age-type fabric frequencies and the relationship to burnishing and vessel counts

Only one, or a few, local clay sources seems likely, and there is no direct evidence from the samples examined to indicate that these dominant wares were being imported from further afield in areas characterised by very different raw materials. This picture is broadly consistent with the model of local production and distribution forwarded by Morris (1994; 1996) for the Middle Iron Age in Eastern England, but largely untested by systematic petrographical examination. Macroscopically, the variety and relative frequency of these fabrics is certainly typical of this period in Suffolk and other parts of East Anglia, which lends further weight to Morris' conclusions. The same can also be said of the range of vessel forms identified, which are widely paralleled at the regional scale. In general, these comprised a variety of ovoid and globular jars and bowls, most of which display weakly-pronounced shoulders and short necks terminating in either rounded, flat-topped, everted, beaded or externally thickened rims. In total, just over a third of the vessels (ninety-three by vessel count) in the assemblage could be assigned to form, including 184 sherds, weighing 48616g (Table 4.15).

Shouldered vessels of Form A, B, D and E dominated the group; notably the slack-shouldered jars of Form A which made up a quarter of the classified vessels. These tended to have ovoid bodies, and were found in a range of fabrics and rim sizes. Two of these jars retained complete profiles, including a burnished pin-dot decorated vessel from pit 20868 (not shown on plan; Fig. 4.8, no. 12), and a plain, burnished vessel from pit 15271 (Fig. 4.9, no. 18). Globular and ovoid vessels of Forms K and L were the second most common, and generally comprised small pots with mouth diameters under 15cm. The Form K varieties had no distinct neck-zone. These comprised

squat, tub-shaped vessels, convex-walled jars, and even the occasional cup. By contrast, most of the Form L pots displayed rounded bodies with distinct, but stunted, rims. Some resemble the globular bowls of Form M/N, which have bulbous or 'fish-bowl'-shaped profiles. A few of these pots also share affinities with the group of S-shaped globular jars and bowls of Form F/G in the assemblage. Amongst the latter was a complete profile of a deep, burnished bowl from pit 17218 (Fig. 4.9, 21), whose body was decorated with two rows of grooved, concentric ovals, with single impressed dots at their centre. These were framed by a row of impressed dots along the neck and foot of the vessel.

Most form-assigned vessels had small mouth-diameters, with only eight measuring over 18cm. Overall, the rim diameter of fifty-six vessel could be established in the assemblage (fifty-two of which belonged to form-assigned vessels), with a clear peak in the representation of pots with diameters between 12–17cm (Figure 4.12). This trend is quite common, and is thought to reflect the higher breakage and deposition-rate of smaller cooking and serving vessels. Such pots were probably used and handled on a day-to-day basis, whereas larger vessels, such as storage jars, may have moved, and ultimately broken less frequently (Hill 1995, 129–30; Hill and Horne 2003, 182).

Surface treatment and decoration
A total of 704 sherds (11770g) were burnished or polished, and represented 54% of the assemblage by sherd count or weight. This figure is high for Middle Iron Age pottery groups, but is matched in a nearby assemblage at Low Park Corner, Chippenham, Cambridgeshire (Brudenell 2013), perhaps suggesting a local preference

Form	Description	MNV	MNV burnished	No/Wt (g) sherds	Rim diameter range
A	Slack shouldered vessels with short upright necks	25	15	63/1170	9-20cm
B	Jars with pronounced rounded shoulders and short off-set upright necks. Constricted mouth.	3	3	9/348	12-16cm
D	Slack shouldered vessels with out-turned necks	10	5	18/706	14-22cm
E	Vessels with a high rounded shoulder and upright neck	4	1	4/202	14-22cm
F/G	Bowls or globular jars with an S-shaped profile	10	9	25/875	13-22cm
K	Ovoid or globular vessels with no distinct neck zone	11	3	23/493	10-14cm
L	Ovoid or globular bowls and squat jars with no distinct neck zone, but a clearly defined rim	21	15	25/561	11-20cm
M/N	Globular 'fish-bowl'-shaped vessels with slightly beaded or everted rims	7	5	14/409	8-14cm
P	Flared walled vessels with no distinct shoulder	1	1	2/80	21cm
Misc.	Shouldered cup with in-turned neck	1	1	1/17	-
Total		**93**	**58**	**184/4861**	**8-22cm**

MNV = minimum number of vessels

Table 4.15 Quantification of Middle Iron Age-type vessel forms. The descriptions are a simplified version of those fully published by Hill and Horne (2003, 174) and Hill and Braddock (2006, 155–156)

for pots with a lustrous surface finish. Decoration was also prolific, with 109 sherds bearing different forms of ornamentation (1949g). The un-burnished sherds were mainly scored (twenty-nine sherds, 544g), or had fingertip/nail impressions on the rims (nine sherds, 248g; nine different vessel rims). Three of the scored sherds (58g, *e.g.* Fig. 4.10, no. 28) were in shell-tempered fabrics typical of pots belonging to the East Midland Scored Ware tradition (Elsdon 1992). These are almost certainly non-local vessels, and may have been acquired through exchange networks with communities to the west, around the southern and western fen-basin.

More extraordinary, however, is the wide array of tooled decoration displayed on the burnished sherds. Leaving aside the rim of a form P-ornamented vessel with fingertip impressions and stab-marks (possibly executed with a bone; two sherds 40g; Fig. 4.10, no. 32), there were sixty-eight burnished sherds (1009g) with grooved, incised and/or dot-impressed decoration on their surfaces; many forming parts of complex curvilinear and geometric patterns (*e.g.* Fig 4.10, nos 35–39, with some of the dot-decorated sherds having white inlay (*e.g.* Fig. 4.10, no. 39). Although the size of the fragments makes motifs difficult to reconstruct in full, they belong to a 'late La Tène-style' decorative tradition which seems to emerge in the 2nd or 1st century BC in Eastern England (Hill and Horne 2003, 180). The collection is one of the largest recovered from a single site in East Anglia (eclipsed only

by Mucking; Brudenell forthcoming), and is regionally significant.

Deposition
The pottery from the Period 3 contexts derived from a fairly limited range of features, dominated by pits (see above). In general, the vast majority (75%) of feature assemblages comprised small groups of pottery weighing less than 250g. These contained just a handful of sherds each, often derived from different vessels. The character of the medium-sized deposits was broadly similar, although three pits in this category yielded complete vessel profiles (pits 15271, 17218 and 20868, not shown on plan); two being highly decorated late La Tène-style pots. These appear to have been singled out for formal treatment in deposition, possibly because they were ornamented.

More infrequent still were the large deposits, all of which yielded over 500g of material (Table 4.16). These derived from just 9% of pottery-bearing Period 3 features, but contained 40% of sherds in the non-residual assemblage (46% by weight). Pit 16063 was the only one to contain a complete vessel profile. However, all contained fragments of multiple vessels, most with refitting sherds within the deposits. With the exception of Ditch 5, they also displayed mean sherd weights above the assemblage average, and were generally characterised by 'fresh'/unabraded medium sized sherds.

Feature	No/Wt (g) sherds	MNV	No. refits	MSW	% Small (<4cm)	% Medium (4-8cm)	% Large (>8cm)
Pit* 15234	32/673	9	9	21.0	22	69	9
Pit 16063	63/1241	7	14	19.7	41	49	10
Pit 19215	61/1175	11	10	19.3	48	49	3
Pit 20153	43/736	14	-	17.1	37	56	7
Pit 21275	34/789	9	10	23.2	38	50	12
Ditch 5	57/855	12	-	15.0	51	47	2

* denotes assemblages associated with radiocarbon dates

Table 4.16 Composition of large-sized Period 3 assemblages

Fabric Type	Fabric Group	No/Wt sherds	% of fabric (by wt.)	No/Wt Burnished	% of fabric burnished (by Wt)	No/Wt Wheel-made	MNV	MNV burnished
G1	Grog	6/150	17.6	1/10	6.7	-	-	-
G2	Grog	3/10	1.2	1/4	40.0	3/10	1	-
G3	Grog	8/84	9.9	5/55	65.5	2/30	2	-
Q1	Sand	29/375	44	11/140	37.3	10/95	6	3
Q2	Sand	13/76	8.9	7/46	60.5	8/49	1	1
Q3	Sand	5/56	6.6	5/56	100	3/12	1	1
S1	Shell	1/78	9.2	-	-	-	-	-
S4	Shell	1/23	2.7	-	-	1/23	-	-
Total		**66/852**	**100.1**	**30/311**	**36.5**	**27/219**	**11**	**5**

MNV = minimum number of vessels, calculated as the total number of different rims and bases

Table 4.17 Late Iron Age fabric frequencies and the relationship to burnishing, ceramic technology and vessel counts

The Late Iron Age-type pottery

In most parts of Suffolk, the adoption of wheel-made 'Belgic' pottery and other diagnostic Late Iron Age-type ceramic forms (*i.e.* handmade or wheel-made grog-tempered pots, and combed or rilled jars) was a protracted and piecemeal process, which only began to accelerate in the decades immediately prior to the Roman Conquest (Hill 2002). On most settlements there was no wholesale replacement of the handmade potting traditions of the Middle Iron Age, which persisted alongside the introduction of wheel-made wares and other 'Beligicised' ceramic influences (see discussion above). Though it is often difficult to identify the stage at which these Late Iron Age-type wares were grafted onto the pottery repertoire (since closely datable ceramics such as Gallo-Belgic imports are rare from domestic contexts), they appear to be absent from the region's settlement sites prior to the mid to late 1st century BC (Sealey 2007, 27–31).

In this context, only 66 sherds (852g) of Late Iron Age-type pottery were identified in the assemblage, displaying a MSW of 12.9g (Table 4.17); 58% small sherds; 39% medium; 3% large). The pottery included both handmade and wheel-made sherds (41% by count), in a range of grog (29% by weight), sand (60%) and shell-tempered fabrics (12%). Pottery was recovered from thirty-one contexts relating to a range of features.

Pottery was primarily assigned to this period in cases where sherds were identified as being wheel-made/wheel-finished; grog-tempered, combed and/or decorated, with wide, grooved lines (imitating cordons) or burnished lattices. A few other sherds were distinguished for displaying beaded, or everted, rounded-rim forms typical of 'Belgicised' Late Iron Age wares. Overall, the handmade pottery in this group may date anywhere between the mid–late 1st century BC and mid-1st century AD, and potentially overlapping in currency with some of the Middle Iron Age-type wares discussed above. By contrast, the wheel-made sherds probably date from the early to mid-1st century AD. These tended to have hard-fired, well-refined fabrics; some of which resemble proto-grey wares.

Most of the Late Iron Age-type pottery was residual (see Table 4.10, 42 sherds, 491g). In fact, only thirteen sherds (180g) were recovered from four Period 4 features: Ditch 6 (four sherds, 35g) and pits 18029 (two sherds, 44g), 20403 (three sherds, 67g), 20817 (two sherds, 26g) and 20927 (two sherds, 8g). Few definitive conclusions

can therefore be drawn from the pottery, other than the observation that the activities which resulted in the generation and deposition of ceramic debris were fairly infrequent within the area examined by the excavations.

Discussion

The prehistoric pottery from Mildenhall constitutes a relatively large multi-period assemblage, with significant Late Bronze Age and Middle Iron Age components. The Late Bronze Age assemblage belongs to the Plainware phase of the Post-Deverel Rimbury ceramic tradition (Barrett 1980), conventionally dated *c.* 1100–800 BC. Although modest in size, few well-dated assemblages of this period have been published from Suffolk, so this group represents a significant addition to the county corpus. The key assemblage derived from the fills and re-cuts associated with pit 20238, which yielded fragments from a range of pots typical of the period, including the complete profile of a coarseware bowl which appears to have been carefully deposited. On typo-chronological grounds, the character and forms of the vessels suggest a date-range of *c.* 1000–800 BC (Brudenell 2012), which is broadly corroborated by two of the radiocarbon dates achieved from this complex of features (1004–842 cal. BC (SUERC-48048: 2779 ± 30 BP) and 896–797 cal. BC (SUERC-48047: 2669 ± 30 BP). Typologically, the material finds ready parallels in Suffolk with the published pottery groups from Barnham (Martin 1993) and Game Farm, Brandon (Last 2004), together with a number of currently unpublished assemblages including Hartismere High School, Eye (Percival 2012); Bloodmoor Hill, Carlton Colville (Percival 2013) and Days Road, Capel St Mary (Brudenell 2010).

Although the recovery of a few diagnostic sherds of Early Iron Age pottery indicates sporadic activity at the site the during the early–mid 1st millennium BC, the bulk of the Iron Age pottery was classified as handmade Middle Iron Age-type wares. These were characterised by a range of slack-shouldered jars, globular bowls, and a series of tub-shaped vessels mostly made in dense, sandy fabrics. The main *floruit* of this pottery tradition was between *c.* 350–50 BC in Suffolk, although elements persisted after the 1st-century BC introduction of 'Belgicised' wheel-made forms, fabrics and manufacturing techniques; some of which had little impact on domestic potting practices in this region prior to the first or second quarter of the 1st century AD.

70

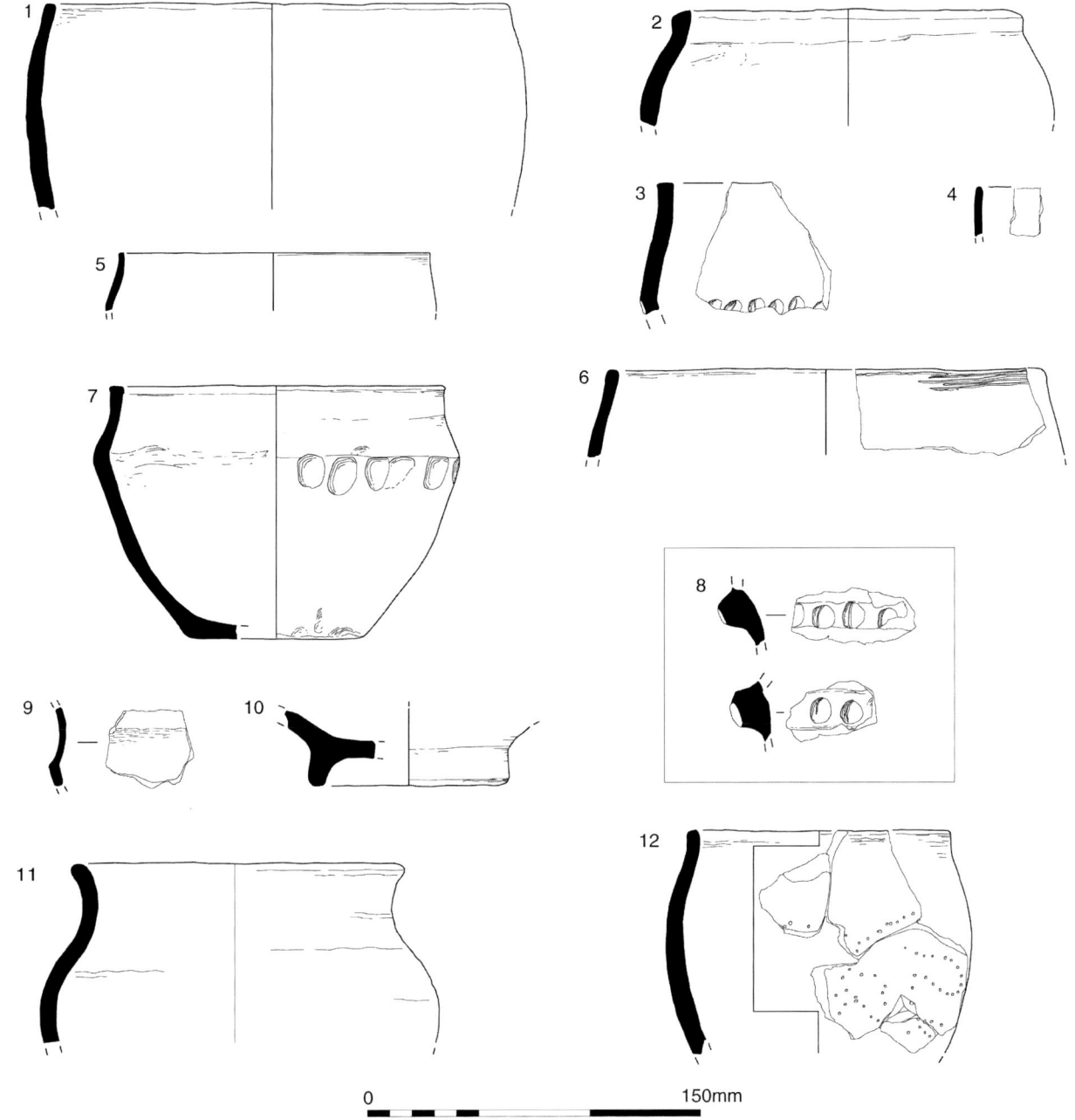

Figure 4.8 Bronze Age and Iron Age pottery (scale 1:3) nos 1–12

More precise dating of Middle Iron Age-type assemblages can therefore be difficult. In this instance, however, there is no reason to suspect an especially late (AD) date, or extended currency, for this material. Indeed, given the repertoire of vessel forms recovered, coupled with the presence of late La Tène-style decorated sherds, a date centred on the second to first centuries BC seems appropriate. To some extent this is corroborated by the two radiocarbon dates achieved for pit 15234: 361–112 cal. BC (SUERC-48069: 2166 ± 30 BP) and 353–56 cal. BC (SUERC-48070: 2140 ± 30 BP). It would also accord well with the date assigned to typologically comparable assemblages from Bridge House Dairies, just c. 0.5km to the southwest (Peachey 2010); pottery from Low Parks, Chippenham (c. 7km southwest, Brudenell 2013), and the

published Phase II Iron Age assemblage from West Stow (c. 12km southwest, Martin 1989, 68).

Interestingly, all three of these sites yielded sherds of late La Tène-style decorated pottery, but not in the quantities recovered from Recreation Way. Relative to the size of the assemblage, Recreation Way has a surprising number and variety of sherds from late La Tène-style decorated finewares, although quite what this means in social terms is difficult to interpret (i.e. are these special-purpose pots or status ceramics?). While very little work has been conducted on the decorative traditions of the later Iron Age in northern East Anglia, it is now evident that a variety of different motifs were employed on the pots, some being more formal in design than others. Judging by recent discoveries, diversity appears to be the common theme. In fact, late La Tène-style ornamented

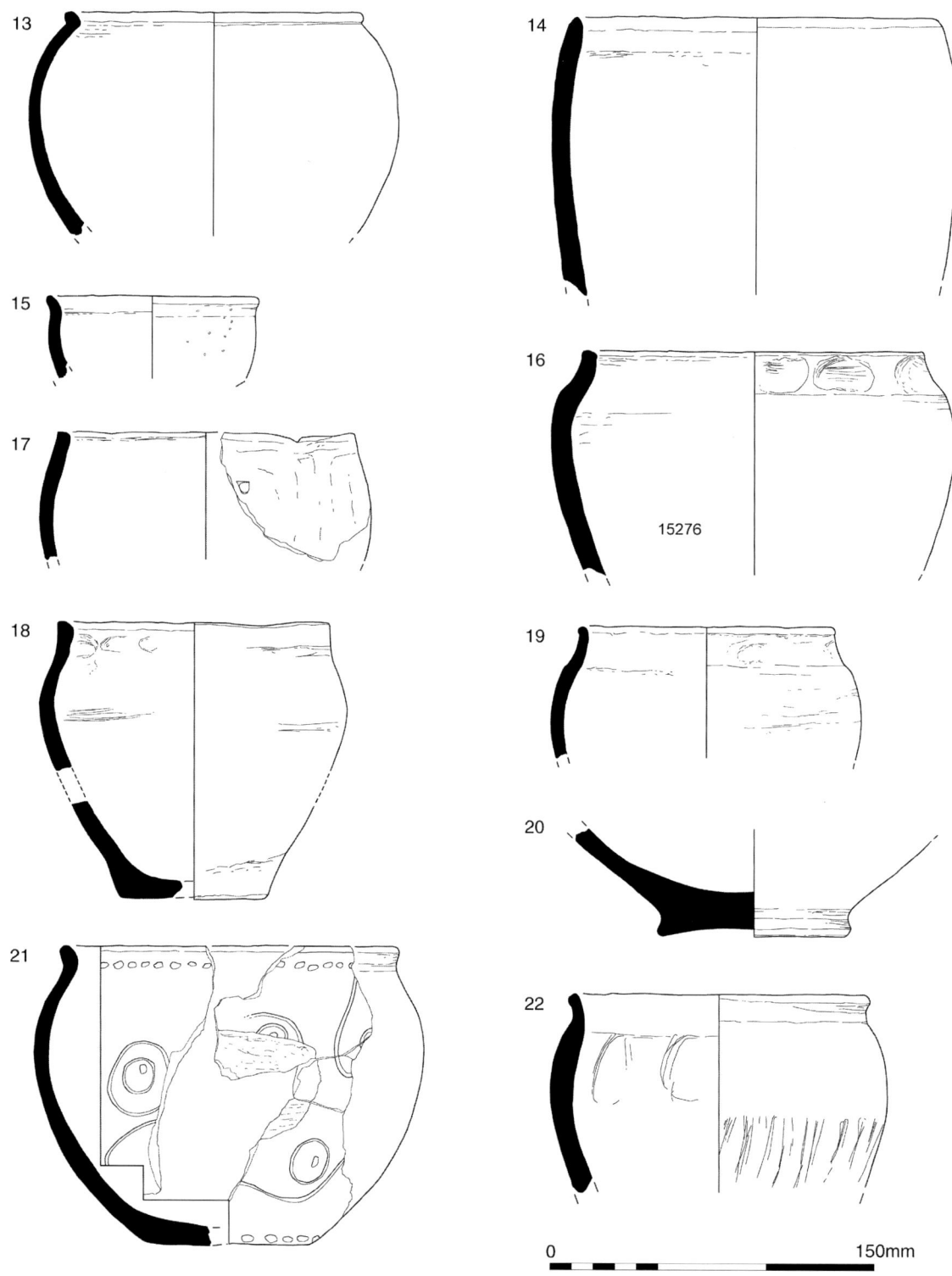

Figure 4.9 Iron Age pottery (scale 1:3) nos 13–22

pots from southern Cambridgeshire, Suffolk and Norfolk display a range of motifs with only passing affinities to the better-known decorative traditions recorded in parts of Northamptonshire, Lincolnshire, southeast Essex, or even the Glastonbury wares from southwest Britain (for an overview and other discussions see Brown 1991; Elsdon 1975; Hill and Horne 2003, 180; Knight 2002, 131–3).

Some of the East Anglian examples are no doubt imports from these areas, although the petrographic study conducted here suggests that vessels in this tradition were also being made and distributed at a local level. Indeed, given the various design grammars evident in published pots from Addenbrooke's (Cra'ster 1969; Webley and Anderson 2008, 68, fig. 2.8, no. 1), West Stow (West 1989, 65 fig. 48) and Wardy Hill (Hill and Horne 2003, 155, fig. 80), amongst others, it is perhaps hard to argue that a singular 'East Anglian style' ever existed. Instead, local potters perhaps imitated and adapted a variety of patterns

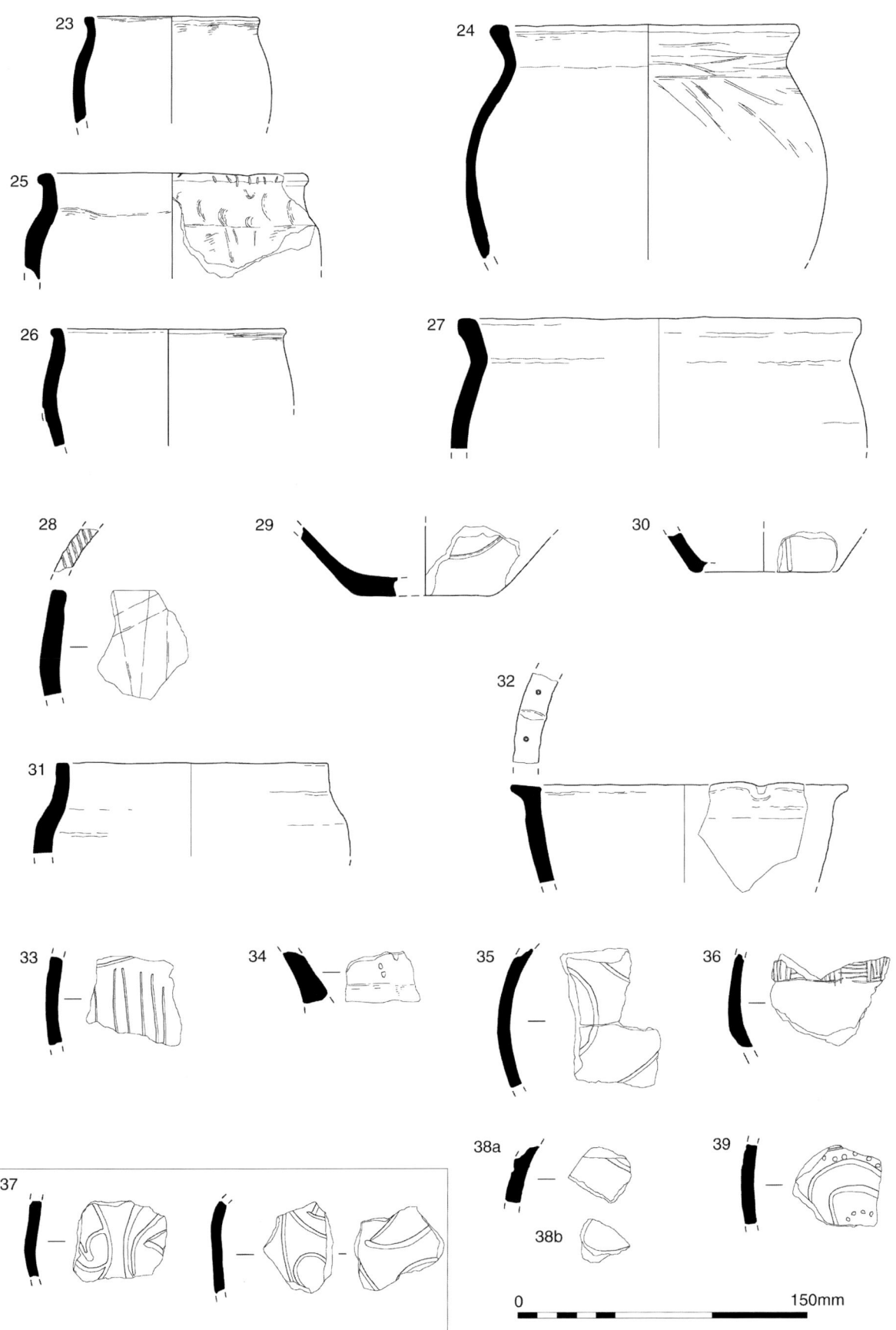

Figure 4.10 Iron Age pottery (scale 1:3) nos 23–39

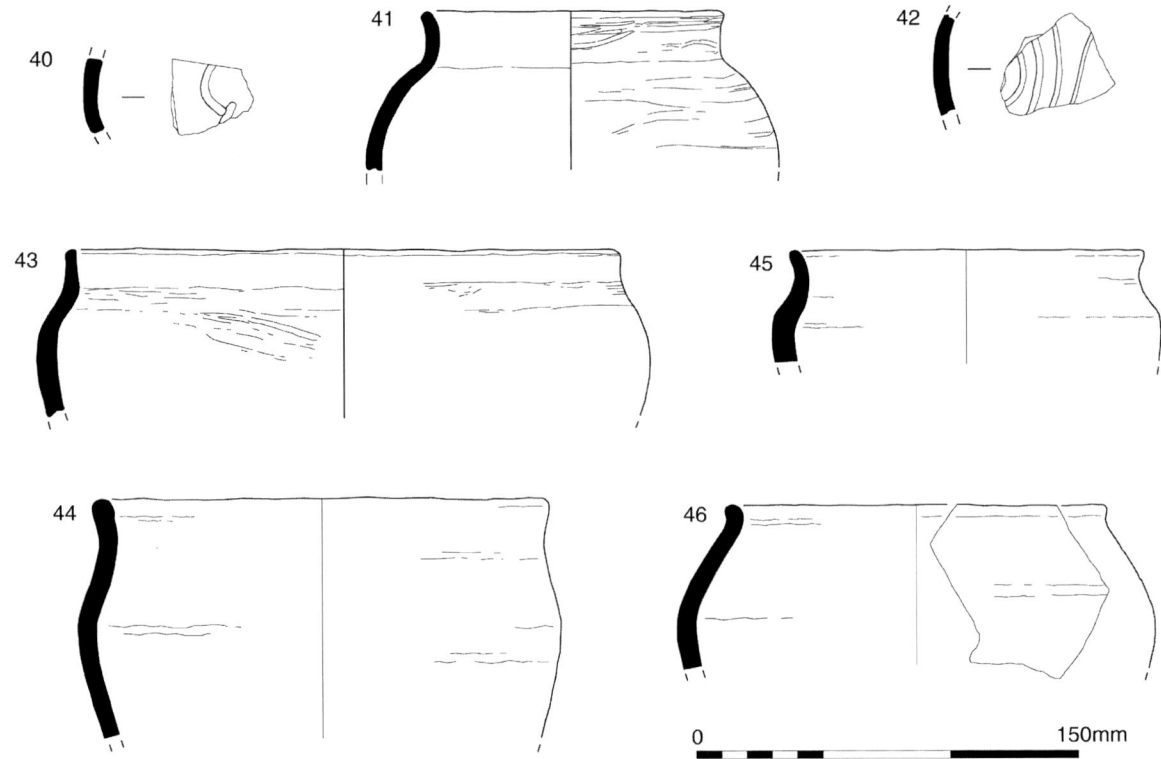

Figure 4.11 Iron Age pottery (scale 1:3) nos 40–46

and techniques common to other regions (and alternative mediums, such as metalwork), thus creating a multiplicity of different sub-regional styles. However, these do not appear to have persisted much beyond the 1st century BC in the region, coming to an end with, or perhaps soon after, the introduction of 'Belgic' pottery. At Recreation Way, the assemblage of Belgic-related ceramics and other Late Iron Age-type wares was relatively small, which suggests that the main focus of the settlement after *c.* 50 BC lay beyond the excavation area.

Illustrated vessels
(Figs 4.8–4.11)

Late Bronze Age
Fig. 4.8

1. Vessel 3 (Rim 21cm). Fabric FQ2, Class I, Form B. Period 3; fill 21238 of Ditch 21197.
2. Vessel 51. Fabric F1, Class I, Form F. Period 2; fills 20319, 20336 and 20338, pit 20238 (and associated re-cuts).
3. Vessel 58. Fabric F2, Fingertip impressed shoulder, Class I, Form G. Period 2; fill 20319, pit 20238.
4. Vessel 61. Fabric F4, Class V, Form S. Period 2; fill 20319, pit 20238.
5. Vessel 68 (Rim 14cm). Fabric FQ4, Burnished, Class IV, Form K. Period 2; fill 20319, pit 20238.
6. Vessel 72 (Rim 20cm). Fabric FQ3, Class I, Form D. Period 2; fill 20319, pit 20238.
7. Vessel 76 (Rim 15cm, base 8cm). Fabric F2, Class III, Form M. Period 2; fill 20335, pit 20238 (and associated re-cuts).
8. Fabric F1, Neck cordon with fingertip impressions. Period 7; fill 3082, Ditch 23 and Period 2; fill 20320, pit 20238 (and associated re-cuts).

Early Iron Age
9. Fabric F2. Period 5; layer 3147, Area 3.

10. Vessel 217 (Base 9cm). Fabric FQ2, burnished. Period 9 (Modern); fill 20516, pit 20513.

Middle Iron Age-type ceramics
11. Vessel 237 (Rim 15cm). Fabric Q1, burnished, Form F/G (Hill and Horne, 2003). Period 3; fill 20155, pit 20153.
12. Vessel 215 (Rim 15cm, base 8cm). Fabric Q3, burnished, pin-dot decorated body, Form A (Hill and Horne, 2003). Period 3; fill 20869, pit 20868.

Fig. 4.9
13. Vessel 7 (Rim 14cm). Fabric Q1, Burnished, Form M (Hill and Horne, 2003). Period 3; fill 21258, pit 21256.
14. Vessel 16. Fabric Q1, burnished, Form K (Hill and Horne, 2003). Period 3; fill 21276, pit 21275.
15. Vessel 37 (Rim 8cm). Fabric Q1, burnished, pin-dot decorated body, Form M (Hill and Horne, 2003). Period 3, fill 15033, pit 15031.
16. Vessel 48 (Rim 16cm). Fabric Q1, burnished, Form B (Hill and Horne, 2003). Period 3; fill 15276, pit 15234.
17. Vessel 49 (Rim 12cm). Fabric Q1, Form K (Hill and Horne, 2003). Period 3; fill 15276, pit 15234.
18. Vessel 84 (Rim 13, base 7cm). Fabric Q3, burnished, Form A (Hill and Horne, 2003). Period 3; fill 15270, pit 15271.
19. Vessel 85 (Rim 11cm). Fabric Q3, Form M (Hill and Horne, 2003). Period 3; fill 15270, pit 15271.
20. Vessel 103 (Base 8cm). Fabric Q1, burnished. Period 3; fill 16006, pit 16005.
21. Vessel 117 (Rim 15cm, base 7cm). Fabric Q4, burnished, grooved and dot impressed, Form F/G (Hill and Horne, 2003). Period 3; fill 17219, pit 17218.
22. Vessel 123 (Rim 14cm). Fabric Q4, Form D (Hill and Horne, 2003). Period 3; fill 18030, pit 18031.

Fig. 4.10
23. Vessel 127 (Rim 9cm). Fabric Q2, burnished, Form A (Hill and Horne, 2003). Period 3; fill 19210, pit 19215 and fill 19220, pit 19088.
24. Vessel 129 (Rim 16cm). Fabric QVE1, burnished, Hill Form F/G (Hill and Horne, 2003). Period 7; fill 19121, pit 19119.

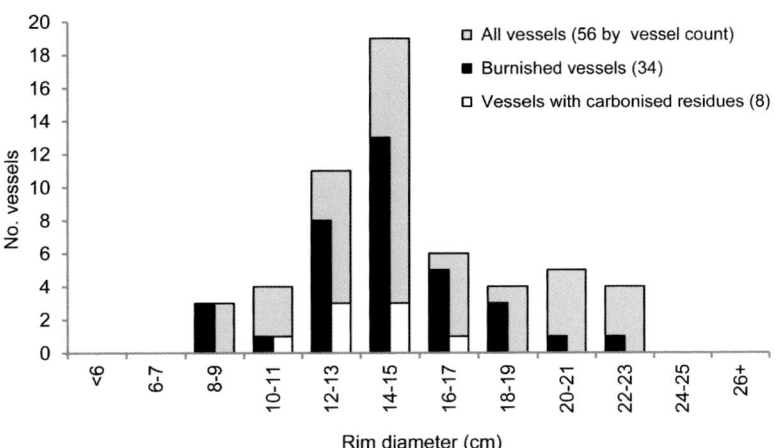

Figure 4.12 Middle Iron Age rim sizes and the relationship to burnishing and carbonised residues. Residues were recorded on 100 sherds (2441g) in the assemblage

25. Vessel 134 (Rim 14cm). Fabric QVE3, Fingernail impressed rim-top, Form E (Hill and Horne, 2003). Period 7; fill 19121, pit 19119.

26. Vessel 137 (Rim 12cm). Fabric Q4, Burnished, Form L (Hill and Horne, 2003). Period 7; fill 19095, pit 19094.

27. Vessel 152 (Rim 21cm). Fabric Q1, Fingernail impressed rim-top, Form F/G (Hill and Horne, 2003). Period 9; fill 20051, pit 20050.

28. Vessel 158. Fabric S3, Fingernail impressed rim-top and scored body, Form K (Hill and Horne, 2003). Period 3, fill 20086, pit 20085.

29. Vessel 167 (Base 7cm). Fabric Q1, burnished, grooved curvilinear line on body. Period 3, fill 20590, pit 20153.

30. Vessel 178 (Base 6cm). Fabric Q3, burnished, lightly grooved vertical line on body and base. Period 3; fill 20365, pit 20370.

31. Vessel 187 (Rim 14cm). Fabric Q2, burnished, Form E (Hill and Horne, 2003). Period 3; fill 20768, pit 20759.

32. Vessel 206 (Rim 21). Fabric Q1, burnished, fingertip marks and (bone?) impressed dots on rim-top, Form P (Hill and Horne, 2003). Period 7; fill 20792 of pit 21005 and deposit 21003.

33. Fabric Q1, scored body. Period 3; fill 15130, pit 15129.

34. Fabric S5, burnished, impressed dots on body. Period 3; fill 15130, pit 15129.

35. Fabric Q2, burnished, grooved arching lines on body. Period 3; fill 19214, pit 19215.

36. Fabric Q1, burnished, alternate panels of lightly incised vertical and horizontal lines on body. Period 3; fill 20086, pit 20085 and fill 20387, pit 20386.

37. Fabric Q2, burnished, grooved curvilinear lines on shoulder. Period 3; fill 20125 and 20126, pit 20119.

38. Fabric Q4, burnished, grooved curvilinear line on body. Period 3; fill 20265, pit 20085.

39. Fabric Q1, burnished, grooved curvilinear lines with chalk-filled punched dots on body. Period 3; fill 20587, pit 20153.

Fig. 4.11

40. Fabric Q2, burnished, grooved curvilinear lines on shoulder. Period 3; fill 20588, pit 20153.

42. Fabric Q1, Burnished, Lightly grooved curvilinear lines on body. Period 3; fill 16065, pit 16063.

43. Fabric Q1, Hill Form E (Rim 22cm). Period 3; fill 16065, pit 16063.

44. Fabric QCH1, Burnished, Hill form F/G (Rim 18cm). Period 3; fill 20931, pit 20927.

45. Fabric Q1, Burnished, Hill Form D (Rim 14cm). Period 4; context 20792, silting deposit.

46. Fabric Q2, Burnished, Hill Form M (Rim 14cm). Period 4; context 20792, silting deposit.

Late Iron Age-type

41. Vessel 122 (Rim 12cm). Fabric Q3, burnished, Form F/G (Hill and Horne, 2003). Period 4; fill 18027, pit 18029.

VIII. Roman pottery
by E.R. McSloy, with a contribution by G. Monteil

Introduction
Roman pottery amounting to 1723 sherds (23.8kg) was recovered from 432 separate deposits (Table 4.18). The bulk of the assemblage was hand-recovered with seventy-seven sherds (172g) retrieved from bulk soil samples.

The Roman pottery has been sorted into fabrics and quantified according to sherd count, weight and rim EVEs (Estimated Vessel Equivalents). A longer version of this report containing full fabric descriptions for local/unsourced fabrics is contained in the archive. A record of vessel form, typically from vessel rim sherds has also been made together with evidence for use as carbonised and other residues. The common Roman traded wares present in the assemblage were recorded with reference to the National Roman reference collection codes (Tomber and Dore 1998).

Roman activity was largely confined to the northeast and southern parts of the site with the majority of pottery associated with a sequence of enclosures in Area 3 and dispersed ditches/pits on the higher ground. The post-Roman activity across the site has resulted in high levels of disturbance and 691 sherds (37% of the Roman group) were re-deposited, occurring in deposits allocated to Phases 6–9. The bulk of material (from the excavation) was derived from the fills of 'negative' features; primarily from ditches (557 sherds or 34.4%) and pits/postholes (425 sherds or 26.2). Sherd count per deposit is overall low, averaging under four sherds and with only two deposits (17084: fill of drying oven 17048 and 20792: silting layer) producing in excess of fifty sherds.

Condition
A sizeable re-deposited component to the assemblage is not obviously reflected in its condition; only a small proportion of the group (sixty-four sherds or 2.9%) was recorded as abraded and the mean sherd weight is moderately high for a Roman group at 14g. Preservation of shell or limestone inclusions is good, probably largely as the result of the calcareous soils. Surface treatments such as burnishing survive well and carbonised and limey residues also survive although incidence is low overall (129 sherds or 8%).

Source	Fab. Gp.	fabric	Description	Ct.	Wt(g)	EVEs
Local/uncertain (transitional)	GROG	GROG	Wheelthrown grog-tempered	18	281	.13
	GROG	GROGbuff	Harder/pinkish grog-tempered	2	48	-
	SILTY	SILTY	Silty ware (Gallo-Belgic imitations)	3	23	-
Local/uncertain (Romano-British)	OXID	OXID	Unsourced oxidised wares	14	238	.17
	OXID	OXIDf	Unsourced oxidised wares (finer)	10	85	.20
	OXWS	FFws	Flagon fabric, white-slipped	2	10	0
	REDU	BSb	Dark-firing; sandy; highly burnished	35	377	.73
	REDU	BSc	Black sandy; coarse	120	1135	1.36
	REDU	GWc	Coarse sandy greyware	364	4972	3.48
	REDU	GWc ls	Coarse sandy greyware with sparse limestone	18	413	.09
	REDU	GWf	Greyware, fine, hard; iron grey throughout	87	1121	1.84
	REDU	GWf f	Greyware, fine with flint incs	90	620	.74
	REDU	GWfbs	Greyware, fine, black surfaces	102	973	.62
	REDU	GWg	Greyware with grog	2	331	.12
	REDU	Gwhi	Hard, paler core; - Hadham?	4	34	.17
	REDUm	GWfm	fine greyware, micaceous pale grey throughout	152	1506	1.21
	REDUm	GWm	Sandy grey micaceous	141	1395	1.86
	MICAD	MICAD	Mica-dusted ware (Pakenham?)	1	10	-
	MSC CC	MSC CC	Unsourced colour-coated wares	17	208	-
Regional	BB1	DOR BB1*	Dorset Black-Burnished ware	11	77	-
	BB2	COL BB2*	Colchester Black-Burnished	5	66	-
	COL CC	COL CC*	Colchester Colour-Coated ware	8	55	.35
	HAD OX	HAD OX*	Hadham oxidised	93	840	1.42
	HAD OX	HAD Oxm	Hadham oxidised (mortaria)	1	21	-
	LNV CC	LNV CC*	Lower Nene Valley Colour-Coated	87	1455	2.25
	LNV CC	LNV CCm	Lower Nene Valley Colour-Coated (mortaria)	1	10	-
	LNV CC	LNVCCs	Lower Nene Valley Colour-Coated (Stanground?)	4	77	-
	LNV WH	LNV WH*	Lower Nene Valley self-coloured (creamwares)	7	66	-
	LNV CW	LNV WHm	Lower Nene Valley self-coloured (mortaria)	7	251	.30
	LNV GW	LNV GW	Lower Nene Valley greywares	2	44	.03
	HOR RE	HOR RE*	Horningsea greywares	6	284	.15
	OXF RS	OXF RS*	Oxford Red-slipped ware	9	107	.15
	OXF RS	OXF RSm	Oxford Red-slipped ware (mortaria)	1	42	0
	OXF WH	OXF WH*	Oxford whiteware (mortaria)	1	41	.08
	OXF WS	OXF WS*	Oxford white slipped ware (mortaria)	1	27	0
	ROB SH	ROB SH*	Roman Shell-temped ware	149	3943	2.91
	BUFF/WH	BUFFf	fine, buff flagon fabric	24	199	1.12
	BUFF/WH	BUFFg	Buff gritty fabric; grey core	69	1754	.08
	BUFF/WH	BUFFls	Buff gritty fabric; grey core (limestone inclusions)	6	73	-
	BUFF/WH	WH	Unsourced whitewares (Godmanchester?)	11	111	-
Continental	BAT AM	BAT AM*	Baetican amphorae	3	325	-
	KOL CC	KOL CC*	Cologne Colour-Coated ware	1	7	-
	samian	LGF SA*	South Gaulish samian (La Graufesenque)	5	9	-
	samian	LEZ SA2*	Central Gaulish samian (Lezoux)	16	157	.06
	samian	EG SA	East Gaulish samian	3	11	-
	samian	RHZ SA*	East Gaulish samian (Rheinzabern)	10	53	.08
Total				**1723**	**23885**	**21.70**

* Codes equate to National Roman Fabric Reference Collection Codes (Tomber and Dore 1998)

Table 4.18 Roman pottery summary quantification

Generic Form	No	EVEs	%EVEs
Flagon	7	1.27	*5.9*
Beaker	11	.94	*4.3*
Beaker/small jar	4	.43	*2.0*
cup	1	0	-
jar	117	10.06	*45.5*
Jar (large storage)	18	1.74	*8.0*
Jar or bowl	3	.20	*0.9*
bowl	48	3.12	*14.4*
'bowl-jar'	7	.74	*3.4*
'Castor Box'	2	.58	*2.7*
Dish	32	1.98	*9.1*
Lid	1	.05	*0.2*
Mortarium	6	.38	*1.8*
Platter	2	.18	*0.8*
Strainer	1	0	-
Total	**260**	**21.67**	-

EVE = Estimated Vessel Equivalent

Table 4.19 Roman vessel forms summary

Assemblage composition
(Tables 4.18 and 4.19)
The large bulk of the assemblage (65% by count) comprised reduced coarsewares which for the most part are insufficiently distinct in their fabric or form range to be able to indicate a specific source. The highly micaceous greywares (types GWfm; GWm) are however representative of a regional tradition, and equivalent types dominate Roman assemblages from the area, and extending into Norfolk (Rogerson 1977, 172). Kilns identified in the area of Wattisfield, Suffolk, *c.*30km to the east of Mildenhall produced visually similar micaceous greywares, as well as a range of finewares (below). Kilns at West Stow, *c.* 25km to the southeast (West 1989), also produced micaceous grey and white/buff-firing fabrics and may be represented among the Mildenhall material. There is some overlap in vessel forms across the earlier Roman groups and the West Stow kiln groups, particularly amongst the barbotine dot panel-decorated and rusticated beakers/jars (Fig. 4.13, no. 11). The compass-scribed and other 'London ware' style vessels most associated with the West Stow kilns do not however occur. No certain source can be asserted for the bulk of the non-micaceous and largely nondescript greywares and oxidised types which form the bulk of the Roman assemblage. The area to the west of Mildenhall and south of the fen edge is perhaps a likely source. Horningsea greywares (HOR RE), manufactured further (*c.* 30km) to the west, are poorly represented, occurring as the distinctive large storage jars with bifid rims (Evans 1991).

Roman shell-tempered wares make up only *c.* 8% of the assemblage total, although these appear to be more significant among Late Roman groups (below). More than one source is likely, with some evidence for a change over time; a thicker, coarser, and typically red/brown-firing fabric occurs among some earlier Roman groups including that from drying oven 17048 (Fig. 4.13, no. 7). The coarser earlier fabric resembles material commonly encountered from the area of Peterborough and described as 'local' from Orton Hall Farm (Perrin 1996). Thinner-walled vessels in a finer, typically dark, grey/brown-firing fabric are probably products of kilns at Harrold, north Bedfordshire (Brown 1994), *c.* 90km to the west. A few vessels, consisting of channel-rimmed jar forms (Fig. 4.13, no. 6) resemble the early Roman products from this source. The majority are representative of late (4th-century) production, the period which sees an expansion of this industry with its products very widely distributed (*ibid.*). Forms consist of necked jars with rilled bodies and overhanging rims (Fig. 4.13, no. 19).

Non-sigillata finewares are uncommon in the earlier/middle Roman context groups, largely limited to colour-coated mica-dusted and white-slipped fabrics. Among the colour-coated types are probable Colchester products consisting of bag-shaped/cornice-rim beakers (Fig. 4.13, no. 1). The kilns at Pakenham, Suffolk, *c.* 25km to the south-east of Mildenhall, may be the source for some at least of the unidentifiable colour-coated ware sherds, and also for mica-dusted vessel no. 3 (Tomber and Dore 1998, 182). The earliest (beaker) products in Lower Nene Valley Colour-Coated wares are absent and this ware type may not have been common before the 3rd century AD.

Significant differences are apparent across the Early/Middle and Late Roman groups in terms of the abundance of regionally-imported finewares and mortaria (Table 4.19). The location of Mildenhall is the main governing factor in the relative abundance of Lower Nene Valley, Hadham and Oxford region wares, the latter type being least common. The abundance of Hadham oxidised wares (ninety-two sherds or 5.7% of the total) may in part reflect chronology, this type being most widespread in the mid and later 4th century. The Hadham ware group is a typically 'late' assemblage comprising a mix of jars/'bowl-jars' (Fig. 4.13, nos 17–18), flagons (Fig. 4.13, no. 20) and fineware bowls, including vessels with 'Romano-Saxon' style traits (Fig. 4.13, no. 22). Forms among Lower Nene Valley Colour-Coated wares include few beakers and are mainly the 'coarseware' vessel classes (jars, conical flanged bowls and plain-rim dishes), and simplified 'Castor box' forms which typify late assemblages. A late wide platter in this fabric (Fig. 4.13, no. 23) is a relatively uncommon form supportive of dating into the second half of the 4th century. The Lower Nene supplied the majority of mortaria identified from the site; the remainder from Oxfordshire and one possible Hadham vessel.

Continental imports are sparsely represented, consisting of Gaulish samian and occasional sherds of Cologne Colour-Coated ware and amphorae. The samian amounts to 33 sherds, or 2% of the total, and includes examples from each of the production regions (South, Central and East Gaul). South Gaulish (La Graufesenque) vessels are earliest, and date to the mid-1st to early 2nd centuries, with the one decorated vessel, a Dragendorf form 37 bowl (see below) of the late Flavian or early Trajanic period. The Central and East Gaulish vessels are mostly or entirely 2nd century in date. The few identifiable vessel forms (Dr 31, 32, 33) are suggestive of mid/late Antonine dating, and a decorated Rheinzabern vessel is also of this period. The stamped Central Gaulish vessel, also of Antonine date, is noteworthy as only the second instance of the potter (*Alubus* of Lezoux) to be recorded (Hartley and Dickinson 2008, 160). A cup (form Dr 33) from layer 4024 features a scratched ownership mark in the form of a cross close to the base angle.

Samian catalogue
by G. Monteil

Decorated sherds

Bodysherd (bowl) Dr 37, La Graufesenque, 4g. Partial decoration showing a split panel separated by a straight horizontal line with a large dog with collar running left on top of a grass tuft and the top of a festoon which seems to be made out of chevrons. A number of late South Gaulish potters used these motifs: *Biragillus* i (Mees 1995, Taf 14, no.1) for the grass tuft, the horizontal line and the festoon, *Mercator* i (*ibid.*, dog on Taf 128, no.1; grass tuft on Taf 135, no.9 and horizontal line on Taf 130, no.1), *Sabinus* iv (*ibid.*, dog and grass tuft Taf 179, no. 1). AD 80–110. Area 3; Period 5, pit 3725, fill 3722.

Bodysherd (bowl) Dr 37, Rheinzabern. Joins with a bodysherd from deposit 5168 (below). Wild boar with a particularly detailed hide, type T70 (Ricken and Fisher 1963) known for *Cobnertus* iv (Cobnertus I style). See fill 5168 sherd below for rest of decoration. Area 3; Period 5, layer 3917.

Two joining rim fragments with top of ovolo, one bodysherd with ovolo and wavy border (joins with layer 3917 sherd) and one bodysherd with medallion, roped border, mask and panther, Dr 37, Rheinzabern. The ovolo is E44, the wavy border O248. The double circle medallion is the size of K19a and contains sea-horse T190, the vertical roped border is O242, the mask M16 and the tail and back legs are the ones of panther T32. All of these motifs are known for *Cobnertus* iv (Cobnertus I style, Ricken and Fisher 1963, Taf.21, nos 9, 11). AD 155–180. See 3917 above for joining fragment. Area 3; Period 5, pit 5169, fill 5168.

Stamps

Alubus, 1a, AL [ ] MAN, three joining base fragments from a Dr 31, Lezoux, Antonine (*c.* AD 138–193) (Hartley and Dickinson 2008, 160). 110g, base EVEs=0.83, diam.=90mm. This is the second example of this potter's stamp known to date; the other was recovered on the base of a Dr 38 or 44 in Wilcote, Oxon (*ibid.*). The vessel is heavily burnt but shows very little wear on the footring and appears to have been trimmed all around the base. Area 3; Period 5, Ditch 7, fill 3782.

Stratigraphy: Early and Middle Roman c. 70–200/250 AD

Pottery from the silting/soil formation, and an episode of deliberate infilling in Ditch 1, amounted to 115 sherds (1.48kg/1.33 EVEs) (Table 4.20). Greyware types dominate (seventy-six sherds), although micaceous types are relatively uncommon (twenty-one sherds). Represented forms are mainly jars, and include neck-less forms derived from Black-Burnished ware cooking pots. Occasional sherds of grogged wares hint at some accumulation of material from the mid/later 1st century AD. The influence of Black-Burnished ware apparent in some of the greywares, together with sherds of Central Gaulish samian (deposit 4024) and a clay-roughcasted beaker sherd in fabric MSC CC (deposit 4023), support continuation well into the 2nd century AD.

Limited evidence for Earlier Roman activity was identified from Area 3, mainly from Ditch 7, (fifty-seven sherds/832g/0.08 EVEs). In common with the Ditch 1 group on the higher ground, greywares are dominant (forty-one sherds), though micaceous types (REDUm) are in this instance prevalent (thirty sherds). Sherds of South Gaulish samian date before *c.* 110 AD. However a Central Gaulish form 31 bowl (Ditch 7, fill 3782) and adjoining sherds from an East Gaulish form 37 bowl (pit 5169, fill 5168) are both mid/late Antonine in date (see samian catalogue above).

Pottery from Enclosure E amounted to forty-one sherds (661g/0.57 EVEs). As with the larger groups discussed above, greywares and buff-firing types are common and occur mostly as jars. There are few closely-datable elements in this group, though the absence of Late Roman types is considered significant. A Central Gaulish

samian form 32 dish from Ditch 32 supports dating in the second half of the 2nd century.

Pottery from drying ovens 17028 and 17048 amounted to 146 sherds (1501g)/1.12 EVEs). Reduced coarsewares are strongly dominant (129 sherds), the remainder consisting of sherds in shell-tempered wares. Forms are a mix of necked jars and dishes with moulded/bead-like rims, the latter probably related to 2nd-century black-burnished ware classes.

Earlier Roman material is represented among the loosely-grouped activity (219 sherds (2699g) from pits/postholes 4009, 17081, 17133, 17152, 17339, 17434, 20399, 20401, 20334, 20637, 20666, 20723, 20731, 21184, 21395, 21639 and gully/ditch 20059, 20726, 20861) located across the higher ground. Micaceous greywares predominate and include forms most likely of 2nd-century date (Fig. 4.13, nos 9–11).

Stratigraphy: Later Roman: c. 250/70–400+

Pottery amounting to 151 sherds (3.12kg/3.12 EVEs) was associated with the construction/use of Enclosure B in Area 3 (Table 4.20). A proportion, including a large jar in a grog-tempered fabric (Fig. 4.13, no. 2) and colour-coated beaker (Fig. 4.13, no. 1), are probably residual, with the majority of 'date markers' supporting a date after *c.* AD 250. Greyware types make up the bulk of the coarsewares (fifty-five sherds), although shell-tempered wares are also common (twenty-nine sherds). Included among the latter are necked jars with distinctive undercut rims (Fig. 4.13, no. 19) which are characteristic of 4th-century production at Harrold, Bedfordshire (Brown 1994). Further indications of dating of this period come from traded finewares comprising products of the Lower Nene Valley (LNV CC) and Much Hadham (HAD OX). Identifiable vessel forms are 'coarseware' dishes/bowls and a samian form 38-derived bowl in LNV CC and 'bowl-jars' in HAD OX.

Pottery associated with the construction and use of Enclosure A in Area 3 amounted to forty-one sherds (747g/0.67 EVEs) and a further forty-three sherds (1328g/2.29 EVEs) were derived from alluvial deposition above Enclosure A. In both groups, coarsewares comprise a mix of greywares (mainly GWc), and shell-tempered types. The Late Roman traded fineware recorded from Enclosure B also occur and with the addition of Oxford-shire red-slipped wares (OXFRS). The presence of conical flanged bowls in fabric LNV CC, and samian form 38-derived bowls in both OXF RS and HAD OX, support 4th-century dating.

A number of smaller pottery groups from Area 3, relating to Ditch 46 and pits 3815, 3817, 3841, 3856, 3860, 5211, support Late Roman (probably 4th-century) dating. A group of seven sherds from Ditch 8 included a sherd of Oxfordshire mortarium suggesting a date after *c.* 270 AD. Pits located in the northwest of Area 3 also produced seven sherds (137g), and included Hadham oxidised face-flagon (Fig. 4.13, no. 20), a form probably dating to the second half of the 4th century. Discrete pits (3112, 3114 and 3119) pre-dating Period 5 alluvial deposition in Area 3 produced twenty sherds of pottery (167g/0.32 EVEs) including sherds in fabrics LNV CC and HAD OX supporting a date after *c.* AD 270/300.

Dumped deposits in the western part of Area 3 produced small quantities of Roman pottery (three sherds/118g) including a substantially complete miniature bowl

Table 4.20 Roman pottery summary by selected Group. Quantities as sherd count/weight (g)

| Group> | Early/Middle | | | | | | | | | | | | | | | | Late | | | | | | | |
| Fabrics | Ditch 1 | | Area 3 | | Enc. E | | Dr. ov. 17048 | | Other | | Enc. A | | Alluv. above Enc. A | | Enc. B | | Area 3 pits | | Area 17 land div. | | Area 3 dumped | | Area 3 other | |
	Ct	Wt	Ct	Wt	Ct	Wt	Ct	Wt	Ct	Wt	Ct	Wt	Ct	Wt	Ct	Wt	Ct	Wt	Ct	Wt	Ct	Wt	Ct	Wt
GROG	2	23							9	147			3	41	4	187								
OXID	1	4							3	13														
REDU*	68	756	11	410	36	352	111	620	119	1450	16	262	24	340	48	1234	4	108	9	129			2	20
REDUm*	22	132	30	259	9	166	21	227	69	666	2	10	3	37	13	164			6	43			1	7
BB2	2	26																						
BUFF/WH*	21	549	4	11	2	68			7	225	1	10	5	93	7	127								
COLCH CC															8	55								
MSC CC	1	4			1	6					1	2	1	2	2	6								
ROB SH	3	38					17	720	2	42	10	331	4	555	29	944	3	17	1	18				
HAD OX									4	12			10	102	19	249			1	3	1	7		
LNV CC									5	78	7	100	7	81	12	132			1	12	1	109	1	15
LNV CW									1	66			1	63					1	27				
OXF RS											2	24			2	5								
KOL CC											1	7												
Samian	1	24	14	166	1	5					1	1	2	6	7	12					1	2		
BAT AM					1	76																		
Totals	121	1556	59	846	50	673	149	1567	219	2699	41	747	60	1320	151	3115	7	125	19	232	3	118	4	42

* Codes equate to National Roman Fabric Reference Collection Codes (Tomber and Dore 1998). Pottery fabrics description in Table 4.18
Dr. ov. – drying oven, Enc. – Enclosure

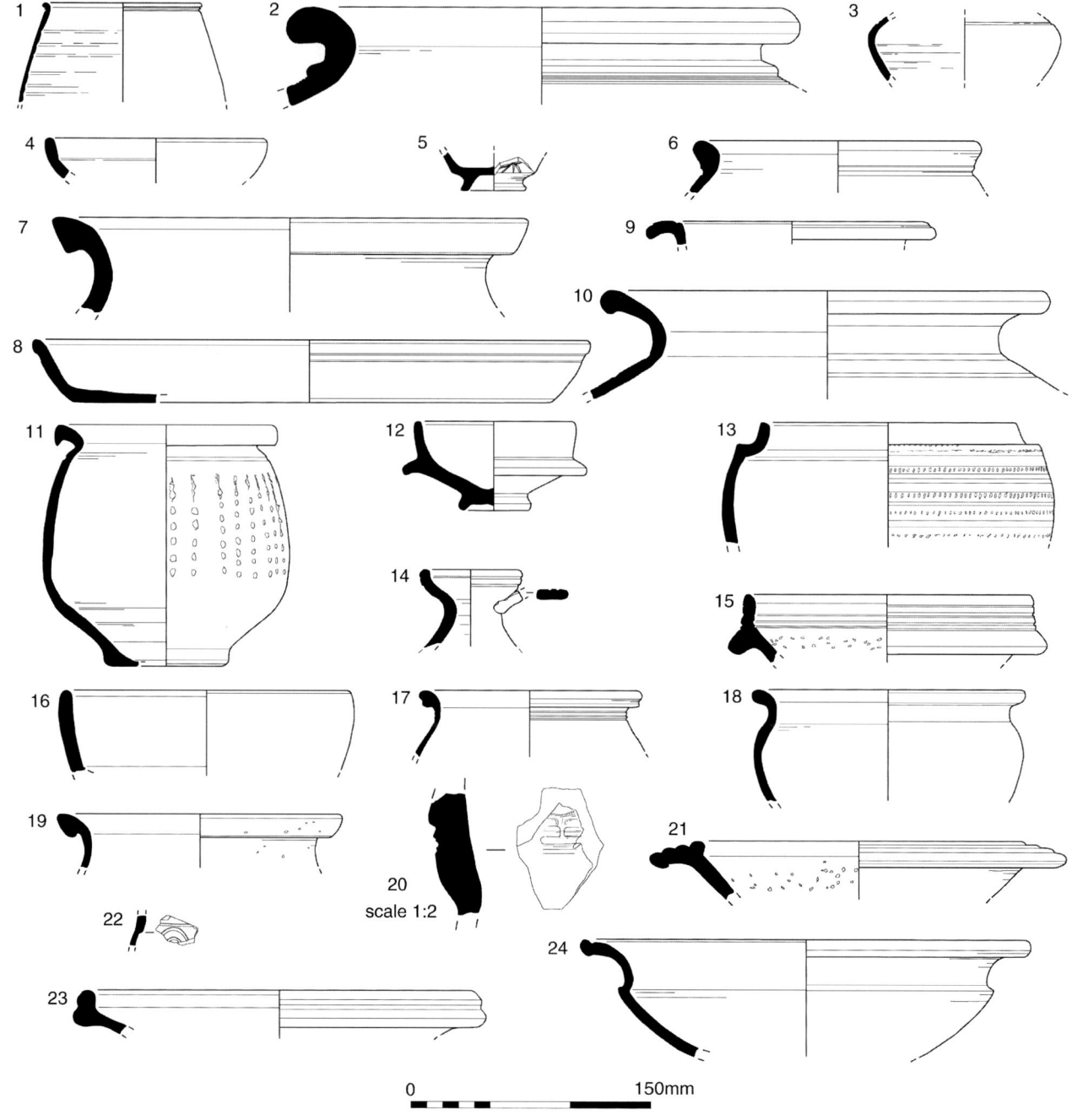

Figure 4.13 Roman pottery (scale 1:4) nos 1–24

in fabric LNV CC (Fig. 4.13; no. 12). Period 5 alluvial deposits in Area 2 and 3 produced thirty-seven sherds (691g), mostly Late Roman in character.

The cluster of features in the north-east part of the higher ground produced some limited evidence for Late Roman activity from land division features (mainly Ditches 42 and 43). Small quantities of pottery, associated with a number of gully, pit and posthole features (in total nineteen sherds/252g/0.32 EVEs), were for the most part broadly datable. Jar/dish forms in fabric LNV CC from posthole 17244, and a mortarium from pit 17638, suggest that at least some of this activity relates to the Late Roman period.

Discussion

In its overall composition, the Roman assemblage is typical for the area and date range. There is limited evidence for activity before *c.* AD 100 and most activity would it seems date to the mid/later 2nd century and 4th centuries. A number of elements support occupation up to the end of the Roman period in Britain. Reduced coarsewares of certain or presumed local manufacture dominate, and there is some indication that micaceous type are commonest in the earlier or mid Roman period. 'Traded' types are uncommon among the earlier groups, but relatively abundant among the Late Roman assemblage.

There is little in the assemblage to indicate higher status. The samian component is small (33 sherds), equivalent to 2% of the total and a level of use consistent with many smaller rural sites. The scarcity of amphorae and specialist forms such as mortaria are similarly consistent with a lower-status community. The increased abundance of 'finewares' in the later Roman period almost certainly reflects wider patterns of pottery supply, and is unlikely to reflect changes in status. The breakdown of vessel forms across the Period (Table 4.19) reveals an assemblage dominated by jars and other utilitarian forms (the majority of dishes/bowls are classes most likely used for food preparation or cooking).

Illustrated vessels
(Fig. 4.13)

1   Fabric MSC CC (prob. Colchester). Bag-shaped beaker with cornice rim. Area 3; Period 5, ditch 3769, fill 3768.

2   Fabric GWg. Large, necked jar with cordon. Area 3; Unphased.

3   Fabric MICAd. Bowl or cup? Area 3; Period 5, Ditch 15, fill 3094.

4   Fabric GWfm; platter/dish. Period 5, Ditch 1, fill E308 (Evaluation Trench 3).

5   Fabric LEZ SA2. Cup (Dr 33) with scratched grafitto. Period 5, Ditch 1, silting 4024.

6   Fabric ROB SH. Channel rim/lid-seated jar. Period 5, Ditch 1, silting. 4030.

7   Fabric ROB SH. Large necked jar. Period 5, tertiary fill 17049 of drying oven 17048.

8   Fabric GWfm. Dish with bead-like rim and base chamfer. Period 5, drying oven 17048, fill 17077.

9   Fabric GWfm. Dish or bowl with flat, grooved rim. Period 5, gully fill 20725.

10 Fabric GWc. Large necked jar. Period 5, gully fill 20725.

11 Fabric GWfm. Bag-shaped beaker/small jar with barbotine dot decoration. Period 5, gully fill 20724.

12 Fabric LNVCC. Miniature bowl copying samian Dr 38. Wear pattern to interior suggests use as mortar. Area 3; Period 5, layer 5153.

13 Fabric LNVCC. Late style 'Castor Box'. Area 3; Period 5, layer 5131.

14 Fabric BUFFf. Flagon with cupped rim. Area 3; Period 5, layer 3187 (alluvium above Enclosure A).

15 Fabric LNVWHm. Mortarium collared/wall-sided with multiple grooves (cf. Hartley and Perrin 1999, fig. 77, M22/23). Area 3; Period 5, layer 3187 (alluvium above Enclosure A).

16 Fabric LNVCC. Plain-rimmed dish. Area 3; Period 5, Ditch 9 fill 3660.

17 Fabric HAD OX. Necked jar with bifid rim. Area 3; Period 5, Ditch 9 fill 3710.

18 Fabric HAD OX. 'Bowl-jar'. Area 3; Period 5, Ditch 10 fill 3171.

19 Fabric ROB SH. Necked jar (undercut rim). Area 3; Period 5, Ditch 17 fill 3215.

20 Fabric HAD OX. Face-neck flagon (cf. Symonds and Wade 1999, nos 155/6). Area 3; Period 5, (Pits northeast of Area 3) fill 3839.

21 Fabric LNV WH. Mortarium with flat reeded rim (cf. Howe et al. 1980, fig. 8; no. 102). Period 5, posthole fill 17436.

22 Fabric HAD OX ?bowl sherd with stamped/bossed 'Romano-Saxon' style decoration. Period 7, residual in pit fill 15290.

23 Fabric LNV CC. Platter (cf. Howe et al. 1980, no. 88). Unstratified Trench 11.

24 Bowl in imitation of samian form 36 (cf. Symonds and Wade 1999, nos 111–15). Unstratified Trench 13. Fabric HAD OX.

IX. Post-Roman pottery
by Sue Anderson

Introduction
A total of 1,668 sherds of pottery, weighing 23,759g, was collected from 330 contexts in 242 features and 49 layers. Table 4.21 shows the quantification of post-Roman pottery by fabric. A more detailed report, including fabric descriptions, is available in the archive.

Quantification was carried out using sherd count, weight and estimated vessel equivalent (EVE). The minimum number of vessels (MNV) within each context was also recorded, but cross-fitting was not attempted unless particularly distinctive vessels were observed in more than one context. A full quantification by fabric, context and feature is available in archive. All fabric codes were assigned from the Suffolk post-Roman fabric series (Anderson 2016). Early Saxon fabric groups have been characterised by major inclusions, and form terminology and dating for Early Saxon pottery follows Myres (1977) and Hamerow (1993). Thetford-type ware fabrics are based on Dallas (1984), and forms on Anderson (2004). Form terminology for medieval pottery is based on MPRG (1998).

Early Saxon (broadly 5th–7th centuries)
Thirty-four sherds of handmade pottery were probably of Early Saxon date. The range of fabrics in this group, including grass-tempered, sandy, calcareous and granitic tempered sherds is comparable with other Early Saxon groups in the area. At this site, organic-tempered fabrics dominated by sherd count and MNV, and there were also fairly high proportions of fine and medium sandy fabrics, but all fabric types produced less than ten sherds each. Organic-tempering is thought to be a late development in Essex (Hamerow 1993, 31), and Suffolk (Keith Wade, pers. comm.). Radiocarbon dating at Bloodmoor Hill, Carlton Colville, has suggested that granite-tempered pottery there was probably in use during the 6th century, and organic-tempered pottery from the mid 6th century onwards (Marshall et al. 2009, 328–9).

Seven rimsherds were present, representing six jars and a small bowl, but the sherds were too small to identify vessel types in more detail. One flat base was identified in alluvial deposit 3596. Several vessels had signs of surface treatment in the form of smoothing or burnishing. A small body sherd from the fill of pit 20115 was decorated with incised horizontal and vertical lines, and a larger piece in a different fabric from the fill of pit 20569 also had an incised horizontal line.

Middle Saxon pottery (broadly 8th–9th centuries)
Eighty sherds of Ipswich Ware were identified, including eleven jar rims (four type A, two type C, four type E and one type G; West 1963) and several base fragments (all sagging). Girth-grooving of the upper half of the vessel was frequent, and two vessels showed signs of burnishing/smoothing.

Late Saxon pottery (late 9th–11th centuries)
The relatively large Late Saxon assemblage was dominated by Thetford-type ware. Much of this group was in fabrics which are typical of Thetford itself (Dallas 1984), although a few sherds were in fabrics which probably represent local rural production sites.

It was possible to identify sixty-seven of the Late Saxon vessels to basic forms from their rims or from other characteristics, e.g. some vessels in the various Thetford-type fabrics could be identified from body sherds. Amongst the Thetford-type wares, there were twenty-seven medium and large jars, one spouted pitcher, two handled jars, and two large storage jars. Two rims were from jars of uncertain type. Twelve large storage vessels were identified from body sherds. A further twelve St

Description	Fabric	No	Wt/g	EVE	MNV
Early Saxon grass tempered	ESO1	10	78		9
Early Saxon grass and sand tempered	ESO2	2	35	0.08	2
Early Saxon coarse quartz tempering	ESCQ	1	8		1
Early Saxon medium sand tempering	ESMS	8	85	0.21	7
Early Saxon fine sand tempering	ESFS	6	170	0.10	6
Early Saxon very fine sand and abundant white mica	ESSM	1	2		1
Early Saxon grog and sand tempering	ESGS	1	3		1
Early Saxon granitic tempering	ESCF	2	6	0.06	2
Early Saxon sparse chalk in a fine to medium sandy matrix	ESSC	3	52		3
Total Early Anglo-Saxon				**0.45**	
Gritty Ipswich Ware (Group 2)	GIPS	18	454	0.50	17
Sandy Ipswich Ware (Group 1)	SIPS	62	1706	1.00	36
Total Middle Saxon				**1.50**	
Thetford-type ware	THET	385	5429	3.31	298
Thetford Ware (Grimston)	THETG	70	1840	0.61	41
'Early medieval' sandwich wares	EMSW	7	53		6
Stamford Ware Fabric A	STAMA	11	95	0.14	9
St Neots Ware	STNE	69	641	1.27	63
Saxo-Norman wares (general)	SXNO	2	21		2
Total				**5.33**	
Early medieval ware	EMW	241	1825	1.45	186
S Cambridgeshire (Essex?) sandy EMW	EMW1	61	817	0.40	36
Early medieval ware gritty	EMWG	7	51		6
Early medieval ware chalky	EMWC	4	28		4
Early medieval ware shelly	EMWS	7	46		3
Early medieval ware micaceous	EMWM	11	176		11
Yarmouth-type ware	YAR	12	88	0.07	10
Yarmouth-type non-calcareous	YARN	5	40		4
Early medieval sparse shelly ware	EMWSS	4	46	0.03	4
Early medieval sparse shell and coarse quartz	EMWSG	6	215	0.15	2
Stamford Ware Fabric B	STAMB	4	31		4
St Neots Ware Developed	STND	7	29		5
Total Late Saxon				**2.10**	
Medieval coarseware 1	MCW1	163	3220	1.72	94
Medieval coarseware 2	MCW2	98	1253	0.73	56
Medieval coarseware 3	MCW3	10	167		6
Medieval coarseware 4	MCW4	6	40		5
Medieval coarseware 5	MCW5	29	513	0.51	13
Medieval coarseware gritty	MCWG	5	94	0.15	4
Grimston coarseware	GRCW	10	288	0.05	6
Local medieval unglazed	LMU	2	23		2
Medieval coarseware micaceous	MCWM	7	57		7
Bury sandy fine ware	BSFW	16	172	0.23	14
Bury coarse sandy ware	BCSW	32	407	0.40	27
Bury medieval coarseware	BMCW	52	1065	0.83	40
Bury medieval coarseware gritty	BMCWG	1	26		1
Hedingham coarseware	HCW	2	43	0.10	2
Bury medieval shelly ware	BMSW	5	139	0.35	4
Ely coarseware	ELCW	42	592	0.70	31
Mildenhall-type coarseware	MILW	10	89	0.22	9
Hunts calcareous medieval coarseware	HFSW	3	110	0.08	2
Lyveden-Stanion Coarseware	LSCW	3	7	0.05	1
Unprovenanced glazed	UPG	4	55		3
Grimston-type ware	GRIM	3	19		3
Mill Green Ware	MGW	1	2		1
Hedingham Ware	HFW1	19	197		18
Essex sandy orange wares	ESOW	3	101	0.22	2
Ely Glazed Ware	ELYG	16	148		10
Total medieval				**6.34**	

Fabric	Code				
Late medieval and transitional	LMT	7	129	0.05	5
Late Grimston-type ware	GRIL	1	2	0.11	1
LMT Cambridgeshire sparse calcareous type	LMTC	3	5		3
Glazed red earthenware	GRE	13	138	0.16	13
West Norfolk Bichrome	WNBC	1	3		1
Speckle-glazed Ware	SPEC	2	10		1
Non-local post-medieval earthenwares	NLPM	1	22		1
Post-medieval slipwares	PMSW	3	31		2
Westerwald Stoneware	GSW5	1	2		1
Total late medieval and post-medieval				**0.32**	
Late post-medieval unglazed earthenwares	LPME	4	28	0.06	2
Industrial Slipware	INDS	1	39		1
Refined white earthenwares	REFW	16	101	0.17	15
English Stoneware	ESW	6	235		2
Porcelain	PORC	2	4	0.21	2
Staffordshire white salt-glazed stonewares	SWSW	1	9		1
Late slipped redware	LSRW	4	46	0.10	3
Total modern				**0.54**	
Unidentified		33	58		9
Totals		**1668**	**23759**	**16.58**	**1203**

Table 4.21 Post-Roman pottery quantification by fabric

Neots Ware jars were present. Jars in all fabrics were generally typical of the Late Saxon tradition and all of the common rim types were represented (Anderson 2004, fig. 43). The most frequent rim type in this group were rounded wedge (Type 6) and parallel sided (Type 4), suggesting that 'intermediate' (later 10th to mid-11th century) and 'late' (11th-century) groups were more common.

Only six bowls were identified in this group, the main types being St Neots bowls (four examples, inturned rims), a Dallas (1984) type BB6? (one example, Type 4 rim), and an uncertain type (one example, cavetto rim). Other vessels were less frequent, but included a Thetford-type costrel with flaring rim. One Stamford Ware vessel from pit 15215 was a crucible with a thin layer of soot externally but no metalworking residue, and there was also a Stamford Ware costrel with a flat-topped everted rim in pit 19153.

Decoration was very sparse on these vessels. Eleven vessels had rouletted decoration in the form of diamond, rectangular or square lattices. An unusual Thetford-type jar with a flanged rim had incised wavy line decoration. One bowl had a thumbed rim, and a Grimston Thetford-type vessel had a thumbed and stabbed handle. The most frequent form of surface treatment, however, was the application of thumbed strips to large storage vessels, although this may have been intended more for strengthening rather than as true decoration. Applied strips were recorded on eighteen vessels, and combed wavy lines were seen on two of these. Four of the Stamford Ware vessels were glazed, with the costrel having yellow glaze on the inner and outer surfaces.

Early medieval pottery (11th–13th centuries)
Early medieval wares are generally defined as handmade wares which first appeared in the 11th century and continued to be made into the 13th century in rural parts of East Anglia. Sometimes pots were finished on a turntable and many have wheelmade rims luted onto handmade bodies; rim forms suggest that this technique probably started in the 12th century in most areas. These handmade wares can be considered transitional between the Late Saxon and medieval wheelmade traditions, and their use overlaps with both period groups.

The group was dominated by the fine to medium sandy fabric which is typically found in Norfolk and north Suffolk. Most sherds were thin-walled and probably from jars with simple everted rims – sixteen such rims were present, making them the most common form in this group. Other relatively early types included lid-seated everted, tapering, and upright beaded, plain and thickened types, each represented by a single example. A few more developed rims were also present, including wedged, hammerhead and flat-topped everted types, again one of each type. Of the early medieval coarsewares, twenty-five rims were identifiable as jars. Three bowls and a spouted pitcher were also identified. One of the bowls was pierced below the rim (Fig. 4.14, no.1).

Decoration was not common. Seven rims were thumbed, two vessels appeared to have sparse shell-dusting, five had shallow girth-grooving, two had incised horizontal lines, one had combed wavy lines and one was possibly burnished. Three Stamford Ware body sherds were glazed with clear, yellow or copper green glazes, the latter having incised horizontal lines.

Illustrated vessels
1. EMW1 bowl, square beaded rim. Pit fill 15188, G113, Period 7. (Fig. 4.14, no.1)

Medieval wares (12th–14th centuries)

Coarsewares
Medieval coarsewares are wheelmade wares which are generally of 12th–14th-century date. Most in this group were well-fired and fully reduced to pale to dark greys, although oxidised wares were also found. This large group was dominated by coarsewares, the majority of which were unprovenanced.

The range of coarseware fabrics present during the high medieval period is broad and many of them are currently unprovenanced. It was possible to identify some wares which were probably made in or around Bury St Edmunds, at Hedingham in Essex, at Ely in Cambridgeshire and in the Huntingdon area. A few sherds are similar to a group identified as 'Mildenhall ware' (during the Fenland Survey), which was thought to contain some wasters. Studies of other rural sites in the region have shown that most pottery was sourced from production sites within a 25-mile radius (Anderson 2006) and this site appears to follow the pattern, although small quantities seem to have come from further afield.

The range of forms present in the high medieval group comprised jars, bowls, jugs and a lamp. The rim forms indicated that the assemblage continued into the 14th century, although the majority of datable types belonged to the 12th and 13th centuries. Rims of Essex and Cambridgeshire types are present as well as Suffolk examples. The Essex forms are relatively closely datable due to work at Rivenhall (Drury 1993).

In total there were sixty-two rims (based on MNVs) in the medieval coarseware group. The wheelmade medieval coarsewares included a similar range of rim types to the early medieval wares, emphasising their overlap. The majority of vessels were jars (Fig. 4.14, nos 4–13), with only eleven bowls (Fig. 4.14, nos 2–3), five jugs (Fig. 4.14, nos 14–15), a dish and a lamp. The most common jar rim forms in this group were the upright beaded and everted beaded types of 12th/13th-century date, and the square-beaded everted type which is probably 13th/14th-century, although in this group the forms are not close enough to late medieval types to suggest that they extend far into the 14th century. Bowl and dish rim forms in this group were generally simple forms of probable early date (inturned, beaded, upright flat-topped), but a few slightly later (13th century?) types were also present. Of the five jugs, two were early types with everted and upright beaded forms, and three were more developed types, although none was probably later than the 13th century.

Thirty-four vessels in this group had some form of decoration, some having more than one type. The most common types were applied thumbed strips, combed or incised wavy lines, finger-tip impressions, combed or incised horizontal lines, sparse shell-dusting and shallow girth-grooving. Three vessels had thumbed rims and one had a thumbed and stabbed handle. One bowl had a horizontal cordon.

Glazed wares
Glazed wares formed 8.5% of the high medieval group (based on sherd count). This is an average proportion for a rural site. For example, contemporary groups from Cedars Park, Stowmarket, and Days Road, Capel St Mary both produced 9% (Anderson 2016; Anderson 2011). Smaller urban centres tend to produce slightly more, for example at Clare Castle glazed wares represented 10.5% of the medieval sherd count (Anderson 2013a), and at Castle Hill, Orford the figure was 13% (Anderson 2001). Urban sites in the centre of Bury St Edmunds, however, often produce between 20–40%. The majority of glazed wares in this group were from Hedingham and Ely, with only a few from Grimston. The latter seems to have taken over from Hedingham Ware during the 13th century in Bury St Edmunds, and the small quantities of it at this site may

reflect a decline prior to the 14th century, which is also suggested by the coarseware rim forms.

Three types of unprovenanced glazed wares were present: a fine pale grey with dark green glaze, a white to pale pink fabric with abundant fine pink and red sand with light green glaze and brown slip stripes, and a fine orange fabric with occasional fine calcareous inclusions, white slip and clear glaze. The latter may be Cambridgeshire sgraffito.

All identifiable forms were jugs, but only two rims (one with a handle) were present, both in Essex Sandy Orange Ware, and there was one other handle in Hedingham Ware.

Glazes were typical of the fabrics, with most being lead or copper green, but with some Hedingham and other Essex wares having clear or orange lead glaze. Decoration other than glaze was rare, but included white or brown slip lines, narrow applied strips, and all-over white slip.

Illustrated vessels
(Fig. 4.14)
2   MCW5 flaring sided bowl, beaded rim. Handmade, wheel-finished? Period 7, Ditch 23, fill 3052.
3   MCW5 bowl with horizontal cordon, upright flat-topped rim. Period 7, Area 3, silting deposit 3028.
4   BCSW jar, tapering everted rim, applied thumbed strips. Period 7, pit 15185, fill 15188.
5   BMSW jar, upright square-beaded rim, possibly handmade body? Period 7, pit 4086, fill 4085.
6   BMCW jar, everted beaded rim, shallow girth-grooving. Period 7, pit 20429, fill 20419, Pit Group 1.
7   MCW1 jar, upright flat-topped rim, very sparse shell-dusting? Period 7, pit 15178, fill 15177.
8   MCW1 jar, square beaded rim, applied thumbed strips. Period 7, layer 3195.
9   MCW1 jar, squared rim, applied thumbed strips and fingertip impressions. 20573 fill of gully 20574 and 20871 fill of pit 20870.
10 MCW2 jar, everted beaded rim. Period 7, pit 15178, fill 15177.
11 MCW5 jar, lid-seated everted rim with thumbed edge, surfaces pale grey, form similar to some Grimston coarsewares. Period 7, layer 2113.
12 BMCW jar, upright everted rim. Period 7, pit 20476, fill 20474.
13 HFSW jar, flat-topped everted rim with combed wavy line decoration, combed lines on body. Period 7, clay dump 3080.
14 BCSW jug, square beaded rim. Period 7, pit 20153, fill 20198.
15 MCW1 jug. thickened/beaded everted rim with thumbed decoration. Period 7, pit 20429, fill 20419, Pit Group.

Late and post-medieval pottery (late 14th–18th century)
Most pottery in this group comprised local and regional redwares. There was clearly a decline in pottery use on this site from the 14th century onwards, and whilst some of the late medieval wares could be contemporary with the very latest occupation on the site, it is likely that much of this small group arrived at the site during manuring activity. The range of identifiable vessels included a jug, two jars, a bowl/pancheon and a mug. At least some of the sherds have parallels amongst the post-medieval wares produced in Ely (Cessford et al. 2006).

Modern ceramics (late 18th century+)
The small quantity of modern pottery included sherds of slipped redware bowls, pieces of plantpot, fragments of refined whiteware table wares, stoneware storage vessels and some fragments of decorated porcelain. Like the earlier post-medieval material, this small group was

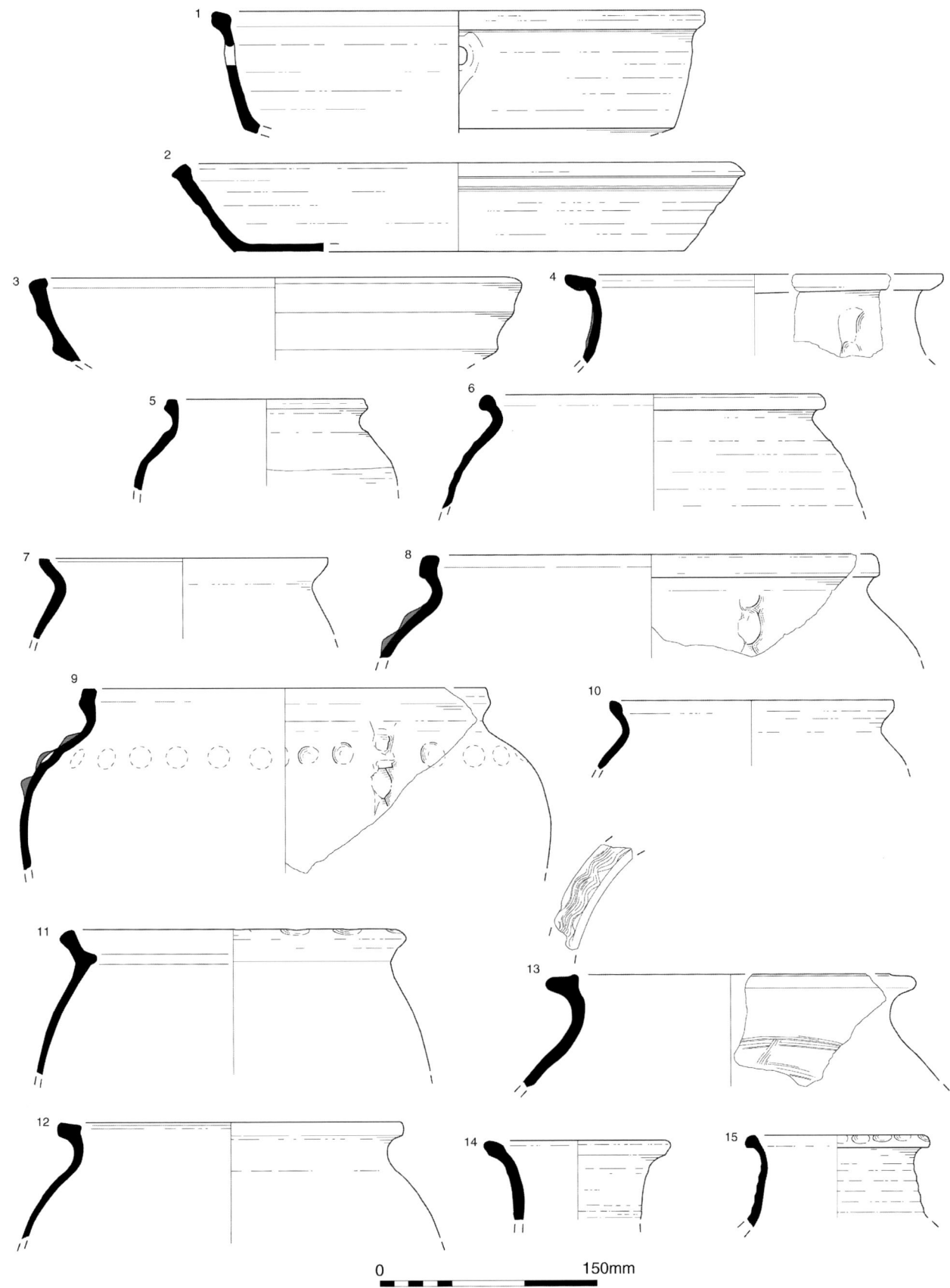

Figure 4.14 Post-Roman pottery (scale 1:4) nos1–15

probably dispersed across the field as a component of 'night soil'.

Modern pottery was largely recovered from Period 9 (twenty-nine sherds), but a few sherds were intrusive in Periods 3, 5 and 7. Like the post-medieval wares, there was no particular spatial patterning in this group.

Pottery by site period
A summary of the pottery by site period is provided in Table 4.22. The largest group was from Period 7 (medieval). Some post-Roman sherds were intrusive in earlier features and there was some residual material in Period 7. For example many Middle Saxon and most Late Saxon sherds were recovered from medieval contexts. Only the post-Roman periods are discussed here.

Period 6 – Saxon
Ninety-one of the ninety-nine sherds recovered from features of this period were of Saxon date. Fourteen were Early Saxon, thirty-six were Middle Saxon and forty-one were Late Saxon. The other sherds were three early medieval and three medieval wares, and two unidentified. The largest groups were from pits and other features on the east side of the site (forty-one sherds), with an additional eighteen sherds from pit 20405 (probably Middle Saxon); a further nineteen sherds of mixed dates were from the margins of the floodplain at the south end of the site.

Period 7 – Medieval
A total of 1332 sherds were recovered from features assigned to this period. They were recovered from a range of features including pits, postholes, ditches, a grave, an animal burial, wells and a corn-dryer. Alluvial and dump layers also contained small quantities. The majority of sherds were recovered from the pits and ditches, as described below.

Ditches and land divisions
Eleven groups relating to ditches and associated features, and a fenceline, contained a total of 271 sherds (3578g) of 181 vessels. Eleven sherds were certainly residual in this phase (two Early and nine Middle Saxon) and two were unidentified. Eighty-seven sherds of sixty-six Late Saxon vessels could represent early deposits in some of the ditches, perhaps indicating an 11th-century inception for some, but many of these were probably also residual. In general, early medieval sherds occurred in the same contexts, and totalled fifty-five sherds from forty-seven

vessels. The largest period group in these features was the medieval pottery, which totalled 116 sherds from only fifty-five vessels. No intrusive later sherds were identified. Where diagnostic medieval rim forms and fabrics were present, it was possible to suggest a 12th-century date for Ditch 34, a 12th/13th-century date for the fills in Ditches 2, 3, 24, 27 and 35, and a 13th-century date for the majority of cut features enclosed by these ditches.

Pit groups and quarry pits
Seven groups relating to pit groups and quarry pits produced a total of 599 sherds (8947g) of 439 vessels. They were recovered from a total of forty-nine features, providing an average of only twelve sherds per pit. The largest group from a single feature was 135 sherds, with most pits containing only a handful of pottery. Five Early and six Middle Saxon sherds were residual, and four sherds were unidentified. There were six late medieval sherds from the cluster of medieval pits in the north-west corner of the site. One post-medieval and one modern sherd were intrusive. Late Saxon and early medieval wares totalled 193 and 174 sherds respectively. Several pits, notably some pits to the west of Ditch 2, contained only material of this date range, suggesting that some of the pits were of 11th/12th-century date. Others contained a high proportion of this material and probably originated in the early medieval period, but continued in use during the 12th/13th centuries. Alternatively there was a very high degree of residuality in these pits. A few of the pits may be of later date, particularly those in Pit Group 5 which are potentially of 13th/14th-century date. In addition to these pits, nineteen isolated pits and nine postholes produced 77 sherds ranging from Early Saxon to 13th/14th-century in date, but only two of these pits contained more than five sherds.

Other features
Very little pottery was recovered from kiln 20044. Four Late Saxon and early medieval sherds were recovered from rake-out deposits and the kiln lining, and the lining and rake-out also contained two sherds of medieval coarseware. Fragments from topsoil slumping in the top of the kiln were late medieval and modern.

The fill of corn-dryer 17182 produced a tiny fragment of early medieval ware from a sample, and a fragment of Thetford-type ware from an associated pit. A further five sherds came from other corn-dryer fills and comprised Grimston Thetford ware, early medieval and medieval coarsewares.

Three wells (17337, 17156, 20151) all contained a high proportion of Late Saxon pottery, suggesting that they may have been in use in this period, but their fills also contained high medieval wares suggesting that 17156 and 20151 were probably filled in during the 12th or early 13th century, and 17337 may have remained at least partly open into the late 14th/15th century.

A grave and an animal burial both contained small amounts of Late Saxon to medieval wares, and the grave also produced two sherds of Early Saxon pottery.

Alluvial deposits
Fifty sherds were recovered from alluvium and peat layers on the floodplain edge. The majority of pottery from these deposits was of high medieval date, with two late medieval sherds found in layer 2058. Only three sherds were early

Pot period	P.1	P.2	P.3	P.5	P.6	P.7	P.9	Un
ESax	1	1		3	14	13	2	
MSax			3	1	36	37	3	
LSax		4	7	6	41	445	40	1
EMed			10	2	3	326	28	
Med			7	1	3	467	55	9
LMed						10		1
PMed	1			1		1	16	1
Mod			1	1		3	30	
Un					2	30	1	
Totals	**2**	**5**	**28**	**15**	**99**	**1332**	**175**	**12**

Table 4.22 Post-Roman pottery types present by period (sherd count)

86

medieval, and one Middle Saxon sherd was found, but there was no Late Saxon pottery in these layers.

Dumping and land reclamation
Seventy-nine sherds ranging from Early Saxon to medieval date were found in deposits above the medieval alluvial layers. Most of the sherds from these deposits were medieval and the range of wares suggested a 13th/14th-century date.

Summary and discussion
A small quantity of pottery was of Early Saxon date and there was a slightly larger assemblage of Middle Saxon material. Both groups were largely residual in medieval contexts. At the other end of the assemblage's date range, small quantities of late medieval, post-medieval and modern pottery probably post-date any occupation on the site and are likely to be related to manuring of open fields. The bulk of the assemblage is of Late Saxon, early and high medieval date and was found in contexts assigned to Period 7.

The majority of the assemblage was recovered from pits and linear features, with smaller quantities being derived from postholes and other negative features. However, only one feature (pit 20569) produced more than 100 sherds, whilst 182 features contained less than ten sherds. Although more than two-thirds of the assemblage came from the northern half of the site, there were no particular concentrations of finds. With a few exceptions, it seems likely that most of these sherds were incorporated into features accidentally. Larger quantities may be evidence for deliberate rubbish disposal in pits, particularly in the large quarry pits and wells, which seem to have been used for this purpose once their primary function was completed.

The small group of Early Saxon pottery included a variety of fabrics, some of which were probably relatively late and could be contemporary with the Middle Saxon Ipswich Ware from the site. Assemblages from nearby Early Saxon sites such as West Stow Museum Store (Anderson 2013b) have produced a similar range of fabrics, although the proportions differ significantly. In terms of fabric distribution, the closest large group from Suffolk is the assemblage from the Eriswell settlement site ERL101 (Anderson 2005), which produced most of the same fabrics in similar proportions. The group is too small to indicate occupation on the site at this period and the sherds may have been spread on open fields with manure.

Middle Saxon Ipswich Ware has not previously been found in any great quantities in Mildenhall parish, although it does occasionally turn up at sites on Lakenheath airbase, with one large assemblage coming from the Consolidated Support site ERL116 (Anderson 2003). The largest assemblage of this material from this part of Suffolk was found at Brandon, a high status Middle Saxon settlement on Staunch Meadow (Tester *et al.* 2014). Smaller quantities have also been recorded in Thetford, most recently at Brandon Road (Blinkhorn 2010) and previously at Redcastle Furze (Knocker 1967, 137), and at Ely (Blinkhorn 2012, table 26). An overland route from Ipswich could have passed through the Norfolk and Suffolk settlements on the way to Brandon, which would have been the biggest consumer of such pottery in this part of Suffolk at the time. Alternatively, Brandon may have

been the focus for a market, and Ipswich Ware vessels may have been distributed into the fens and south-west Norfolk from there. Blinkhorn suggests that the presence of Ipswich Ware in smaller rural Middle Saxon settlements, whilst not necessarily an indicator of high status, is often associated with specialised craft production (Blinkhorn 2012, 99).

Late Saxon pottery formed the largest period group at the site, despite the lack of much evidence for features of this date. It was dominated by Thetford-type ware and local variants (including THETG and EMSW), making up 85% of the period total. St Neots Ware made up 13%, and Stamford Ware 2%. These proportions are within the range which would be expected for this area, when compared with surrounding settlements. In Thetford itself, Thetford Ware from the Knocker excavations made up 96% of the Late Saxon assemblage, with St Neots Ware providing 3% and Stamford Ware 1% (Dallas 1984, 118, 123–4), and the same proportions were found at the Late Saxon site at Brandon Sports Centre (BRD 071; Tester *et al.* 2014). Other sites in Thetford have produced much higher proportions of St Neots Ware (*e.g.* Mill Lane, 7% (Anderson 2004) and site 1092, 29% (Dallas 1984, 126–7)), but it is suggested that site 1092 was of 11th-century date. St Neots Ware is thought to have arrived in Thetford, and elsewhere in the fens (*e.g.* Ely and Soham, Spoerry 2016) in the second half of the Late Saxon period. Further to the west, St Neots Ware was more frequent, with an overall proportion at Ely sites of 34% (Thetford-type ware 63%, Stamford Ware 3%; Spoerry 2016) and at Cherry Hinton of 62% (Thetford-type ware 36%, Stamford Ware 2%; *ibid*). Spoerry suggests that St Neots Ware may have been distributed with greatest ease along the River Great Ouse, and it is more frequent in fenland sites close to this waterway. Potentially it could have reached Mildenhall via the River Lark, with Stamford Ware following a similar route. However, it seems likely that Thetford Ware reached the settlement overland, perhaps travelling along the Icknield way for part of the route, and perhaps the other non-local wares came with it. The higher proportion of St Neots Ware at the Mildenhall site may simply reflect the broadly late 10th and 11th- century date of most of the identifiable Late Saxon forms here.

Early and high medieval pottery was broadly of later 11th to 13th-century date, with only a few diagnostic sherds which could stretch the date range into the 14th century. This group includes both the handmade wares (some of which had wheel-finished rims) classified as 'early medieval' and the wheelmade greywares classified as 'medieval'. Although the handmade and wheelmade fabrics have been separated for the purposes of classification, it is likely that they were broadly contemporary and simply represent the output of different potters or production sites using different techniques. The fabrics are very similar in both types, being distinguished largely on the basis of coarseness of the sandy inclusions and evidence of hand-building, and it is likely that they were made at potteries located on similar geological deposits. A few calcareous-tempered wares were present, but these were less common than the sandy types.

There are few rural fenland assemblages currently available with which to compare the early medieval wares. Evidence from Ely suggests that Thetford Ware use had ceased before the 12th century, but St Neots Ware continued, and Ely Ware now dominated (Spoerry 2016).

Some of the Ely Ware bowls in the Mildenhall assemblage could be of this early date. In Thetford, the fine to medium sandy thin-walled wares predominate, although quantities in most assemblages are small. Mill Lane produced a similar quantity of early medieval pottery to the Mildenhall site, and the distribution of fabrics is almost identical, but the Cambridgeshire fabric EMW1 was not identified at Mill Lane, whilst early medieval Stamford Ware was significantly more frequent there (Anderson 2004). Even though Thetford had stopped producing wheelmade vessels of high quality, it was still the main urban centre in this part of East Anglia and it is likely that much of the 11th/12th-century pottery in the Mildenhall assemblage came through or from the town, with other pottery arriving at the site from across the fens.

Large high medieval assemblages are even less common in this part of the region. This is the first large assemblage of medieval pottery to have been excavated in Mildenhall, and one of the few west of Bury St Edmunds (within Suffolk). Two aspects are of particular significance: firstly the lack of so-called 'Mildenhall ware', suggesting that the few sherds collected during the Fenland Survey may have been made elsewhere (perhaps locally to Ely); secondly the presence of wares which had previously mainly been found in Bury St Edmunds and which are rare at rural sites to the north, south and east of the town. This suggests direct links with the town during the high medieval period.

Most of the Mildenhall coarsewares are unprovenanced, but MCW1 shows similarities in fabric to Thetford Ware, and the fabric of some wheelmade medieval greywares from the town does seem to suggest that there was a minor rekindling of the pottery industry somewhere in the vicinity during the medieval period. Other unprovenanced medieval coarsewares in the Mildenhall assemblage are similar to wares found in Bury and in east Suffolk, and there were certainly some Bury wares in the assemblage. Other provenanced pottery of this date included material which had travelled from north-west Norfolk, Cambridgeshire, Huntingdon, Essex, and even Northamptonshire, but there were no imported wares. Glazed wares were relatively infrequent in the assemblage, but as a proportion of the high medieval group, this assemblage is comparable with other rural medieval sites in Suffolk, particularly those which appear to have declined towards the end of the 13th or in the early 14th century.

Again the main comparable evidence is from the urban centres at Ely and Thetford. The small group from Mill Lane, Thetford, was dominated by Bury wares, Norfolk LMU and Grimston coarseware. Ely, of course, had its own pottery producers and assemblages there are dominated by Ely Ware, but pottery from Norfolk, Essex, Buckinghamshire, Northamptonshire and Lincolnshire is also present, as well as imported wares. It is likely that the main markets serving Mildenhall were those in Thetford, Bury St Edmunds and, to a lesser extent, Ely. The more 'exotic' wares from Norfolk, Essex and the west could have reached Mildenhall via these three towns.

The small quantities of late medieval and later pottery suggest that any intensive activity had declined by the late 14th century if not before. This group is typical of the periods it belongs to, but too small for further interpretation.

X. Fired clay
by E.R. McSloy

Clay weights

A complete triangular weight with perforations across all three corners was retrieved from pit 16063. This and two fragmentary examples from the same feature are illustrated. Further, more fragmentary weights, probably of triangular form, were recorded from Period 3 pits 19215, 19114 and (residual within) Period 6 Ditch 20947 (Enclosure D).

Triangular clay weights are common finds from Iron Age sites, and are typically interpreted as for use with vertical, warp-weighted looms. Good parallels can be found from the major Iron Age sites at Danebury and Winnall Down in Hampshire (Poole 1984; Bates and Winham 1985).

(Fig. 4.15)

1 Complete. Triangular/tri-perforated form (one side is rounded). Round perforations at each angle (8–10mm diam.). Soft, pale buff fabric with sparse chalk and small stones. Each side c. 140mm; thickness 75mm; weight 1241g. Area 16; Period 3, pit 16063 (16065).

2 Fragment. Triangular form. One surviving round perforation through angle (10mm diam.). Hard red-orange fabric with common chalk and flint pebbles 6–9mm. Thickness 65mm. Area 16; Period 3, pit 16063 (16064).

3 Fragment, broken longitudinally. Triangular form. Two partial round perforations through two surviving angles. Fabric as no. 2. Area 16; Period 3, pit 16063 (16064).

XI. Worked bone and antler
by E.R. McSloy

A total of twenty-five objects of worked bone or antler were recorded, the majority coming from Period 3 (Iron Age)-phased deposits (Table 4.23). The catalogue of illustrated material presented below omits some waste or incomplete items (Figs 4.16–18). Evidence for bone working occurs in the form of waste pieces, incomplete items and trial pieces (Fig. 4.17; nos 17–18), and is limited to Period 3 deposits. Unless otherwise stated, identification of animal species/element is by J. Geber.

Published Iron Age groups of worked bone which are comparably large and diverse are relatively rare from the region. For this reason, many of the parallels quoted for objects are from southern and western Britain, and particularly from among the large and well-published assemblages from Danebury, Hants (Sellwood 1984; Cunliffe and Poole 1991).

The worked bone catalogue is organised by period and functional categories, which are based on Crummy's divisions (1983). Over half of the items considered to date to the Late Prehistoric period (10 from 19) can be associated with varying degrees of certainty with textiles. In most respects, the assemblage reflects the function-related groupings seen at central-southern English 'hillforts', and those from the Somerset Levels. A perhaps significant absence, particularly given the size and preservation of the faunal remains, is that of the bone gouges/points made from sheep longbones which were common at Danebury, Glastonbury and Maiden Castle (Sellwood 1984, 385–7).

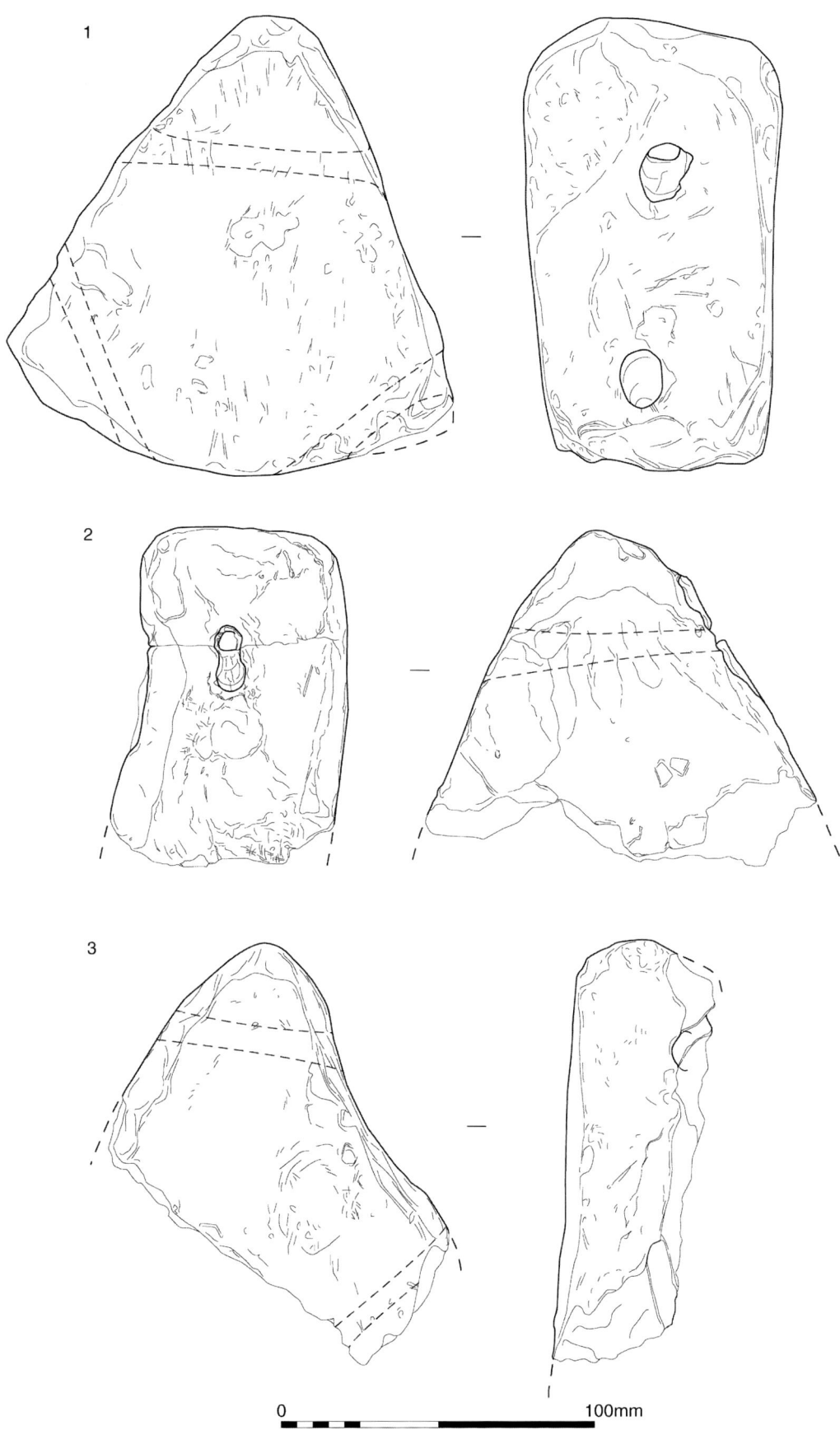

Figure 4.15 Fired clay objects (scale 1:2) nos 1–3

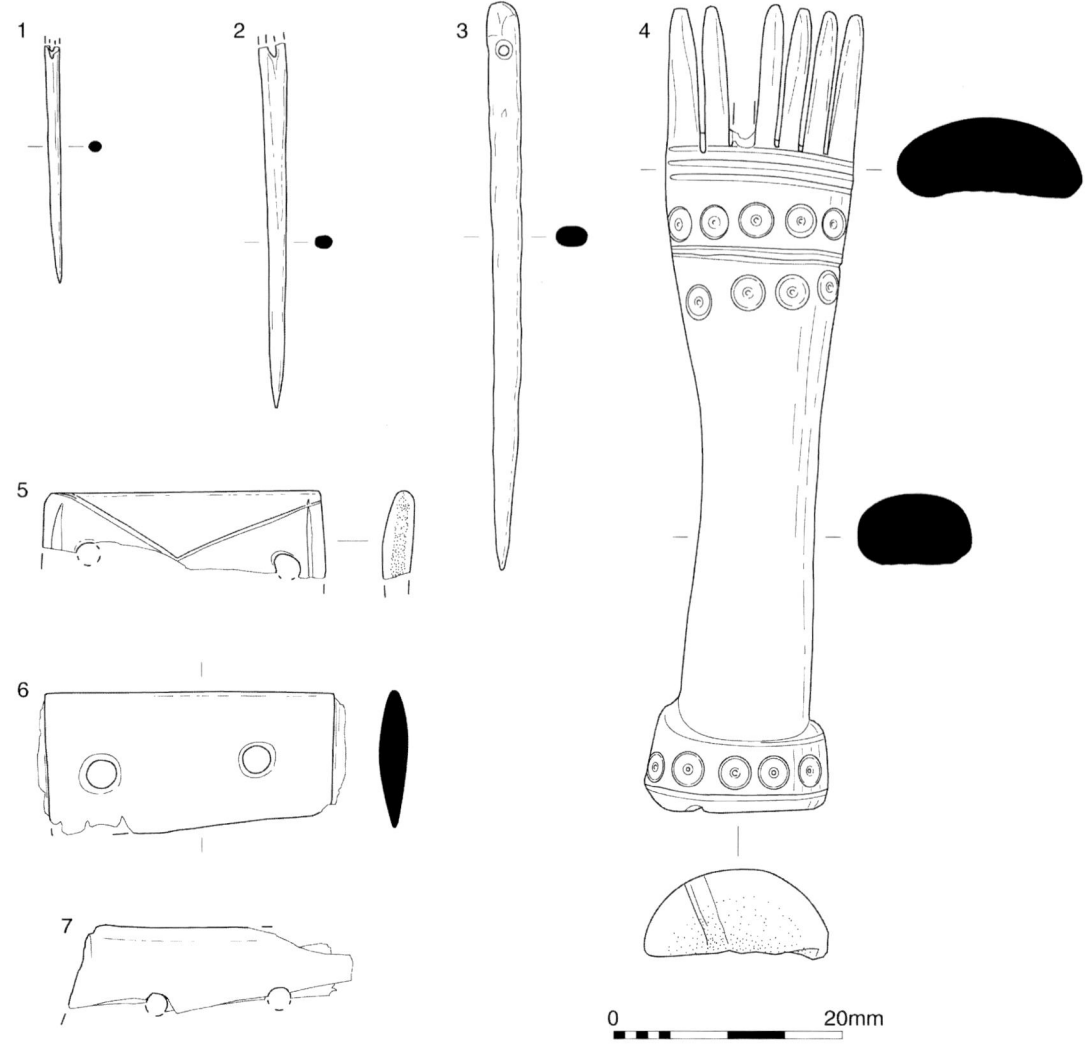

Figure 4.16 Worked bone (scale 2:3) nos 1–7

Late Bronze Age
(Fig. 4.16)

Crafts/textiles

1 Needle fragment, broken at the 'eye'. From a splinter of bone, with oval section. The surfaces are polished from use. Late Bronze Age bone needles are uncommon, although they are known from Runnymede Bridge (Needham and Serjeantson 1996, fig. 101), and the Marlborough Downs (Gingell 1992, 114–5, nos 2 and 17). The elongated eye is not a feature of these examples, although it is known with Iron Age finds from Danebury (Sellwood 1984, fig. 7.32). Surviving length 48mm; width 2mm; thickness 1.5mm. Period 2, pit 22063 (fill 20337).

Iron Age
(Fig. 4.16)

Crafts/textiles

2 Needle fragment, broken at the 'eye', which is of elongated form. Probably bird. As noted above, the form of the eye is typical of Iron Age needles. Surviving length 73mm. Period 3, pit 20085 (fill 20159).

3 Needle. Complete, from splinter of bone, sub-square in section. The surfaces exhibit a high polish from use. Simple, rounded head. The eye round and bored from either face, resulting in bi-conical profile. Medieval needles are invariably of metal, and no. 3 is almost certainly a re-deposited object, of earlier Saxon, or most likely Iron Age, date. Examples from Meare, Somerset (Coles 1987, fig. 3.3), and Danebury, Hants (Cunliffe and Poole 1991, fig. 7.31, no. 3.277) are similar. Length 125mm. Period 7, Ditch 3940/Ditch 24 (fill 3941).

4 Weaving comb. Probably from horse metapodial. The inside (undecorated) face exposes the trabecular structure of the bone. Six of the original seven teeth are present, and these are of approximately equal length. The notches between are regular and U-shaped. The butt falls within Sellwood's 'Square or rectangular enlargement' category, as used for classification at Danebury (Sellwood 1984, 371). In this instance, the rectangular expansion is asymmetric, extending part-way up one side of the shaft. Decoration is restricted to the butt, and to the portion below the dentate end. This consists of triple (lateral) grooves below the teeth, and rows of compass-scribed 'ring-and-dot', separated by double, lateral grooves. Decoration to the butt consists of a row of ring and dot between single grooves. Most discussions of the dating and function of combs are based on groups from the south and west. Sellwood (1984, 375) noted a significant concentration of square/rectangular-butted forms in association with the latest (Iron Age) ceramic phases. There is also

Functional	<>	2	3	5	6	7
Fasteners			2			1
Personal adornment/dress	1					
Textiles		1	5	2		3
Toilet/pharmaceutical (modern tongue-depressor)	1					1
Tools			2			
indeterminate	1		2	1	1	1

Table 4.23 Worked bone objects summary by function/period

the suggestion, based on an absence of similar forms from western British sites, that the square/rectangular-butted group may have an eastern British distribution. Length 159mm; width at dentate end 40mm; thickness 19mm. Period 3, pit 19198 (fill 19214).

Object no. 5, together with undecorated examples, nos 6 and 7, are tentatively suggested as weaving tablets, although other uses are possible (below). An object of similar form, though undecorated, occurs from Danebury (Sellwood 1984, fig. 7.39, no. 3.210). Weaving tablets were in use since at least the early Iron Age and were used in the production of decorative cloth strips. Although tablets with four perforations are more common, examples with two are known (Hodges 1976, 137). The notches noted with no. 6 may relate to function, and argue against use as a weaving tablet. An alternative use as a bobbin or thread-winder is possible.

(Fig. 4.17)

5 Fragmentary object from cattle rib. Rectangular, with smoothed ends. There are two irregular perforations close to the ends, and central to the length of the rib. Decoration consists of groves inset from, and parallel to, the ends, and a incised saltire cross – a scheme seen frequently on weaving combs (Coles 1987, fig. 3.46, no. H76). The surfaces are polished from use, and the perforations worn. Length 55mm. Period 3m pit 20085 (fill 20086).

6 Rectangular object from cattle rib. Rectangular, with rough, knife-cut ends and undecorated. The surfaces are smoothed from use. Two circular perforations positioned at centreline of rib. There are a series of notches cut or worn to one edge below one perforation. Length 62mm; width 29–25mm. Period 5, layer 20792.

7 Fragmentary object from cattle rib. Two circular perforations at centreline of rib. Length 55mm. Period 7, pit 19161 (fill 19160).

Object nos 8–10 are of the same form, adapted from sheep metacarpals (no. 8) and metatarsals (nos 9 and 10), and seemingly representing different stages of manufacture. Comparable objects occur among the larger worked bone assemblages from the major Iron Age sites. Discussion of function has centred on associations with textiles, and possible use as bobbins to hold spun yarn, and with the thread end held through the central hole. Significantly the one 'finished' object, no. 8, exhibits wear to the central perforation and a degree of surface polish, which would be consistent with use in this way.

(Fig. 4.17)

8 Fragment from sheep metacarpal. Central, transverse circular perforation, approximately central to the shaft. Wear/polish to the hole and surfaces. Surviving length 80mm. Period 3, pit 15234 (fill 15276).

9 Complete (juvenile) sheep metatarsal. A circular perforation, approximately central to the shaft, has been drilled from the ventral surface only, and into the central cavity of the bone. Length 106mm. Period 3, layer 19206.

10 Complete (mature) sheep metatarsal. A circular perforation approximately central to the shaft, has been begun from the ventral surface, but not completed. Length 110mm. Period 5, layer 21092.

Fasteners

11 Toggle. From a large mammal longbone, the ends of which are smoothed. The single perforation is approximately central. Decoration consists of a double line of incised grooves at each end, and multiple rows of double ring and dot. By far the largest group (46) of toggles is from Danebury, the majority (36) coming from the latest Iron Age Ceramic phases. The form of some of the Danebury examples is very similar to no.11 (Cunliffe and Poole 1991, 358, no. 3.263). Length 39mm; width 31mm; thickness 23mm. Period 3, pit 21031 (fill 21032).

12 Probably a toggle fragment. From large mammal longbone. As with no. 11, the ends are smoothed, though this example is unadorned. Length 28mm. Period 3 pit 21398 (fill 21406).

13 Toggle. Probably red deer antler. Cylindrical form, lightly waisted, with slot-like rectangular perforation. Smooth from use. Antler toggles of the same form as no. 13 are known from a number of sites, including Cadbury, Somerset (Britnell 2000, 202; fig 97 nos 13 and

14), Meare (Coles 1987, fig. 3.26) and Danebury (Cunliffe and Poole 1991, fig. 7.37, no. 3.362). Length 55mm. Period 7 gully 16059 (fill 16060).

14 Perforated canine tooth (dog or wolf). Finds of pierced canine teeth were common from Late Iron Age contexts from Meare, Somerset (Coles 1987), and of early Roman date from Colchester (Crummy 1983, no.1803) and Baldock (Stead and Rigby 1986, no. 676). Examples are also known of earlier Saxon date (Evison 1994, 148, fig. 28 4B). Use as toggles or pendants are possible. Length 42mm. Area 20. Unstratified.

Tools/handles

15 Awl/point. Tibiotarsus from fowl (id. by A. Clark), knife-trimmed to a point at the proximal end. Crudely sharpened bone points are a feature of Iron Age worked bone assemblages, a large number for example coming from Danebury (Cunliffe and Poole 1991, 359–66). The use of bird bone is unusual, although probably a reflection of the available resource (Chapter 5.IV). Length 89mm. Period 3 pit 20370 (fill 20367).

16 Handle. Red deer antler. Roughly-trimmed and smoothed from use. The narrower end features a small, circular hole for a tang. Iron gouge no. 12 (Chapter 4.II) was also recorded from deposit 19089. The two items are probably from the same tool and have been illustrated together on Fig. 4.2. Length 66mm; diam. 25–19mm. Period 3, pit 19088 (fill 19089).

'Trial pieces'

17 Fragment of horse radius (proximal). One surface with one complete, and one partial, compass-scribed double ring-and-dot motifs. Surviving width 78mm. Period 3, Ditch 21197/Ditch 5 (fill 21629).

18 Larger mammal ulna fragment. May be part of a functional object, although the irregularity of its underside makes this unlikely. The adapted surface exhibits three complete, and one partial compass-scribed double ring-and-dot motifs. Surviving length 66mm. Period 3 pit 20392 (fill 20393).

Uncertain

19 Sheep metatarsal. Perforated through the proximal end. Sheep longbones modified in this way and of Iron Age date occur from Danebury (Cunliffe and Poole 1991, fig. 7.34, nos 3.347–8). Their function is unknown. Surviving length 113mm. Period 7, gully 2096 (fill 2100).

Post-Roman

Textiles

20 Bone-point fragment, with sub-square section and polished surfaces. Possibly a pin-beater, an implement class known to be associated with weaving, and possibly utilised for unpicking knots or tangles. Most are earlier Anglo-Saxon in date, although Late Saxon/medieval examples are known (MacGregor 1985, 186–89). Surviving length 36mm; width 8.5mm; thickness 5mm. Period 6, pit 20870 (fill 20871).

Toilet/pharmaceutical
(Fig. 4.18)

21 Bone comb. Fragmentary, of single-sided composite class, with four from the probable five iron rivets in place. Decoration consists of repeated diagonal incised lines to the outer (approximately) one third of the connecting plate, and a 'spine' of incised diagonal line contained within a double-grooved border. Sufficient survives to identify it as of Ashby's Type 7 (2007, 3–4). These are characterised by deep, plano-convex connecting plates which can (as here) be concavo-convex in form, and feature simple decoration. The suggested dating, based on groups including that from Coppergate in York, is c. 900–1100 AD (Ashby 2007). Surviving length 101mm; width (comb plate) 37mm. Period 7, pit 19060 (fill 19000).

22 Small fragment from composite bone comb strengthening-plate. A portion of one circular rivet hole is present. A series of six incised lines have resulted from the cutting of the teeth, and can commonly be seen on objects of this class. Surviving length 18mm. Unstratified.

Uncertain

23 Pig fibula fragment adapted at distal end to form a spatulate terminal. Unfinished pin/needle or possibly implement for burnishing/decorating pottery. Surviving length 49mm. Period 6 pit 20405 (fill 20407).

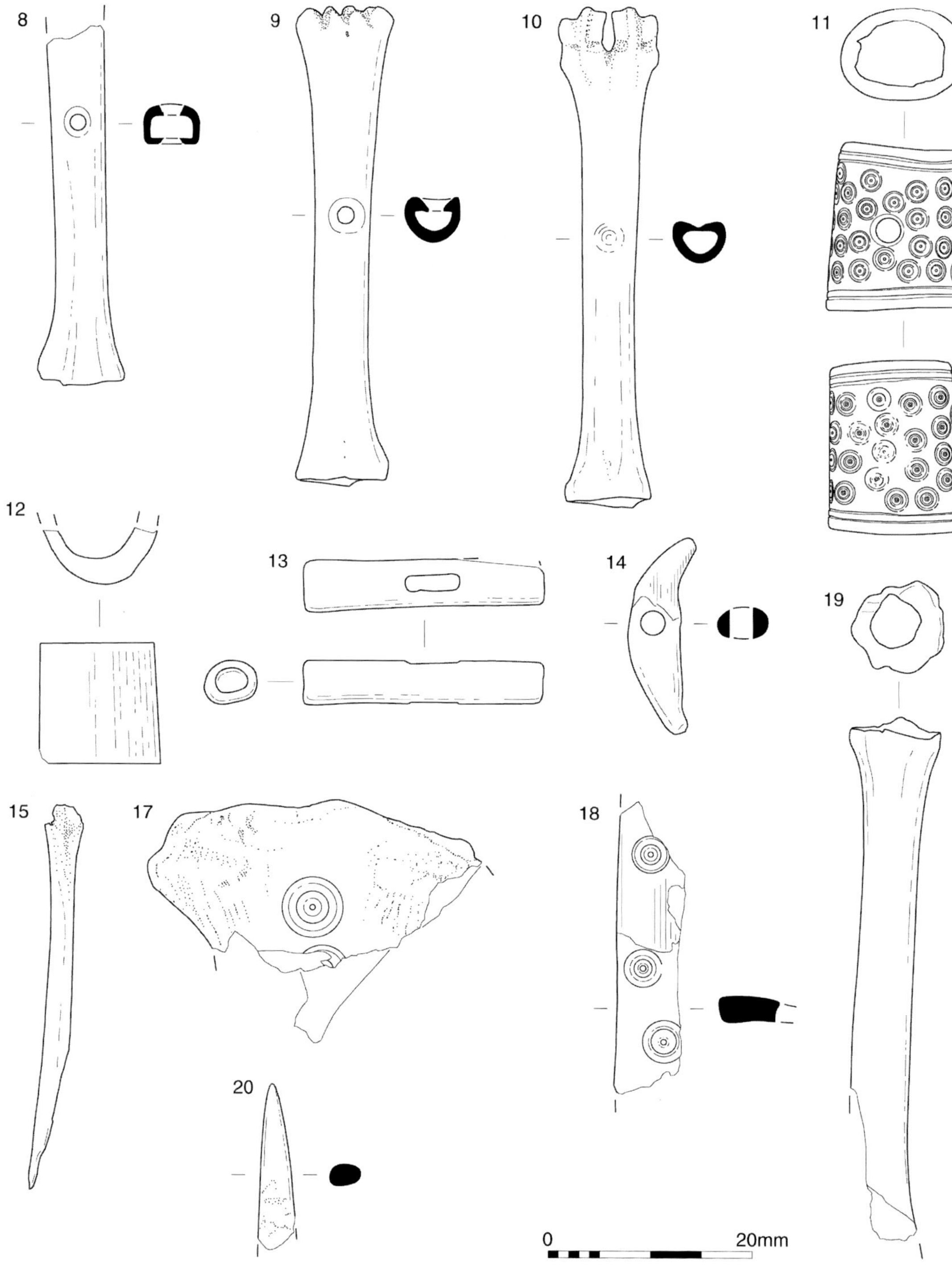

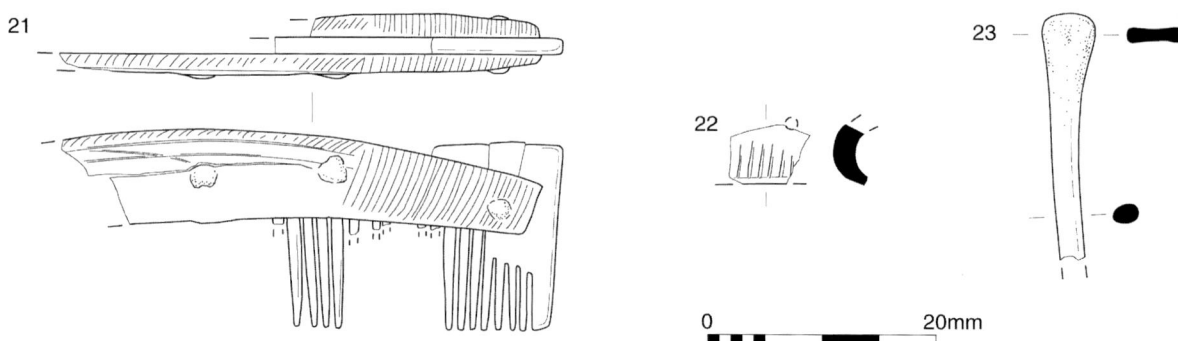

Figure 4.17 Worked bone (scale 2:3) nos 8–20 (no. 16 shown on Fig. 4.2)

Figure 4.18 Worked bone (scale 2:3) nos 21–23

Chapter 5. Zoological and Environmental Evidence

I. Radiocarbon dating
by Sarah Cobain

Introduction
A total of 27 Accelerator Mass Spectrometry (AMS) radiocarbon measurements were obtained using single fragments of charred or waterlogged plant macrofossils, charcoal, animal bone and human bone. The samples were prepared and measured during September 2013 and March 2014 at Scottish Universities Environmental Research Centre (SUERC). The aim of the dating programme was to establish dates for artefact-free features and inhumation burials recovered on site and to ascertain whether increased precision could be achieved by Bayesian modelling of the radiocarbon dates.

Methodology
The samples were successfully dated using the AMS method. Where possible, the use of single fragments of material eliminated the risk of combining material of different ages in the same sample. Care was also taken to ensure that material was selected from secure deposits to reduce the risk of residual or intrusive material, where this was not possible, paired samples were used to confirm radiocarbon measurements. The uncalibrated dates are conventional radiocarbon ages (BP). The radiocarbon ages were calibrated by using the University of Oxford Radiocarbon Accelerator Unit calibration programme OxCal 4.2 (Bronk Ramsey 2009) using the IntCal13 dataset (Reimer *et al.* 2013) (Fig. 5.1).

Results and discussion
Full radiocarbon measurements and calibrations to 95.4% and 68.2% probability are listed in Table 5.1.

Late Bronze Age
Human bone recovered from second fill 20338 within recut 22063 of pit 20238 (first recut) provided a Late Bronze Age date. A charred barley grain from second fill 20336 within recut 22064 of pit 20238 (second recut) also dated to the Late Bronze Age, although a conflicting date from animal bone from this fill provided an early medieval date. Since finds from this deposit suggest a Late Bronze Age date, this animal bone is thought to be intrusive.

Datable material from palaeochannel 3617 was limited, restricted to the top two fills (3612 and 3593) and it was acknowledged there was a risk of residual or intrusive material within these fills. Initially paired dates were recovered from waterlogged plant remains within fill 3612 which provided a Late Bronze Age to Early Iron Age date and a Roman date. Suspecting that the material yielding the Roman date was intrusive, material from uppermost fill 3593 was dated and provided a Late Bronze Age date.

Middle Iron Age to Late Iron Age
Paired dates were undertaken from fills 20587 and 20589 within pit 20153, and fill 15281 within pit 15234, all yielding Middle to Late Iron Age dates. Single dates from fill 22047 within Ditch 6 slot 21979, inhumation burial 22028 within Ditch 6, sheep skeleton 20292 within pit cut 20290, inhumation burial 21386 within Ditch 5 and silting deposit 3663 all provided Middle to Late Iron Age dates.

Late Iron Age to Early Roman
Bone from dog skeleton 22027 within Ditch 6 yielded a Late Iron Age to Early Roman date.

Roman
Human bone from inhumation burials 21080 and 21921 within Ditch 5 and inhumation burial 20808 within grave 20809 and a charred barley grain from fill 17034 within posthole 17019 all provided Roman dates.

Saxon
A charcoal fragment and a charred rye grain recovered from fill 2091 within pit 2095 and a rye grain from fill 5213 within pit 5211 all produced Saxon dates.

Medieval
Two dates from a charred seed and charcoal fragment from fill 20047 within kiln 20044 yielded medieval dates.

Bayesian analysis
Consideration was given to undertaking Bayesian analysis to improve the precision of the radiocarbon dates. Establishing a chronology for the double-ditched Iron Age enclosure, and a relative chronology in relation the more massive Ditch 6 on the east side of the excavated area were identified as objectives of the site analysis, and were one of the few aspects of the archaeological record to hold deep stratigraphic sequences. Despite the depth of stratigraphy, conventional dating evidence from the sequences was sparse, and where present, offered insufficient refinement for an intra-site chronology. A small number of radiocarbon dates obtained from material within these sequences provided Middle to late Iron Age dates. Frances Healy of the University of Cardiff was asked to assess the available dating evidence for Bayesian analysis, and to discuss the potential of additional material to provide additional dates. From this assessment she observed that the existing Iron Age dates from the ditches all coincided with 'wiggles' in the calibration curve which extended their calibrated ranges, and that this would also reduce the precision of any further dates. At this stage the archaeological record was examined for additional material (for example articulated bones, antler tools left near to the base of features, carbonised residues adhering to groups of pot sherds representing a single pot or single fragments of short lived charred plant remains from secure

Feature	Lab No.	Material	δ13C	δ13N	C/N ratio	Conventional Radiocarbon Age	Calibrated dates 95.4% probability	Calibrated dates 68.2% probability
Context 20338 Pit 20238	SUERC-48048	Human bone: Adult frontal bone	-20.3‰	9.8‰	3.3	2779 ± 30yr BP	1003–844 cal BC (95.4%)	979–895 cal BC (68.2%)
Context 3593 Palaeochannel 3617	SUERC-50899	Waterlogged seed: Sedge sp. x 5 (Carex sp.)	-25.0‰	-	-	2739 ± 26yr BP	931–821 cal BC (95.4%)	904–842 cal BC (68.2%)
Context 20336 Pit 20238	SUERC-48047	Charred seed: Barley grain (Hordeum vulgare)	-24.3‰	-	-	2669 ± 30yr BP	895–798 cal BC (95.4%)	841–801 cal BC (68.2%)
Context 3612 Palaeochannel 3617	SUERC-48045	Waterlogged seeds: Sedge sp. x 5 (Carex)	-25.0‰ assumed	-	-	2562 ± 30yr BP	806–747 cal BC (61.7%) 686–666 cal BC (15.0%) 643–554 cal BC (14.4%)	801–757 cal BC (64.3%) 679–672 cal BC (3.9%)
Context 20587 Pit 20153	SUERC-48056	Charcoal: Cherry sp. (Prunus)	-25.2‰	-	-	2209 ± 30yr BP	371–198 cal BC (95.4%)	358–347 cal BC (7.2%) 320–276 cal BC (27.9%) 259–206 cal BC (33.1%)
Context 22047 Ditch 21979	SUERC-50896	Animal bone: Horse tooth	-22.1‰	5.2‰	3.3	2193 ± 28yr BP	361–185 cal BC (95.4%)	356–287 cal BC (46.6%) 234–201 cal BC (21.6%)
Context 20589 Pit 20153	SUERC-50897	Charcoal: Alder/hazel (Alnus glutinosa/Corylus avellana)	-25.1‰	-	-	2170 ± 29yr BP	360–271 cal BC (49.3%) 264–159 cal BC (44.1%) 133–118 cal BC (2.0%)	352–298 cal BC (40.2%) 228–221 cal BC (3.7%) 211–176 cal BC (24.3%)
Context 15281 Pit 15234	SUERC-48069	Charred seed: Barley (Hordeum vulgare)	-23.9‰	-	-	2166 ± 30yr BP	359–273 cal BC (45.7%) 262–151 cal BC (45.8%) 137–114 cal BC (3.9%)	352–297 cal BC (37.6%) 228–221 cal BC (3.3%) 211–172 cal BC (27.3%)
Context 15281 Pit 15234	SUERC-48070	Charcoal: Hazel (Corylus avellana)	-25.8‰	-	-	2140 ± 30yr BP	353–295 cal BC (19.5%) 230–220 cal BC (1.5%) 213–88 cal BC (71.2%) 77–57 cal BC (3.2%)	345–322 cal BC (11.0%) 206–149 cal BC (42.2%) 141–112 cal BC (15.0%)
Context 22028 Skeleton Ditch 6	SUERC-48064	Human bone: Neonate skull vault	-21.0‰	12.0‰	3.3	2137 ± 30yr BP	352–298 cal BC (16.6%) 229–221 cal BC (1.0%) 211–86 cal BC (73.6%) 80–55 cal BC (4.3%)	342–327 cal BC (6.8%) 204–112 cal BC (61.4%)
Context 20292 Sheep skeleton Pit 20290	SUERC-48074	Animal bone: Sheep cervical vertebra	-21.3‰	6.5‰	3.5	2133 ± 30yr BP	351–303 cal BC (12.9%) 210–54 cal BC (82.5%)	204–107 cal BC (68.2%)
Context 20589 Pit 20153	SUERC-50898	Charred seed: Spelt wheat (Triticum spelta)	-22.8‰	-	-	2128 ± 30yr BP	350–312 cal BC (8.9%) 209–52 cal BC (86.5%)	201–106 cal BC (68.2%)
Context 20587 Pit 20153	SUERC-48055	Animal bone: Pig temporal bone	-22.3‰	8.4‰	3.3	2115 ± 30yr BP	341–328 cal BC (1.9%) 205–49 cal BC (93.5%)	191–101 cal BC (68.2%)
Context 21386 Skeleton Ditch 5	SUERC-48057	Human bone: Adult frontal bone	-20.5‰	10.5‰	3.2	2115 ± 30yr BP	341–328 cal BC (1.9%) 205–49 cal BC (93.5%)	191–101cal BC (68.2%)

Feature	Lab No.	Material	δ13C	δ 13N	C/N ratio	Conventional Radiocarbon Age	Calibrated dates 95.4% probability	Calibrated dates 68.2% probability
Context 3663 Silting deposit	SUERC-48049	Animal bone: Horse maxilla	-22.8‰	5.9‰	3.4	2093 ± 30 yr BP	194–44 cal BC (95.4%)	166–89 cal BC (55.3%) 76–57 cal BC (12.9%)
Context 22027 Dog Skeleton Ditch 6	SUERC-48060	Animal bone: Dog coxae	-20.4‰	10.4‰	3.2	2017 ± 30 yr BP	101 cal BC–60 cal AD (95.4%)	48 cal BC–22 cal AD (68.2%)
Context 21080 Skeleton Ditch 5	SUERC-48059	Human bone: Left scapula	-19.7‰	10.8‰	3.2	1856 ± 30 yr BP	81–234 cal AD (95.4%)	125–216 cal AD (68.2%)
Context 21921 Skeleton Ditch 5	SUERC-48058	Human bone: Adult fibula	-19.7‰	10.2‰	3.2	1840 ± 30 yr BP	86–242 cal AD (95.4%)	133–216 cal AD (68.2%)
Context 20808 Skeleton	SUERC-48066	Human bone Infant right petrous temporal	-19.1‰	12.0‰	3.2	1830 ± 30 yr BP	86–109 cal AD (3.5%) 117–252 cal AD (91.7%) 307–311 cal AD (0.5%)	137–220 cal AD (68.2%)
Context 3612 Palaeochannel 3617	SUERC-48044	Waterlogged seeds: Elder sp. x 5 (*Sambucus nigra*)	-25.3‰	-	-	1789 ± 30 yr BP	134–264 cal AD (67.5%) 275–330 cal AD (27.9%)	145–150 cal AD (1.9%) 170–194 cal AD (10.2%) 210–259 cal AD (34.1%) 282–300 cal AD (22.1%)
Context 17034 Posthole 17019	SUERC-48065	Charred seed: Barley (*Hordeum vulgare*)	-25.0‰ assumed	-	-	1635 ± 30 yr BP	340–438 cal AD (69.6%) 443–474 cal AD (5.6%) 486–535 cal AD (20.1%)	382–430 cal AD (55.0%) 493–510 cal AD (8.5%) 518–528 cal AD (4.6%)
Context 20336 Pit 20238	SUERC-48046	Animal bone: Cattle femur	-21.7‰	6.9‰	3.3	1303 ± 30 yr BP	658–730 cal AD (65.3%) 736–770 cal AD (30.1%)	667–711 cal AD (47.4%) 745–764 cal AD (20.8%)
Context 2091 Pit 2095	SUERC-48050	Charred seed: Rye grain (*Secale cereale*)	-21.9‰	-	-	1245 ± 30 yr BP	680–870 cal AD (68.3%) 788–874 cal AD (27.1%)	687–777 cal AD (65.4%) 794–800 cal AD (2.8%)
Context 2091 Pit 2095	SUERC-48054	Charcoal: Field maple (*Acer campestre*)	-29.4‰	-	-	1193 ± 30 yr BP	721–741 cal AD (3.6%) 766–897 cal AD (89.1%) 926–943 cal AD (2.7%)	778–782 cal AD (2.6%) 787–876 cal AD (65.6%)
Context 5213 Pit 5211	SUERC-50900	Charred seed: Rye (*Secale cereale*)	-22.0‰	-	-	1094 ± 29 yr BP	891–1014 cal AD (95.4%)	899–923 cal AD (25.6%) 947–987 cal AD (42.6%)
Context 20047 Kiln 20044	SUERC-48067	Charcoal: Hawthorn/rowan /crab apple (*Crataegus monogyna/Sorbus/ Malus sylvestris*)	-25.9‰	-	-	910 ± 30 yr BP	1033–1190 cal AD (94.0%) 1198–1204 cal AD (1.4%)	1045–1095 cal AD (39.7%) 1120–1142 cal AD (16.1%) 1147–1163 cal AD (12.4%)
Context 20047 Kiln 20044	SUERC-48068	Charred seed: Barley (*Hordeum vulgare*)	-23.3‰	-	-	377 ± 30 yr BP	1445–1526 cal AD (59.6%) 1556–1633 cal AD (35.8%)	1452–1515 cal AD (52.4%) 1598–1618 cal AD (15.8%)

Table 5.1 Conventional radiocarbon ages and calibrated dates

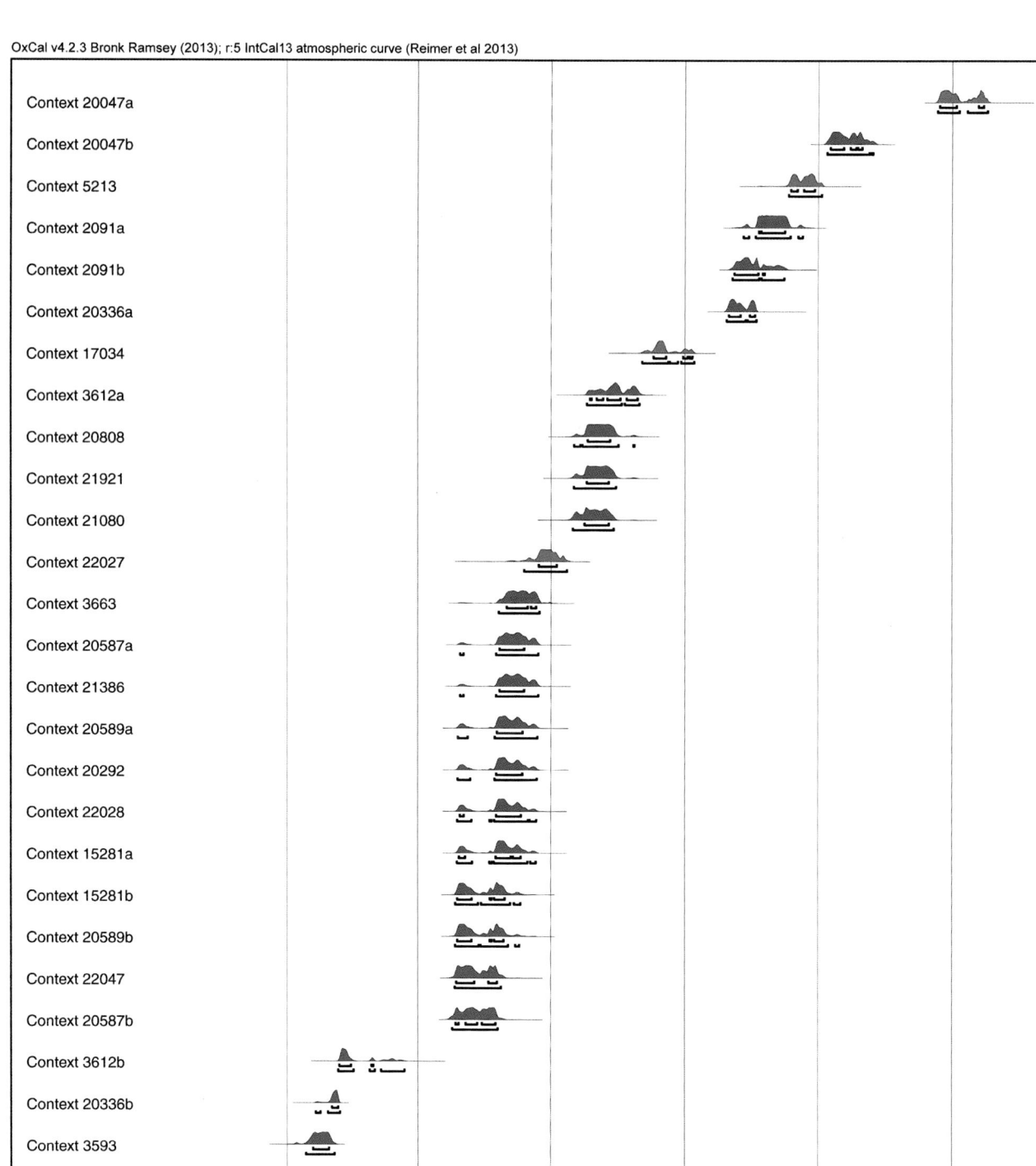

Figure 5.1 Radiocarbon dates calibrated using OxCal 4.2 (Bronk Ramsey 2009) and the IntCal13 dataset (Reimer *et al.* 2013)

deposits (hearths, discrete and deliberate dumps of waste material)) to provide the necessary number of radiocarbon dates for the modelling to work. No suitable material was available, and it was agreed that despite the fact the site has complex and clearly recorded stratigraphy, there was insufficient suitable material recovered to pursue this course. This being the case, no further statistical analysis beyond calibration of the conventional radiocarbon ages was undertaken.

Sample	Declination (°)	Inclination (°)	MAD (°)	Temperature(°C)
1A	20.6	69.6	2.3	180-360
1B	1.5	75.7	Mean direction	Sample broke at 170°C
1C	17.3	72.5	1.3	180-360
1D	18.6	75.3	1.5	180-560
2A	0.3	79	2.9	320-560
2B	349.6	69.9	3.1	360-560
2E	11.2	65.9	1.6	100-560
3A	335.7	67.7	1.0	100-380
3B	341.7	76.1	0.9	250-510
3C	333.4	73.8	1.9	100-450
4A	351	70.9	4.3	100-360
5A	11.4	74.3	2.1	270-450
5B	24	71.9	1.3	100-500
6A	12.6	69.7	3.4	250-560
6B	4.1	72.4	1.5	0-560
6C	0	63.4	1.4	270-500
7A	329.3	14.4	2.4	100-470
8	341.3	76.1	1.1	0-380

Table 5.2 Direction of characteristic remanence for selected samples along with maximum angle of deviation (MAD) and temperature range of selected components

II. Archaeomagnetic dating
by Neil Suttie

Hearth 22058 was circular, approximately 2m in diameter, and of fired reddish-orange clay. Around the perimeter of the hearth was a ring of heat-affected stones. These were mainly flints measuring a few centimetres across, and rounded pebbles and cobbles of pink quartzite of the type commonly found on river-beds. The feature was sampled for the purpose of archaeomagnetic dating on 22 November 2010.

As there was some pressure to finish the sampling quickly, it was decided to sample the feature by taking oriented monoliths, 10–20cm across, set in plaster. The advantage of this method was that a reasonable amount of material could be quickly removed, however there are fewer independently oriented samples than may be acquired using other methods. In total, eight individual monoliths were taken. Plaster of Paris was mixed and poured over a part of the feature, and its surface levelled using a sheet of Perspex and a bubble level. Once dry, a magnetic compass was used to mark the position of north on the plaster. Owing to prevailing conditions, a sunsight could not be used, and there is therefore a small possibility that the results given here could have been affected by the presence of local field irregularities, although there was no indication of these. Five samples were taken from the stony edge of the feature, and three from the fired clay in the middle. Blocks 3, 4, 5, 7 and 8 contained stones set into the fired clay, while blocks 1, 2 and 6 consisted of fired clay from the central area. In the laboratory, blocks 1, 2 and 6 were cut into 2cm cubes; four from block 1, five from sample 2 and three from block 6. A total of eleven one-inch cores were drilled from the stones in the remaining blocks. The flints tended to fracture during drilling, and so did not produce well-oriented cores.

In total, twenty-three subsamples were subjected to incremental thermal demagnetisation up to 560°C, or until completely demagnetised. Several samples, especially those from the stone edge of the hearth, possessed more than one component of magnetisation. In total, a characteristic remanent magnetisation was identified in eighteen samples. Table 5.2 gives the characteristic direction in addition to the temperature over which it was taken, and the maximum angle of deviation (MAD) of the isolated component (Kirschvink 1980). The directions are shown as a circular plot in Figure 5.2. Sample 7A is a clear outlier, and it is likely that this flint was moved after cooling. Of the original twenty-three samples, the remaining seventeen are used to determine the direction of the geomagnetic field when the feature was last fired. The International Geomagnetic Reference Field gives the local declination as 1.6°W at the time of sampling. Correcting the values in Table 5.2 by this amount yields a mean direction of 0.3°W, with an inclination of 72.6° and an α_{95} of 2.8°, for the seventeen selected samples.

To date the firing of the feature, the mean direction is compared with a reference curve. At the time of writing the British calibration curve is not very well constrained for the Iron Age, and it was decided use the French secular variation curve of Gallet et al. (2002). Results are displayed using the software of Pavón-Carrasco et al. (2011) in terms of Bayesian confidence intervals following Lanos (2004) in Figure 5.3. The estimated 95% confidence interval for the date of firing covers three possible age-ranges: 450–70BC, 550–810AD, as well as a post-medieval date, which seems unlikely on archaeological grounds. The archaeomagnetic results are summarised below.

Site latitude 52.34°N, longitude 0.51°E
N=17/23
Declination = -0.3° Inclination = 72.6° α_{95} = 2.8°
Date of last firing
450–70BC, 550–810AD, 1610–1730AD (95%)

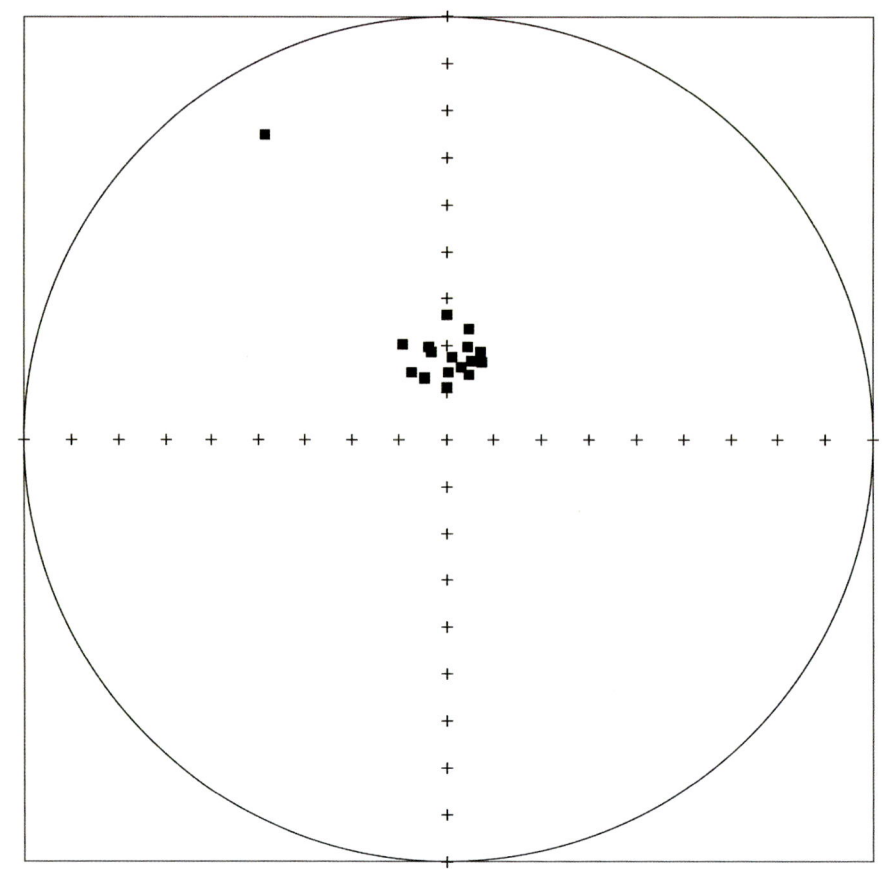

Figure 5.2 Azimuthal projection of the 18 directions given in Table 5.2

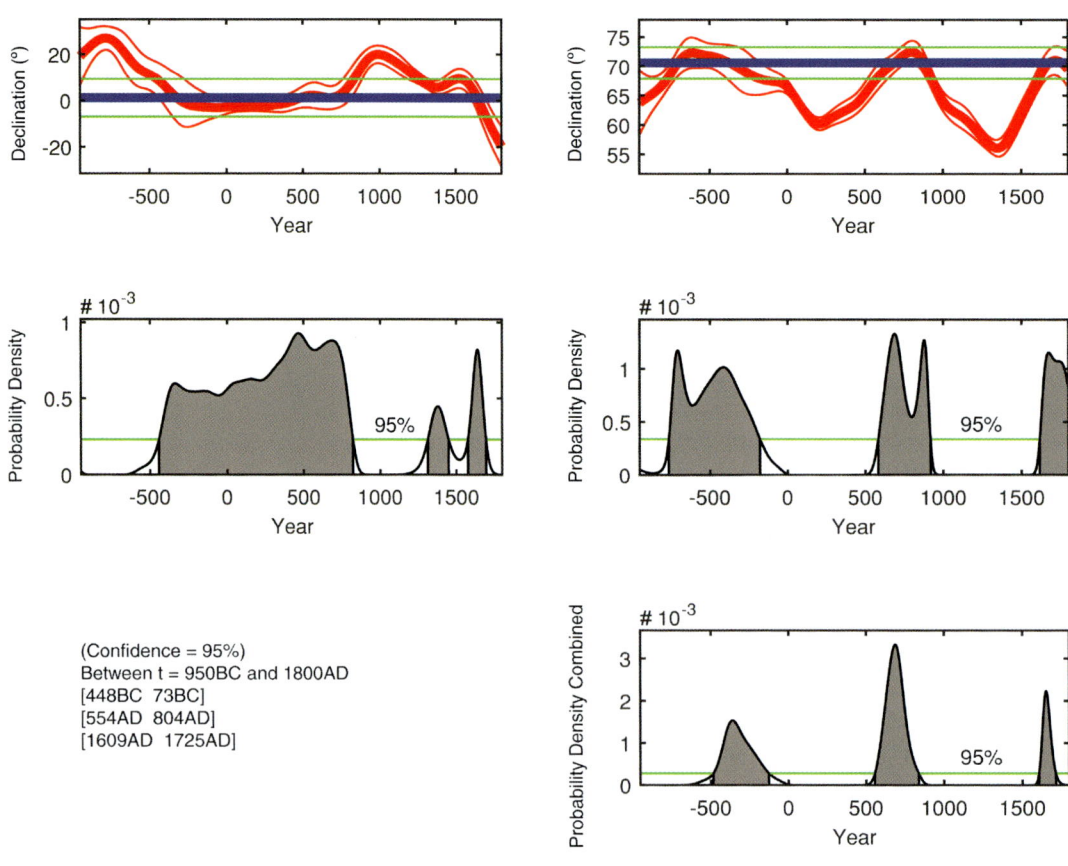

(Confidence = 95%)
Between t = 950BC and 1800AD
[448BC 73BC]
[554AD 804AD]
[1609AD 1725AD]

Figure 5.3 Estimated 95% confidence ranges for the date of last firing. Results are displayed using the software of Pavón-Carrasco (2011) in terms of Bayesian confidence intervals following Lanos (2004)

Skeleton	Period	Completeness	Age	Sex	Stature	Pathology
21386	3	10%	26–35 years	M	-	Caries (2/32), calculus (23/32)
22028	4	75%	39–41 weeks *in utero*	?	-	-
17085	5	10%	31 weeks *in utero*	?	-	-
20808	5	40%	36–38 weeks *in utero*	?	-	-
20812	5	80%	5–6 years	?	-	-
21080	5	85%	26–35 years	M	171cm	Caries (7/20), calculus (7/20), periapical lesions (3/15), AMTL (1/15), SDJD, DJD, trauma
21921	5	75%	= 45 years	M	172cm	Caries (1/1), periapical lesions (1/7), AMTL (4/7), SDJD, osteoid osteoma, periostitis
2019	6	75%	17–18 years	F	-	Calculus (5/11), osteomyelitis
20979	?	20%	37–38 weeks *in utero*	?	-	-
22070	?	80%	12–14 years	?	-	-
22071	?	10%	36–45 years	M	-	DJD
22072	?	50%	26–35 years	M	172cm	Caries (6/14), calculus (9/14), periapical lesions (3/20), SDJD

Period 3 = Middle Iron Age; Period 4 = Late Iron Age; Period 5 = Roman; Period 6 = Saxon; Period ? = Undated; AMTL = antemortem tooth loss; DJD = degenerative joint disease; SDJD = spinal degenerative joint disease

Table 5.3 Summary table of analysed human skeletons from Mildenhall

III. The human bone
by Jonny Geber

Summary
Human remains were recovered from twenty-nine contexts. These comprised twelve skeletons or re-associated, co-mingled remains (Table 5.3), and 144 disarticulated bones. The deposits span in date from the Late Bronze Age (Period 2) to the Saxon period (Period 6). Some co-mingled skeletons and charnel were recovered from later deposits, and are likely to be re-depositions of burials disturbed in antiquity. The remains were very well preserved, and had only suffered minor degrees of post-depositional fragmentation and surface erosion. All but one skeleton was analysed by the author. A single foetal skeleton (17085) was analysed by Andrew Clarke of Cotswold Archaeology, and the results incorporated into this text. This report is accompanied by a grave catalogue. The full details of each analysed skeleton and other elements of a research level archive will be made available for this project in due course through the Archaeology Data Service at http://ads.ahds.ac.uk.

Methodology
The methods chosen for the analysis of these remains are in concordance with standard practice as recommended by Buikstra and Ubelaker (1994) and Brickley and McKinley (2004). Neonatal skeletons were aged using the dimensions of the basal and lateral parts of the occipital bone (Redfield 1970) and the greatest length of the long bones (Scheuer *et al.* 1980). Juveniles were aged from the stage of dental development and eruption (Broadbent *et al.* 1975; Liversidge *et al.* 1998). Adults were aged based on joint surface morphology (Brooks and Suchey 1990; Lovejoy *et al.* 1985; Todd 1921a; 1921b), sutural obliteration (Meindl and Lovejoy 1985), and dental attrition (Brothwell 1981). Each individual was thereafter assigned an appropriate age category: foetal (< 38 weeks *in utero*), neonate (~ birth), infant (0–1 years), young child

(2–5 years), older child (6–12 years), adolescent (13–17 years), young adult (18–25 years), early middle adult (26–35 years), late middle adult (36–45 years), and older adult (= 46 years).

Sex determination of the adult skeletons was conducted using the descriptions by Sjøvold (1988), and osteometrics (Bass 1995). The masculinity and femininity were scored according to the following division: hyperfeminine (–2), feminine (–1), indeterminable sex (0), masculine (+1) and hypermasculine (+2). Both cranial and post-cranial measurements were taken in accordance to Brothwell (1981). Living stature was estimated using the methods developed by Trotter and Gleser (1952 and 1958) and Sjøvold (1990). Cranial and post-cranial non-metric traits are scored following the descriptions by Berry and Berry (1967) and Finnegan (1978).

Results

Minimum number of individuals
As an unknown proportion of the disarticulated material is likely have been re-deposited from much earlier contexts into later ones, there is no value in attempting to quantify this material by chronology. The disarticulated material on its own represented the remains of a minimum of ten individuals: one neonate, three infants, one child, one adolescent, and four adults of which one was male and another female. When considering the entire human bone material, irrespective of whether they were articulated or disarticulated, there was a minimum of eighteen individuals represented in the assemblage: one foetus, two neonates, five infants, one child, two adolescents, and seven adults of which four could be sexed as male and one as female. The fact that the total MNI of the entire assemblage exceeded the number of articulated and re-associated skeletal remains suggests that there were additional burials on the site which have been disturbed in antiquity. The disarticulated material is not discussed further; osteological data relating to it are available via the site archive or directly from the author.

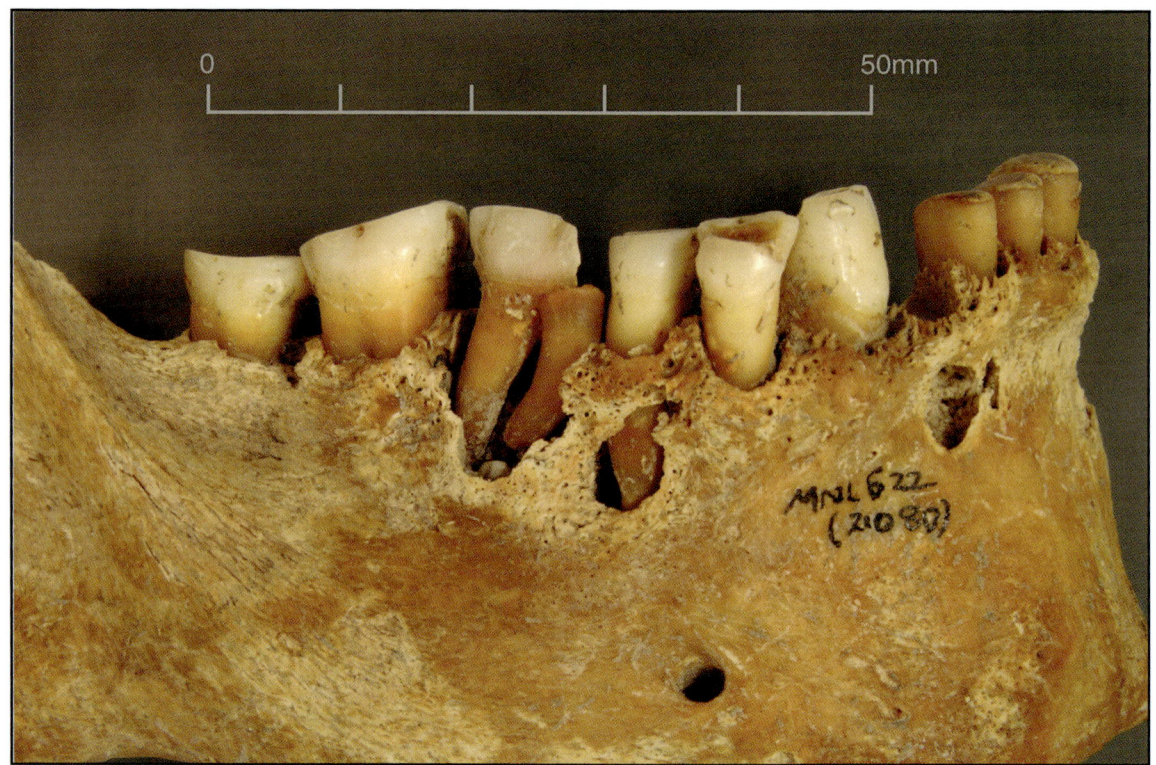

Figure 5.4 Approximal caries, periapical abscesses and slight calculus deposits on the left mandibular dentition of Roman adult male skeleton 21080

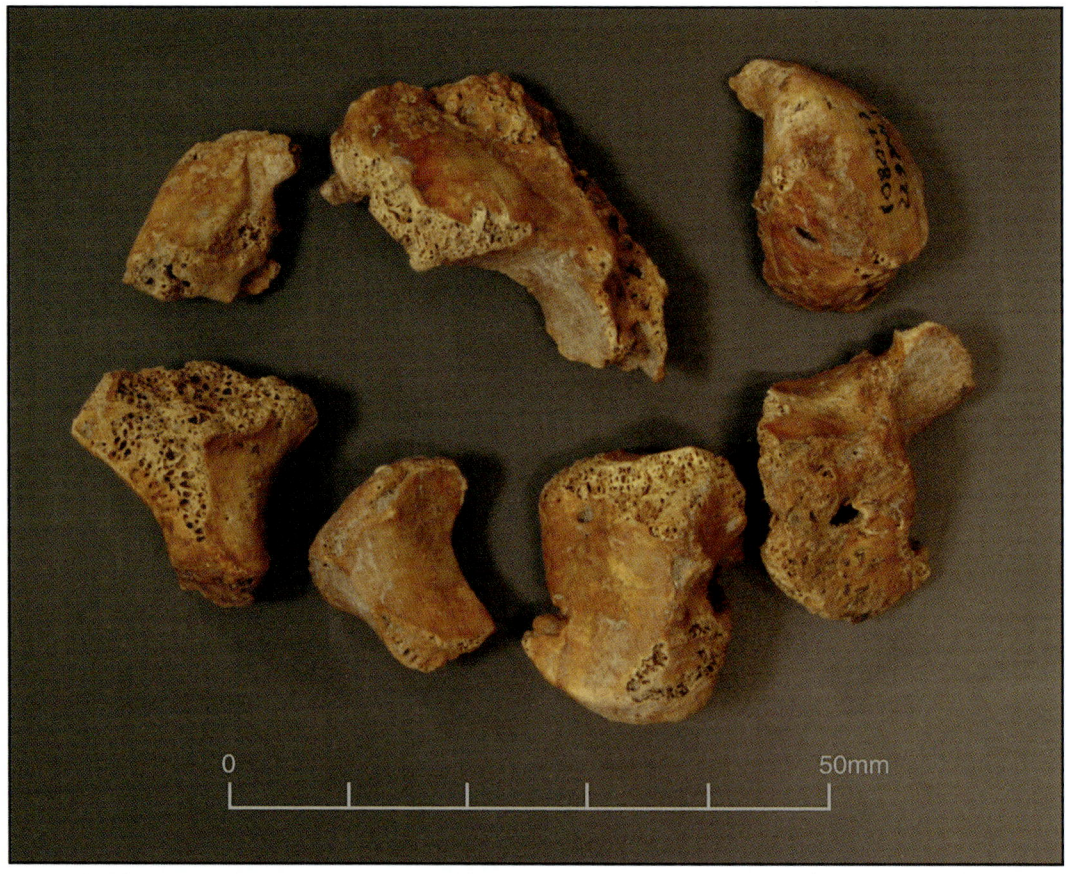

Figure 5.5 Probable crush fracture of the scaphoid and degeneration of the carpals in the left wrist of Roman adult male skeleton 21080

Late Bronze Age (Period 2)

The only remains of confirmed Bronze Age date were a collection of inhumed adult human remains found in the fills (20338 and 21397) of pit 20238, later re-cut as 22063. These comprised a frontal bone (possibly from a male individual), a right humerus, and the diaphysis of a left tibia in 20338, and the diaphysis of a fibula in 21397. It is possible that all the bones derive from the same individual. The context in which they were found (see Chapter 2.II), and the fact that only partial remains were recovered, would suggest that they represent redeposited charnel rather than an intentional formal burial, although this possibility cannot be completely discarded.

Mid- to Late Iron Age (Period 3–4)

Two burials were within Iron Age ditches. Skeleton 21386 (Period 3) was that of an early middle adult male, buried within Ditch 5. All that remained was the skull and the two first cervical vertebrae. It is possible that this burial represent a decapitated skull, although no evidence of perimortem trauma was identified on the remains. The skull was well preserved, and displayed a dolichocranic (long-headed) shape. The only pathologies observed were moderate occlusal caries on the second and third left mandibular molars, and the teeth also displayed very slight calculus (mineralised plaque) deposits. The skull was radiocarbon dated to 341–49 BC (SUERC–48057; 2115±30BP).

The neonatal skeleton 22028 (Period 4) was nearly complete, and was found buried in a supine position with the head to the east within Ditch 6. No pathological markers were observed on the bones. The remains were radiocarbon dated to 352–55 BC (SUERC–48064; 2137±30BP).

Roman (Period 5)

Six burials date to the Roman period. Third trimester foetal remains were found within the fill 17085 of corn dryer 17048. What remained were fragments of the radii, the right ulna, a hand phalanx, a right ilium, the femora and tibiae. It is unclear whether this is a primary burial, or secondary deposits from a disturbed context elsewhere. A second non-adult was that of a 5–6 year old child (20812) buried in a crouched position on the left side with the head to the north. A single coffin nail was found adjacent to this burial, which suggest it was placed in a coffin. The bones were moderately well preserved, and displayed no evidence of pathology.

The third Roman period skeleton (21080) was that of an early middle adult male. The bones were very well preserved, and the skeleton virtually complete. This burial was apparently placed in a hollow orientated north to south. No cut was identified, but seven nails recovered from the deposits above suggest a coffin may have been used (Chapter 4.II). Living stature was estimated to be 1.71m (5ft 7½ inches), which is about 2cm (1 inch) taller than the average male stature in Roman Britain (see Roberts and Cox 2003). The individual displayed caries which primarily affected the premolar and molar teeth in seven of the twenty available teeth. Occlusal lesions were also observed on two incisors, which are quite rare locations for caries in archaeological skeletons. These may have been caused by trauma or excessive extra-masticatory wear, the latter which was indicated from the considerable wear of the incisor teeth from both

the maxillae and the mandible. Three of the carious molar tooth sockets (alveoli) in the mandible displayed periapical abscesses. These abscesses are the result of a pus build-up due to an infection of the tooth root, which eventually breaks through the bone and results in a circular perforation, and it can potentially result in serious complications (Robertson and Smith 2009). In this particular case, it is clear that the severe carious lesions provided an entry point of infection of these particular molar teeth (Fig. 5.4). One mandibular molar had been lost antemortem, probably due to dental caries. This dentition did also display slight calculus deposits of the mandibular teeth.

Skeleton 21080 displayed the most skeletal degeneration of the joints of all the analysed skeletons from Mildenhall. Indications of vertebral osteophytosis of the lumbar spine were observed. This is the most common of the spinal degenerative joint disorders in the human skeletons, and is present in more than 90% of all individuals over the age of 60 years in a modern population (Møller-Christensen 1958). It is generally caused by wear-and-tear and compression of the intervertebral discs, and is therefore more commonly observed in older individuals. The skeleton also displayed ossified ligamentum flavum of four thoracic vertebrae. This condition is primarily degenerative, but may also relate to specific myelopathies such as DISH (Diffuse Idiopathic Skeletal Hyperostosis) (Kudo *et al.* 1983; Williams *et al.* 1982). Further activity related skeletal changes in this skeleton were also evident from a bone formation (enthesophyte) at the attachment of the *brachialis* muscle of the left arm. This muscle is used for the flexion of the elbow, and is one of the strongest muscles involved for that movement.

Joint degeneration was also observed in the left wrist, the right hip joint and the left ankle, all of these cases are likely to be secondary to trauma. The left wrist displayed a probable crush fracture involving the scaphoid bone. This had resulted in a severe osteophytic build-up at the anterior margin, and considerable eburnation (direct bone-to-bone contact wear resulting in a polished and dense surface) on the inferior articular facet. Marginal bone formation or osteophytosis was also observed on the lunate bone, and illustrates displacement and instability of the carpal bones (Fig. 5.5). An articular fracture was also observed at the base of the malleolus process, which is part of the ankle, of the right tibia. Although the fracture was well healed, it seems most likely that the trauma would have resulted in secondary degeneration, as osteophytosis and eburnation was observed on the process, and osteophytosis was also observed in the right hip joint and the ankle of the left foot, which suggest this individual tried to adapt to the pain in the right ankle by assuming a different walking posture.

The fourth burial was that of an older adult male (21921). The skeleton was nearly complete and in very good condition, with an estimated living stature of 1.72m (5ft 8 inches). Only the left maxilla remained from the dentition, which displayed a moderate granuloma, which is a soft tissue inflammation (Ogden 2008), at the left maxillary canine tooth socket. The tooth in question was severely affected by caries, and only the root remained. Four teeth had been lost antemortem. Despite the older age of this individual, the only observed evidence of joint disease in the skeleton was vertebral osteophytosis of the

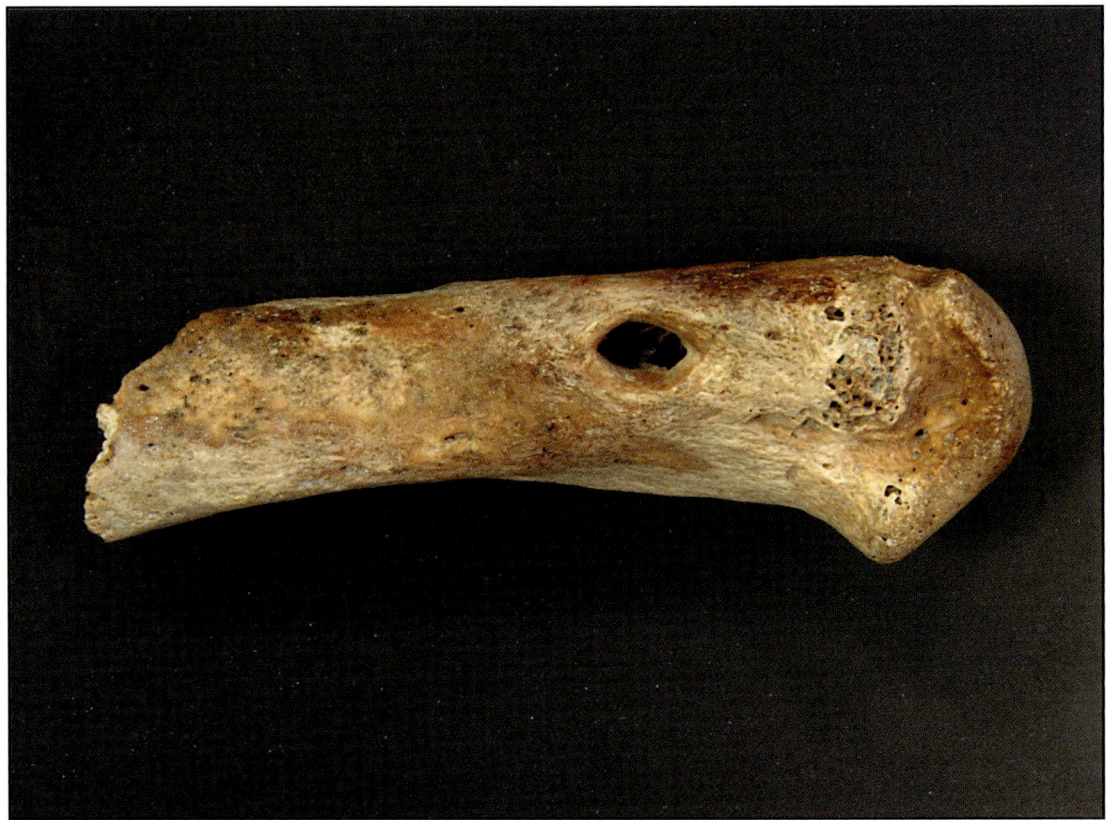

Figure 5.6 Osteomyelitic cloaca on the mid-diaphysis of the fourth metacarpal in the right hand of early medieval adolescent female skeleton 2019

bodies of the lower lumbar and first sacral vertebrae. This individual also displayed an osteoid osteoma that was present on the mid-shaft of the right femur. This pathological marker is a benign tumour, which tends to be particularly common in males, of which the femur is a frequent location. The condition is potentially painful (Campanacci *et al*. 1998).

Plaques of striated periostitis were also observed on the tibiae and the left fibula, with some cortical thickening noted on the right sided bone. As this particular bone is located close to the skin surface, this condition may have been caused by infection resulting from injury (Ortner 2003). Periostitis of the lower leg bones, is however also commonly observed in metabolic disorders such as scurvy, caused by Vitamin C and results in microtrauma and haemorrhage at the site of muscle attachments (Geber and Murphy 2012).

The fifth skeleton of Roman date was a partial neonate (20808) which had evidently been disturbed in antiquity and re-deposited into a pit during the medieval period (Period 7). The bones were radiocarbon dated to AD86–311 (SUERC–48066; 1830±30BP).

Neonatal remains were also recovered from pit 20977. The skeleton (20979) was incomplete and only comprised fragments of the facial bones, three vertebrae, six ribs and parts of the left arm and leg.

Saxon (Period 6)
One single early medieval burial was discovered on the site. This was the remains of a late adolescent female (2019) aged between 17 and 18 years at the time of death, and the bones were in excellent condition. This individual displayed a vertebral anomaly during which the coccyx is

fused with the last sacral segment. It is usually asymptomatic, but is more common in males than in females which make this case interesting (Scheuer and Black 2000). Five out of eleven available mandibular teeth were affected by calculus, but overall very slight and probably of no noteworthy health implications for this individual.

A more serious health condition was however presented by a case of well healed osteomyelitis observed on the diaphysis of the fourth metacarpal of the right hand (Fig. 5.6). Osteomyelitis is a bone infection which can be introduced via the bloodstream (haematogenous osteomyelitis), or locally through either a soft tissue wound or direct exposure of bone. The infection involves the medullar cavity of the bone, where the build-up of pus eventually erupts through the bone via an opening called a cloaca (Schwartz 1995, 231–2). Osteomyelitis in tubular bones is a common feature of tuberculosis in non-adult individuals (Tuli 2004), and the disease is a possible cause for the lesion in this skeleton. It may however also simply be localised injury which became infected.

Medieval (Period 7)
The remains of three individuals were recovered from the fill (21003) of pit feature 21005. All three skeletons were recovered as disarticulated and co-mingled remains, but could easily be re-associated during the post-excavation analysis. The pit feature is of medieval date (Period 7), but the bones may be of much earlier date.

One of these skeletons was the remains of an unsexed adolescent individual (22070) which is estimated to have been between 12 and 14 years of age at the time of death. The skeleton was virtually complete and very well preserved, and no pathological markers were identified in the remains. The second individual (22071) was that of a late middle adult male, and comprised only parts of the left shoulder joint, the coxae and the left femur. This skeleton displayed slight degeneration of the left hip joint.

About half remained of the third skeleton (22072), an early middle adult male, with a living stature about 1.72m (5ft 7½ inches). This individual suffered dental disease displayed as considerable carious lesions on the left maxillary second premolar and molar teeth, as well as moderate lesions on the right mandibular second premolar and first molar tooth. The crowns of the second and third maxillary molars were completely destroyed, with only the roots of the teeth remaining. The caries in this dentition had resulted in periapical abscesses of three teeth. Calculus deposits were present on six maxillary teeth and three mandibular teeth.

Discussion

As the remains span a wide chronological range, and only comprise twelve skeletons in total, it is not possible to detect any temporal changes in skeletal characteristics from these burials. The non-adult to adult ratio in the articulated and re-associated co-mingled remains (7:5) was virtually the same as observed in the disarticulated bones (6:4), which suggest that the additional but destroyed burials on the site were not dominated by a particular age category. The apparent lack of adult burials is interesting, although the dominance of non-adult skeletons may simply be reflection of the excellent degree of bone preservation which has favoured the survival of foetal, neonatal and infant bones that are very fragile and generally underrepresented on archaeological sites. Of the adults, one individual could be sexed as female and four as males. Three of the four males were dated to the Roman period.

The skeletal pathological changes are all of conditions commonly observed in archaeological populations. Dental disease was observed in five skeletons dating from all periods. Dental caries was observed in the dentitions of four of these individuals, with prevalence rates of number of teeth affected ranging from 35% to 72%. Other than causing pain and discomfort, carious cavities in teeth can potentially provide an entry point for infection, and as such can lead to serious health condition even though the pathology on its own is not life-threatening (Larsen 2002, 123). Joint disease is another commonly diagnosed condition from archaeological skeletons, and it was present in three out of five adults. None of the observed degenerative pathological markers were considerable in these skeletons.

Periosteal lesions were observed on the lower leg bones of older adult male skeleton 21921 dating to the Roman period, which may relate to infectious disease and metabolic disorders. As a general stress marker, it indicates that this individual had been exposed to a condition long enough to form osseous lesions. This may also mean that a proportion of the other skeletons with no periosteal lesions present could very well have suffered infectious and metabolic disease, but died before these were manifested skeletally (see Wood *et al.* 1992). The osteomyelitis observed in the hand bones of early medieval adolescent female skeleton 2019 probably represents the most severe pathological condition in this group. It was however inactive at the time of death, and is unlikely to relate to the cause of death of this individual.

The human remains from Mildenhall have added greatly to our understanding of the multi-period use of a site for human burial. The bones are well preserved, and hold the potential for future scientific study, such as aDNA and additional stable isotope analyses. These type of studies are not only of great archaeological and historical interest, but also significant for the study of palaeopathology and evolution of disease and skeletal manifestations of pathological processes.

IV. Mammal and bird bone
by L. Higbee

Introduction
The assemblage comprises 21,135 fragments of animal bone, with a combined weight of 312.405kg. Over half of this material (11,887 fragments or 56%) was identifiable to species and skeletal element. Bone fragments were recovered from all periods with the exception of Period 8 (Post-medieval). The quantity of material from each period varies considerably — large stratified groups were recovered from Periods 3 (Middle Iron Age, 25% of the total) and 7 (Medieval, *c.* 26%), with more modest groups from Periods 4 (Late Iron Age, 7%), 5 (Roman, 14%), 6 (Saxon, 14%), and 9 (modern, 7%), and small groups from Periods 1 (Geological features, 0.2%), and 2 (Bronze Age, 1.7%). The entire assemblage is quantified in Table 5.4 by species and period. The NISP (number of identified specimens present) presented in Table 5.4 have been adjusted to take account of a small number of complete and part skeletons (or ABGs), and these are detailed in Table 5.5. This report does not include analysis of Period 9 (modern) other than a quantification of the number of species present. Tables showing details of the analysis of size, shape and sex of sheep and cattle are available in the archive. The report is based on quantification and analysis by Jonny Geber.

Methods
All anatomical elements were identified to species where possible, any unidentifiable fragments were assigned to general size or taxonomic categories (*e.g.* large mammal, aves etc.). Where appropriate the following information was recorded for each fragment; element, anatomical zone (after Serjeantson 1996, 195–200; Cohen and Serjeantson 1996, 110–12), anatomical position, epiphyseal fusion state (after O'Connor 1989), tooth eruption/wear (after Grant 1982; Halstead 1985; Hambleton 1999; Payne 1973), butchery marks, metrical data (after von den Driesch 1976; Payne and Bull 1988), gnawing, burning, surface condition, pathology and non-metric traits.

This information was directly recorded into a spreadsheet (in MS Excel) and cross-referenced with relevant contextual information. The site archive includes the raw data, a detailed methods statement, and additional tables, figures and appendices of summary data.

Caprines (sheep and goat) were differentiated based on the morphological criteria of Boessneck (1969), Halstead *et al.* (2002), Payne (1985), and Prummel and Frisch (1986). The majority (98%) of the positively differentiated caprine bones belong to sheep, therefore this term will be used throughout the report to refer to all undifferentiated caprine bones. Sex was determined from

Species					Period					
	1	2	3	4	5	6	7	9	UD/US	Total
cattle	11	69	1257	371	619	892	1100	238	53	4610
sheep/goat	4	43	2119	393	619	450	883	482	83	5076
sheep	1	1	125	18	19	22	69	14	1	270
goat			3				3			6
pig	3	4	361	77	81	134	248	85	15	1008
horse	5	5	40	35	75	33	103	85	4	385
dog	1	1	18	5	74	11	110	4	2	226
cat			3		2	5	4	1		15
red deer			7	1	13			4		25
roe deer	1	2			1		1		1	6
deer					1					1
fox					13					13
hare	1		2		1		2			6
polecat			1							1
badger							1			1
hedgehog							1			1
mole							4			4
field vole					2					2
wood mouse			10							10
shrew					1		1			2
domestic fowl			2	1	2	17	20	20		62
goose			3	1	3	6	11	11	2	37
duck			1		4	2				7
teal		2	1							3
plover/lapwing						1	1	1	1	4
mute swan			1				1	1		3
crane			5		1	2				8
buzzard			4							4
crow			6	1		1				8
passeridae/turdidae					6	1	6	6		19
frog/toad	1	28	2		15	5	12	1		64
Total identified	**28**	**155**	**3970**	**904**	**1552**	**1582**	**2581**	**953**	**162**	**11887**
large mammal	4	72	579	213	527	476	1041	161	55	3128
medium mammal	4	119	769	163	478	344	762	292	49	2980
small mammal			4		26	8	24	1		63
mammal	13	16	846	226	301	590	983	64	1	3040
aves		1	5	1	1	7	11	11		37
Total unidentified	**21**	**208**	**2203**	**603**	**1333**	**1425**	**2821**	**529**	**105**	**9248**
Overall total	**49**	**363**	**6173**	**1507**	**2885**	**3007**	**5402**	**1482**	**267**	**21135**
Overall % total	**0.2**	**1.7**	**29.2**	**7.1**	**14**	**14**	**25.5**	**7**	**1.3**	**100**

UD = undated and US = unstratified
Note: the fragment counts for Periods 4, 5 and 7 have been adjusted to take account of part/complete skeletons (see Table 5.5)

Table 5.4 Number of identified specimens present (or NISP) by Period

Period	Context	Feature	feature	NISP	Comments
4	22027	21979	Ditch 6	204	dog - complete skeleton
5	17085	17048	corn drier	19	cat - part skeleton
7	3024	3023	pit	102	horse - complete skeleton
7	20292	20290	pit	136	sheep - complete skeleton

Table 5.5 List of associated bone groups (or ABGs)

feature / deposit	Period								
	1 %	2 %	3 %	4 %	5 %	6 %	7 %	9 %	Total %
pit		90	81.4	67	24.7	66	54.1	60	**62**
ditch		1.5	10	11.9	26	9	20.2	3	**14**
layer	100		0.6		35.5	13	11.2	21	**11.6**
posthole		8.5	0.8	20.9	6.8	7.2	2.8	1.8	**5**
grave			7.2		1.5	0.6			**2**
gully					0.8	3	7.5	1.5	**2.6**
other				0.2	4.7	1.2	4.2	12.7	**2.8**
Total	**100**	**100**	**100**	**100**	**100**	**100**	**100**	**100**	**100**

Table 5.6 Distribution of animal bone by feature/deposit type and Period

the presence/morphology of canine teeth in horses and pigs (Schmid 1972), from humerus morphology and baculum bones in dogs (Ruscillo 2006), and from pelvic features in cattle and caprines (Greenfield 2006).

Withers height estimates for the main domesticates follow the conversion factors of Matolcsi for cattle, Teichert for sheep and pig (see von den Driesch and Boessneck 1974), May (1985) for horse, and Harcourt (1974, 154) for dog.

Quantification methods applied to the assemblage include the number of identified specimens (NISP), minimum number of elements (MNE, calculated on the bases of anatomical position and zone counts), and minimum number of individuals (MNI). As an additional means of assessing the relative importance of livestock species, meat weight estimates (MWE) were also calculated. These are based on the midpoints from the Manching dataset of live weights (Boessneck *et al.* 1971 and following Bourdillon and Coy 1980; Bond and O'Connor 1999; Dobney *et al.* 2007). The mid-point values are 275kg for cattle, 37.5kg for sheep, and 85kg for pig.

Results

Preservation and fragmentation

Bone preservation is generally good to fair — most fragments have intact cortical surfaces, displaying little or no signs of weathering, and fine details such as knife cuts are clear and easily observed. Poorly preserved fragments were also recorded but account for only *c.* 2% of the total assemblage. Over half of all the poorly preserved fragments were from contexts assigned to Periods 3 (27%) and 7 (28%). These poorly preserved fragments were retrieved from the same contexts as well-preserved bones, which suggests that the poorly preserved bones are probably residual, having been re-deposited after a period of surface exposure. However, in some instances differences in bone preservation within individual contexts were due to the presence of bones from immature animals, which are more fragile and prone to deterioration than bones from adult animals.

Gnaw marks were recorded on less than 1% of post-cranial bones. This is a very low level and suggests that bone waste was rapidly buried after disposal so that scavengers such as domestic dogs were unable to access the material. The low rate of canid gnawing, coupled with the generally good state of bone preservation, indicates

that the site was kept relatively clear of surface detritus and that bones were not left to accumulate in midden heaps before being deposited into open features.

Bone fragmentation was assessed using anatomical zone counts for post-cranial bones from livestock species. This indicates that shaft fragments are more numerous than the ends of long bones, that there are fewer complete or near complete cattle bones in the assemblage than sheep or pig bones, and that there is very little difference in the degree of fragmentation between periods. The data also clearly demonstrates what can be considered a normal pattern of fragmentation based on the density of different types of skeletal elements. For example skulls, ribs and scapulae are highly fragmented, while small compact bones such as phalanges are generally complete.

Similar analysis of the proportion of loose teeth relative to teeth retained in mandibles indicates that sheep and pig mandibles are more fragmented than cattle mandibles. However, this probably reflects that fact that more sheep and pigs were culled at an earlier age than cattle, and immature mandibles fragment more easily than adult mandibles.

Spatial distribution

Most (46%) of the animal bone comes from the east side of the site on the higher ground, while modest amounts were recovered across the rest of the site. Pit fills were by far the richest bone deposits on the site and produced 62% of the total assemblage (Table 5.6). This pattern is consistent for most periods with the exception of Periods 1 and 5. The Period 1 pattern reflects the limited range of deposits, and is all from alluvial and silting deposits associated with palaeochannel 3617, and the Period 5 material was more evenly distributed across pits, ditches and layers, including dump deposits associated with episodes of land reclamation. Overall, 14% of fragments were recovered from ditches and a further *c.* 12% from layers. Bone was also recovered from a number of minor feature types including postholes, graves, gullies, corn dryers and a well.

The pit assemblages were dominated by cattle and sheep bones, and the proportional representation of these species is broadly consistent with their overall frequency for each period (Table 5.7). There is one notable exception to this: the medieval (Period 7) assemblage is dominated by cattle bones (43% NISP), but this is not reflected in the composition of the assemblage from Period 7 pits, which include near equal amounts of sheep and cattle bones. The

Pits	Period						
	2	3	4	5	6	7	9
Species	%	%	%	%	%	%	%
cattle	56.4	31.5	32.5	33	51.5	39.8	14.5
sheep	33.6	56.3	54.9	38.5	34	42.8	68.4
pig	1	9.8	8.8	9	9.3	9.3	9.4
other domestic mammal	4.5	1.3	3	16.8	2.2	7	7.2
wild mammal	1.8	0.3	0.3	-	-	0.1	-
bird	2.7	0.8	0.5	2.7	3	1	0.5
Total	**100**	**100**	**100**	**100**	**100**	**100**	**100**

Ditches	2	3	4	5	6	7	9
Species	%	%	%	%	%	%	%
cattle	33.3	35	55	66.8	48	48.3	-
sheep	33.3	57	35.2	27.2	35.5	31.8	-
pig	33.3	6	3.3	2.3	13.9	11.1	-
other domestic mammal	-	2	5.7	2.5	0.6	6.7	-
other wild mammal	-	-	-	0.3	-	0.4	50
bird	-	-	0.8	0.9	2	1.7	50
Total	**100**	**100**	**100**	**100**	**100**	**100**	**100**

Table 5.7 Distribution of animal bone species and Period for two main feature types

proportion of pig bones from pits was fairly consistent between periods, at *c*. 9% NISP. The Period 5 Roman pits include the highest proportion of bones from other domestic species, mostly horse and dog. The earlier pits (*i.e.* Periods 2 to 4, Prehistoric to Late Iron Age) all include bones from wild mammals, but there are none from later pits. Finally the Iron Age Period 3 pit assemblages include the most diverse range of bird species.

The animal bone assemblage from Period 2 pit 20238 is worthy of further note due to its association with human bone and a large amount of pottery. Most (46%) of the animal bone from this feature was recovered from fill 20319, with small amounts from nine other fills. The pit assemblage is dominated by cattle bones, including both cranial and post-cranial elements and these are from a minimum of three different animals. The assemblage also includes the remains from at least two sheep, four bones from a horse, two roe deer metatarsals, the canine from a female pig, and a dog mandible. The composition of the assemblage suggests that it is a random accumulation of waste material from different stages in the carcass reduction sequence.

The ditch assemblages were less diverse in terms of species range, and largely dominated by cattle bones. The one notable exception to this was the Period 3 ditches, which include a high proportion of sheep bones, a general reflection of the clear dominance of this species in the overall assemblage for this period (see Table 5.4).

The assemblages from both pits and ditches include a range of different body parts, which suggests that there was little or no separation of waste material from different sources. Domestic refuse was disposed of in the same way as butchery waste, and the by-products of industrial or craft-type activities such as tanning and horn-working. Cranial fragments (*i.e.* skull, mandible, loose teeth, horn cores), and skeletal elements from the torso (*i.e.* ribs and vertebrae) were amongst the most common components recovered from pits and ditches. However, as previously stated these categories include elements that are prone to high rates of fragmentation, and will therefore be over-represented in the NISP counts used for this analysis. Long bones from the fore- and hind-quarters are equally well represented in both pits and ditches, accounting for between 26%–41% of fragments. Period 6 and 7 pits and ditches include slightly more bones from the forequarter than the hindquarter, and this could reflect differences in the selection or procurement of meat joints, or changing patterns of butchery and refuse disposal. Foot bones account for between 11%–19% of the animal bones recovered from these features, with the highest percentage recorded for Period 7 pits, and this could suggest that these features include proportionally more butchery waste than earlier pits.

Species represented
Fifty-six percent of fragments are identifiable to species and skeletal element. The proportion of identified bones from each of the eight periods varies from 48% to 64%. Bones from livestock species dominate the assemblage, and account for *c*. 92% NISP, or between 68%–97% NISP per period. Sheep are the most common species overall and account for 45% NISP, followed by cattle (49% NISP), and then pig (8.5% NISP). Changes in the relative importance of livestock between periods are described below.

Horse, dog and cat bone were also identified and together these domestic mammals account for *c*. 5% NISP. The proportion varies between periods from 1.5%–10%, and cat bones were present in some but not all periods (see Table 5.4). Bones from wild mammals make-up less than 1% NISP, and include red and roe deer, fox, hare, polecat, badger, hedgehog, mole, and a range of rodent species.

The assemblage also includes both domestic and wild bird species, which together account for 1.3% NISP. The most common bird species are domestic fowl and goose.

| | | Period | | | | | | | | | | | |
| | 3 | | 4 | | 5 | | 6 | | 7 | | 9 | |
NISP	N	%	N	%	N	%	N	%	N	%	N	%
cattle	1257	32.5	371	43.2	619	46.3	892	59.5	1100	47.8	238	29
sheep	2244	58.1	411	47.8	638	47.7	472	31.5	952	41.4	496	60.6
pig	361	9.4	77	9	81	6	134	9	248	10.8	85	10.4
Total	3862	100	859	100	1338	100	1498	100	2300	100	819	100

| | 3 | | 4 | | 5 | | 6 | | 7 | | 9 | |
MNE	N	%	N	%	N	%	N	%	N	%	N	%
cattle	412	22.8	111	31.4	178	26.4	374	49.8	434	38.5	96	26.8
sheep	1174	64.9	204	57.8	440	65	293	39	549	48.7	212	59
pig	222	12.3	38	10.8	58	8.6	84	11.2	144	12.8	51	14.2
Total	1808	100	353	100	676	100	751	100	1127	100	359	100

| | 3 | | 4 | | 5 | | 6 | | 7 | | 9 | |
MNI	N	%	N	%	N	%	N	%	N	%	N	%
cattle	21	18.7	7	24.1	11	21.6	15	34	21	30	6	27.3
sheep	75	67	17	58.7	35	68.6	21	47.8	37	52.9	13	59
pig	16	14.3	5	17.2	5	9.8	8	18.2	12	17.1	3	13.7
Total	112	100	29	100	51	100	44	100	70	100	22	100

| | 3 | | 4 | | 5 | | 6 | | 7 | | 9 | |
MWE	N	%	N	%	N	%	N	%	N	%	N	%
cattle	5775	58	1925	64.4	3025	63.5	4125	73.8	5775	70.6	1650	69
sheep	2812	28.3	637	21.4	1312	27.6	787	14	1387	17	487	20.4
pig	1360	13.7	425	14.2	425	8.9	680	12.2	1020	12.4	255	10.6
Total	9947	100	2987	100	4762	100	5592	100	8182	100	2392	100

NISP= number of identified specimens present
MNE= minimum number of elements
MNI= minimum number of individuals
MWE= meat weight estimates

Table 5.8 Relative frequency of livestock species by number and percentage NISP, MNE, MNI and MWE

Less common species include ducks (mallard and teal), plover/lapwing, mute swan, and crane, crow, buzzard, and small garden birds (*passeridae* and *turdidae sp.*). Amphibian bones were also recovered from a small number of features.

Species considered part of the general environmental background noise to the site, such as rodents, amphibians, badgers and moles, have been excluded from any further discussion. The general interpretation of these species is that they represent the remains of animals that have either fallen into open features or burrowed through archaeological deposits.

Relative importance of livestock species

Hambleton (1999, 39–40) has demonstrated that the optimum sample size needed to provide a reliable assessment of the relative importance of livestock species is an NISP count over 300 and a MNI count over thirty. Periods 3 to 9 all exceed the recommended minimum NISP count required for this type of analysis, and most also exceed the minimum MNI count. Periods 4 and 9, however, both have MNI counts below thirty, which means that this method of assessing relative importance is likely to be less accurate than for other periods. The small animal bone assemblages from Periods 1 and 2 have been excluded from this analysis for obvious reasons. It is however worth noting that cattle bones are common in both assemblages, followed by sheep and then pig.

It is clear that there is some variation in the relative importance of livestock throughout the sequence of occupation (Table 5.8 and Fig. 5.7). The NISP (58% and 48%), MNE (65% and 58%) and MNI (67% and 59%) counts for Periods 3 and 4 all indicate that the pastoral economy was primarily based on sheep-farming, and sheep-dominated assemblages are a common feature of many Middle and Late Iron Age sites in the region (see Hambleton 1999, 46). For Periods 5, 6 and 7 the three standard quantification methods (NISP, MNE and MNI) all give slightly different results. The differences between these results indicate that cattle bones are more fragmented than sheep bones, therefore NISP counts for cattle are higher than for sheep, therefore the latter two quantification methods (MNE and MNI) are considered to provide a more accurate indication of species proportions.

In Period 5 sheep bones were only marginally more common than cattle bones, at 48% NISP compared to 46% NISP for cattle. However, according to both MNE and MNI, sheep were clearly the dominant species, and account for 65%–69% of livestock. According to NISP and MNE, cattle were the dominant species in the Period 6 assemblage, accounting for 50%–60% of livestock, however, MNI (49%) suggests that there were more sheep

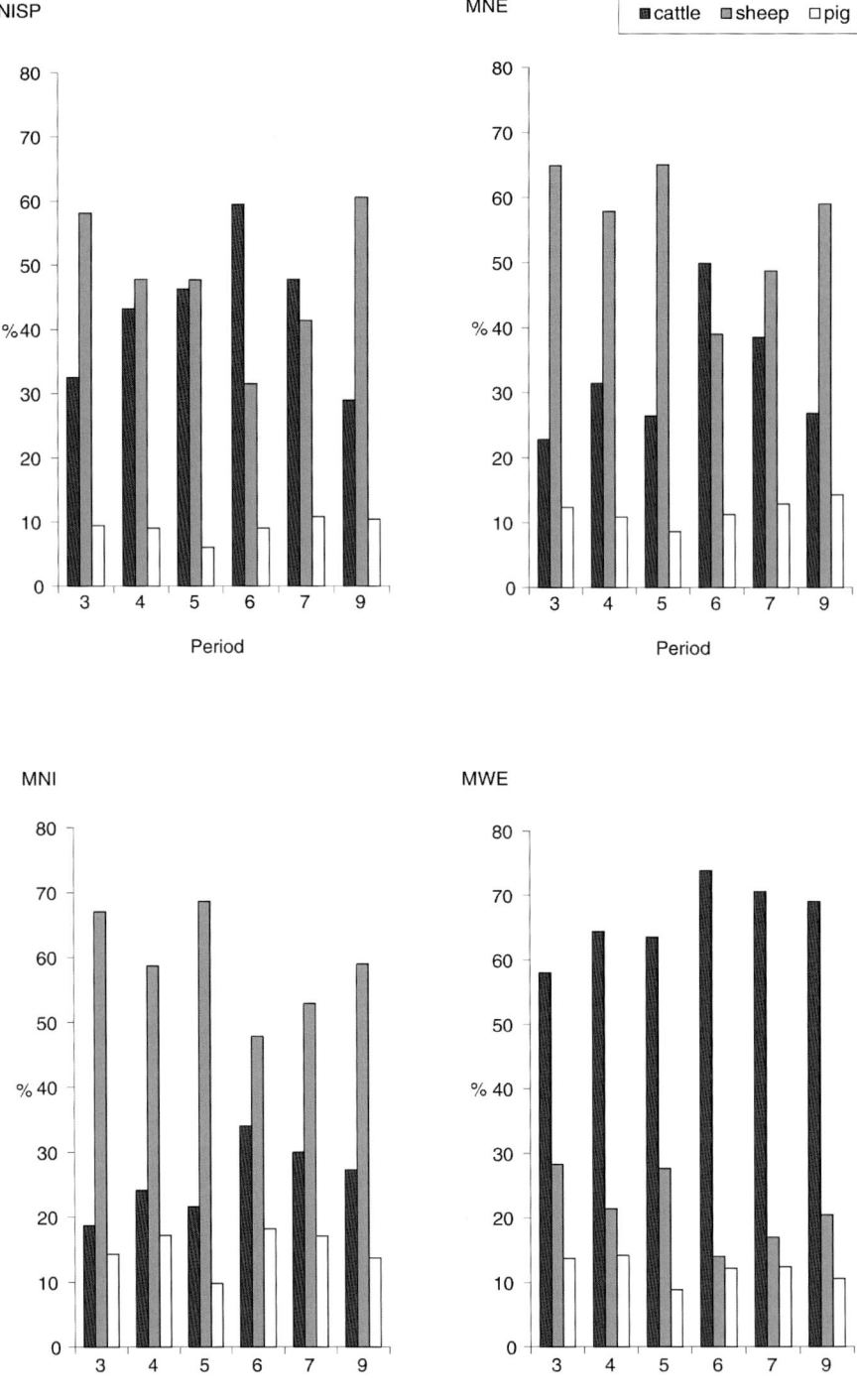

Figure 5.7 Relative importance of livestock species by Period

in the assemblage than cattle. Likewise for Period 7, which NISP (48%) suggests is cattle-dominated, but both the MNE (49%) and MNI (53%) results include more sheep.

Regardless of the number and proportion of sheep bones in the assemblage it is clear that cattle, by virtue of their greater size, provided most of the animal-based protein consumed at the site during all periods in the occupation sequence. Meat weight estimates (MWE) indicate that beef formed 58%–74% of the meat diet, compared to 14%–28% for mutton and just 9%–14% for pork.

Taking all the above information into account, it would seem that for most of the occupation sequence, the pastoral economy of the site was one based primarily on sheep-farming. Based on MNE counts, which have been assessed to be more accurate than NISP counts, sheep accounted for 49%–65% of livestock during much of the site occupation sequence, and it is only in Period 6 that cattle were the mainstay of the pastoral economy, accounting for 50% of livestock. However, based on MNI counts there is no significant change in the pastoral economy of the site between periods.

Livestock

Sheep/goat

Every effort was made to try and distinguish between sheep and goat bones. Only six goat bones were positively identified, compared to 270 positively identified sheep bones, a ratio of 1 in 45. For this reason the large group of undifferentiated caprine bones are considered more likely to be sheep bones than goat.

Goat bones were from three separate Period 3 pits, and include a metacarpal and two left frontal bones (*i.e.* skull) complete with horn cores. The other goat bones, two metacarpals and a horn core are from three separate Period 7 contexts, including horse burial 3023, pit 17223 and silting layer 3625.

Body parts

All parts of the sheep carcass are present in the assemblage, which suggests that live sheep were brought to the site from the surrounding fields to be slaughtered and butchered for local consumption. A few of the smaller elements such as ankle bones and phalanges are absent or under-represented. This is a common issue with hand-recovered assemblages, and is to some extent redressed by the small sieved assemblage.

Tibiae were the most common type of skeletal element in all periods. Other common elements include the mandible, radius, metacarpals and metatarsals. Many of these bones including the distal end of the tibia, which is more common than the proximal end, are considered to have low meat value and/or represent waste elements that are generally discarded at the primary butchery stage. However, these elements are all relatively robust bones that generally show a good survival and recovery rate in most assemblages of animal bone.

As previously indicated most of the sheep bones were derived from pits and ditches, and particularly large concentrations were noted from pits 1534, 16005, 16063, 20153, 20370 (Period 3), 20759 (Period 4), 20405 (Period 6), 16132, 21005 (Period 7), 16122 and 20513 (Period 9). The composition of the waste from these pits indicates that the bones derive from different stages in the carcass reduction sequence. This fits with general observations regarding the mixed nature of bone deposits. It is also worth mentioning the complete sheep skeleton from Period 7 feature 20290 (Table 5.5).

Mortality profiles

Reconstructed mortality profiles for each period are based on mandibles retaining two or more teeth with recordable wear. The sample sizes vary significantly; Period 3 has the largest sample of mandibles, followed by Period 5, and then Periods 4, 6 and 9, which all have sample sizes of less than 20 mandibles. Mandibles from the two youngest age groups (MWS A and B) are largely absent from most of the samples. As previously indicated the mandibles of immature animals tend to fragment easily, and this could account for their absence in the samples. However, the number of unworn or lightly worn loose deciduous fourth premolars in the assemblage is also quite low, which would seem to suggest that the age range of sheep as represented by mandibles is fairly accurate.

A total of 103 mandibles was recovered from Period 3 contexts. The mortality profile reconstructed from this data shows a main peak of slaughter amongst sheep between the ages of 1 and 2 years, and secondary peaks at 3–4 years and 4–6 years (MWS (mandible wear stages) D, F and G). Closer inspection of this data reveals that 50% of sheep were slaughtered at or before the age of 1–2 years, and only 20% survived beyond 3–4 years. This pattern is consistent with an intensive strategy geared towards prime meat production, and also one in which wool production is likely to have been of some significance.

The small sample of data from Period 4 shows a main peak of slaughter amongst sheep between the ages of 3 and 4 years, and a minor peak amongst sheep in the 1–2 year old category (MWS D and F). The proportion of sheep surviving beyond 1–2 years is higher than in Period 3, at 57%, and this suggests that prime meat production was still important but the husbandry strategy was less intensive than in the preceding period, perhaps because secondary products were also of some significance.

The mortality profile for Period 5 mandibles shows a fairly even spread across age classes and this is reflected in the smooth shape of the survival curve. Minor peaks of slaughter are apparent amongst sheep aged 3–4 years and 4–6 years (MWS F and G). However the proportion of sheep surviving beyond 1–2 years and 3–4 years is higher than in earlier periods, at 70% and 30% respectively. This pattern suggests a less intensive mixed husbandry strategy than in previous periods.

The small sample of mandibles from Period 6 contexts shows a main peak of slaughter amongst lambs aged between 6 and 12 months (MWS C). Almost 30% of sheep died or were slaughtered in their first year of life, a much higher proportion than in any of the other periods. Natural mortalities amongst lambs are to be expected and this might account for some of the deaths, however if these animals were slaughtered as part of the husbandry strategy then it is likely that this was a deliberate policy to reduce the size of the flock down to one that could be easily provisioned with fodder over the winter months. This type of strategy is one that is thought to work well as part of a mixed agricultural system (see Hambleton 1999, 70).

The Period 7 sample includes 32 mandibles, and these indicate a main peak of slaughter at 3–4 years, with minor peaks at 6–12 months and 4–6 years (MWS C, F and G). Fewer lambs died or were slaughtered than in the previous period. The proportion of sheep surviving beyond prime meat age is quite high at 62%, and the proportion surviving beyond 3–4 years is similar to the preceding period at 25%. The mortality profile suggests a mixed husbandry strategy, in which wool production is likely to have been of prime importance. This strategy also probably involved a deliberate autumn kill policy to reduce the size of the flock before winter and is likely to have complemented arable cultivation strategies (Hambleton 1999, 70).

Epiphyseal fusion data was also collated to provide additional information about slaughter patterns, but is generally considered to be less accurate than MWS data. Between 54% and 73% of sheep post-cranial bones recovered from the site have fused epiphysis, and the fusion data broadly corresponds to the mortality patterns recorded from mandibles. For example, the fusion data for Period 3 indicates that *c.* 50% of sheep were slaughtered between the ages of 1 and 2 years (intermediate fusion category), and *c.* 34% between 3 and 4 years — the same basic proportions as represented by the MWS data. There are of course exceptions to this, for example the Period 9 fusion data indicates that *c.* 75% of sheep were slaughtered before the age of 1–2 years, a much higher kill-off rate than suggested by MWS data. Neonatal sheep remains were recovered from most of the main periods, but in particular Periods 3, 5 and 7. This evidence indicates that pregnant ewes were kept close to the site during the winter months and into the spring lambing season.

Butchery
Butchery evidence was recorded on only 132 sheep bones in the whole assemblage. Over half (55%) of this evidence was recorded on sheep bones from Period 3 pits. Knife cuts were noted on *c.* 30% of bones and are consistent with skinning, disarticulation and filleting. Chop marks were also noted, and these marks generally relate to primary disarticulation of the carcass and secondary reduction into meat joints. Skulls were split open along the sagittal line, presumably in order to access the brain tissue. A small number of horn cores had been removed from the frontal bone by chopping through the base. These were undoubtedly removed so that the outer sheath could be used as a raw material. Saw mark evidence noted on one horn core indicates that the outer sheath was probably cut to size while still attached to the horn core.

Size, shape and sex
Withers height estimates indicate that there was little change in the overall stature of sheep between periods. The mean height estimate ranges from 0.55m–0.59m. Similarly comparison between periods using the mean values for common measurements such as shaft diameter (or SD), and distal breadth (or Bd), failed to find any significant differences (see summary descriptive statistics tables in archive).

Examination of the length and width of lower third molars indicates a general increase in the size of sheep teeth over time. Indeed some of the Period 5 (Roman) third molars are comparable in size or larger than those from Periods 7 (medieval). As teeth are not affected by sexual dimorphism, the size changes are likely to be due to improvement in husbandry and genetic diversity brought about by selective breeding.

Analysis of the size and shape of sheep metacarpals and metatarsals indicates that there is considerable variation both within and between periods, and the most likely explanation for this is sexual dimorphism, coupled with general changes in stature and conformation due to more general improvements in husbandry and genetic diversity. Only Periods 3 and 7 had sufficient numbers of pelvises to provide an estimate of the sex ratio of the flock, and the majority (69%–71%) of these are from ewes, although the presence of male castrates cannot be discounted.

Cattle

Body parts
All parts of the cattle carcass are present in the assemblage, which suggests that like sheep, live cattle were also brought to the site from the surrounding fields to be slaughtered and butchered for local consumption. Recovery methods do not appear to have such a biasing effect on the cattle bone assemblage as they had on the sheep bone assemblage, and although small elements such as ankle bones and phalanges are slightly under-represented there are no absences.

Common skeletal elements include the humerus (Periods 3, and 5), metacarpal (Period 4), mandible (Periods 6 and 7), and horn core (Period 6). In periods where the humerus is the most common element, the number of scapulae is also relatively high, which could suggest that there was a preference for shoulder joints of beef. Most of the other common elements are generally discarded at the primary butchery stage, or represent by-products from horn-working. Again, these elements are all relatively robust bones and generally show a good survival and recovery rate in most assemblages of animal bone.

Most cattle bones were derived from pits and ditches (Table 5.7), and ditch assemblages include proportionally more cattle bones than sheep bones. Large concentrations of cattle bones were noted from pits 20238 (Period 2), 16063 (Period 3), 20405 (Period 6), and Ditch 6 (Period 7). The composition of the waste from these features indicates that the bones derive from different stages in the carcass reduction sequence, which fits with general observations regarding the mixed nature of bone deposits.

Mortality profiles
A total of seventy-seven complete or near complete cattle mandibles were recovered from the site. Only Periods 3, 5, 6 and 7 include sufficient numbers to allow mortality profiles to be reconstructed from mandible wear stages (MWS). Mandibles from the two youngest age classes are under-represented, and are also not well-represented in the age-data for loose deciduous fourth premolars. Three of the four mandibles recovered from Period 2 contexts are from calves aged 8–18 months and the other is from an individual aged 18–30 months (MWS C and D). This limited data suggests that dairy products are likely to have been more important than meat production. The Period 3 mortality profile, based upon a sample of just thirteen mandibles, shows a spread of data across age classes (MWS C–H) with a minor peak in slaughter amongst senile cattle (MWS I). This pattern suggests that cattle were primarily managed for secondary products and used as traction animals, particularly since few cattle were slaughtered at the optimum age for prime beef.

Four mandibles were recovered from Period 4 contexts; they include two mandibles from young calves aged 1–8 months, an older calf aged 8–18 months and a young adult (MWS B, C and F). The data is limited but again suggests that secondary products were of some importance.

A sample of twelve mandibles from Period 5 shows minor peaks of slaughter at 18–30 months and amongst adult cattle (MWS D and G). This pattern is consistent with mixed husbandry strategy in which calves were slaughtered to free up milk for human consumption, a small proportion of male cattle were slaughtered at the optimum age for prime beef (MWS D and E) and adult cows were maintained for milk production and breeding purposes.

The relatively large sample of mandibles from Period 6 contexts shows a main peak of slaughter amongst adult cattle (MWS G) that suggests that cattle were primarily managed for secondary products and as traction animals.

The relatively large sample of mandibles from Period 7 contexts shows a main peak of slaughter amongst cattle aged 18–30 months and a minor peak amongst senile cattle (MWS D and I). This pattern is consistent with a mixed husbandry strategy geared towards prime beef and secondary products. One adult (MWS G) mandible was recovered from a Period 9 context.

Epiphyseal fusion data again largely confirms the mortality pattern suggested by mandibles, and provides more information for those periods with few mandibles. For Period 2 the fusion data indicate that most of the post-cranial bones are from skeletally mature animals over the age of three years. This age class is also better represented in the fusion data for Period 4 than the mandible data indicate.

Neonatal calf bones were recovered from most of the main periods, but in particular Period 3 pits. This evidence suggests that pregnant cows were kept close to the site during the spring calving season, and might even have been housed over the winter months.

Butchery

Butchery marks were noted on 199 cattle bones in the entire assemblage, and the majority were recovered on bones from Periods 3 (38%) and 7 (22%). Chop marks are more common than cut marks, and were recorded at major joint surfaces and on the mid-shafts of long bones. The distribution of these marks indicate that heavy chopping tools such as cleavers were used to disarticulate large carcasses and reduce them into more manageable joints for the purposes of storage, transportation and cooking. Skulls were split along the sagittal line to gain access to the brain tissue, and there was also some evidence for decapitation on the occipital condyles of two skulls from Period 6. Horn cores were removed from the frontal bone by chopping through the base. A small number of vertebrae had been split down the mid-line (i.e. dorso-ventrally), indicating that cattle carcasses, or at least racks of beef were often split into sides. A distinct pattern of butchery marks was noted on a small number of scapulae from Periods 3, 4, and 7. This type of butchery is often seen on shoulder joints that have been cured by a process of hot or cold smoking (see Dobney et al. 1996, 26–27). Trimming the distal end and removing the spine allows the smoke or brine to penetrate deep into the muscle tissue, preserving the meat so that it can be stored for later use. When eaten the meat is simply filleted off the bone, which results in numerous nick and cut marks on the blade. This type of evidence is often seen on Roman cattle scapulae, but there are none from Period 5 at Mildenhall.

Size, shape and sex

The withers (or shoulder) height of cattle increased throughout the occupation sequence, from a mean height of c. 1.11m in Period 3 to 1.16m in Period 7 (Table 5.9). The height estimates range from 0.98m to c. 1.52m, and Period 6 showed the widest variation in cattle stature. The very large animal recorded in the Period 6 assemblage is almost definitely a bull.

Detailed analysis of the size and shape of these metacarpals and metatarsals from Periods 3, 5, 6 and 7 (figures available in the archive) shows some separation of the data into at least two distinct clusters which can be interpreted as an indication that the sample includes both male and female. Some of the bone from Periods 5 and 6 are particularly large, and that this could indicate a general increase in the size of cattle due to improvements in

husbandry and/or genetic diversity rather than merely reflecting sexual dimorphism (see Albarella et al. 2008; Murphy et al. 2000).

Cattle horn cores are also sexual dimorphic, and their cross-sectional shape at the base varies accordingly. The cross-sectional shape of female cattle horn cores is generally oval, while male horn cores are round. Male castrates usually fall between these two categories when both size and shape are assessed together. Measurements of the basal circumference, and minimum and maximum widths indicate that the sample includes horn cores from both sexes, and revealing that female cattle are in the majority, particularly during Period 6. This fits with the mortality profile for this period which indicated that cattle were primarily managed for secondary products such as milk.

Cattle astragali are one of the main weight-bearing bones in the hindquarter and generally survive intact. Measurements of lateral length and distal breadth show a general increase in the size of cattle throughout the occupation sequence and reveals that some of the Period 5 and 6 cattle were larger and more robust than those bred under modern farming practices. These changes could indicate improvements to husbandry and/or greater genetic diversity than in previous periods. However, it could equally indicate the presence of one or two large bulls in the data sample.

Species	Period	N	M	Min	Max
sheep	3	20	0.57	0.53	0.62
	4	3	0.57	0.56	0.59
	5	1	-	-	0.55
	6	14	0.59	0.55	0.67
	7	11	0.55	0.51	0.60
	9	6	0.56	0.52	0.60
cattle	3	14	109.51	97.98	121.61
	4	3	113.48	110.36	117.11
	5	6	110.56	101.34	123.17
	6	23	115.76	103.01	151.59
	7	21	116.43	100.13	129.13
	9	6	120.10	114.18	120.90
pig	3	6	0.72	0.66	0.74
	4	1	-	-	0.72
	6	1	-	-	0.88
	7	4	0.69	0.63	0.75
	9	1	-	-	0.73
horse	1	1	-	-	118.38
	3	3	130.28	124.77	137.72
	5	3	133.40	119.45	144.07
	6	2	137.92	136.07	139.77
	7	7	150.54	134.20	159.30
	9	9	144.10	119.09	161.26
dog	3	1	-	-	0.53
	4	9	55.17	0.54	0.57
	5	2	0.62	0.60	0.64
	6	3	0.52	0.36	0.61
	7	9	0.46	0.30	0.55

Table 5.9 Withers (or shoulder) height estimates for common species by Period

Pig

Body parts

The body-part data for pigs was only assessed for those periods with a NISP count for this species of 100+; these include Periods 3, 6 and 7. The data indicated that all parts of the pig carcass are represented in these assemblages, and any absences or under-representations are likely to be the product of recovery methods and small sample size. Pigs, like other livestock, were therefore brought to the site to be butchered for local consumption. Small numbers of pigs might even have been kept within occupation areas, where they could be fed on scraps and general food refuse, thereby negating the need to remove waste away from domestic areas (see for example Rixson 2000, 115; Albarella 2006, 79).

Common skeletal elements include the humerus (Periods 3 and 7), and tibia (Period 6). As in the cattle bone assemblage, in those periods where the humerus is common, the number of scapulae is also relatively high, which again could indicate a preference for shoulder joints, but could also indicate that these joints were cured for long-term storage.

Mortality profiles

Periods 3 and 7 include sufficient numbers of pig mandibles to allow mortality profiles to be reconstructed. The mortality profile for Period 3, shows a peak of slaughter at 14–21 months, a second peak at 21–27 months (MWS D and E), and a minor peak at 7–14 months. The mortality profile for Period 7, shows a peak of slaughter amongst older animals aged 21–27 months, a second peak at 14–21 months and a minor peak at 7–14 months (MWS C, D and E). All of the mandibles from the other periods with small samples are from animals in the same age classes; the majority fall into MWS D and E, and there is a fairly even split between these categories for each period.

The mortality pattern reflects the fact that pigs provide no secondary products, reach full body weight quickly and have large litters. These characteristics mean that pigs are generally slaughtered at a younger age than other livestock, usually as part of an intensive husbandry strategy to produce meat. Sixty percent of the mandibles from Period 3 and 33% of those from Period 7 fall into the 14–21 months age group, and pigs of this age group are generally considered to make the best porkers and baconers (Campbell 2000, 165; Albarella 2006, 83). Half of the mandibles from Period 7, and 35% of those from Period 3 fall into the 21–27 month age group. This is the age at which pigs reach full body weight. It therefore makes sense to slaughter them around this time so that no further resources are wasted maintaining animals that will provide no additional return. The epipyseal fusion data for pigs confirms the mortality pattern recorded from mandibles. Foetal and neonatal pig bones were recovered from Periods 3, 4, 5 and 7. The evidence suggests that these animals were kept in close proximity to the site.

Butchery

Butchery marks were noted on twenty-eight pig bones, the majority (57%) were recorded on bones from Period 3, with small numbers from Periods 6, and 7. Pig skulls, like those of other livestock, were also split along the sagittal line.

Size and shape

The sample of pig bone measurements is too small to provide any meaningful information regarding changes in size or conformation between periods. Withers height estimates (Table 5.9) range from 0.63m (Period 7) to 0.88m (Period 6).

Horse

A total of 385 horse bones were recovered from the site and these account for *c.* 3% NISP. A small number of horse bones were recovered from Period 1 layers, and two pits, 20238 and 2042, assigned to Period 2. The Period 3 assemblage includes forty identified horse bones (*c.* 3% NISP), most of which were recovered from pits (Table 5.7). The remains are from a minimum of three different animals, all mature adults of between 12.1hh to 13.2hh (or 1.25m–1.38m; Table 5.9). The Period 4 assemblage includes thirty-five horse bones (4% NISP), and these were recovered from a variety of different features (Table 5.6). The bones are from at least three different animals, one of which is a juvenile. The Period 5 assemblage includes seventy-five horse bones (5% NISP), most of which are from layers and ditches, including enclosure ditches A and B. The bones are from a minimum of three different animals, all adults of between 11.3hh to 14.1hh (or 1.19m–1.44m). The Period 6 assemblage includes thirty-three horse bones (2% NISP), most of which are from pits, in particular pit 20405. The remains are from a minimum of three different animals, they include the mandible of a juvenile from alluvial layer 2039, and the scattered remains of at least two adults of similar stature, at *c.* 13.3hh to 14hh (or 1.36m–1.40m). The Period 7 assemblage includes 204 horse bones (4% NISP). This figure includes 102 fragments that belong to a near complete skeleton from pit 3023. The skeleton is that of a mature adult animal with an estimated withers height of *c.* 15.2hh (or 1.57m). The disarticulated horse bones are all from adult animals and these range in stature from 13.1hh to 15.3hh (or 1.34m–1.59m).

Dog

The assemblage includes 385 dog bones (or 1.9% NISP), and the proportion of dog bones per period varies from 0.5% (Period 3) to 4.7% (Period 5). The single dog bones recovered from Periods 1 and 2 are both mandibles, and these are from medium-sized adult animals. Eighteen dog bones were recovered from fifteen separate features assigned to Period 3, mostly pits but also a few ditches, and a posthole. The remains are from at least three different animals, including an adult male, a juvenile aged less than 1.5 years, and puppy aged 2–5 months. The Period 4 assemblage includes 208 dog bones, however 204 of these belong to a complete skeleton (SK 22027) from Ditch 6, which was associated with human skeleton SK 22028. The dog skeleton is that of an adult male with an estimated shoulder height of 0.55m (Table 5.9).

Seventy-four dog bones were recovered from Period 5 pits. The remains found in grave 21094 are small fragments of skull, and are probably just incidental inclusions within the backfill of the grave. Layer 3214 includes bones from the hindquarters of at least two different animals, while pit 3836 includes a range of body parts from at least two other animals. All other bones are from adult animals and these range in stature from 0.60m–0.64m. The dog bones from Period 6 are from an adult male and a juvenile animal. These animals range in stature from 0.36m–0.61m. The relatively large group of dog bones from Period 7 are mostly from layers. They include the remains from at least four adults and a juvenile animal. These animals range in size from 0.30m–0.55m.

Cat

A small number of cat bones were identified from Periods 2, 5, 6, and 7. Most are isolated bone elements but a few associated groups were also noted. These include a pair of mandibles from pit 20405 and a part skeleton from Period 5 corn dryer 17048. The remains from the corn dryer are those of an immature animal and include the left radius, and a few vertebrae and ribs. Whole or partial remains of cats have been recorded from a few Roman ovens, notable examples include one in the backfill of an oven on the site at Owslebury in Hampshire (see Morris 2011, 73), and one from the backfill of a malting oven/grain dryer in Area B at East Anton, near Andover in Hampshire (Higbee 2013c).

Deer

Both native species of deer, red and roe deer, have been identified from the assemblage. Red deer remains were more common than those of roe deer and were identified from Periods 3, 4, and 5. The remains of red deer include pieces of antler (56%) and post-cranial bones. Many of these pieces show signs of having been cut through with a saw either to remove tines or flat, regular pieces for object manufacture. Off-cuts from antler-working were noted from all four periods, however most of this material comes from Period 3 pits 15129 and 16128, and Period 5 layers 4044 and 20792. The roe deer remains include a mandible and several metatarsals and these were identified from contexts assigned to Periods 1, 2, 5 and 7.

Other mammals

Thirteen fox bones were recovered from Period 5 layer 21092. The remains include a fragmented skull, three pairs of mandibles, a left ulna and several vertebrae. It is likely that these remains were washed in from elsewhere during an episode of flooding.

A small number of hare bones were identified from Periods 1, 3, 5 and 7. The remains include a mandible, two humeri and several metapodials, and these are from both adult and juvenile animals. It is likely that hares were occasionally trapped for their pelts and as an additional source of meat.

Single bones from a polecat (Period 4), badger and hedgehog (both Period 7) were also identified, as were four bones from a mole and numerous rodent bones.

Birds

The bird bones account for only 1.3% NISP but include a range of both domestic and wild species. Domestic fowl was the most common bird species accounting for 40% of the bird bone assemblage. The numbers were very low in the earliest periods, but increase from Period 6 onwards. Most of the domestic fowl bones are from adult birds, which suggests that domestic fowl were primarily kept for their eggs.

Geese were the second most common bird species, accounting for 24% of the bird bone assemblage. Only a few bones were recovered from the Periods 3–5 and the numbers increase from Period 6. All of the goose bones are from adult birds, and again this suggests that egg

production was important. Eighty-six percent of all the goose bones recovered from the site are from the wing of the bird. This extreme bias in skeletal element representation could simply be a product of survival and recovery, or could indicate that the wings were treated differently from the rest of the carcass, perhaps because the flight feathers were used to fletch arrows.

The assemblage also includes bones from a number of common wetland species, and these are all likely to have been exploited as an additional source of meat. The identified species include ducks, both mallard and teal, ground-nesting birds, such as plover or lapwing, and large water birds, such as mute swan and crane (see Table 5.4). The Period 3 crane bones are from pits 15234 and 19093, which lie in close proximity to each other on the west side of the site. These bones could potentially be from the same bird since there are no repeated elements.

Other identified bird species include birds that commonly fill the scavenger niche around settlement sites, such crow and buzzard, and also small garden birds belonging to the *passeridae* and *turdidae* families, that once lived in trees and hedgerows in fields around the site.

All of these bird species have previously been recorded from a number of contemporary sites in Suffolk (Crabtree 1994; 1989; 1990 and 2012; Jones and Serjeantson 1983) and the wider region (Davis 2003; Evans and Serjeantson 1988; Luff 1993; Stallibrass 1996).

Discussion

Livestock dominate the assemblages from each period of occupation, and it is their relative importance to the pastoral economy of the site that is the main focus for discussion in the following sections. Inter-site analysis was carried out in order to understand how the assemblage from Recreation Way fits with regional trends for each period and to address where possible the research potential of the assemblage. The corpus of comparative data was restricted to sites in the East of England (*i.e.* Bedfordshire, Buckinghamshire, Cambridgeshire, Essex, Hertfordshire, Norfolk and Suffolk) with animal bone assemblages that have a NISP count for livestock species of 300+. A total of eighty-eight sites were included in the survey and these are listed in the archive. Due to the scarcity of published data for Late Bronze Age animal bone assemblages from the region, sites in other regions with large and informative assemblages have also been included.

Period 2 Late Bronze Age

Most of the 155 identified bones recovered from Late Bronze Age contexts are from cattle and sheep. In terms of relative numbers, cattle were clearly of prime importance, and accounted for 59% of all livestock. Unfortunately age information was limited, but the presence of three mandibles from calves aged 8–18 months suggests that cattle might have been managed for milk production. Comparative data indicates that at some regional sites with high cattle bone frequencies such as Springfield in Essex (Wade 2000), and Billingborough in Lincolnshire (Iles 2001), the husbandry strategy was geared towards secondary products, while at West Row Fen in Mildenhall (Olsen 1994), where cattle account for 57% (by NISP) of livestock, the high survival rate amongst adult and senile animals indicates that cattle were primarily kept for meat and as draft animals rather than for their dairy products

(Olsen 1994, 144). It is however worth noting that in general the Late Bronze Age pastoral economy in England appears to be one based on sheep-farming (see for example Pryor 1996). This is based on the large assemblages of animal bone from midden deposits at Potterne in Wiltshire (Locker 2000) and Runnymede Bridge in Surrey (Serjeantson 1996).

A large proportion of the Late Bronze Age assemblage comes from pit 20238, and was found in association with human remains and a large amount of pottery. The composition of the animal bone assemblage from 20238 suggests that it is a random accumulation of waste material from different stages in the carcass reduction sequence, and apart from the quantity of bone, it is indistinct from the other Late Bronze Age pit assemblages or indeed those from later periods. However it clearly contained a complex sequence of deposits that could be interpreted as having structure and meaning beyond the mundane activity of refuse disposal.

Period 3 Middle Iron Age
The Middle Iron Age assemblage is relatively large and comprises 3970 identified bones, the vast majority of which were from livestock species. Sheep accounted for 58% of livestock, most were ewes or male castrates, which the mortality profile suggests were intensively managed for prime meat, with wool production a secondary consideration. Loom weights and a weaving comb were recovered from the site, so despite only being a secondary aim it would appear that any wool produced was at least being used locally to produce textiles. Cattle were of secondary importance to the pastoral economy of the site, their bones account for *c.* 33% NISP, and it would appear that the management strategy was geared towards milk and possibly traction, since most cattle are older females.

In her review of Iron Age animal husbandry regimes, Hambleton (1999, 46) states that *'there is a notable amount of intra-region variation in species proportions within the Eastern samples, particularly with regards to the relative importance of sheep and cattle'*. However, most of the Middle Iron Age sites surveyed for this report have high sheep bone frequencies between 51% and 68%. These include Great Barford and Fairfield Park in Bedfordshire (Holmes 2007a and 2007b), and Haddenham V and Earith in Cambridgeshire (Serjeantson 2006; Higbee 2013a), while the assemblage from the open settlement at Pennyland in Buckinghamshire (Holmes 1993) is dominated by cattle bones (62%). The mortality profiles for sheep and cattle from these Middle Iron Age sites are broadly similar to those for Mildenhall. At both Great Barford and Fairfield Park, sheep were intensively managed for prime meat, while at both Haddenham and Pennyland the high rates of mortality amongst yearlings indicated a winter kill strategy. This strategy complements arable cultivation and has been recorded at a wide range of Iron Age sites in the region (Hambleton 1999, 70, 73–4). Serjeantson (2006, 220) suggests that at Haddenham V the mortality profile, which also includes a high number of old adult sheep, is in keeping with an economy in which wool production is important. She stresses that wool was an important commodity in the Iron Age economy of Britain, and could be used for exchange and payment of dues after it had been transformed into woven cloth. The mortality profiles for cattle generally indicate these

animals were managed for secondary products and as traction animals.

There is limited evidence for the exploitation of deer, hare and birds, including wetland species including cranes. Most Iron Age sites in the region that are located on the edge of the wetlands include at least some evidence for the exploitation of wetland resources (see for example Evans and Serjeantson 1988).

Period 4 Late Iron Age
The Late Iron Age economy was also based primarily on sheep farming. Based on NISP sheep accounted for 47% of livestock, marginally more than cattle (43%), however cattle bones were generally more fragmented than sheep bones, therefore when MNE counts are considered it is clear that sheep were the dominant species, accounting for 58% of livestock. Mortality profiles indicate that sheep were less intensively managed for meat production than in the Middle Iron Age, probably due to a gradual shift in emphasis towards wool production. The age information for cattle is quite limited but suggests that secondary products were important.

As indicated above, there is considerable variation in Iron Age husbandry regimes within the region. Many of the regional sites surveyed for this report have high sheep bone frequencies (45%–65%) including the enclosed settlement at Burgh in Suffolk (Jones *et al.* 1988), while others have high cattle bone frequencies, for example Cedars Park, Stowmarket in Suffolk (Cussans and Philips 2016). Two of the regional sites have extremely high sheep bone counts (89%–99%), however both are temple sites (Legge *et al.* 2000; Legge and Dorrington 1985), and cannot therefore be considered to be truly representative of the wider economy. The major Late Iron Age settlement complexes at Puckeridge-Braughing (Croft 1979) and Skeleton Green (Ashdown and Evans 1981) in Hertfordshire, have higher pig bone frequencies (34%–49%) than other types of regional sites. It is considered that these more 'urban' settlements probably acted as consumers rather than producers, and generally show more evidence of Roman influences, including the dietary preference for pork, than contemporary rural sites (Hambleton 1999, 56).

The mortality patterns for sheep show some regional consistency and generally indicate that these animals were managed in a way that would complement arable farming. This involved reducing stock densities before winter and grazing sheep on stubble fields for the direct application of manure (Hambleton 1999, 70). As part of this strategy yearlings were exploited for meat, while older animals were retained for wool. For example at Cedars Park in Suffolk (Cussans and Philips 2016), two main peaks in slaughter were noted, one at 6–12 months and the other at 4–6 years, indicating a winter cull strategy and an emphasis on wool, and a similar pattern was noted at Burgh in Suffolk (Jones *et al.* 1988). Cattle mortality profiles from other sites in the region indicate a mixed rather than a specialist husbandry strategy, with the scope to alter the emphasis on different products (Hambleton 1999, 82 and 89).

Period 5 Roman
Due to a lack of refined dating evidence the Roman assemblage can only be discussed in broad terms. Based on NISP the assemblage includes near equal numbers of

sheep and cattle, however like the Period 4 assemblage, cattle bones were more fragmented than sheep bones, therefore the MNE counts were considered to be more accurate. The MNE results suggest that the Roman economy was based primarily on sheep-farming, with sheep accounting for 65% of livestock, compared to only 26% for cattle. In general terms this represents a continuation of the local Iron Age economy and is typical of rural settlements, which were generally less affected by Romanising influences on diet, than villa estates and urban centres which tend to have higher cattle bone frequencies (see King 1978, 1984 and 1999; Grant 1989).

The corpus of published data for Roman sites in the region is large in comparison to other periods, which means that it is possible to get a much better understanding of the regional trends in animal husbandry strategies. Of the forty-one Roman sites surveyed, only a small proportion (17%) have sheep bone frequencies of over 45% NISP similar to Mildenhall. These sites are mostly rural settlements and include West Stow in Suffolk (Crabtree 1990), Great Barford in Bedfordshire (Holmes 2007a), Langdale Hale, Grandford, Orton Hall Farm and Stonea in Cambridgeshire (Higbee 2013b; Stallibrass 1982 and 1996), and Puckeridge-Braughing in Hertfordshire (Fifield 1988). Roman sites in the region with high cattle bone frequencies include several towns, for example Braintree, Chelmsford and Colchester in Essex (Smoothy 1993; Luff 1988 and 1993), and Scole-Dickleburgh and Wixoe in Suffolk (Baker 2014; Faine pers. comm.), but also some rural settlements including Cedars Park and Hartismere School in Suffolk (Cussans and Philips 2016; Higbee forthcoming a). There is clearly a considerable degree of variation in species proportions between Roman sites in the region, and while rural sites tend to have higher sheep bone frequencies than urban sites, this is not always the case and there are clearly local factors influencing animal husbandry regimes at individual sites.

The mortality profiles for sheep and cattle from Roman Mildenhall suggest that both were managed as part of a mixed husbandry strategy, perhaps with a slight emphasis on secondary products. It is also likely that older cattle were maintained for use as traction animals, since many of the regional sites including Cedars Park, Hacheston and Eye in Suffolk (Cussans and Philips 2016; King 2004; Higbee forthcoming a) show significant numbers of cattle were maintained beyond the optimum age for prime beef. This pattern would fit with the use of cattle as traction animals, and other evidence for agricultural intensification and the expansion of arable farming into previously uncultivated areas during the Roman period in England (Thomas and Stallibrass 2008, 10).

Period 6 Saxon
Both NISP (60%) and MNE (50%) counts indicate that the pastoral economy of the site during the Saxon period was largely based on cattle-farming. Contemporary regional sites with high cattle bone frequencies (45%–84%) include the Early Saxon settlements at Bloodmoor Hill in Suffolk (Higbee 2009), and Orton Hall Farm in Cambridgeshire (King 1996), as well as several Middle and Late Saxon urban sites including Ipswich in Suffolk (Crabtree 2012), and Norwich (Albarella *et al.* 2009) and Thetford in Norfolk (Albarella 2004; Jones 1984 and

1993; Powell and Clark 2002; Wilson 1995). However most of the other regional sites, including the large Early Saxon assemblage from West Stow in Suffolk (Crabtree 1989), have high sheep bone frequencies, which suggests that variations in animal husbandry regimes are not determined by site type or chronology. There is also some evidence that certain sites in the region adopted more specialist economic strategies, these include the Early Saxon site at Bloodmoor Hill (Higbee 2009), and the Middle Saxon sites at Brandon in Suffolk and Wicken Bonhunt in Essex (Crabtree 1994, 50; 1996, 72–73; 2012). The rise of these specialised rural producer sites has been linked to the development of estate centres and *wic* or emporia sites such as Ipswich, as centres of craft production and trade.

Period 7 medieval
Based on NISP cattle bones were marginally more common than sheep, at 48% compared to 41%, however cattle bones were generally more fragmented than sheep bones, therefore when MNE counts are considered the relative importance of sheep increases to 49% compared to just 39% for cattle. The data set of comparative sites from the region suggested that medieval rural assemblages, and high medieval urban assemblages are generally sheep-dominated, whilst late medieval urban assemblages generally have near equal proportions of cattle and sheep, and a similar pattern was noted by Sykes (2006, 62).

The East Anglian region has a long tradition of sheep farming (Sykes 2007, 29), and this established farming regime is likely to have become more significant during the medieval period due to the economic importance of the wool trade (see Lloyd 2005). In the early medieval period wool was exported to Europe from eastern seaports such as King's Lynn and Boston, but by the late medieval period this was replaced by woollen textiles produced in towns and villages such as Lavenham in Suffolk and Worstead in Norfolk. The revenues brought in by the export of cloth allowed the region to prosper throughout the 14th and 15th centuries.

Conclusions
The pattern of livestock farming established during the Middle Iron Age persisted throughout much of the site's occupation sequence, albeit with minor alterations in strategy. The general characteristics of the assemblage with its low species diversity, overwhelming reliance on domestic sources of meat, and a mixed husbandry regime suggests the area had a well-balanced and self-sufficient agricultural economy based primarily on sheep-farming to produce wool. Cattle were also important for meat and milk, and provided the means by which much of the land was ploughed for arable cultivation.

V. Fish bone
by Philip Armitage

Introduction
Examination of 379 fish bones from sieved samples from pits, ditches, gullies and other deposits dating from the Iron Age (Period 3) to the medieval period (Period 7), has resulted in the identification of 218 specimens (57.5%/total) representing the remains of six species (Table 5.10). Identifications were made using the author's

Taxon	Common name	Period 1	Period 3	Period 4	Period 5	Period 6	Period 7	Totals
Anguilla anguilla	freshwater eel	1	1	-	41	28	74	145
Rutilus rutilus	roach	-	-	-	-	1	1	2
Cyprinidae	cyprinids (carp family)	-	-	1	3	7	20	31
Esox lucius	pike	-	-	-	2	1	6	9
Gasterosteidae	sticklebacks	-	-	-	2	-	16	18
Clupea harengus	herring	-	-	-	2	2	8	12
cf.Platichthys flesus	cf.flounder	-	-	-	-	-	1	1
		-	-	-	-	-	-	-
unidentified		3	1	-	8	44	105	161
Totals		4	2	1	58	83	231	379

Table 5.10 Summary counts of identified fish bone specimens (NISP) from each period

modern comparative osteological collections. Reference was also made to Libois and Hallet-Libois (1988), Libois *et al.* 1987, Newdick (1979), Radu (2005) and Wouters *et al.* (2007). The anatomical distributions for the major deposits reveal a preponderance of vertebrae. The complete data sets of recorded anatomies for each species represented from each context and period are in the site archive.

Analysis

Although a few specimens were well-preserved, the overall majority were in a fragmented state owing to post-depositional attritional damage. Despite this damage it proved possible to obtain measurements (in mm), using Draper dial calipers (graduated 0.02 mm), on the pelves of two 3-spined sticklebacks (*Gasterosteus aculeatus*) following the system of Prenda *et al.* (2002, fig. 2, 21), also on a freshwater eel (*Anguilla anguilla*) articular, following the system of Libois *et al.* (1987, fig. 2, 4) and roach (*Rutilus rutilus*) pharyngeal bone (system of Libois and Hallet-Libois (1988, fig.2, C). From these data, the size (TL, total length) of each fish could be calculated based on regression formulae.

Whilst the larger of the two sticklebacks whose total lengths were calculated was of a size close to the adult average of 4–5cm (see Newdick 1979, 82), the smaller individual probably was an immature fish. The eel represented by the articular was slightly below the average of 40cm for mature individuals (Libois *et al.* 1987, 88). Only a few of the cyprinid fish represented in the samples were of large, or even of moderate size; most of the bones examined apparently derived from very small, immature individuals. Pike bones were also notably from small fish; with the exception of the two precaudal vertebrae (context 15446, fill of Period 7 medieval posthole 15447) that are from a fish closely comparable in size to a modern adult pike of TL 45.7cm.

Interpretation and discussion

No detailed interpretation of the fish bones from the Iron Age (Periods 3 and 4) was feasible owing to the extremely small samples available; the following interpretation and discussion therefore focuses on the Roman (Period 5), Saxon (Period 6) and medieval (Period 7) assemblages.

Not all the fish bone represents human food waste. In the case of the sticklebacks, their presence in the Roman and medieval alluvial deposits, ditches and gullies indicate these fish may have once formed part of the natural aquatic fauna in these features. Where their bones

occurred in the medieval pit fills, in association with domestic/household food debris, it is possible that the sticklebacks had instead been the prey of predatory fish such as pike. In preparation for cooking/consuming of the pike by the local inhabitants, these fish would have been gutted and the stomach contents (including the sticklebacks) discarded along with other kitchen waste. Pike will also eat small cyprinids, which would provide one explanation (in the same manner as the sticklebacks) for their presence at the site. The bones of the larger cyprinids however may well represent remains of fish consumed by the human inhabitants, whilst the preponderance of freshwater eel bones in all three Periods (5, 6 and 7) suggests this fish — probably sourced locally from the River Lark or nearby fenlands — was an important component in the local human diet. Apart from the single flatfish (flounder vertebrae, fill of Period 7 posthole 15439) there is a notable absence of evidence for the consumption of marine fish. Although the site is inland, the east coast fisheries were not so distant as to prevent supplies of fresh sea fish reaching the local market in the medieval period. However, such fish, especially flatfish (flounder and plaice) were only within the affordable price range of the more wealthy households (Serjeantson and Woolgar 2006, 117). Therefore the virtual absence of marine fish at the Mildenhall site would seem to suggest the local inhabitants were not well-to-do. If this was the situation, the presence of pike among the recovered food waste from Period 7 deposits is somewhat puzzling as mature pike was an expensive luxury in medieval times and could cost the equivalent of two pigs or as much as the weekly wages of a skilled craftsman (Labarge 1965, 81; Dyer 2000, 108), and the price of even a small pike, known as a pickerel, was more than a fat capon (Yarrell 1836, 384). There is therefore an apparent ambivalence of the medieval fish bone evidence, and it is not possible to establish the socio-economic status of the local inhabitants based on this material alone.

VI. Insect remains
by David Smith

Introduction

The insect faunas described in this report come from six of the bulk samples taken from various sections excavated through a series of buried soil horizons and thin peats that covered the south-eastern corner of Areas 2 and 3 of the

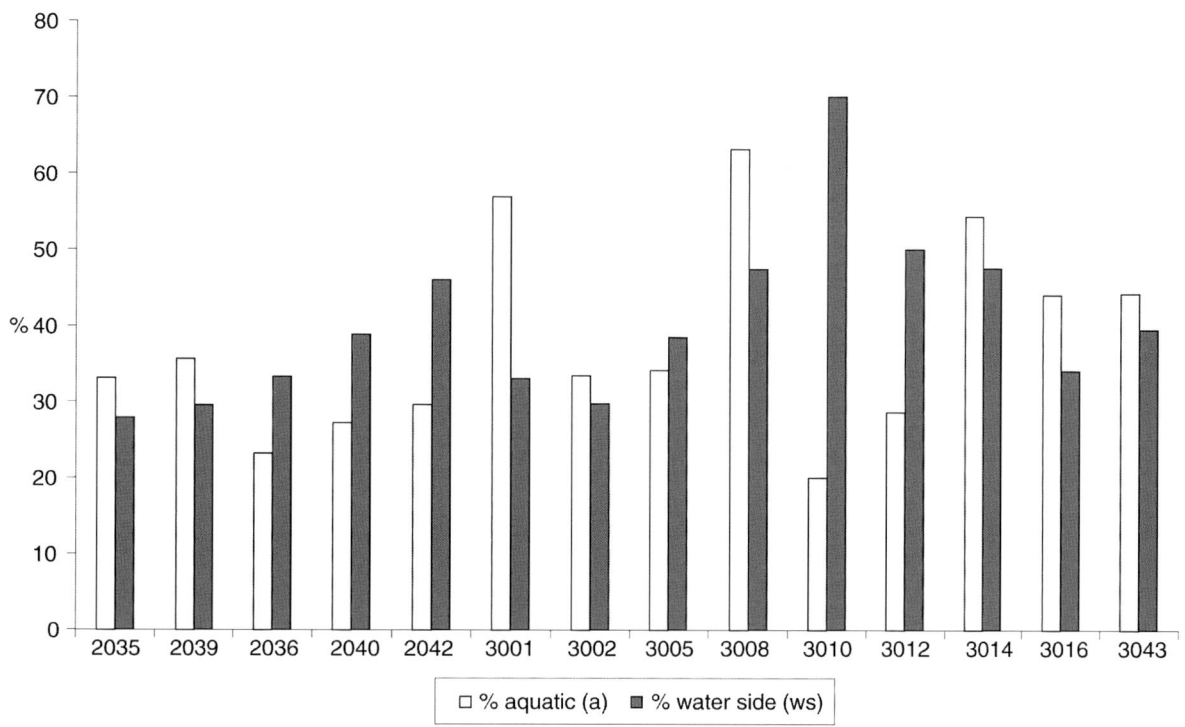

Figure 5.8 The proportions of the aquatic ecological groups of Coleoptera

site. One sample is dated to the Saxon period (Period 6), and the remaining samples are medieval in date (Period 7).

Standard laboratory methods for archaeoentomological analysis were used and nomenclature for Coleoptera follows Lucht (1987). The full specialist report is available in archive. The full list of the insects recovered is presented in Table 5.11 (see Appendix 2).

The majority of the insect remains recovered are beetles (Coleoptera), with true bugs (Hemiptera), ants (Formicoidea) and flies (Diptera) occurring in much smaller numbers.

The insect faunas recovered

Area 2
Five insect faunas came from Area 2. Sample 2042 was from a Saxon alluvial layer 2086 from Period 6. The remaining samples were medieval (Period 7). Two samples 2036/2040 were from the buried soil 2051. Samples 2035/2039 were from a thin band of peat 2050 that sealed 2051. All of the insect faunas are essentially similar in nature suggesting that the landscape remained relatively stable during the period of soil and peat formation.

The insect faunas are dominated by 'water beetles' and taxa associated with stands of waterside vegetation (ecological groups 'a' and 'ws' in Table 5.12 and Figure 5.8). The 'water beetles' recovered, mainly a range of Gyrinidae, Dytiscidae, Hydreanidae and Hydrophilidae (see Table 5.11, Appendix 2), often are associated with shallow water; such as fresh water marshes, puddles, ponds and field drains (Hansen 1986; Nilsson and Holmen 1995, Foster and Friday 2011).

Waterside vegetation also occurred in the area which included common club rush, bulrush, water reed, reed sweet grass and erect bur reed (the food plants of *Donacia clavipes, Donacia cineraria* and *Plateumaris braccata*

Notaris acridulus and of *Donacia marginata* respectively: Koch 1992). The insect remains also suggest that more open areas of water were present, which supported a range of floating aquatic plants, including white and yellow water lillies, duckweed and water milfoils (the food plants of *Donacia crassipes, Tanysphyrus lemnae* and *Eubrychius velutus* respectively: Koch 1992).

A wide range of both Carabidae 'ground beetles' and Staphylinidae 'rove beetles' recovered are associated with saturated or muddy ground, often located by water (including *Elaphrus* spp., *Pterostichus gracilis, P. niger, Agonum gracile,* the *Lesteva* and *Platystethus* taxa recovered: Lindroth 1974; Luff 2007; Duff 2012, Lott 2009).

The local terrestrial environment appears to be dominated by pasture and grassland. This is indicated by the recovery of a range of 'dung beetles', including the Scarabaeidae 'dung beetles' *Onthophagus joannae,* a range of *Aphodius* species and the 'dor beetle', *Geotrupes* spp. and the small staphylinid *Platystethus arenarius* all of which are associated with herbivore dung in pasture (Jessop 1986, Lott 2009). Taken together indicators for pasture dung account for 12% – 23.6 % of the terrestrial fauna recovered. Similarly, though not exclusive to animal dung, *Cercyon analis* and the range of Histeridae beetles recovered will also live and feed in such material (Duff 2012). Perhaps the strongest indicator for the presence of grazing animals in the area is the recovery of two puparia of the 'sheep ked' *Melophagus ovinus.* This is a parasite of sheep and has been used in the archaeological record to indicate the presence of sheep in the landscape and wool processing when found in settlement (Buckland and Perry 1989; Hall and Kenwood 2003).

Other indicators for grassland are several of the Carabidae 'ground beetles' and the Elateridae 'click beetles' listed in Table 5.11 (Appendix 2). A number of the phytophage species recovered also are common in

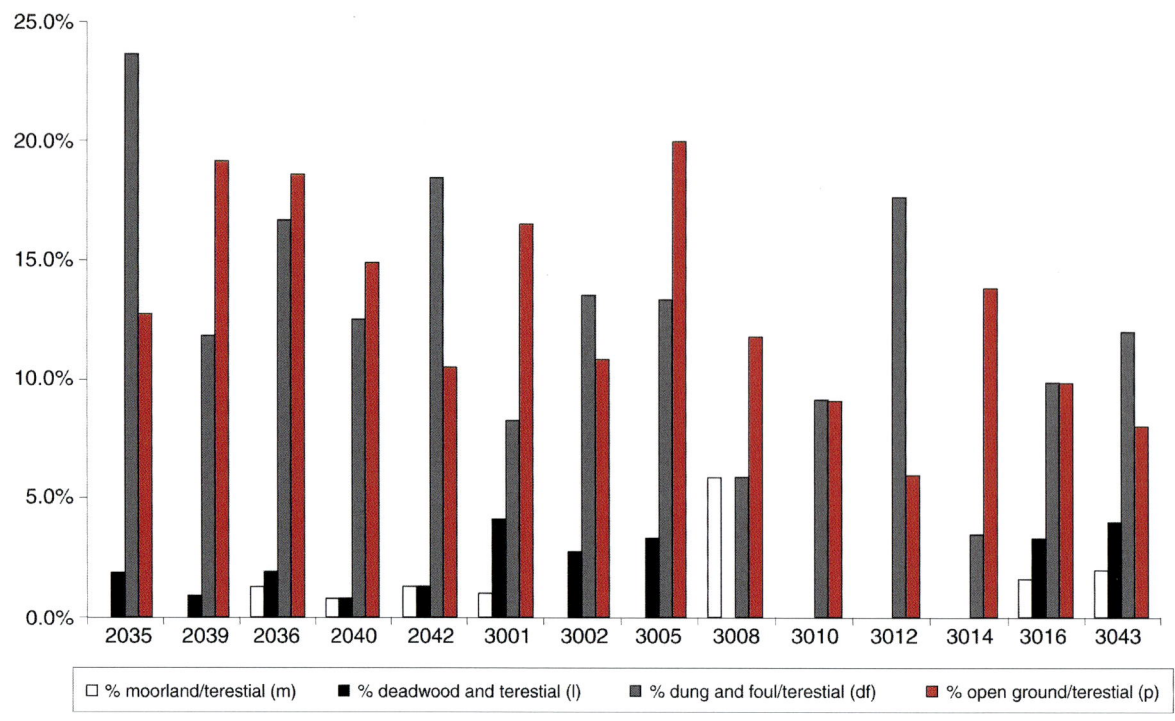

Figure 5.9 The proportions of the terrestrial ecological grouping of Coleoptera

grassland where they feed on a range of grassland plants such as vetches, clover, hairbells and plantain (the food plants of *Apion ?craccae*, *Sitona suturalis* and *Hypera* spp. *Mairus campanulae*, *Mecinus pyraster, Gymnetron labile* and *G. pascuorum* respectively: Koch 1992; Morris 2008). Several beetles also suggest that stinging nettle grew in the area, since it is the food plant of *Brachypterus urticae, Apion urticarium* and *Cidnorhynus quadrimaculatus* (Koch 1992; Morris 2008). Common mallow is indicated by *Apion aeneum*. There also is the suggestion that heather may have grown in the area, since this is the food plant of *Micrelus ericae* (Koch 1992; Morris 2008). Several individuals of the 'garden chaffer' *Phyllopertha horticola* also were recovered. This is a species which, as a larva, feeds on the roots of grass, especially in pasture (Jessop 1986).

In addition to indicators for grassland/pasture, there are very few species of insects recovered that indicate woodland (ecological group 'l' in Table 5.12 and Figure 5.9). These are limited to single individuals of species, such as *Nemadus colonoides* and *Platypus cylindrus,* the 'common woodworm' *Anobium punctatum*, the 'powder post' beetle *Lyctus linearis* and the 'wood borer beetle' *Ptilinus pectinicornis*. The bark beetle *Phloeophthorus rhododactylus* is directly associated with broom.

A very small number of species recovered are common in human habitation, for example the woodworm, powder post and wood borer beetle mentioned above, *Xylodromus concinnus, Monotoma* spp., *Cryptophagidae, Lathridiidae, Ptinus* spp. and *Aglenus brunneus*. These all have been described by Kenward (Kenward and Hall 1995), perhaps misleadingly, as the 'house fauna' and their presence may suggest that a limited amount of settlement waste, animal fodder or bedding may have been in this area.

Area 3

Insect faunas were recovered from two locations in Area 3. Sample 3001 (context 3009) and samples 3002, 3005 3008, 3010, 3012, 3014 and 3016 (context 3016) came from a sequence of peats in the centre of this area that appeared to seal many of the medieval features. Sample 3043 (context 3870) was from a similar thinner spread of peat in the western part of Area 3. The insect remains from both parts of Area 3 were very similar in their nature suggesting that the landscape and environment remained relatively stable throughout this period.

The insect faunas from Area 3 contained many of the same taxa as seen in the deposits from Area 2. Again a range of Dytsicidae, Hydreanidae and Hydrophilidae 'water beetles' dominate indicating that freshwater marsh was present in this area. Stands of waterside vegetation, including water reed, bulrush and reed sweet grass along with a range of floating plants such as water lily and duckweed grew in this area as well. This is indicated by the recovery of a similar range of *Donacia* and *Plateumaris* 'reed beetles' and weevils as were seen in Area 2. The waterside nature of this environment also is confirmed by the recovery of several specimens of the 'ground beetle' *Odacantha melanura* which is also normally associated with stands of water reed (Luff 2007).

Beyond this immediately local, swampy area there are strong indications for a largely cleared landscape of grassland and pasture. Again, grassland and grazing animals are suggested by a range of dung beetles such as *Geotrupes* spp., *Aphodius contaminatus, A. sphacelatus* or *A. prodromus* and *A. porcus* and plant feeding weevils such as *Sitona flavescens* associated with clover, *Larinus planus* with thistles, *Cidnorhynus quadrimaculatus* with stinging nettle and *Gymnetron* spp. with plantain.

Insects associated with woodland are underrepresented in both sets of samples and are limited to several individuals of the 'nut weevil' *Curculio* spp. and a single individual of the 'leaf miner' *Rhynchaenus* spp. in context 3016 and the 'woodworm' *Anobium punctatum* and the weevil *Rhampus pulicarius* recoved from context 3870, the latter species is associated with willow. The lack of species directly associated with woodland suggests that the landscape was essentially cleared and open.

Discussion

The insect faunas from deposits at Mildenhall indicate that the landscape surrounding Areas 2 and 3 throughout the Saxon and Medieval periods contained areas of shallow, slow-flowing freshwater marsh. This may suggest that this area of the site was subject to seasonal flooding, if not a rising water table during this time. All of the faunas studied strongly suggest that grassland and grazing animals occurred in the vicinity of both areas of the site and that the landscape essentially was cleared of woodland. Though dung beetles are a substantial part of the terrestrial fauna recovered in both areas (see ecological group 'df' in Table 5.12 and Figure 5.9) they are not as dominant as seen at a range of other archaeological sites where the levels of grazing are thought to have been high or a determining factor in the landscape (*i.e.* Robinson 1979, 1983; Lewis *et al.* 2006; Smith 2011a). A number of recent modern studies have indicated that the relative proportions of 'dung beetles' fairly reliably indicate the relative extent of grazing in an area and whether this was occurring directly or adjacent to the site (Smith *et al.* 2010). This may suggest that grazing was limited at Mildenhall or, more probably, occurred further away from the site. The recovery of sheep keds in Area 2 clearly indicates that sheep were, however, grazing in the area of the site.

There are very few insect faunas from archaeological sites in Suffolk and Norfolk (Buckland and Buckland 2006; Hall 2008: *Environmental Archaeology Bibliography*) with most work coming from either a range of Pleistocene sites (*e.g.* Coope 2006; 2010), the Bronze Age trackways at Beccles (Smith 2011b) and a limited amount of work on urban medieval deposits from Norwich (*e.g.* Kenward and Allison 1994) and Ipswich (*e.g.* Kenward 1987). At present the insect faunas from Mildenhall are the only archaeoentomological assemblage from East Anglia to come from rural medieval deposits. Nationally most medieval insect faunas come from urban locations (*e.g.* Kenward and Hall 1995; Smith 2012) and not from rural landscapes; therefore, this assemblage is of national importance and the Mildenhall archaeoentomological data can serve as a baseline for other work from rural medieval environments in future.

VII. Palaeoenvironment and land-use: the sediment and land snails
by Michael J. Allen

Summary
A series of eighteen monoliths containing undisturbed sediment was taken from a series of nine sampled sequences, from which bulk samples were also obtained (Fig. 5.10). Samples through the alluvial sequences were taken with the assistance of Richard Payne of ARCA, who visited the site during excavation and provided advice. Following assessment, a series of sampled sediment profiles were examined for geoarchaeology (sediment record) and pollen, and a suite of eleven samples were

Sample number	2035	2039	2036	2040	2042	3001	3002	3005	3008	3010	3012	3014	3016	3043
Total number of individuals	79	163	217	191	122	176	54	47	38	20	28	59	100	86
Total number of taxa	44	77	94	80	69	82	32	31	27	14	15	38	60	58
% aquatic (a)	16.5%	17.8%	11.5%	13.6%	14.8%	28.4%	16.7%	17.0%	31.6%	10.0%	14.3%	27.1%	22.0%	22.1%
% water side (ws)	13.9%	14.7%	16.6%	19.4%	23.0%	16.5%	14.8%	19.1%	23.7%	35.0%	25.0%	23.7%	17.0%	19.8%
% moorland/ terrestrial (m)	0.0%	0.0%	1.3%	0.8%	1.3%	1.0%	0.0%	0.0%	5.9%	0.0%	0.0%	0.0%	1.6%	2.0%
% deadwood and treeleaf (l)	1.8%	0.9%	1.9%	0.8%	1.3%	4.1%	2.7%	3.3%	0.0%	0.0%	0.0%	0.0%	3.3%	4.0%
% dung and foul/ terrestrial (df)	23.6%	11.8%	16.7%	12.5%	18.4%	8.2%	13.5%	13.3%	5.9%	9.1%	17.6%	3.4%	9.8%	12.0%
% open ground/ terrestrial (p)	12.7%	19.1%	18.6%	14.8%	10.5%	16.5%	10.8%	20.0%	11.8%	9.1%	5.9%	13.8%	9.8%	8.0%

Table 5.12 The proportions of the ecological grouping of Coleoptera.

119

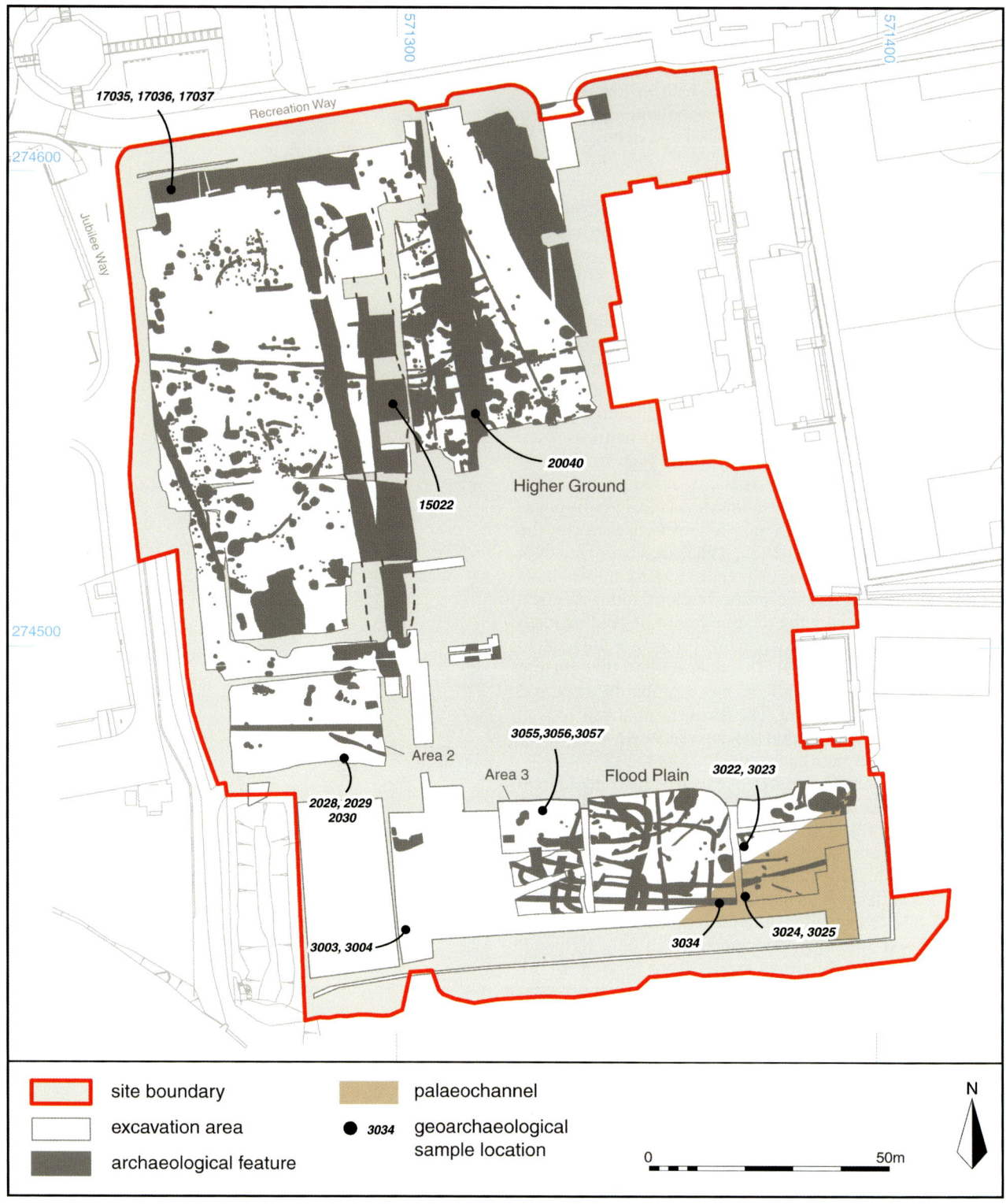

Figure 5.10 Location of geoarchaeological samples

analysed for snails. A series of eighteen monoliths was initially examined and described, and two sequences through medieval alluvium and peat (monoliths 3022–3023) and the prehistoric to medieval alluvium (monoliths 3055–57) were examined in more detail.

Topography, geology and soils
The site lies on the northern side of the river Lark. A limited area of level floodplain is present immediately adjacent to the water course, and the land rises clearly but

gently northwards, from the peat and valley alluvium onto the Middle Chalk. Pelo-alluvial soils and gleyic alluvial sandy brown earths are mapped in the valley, and typical brown calcareous earths (Swaffham Prior Association) over the Middle Chalk.

In the wider landscape we can see that the Lark valley traverses Cretaceous Chalk through most of its course above Mildenhall. However, the Lark valley does contain a buried Pleistocene channel, the base of which is at a level of -40m OD (Bridgland and Lewis 1991), and is a part of

Monolith	contexts	Profile summary – archaeologist's descriptions	Associated samples
Alluvial sequences			
3034	3593, 3612, 3613	Period 2 Late Bronze Age – Palaeochannel 3617	snails, pollen
3055	5118, 5203, 5128, 5131	Alluvial sequence prehistoric to medieval	-
3056	5131, 5233, 5234, 5128	Alluvial sequence prehistoric to medieval	-
3057	5234, 5235, 5236, 5241	Alluvial sequence prehistoric to medieval	-
3022	3080, 3081, 3083	Alluvial sequence Roman to medieval	-
3023	3083, 3131, 3250, 3251, 3147	Alluvial sequence Roman to medieval	-
3024	3080, 3081, 3130, 3083, 3131	Alluvial sequence Roman to medieval	-
3025	3130, 3083, 3131, 3249, 3252	Alluvial sequence Roman to medieva	-
3003	3015, 3016	Medieval 'peat'	pollen
3004	3016	Medieval 'peat'	pollen
2028	2049, 2010, 2050, 2051	Medieval 'peat' over alluvium sequence base Anglo Saxon	-
2029	2051, 2039	Medieval 'peat' over alluvium sequence base Anglo Saxon	-
2030	2051, 2039, 2086	Medieval 'peat' over alluvium sequence base Anglo Saxon	-
Ditch sequences			
20040	20541, 21186, 21272	Ditch 20496: M-LIA bank and soil dump	-
17035	17383	Ditch 1 [17384]: Medieval soils/turf	snails
17036	17383, 17382	Ditch 1 [17384]: Medieval soils/turf	snails
17037	17393	Ditch 1 [17384]: Medieval soils/turf	-
15022	15582, 15416, 15581	Ditch 15415: Medieval ditch turf	-

Table 5.13 List of monolith samples with sampled contexts, profile and phase summary

the buried valley system called the 'Lark Valley Complex' and contains a series of quartzose gravels. Other Pleistocene sediments include till, glaciofluvial outwash, fluvial sands (*e.g.* Warren Hill sands, Wymer *et al.* 1991), and gravels, silts and clays, solifluction deposits and coversands. These are all significant as they may occur as primary or redeposited sediments in the Lark valley floodplain at Mildenhall.

Geoarchaeology
The monoliths for each profile were laid out in spatial orientation to each other, following the field section drawings. The exposed surfaces were cleaned and the upper surface sediment removed to expose clean, unsmeared and unweathered surfaces. These were described following pedological notation given by Hodgson (1976) and ditch infill sequence terminology outlined by Evans (1972), Limbrey (1975) and Allen (1995a). The sequences were examined with section/profile data provided by the archaeologists and with the specific sample-orientated questions and the aims given below. The monolith samples are listed in Table 5.13 by profile and divided into the sampled ditch sequences, and the alluvial and palaeochannel profiles.

Five alluvial sequences were sampled; three of which included a deposit described as 'peat', which were sampled to define deposition character of the alluvial and sediments, and in particular the nature of the 'peat'

deposits. Other sampled alluvial sequences provided important or long time-frame records of potential changes in the history of the floodplain or channel.

Alluvial sequences sampling medieval 'peat' 3081 (monoliths 3022, 3023, 3024 and 3025)
(Tables 5.16, 5.19)
Two sequences were sampled and described; that in monoliths 3024 and 3025 (Table 5.19), and that in 3022 and 3023 (Table 5.16). In both, context 3081 is present, and is described as 'silty peaty clay', although the nature of the full sequence required explanation. The basal deposit 3251 is a sand with some gravel and may relate to higher-energy floodplain events, possibly relating to late glacial gravel meltwaters, or early post-glacial fluvial environments. Deposits above this are sands and gravels 3252 or sands, fluvially sorted from deposits below them (3131, 3147). Some possible channels are present, infilled with silty clay loams 3249, and sandy silts 3131, which mark the onset of a fine-grained alluvial facies which is defined by the dark-grey sandy silts 3083 and 3130. A very dark greyish-brown to very dark grey humic silty clay 3081 is present within both sampled sequences, but is more pronounced at the location sampled by monolith 3022. This is a minerogenic humic silt, with some evidence of waterlogging and local highly humifed peat. It is calcareous or shows distinct flushes of calcium carbonate, indicating that pollen preservation is likely to

Monolith sequence: 3055, 3056, 3057				Archaeological question: Nature of the deposits and deposition – anthropogenic vs natural and retting potential
Depth (cm)	*context*	*Phase*	-	*Description and interpretation*
0–32	-	-	-	Monolith sample disturbed but descriptions made but no *in situ* structure recorded
0–12	5118a	Medieval	Humic slightly stony silt	Grey (10YR 5/1) silt with rare small and very rare medium chalk pieces [some compact possibly medium blocky structure possibly present] Overbank alluvium
12–28	5118b	Medieval	Humic	Dark grey (10YR 3/1) silt with clear moderate, medium blocky structure, rare and small chalk pieces [sediment disturbed] Overbank alluvium
28–31	?5203	Medieval	Humic	Dark grey (10YR 5/1) humic silt, rare small chalk pieces, possible large crumb structure [very disturbed monolith sample], ?abrupt boundary It is not possible to determine if this is a turf, but no pedogenesis beneath so this is probably an alluvial humic inwash — overbank alluvium
31–42	5128	Medieval	Humic	Very dark greyish brown to dark greyish brown (10YR 3/2–4/2) silty clay loam with rare medium chalk, no structure discernible — fine terrestrial shells present, clear boundary Humic overbank alluvium
42–63	5131	Roman	Humic	As above but denser and firmer — Very dark greyish brown to dark greyish brown (10YR 3/2–4/2) silty clay loam with rare medium chalk, v rare shells fragments, no structure discernible
63–65	5233	Prehistoric/ Iron Age	Stone-free mineral silt	— at 63cm a fine chalk lens
65–76	5234a	Prehistoric	Stone-free	Dark greyish brown (10YR 4/2) calcareous silt to silt loam with rare medium stones, common chalk flecks, clear boundary Humic overbank alluvium
76–97	5234b	Prehistoric	Stone-free	Grey (10YR 6/1–5/1) compact stone-free calcareous silt, some weak incipient structure noted, abrupt boundary
97–101	5235	Prehistoric	Stone-free	Brownish yellow (10YR 6/6) fine sand lens with rare small subrounded flint and chalk pieces, abrupt boundary Sand inwash event
101–121	5236	Prehistoric	Stone-free	Grey (10YR 5/1) stone-free compact sandy silt loam
121–130+	5241	Prehistoric	Stone-free	Grey to dark grey (10YR 5/1–4/1) darker sandy silt

Table 5.14 Periods 1–3 to Period 7 alluvial sequence

be poor. This probably formed in wet low-lying floodplain environments, with pools of standing water fed by overbank flooding events depositing sand, and fine stones. It is sealed by a humic alluvial soil 3080.

Medieval alluvial sequences (monoliths 3055, 3056, 3057) (Fig 5.11, Table 5.14)
Three monoliths sampled 1.30m of profile, with relatively complex stratigraphy (Fig 5.11). Portions of the upper part of the profile, especially context 5118, but also contexts 5128 and 5131, were considered as possible medieval dump horizons, whilst the underlying contexts 5234 and 5236 were considered to have formed 'naturally'. The field section drawings, however, indicate fairly large-scale linear and horizontal deposition of all the contexts sampled.

As with other alluvial sequences, the basal deposits sampled were sandier facies 5241. Overlying this were grey and greyish-brown silt loams (5236 and 5234), separated by a thin band of fine sand inwash 5235. These represent overbank alluvial facies separated by a sandy flood deposit, indicating episodic higher-energy isolated floodplain inundation events. The finer-grained alluvial facies 5236 and 5234) were compact and calcareous, with some evidence of soil formation indicating alluvial soils developing on a floodplain. They become more calcareous over time, and were sealed by a fine (20mm thick) chalk lens. This too may represent an alluvial outwash event, or could represent the deposition of chalk on the floodplain

for liming or to make surfaces in, or across, the floodplain. These deposits are cut by channel or ditch 5111.

Contexts above this (5131 and 5128) show no evidence on visual inspection of mass deposition by anthropogenic means. They are weakly calcareous, homogenous silty loams probably largely derived from overbank flooding in the floodplain environments and development of alluvial soils. Some terrestrial shells are present, but samples have been not been taken or assessed for snails from these deposits. Pollen survival is unlikely, due to the biotic mixing and calcareous base-rich nature of the deposits. These deposits are cut by channel or ditch 5232.

A thin horizon 5203 occurs across this alluvial stratigraphy, and is recorded elsewhere as overlying a Roman or Saxon 'chalk-rich layer 5200'. It was recorded at 70mm thick in monolith 3055, but was disturbed and did not survive in the sample as intact undisturbed sediments (Table 5.14). Although possible, it seems unlikely that this is a turf horizon, and may represent inwash or more humic, nutrient-rich muddy deposits as a result of overbank flooding in which some soil formation occurred and vegetation grew. The upper context, 5118, was severely disturbed in the sample, but probably represents an alluvial soil which developed in overbank floodplain alluvium. The presence of thin inwash deposits (e.g. contexts 5235, 5233 and 5203) indicate seasonal alluvial flood deposit events of slightly higher energy, but their preserved presence indicates their burial by ensuing

Depth (cm)	context	Sub samples (pollen)	Description and interpretation
0–8	3593	4cm	Very dark greyish brown (10YR 3/2) humic sandy silt loam, rare medium chalk pieces, no structure observed, clear boundary Humic channel alluvium
8–23	3593	8cm 12cm 16cm 20cm	Dark brown (10YR 3/3) humic silty loam, stone-free, rare fine, waterlogged wood/plant matter present, clear boundary Humic channel alluvium
23–34	3612	24cm 32cm 40cm	Dark brown (10YR 3/3) sandy humic silt, rare very small stones. Less waterlogged plant matter present than above, clear to gradual boundary Not peat but a humic alluvial soil/humic channel fill
44–50+	3613	48cm	Pale brown (10YR 6/3) to light brownish grey (10YR 6/2) medium to fine sand with rare very small stones Sandy channel fill

Table 5.15 Period 2 Late Bronze Age, fill 3612 Palaeochannel 3617

floodplain alluviation, suggesting a relatively dynamic floodplain environment.

Palaeochannel 3617
(Table 5.15)
In contrast to the accumulatory alluvial sequences sampled, one sequence through 'sandy peats' in palaeochannel 3617 was sampled (monolith 3034), and the deposits are considered to be 'natural' and pre-date even the Period 2 Late Bronze Age activity on site (Table 5.15). The aim of sampling was to recover dating evidence and information about the formation of these deposits; the upper contact of these 'peat' deposits with the overlying context 3598 was not sampled. Deposits 3612 and 3593, described as 'peat', overlay fine sand 3613, probably a well-sorted early channel-bed deposit. The deposits above are waterlogged minerogenic sandy humic silts, with waterlogged plant matter and wood present, particularly in the lower portion of 3593. These represent humic channel infill deposits, which accumulated as water flow decreased and vegetation growth within the channel increased. They are, therefore, relating to the last phases of the infilling channel, rather than during its phase of a free-flowing water course.

Medieval 'peat' 2050 over alluvium (monoliths 2028, 2029, 2030)
A sequence of 1.30m of sediment was sampled and described (Table 5.20). The basal deposit sampled (2086) was a compact, calcareous gravel, representing a high-energy, possibly channel, or near channel, deposit. The unsorted deposits above are typical of broadly-banded overbank floodplain alluvium (2039), with a broadly-banded sandier, slightly humic, possible floodplain alluvium (2051) above. Deposited and formed over this is a black, greasy stone-free humic silt (2050) described in the field as peat. It contains no vegetative material even when examined with hand lens and low power stereo-binocular microscope, and is largely minerogenic 'gyttja' comprising a fine-grained, nutrient-rich organic mud, typical of slow-moving or closed bodies of water. It is possible that this deposit may be related to flax-retting pools.

Cessation of deposition of this gyttja was followed by alluviation (overbank floodplain alluvium) and soil formation (pedogenesis). There is no obvious evidence of

continued deposition of the fine-grained nutrient-rich mud (2050), indicating a change in land-use and of floodplain environments. The upper deposit sampled (2007) is an overbank floodplain alluvium, with evidence of both soil formation and disturbance.

Medieval 'peat' 3016 (monoliths 3003, 3004)
(Table 5.22)
The upper portion of an exposed 'peat' (3016) was sampled in two overlapping monoliths (50cm in monolith

Figure 5.11 The alluvial sequence showing pre-Roman minerogenic silts overlain by humic floodplain soils

Monolith sequence: 3022, 3023				Archaeological question: Nature of the deposits — anthropogenic vs natural and retting potential
Depth (cm)	context	Phase	-	Description and interpretation
0–18	3080	Medieval	Humic slightly stony silt	Dark grey (10YR 4/1) firm, dense sandy silt, with rare medium chalk pieces at top of sampled sequence (0–3cm), then rare small and fine chalk pieces, clear to abrupt boundary Humic alluvium / alluvial soil
18–30	3081	Medieval	Humic slightly stony silt	Very dark grey (10YR 3/1) dense humic silty clay, firm and stiff stone-free, no structure evidence, but some reprecipitated or redeposited calcium carbonate within drying cracks, abrupt boundary. Called peat by archaeologists but is a fine-grained humic silt settled in fluvial/aqueous conditions (almost a gyttja)
30–73	3083	Roman	Humic slightly stony silt	Dark grey (10YR 4/1) sandy silt, rare small chalk pieces, many very small chalk flecks, some large at base of context Alluvial facies
73–77	transition	Roman	-	Transition – weathered interface
77–81	3131/3147	Roman	Stone-free mineral silt/ sands	Light yellowish brown (10YR 6/4) silty sand, rare small and medium chalk pieces Sorted/weathered parent material
81–84+	3251	Roman	Stone-free	Light yellowish brown (10YR 6/4) silty sand, many fine flint gravel Parent material

Table 5.16 Period 5 Roman to Period 7 medieval alluvial sequences sampling medieval 'peat' 3081

Monolith sequence: 17035, 17036, 17039			Archaeological question:
Depth (cm)	context	Phase	Description and interpretation
0–11	17380	Iron Age	0-6cm void. White (2.5Y 8/1) chalk marl with common small and medium chalk pieces, evidence of other large chalk pieces missing, abrupt boundary Dump — damp derived slump — backfill
11–38	17381	Iron Age	Dark yellowish brown (10YR 4/4) sandy silt loam, rare chalk pieces, no structure, clear to abrupt boundary B horizon (subsoil) derived material
38–69	17382	Iron Age	Abundant loose medium and large chalk pieces no matrix, abrupt boundary Chalk dump
69–143	17305	Iron Age	Dark yellowish brown (10YR 4/6) essentially stone-free sandy silt loam, some chalk inclusions at base Soil derived fill — no chalky primary fill present

Table 5.17 Period 3 Middle Iron Age Ditch 1, slot/intervention 17384

Monolith sequence: 20040			Archaeological question: Infill history and materials
Depth (cm)	context	Phase	Description and interpretation
0–13	?	Iron Age	Abundant medium and rare large chalk pieces in a dark brown (10YR 3/3) calcareous silt loam with very many small chalk flecks, sharp boundary. Dump possibly 20542
13–27	20541	Iron Age	Dark greyish brown to greyish brown (10YR 4/2–3//2) calcareous silt to silt loam with rare small and medium chalk pieces, abrupt boundary Material derived from B horizon or A/B horizon — no evidence of in situ turf or pedogenesis in small 'window' provided by monolith samples
27–36	21186	Iron Age	Abundant small and medium chalk pieces in a light brownish grey (10YR 6/2) calcareous silt Chalk primary fill or dump
36–50+	21186/ 21272	Iron Age	Brown (10YR 5/3) calcareous silt, common small chalk pieces, rare charcoal flecks/pieces

Table 5.18 Period 3 Middle Iron Age Ditch 5 intervention/slot 20496

Monolith sequence: 3024, 3025			Archaeological question: Nature of the deposits — anthropogenic vs natural and retting potential
Depth (cm)	context	Phase	Description and interpretation
0–12	3080	-	missing
`12–24	3081	Medieval	Very dark greyish brown (10YR 3/2) loose weak silty humic loam loose, and weak, clear boundary — not as clearly defined as in 3022, more redeposited calcium carbonate that in 3022 Called peat by archaeologists but is a fine-grained humic silt settled in fluvial/aqueous conditions
24–38	3130	Medieval	Dark grey (10YR 4/1) sandy silt, largely stone-free excepting fine chalk flecks Alluvial facies
38–46	3183	Roman	Dark grey (10YR 4/1) sandy silt, with rare small stones (as above but rare stones)
46–53	3131	Roman	(10YR 3/2) Firm sandy silt, rare stones Sandy silt overbank alluvium
53–75	3249	Roman	Yellowish brown (10YR 5/6) silty clay loam,
75–84+	3252	Roman	Brown (10YR 4/3) coarse sand rare stones slightly humic Weathered/mixed parent material

Table 5.19 Period 5 Roman to Period 7 medieval alluvial sequences sampling medieval 'peat' 3081

Monolith sequence: 2028, 2029, 2030			Archaeological question:
Depth (cm)	context	Phase	Description and interpretation
0–9	2007	-	Dark grey to very dark grey (10YR 4/1–5/1) silty loam, unsorted some fine chalk pieces, weak blocky structure, clear boundary Overbank alluvium, some pedogenesis and disturbance
9–24	2010	Medieval	Dark grey (10YR 4/1) silty loam as above, but with many fine and very small stones, clear to abrupt boundary
18–27	2050	Medieval	Black (10YR 2/1) greasy stone-free humic silt (to silty clay) (described as peaty), clear to abrupt boundary Sorted humic silt nutrient-rich mud — gyttja — slow aqueous deposition
27–35	2051a	Medieval	Yellowish brown (10YR 5/4) humic fine sandy loam, with a zone of gleying
35–54	2051b	Medieval	Very dark greyish brown (10YR 3/2) slightly humic silty clay loam, stone-free, broadly banded, abrupt boundary
54–86	2039	Saxon	Brown (10YR 4/3) fine sandy loam , common small stones clear to abrupt boundary
81–106	2039	Saxon	Yellowish brown(10YR 5/4) sandy loam, many small chalk flecks, clear boundary
106–110+	2086	Saxon	Compact calcareous gravel and calcareous sandy matrix Alluvial — possible channel or near channel deposits

Table 5.20 Period 6–7 Saxon alluvium to medieval 'peat' 2050

Monolith sequence: 15022			Archaeological question: Is 15416 a turfline?
Depth (cm)	context	Phase	Description and interpretation
0–9	15417	Medieval	Void
9–35	15416	Medieval	Dark greyish brown (10YR 4/3) calcareous silty clay loam, many very fine chalk flecks, otherwise essentially stone-free, massive, clear boundary A or B horizon soil material, not turf per se or likely to be stacked turfs or a developed soil
35–44	15582	Medieval	Compact small and medium chalk pieces in a light brownish grey (10YR 6/2) silty loam, clear boundary Primary fill
44–50+	15581	Medieval	Brown (10YR 5/3) calcareous silty loam, some chalk pieces Primary fill

Table 5.21 Period 7 medieval Ditch 2 intervention/slot 15415

Monolith sequence: 3003, 3004 (30–55cm)			Archaeological question: Nature of the deposits — retting potential
Depth (cm)	context	Sub samples (pollen)	Description and interpretation
0–0.5	3015	-	Dark dark greyish brown calcareous silty clay, stone-free, abrupt boundary
0.5–4.5	3015	-	White small and medium chalk with no matrix, sharp boundary
4.5–55+	3016	6cm 18cm 30cm 42cm 54cm	4.5–55cm very dark grey to black (10YR 3/1–2/1) dense humic silty (peat), with fine sand inclusions, rare stones From 4.5 to 17.5cm humified oxidised dark reddish brown peat, finely but weakly laminated or bedded, some roots and vegetative material From 44cm black humified silty peat rare plant matter Humified silty peat

Table 5.22 Period 7 medieval 'peat' 3016

3003 and 25cm in monolith 3004) (Table 5.22). The basal contact of this deposit was not sampled. This deposit is in excess of 50cm thick, and is very dark grey to black, dense humic silty peat. It has formed *in situ* by the decay of vegetation in anaerobic, waterlogged conditions, with plant matter and wood preserved in the upper portion at least. The presence of sand, stones and some minerogenic silt indicate some alluvial inwash, probably by flooding. The silty peat is capped by a deliberate dump of chalk and chalky marl (3015).

Discussion
The majority of the deposits sampled in the alluvial sequences are overbank alluvium. Most are underlain by sands or sands and gravels thought to have derived from late glacial, or early post-glacial, outwash rivers. These were overlain by minerogenic sands or silts, which were dated as pre-Roman and Iron Age, or earlier. Most of the deposits described as 'peat' or 'peaty' in the field are alluvial minerogenic humic silts, rather than peats, and are of Medieval or Roman date. These are, therefore, transported and deposited sediments, rather than evidence of *in-situ* peat development. This represents gradual incremental development of floodplain alluvial soils, by seasonal flooding. Some occasional higher-energy flooding events are also indicated. The deposits become more calcareous over time, possibly suggesting the thinning of chalky soils on the slopes within the catchment of the Lark.

In situ peat and minerogenic silty peats were only identified in one sequence, where medieval context 3016 is a peat. One deposit of a fine-grained nutrient-rich mud or gyttja (context 2050) indicates the presence of still water, possibly a pool that may be related to flax-retting.

It is clear, however, that there is major change from the pre-Roman deposition of minerogenic fine sands and silts to Roman and principally medieval humic overbank floodplain deposits, with humic pasture soils developing in probably seasonally wetland conditions.

Ditch fill sequences
All of the sampled ditch sequences were consistent, in that typical primary, secondary and tertiary infills were not immediately identifiable. In particular, the loose chalk rubbles typical of primary fills were largely absent, indicating either that the ditches had been cleaned out after the ditch sides had become stable, or that the chalk is particularly hard, strongly structured, and not prone to such extensive weathering as elsewhere. A humic

soil-material fill or layer was common to all three sampled profiles of both Iron Age and medieval date.

Period 3 Middle Iron Age Ditch 5 intervention/slot 20496 (Table 5.18)
A monolith through a sequence of ditch fills sampled the full profile of context 20541 (Table 5.18), thought by the excavators to be 'original soil surface ... slumping into the ... ditch'. The material is an unsorted, soil-derived deposit, and like the others sampled, no structure, earthworm-worked zones, banding or evidence of soil development or weathering of the contact zone below, was present to indicate *in-situ* soil development.

Period 7 medieval Ditch 2 intervention/slot 15415 (Table 5.21)
A series of soil-based chalky primary fills occur, of which two were sampled and described (15581 and 15582) (Table 5.21). A distinctive context (15416) was considered in the field by the excavators to be a 'turf-line deposit'. This certainly comprises calcareous 'topsoil' material derived from humic rendzina soils (A horizon material) of calcareous brown earths (A and B horizon material), but there are no structures indicating either *in-situ* soil development or banding and stone-free and stony zones suggesting the presence of stacked turves.

Period 3 Middle Iron Age Ditch 1 slot/intervention 17384 (Table 5.17)
The high content of soil matrix in primary fill 17305 is unusual from a chalk-cut ditch. The dense non-matrix supported chalk 17382 that lies above this is unlikely to result from weathering-back of the ditch sides, and is, as noted in the field, likely to comprise deliberated deposited and dumped clean chalk. This was probably recently excavated, or derived from a chalk bank or mound. A dark yellowish-brown sandy loam (context 17381) lies unconformably above the chalk dump, indicating that it had been deposited on, rather than developed in, the chalk dump. Although clearly soil material, its unsorted nature, lack of any pedological structure, evidence of banding, worm-worked horizons (stone-free and stony lenses) both in the monolith sample and as depicted in the field drawings, suggest that this is not a result of either soil formation, or turves stacked in the ditch. It is, however, derived from soil material, and like the examples above, is from A horizon material (rendzina) or A and B horizon material from calcareous brown earths. This earthy deposit is sealed, again unconformably, by dumped chalk and calcareous marl. This suggests episodes of deliberate

backfill from two discrete and individual (albeit close) sources.

Discussion

Overall the sampled ditches all show untypical primary fills, from which we suggest that the chalk here is very hard and slow weathering, or that the ditches have been cleaned out and earlier chalk rubble primary fills removed. The soil material present (*e.g.* 15416, 17381 and 20541) all indicate the presence of deposited or dumped soil material derived from A or A and B horizons from shallow rendzina soils, or calcareous brown earths, respectively.

In situ peat and minerogenic silty peats were only identified in one sequence where medieval context 3016 is a peat. One deposit was a fine-grained nutrient-rich mud or gyttja (context 2050) indicates the presence of still water, possibly a pool that may be related to retting.

It is clear, however, that major change occurred from the pre-Roman deposition of minerogenic fine sands and silts, to Roman and principally medieval humic overbank floodplain deposits, with humic pasture soils developing in probably seasonal wetland conditions.

Land snails (Mollusca)

(Table 5.23)

Flots of the bulk samples processed by standard flotation methods by Cotswold Archaeology were dried and examined under a ×10 – ×30 stereo-binocular microscope. The species present were identified and quantified, and the results are given in Table 5.23. Mollusc nomenclature follows Anderson R. (2005).

Analyses are of shells from the flots only, and some bias may exist, as the residues to 0.5mm may contain identifiable and quantifiable shell fragments, including species less likely to be recovered in the flots (Evans 1972). In colluvial deposits (*e.g.* tertiary ditch fills), the assemblages are frequently more fragmented, and often *c.* 60% of the entire assemblage may be recovered from the residues.

An important consideration is the taphonomy of the assemblages, as some originate from pits and ditches which include species derived from the immediate surroundings, as well as those that might inhabit the micro-environment created by the features. Others relate to overbank flooding of the Lark and floodplain environs (*i.e.* allochthonous), and some may relate to freshwater species inhabiting some of the features (*i.e.* autochthonous), such as larger ditches. Nevertheless, this allows us to attempt to characterise the upper land, the floodplain and the nature of the River Lark itself.

The samples are restricted to single bulk samples from specific contexts, so these samples did not provide an opportunity for examining *change* through time at individual locales. Sequences of small (0.5 litre) subsamples were removed at between 6cm and 10cm contiguous intervals from monoliths through the sequences of the Iron Age Ditch 1 (17384; monoliths 17635–37), the medieval (13–14th century) alluvial sequence (monoliths 3055–3057), the medieval alluvial sequences sampling medieval 'peat' 3081 (monoliths 3022–23). A total of 37 samples were removed (256g–498g), and processed for land snails following standard method (Evans 1972), but unfortunately few samples contained enough shells to offer statistically

viable analysis, and none of the three sampled sequences contained enough samples with shells to examine through time.

As the bulk samples examined were primarily taken for charred remains, they were from largely cultural, rather than palaeo-environmental deposits. Many of the sampled contexts, especially in pits and wells, represent anthropogenically re-deposited or dumped material, rather than natural sedimentation. As such, these contexts may contain material derived from unknown or undefined locations elsewhere (Shackley 1976). Shells may have been introduced from these locations which do not represent the environment of the pit, well or ditch, but are representative of local habitats. Even in naturally accumulated deposits, extraneous shells may be incorporated by overbank flooding events, often including permanently aquatic species ejected from streams or rivers. Interpretation here attempts to take account of these factors and the origin of the snails, especially when considering the nature of the aquatic species.

Sampled sequences

The eleven samples selected for analysis cover the Late Bronze to medieval periods and, importantly, are from the wetter floodplain edge at the south of the site, as well as the higher drier chalk land to the north. Some the changes in the reported assemblages relate to these spatial differences rather than changes through time. The assemblages are principally of terrestrial or freshwater species reflecting this division.

Terrestrial assemblages – the dryland

None contain shade-loving species, and are thus all generally indicative of open-country conditions. Whether the terrestrial elements comprised long grassland, grazed short-turfed grassland or arable were difficult to determine from analysis.

All the terrestrial assemblages from Late Bronze Age to medieval contexts are dominated by open-country species (46–97%). None contain any significant shade-loving fauna, the highest being the 6% represented probably by the microhabitat of the sampled pit. Little significant change can be seen over time (though we are examining only seven samples representing 2,500 years). These assemblages are characterised by the super-abundance of *Pupilla muscorum*, with *Helicella itala*, *Trochulus hispidus* and *Vallonia* spp. This suggests open, dry short grassland (grazed or trampled) conditions (*cf.* Chappell *et al.* 1971), and the general paucity of *Pomatias elegans* and other loose-soil tolerating species suggests that these open, dry conditions do not represent tillage.

Slum species (*Succinea/Oxyloma* and Vertignids including *Vertigo moulinsiana*) occur in some samples (Iron Age pits 16063 and 16101, indicating damp conditions in these features as a result of high groundwater tables and possibly occasional overbank flooding events. One planorbid was recovered from Iron Age Ditch 1 (17384), located at the northerly extreme of the excavation further from the floodplain and the habitat source of the mollusc, the River Lark. The super-abundance of *P. muscorum* is noted in short-turfed grazed grassland, as reported by Allen and Wyles (1994) from Bronze Age barrows at King Barrow Ridge, Wiltshire, but is also a feature of floodplain pasture (Davies 1999; Davies and Grimes 1999; Davies *et al.* 1996). The few intermediate

	6	6	5	2	7	4	4	4	4	3	2
Period	6	6	5	2	7	4	4	4	4	3	2
Feature	Saxon	Saxon	Roman	LBA	Med	IA	IA	IA	IA	MIA	LBA
	Layer	layer	ditch	channel	ditch	pit	pit	pit	ditch	ditch	pit
Feature	-	-	20	-	1	16101	16063	20119	1	1	20238
segment	-	-	3718	3617	17384	-	-	-	15625	17384	-
Context	2086	2086	3717	3593	17383	16100	16064	20127	15692	17381	21320
Sample	2031	2041	3039	3035	17038	16001	16003	20001	15023	17039	20053
Wt (g)/ vol (L)	-	-	-	-	-	-	-	-	-	-	-
MOLLUSCA											
Pomatias elegans (Müller)					+	+					1
Carychium cf. minimum Müller								1 [+1]	1		
Carychium tridentatum (Risso)								2 [+4]			
Carychium sp.					1						
Succinea putris (Linnaeus)			4								
Succinea cf. putris (Linnaeus)			6					1			
Oxyloma elegans (Risso)			1			1					
Oxyloma cf. sarsi (Esmark)			1								
Cochlicopa cf. lubrica (Müller)	2	1	2		5		1			1	2
Cochlicopa cf. lubricella (Porro)					4	1					3
Cochlicopa spp.	1					1				1	
Truncatellina cylindrica (Férussac)									1		
Vertigo antivertigo (Draparnaud)								1			
Vertigo cf. antivertigo (Draparnaud)								2			
Vertigo substriata (Jeffreys)								6			
Vertigo pygmaea (Draparnaud)					2		6	2			
Vertigo cf. pygmaea (Draparnaud)	2										
Vertigo moulinsiana (Dupuy)								3			
Vertigo sp.											1
Pupilla muscorum (Linnaeus)	3		2		418	124	36	123 [+46]	136	471	67 [+2]
Vallonia costata (Müller)					8	1		6	3	16	6
Vallonia pulchella (Müller)						3		[1]	1		
Vallonia cf. pulchella (Müller)					3						1
Vallonia excentrica/pulchella		1	1					9 [+7]			
Vallonia cf. excentrica Sterki	1				34	10	10		6	16	14
Vallonia spp.						2					
Punctum pygmaeum (Draparnaud)								1 [+1]			
Discus rotundatus (Müller)						1					
Vitrina pellucida (Müller)										1	

Table 5.23 Mollusca from analysed samples

Taxon									
Vitrea crystallina (Müller)	–	–	–	–	–	–	–	–	–
Vitrea contracta (Westerlund)	–	–	–	–	–	1	–	–	–
Nesovitrea hammonis (Ström)	–	1	1	–	–	–	1	–	–
Aegopinella nitidula (Drapamaud)	1	–	–	–	[1]	–	–	–	–
Euconulus cf. *fulvus* (Müller)	1	–	–	–	[1]	–	–	–	–
Cecilioides acicula (Müller)	4	–	6	–	277	–	169	68	4
Helicella itala (Linnaeus)	14	–	56	12	66	12 [+3]	5	12	14
Candidula gigaxii (L. Pfeiffer)	–	–	–	–	1	–	2	–	–
Trochulus striolatus (C. Pfeifer)	1	–	–	–	7	–	3	–	–
Trochulus hispidus (Linnaeus)	17	–	12	6	78	15 [+4]	62	48	5
Cepaea spp.	1	–	2	2	2	–	–	–	+
Cornus aspersum (Müller)	–	–	+	–	+	–	+	–	–
FRESH-BRACKISH-WATER									
Valvata cristata Müller	–	–	–	–	–	–	–	–	–
Valvata piscinalis (Müller)	6	–	10	–	–	–	–	–	–
Bithynia tentaculata (Linnaeus)	10 (14)	2 (3)	14 (17)	–	–	–	–	–	–
Galba truncatula (Müller)	3	–	26	–	–	–	–	–	–
Lymnaea stagnalis (Linnaeus)	–	–	7	–	–	–	–	–	–
Planorbis planorbis (Linnaeus)	–	–	24	–	–	–	–	–	–
Planorbis carinatus (Müller)	13	–	27	5	–	1	–	–	–
Planorbis sp.	–	–	8	–	–	–	–	–	–
Anisus leucostoma (Millet)	6	–	202	–	–	–	–	–	–
Anisus vortex (Linnaeus)	–	–	3	–	–	–	–	–	–
Bathyomphalus contortus (Linnaeus)	2	–	–	–	–	–	–	–	–
Gyraulus crista (Linnaeus)	5	–	4	–	–	–	–	–	–
Hippeutis companatus (Linnaeus)	1	–	2	–	–	–	–	–	–
Pisidium nitidum Jeyns	–	–	–	–	–	–	–	–	–
MARINE									
Mytilus edulis	–	–	–	–	+	–	–	–	–
Taxa	16	3	18	2	12	6	18	12	10
Total Freshwater	**46**	**2**	**327**	**5**	**1**	**0**	**0**	**0**	**0**
Total Terrestrial	**30**	**2**	**38**	**1**	**597**	**123**	**256**	**168**	**115**
TOTAL	**76**	**4**	**365**	**6**	**598**	**123**	**256**	**168**	**115**
% freshwater	61	50	90	83	0	0	0	0	0

Figures in square parentheses are [burnt], in round parentheses are (operculum)

Table 5.23 Mollusca from analysed samples

129

and shade-loving species (*Nesovitrea, Vitrea* and *Aegopinella*) in pit 15129 (assessment data), pit 20119, and Ditch 1 cut (17384) hint at slightly more mesic conditions, possibly the micro-habits of the features themselves, but also possibly slightly longer, more mesic grassland. The presence, in Iron Age pit 20119, of the stenotopic marsh-loving species, *Vertigo moulinsiana*, which is commonly associated with *Carex* or *Glyceria maxima* on whose stems it lives (Butot and Neuteboom 1958; Bishop 1974; both quoted by Evans *et al.* 1992, 68), indicates fen environments locally, probably on the floodplain and river margins. This pit contained 9% slum or marsh species, including the obligate marsh species *Vertigo antivertigo*. Their presence in this pit might indicate damp, seasonally wet conditions in the pit, overbank flooding, or the exploitation of riverine resources such as reeds, clay or water, as seen on a number of Iron Age hillfort sites (*e.g.* Allen 1995b).

A number of shells were burnt, especially those from pit 20119, where sixty-nine species were clearly burnt, but also Late Bronze Age pit 20238 contained two burnt shells. These confirm the anthropogenic discard of material into these pits, including burnt soil probably derived from hearths and fires.

Wet land assemblages – the floodplain

Four samples from the Late Bronze Age channel 3617, Roman Ditch 20 and Saxon layer 2086 were analysed (Table 5.23). All analysed assemblages were dominated by aquatic and slum species, and two (Roman Ditch 20 and layer 2086) contained enough shells for palaeo-environmental interpretation.

A sample from the Roman Ditch 20 contained 365 shells, of which 90% were freshwater species. The majority of the few open country species were slum and marsh taxa (*Succinea/Oxyloma* sp.). Apart from the amphibious species *Anisus leucostoma* and *Galba truncatula,* representing 62% of the freshwater assemblage (*cf.* Robinson 1988), the majority of the species are ditch aquatic species occurring in slow-moving plant-rich streams (group 3), and moving-water species found in large streams and ponds, where currents or wind affect water movements (group 4) as defined by Sparks (1961), Sparks and West (1959) and Robinson (1988). Dominant among these were *Bithyna tentaculata,* which is common in large bodies of well-oxygenated and slow-moving water (Kerney 1999), and *Planorbis planorbis* and *P. carinatus,* both of which also inhabit well-vegetated water, and are characteristic of swampy pools and running ditches. The assemblage from the Saxon layer 2086 contains a similar but smaller assemblage. Overall, these suggest a large body of well-vegetated slow-moving water, probably the Lark, which provide much of the source material, combined with *Anisus leucostoma* and possibly *G. truncatula* living on the floodplain pasture (Robinson 1988). The assemblage suggests, however, that the Roman ditch may have contained its own aquatic micro-environs (*P. planorbis* and *P. carinatus*) of shallow, swampy running water.

Discussion

Despite the analysis of just a few single bulk samples, some statements can be made about the nature of the local environment and land-use; change through time in the local environment and land-use is more difficult to elucidate.

Landscape character

The area can be clearly divided into the larger northern portion which was essential dry land, supporting open country with short dry grassland sward. This may have been subject to very occasional large winter floods, and rising groundwater tables in the winter may have made for more mesic conditions, especially in the cut features. The lower floodplain of the Lark to the south suggests a moist, mesic floodplain pasture, with a large well-vegetated, fringed and slow-flowing water of the reed-fringed river itself. Features on the floodplain, including ditches and alluvial layers, indicate seasonal overbank flooding, with probably almost permanent running water in the ditch (Ditch 20) and high general groundwater tables and overbank floodplain alluviation (layer 2086).

Land-use

The drier area was clearly open trampled and grazed short grassland pasture, with no clear evidence of any tillage. The exploitation of riverine resources such as reeds, clay or water, may be seen in the presence of aquatic shells in some of the features in the drier areas further from the Lark.

Change through time

The examination of change through time is very difficult, as two distinct and discrete landscapes have been sparsely sampled across a time-span covering the Late Bronze Age to medieval periods. Nevertheless, there is generally an indication of little change in the higher drier land. With only two statistically viable samples (from Roman and Saxon contexts) from the floodplain, little can be said for this area. What is perhaps remarkable is the consistency in the environment as amplified by the pollen analysis (Scaife, Chapter 5.IX).

Conclusion: landscape, landscape change and land-use

The higher drier land was open, and was dominated with grassland used as pasture, with ash, lime oak and hazel at some distance. The floodplain contained wetter marsh species, with reeds, and marsh arrow grass. Initially the 'floodplain' area was a former wide, low-energy channel, depositing minerogenic silts. By the Roman period, it was a smaller, defined channel, with a wide floodplain with a humic rich pasture soil. The River Lark existed as a large, slow-flowing well-vegetated river, with marginal aquatics and reeds, and pondweed. Although the land snails did not suggest arable cultivations, the presence of cereal pollen may indicate cereal cultivation locally and also the use and preparation of cereals on site.

VIII. Plant macrofossils and charcoal
by Sarah Cobain

Introduction

A total of 245 bulk soil samples were processed and assessed for plant macrofossil and charcoal remains. A total of sixty-six plant macrofossil and forty-five charcoal samples containing quantities of well-preserved material were selected for further analysis.

Methodology

Plant macrofossil and charcoal remains were retrieved by standard flotation procedures (CA 2003). The seeds were identified with reference to Cappers *et al.* (2006), Neef *et al.* (2012), Berggren (1981) and Anderberg (1994). Up to 100 charcoal fragments (>2mm) were identified with reference to Gale and Cutler (2000), Schoch *et al.* (2004) and Wheeler *et al.* (1989). Nomenclature of seed and charcoal and habitat information species follows Stace (1997). Taxa have been identified as one of two possibilities (for example emmer/spelt wheat) where the two species exhibit similar morphology but the seeds are not sufficiently preserved to observe subtle anatomical differences required for full identification. Full methodological details are available in the archive.

Results

(Tables 5.24 and 5.25)

Summary results are displayed in Tables 5.24 and 5.25; full results in tabular form are available in the archive and via the internet.

Discussion

Period 2 Late Bronze Age

Arable agriculture in the Early Bronze Age centred around the cultivation of emmer wheat (*Triticum dicoccum*) and barley (*Hordeum vulgare*). However, from the Early to Middle Bronze Age, spelt wheat (*Triticum spelta*) has been identified on sites in southern England and started to become a dominant crop towards the end of the period (Campbell and Straker 2003, 15, 21; Brown and Murphy 1997, 18). At Mildenhall, this period was represented by very few features, and only the largest of these, pit 20238 contained suitable macrofossil remains for analysis. Samples from fills 20336, 20337 and 20325 within recut 22064 of Late Bronze Age pit 20238 were considered valuable for analysis to provide information regarding the adoption of spelt during the Bronze Age, strategies employed in its cultivation and the methods in which harvested crops were processed. The analysis of just one feature limits interpretational value, as the remains within a single pit may not be representative of the full range of crops cultivated at Mildenhall during the period, however some inferences can be made.

Plant remains from this feature were abundant and well preserved consisting principally of barley, spelt wheat and emmer/spelt wheat cereal grains with a small number of identifiable emmer wheat and oat grains (*Avena*) present. As no floret bases were identified, it was not possible to ascertain whether oat was cultivated or wild, but since the oat and emmer wheat were only identified in small quantities their presence is most likely due to crop contamination and/or weed intrusions. Dominance of spelt wheat and barley is typical of the Late Bronze Age period and has also been seen in sites such as North Shoebury, Essex (Murphy 1995, 148) and within a pit and hearth at Greenfields (Site 27/28), Essex (Carruthers 2007, 378–379). Together with Mildenhall these sites support a regional trend towards more widespread use of spelt wheat towards the end of the Bronze Age (Brown and Murphy 1997, 18).

Cereal chaff included a large number of spelt wheat and emmer/spelt wheat glume bases and a small number of culm nodes, straw and a culm base. The composition of this assemblage is consistent with the processing of grain, on a small scale and as required, prior to cooking — the assemblage, rich in glume bases would be expected from emmer/spelt wheat crops, which require parching to free grains from the spikelets (Hillman 1981, 132–133). A similar chaff and grain composition was found at Greenfields (Site 27/28), Essex (Carruthers 2007, 378–379). Barley is not represented in the chaff assemblage, although barley is one of the principal components of the charred grain assemblage. The absence of barley chaff may be a function of the free-threshing nature of barley where no heat is required, hence no requirement for the crop to come into contact with fire (Hillman 1981, 134–135).

The herbaceous taxa assemblage reveals an interesting mixture of species indicative of arable, disturbed pasture, heathland and marshland environments, comprising fertile and infertile, sandy and heavy clay soils. Species present include arable weeds, such as field gromwell (*Lithospermum arvense*) and corn spurrey (*Spergula arvensis*) which are indicative of fertile and fertile sandy soils respectively; annual knawel (*Scleranthus annuus*) which establishes in infertile sandy soils and stinking chamomile (*Anthemis cotula*) which is indicative of infertile heavy clay soils. Bromes (*Bromus*) is an arable weed which grows in fertile soil, although the large number of these identified may also suggest they were being cultivated for use as fodder. Arable and/or disturbed pasture weeds including black-bindweed (*Fallopia convolvulus*), cleavers (*Galium aparine*), small nettle (*Urtica urens*), knotgrass (*Persicaria*), dock (*Rumex*), mallow (*Malva*), goosefoots (*Chenopodium*) and grassland species including thistles (*Cirsium/Carduus*) were present and indicative of fertile soils. Medick/clover (*Medicago/Trifolium*) seeds were also identified and are usually typical of infertile soil. Heaths (*Erica*) seeds, indicative of infertile heathland soil with a high water table and sedge (*Carex*) suggestive of marshland environments, were also present.

The varied range of environments represented by this plant macrofossil assemblage is expected given the location of the site, split between the northern dry ground and southern floodplain areas associated with the River Lark. The relatively high number of species identified which establish in areas of infertile soil is of interest and may suggest increased pressure on land, and encroachment onto more marginal areas. It is also however possible that some crops were brought in from outside and represent environments from outside of the Mildenhall area. The majority of these taxa are between 0.05–1m in height, averaging approximately 0.5m. Since barley and spelt crops grow to approximately 1.5m in height, it indicates crops were harvested close to the base of the plant. The presence of a single culm base suggests crops may also have been uprooted.

Period 3 Middle Iron Age

Plant remains

The plant remains from this period were examined from pits 15129, 15234, 19215, 19215, 20119, 20153, 21389, grave 21305 and Ditch 39. The assemblages were all similar, consisting dominantly of spelt and emmer/spelt wheat cereal grains followed by barley and smaller number of oat and emmer wheat grains along with a large

	Period 2		Periods 3 and 4		Period 5		Period 6		Period 7	
	Sum	%	Sum	%	Sum	%	Sum	%	Sum	%
Herbaceous taxa	-	-	-	-	-	-	-	-	-	-
HSW	0	0.0	22	3.1	13	16.3	16	1.2	39	2.9
M/WL	16	4.8	23	3.3	6	7.5	91	7.0	100	7.6
A/D*	184	55.1	259	36.7	31	38.8	353	27.0	579	43.7
D/A	77	23.1	328	46.5	16	20.0	596	45.6	330	24.9
E	0	0.0	1	0.1	7	8.8	142	10.9	115	8.7
G/D*	29	8.7	66	9.3	7	8.8	99	7.6	79	6.0
He	28	8.4	7	1.0	0	0.0	10	0.8	82	6.2
Cereals	-	-	-	-	-	-	-	-	-	-
Oat grain	11	2.6	16	5.4	14	2.7	888	4.1	978	7.3
Barley grain	117	27.6	77	25.9	137	26.7	5645	26.0	1999	14.9
Rye grain	0	0.0	0	0.0	82	16.0	4061	18.7	3503	26.1
Free-threshing wheat grain	0	0.0	0	0.0	0	0.0	5488	25.3	5411	40.4
Emmer wheat/spelt wheat grain	163	38.4	138	46.5	196	38.1	47	0.2	49	0.4
Indeterminate cereal grains	133	31.4	66	22.2	85	16.5	5597	25.8	1470	11.0
Cereal chaff	-	-	-	-	-	-	-	-	-	-
Wild-oat palea	0	0.0	0	0.0	0	0.0	2	0.1	1	0.1
Cultivated Oat grain and palea	0	0.0	0	0.0	0	0.0	0	0.0	6	0.5
Cultivated Oat palea	0	0.0	0	0.0	0	0.0	5	0.3	5	0.4
Barley rachis internodes	0	0.0	0	0.0	0	0.0	171	11.2	133	10.5
Barley/Rye rachis	0	0.0	0	0.0	2	0.6	865	56.6	374	29.6
Rye rachis	0	0.0	0	0.0	1	0.3	243	15.9	209	16.5
Free-threshing wheat rachis internode	0	0.0	0	0.0	1	0.3	26	1.7	19	1.5
Bread wheat rachis internode (hexaploid wheat)	0	0.0	0	0.0	0	0.0	27	1.8	45	3.6
Pasta wheat rachis internode (tetraploid wheat)	0	0.0	0	0.0	0	0.0	17	1.1	42	3.3
Spelt wheat glume bases	40	31.0	77	26.9	236	73.5	5	0.3	51	4.0
Emmer wheat glume base	0	0.0	1	0.3	0	0.0	0	0.0	0	0.0
Emmer wheat/ spelt wheat glume bases	82	63.6	203	71.0	69	21.5	3	0.2	23	1.8
Awns	0	0.0	0	0.0	0	0.0	5	0.3	0	0.0
Culm node (whole)	3	2.3	4	1.4	9	2.8	128	8.4	305	24.1
Culm base	1	0.8	1	0.3	0	0.0	7	0.5	11	0.9
Palea	0	0.0	0	0.0	0	0.0	17	1.1	15	1.2
Spikelet fork	0	0.0	1	0.3	0	0.0	0	0.0	0	0.0
Straw	3	2.3	0	0.0	3	0.9	8	0.5	24	1.9
Grand totals										
Total Weeds	334	37.7	706	54.8	80	8.7	1307	5.3	1324	8.3
Total grains	424	47.8	297	23.0	514	56.2	21726	88.5	13410	83.8
Total chaff	129	14.5	286	22.2	321	35.1	1529	6.2	1263	7.9
Total (weeds, grains, chaff)	887	100	1289	100	915	100	24562	100	15997	100

Key

A = arable weeds; D = weeds indicative of disturbed environments (opportunistic species); HSW = hedgerow/scrub/woodland species; M = marshland species; WL = wetland species; G = grassland species; He = heathland species; E = economic species (excluding grain)

*where e.g. A/D, G/D are indicated is acknowledge that whilst these species tend to establish in arable/grassland environments, they will also grow opportunistically if conditions allow.

Table 5.24 Plant macrofossil identifications summary (carbonised material)

Table 5.25 Charcoal identifications summary

| Species | Periods 3 and 4 | | | | Period 5 | | Period 6 | | | | Period 7 | | | |
| | Full analysis | | Broad characterisation | | Broad characterisation | | Full analysis | | Broad characterisation | | Full analysis | | Broad characterisation | |
	Sum	%	Sum	%	Sum	%	Sum	%	Sum	%	Sum	%	Sum	%
Viburnums	0	0.0	1	0.7	0	0.0	0	0.0	0	0.0	0	0.0	2	0.7
Alder r/w	0	0.0	0	0.0	0	0.0	2	0.2	0	0.0	1	0.7	0	0.0
Alder/Hazel	64	13.9	9	6.4	18	30.0	327	36.3	17	28.3	37	24.8	59	21.1
Birches	2	0.4	0	0.0	0	0.0	3	0.3	0	0.0	2	1.3	1	0.4
Hazel	3	0.6	1	0.7	1	1.7	143	15.9	10	16.7	0	0.0	20	7.1
Dogwoods	0	0.0	2	1.4	0	0.0	0	0.0	0	0.0	0	0.0	2	0.7
Gorses/Brooms	1	0.2	2	1.4	0	0.0	0	0.0	0	0.0	0	0.0	5	1.8
Beech	4	0.9	0	0.0	0	0.0	0	0.0	0	0.0	0	0.0	0	0.0
Sessile Oak/ Pedunculate Oak	186	40.3	77	55.0	19	31.7	257	28.6	10	16.7	10	6.7	79	28.2
Ash	56	12.1	26	18.6	7	11.7	32	3.5	11	18.3	8	5.4	5	1.8
Alder Buckthorn	0	0.0	0	0.0	0	0.0	1	0.1	0	0.0	6	4.0	0	0.0
Hawthorn/Rowans/ Crab apple	70	15.2	14	10.0	1	1.7	25	2.8	5	8.3	38	25.5	20	7.1
Cherries	38	8.2	2	1.4	0	0.0	0	0.0	0	0.0	2	1.3	5	1.8
Willows/Poplars	7	1.5	3	2.1	12	20.0	96	10.7	1	1.7	42	28.2	70	25.0
Field maple	31	6.7	3	2.1	2	3.3	13	1.4	6	10.0	3	2.0	12	4.3
Wych Elm	0	0.0	0	0.0	0	0.0	1	0.1	0	0.0	0	0.0	0	0.0
Grand total	462	100	140	100	60	100	900	100	60	100	149	100	280	100

Key
Full analysis = up to 100 fragments of charcoal identified
Broad characterisation = up to 20 fragments of charcoal identified

assemblage of cereal chaff including spelt and emmer/spelt glume bases and culm nodes. A relatively large assemblage of bromes was also identified. This type of assemblage is typical of the Iron Age period (Murphy 1997, 30). A similarly proportioned charred cereal assemblage from ditches, pits and structures at Wardy Hill Ringwork, Coveney, Ely, Cambridgeshire was dominated by glume wheat (emmer/spelt) and barley (Murphy 2003, 102, 108–109) and from pits at Bridge House Dairies, Mildenhall, Suffolk (Livarda 2010, 109) along with sites further afield such as Cresswell Field (Pelling 2011, 524) and Yarnton, Oxfordshire (Stevens 2011, 560) where spelt wheat appeared to be a more dominant crop. Spelt wheat and barley would have been used to produce bread, porridge, pottages, animal fodder and to produce beer.

The move from the Late Bronze Age into the Iron Age at Mildenhall demonstrates a continuation in the cultivation of spelt wheat, with abundance increasing from 38.4% in the Late Bronze Age to 46.5% during the Iron Age and barley decreasing from 27.6% to 25.9%. There is also an increase in the number of oats from 2.6% to 5.4%. This being the case it is possible oat was grown alongside bromes for fodder, although it is equally viable that this increase represents an increase in the presence of oats as weeds in crop fields. Emmer wheat, present in such small quantities continues to be considered as a weed intrusion. Spatially, the pits containing cereal grains, chaff and weeds were clustered across the middle of the high ground, and occurred both within and outside the enclosure. This type of assemblage is typical of crop processing waste. The remains in all these pits were all largely of similar composition although higher concentrations were found within the pits outside the enclosure, which may suggest processing was taking place here or close by.

All of the weeds associated with arable environments, with the exception of mustard/cabbage (*Brassica/Sinapsis*) and black-bindweed, consisted of species measuring 1m or less in height. Since most cereal crops grow to at least 1.2m, it can be assumed that the crops during this period were harvested low down on the plant and the presence of culm bases suggests crops may have been uprooted rather than cut.

The stages of processing that took place on site are difficult to identify, and there are several reasons why the interpretation of the surviving remains is not straightforward. Hulled cereals such as emmer/spelt wheat are usually stored as bulk spikelets and require parching in order to make the cereal chaff brittle and allow grains to be released from their spikelets. During the Iron Age, this would have been done on a small scale over a hearth, as and when grain was required. Free-threshing cereals such as oat, barley and bread-type wheat (*Triticum aestivum/Triticum turgidum/Triticum durum*) do not require parching, as the grains are readily released from the ears by threshing alone (Hillman 1981, 133–134). This means that hulled cereals and their respective cereal chaff have a higher likelihood of becoming accidentally burnt, therefore have a higher representation in carbonised cereal assemblages. The presence of cereal processing waste is not always a direct indication of crop processing, as the cereal processing waste produced in one stage is often used as fuel in a later stage; or for other purposes such as fodder or temper for pottery (Hillman 1981, 133–140), and may have been brought onto site for that purpose.

Cereal processing waste associated with barley and spelt/emmer wheat crop processing may be under- or over-represented in carbonised waste deposits, and for this reason it is difficult to ascertain crop processing techniques and whether spelt wheat or barley would have been the dominant crop during this period.

Taking into account the above limitations, some assertions can be made regarding the emmer/spelt wheat crop processing. The plant macrofossil assemblage consists of almost equal amounts of chaff and cereal grain, but is dominated by herbaceous taxa (primarily arable and arable/disturbed weeds), at a ratio of approximately 1 chaff to 1 cereal element to 2.5 herbaceous taxa. This waste composition may result either from initial threshing and winnowing when the ears of emmer/spelt wheat are broken down into individual spikelets (for storage), or from the pounding and second winnowing stage when the spikelets are taken from storage and parched to release the grains ready for use (milling to make bread/included whole into stews/pottages) (Hillman 1981, 132–134).

Charcoal
Samples retrieved for charcoal analysis from Ditch 39, pits 19215, 20153 and 21389 and grave 21305 were all characterised as deposits of waste material/waste firing debris, most likely associated with crop processing or domestic activities. The dominant species identified was oak (*Quercus robur/Quercus petraea*), with moderate amounts of ash (*Fraxinus excelsior*), hawthorn/rowan/crab apple (*Crataegus monogyna/Sorbus/Malus sylvestris*) and alder/hazel (Alnus glutinosa/Corylus avellana) also present. In addition birch (*Betula*), gorse/broom (*Ulex/Cytisus*), cherry tree species (*Prunus*), willow/poplar (*Salix/Populus*) and field maple (*Acer campestre*) were also identified.

Oak, particularly in the form of charcoal, is regarded as one of the better fuels as it provides a constant high temperature (Harris *et al.* 2003, 13). Hazel, ash, hawthorn/rowan/crab apple, cherry tree species and field maple are also recorded as good fuel woods, although they do not burn for such long periods as oak (Gale and Cutler 2000). This assemblage would be suitable for fuel wood used in temporary or domestic fires, including parching emmer/spelt wheat where lower temperatures are sufficient. Gorse/broom, alder and poplar/willow are ideal to use for kindling as they are anatomically less dense than for example, oak and burn quickly at relatively high temperatures (Gale and Cutler 2000). The presence of heaths seeds may also indicate heaths/heather as a kindling fuel, the fine branches when charred would be unlikely to produce charcoal large enough to identify, but the presence of the seeds indicates it was used. The charcoal from pits 15129, 15234, 19093, 19088, 20160 and 20370 which was broadly characterised, all show a similar assemblage to the fully analysed samples and can be assumed to represent firing debris from domestic activities.

The use of these scrub and hedgerow-type species such as hazel, hawthorn/rowan/crab apple, gorse/broom and cherry species may reflect the increasing pressure on woodland resources, as woodland clearance continued throughout the Iron Age (Rackham 2001, 35) and it is likely the less efficient fuels were collected from unmanaged woodlands/scrub and hedges in order to preserve oak for activities such as iron working, that required much higher temperatures. The trend of woodland clearance is observed in pollen analysis from nearby Diss Mere, Norfolk, where there is a significant drop in the concentration of all tree pollen, especially oak, by the end of the Iron Age (Peglar 1993, 36–37). The charcoal was in general too highly fragmented to ascertain whether large branches/timbers or small branches/brushwood were being used, although there was a small amount of evidence of charcoal fragments with curved growth rings indicating the use of some small branches/twigs.

The herbaceous taxa is dominated by species indicative of arable and disturbed environments (83.2%) with smaller quantities of species indicative of hedgerow/woodland/scrub (3.1%), marshland (3.3%), pasture/disturbed (9.3%) and heathland (1%) environments. This assemblage, as with that from the Late Bronze Age, comprises a mixture of species which establish in fertile, nutrient rich soils such as goosefoots, stitchworts (*Stellaria*) and field gromwell, plus those that like sandy/free draining and infertile soils such as annual knawel and corn spurrey, and also heaths that indicate the continued presence of infertile heathland environments. The percentage of species in each habitat group and the presence of species with similar soil preferences, indicate a continued use of chalk and floodplain areas for cultivation. Taken together, the plant macrofossil and charcoal assemblages suggest that the Iron Age landscape was predominantly arable and pastoral, with fields separated by hedgerows (hawthorn/rowan/crab apple, cherry sp.) and trees, residual stands of scrub woodland including hazel, areas of heathland (gorse/broom, heaths) and marsh (alder carr woodland, willow/poplar) within the flood plain.

Most of the herbaceous taxa identified we consider today as weeds, although some may have nutritional or medicinal value. In particular, there is evidence that goosefoots, docks (*Rumex*) and wild varieties of cabbage/mustard may have been eaten raw as salad, boiled down and used (along with cereals) as pottage in stews and soups and as vegetables similar to spinach (Williams 1963, 716; Behre 2008, 67–8). Poppy (*Papaver*) seeds may have been used to produce oil for cooking. The presence of hazelnut shells may also indicate the gathering of wild food resources although may also be attributed to the occasional hazelnut left on a branch being used as fuel.

In terms of medicinal value, cleavers juices are known to clean the lymphatic system, cleanse wounds and protect against eczema (Press 2002, 62). Stitchworts can be used as an anti-inflammatory for the skin and mustard/cabbage is thought to have a laxative effect (Press 2002, 25, 29, 62). The leaves of drug fumitory (*Fumaria officinalis*) are known to have been distilled and juices used to make potions/cures for arthritis, eczema, scabies, liver disorders and gallstones (Mitich 1997, 843). All these species would have established within the vicinity of the site and may have been collected for consumption or other uses, although larger numbers would be required to confirm use of these species to any certainty.

Period 4 Late Iron Age
The plant macrofossil remains from corn dryer 21830 dating to the Late Iron Age were recovered in small quantities dominated by spelt wheat grains with occasional emmer wheat, oats and barley. This assemblage supports the assertion that spelt wheat continued to be cultivated as a dominant crop throughout the Iron Age and into the Roman period (Murphy 1997, 30). The plant remains are indicative of cereal processing waste, although the small quantity suggests that the corn dryer had been cleaned out after its final use.

Period 5 Roman

Plant remains
Plant macrofossils identified from corn dryers 17048 and 17028, pits 17022 and 3146, posthole 17019, curvilinear gully 2 and silting layer 3083 from this period consisted of a large assemblage of spelt and emmer/spelt wheat and barley cereal grains followed by rye (*Secale cereale*) and a smaller quantity of oats. The cereal chaff identified consisted dominantly of spelt and emmer/spelt wheat glume bases along with a small number of barley/rye rachis, culm nodes and straw. The relative percentage of crops present remain largely similar to the Iron Age with a small drop in the percentage of emmer/spelt wheat from 46.5% to 38.1%, an increase in barley from 25.9% to 26.7%, and the first occurrence of rye, which amounts to 16% of the cereal assemblage.

This type of assemblage is largely typical of Roman assemblages and similar to that from a possible structure associated with malting at Beck Row, Mildenhall, (Fryer 2004, 52). Other Roman sites in the area such as Stebbing Green, Essex (Murphy 1999, 19–21) Rayne Roundabout (Site 33/34) and Strood Hall (Site 9), Essex contained similar plant macrofossil assemblages, rich in spelt and emmer/spelt wheat (Carruthers 2007, A120 CD-Rom). One exception to the typical nature of this assemblage is the presence of rye grains within corn dryer 17048. Rye, whilst known to have been consumed in Britain during the Roman period (Cool 2006, 71), is not commonly found in Roman crop assemblages. There is evidence of small amounts found at Beck Row Mildenhall (Fryer 2004, 52), along with identifications at Yarnton, Oxfordshire (Stevens 2011, 555–557) and Staines, Middlesex (McKinley 2004 cited in Booth *et al.* 2007, 281).

Crops continued to be cultivated and processed on a relatively small scale until the Middle Roman period, when increased scale and efficiency of production were required to support the rising population (military and civilian) and the associated growth of new towns. Changes in land ownership meant that rural areas were supplying not only their own needs, but also those of nearby towns and the army (Parks 2012, 20–22).

This increased scale of processing led to the use of new technology in order to efficiently process crops, including the use of corn dryers (van der Veen 1989, 315). Crop processing activities at the Mildenhall site appear to have had two main areas of focus: one at the north end of the site where corn dryers 17048 and 17028 were located, along with waste dumped in Ditch 31 and residual grain recovered within nearby postholes; the second was within Area 3 where a large number of plant remains were identified within curvilinear Ditch 20 to the west, and pit 3146 and silting layer 3083 to the east. The concentration of waste in Area 3 may indicate a function for Enclosure A and/or B, but as there was no evidence of burning here, it is equally likely that the cereals were being processed on the higher dry land, and waste being dumped in the wetter, more marginal areas adjacent to the River Lark.

As with the Iron Age, interpreting the stages of crop processing is complex. The presence of corn dryers provides direct evidence for the parching and drying of cereal crops, and the relatively large quantities of spelt wheat grains and chaff probably relate to this process. The relatively small number of carbonised weeds suggests spelt spikelets were stored clean. The waste within the corn dryers and also within deposit 3083, curvilinear Ditch 20 and pit 3146 in Area 3 is consistent with the discard of crop processing waste, most likely from parching and pounding.

Because the relative preservation of spelt and barley is affected by the different processing techniques involved, it is not possible to ascertain whether spelt wheat or barley was the dominant crop. Literature suggests that spelt wheat was more prevalent in the Roman period and would have been used primarily to bake bread. Barley has been described as a fodder crop (Wilmott 2001, 103 cited in Britton and Huntley 2011, 42) or in sources such as Polybius' *Histories* as a punishment ration (Shuckburgh 1889, 6, 38 cited in Britton and Huntley 2011, 42). However, evidence is being revealed demonstrating the use of barley as a cereal crop in both Roman military and civilian sites (Britton and Huntley 2011, 42). This being the case it would have been used to produce bread, porridge and pottages as well as animal fodder. No evidence of malting was observed within any of the samples looked at, although the cultivation of barley or spelt for this use cannot be completely ruled out. It is possible that crops from Recreation Way, Mildenhall were transported to Beck Row, Mildenhall for malting, although no evidence for this is available (Fryer 2004, 52). Oats were dominantly used as fodder and may have been combined with bromes for this purpose (Cool 2006, 70–71).

Other plants of economic importance included broad bean (*Vicia faba*) and also coriander (*Coriandrum sativum*) — a possible seed was identified. These types of remains are usually rare in archaeological assemblages as processing techniques do not require any exposure to fire. Broad beans and coriander would have been used alongside wild mustard/cabbages, goosefoots, stitch-worts, docks and nettles (also found in the assemblages), as vegetables and salads, and as pottage in stews and soups (Williams 1963, 716; Behre 2008, 67–8). Broad beans and vetches/peas (*Vicia/Lathyrus*) are also known for their ability to fix nitrogen to the soil thereby fertilising fields. The presence of hazelnut shells and elder (*Sambucus nigra*) seeds may also indicate the gathering of wild food resources, and these may have been used to add additional flavour and nutrition to meals. As discussed for the Iron Age assemblage, cleavers, mustard/cabbage and fumitory can be utilised for their medicinal value and may have been used for cleaning wounds, treating colds and coughs and for treating liver disorders, gall stones and eczema.

The carbonised herbaceous taxa assemblage is consistent with that from arable/disturbed environments including goosefoots, cabbage/mustards, docks, cleavers, knotweeds, vetches/peas, black-bindweed, field gromwell, wild radish (*Raphanistrum raphanistrum*) and corncockle (*Agrostemma githago*). Species indicative of grassland include medicks/clover, ribwort plantain (*Plantago lanceolata*), buttercups (*Ranunculus*) and false-oat grass (*Arrhenatherum elatius*) and may indicate fields used as pasture as well as those used for arable cultivation. A small number of species indicative of hedgerow/woodland/scrub, marshland, and pasture landscape were identified.

In addition to the carbonised plant macrofossil assemblage, deposit 3083, fill 3145 within pit 3146 and fill 3717 within curvilinear Ditch 20 all contained a large number of waterlogged remains which allows a wider interpretation of the landscape during the Roman period. The land adjacent to the River Lark, where deposits 3083, 3145 and 3717 accumulated, contained a large number of plants indicative of marshy areas such as sedges, water plantains (*Alisma*), small balsam (*Impatiens parviflora*), rushes (*Juncus*) and spikerushes (*Eleocharis*). In addition a large number of elder seeds were present. Elder frequently establishes in nutrient rich, wetland environments adjacent to river courses. The absence of any full wetland species suggests these deposits were within a damp environment and periodically inundated, rather than completely waterlogged.

Similar to the charred assemblages, waterlogged goosefoots, knotweeds and docks were identified. In addition, species indicative of arable (corn spurrey, fool's parsley (*Aethusa cynapium*)), disturbed (campions (*Silene*), stitchworts, small nettle) and grassland (chervil (*Chaerophyllum*), thistles, cinquefoils (*Potentilla*)) environments were identified, providing evidence of these environments in the vicinity of the River Lark. The remains would either be washed into deposits/features accumulating in the wetland area by rainfall, or be deliberately deposited via domestic and arable/pastoral waste into these features.

As with the Late Bronze Age and Iron Age assemblages, these waterlogged and charred weed remains reflect a range of soil types and environments, and include species that establish on fertile soils such as black-bindweeds, knotweeds and cleavers, those on fertile and free draining soils for example corn chamomile (*Anthemis arvensis*) and campions, as well as those on infertile soils for example buttercups, medick/clover and fumitories. The indications are that the catchment area for the site in this period (as for earlier periods) covers a wide range of geological zones.

Charcoal

As there were no well-preserved samples from features indicating direct evidence of burning, no full analysis of the charcoal remains from this period was undertaken. However broad characterisation of material from pits 3146, 3844 and 17022 revealed the use of oak, alder/hazel, hazel, hawthorn/rowan/crab apple, willow/poplar and field maple as fuels. This mix of species suggests a range of landscapes similar to the Iron Age which was dominantly arable and pastoral with fields separated by hawthorn/rowan/crab apple hedgerows, but with scrub woodland including hazel, ash and field maple on the higher ground, and marshy areas represented by alder and willow/poplar within the flood plain. The large range of species used is an indicator of the increased pressure on woodland resources. Charcoal from *in-situ* burning events such as burning layers in hearths and kilns would be required to confirm this assertion, as it is possible residual charcoal waste may not represent the full range of species present in the fires.

Plant remains

The onset of the Saxon period saw a significant change in the selection of crops being cultivated with a move from the use of hulled wheats (emmer/spelt) to the use of free-threshing wheat and rye, with barley continuing to feature as an important constituent of the range of cultivated crops. This shift in agricultural regime is reflected at Mildenhall with free-threshing wheat and rye making up 25.3% and 18.7% of the charred cereal assemblages respectively, together with the continued use of barley, making up 26% of assemblage. Oats continue to be represented increasing from 2.7% in the Roman period to 4.1% in the Saxon period. For the first time, identifiable floret bases were preserved, indicating the presence of both wild and cultivated oat (*Avena fatua* and *Avena sativa*). Emmer/spelt wheat was still present but had dropped from 38.1% of the charred cereal assemblage in the Roman period to 0.2% in the Saxon assemblage. This small percentage can be attributed to the germination of remnant seeds from past use of the fields, and if this is the case, it also indicates that at least some of the same fields were used for cultivation in the Roman and Saxon periods. This selection of crops has been recorded in pits, ditches and a well excavated at West Fen Road, Ely, Cambridgeshire (Carruthers 2011, 114–116) as well as sites further afield such as those excavated in the upper Thames Valley with free-threshing wheat, barley, rye and cultivated oat all present (Booth *et al.* 2007, 330).

A wide variety of cereal chaff was identified including barley and rye rachis, free-threshing wheat rachis indicating the cultivation of both bread wheat (hexaploid) (*Triticum aestivum*) and durum wheat (tetraploid) (*Triticum durum*), wild and cultivated oat paleas, emmer/spelt wheat glume bases, culm nodes, culm bases, straw, awns and indeterminate paleas. This mixture of cereal remains and chaff, which make up 94.7% of the charred plant assemblage, is indicative of deliberate dumps of cereal processing waste.

The inclusion of frequent seeds of low growing arable and disturbed ground weed species (corn marigold (*Glebionis segetum*), field gromwell, campions) within the cereal processing waste suggests that crops were harvested low on the stalk, close to the ground and the inclusion of culm bases within the assemblage indicates some crops may have been uprooted rather than cut. The Anglo-Saxon period also saw a vast increase in the presence of more persistent and invasive arable weeds such as corn marigold, scentless mayweed (*Tripleurospermum inodorum*) and corncockle. Corncockle provided a particular challenge as the seed is poisonous and being a similar size to grain, had to be hand-picked from sieves. It is likely that the crops would have required regular weeding to prevent any negative impacts on the growth of the crop.

Spatially, the most significant concentrations of cereal processing waste were concentrated within Area 2 (drying oven 2095, possible drying oven 2028, waste pits 2024, 2065, 2074, 2085, 2089 deposit 2086) and in pit 5211 in the north-west part of Area 3. In addition, a third possible drying oven 2125 may have been used for drying grain, but no samples were recovered from its fill. The mechanism by which this material became charred is uncertain. Unlike hulled cereals which require parching to release

the grain from their spikelets, free-threshing cereals such as bread-type wheat, rye and barley do not require exposure to fire as the grains are readily released from the ears by threshing alone (Hillman 1981, 134–5). As with the assemblages from the earlier periods, the composition of carbonised cereal chaff, weeds and grain does not necessarily always reflect the crop processing stages being undertaken due to the re-use of cereal chaff as fuel, fodder, thatching, flooring and temper. The presence of a mixture of grains, light weeds (*e.g.* corn marigold and cabbage/mustard), heavy weeds (*e.g.* wild radish, perianiths and field gromwell), weed heads (corncockle and corn marigold) and light and heavy chaff (rachis and culm nodes respectively) are suggestive of several processing stages including threshing, winnowing and sieving. It is likely that these stages were all taking place in this area or nearby, and at least some of this waste was being utilised as fuel directly within the drying ovens.

The high concentration of cereal grains compared to chaff or weeds (ratio 16.6:1.2:1 respectively) can be attributed to the denser nature of grain relative to cereal chaff, which makes it more likely to survive exposure to fire, unlike the chaff which would burn to ash more quickly. Two other explanations that may provide reasons for the large amount of charred grain on the site include the grain itself being used as fuel (however, as grain was a valuable commodity, this may be restricted to spoilt crops), accidental fire within the drying ovens, or some kind of catastrophic fire event in this area of the site that led to this concentration of grain. Initial evidence suggests these last two possibilities are less likely, as few of the cereal grains exhibits signs of spoiling (sprouting) and higher levels of scorching and *in situ* burning would be expected if a fire event was the cause.

Once cleaned and processed, free-threshing wheat, barley and rye would have been used to produce bread and in addition barley would have been malted to make ale and used as fodder. The presence of a single sprouted barley grain may indicate the use of barley to produce ale, although a larger assemblage would be required to confirm this, as it is equally possible that this sprouting grain represents part of the crop that has spoiled. Oats, only present in small quantities, may have been used to make porridges, although the mixture of both cultivated and wild oats along with large numbers of bromes is more suggestive of cultivation for fodder rather than human consumption (Hagan 2006, 21–42, 225).

Other remains of economic importance include a small number of charred lentil (*Lens culinaris*) and pea (*Pisum*) seeds and a larger number of vetches/peas. Lentils and peas would have been cultivated for addition to stews and pottages. In times of poor harvest, they may also have been milled along with wheat, barley or oat flour to make bread. The presence of vetches/peas is of interest as, in addition to their possible use in stews/pottages, they were often cultivated as a fodder crop (Stone 2006, 11). Farmers would also then benefit from their nitrogen fixing abilities to help improve the fertility of the soil (Zohary *et al.* 2013, 75), and thereby their presence may be an indicator of the decreasing soil fertility.

Flax (*Linum usitatissimum*) (seeds and capsules, waterlogged and charred) was recovered from alluvium 2086 and drying oven 2095, both in Area 2. Flax seeds are a relatively common find during the Anglo-Saxon period and plants were typically cultivated either for their oil or their fibre. The floodplain of the River Lark would have provided an ideal location for cultivation and retting of flax (Zohary *et al.* 2013, 100–101). However, although the evidence indicates the presence of areas of slow-flowing water, which would be expected in a marshy floodplain area, no direct evidence for retting ponds was identified within the insect, mollusc, pollen or geoarchaeological analyses (see 5.VII Medieval 'peat' 2050). Flax plants are usually harvested for retting when the seeds are still immature (Zohary *et al.* 2013, 101), but the seeds found in this assemblage were mature, and thus at a stage more suitable for linseed oil extraction. It is possible both activities were taking place, but there is no direct evidence for either process.

As described previously, hazelnuts, stitchworts, docks, goosefoots, cabbage/mustard, nettles may all have been exploited as hand-gathered food stuffs. The seed pods and leaves of goose grass can also be used as a substitute for spinach if boiled and their seeds can be roasted and ground down to make a coffee-type drink (Mabey 2007, 70). Water-pepper (*Persicaria hydropiper*) has a very acrid taste and may have been deployed to 'spice' foods (Timson 1966, 817). Elderberries and flowers may have been used in in pies/puddings and also to make flavoured drinks (Aitkinson and Aitkinson 2002, 916). These would all have been exploited to add additional vitamins and minerals to the diet as well as make food more palatable. Fill 2070 within pit 2074 contained some mineralised field gromwell, cabbage/mustard and clover seeds. Plant remains become mineralised when in contact with cess material. This pit mostly contained carbonised crop-processing waste and it is most likely that a small amount of cess material was discarded into the pit, mineralising crop processing waste rather than the pit being utilised as a cess pit.

Some of the species represented in the assemblages have a medicinal value. As stated previously, docks, mustard/cabbage all are known to have healing properties, whilst linseed oil may help gastric problems (PFAF 2014). Elder flowers, leaves and berries also had herbal medicinal uses and were used to treat inflammation, bruises and wounds (Aitkinson and Aitkinson 2002, 916–917). There is conflicting evidence regarding the use of peas/vetches. McGee (1986 cited in Hagen 2006, 47) suggests that beans were offensive as they caused excessive flatulence and for this reason St Jerome forbade nuns from eating them because 'they tickle the genitals' (*in partibus genitalibus titillationes*). On the other hand, stewed in wine, vinegar or water, they are considered of medicinal value for curing a painful stomach (Hagen 2006, 48).

Charcoal
Charcoal from drying oven 2095, possible drying oven 2028 and pits 2023, 2024, 2065, 2074, 2085 and 5211 was fully analysed. The mixture of charcoal and cereal remains found in these features have been characterised as deposits of waste firing-debris associated with crop processing. Fuel was dominated by alder/hazel and hazel followed next in abundance by oak. In addition smaller amounts of ash, alder, alder buckthorn, hawthorn/rowan/crab apple, willow/poplar, field maple and elm were recorded. A detailed analysis was not undertaken on Roman charcoal samples, but comparisons made with Middle Iron Age charcoal reveal a marked decrease in the

amount of oak from 40.3 % to 28.6% and ash from 11.9% to 3.3%, and an increase in alder/hazel from 19.5% to 52.5% and willow/poplar from 1.5% to 10.7% from the Iron Age to the Saxon period. Broad characterisation of samples where the origin of firing debris is less clear backs up these results in showing similar trends. In addition pollen analysis at nearby Diss Mere shows a similar trend with increased representation of shrubby species such as hazel (Peglar 1993, 36–37).

It is possible that the increase in prevalence of scrub and hedgerow species indicates woodland regeneration associated with abandoned farmland at the end of the Roman period (Rackham 2001 42–43). There is however little evidence from the Mildenhall plant macrofossil remains that areas of farmland were left unoccupied at the end of the Roman period as the volume of crop processing being undertaken on site appears to continue to grow and become increasingly intensive. It is possible that these changes may in fact be indicative of increasing pressure on resources with communities having to rely on fuel wood exploited from marginal environments such as wet woodland and hedgerows and scrub woodland. Alternatively, it may simply be a result of the types of burning being undertaken. Fires used for crop drying will not require best quality wood (oak/ash) and brushwood would have been collected from local woodlands/hedgerows. Roundwood fragments and twigs made up 52% of the charcoal assemblage and together with the fragment of burnt twine identified in pit 2028 may suggest use of brushwood bundles for fuel along with crop processing waste. The only exception to this is pit 2028 which contained exclusively oak charcoal. The absence of any *in-situ* burning within this feature discounts the possibility of a burnt *in-situ* post and suggests the assemblage may be attributed to discarded waste from a single burnt timber. Using purely oak as a fuel tends to be reserved for activities that require high temperatures, for example metal working, however the lack of artefactual evidence restricts further interpretation.

A varied assemblage of species was recorded from Period 6 Saxon samples with charred plant and wood assemblages augmented by better preserved and abundant waterlogged plant material preserved within deposits/features located on/close to the River Lark floodplain. Woodland taxa suggest a largely cleared landscape with fields separated by hedgerows mostly consisting of hawthorn/rowan/crab apple, maple, elder and elm, all of which were typical hedgerow species in this region during this period (Barnes and Williamson 2006, 75). The presence of oak suggests residual stands of oak and scrub woodland including ash, elm, hazel, maple and birch (*Betula*) located on higher ground. Alder-carr wet woodland is indicated by the presence of willow/poplar charcoal, bay willow seeds, elder charcoal and alder charcoal and seeds, and would have been present on the floodplain.

Marsh and wetland areas on the floodplain would have been typified with species such as water-plantains, fool's water cress, sedges, cowbane (*Cicuta virosa*), bogbean (*Menyanthes trifoliata*) and horned pondweed (*Zannichellia palustris*). Together with weeds of arable and disturbed ground, plant remains indicate the continuing presence of arable, disturbed ground, grassland, marshland, wetland and hedgerow/woodland/scrub habitats in the area of the site. These taxa, as in previous periods indicate the use of both fertile (goosefoots, field gromwell, pale persicaria (*Persicaria lapathifolia*)) and infertile (cornsalads (*Valerianella*), thorow-wax (*Bupleurum rotundifolium*), corn spurrey) soils. Areas of pasture would have encouraged grassland species such as thistles, hawkweeds (*Hieracium*), cat's ears (*Hypochaeris*), self-heal (*Prunella vulgaris*), buttercups and cinquefoils to establish. Arable/disturbed areas would have seen species such as nettles, cleavers, knotweeds, goosefoots, corncockle, field gromwell, scentless mayweed and corn marigold opportunistically growing alongside crops of grain, pulses, vetches and flax. This landscape reconstruction reflects the results of pollen analysis undertaken at nearby Diss Mere, Norfolk which indicate that this period saw an increase in rye, barley and wheat pollen, along with the presence of flax, vetches/peas and weed pollen indicating a growth in arable agriculture (Peglar 1993, 38–39).

Period 7 medieval

The medieval period saw a similar range of crops cultivated as before. However, the percentage representation of these crops within the charred assemblages differs, with free-threshing wheat grains increasing from 25.3% in the Saxon period to 40.4% in the medieval period; rye increasing from 18.7% to 26.1%, oats increasing from 4.1% to 7.3% and barley decreasing from 26% to 14.9%. A small number of emmer/spelt wheat grains and glume bases were also identified which most likely represent weed intrusion. Eleven oat paleas were positively identified as cultivated oat and only a single palea as wild oat. This may suggest oat was cultivated for human consumption, although continued identification of relatively large numbers of bromes seeds suggests the sustained use of oats and bromes for fodder. A total of forty-five bread wheat (hexaploid) and forty-three durum wheat (tetraploid) rachis were identified suggesting equal cultivation of both types of free-threshing wheat. In addition barley and rye rachis, culm nodes, straw, and indeterminate paleas were identified. Samples from settlement activity at Blatches (Site 24), Essex and Stebbingford Farm, Essex (Sites 25–26 and 51–52) (Carruthers 2007, CD rom) indicate cultivation of a similar range of crops and at Blatches, a dominance of free-threshing wheat with similar 1:1 ratios of bread-type and rivet-type wheat represented.

Comparable to Saxon Period 6, a range of low growing weeds associated with crop cultivation such as thorow-wax, scentless mayweed and field gromwell were identified, suggesting that crops continued to be harvested close to the base, or, as a small number of culm bases were identified, uprooted prior to further processing. There were several areas of crop processing activity identified across the site. Spatial analysis of assessment results shows a cluster of pits/postholes including 15245, 15259, 15265 and 15477 on the higher ground west of Ditch 2 containing small numbers of carbonised cereal remains. These pits/postholes may have formed some type of windbreak or structure allowing winnowing/threshing to take place. The poor preservation of these remains means it is not possible to ascertain the type of activity taking place. Waste material within pit 15315 and Ditch 2 (cut 15415) also contained moderate numbers of charred cereals and are likely deposits of crop processing waste,

perhaps from activity undertaken in the shelter of the windbreak.

The largest concentrations of discarded cereal remains and chaff are located within deposits 2050, 2051, 2055, 2115 and 2122 at the southern edge of Area 2 and within Ditch 24, Ditch 47, pit 3948 and spreads 3949 and 3989 in Area 3. There is little direct evidence in this area for burning *in-situ* by which these plant remains could have become charred, however further up slope on the dry ground, corn dryer 17182 in the north-west corner of the site, and pit/hearth 20755 (part of Pit Group 7) may have been used for drying crops, and the subsequent waste disposed of in these marginal wetland areas. The assemblage of crop processing waste within Areas 2 and 3 consisted of cereal chaff and weeds indicative of various stages of crop processing. These included large amounts of heavy chaff/seeds (culm nodes, straw, corncockle seeds, wild radish perianths), along with lighter chaff (barley, rye and bread/durum wheat rachis, cultivated oat paleas and campion and goosefoot seeds). This chaff and seed waste is likely to have originated from the threshing, raking, winnowing and sieving stages of processing undertaken on drier areas of the site, after which the useful elements were extracted for use as fodder, animal bedding, thatching and temper, and the remaining waste subsequently used as fuel. The larger amounts of grain identified may have come from accidental losses during kiln drying or the use of spoiled grain as fuel.

Pollen assessment revealed the presence of *Cannabis*-type (hemp) pollen within an evaluation monolith sample (Geary 2010, 3–4). During the excavation, the evaluation trench was re-opened and a bulk soil sample taken from the equivalent location but unfortunately no *Cannabis*-type seeds or vegetative remains were identified. The process of hemp retting is very similar to that for flax with hemp plants being harvested and soaked in water to extract fibres for textile production. The floodplain of the River Lark would facilitate this process (as identified above in VI Insect remains and VII Palaeoenvironment) with the presence of slow-moving water and pools which would be ideal for retting. The evaluation deposits were considered to be of significance, as they contained a high percentage of *Cannabis*-type pollen (98% and 42% respectively). Geary (2010, 3–4) states that these percentages represent the highest reported values for *Cannabis*-type pollen within an archaeological deposit. As hemp for retting is harvested when the plant is flowering, large amounts of pollen are deposited within the retting pools, which is the reason hemp pollen signatures of this concentration strongly indicate retting (Geary *et al.* 2005, 318) and despite the lack of vegetative evidence, the concentration here strongly suggests hemp retting was taking place, either on site or close by. Evidence from Mildenhall together with that from other nearby sites such as Thompson Common, Thetford, Norfolk and Bugg's Hole, Thelnetham, Suffolk where *Cannabis*-type pollen was found in concentrations suggestive of hemp cultivation and processing (Grieg *et al.* 1981 506–507), supports documentary evidence that hemp was widely cultivated in this area of eastern England during the medieval period (Geary *et al.* 2005, 321).

The presence of charred and waterlogged mature flax seeds and capsules indicate the continued cultivating of flax for fibre production and/or linseed oil.

In addition to cereal crops, broad beans (*Vicia faba*), peas and vetches/peas continued to be represented in the medieval period and would have been used to augment the diet as additions to stews and pottages and vetches/peas would have also been used as fodder and to improve soil quality. Examples of these types of crops have been found at Blatches (Site 24), Essex (Carruthers 2007, CD rom). In general the assemblage shows a range of local herbaceous taxa similar to that from Saxon Period 6 that continued to be harvested as a source of wild foodstuff for consumption and medicinal use, with hazelnuts, stitchworts, docks, goosefoots, cabbage/mustard, goosefoots, elderberries, flax and nettles all present. In addition a single mineralised fig (*Ficus carica*) seed and a small number of waterlogged fig seeds were identified. The small quantity identified means that although it is not possible to ascertain whether they were being grown on site or imported, they were certainly consumed. The mineralised fig seed along with mineralised cabbage/mustard seeds suggest disposal of cess waste within well 17156, although mineralised remains are not identified in sufficient volume to suggest use of this feature as a cess pit. Fig, flax, peas, beans and vetches were also identified in medieval settlement activity at Long Causeway, Peterborough, Cambridgeshire (Monckton and Grinter 1997, 11–17).

The charcoal from kiln 20044 was dominated by alder/hazel, hawthorn/rowan/crab apple and willow/poplar fragments with smaller quantities of oak, ash, alder buckthorn, cherry, field maple and birch represented. Whilst it is not possible to ascertain which type of activity was being undertaken within the kiln, the absence of oak as a dominant fuel discounts any activities which require high temperatures such as metal-working. Since the charcoal within this feature is largely similar to that from deposits associated with crop processing waste, it can be tentatively suggested that at least one function of this kiln is crop drying. The high fragment counts of scrub/hedgerow species such as hawthorn/rowan/crab apple, willow/poplar and alder/hazel compared to pre-Saxon periods suggests that woodland resources were becoming scarce and difficult to obtain, and therefore different types of wood were being exploited. Woodlands had become increasingly depleted and ownership and rights were far more complicated than today (Rackham 2001, 62). Woodlands were intensively managed with coppicing and pollarding. Due to the highly fragmentary nature of the charcoal samples, there was no evidence of roundwood fragments with indicators of fast growth, hence no direct evidence for woodland management, however it is very likely that it was taking place during this period. It is difficult to ascertain where the fuel came from as it could have been locally harvested from common land or hedgerows or been brought in from outside. The large quantity of hawthorn/rowan/crab apple, alder/hazel and willow/poplar charcoal suggests that at least some of the fuel wood was being collected locally from hedgerows.

The preservation of a wide assemblage of charred and waterlogged plant remains and charcoal has given a good opportunity for the reconstruction of the local environment during the medieval period and indicates it remains largely unchanged from the Saxon period — with a range of hedgerow/scrub/woodland, arable, disturbed, grassland, heathland and marsh/wetland areas growing alongside cereal and fodder crops and possible crops of flax, hemp and beans/pulses. In terms of percentage of herbaceous taxa by period, marshland/wetland and grassland seeds remains almost constant between the Saxon and medieval periods at approx. 7% each. Hedgerow/woodland /scrub increase from 1.2% to 2.9% and heathland species increase from 0.8% to 6.2%. The largest change is seen in the percentage of weeds indicative of arable and disturbed environments. The number of weeds indicative of arable environments increased from 27.0% to 43.7% with an associated decrease in opportunistic weeds from 45.6% to 24.9%. This may indicate an increase in the intensity of arable cultivation or may suggest that efforts to eliminate weeds from arable fields were not successful in keeping up with the rapid rate of arable weed germination. The increase in percentage of species indicative of heathland environments may suggest increased pressure on resources, and the use of otherwise marginal land.

IX. Pollen
by Rob Scaife with Michael J. Allen

Summary
Preliminary pollen analysis of sequences from the palaeochannel (3617) with sandy peat (3012) from monolith 3034, and assessment of the medieval peat 3016 from monoliths 3003 and 3004, has established that the peat contexts contained sub-fossil pollen and spores from which data on the vegetation and environment of the site could be established (Scaife 2014). More detailed analysis has only been carried out on the palaeochannel sequence 3612, which is dated to the Late Bronze Age. Additional pollen analysis has produced a diverse range of pollen taxa, demonstrating a predominantly pastoral agricultural environment within a deforested landscape.

Pollen procedures
Samples of 1.5ml volume were processed using standard techniques for the extraction of the sub-fossil pollen and spores (Moore and Webb 1978; Moore *et al.* 1991). The sub-fossil pollen and spores were identified and counted using an Olympus biological research microscope, fitted with Leitz optics. Total pollen counts of up to 700 grains per sample were made, and a pollen diagram plotted, using Tilia and Tilia Graph (Figs 5.12 and 5.13). Percentages for (3612) monolith 3034 (Fig. 5.12) have been calculated as follows:

Sum =	% total dry land pollen (tdlp)
Marsh/aquatic =	% tdlp + sum of marsh/aquatics
Spores =	% tdlp + sum of spores
Misc. =	% tdlp + sum of misc. taxa

Medieval peat 3016, (monoliths 3003–4) (Fig. 5.13) has been calculated as a percentage of total pollen because of the almost sole presence of Cyperaceae pollen. Calculations based on the above (norm) would be meaningless for samples in the upper, sedge-dominated levels.

Taxonomy, in general, follows that of Moore and Webb (1978) modified according to Bennett *et al.* (1994) for pollen types, and Stace (1992) for plant descriptions. These procedures were carried out in the Palaeoecology Laboratory of the Department of Geography, University of Southampton.

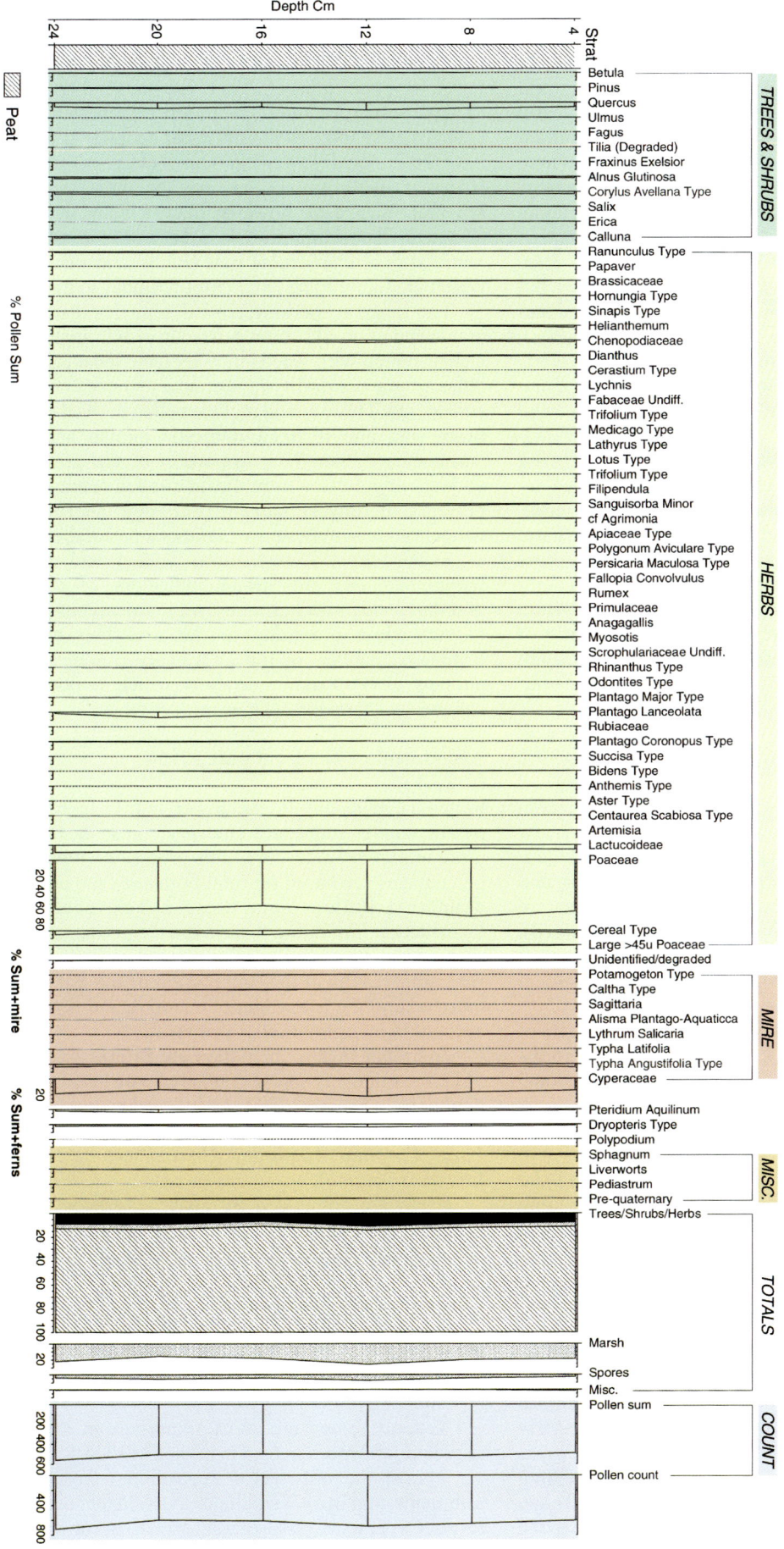

Figure 5.12 Pollen histogram Period 2: Late Bronze Age palaeochannel fill 3612 (monolith 3034)

141

Late Bronze Age palaeochannel fill 3612
(Fig. 5.12)

A preliminary examination (Scaife 2014), showed that the mineral sediments underlying the base of the peat at 24cm were devoid of pollen. The overlying peat, however, contains pollen that varies greatly in preservation and numbers. Overall, the pollen sequence shows little stratigraphical change and, as such, no local pollen assemblage zones have been assigned to the profile. There are few trees and shrubs, and a dominance of pollen from wetland plants and the vegetation of the surrounding zone. The palynological characteristics are as follows.

Trees and shrubs comprise *Quercus* (oak; to 8%), *Alnus* (alder; to 2%) and *Corylus avellana* type (hazel, but may include bog myrtle; to 4%). There are also occasional occurrences of *Betula (*birch*), Pinus* (pine), *Ulmus* (elm), *Tilia* (lime/linden), and *Fraxinus (ash) and Fagus* (beech).

Dwarf shrubs are represented by occasional *Erica* (heather), and continuous but small numbers of *Calluna* (ling).

Herbs are dominant, with Poaceae (grasses) being most important (to 72%). These are accompanied by cereal pollen, with greater numbers at *c.*16cm (7–8%). Also with continuous presence, but in small numbers are, Ranunculaceae (buttercups), Chenopodiaceae (goosefoot and oraches), *Rumex* (docks), *Plantago lanceolata* (ribwort plantain; 6%) and Lactucoideae (dandelion types; 10%). In addition, there is a range of other herbs of grassland and arable or disturbed ground. Of interest are the calcareous-favouring *Helianthemum* and *Sanguisorba minor.*

Wetland herbs are also important, with consistent presence and high values of Cyperaceae (sedges; to 30% at 12cm). There are also small numbers of other mire and marginal aquatics, including *Caltha* type (marsh marigold), *Sagittaria sagittifolia* (arrowhead), *Typha latifolia* (common reed-mace), *Typha angustifolia/Sparganium*-type (lesser reedmace and/or bur reed), and *Lythrum salicaria* (purple loosestrife). Aquatic taxa are also present, with *Potamogeton*-type (pondweed), although this may also be *Triglochin* (marsh arrowgrass) and cysts of algal *Pediastrum*. There are also occasional *Sphagnum* moss spores in the upper levels.

There are few fern spores, with only small numbers of *Pteridium aquilinum* (bracken) and monolete forms (*Dryopteris* type/typical ferns), and occasional *Polypodium.*

The inferred vegetation

The pollen data can be viewed in terms of the on-site vegetation, and that which relates to the surrounding landscape, including the near-local and more regional inputs.

The on-site environment

On site, herb fen is seen, with high sedge (Cyperaceae) values, occasional bur reed and/or lesser reed mace (*Typha angustifolia* type), common reedmace (*Typha latifolia*), arrowhead (*Sagittaria sagittifolia*), water plantain (*Alisma plantago-aquatica*), and purple loosestrife (*Lythrum salicaria*) along with a proportion of the grass pollen (Poaceae). There is some evidence for standing water with occasional pondweed (*Potamogeton*) and algal *Pediastrum* at *c.*16cm and, as such, it appears that herb fen

probably covered the site. This pertained throughout the period represented by the sediment.

The off-site environment

It is clear that the landscape was predominantly open, with few, if any, trees present. Ash (*Fraxinus*) and lime (*Tilia*), as small pollen producers, are poorly represented in pollen assemblages, and it is possible that occasional trees may have been locally present. Oak (*Quercus*) and hazel (*Corylus avellana*), pollen are the most represented arboreal taxa and are, however, likely to come from farther afield. This is certainly the case with the very small numbers of birch (*Betula*), pine (*Pinus*) and alder (*Alnus*), which are likely to be from extra-regional sources.

The range of herbs recorded suggests that a mixed arable and pastoral habitat existed in proximity to the site. Cereal pollen with weeds may indicate local cultivation, although the possibility of secondary sources needs to be considered. These would include pollen derived from crop processing and dumped domestic human and animal waste etc.. Although a proportion of the grass pollen undoubtedly derives from the on-site fen community, the presence of ribwort plantain (*Plantago lanceolata*) and dandelion/daisy types also suggests a pastoral economy.

Salad burnet (*Sanguisorba minor*) and rock-rose (*Helianthemum*) are strong indicators of calcareous grassland and as such, suggest some calcareous lithology in very close proximity to the site. This may have comprised patches of glacial Chalky Boulder Clay, or perhaps anthropogenic deposits which imported such calcareous character, such as middens.

Assessment of medieval peat 3016
(Fig 5.13)

Pollen is abundant in the lower humic levels of this palaeochannel sequence, but very sparse in the upper, more minerogenic levels of this profile. As noted above, percentages are based on total pollen, as the bulk of the countable pollen from these upper levels are of Cyperaceae. Excluding these from the pollen sum would give unreal percentages of the usual pollen sum taxa. Here, this results in the suppression of the Poaceae, and other taxa in the lower humic material, and is taken into account in interpretation of this profile.

Trees and shrubs, as in the Late Bronze Age channel 3612, are relatively sparse compared with herbs which are dominant. *Quercus* (7%) and *Corylus avellana* type (3–4%) are most important, with small numbers of *Betula, Pinus, Carpinus, Fagus* and *Alnus*. There are occasional Ericales (*Calluna*).

Herbs are dominated by Poaceae, especially in the lowest sample (56%), where Cyperaceae (sedges) have not reduced the within-sum percentage. Other taxa include plants of pasture, *Ranunculus* (buttercups), Fabaceae spp. (vetches/trefoils etc.), *Rumex* (docks), Lactucoideae, *Plantago lanceolata* and arable habitats with Cereal pollen, Chenopodiaceae (goosefoots and oraches), Brassicaceae (charlocks), *Persicaria maculosa* type and *Artemisia* (mugwort).

Wetland plants are most important in this pollen sequence, and more so than in monolith 3034. Cyperaceae are almost the only taxon recovered from the upper sediments, and in only small numbers. In the lower humic levels, Cyperaceae (70% of total pollen) occur with *Typha angustifolia* type (bur reed and/or reed mace) and pollen

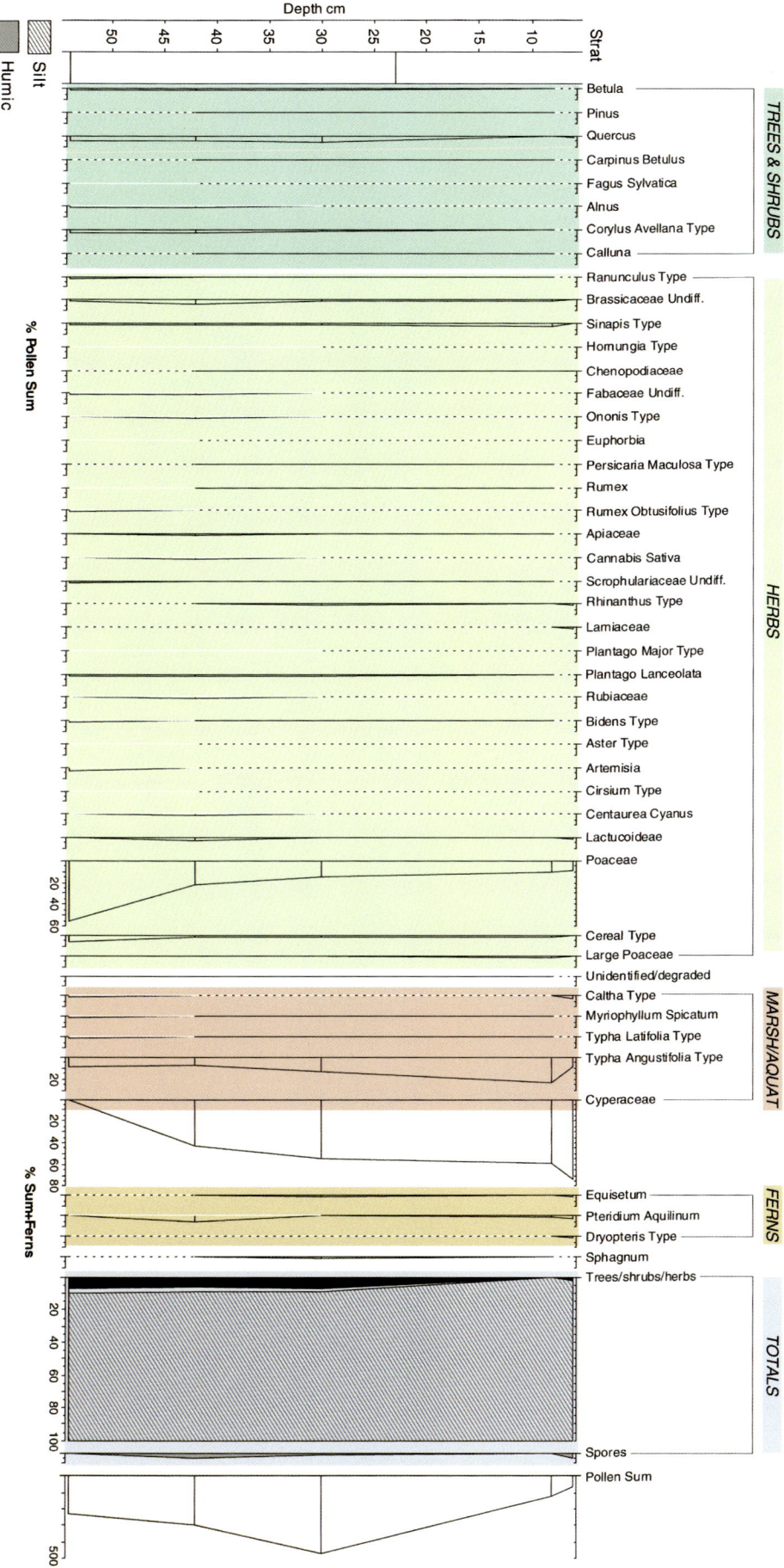

Figure 5.13 Pollen histogram Period 7: medieval 'peat' 3016 (monoliths 3003 and 3004)

143

of the aquatic, *Myriophyllum spicatum (water milfoil)*. Small numbers of *Sphagnum* (bog moss) spores are also present.

The inferred vegetation

The overall palynological characteristics of this profile are very similar to those of the Late Bronze Age channel 3612, with only minor differences in the tree pollen including occasional *Carpinus* (hornbeam) and *Fagus* (beech). The latter is poorly represented in pollen spectra, and may have been local to the site. The other tree taxa are likely to be from more regional sources. Herbs predominate, again with a mixture of arable and pasture indicators suggesting mixed agricultural practices. The strong representation of Cyperaceae with grasses and bur reed and/or reedmace suggest a rich fen environment with water milfoil, indicating some areas of standing water on site.

Conclusions

Overall, the pollen assemblages are dominated by herbs of largely pastoral affinity, with some cereal pollen and weeds of disturbed ground. There are few trees and shrubs, suggesting an open landscape with mixed agricultural habitat at least in proximity to the site. The on-site habitat was one of open grass-sedge fen, with some standing water.

Chapter 6. Discussion and Synthesis

I. The Late Bronze Age and Iron Age periods
by Andrew Mudd

Late Bronze Age occupation

There is clear, if limited, evidence for occupation on the site in the Late Bronze Age, which principally derives from a substantial pit (20238), with a light scatter of re-deposited pottery recovered from later features. The date of the initial digging of the pit is not well defined, but was probably before 1000 BC on the basis of radiocarbon dating from the middle fill (within recut 22063). Although it contained no waterlogged material, a pit of this size is likely to have been a waterhole, a feature that is characteristic of the 2nd millennium BC on the river terraces and fen edge of the region, and elsewhere, and an important provision for the development of permanent settlement (Evans 2013, 110–14). Although waterholes do not appear to be characteristic of the eastern fen-edge at this time (Brudenell 2011a, 22), several were found at West Row Fen, with traces of wooden linings and other waterlogged remains (Martin and Murphy 1988, 355). Recent work has shown the near-ubiquity of later Bronze Age sites near watercourses in the region (Brudenell 2011a), and so the presence of features of this date is not unexpected here. The nature of this settlement is, however, difficult to characterise, and this is a problem encountered more widely throughout the region. The quantity of domestic material dumped in the waterhole-pit after it went out of use offers a good indication of occupation close by, although the absence of ditches and structural postholes renders impossible any detailed interpretation of the form of settlement at this time. It is possible, and perhaps even likely in view of the intensity of Iron Age and later occupation, that a more extensive and well-defined settlement has been lost to truncation. However, in some respects this formlessness is also characteristic of sites of this period, which often remain spatially undefinable at the local scale and with a tendency to merge into one another. Even when exposed on the large scale, and structured by field systems and droveways, as at Colne Fen, Earith (Fig. 6.1), settlement of the 2nd millennium BC can remain disparate and unfocused (Evans 2013, 111). Roundhouses here, throughout the Bronze Age, were identified by irregular, sub-circular or quasi-circular arrangements of postholes that displayed no regularity of pattern, and ground-plans in most cases appear to be notional. This poverty of definition may suggest that settlement was seasonal and transitory at this time, but while the nature of Bronze Age settlement is a subject of debate, this view is not widely held (Evans 2013, 113).

The site at West Row Fen, 3km to the west, (Fig. 6.1) lay on a sandy ridge at an elevation of only 2–3m AOD, and consisted of scattered pits and traces of posthole buildings. It was dated to the later part of the Early Bronze Age, and seems to have been abandoned by the Middle Bronze Age in response to wetter conditions, and therefore is slightly earlier in date than Recreation Way.

The rising Fenland water-table, a consequence of marine transgression which resulted in a considerable loss of land between c. 3000 BC and 1600 BC (Waller 1994, 70, figs 5.16–5.19), appears to provide the environmental context for the appearance of later Bronze Age settlement on drier ground at Mildenhall, at an elevation of c. 12.5–8m AOD. The quantity of finds from pit 20238 at Recreation Way, which included charred cereals and animal bones, suggest that this feature was related to a farming settlement. Like West Row Fen, cattle were the dominant species, with sheep also present. The presence of calves on both sites suggests a continued interest in cattle breeding, and possibly milk production (Higbee, Chapter 5.IV). Charred plant remains show that spelt was the dominant cereal, and it appears to have replaced emmer wheat as the favoured species, which was more common than spelt at West Row Fen. Barley was present at both sites. The recovery of waterlogged flax seeds, and perhaps also stems, at West Row Fen shows that one of the functions of the waterholes there was for flax-retting. There was no evidence for this at Recreation Way during the Bronze Age, although it is possible that waterholes were used in this way without any evidence for this activity surviving. Waterlogged flax came from a Late Bronze Age pit at Small Mead Farm, Berkshire, in the Middle Thames Valley (Campbell 1992, 105–7), and flax pollen has been found in a Middle Bronze Age waterhole at Pode Hole Quarry, Cambridgeshire (Langdon and Scaife 2009), although the evidence is otherwise rare. Other charred seeds from Recreation Way include a wide range of wild seeds indicative of both arable and pasture land uses, and a diversity of soils (Cobain, Chapter 5.VIII). It seems that the Late Bronze Age settlement, while of indiscernible form, established a regime of farming that continued little-changed into the Iron Age.

A radiocarbon date from later in the deposit sequence in pit 20238 at Recreation Way, indicates occupation in the 8th century BC (SUERC-48047), although there was no Early Iron Age pottery from this feature, and very little from the site as a whole (Brudenell, Chapter 4.VII), so it appears that occupation may have ceased shortly after this time. There is no firm evidence of renewed settlement until around 350 BC, or a little earlier, when Middle Iron Age pottery was current, although there are a few diagnostic Early Iron Age sherds from elsewhere on the site which suggest sporadic activity during the intervening 300–400 years. This disjunction of settlement evidence is of unclear significance in the regional context, although it can perhaps be related to much wider transitions in the earlier Iron Age, which have been linked to the abandonment of a social value system based on a bronze metal 'standard', and the new political structures that emerged from c. 800 BC (Needham 2007).

Iron Age fort

The Middle Iron Age occupation at Recreation Way took the form of a large, rectangular double-ditched enclosure of fort-like dimensions. This was associated with a large number of pits, most of which were situated well within the enclosure (at least 10m from the inner edge of the inner ditch), suggesting the contemporaneous presence of a fairly substantial internal bank. Only part of this enclosure was revealed, and its overall form remains conjectural. The term 'fort' rather than 'enclosure' is used hereafter in this discussion to draw attention to the unusually large double ditches which, had they survived as earthworks with associated banks, would have been interpreted without hesitation as being defensive in character. While there is no evidence to indicate that they were specifically designed to repel attack, recent interpretations of Iron Age fortifications have drawn attention to the possibly symbolic aspects of defensive architecture, and it is considered probable that these defences may have been intended to communicate the image of a secure place, rather than to defend the space enclosed. The north-south arm of the inner ditch (Ditch 1) was c. 100m long, 7–8m wide, with an average depth of c. 3.5m. A southern terminal suggests the existence of an entranceway in the south-east of the enclosure. There was no east-west return forming a southern boundary to correspond with the northern boundary ditch, and it is considered likely that the southern boundary was a natural one formed by a channel of the River Lark, or at least by the marshy floodplain of this channel. The notion that the defensive architecture of the fort may have been as much concerned with display as with military defence is underlined by the apparent absence of southern ditches, although it is not possible to accurately define the defensive qualities of the River Lark and its floodplain at this point, or the possible presence of a palisade. The 'marsh-fort' at Sutton Common, South Yorkshire, shows that elaborate defensive architecture was sometimes positioned very selectively; multivallate defences on the eastern side of this fort were accompanied by a complete absence of ditches on the western marshy side (Van de Noort et al. 2007). At Recreation Way the external ditch, 11m to the east, was less completely defined, but was shown to be slightly smaller. Given an unquantifiable degree of vertical truncation to the site, it can be assumed that both ditches were originally somewhat larger. There was a heavily-truncated earlier ditch (Ditch 39), which appears to have been a precursor to Ditch 1 on a much smaller scale. However, if this did comprise part of an earlier enclosure on the same layout, its course as well as its date are irrecoverable. The dating of the doubled-ditched fort cannot be estimated more accurately than c. 350–100 BC, based on the characteristics of the pottery; the radiocarbon dating undertaken offered no greater precision.

The backfills of these ditches showed some variation and indications of complexity, although there is no indication that they outlived the 1st century BC. The inner ditch was deliberately infilled, possibly by slighting the earthwork defences, but subsequently the north-south arm was at least partially recut to a shallower depth, and left to silt-up naturally. The outer ditch (Ditch 5) was also deliberately filled with mixed, chalky rubble, but a series of compacted chalk layers above this levelling deposit indicate its use as a pathway. It is possible that this was in use at the same time as the recut of Ditch 1, and both were of a broad, shallow form. This would seem to be the context of the parallel ditches forming an entranceway into Ditch 5, which were substantial and may represent the foundations of a gate structure. While the dating is not

secure, this architectural form fits better with an Iron Age date than with any Roman-period use of the site. Eventually, the pathway within Ditch 5 was put out of use by infilling, although the dating of this event is not clear. Later still, large pits, 21066 and 20759, are thought likely to have been quarries for chalk extraction from under the former external bank, and from the backfill of Ditch 5. A similar pit (21389) lay to the east. The dating of these features is also not altogether clear, but they appear to have been pre-Roman in date, and a Late Iron Age association with construction relating to the Late Iron Age defensive ditch would seem to offer a likely context. There was therefore a period of modification to the area of the Middle Iron Age defences, following their slighting, which involved the deliberate use of Ditch 5 as a pathway. Ditch 1 probably remained open as a hollow (Roman pottery was recovered from the upper silting), although any defensive role seems unlikely in view of its shallow profile. This period of activity may have been contemporary with either the Middle Iron Age occupation or the Late Iron Age defensive ditch (Ditch 6), although it is not possible to confirm this, as modern truncation will have removed any relationship between the Ditch 6 bank deposits and any internal features, as well as removing the upper fills of the features, which might otherwise have provided terminal dating evidence. Ditch 6 can therefore be interpreted as a replacement for Ditches 1 and 5 on a larger scale, although its overall course is not known, and as it is not even clear on which side the bank lay, such an interpretation must remain tentative.

The dimensions of the ditches of the Middle Iron Age fort invite comparisons with others in East Anglia, although it must be said that these have received minimal archaeological attention, and their dating is often insecure (Davies et al. 1991, 69; Martin 1988). Warham Camp (Fig. 6.1), a bivallate fort, has an inner ditch recorded to be 30 feet (9.14m) wide and 12 feet (3.66m) deep. The distance between the ditches (and the basal width of both embankments) is about 12m (Gray 1933, sectional diagrams). The internal size of the Recreation Way enclosure is, however, relatively small. Warham is 193m in diameter (Davies et al. 1991, 59–61), and Burgh, Suffolk (Fig. 6.1), is much larger at 290 by 240m (Martin 1988, 1). The double-ditched, rectangular form of Recreation Way is similar to Burgh, and the ditches are also of similar dimensions. Burgh's Late Iron Age and Roman date does perhaps equate it with the Late Iron Age occupation at Recreation Way, although, apart from its massive ditch, there is little evidence from Recreation Way for comparison. There were certainly no Late Iron Age pre-conquest imports of the kind that has allowed Burgh to be interpreted as a 'minor oppidum' (Martin 1988, 72). The enclosure at Barnham, south of Thetford (Fig. 6.1), has closer similarities to Middle Iron Age Recreation Way, both in its size (about 1ha) and dating, and its ditches were only slightly smaller (Martin 1979; 1993). There is some suggestion, however, that Barnham, with its human and equine remains, was a special, non-domestic enclosure (Martin 1999, 60–2), and it has been compared with the unique and possibly elite Fison Way enclosure as a primarily ritual site in a marginal upland setting (Hill 1999, 197). In its topographic location Recreation Way has far more in common with many of the Norfolk forts which have, as has been remarked, distinctive river valley and river-crossing locations, but

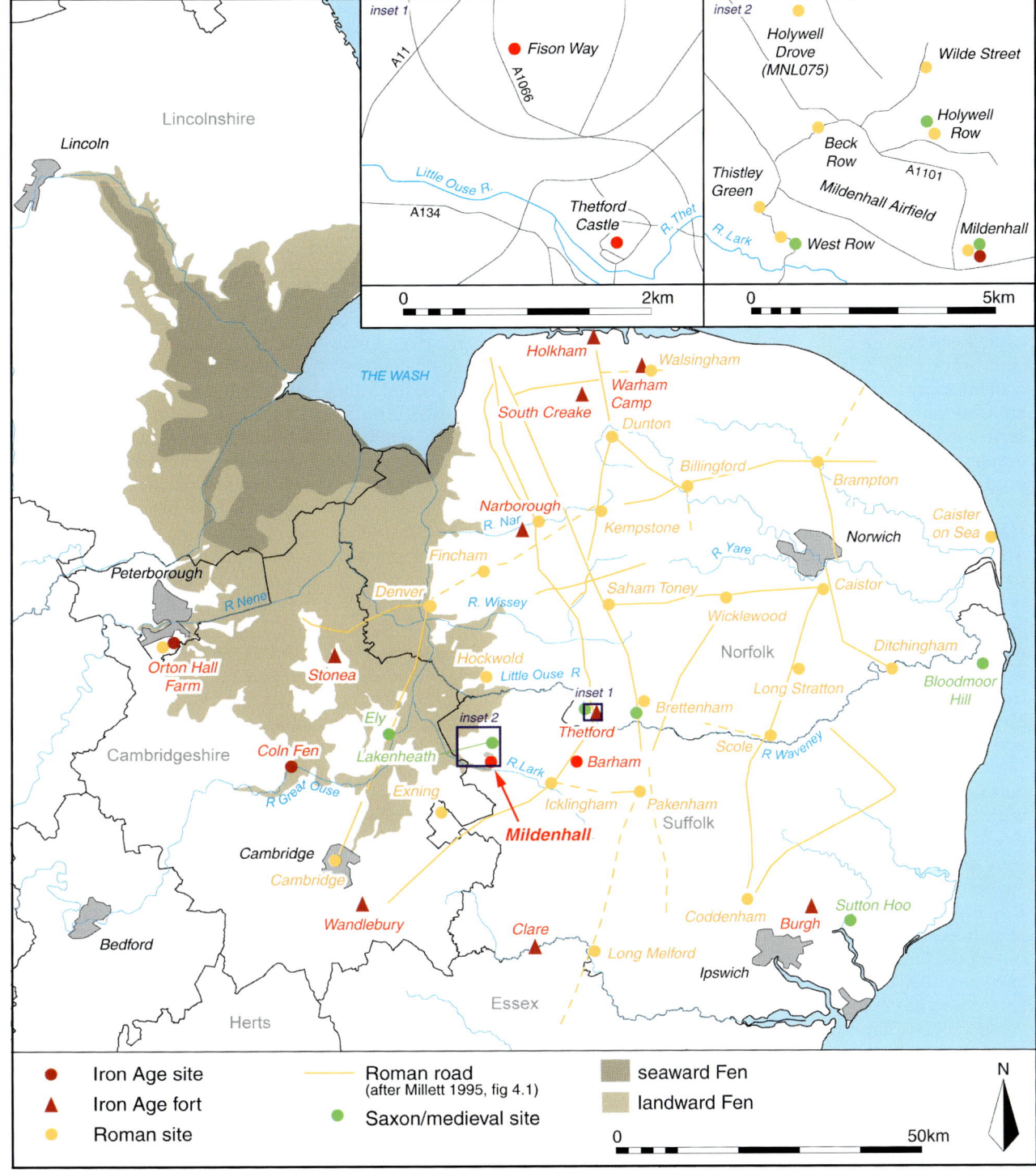

Figure 6.1 Iron Age, Roman, Saxon and medieval sites in East Anglia referenced in the text

which may have enjoyed a similar defensive capacity to hilltop forts through substituting difficulty of approach across a river valley for that of a hill gradient (Gregory and Rogerson 1991, 69). Warham Camp, adjacent to the River Stiffkey, offers a close comparison in this respect, while the fort at Narborough is also relevant, being strategically placed close to the crossing of the Nar by the Icknield Way (Fig. 6.1). Like the Lark, the Nar valley opens westward into the Fens. The fort at Thetford Castle was sited in a similar fashion, on the valley edge overlooking the rivers Thet and Little Ouse. These forts tend to conform to a pattern, and a possible 'strategic line' of Icenian forts along the Fen edge and north Norfolk coast has previously been mooted (Gregory and Rogerson 1991, 69). However, while Recreation Way fits this distribution rather neatly, it is still not clear whether all these forts were actually contemporary with each other, or reflected regional political concerns. In the present state of knowledge, it seems more likely that the forts reflected more local developments, with a principal common factor being the need to control points of passage.

Iron Age occupation evidence

The findings from the excavations at Recreation Way have provided little evidence for the inhabitants of the fort, nor is it clear that it was intended to protect communities or assets within it. There were no identified posthole or ring-gully houses, and, despite the complications of dating and interpretation inherent in a multi-period and truncated site, such absence appears to be genuine since no postholes and roundhouse gullies, survived from later periods. The quantity of finds does, however, indicate settlement close by. Houses may have been present outside the area excavated, or have been shallow-founded with any evidence therefore lost to truncation. A moderately dense distribution of pits within the fort (set back from the conjectured line of the bank), perhaps suggests that houses were built in a separate zone within it. It is also possible that occupation lay on the outside, and attention can be drawn to the presence of Middle Iron Age pits to the east of the defensive ditches, which seem to have been contemporary with them. In this respect, the fort may have had something in common with contemporary farming settlement enclosures of more usual form, where settlement took place both inside and outside the enclosed space. From Sutton Common, it is also apparent that fortifications could be constructed solely to 'protect' stores of crops, and any associated settlement, apparently absent from within the fort, is presumed to have lain on the higher ground (Van de Noort *et al.* 2007, 85). This offers a possible explanation for the absence of structures associated with the pits at Recreation Way, although this is not considered to be a plausible one in this instance, given the quantity of refuse deposited in the pits, which suggests infilling from nearby middens. The evidence in the interior is not dissimilar to that from the large Middle Iron Age site on the opposite side of the River Lark at Bridge House Dairies (Figs 1.1 and 6.2). Here, over 100 pits, spread in clusters over *c.*1.1ha, provided clear evidence of domestic settlement, although the absence of any evidence for houses suggested that the focus of settlement lay beyond the site to the east (Woolhouse 2010, 121–3). On assessing the evidence from a settlement on this scale, however, it appears more probable that the evidence of roundhouses

has simply been lost. With shallow-founded stake or mass-wall construction, and without the need for eaves drainage gullies in a free-draining sand and chalk substrate, it seems entirely possible that any structural evidence would not have survived the effects of ploughing, even to a moderate depth.

Bridge House Dairies offers an insight into an extensive and unconstrained Iron Age settlement, which might be typical of the region (Martin 1999, 49–51; Ashwin 1999, 104–5), with the absence of ditched enclosures accounting for their relative invisibility in archaeological prospection (Bryant 2000, 14; Cunliffe 2005, 265; but see Tremlett 2011 for examples of enclosures and land division, particularly on major interfluves). Quite similar evidence of Iron Age settlement comes from Harford Farm, Caistor St Edmunds, and Valley Belt, Trowse, Norwich (Ashwin and Bates 2000). Both settlements were diffuse, and neither was fully defined. The evidence for houses at Harford Farm consisted solely of a small number of posthole rings, some postholes being very shallow. It can be appreciated that, in the case of Structure 3004, for instance, the loss of another 20cm of ground-depth to ploughing would have removed all trace of the posthole ring (Ashwin and Bates 2000, 95 and fig. 80). Ring-gullies here may have defined other structures, but these were small (5–6m across at most), and likely to have been rick-stands or ancillary buildings (ibid.). Valley Belt, Trowse consisted of a spread of pits and postholes over about 2ha, without evidence of domestic buildings. Both sites show that Middle Iron Age roundhouses may be difficult or impossible to define, a situation that would be typical more widely elsewhere in southern England were it not for the common presence of encircling eaves-drainage gullies. Both these sites also show that unbounded settlements may be typical of the lighter soils of the region, and they pose particular problems of interpretation. Ashwin and Bates thought that Valley Belt may not have been a settlement, but an area 'frequented for a variety of agricultural and craft activities' (2000, 189), and at both Bridge House Dairies and Valley Belt, the settlement core may have lain outside the areas excavated. Intuitively, such explanations become less tenable the more frequently they are invoked, and it seems more likely that the poor archaeological definition of Middle Iron Age settlement may simply be a reflection of the specific traditions and social practices of the inhabitants of the region. It may be more appropriate to use the concept of 'zones of settlement' rather than discrete sites, and at Mildenhall this view would see the Recreation Way and Bridge House Dairies occupation as a settlement zone at a probable crossing point of the River Lark, and perhaps with connections west and east, both to the Fenland edge and to the drier, chalky, sandy uplands. The discovery that the settlement area was both unbounded (the enclosures and droveways at Bridge House Dairies are likely to have been peripheral stock-management features), but juxtaposed with a fort at Recreation Way, is an interesting conundrum, implying that the lower-level security provided by house/household compound enclosures was not seen as being of particular value, but that a fortification was needed for the protection of the group or part of it. Hill (1999, 197) has suggested that communal and ritual concerns may have been the primary motive for fort construction in the region and has remarked upon the possible boundary locations of such sites. This may be significant at Mildenhall where the River Lark has been proposed as an Iron Age tribal boundary on the basis of the distribution of coins and other finds (Martin 1999, 84–6 and figs 3.22–3.23).

The pits at Recreation Way showed some variation in form, and there was little evidence for their primary use. The large Group 1 and Group 3 pits are likely to have been used for grain storage. Burnt grain at the base of pit 19088 may have derived from the *in situ* burning of spoiled or left-over wheat and barley. Elsewhere, all the material within the pits was most likely derived from backfilling. There were also rectangular pits of various sizes, with no clear indications of original use, although again storage seems likely. Sub-rectangular pits formed a distinct class at Danebury, and have been likened to cellars for cold storage, sometimes being located within roundhouses (Cunliffe and Poole 1991, 161). Two clay-lined pits were presumably intended to hold water. Mould and crucible fragments from the casting of copper-alloy items came from pit 15129, although it is not clear that the clay lining of this pit bore any functional relation to bronze-working, and it is likely that the association was a random one.

Finds from the pits included varied, and usually moderate, quantities of pottery and animal bone, the latter showing a mixture of food and butchery waste from the usual domestic species. The pottery assemblage displayed an unusually high proportion of burnished and decorated wares (Brudenell, Chapter 4.VII). This is a regional characteristic, and was also noted at the neighbouring Bridge House Dairies site. The Recreation Way 'late La Tène' decorated assemblage is one of the largest recorded in East Anglia, and it is possible that this was an indicator of unusual status, perhaps associated with ritual activities (Brudenell, Chapter 4.VII). In some cases, decorated vessels may have been formally deposited – vessels with complete profiles were recorded from pits 15271, 17218 and 20868, although but there were no identified groups or combinations of materials that could be identified as being obviously placed or 'structured'.

Prehistoric burials

Grave 21305, cut well within the fill of Ditch 5, contained the skull and first two cervical vertebrae of an adult male. The presence of cervical vertebrae makes it likely that this represents a decapitation, although there were no marks of trauma to indicate any peri-mortem severance of the head. The absence of any other bones in a grave sufficiently large to have accommodated a full skeleton raises a number of questions of taphonomy and burial context. In view of the good preservation of the skull, and more generally of human remains on the site, it appears highly unlikely that the rest of the skeleton had weathered away in such a selective manner. It is also significant that the mandible and vertebrae were found apart from the cranium, strongly suggesting manipulation of the body after at least partial decomposition. The interpretation of human remains from Iron Age sites is the subject of an extensive literature, which has included interpretations of 'head rituals' which cover a wide spectrum, from post-mortem ritual manipulations to warfare and violent retribution (e.g. Green 2001, chapter 5; Craig *et al.* 2005). At South Cadbury, Somerset, it has been argued that some victims of the 'massacre deposit' were beheaded, 'and the severed heads of the vanquished displayed at some conspicuous point on the devastated gate' (Woodward and

Hill 2000, 111), while the cranium found near the entrance to Stanwick (Yorkshire), severed at the level of the fourth cervical vertebra, shows clear evidence of decapitation, and may also have been displayed (Craig *et al.* 2005, 167). Craig *et al.* have reviewed the evidence from Danebury, and make a case for similar practices there in a small number of cases (2005, 167). In the eastern region, a human skull (probably male and lacking the lower jaw) comes from the 'ritual pit' or possible entrance terminal of the inner ditch at Burgh (Martin 1988, 10–12). Further north, in a context that may have been similar, the Sutton Common 'marsh-fort' produced two skulls from the base of the northern terminal of the outer ditch. One of these, with the second cervical vertebra present, is likely to have been fleshed, while the other, which was without the mandible, may not have been (Knüsel 2007, 139). It has been speculated that these examples may represent victims of sacrifice, or slain enemies (Van de Noort and Collis 2007, 182–3), although, it would be very difficult to make a distinction between these and the dismemberment of a dead body in a ritual context from archaeological and osteological evidence. At Recreation Way, the lack of trauma and the evidence for post-mortem manipulation perhaps indicate decapitation in a non-violent context. In a broader sense, the incorporation of a human head or skull within the defences of the putative fort at Recreation Way, and at Burgh, could be interpreted as an act of symbolic reinforcement. Through this process, boundaries were invested with greater security, their crossing became perceived as more dangerous, and the defended settlement afforded greater protection.

The Late Iron Age defensive ditch

The discovery of a massive ditch (Ditch 6, 11m wide and 4m deep), dating to the Late Iron Age, provides an insight into a major feature of regional significance, even though its extent, context and purpose were not apparent in these excavations. The ditch yielded grog-tempered, wheelthrown pottery from its middle and upper fills, and its uppermost fills contained pottery dating to the 1st century AD. The date of its construction can only be approximated to the early to mid-1st century BC. The best evidence is provided by a radiocarbon date from an infant burial in the lower part of the ditch, which, at 352–55 cal. BC, falls within the broader Middle Iron Age range of the earlier broad-ditched enclosure. This implies that Ditch 6 was a fairly immediate undertaking following the demise of the Middle Iron Age 'fort', and appears to have been a direct replacement for it, albeit on a slightly different alignment. The ditch is at least as extensive as those at Warham Camp, with which it appears to be broadly contemporary. Excavation provided no indication of a bank, which may have lain on either the western or eastern side. In contrast with the Middle Iron Age phase of occupation at Recreation Way, there is no good evidence of contemporary settlement associated with the Late Iron Age ditch. While regional studies make it apparent that Middle Iron Age handmade wares continued to be used concurrently with diagnostic Late Iron Age wares (Brudenell, Chapter 4.VII), there do not appear to have been any other significant Late Iron Age features here, and it seems probable that occupation shifted away from the site in the later 1st century BC.

It seems clear that the defensive architecture and function of the Middle Iron Age fort was elaborated upon by this construction. The Late Iron Age ditch suggests that any contemporary 'settlement zone' in and around Mildenhall could be seen as attaining a significant status, possibly even one of a 'territorial oppidum', a type of centre that has so far eluded identification in Icenian territory, but which elsewhere, particularly in south-east England, is defined by massive, but discontinuous, 'dykes' which partly make use of natural landscape features (Cunliffe 2005, 198). It can be suggested that this zone of settlement included the 'peninsula' occupation at the Bridge House Dairies site, where Late Iron Age pits were recorded in the same general area as the Middle Iron Age ones (Woolhouse 2010, 27). At present, both sites lack material indications of status, but such evidence may lie elsewhere within the putative socio-political 'territory' for which the defended settlement provided a focus. Mildenhall lies on the western edge of the Icenian upland, with Fenland to the west and the River Lark as a possible tribal boundary, and some level of strategic importance during this period seems highly probable.

A defensive boundary ditch, whatever its overall form, is a feature which emphasises the importance of the region in the late pre-Roman Iron Age. Such importance has been suggested by other findings from Mildenhall, and here attention should be drawn to what appears to have been an exceptional inhumation burial discovered in 1812 (Fox 1923, 81). This was apparently accompanied by a long iron sword, an axe and a gold torc, and flanked by the skeletons of two horses. The location and details of this burial were unfortunately poorly recorded (Cunliffe 2005, 549–50), although it has been approximately located by the Suffolk HER (ref. MNL Misc MSF9311), to an area some 2.5km to the north-west of Recreation Way (Fig. 6.2). More widely, a major centre at Thetford or Mildenhall may have provided a political context for the rich find of silverware from Hockwold, dated to the late 1st century BC. This was of Italian manufacture, and most probably a diplomatic gift of a direct or indirect nature (Salway 1993, 30). A socio-political centre at Mildenhall has a possible context in the inter-tribal conflicts in southern and eastern Britain, which are thought to have occurred at around the time of Caesar's expeditions in 55 and 54 BC. Caesar's own account of this time refers to the submission of the Cenimagni, who can probably be linked to a branch of the Iceni (Potter and Johns 1992, 35). In the proto-historical framework for this period, an enhanced fortification at Mildenhall may be specifically linked to the expansion of the Catuvellauni, whose influence has been detected well to the west in the lands of the Dobunni (Salway 1993, 35), and who plausibly remained antagonistic towards the Iceni in the century or so before the Roman conquest.

II. The Late Iron Age and Roman periods
by Neil Holbrook

In the Late Iron Age, the focus of activity shifted to the east of the excavated area onto the higher ground. Ditch 6 was c.11m wide and 4m deep, a slight curvature suggesting that it enclosed a settlement to the east, rather than serving as a linear dyke. Ditch 6 is comparable in scale to many of those defining hillforts and contemporary circular defended enclosures in Cambridgeshire (Evans 2000). Future work may confirm that a Late Iron Age fort which dominated a crossing of the River Lark lies beneath

modern Mildenhall. As had been the case in the Middle Iron Age, there is no evidence for the exploitation of the floodplain bordering the river at this time. It is difficult to pin down the date of this Late Iron Age activity, other than that it lies within a relatively broad range extending from the mid to late 1st century BC to the mid-1st century AD. A single worn potin coin, issued c. 50–45 BC, was recovered from the site.

Both the high ground and the lower floodplain were exploited for agriculture in the Roman period. Presumably, the defended Late Iron Age settlement had been abandoned before, or shortly after, the Roman conquest, to be replaced by a farmstead. The main focus of this settlement clearly lay beyond the excavation area, with only more peripheral areas being subject to excavation. What can be said about its economy and chronology is therefore necessarily limited. The pottery assemblage indicates activity on the site from the mid/later 1st century AD, but it is not possible on present evidence to determine whether activity was continuous from the adjacent Late Iron Age settlement defined by Ditch 6, or whether there was a break or shift in settlement focus at this time. Farming activity and, by inference, nearby occupation continued until at least the second half of the 4th century. There is little indication of high status apparent in the pottery assemblage; the small quantity of samian ware recovered, and the scarcity of forms such as mortaria and amphora, are consistent with a lower-status rural community. There is a slight increase in the amount of finewares in 4th-century deposits, although this more probably reflects changes in the local pattern of pottery supply rather than any enhanced settlement status at this time.

The number of excavated features on the higher ground was relatively modest, comprising two drying ovens, an agricultural enclosure, a small number of other ditches and pits, and five inhumation burials. Activity in the 1st and 2nd centuries was largely confined to a small area at the northern end of the higher ground, where drying ovens 17028 and 17048 both produced charred cereal processing waste. Enclosure E was probably used for stock management, to judge from the lack of internal features. Various other ditches, pits, postholes and stakeholes were found, although it is difficult to identify structures with certainty (a partial ring of postholes might conceivably represent part of a roundhouse).

Three Roman-period inhumation burials consisted of two adult males buried in wooden coffins and an un-coffined inhumation of a child. These burials lay in close proximity to one another towards the south-east corner of Enclosure E. In addition, the partial remains of two neonates were recovered from pits. Radiocarbon dates indicate that the burials date to the 2nd or 3rd century AD. Dispersed inhumation burials, often placed close to boundaries, are now recognised as a typical aspect of Roman-period rural settlements in Britain, and their discovery here occasions little surprise.

The lower floodplain on the edge of the chalk bedrock was utilised for the first time in the Roman period, although the area was still liable to periodic flooding to judge from evidence of episodes of silt deposition. The first phase of activity on the floodplain dates to the late 1st to mid-2nd century AD, although there was a marked intensification in use in the late 3rd and 4th centuries, with the construction of a series of agricultural enclosures.

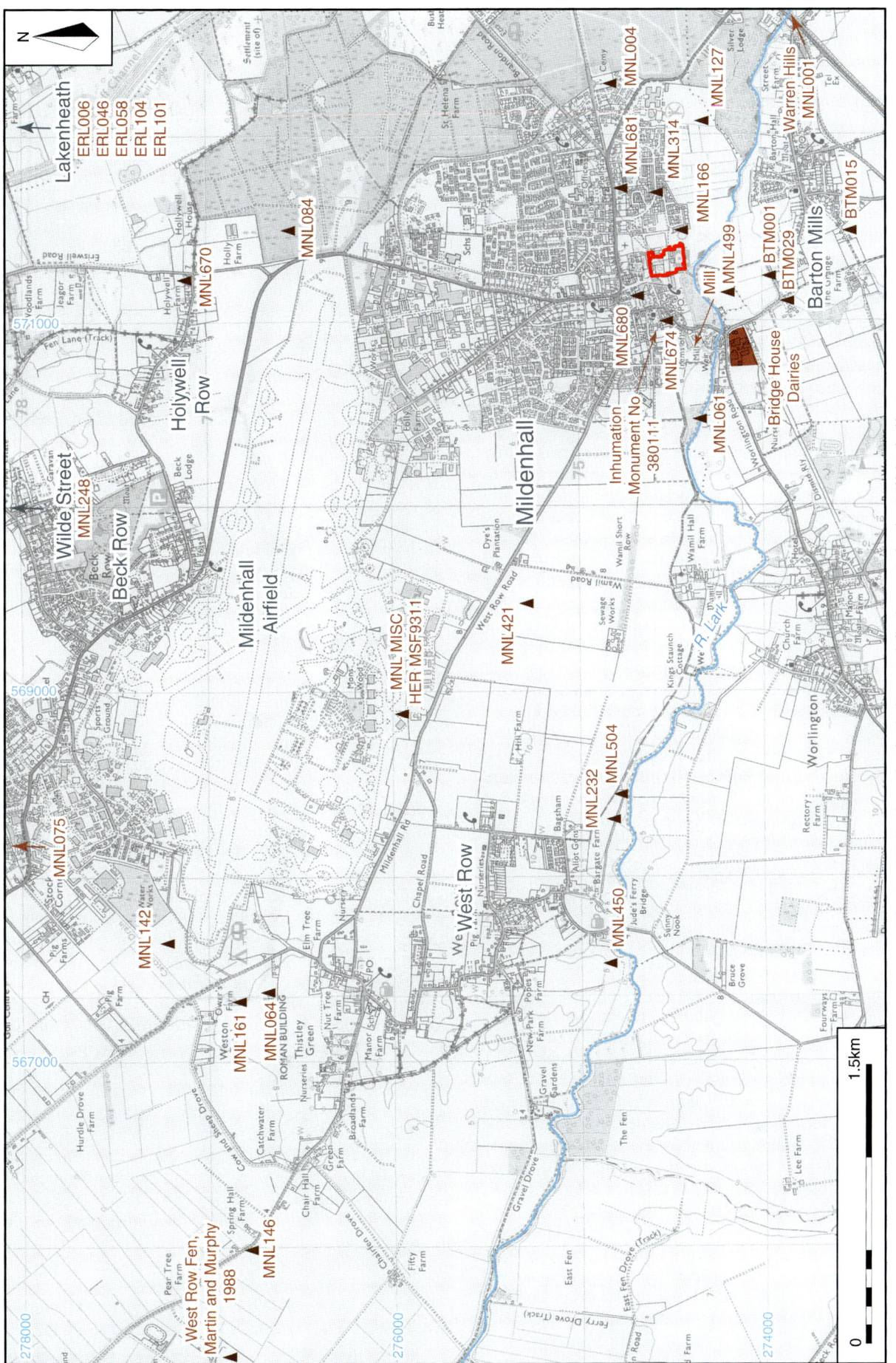

Figure 6.2 Archaeological sites and finds spots in the Mildenhall area

These were probably used for the corralling of stock, which grazed in summer on the lush grasslands bordering the River Lark. Evidence for the local quarrying of chalk may reflect localised attempts to counteract the effects of flooding through the dumping of chalk rubble.

The overall impression gained from the excavated evidence is of a farmstead close to a fording-point of the River Lark. The settlement was involved in mixed farming, with arable crops (spelt wheat and barley) being dried in ovens, and stock corralled in enclosures. The animal bone assemblage recovered from the site indicates that sheep were the predominant species slaughtered on site during the Roman period, as had been the case during the Middle and Late Iron Age periods. Finds of iron slag from one feature also indicate that iron-working played a role in the economy of the settlement, although the small quantity of slag recovered suggests that it did not occur on any scale within the vicinity of the excavated area.

The presence of a Roman settlement on the north bank of the Lark, beneath the centre of historic Mildenhall, has been previously suggested by recorded chance finds of Roman pottery and a coin. We now know more of the character of this occupation, although the core of the settlement remains to be examined. We may reasonably assume that the original ford across the Lark lay close to the present bridging-point, and occupation on the opposite south bank of the river has been demonstrated by metal-detecting finds and a cremation burial at Barton Mills (BTM 001/015/029; Fig. 6.2).

The evidence from archaeological investigations and chance finds suggests that the resources of the surrounding area were heavily exploited during this period. The settlement at Recreation Way was probably one of many similar small farms which exploited the chalk soils and river floodplains in practicing a mixed economy. Drainage schemes and improved climatic conditions contributed to an intensification of settlement and agricultural activity in the region. Gurney (1995), discussing evidence from Norfolk, observed that a picture was emerging of a virtually continuous band of occupation along the Fen edge at this time. In the Mildenhall region, this is notable from the number of sites recorded to the west of Mildenhall, notably at Mildenhall Airfield, and running north along the fen edge to RAF Lakenheath (Fig. 6.1). Amongst these, there is evidence for some higher-status sites, including the probable villa site excavated by T.C. Lethbridge in 1932 at Thistley Green, which has been suggested as possibly the true location of the Mildenhall treasure (Hobbs 2016, 290; MNL 064, MNL 146, MNL161) (Fig. 6.2). Other evidence includes some large aisled, post-built structures, possibly representing granaries or maltings, such as the well-excavated example at Beck Row (Bales 2004), and two similar structures at Wilde Street (MNL 248). A tessellated floor and other evidence for high-status occupation, including numerous finds of metalwork, amphora and other imported goods, suggest the location of another possible villa site at Skelton's Farm (MNL 075), to the north of Beck Row (Fig. 6.2). This accumulation of evidence suggests a settlement landscape which was divided into a series of large wealthy estates, each comprising a series of tenanted farms administered from a villa complex, where produce was processed and redistributed. There is currently insufficient evidence to show whether the farmstead at Recreation Way was integral to this system, or operated as a small, independent farming community.

III. The Saxon period
by Mary Alexander

The evidence for the Early Saxon period is difficult to interpret. A certain amount of evidence for activity of this period is likely to have gone undetected amongst undated features, particularly within the principal area of the site on the higher ground. The dating of Early Saxon activity has been principally achieved on the basis of the pottery assemblage, with a small number of sherds in a variety of fabrics broadly dated to a 5th–7th-century range. However, more precise dating was precluded by the longevity of certain fabrics, some of which may run into the Middle Saxon period. Without doubt, some of the Roman pottery recorded in isolated features is residual, and this may equally be the case for some features at the upper end of the Roman stratigraphic sequence. As would be expected from a multi-period site, residuality is a prevailing issue. The distribution of residual pottery indicates a concentration of Early Saxon activity in the middle part of the higher ground, although only one pit, 2015, lying to the south in Area 3, contained pottery which was exclusively of Early Saxon date. With such a small number of features containing only early pottery, some of which may in fact be Middle Saxon, it is probable that the majority of the Early Saxon pottery owes its presence to the manuring of fields, as Anderson suggests (Chapter 4.IX).

Distinguishing Saxon activity from that of the later Roman period was easier in Area 3 and the parts of Area 2 where post-Roman alluviation provided the horizontal stratigraphy largely missing in the more truncated levels on the higher ground. The alluvial layers in Area 3, and the edge of Area 2, can be linked to a peak in overbank sedimentation in Roman floodplain environments (Lewin 2010, 277), and this is supported by the results of geoarchaeological analysis (Allen, Chapter 5.VII). In Area 3, some of the scatter of pits, stakeholes and gullies cutting the alluvial layers that post-date the Roman field system had an Early and Middle Saxon date which attested to minimal and sporadic use of the area when ground conditions were favourable. Opportunities for summer grazing may also be envisaged, although obviously no evidence for this survived. However, the prevailing conditions were those of regular inundation, and the local population was presumably too small or too under-resourced at this time to either maintain or undertake drainage works. The evident pattern at Recreation Way reflects a wider picture across East Anglia, which suffered from the effects of rising sea levels from the 4th to the 7th centuries, combined with land subsidence which resulted in incursion of the sea from the Wash. This, coupled with a widespread failure to maintain Roman drainage systems, resulted in the abandonment of many lower-lying areas (Hallam 1961, Lamb 1982).

Ditch 4, dating to the 8th or 9th century, represents a significant boundary, and may denote the first new demarcation of land following the Roman period, although there are indications that Iron Age Ditch 6 was still present as a sizeable linear hollow and must therefore have had some significance in terms of access and land use. On the other hand, there is no evidence to suggest that the alignment of Iron Age Ditches 1 and 5 influenced the subsequent demarcation of land, and they must have been fully levelled during the preceding Roman period (the single sherd of 8th/9th-century pottery from the upper fill of Ditch 1 must be considered intrusive). Ditch 4 appears to have gone out of use in the 8th or 9th century.

The steep, V-shaped profile of Ditch 4 may have served a defensive role, and a similar profile was noted with the early 8th-century enclosure ditch at Brandon Road, Thetford (Atkins and Connor 2010, 19). Although there are no other substantial boundary ditches with 8th to 9th-century dating, it is possible that Ditches 2 and 3 are pre-conquest in origin, given their similar alignment to Ditch 4. Dating evidence from Ditch 2 in particular is sparse, and belongs to the period of its final re-modelling. This would imply a width of 40–60m for the field divisions, which is consistent with contemporary rural settlements in the region, such as West Fen Road, Ely (Mortimer *et al.* 2005) and Brandon Road, Thetford (Atkins and Connor 2010) (Fig. 6.1). At Brandon Road, the 8th-century enclosure ditch was of a similar steep-sided V-shaped profile to that of Ditch 4.

There is no surviving evidence of Middle Saxon activity to the east of Ditch 4 other than possibly the hearth, 22058, which was constructed in the soft fills of Ditch 6 and utilised the shelter provided by the sunken ground. One of the two most probable date-ranges provided by archaeomagnetic samples spans the Early and Middle Saxon period, (550–810 AD); the other falls in the Iron Age (Suttie, Chapter 5.II this report), and on stratigraphic grounds this dating remains ambiguous.

Immediately to the west of Ditch 4, there are enigmatic signs of subdivision in the undated gully 17087 and Ditch 20133, and in Ditch 20491 and gully 21674 further to the south. More substantial is the curvilinear gully of Enclosure D, which enclosed an area at least 14m long by 4m wide, and probably originally wider. The parallel line of undated postholes enclosed within Enclosure D may represent a contemporary building structure, or simply a fenceline. There are many examples of this type of enclosure, dating from both the Roman and Saxon periods. Some of these are known to have enclosed buildings and are therefore interpreted as domestic enclosures. Contemporary examples can be found at West Fen Road, Ely (Mortimer *et al.* 2005), and Redcastle Furze, Thetford (Andrews 1995). More frequently, however, these enclosures are interpreted as small paddocks or stock enclosures. No clear indications of structures survive from this period; although there was an enigmatic cluster of substantial postholes spanning Ditch 4 at its southern end. These were clearly substantial enough to support walls and a roof, but any ground-plan remains unclear, and given that they are undated it is possible they were associated with the post-conquest kiln.

Despite the absence of domestic structures, the waste material from pits in the eastern part of the site included domestic waste in quantities that are unlikely to have travelled far from their source. Material from cut features across the site confirmed a range of activities in which some degree of zoning was apparent. The very large deposits of bone in pit 20405 immediately to the south of Enclosure D, and the smaller assemblage in pit 20772 to the east of the enclosure represent all stages of the butchery process. The juxtaposition of these features to Enclosure D might suggest the corralling of livestock on

site for butchery and processing, as the slaughter of livestock brought in on the hoof was clearly indicated by components of the bone assemblage. Much of the livestock was probably grazed on the neighbouring water meadows of the River Lark. The same composition of butchery waste was found in the bone-rich deposits at the edge of the floodplain in Area 2; the pottery incorporated in these deposits is an indication that this locale was used for deposition both in the Saxon and medieval periods, and possibly earlier. The large steep-sided pit (20405) immediately to the south of Enclosure D deserves further investigation. It is unique amongst the pits on site, and its form is not paralleled on other contemporary sites in the surrounding area.

The area was clearly within easy access of settlement, attested by the siting of a cluster of features including the drying ovens 2095 and 2125, which were situated at the southern edge of the high ground. Charred remains from these features indicate the range of activities associated with crop processing, including threshing, winnowing and sieving, that is likely to have taken place here, or nearby. The charred remains within the drying ovens appear to have been used as fuel, and it is possible that the ovens themselves were malting kilns for the production of beer. A rather similar structure was excavated at Redcastle Furze, Thetford, (Structure 2020, Andrews 1995), although a somewhat later date in the 12th–early 13th century was suggested for this feature. The harvested crops could have been transported to this location by river, or have continued onwards by river transport after processing. A scatter of Niedermendig lava fragments may relate to the milling of cereals with domestic rotary querns, or from milling on a larger scale.

There is little evidence for any other activities on site. Evidence for iron-working included smithing-hearth cake fragments, slag and hammerscale, but with no discernible working area, unless the large amounts of hammerscale in pit 16069 on the west side of the site denoted a focus. Iron-smithing was undertaken on a small scale at most rural settlements at this time, but given the levels of fire risk involved, it was generally carried out at a safe distance from domestic dwellings.

There are indications that the livestock were integral to a well-managed, mixed agricultural economy. Cattle sizes may have exceeded modern averages, and in addition to providing a primary source of protein, were also kept for traction and dairy production. Sheep age-at-death statistics suggest a degree of flock reduction during the winter months to reduce requirements for winter fodder, a strategy which will have released land for arable cultivation. The sheep bone assemblage indicates that wool production was also an important element of the economy. The pair of shears recorded from Area 2 is indicative of shearing, but the only evidence of textile production was a single pin-beater, and this activity is likely to have taken place elsewhere. Crummy (2002) argues that wool production increased in the Middle Saxon period, and that textile production moved from the domestic sphere towards more specialised centres. The incidence of both pig and domestic fowl bones increase during this period, compared with the preceding Roman period. Pigs comprised a third element of meat consumption, although domestic fowl were kept primarily for egg production. Locally-caught eels also represented an important source of protein, but surprisingly marine fish were almost absent, indicating a lack of trade in this commodity despite established access routes along the Rivers Lark and Ouse to the sea. Overland routes are suggested for much of the Saxon pottery wares, and only the transportation of Stamford Ware from the Late Saxon period is thought to have utilised inland waterways. In general, there is little evidence for trade at this time, or for the acquisition of high-status or luxury items.

The range of crops recorded reflects a shift during this period to free-threshing wheat and rye which, along with barley, constituted the principal components of the agricultural economy, and one that is typical of the region (Cobain, Chapter 5.VIII and Murphy 1997). Additional crops were also cultivated in the area, both for food and medicinal purposes, and the plant evidence revealed the wide range of environments which were available for exploitation at this time. The general impression from the environmental evidence is for an intensification of arable agriculture, with some indication from charcoal evidence that there was pressure on land by the Middle Saxon period, if not earlier. It would appear that the site at Recreation Way lies on the margins of a small rural settlement for which economic conditions were reasonably favourable, but it was not wealthy, and offers no particular signs of specialisation or status. If the settlement produced any agricultural surplus, this is likely to have been in the form of wool.

There are few clues to any aspect of settlement life beyond subsistence. A chalk gaming-piece, which may be Anglo-Scandinavian in origin, is the only artefact associated with leisure. The isolated burial on the edge of the higher ground in Area 2 may be of Saxon date. Single burials of this type are periodically found in settlement locations in this period, and various explanations for this phenomena have been considered, including 'deviant' burials (for disease or crime) (Reynolds 2009), or the use of burial as a way of laying claim to land and establishing ancestral rights, conferring a spiritual dimension to an occupied area, or recognising boundaries (Lucy 2000; Reynolds 2002). In this case, the location of the burial on the margins of the drier ground may be significant in asserting rights to the floodplain, below.

Hamerow (2006) has classified human remains within settlements as one aspect of the phenomenon of 'special deposits', which also include animal remains. She notes that deposits found in direct association with entrances and boundaries may signify the termination of the use of a feature or, more rarely, a foundation deposit. In contrast to the interpretations of deposits on prehistoric sites (see Hill 1995), the spiritual or ritual aspect of deposition is often overlooked in excavations of this period. The examples she studied were predominantly from ditches and sunken-featured buildings (SFBs); a later study and re-appraisal of this subject included later Saxon examples, predominantly from pits (Morris and Jarvis 2011). This re-appraisal also included a consideration of the actions or processes that characterised the material before it was deposited (ibid., 76). In the light of these studies, it is worth noting the upturned cattle skull in Enclosure D, and the large deposits of animal bone in the nearby pit 20405, close to a possible entranceway into the enclosure. From the majority of animal bone deposits identified as 'special' in Hamerow's study, those of cattle predominate, and in this context, the cattle skull in the base of Enclosure D and the cattle remains which dominate the assemblage from

pit 20405 assume particular significance. Without taking such an interpretation too far, both of these deposits may have had a particular cultural significance for those who created them, although their specific meaning must remain a matter of speculation.

Early Saxon settlement favoured lighter soils (Mudd 2002, 3), with easy access to rivers. It is also apparent that settlement was on a small scale and frequently shifted within its locale, sometimes within the span of two generations (Hamerow 1991, 12; West 1985, 151–2). This is a factor which may have contributed to an impression of population decline in the post-Roman period (Williamson 2005, 17), an impression abetted by a lack of surviving remains of material culture on small, low-status settlements. In fact Scull (1992, 10) argues that a comparison of the Roman and Early Saxon cemetery evidence in East Anglia actually suggests an increase of population during this period. In this respect it is interesting to note the number of cemeteries that have been recorded in the Mildenhall area. Of these, over 120 burials have been excavated from an Early Saxon cemetery at Holywell Row. Lethbridge, excavating in 1929, considered this to be only a part of a larger burial ground (Lethbridge 1931; MNL 084; Fig. 6.2). This burial ground is approximately 0.5km from another large Early Saxon cemetery of possibly comparable size, which was first discovered in the 1950s at Lakenheath Airbase, Little Eriswell (Figs 6.1 and 6.2) (ERL 006, ERL 046, ERL 058, ERL 104), later excavations to the south of this cemetery located an Early Saxon settlement identified by a total of four sunken-featured buildings (ERL 101). A smaller burial ground containing both inhumation and cremation burials was found in the 19th century in and around an Early Bronze Age barrow cemetery at Warren Hills, approximately 3km to the east of Recreation Way (Prigg 1874; MNL 001; Fig. 6.2). Metal detecting in the 1970s and 1990s suggested another location for a cemetery and possibly settlement at West Row, 3km to the west of Mildenhall on the north bank of the River Lark (MNL 232, MNL 450, MNL 504; Fig. 6.2).

Other findspots of Early Saxon metalwork to the northwest, and west, of Mildenhall may denote further cemeteries, or possibly settlements (e.g. MNL 142, MNL MISC/HER MSF9311; Fig. 6.2). Other than metalwork finds, evidence for the settlements that these cemeteries served remains elusive. Smaller excavations to the west and east of the Recreation Way site have also shown negative results (MNL 674, MNL 680, MNL 681; Fig. 6.2). An isolated burial found in the core of the medieval town (Monument no 380111 NRHE; Fig. 6.2), represents the only possible Saxon evidence from this area (see below). To the south of the River Lark, at Bridge House Dairies, open-area excavation proved that at least in this area there was no sign of settlement between the Iron Age and post-medieval periods (Woolhouse 2010) (Fig. 6.2), and fieldwalking in the area (e.g. MNL 499; Fig. 6.2) would appear to support this. Further south at Grange Lane, Barton Mills, where a 6th-century cruciform brooch had previously been found, undated ditches and pits were located, although surface finds suggest that these features could equally be Roman or early medieval in date (12th–13th century) (BTM 015). Pottery of mid-9th to 11th-century date was found amongst much larger quantities of Roman pottery during fieldwalking in fields between West Row and Mildenhall (MNL 421; Fig. 6.2).

This would appear to be a possible location for a Late Saxon settlement which occupied land formerly settled in the Roman period.

At Brandon Road in Thetford, Early Saxon settlement occurred within the former Roman settlement, and although continuity of occupation could not be demonstrated, the alignment of boundaries suggested some residual Roman influence. The author suggested that this may reflect a trend previously noted around the Thetford area (Atkins and Connor 2010, 109). Some Roman sites within the wider East Anglian region are known to have been re-occupied at a later date. At both Kilverstone and Brettenham, just east of Thetford, pottery suggests an interval of at least a century between Roman and Saxon occupation (Tipper in Garrow *et al.* 2006; Mudd 2002), and Orton Hall Farm, Cambs (Mackreth 1996) provides a similar example (Fig. 6.1). At Bloodmoor Hill, Suffolk (Fig. 6.1) the gap is approximately 250 years between earlier Roman remains and the 6th-century inception of Saxon settlement, leading the authors to observe that these Saxon sites are 'coincident, but not necessarily continuous with their Roman predecessors' (Lucy *et al.* 2009, 428). This is an observation that may well hold true for the activity in Period 6 at Recreation Way. Here, it is difficult to judge the extent to which Roman settlement influenced subsequent patterns of occupation and land-use in the immediate aftermath of the Roman period. Surviving evidence from the 5th-6th centuries is sparse, either denoting settlement on a very small scale, or a settlement close by but periodically shifting within the immediate locale. The extent to which the vestiges of earlier boundaries influenced field division in the Middle Saxon period, and how far the lie of the land and the practicalities of drainage determined field alignments, is hard to assess.

What is apparent at Recreation Way is that, despite worsening conditions in the southern part of the site, the area continued to be used and more heavily exploited into the Middle Saxon period, no doubt as part of a rural community which in some respects differed little from those which had farmed there in the Roman period. The general picture from Mildenhall and surrounding parishes is that occupation in all periods hugged the fen edge. Topographical, geological and environmental determinants must have played an essential part in locating, or relocating, settlements, and in their eventual economic success. Political factors may also have played an increasing role in both the location and economic fortunes of the settlements in the Mildenhall area at this time, although their impact is difficult to assess from the evidence at Recreation Way. At Brandon Road, Thetford, the abandonment of the settlement has been linked to the defeat of King Edmund at Thetford in 869, and to subsequent settlement changes under Danish occupancy (Atkins and Connor 2010). Within the more outlying rural areas, including Mildenhall, the impact of political change was possibly less. At Recreation Way, the use of the area appears to have been continuous from the 8th or 9th centuries through to a decline in the 14th century, despite the political turbulence of these times. Ditch 4, the only possible feature of this period with a defensive character, may equally have been constructed as an effective barrier for livestock.

IV. Medieval
by Mary Alexander

Climatically, the early medieval and Late Saxon periods fall within the so-called 'Medieval Warm Period' *c.*900–1400, but it was not necessarily a drier period, and records suggest that there was considerable fluctuation within the overall trend, with some years experiencing cold or even severe winters (Ogilvie and Farmer 1997). Rising sea-levels in the later medieval period (Hallam 1961, 152–3) were accompanied by a peak in overbank sedimentation in lowland areas in the late 13th to 15th centuries (Lewin 2010) 277. It is apparent from the deposition sequence in Area 3 that a wet floodplain environment prevailed, the early trackway suggests seasonal grazing, later ditches and dumped deposits show that measures were taken to drain the area. These attempts were repeated, possibly as a response to increasing pressure on land, although the area continued to be flooded on a periodic basis, probably until the canalisation of the river in the early 18th century.

Early in the excavation at Recreation Way, Ditch 2 was originally interpreted as the eastern boundary of the medieval settlement at Mildenhall, and a marked difference in the nature of the excavated evidence to the east and west of this boundary was anticipated. But as excavation continued, it became apparent that use of land to the west of Ditch 2 did not differ significantly from that to the east, in that evidence survived in both areas of activities commonly undertaken within the peripheries of village or rural settlement. However, the size and depth of the ditch (despite the post-medieval and modern truncation) suggest that the feature was of some importance, and that with a bank this would have presented a considerable obstacle to entry from the east, other than through the entrance way to the north-east, which was later blocked.

Ditch 3 divides the area to the west of Ditch 2 into a long strip of land; the less substantial and discontinuous Ditch 35 appears to divide two zones of activity, while evidence of other minor subdivisions may have been lost to truncation. Dating from Ditches 2, 3 and 35 suggests that this arrangement prevailed from the 11th to the 13th centuries, and only later, in the 14th century, was this area subdivided by the east-west boundary of Ditches 38 and 39. As discussed above, it remains possible, but entirely conjectural, that Ditch 2 was initially a smaller ditch which was dug as part of land divisions in the pre-conquest period, when Ditch 4 played a major role as a deterrent to ingress from the east. In size and location, Ditch 2 would be considered a good candidate for the eastern arm of a town ditch referred to as the Baille or Bayle in 15th and early 16th-century sources, although the dating evidence and the presence of the east-west boundary which cuts through the backfill of Ditch 2 mitigates against this possibility, unless these sources preserve a reference of considerable antiquity.

Post-medieval and modern truncation has depleted the evidence from this period, and has no doubt created a bias in favour of the more robust cut features, although some of the surviving evidence points to distinct zones of activity. The largest of the surviving features, the chalk extraction pits found towards the south-west of the higher ground, may have been cut to supply the kiln, 20044. This conforms in its shape and surviving internal details to a type of medieval lime-kiln known as a 'Flare' or 'periodic' kiln, which took a single charge of raw material (in this case probably chalk), which required cooling and unloading before the kiln was re-loaded. 'Perpetual' kilns, that evolved to burn and process lime continuously, tend to be a later medieval development, which continued into the industrial age (Williams 2004). The kiln chamber would have been walled above ground, using chalk or stone blocks, and open at the top. The higher of the two internal ledges probably held the chamber walls, the lower ledge supporting a vault of chalk blocks to protect the material above from the fire source. These surviving structural details indicate that the kiln was of a type designed to produce good-quality lime, unmixed with ash, which would have been deployed variously for lime-wash for walls, bleaching paper, preparing hides for tanning, disinfectant, or in medicine (EH 2011, 2), rather than as a building material. There may be a connection between the lime kiln and the bone-rich deposits in Area 2, as some elements of this mixed assemblage may derive from the preparation of hides for tanning. Lime production, which was a smelly and dangerous process, took place over several days, and was thus suited to locations some distance away from settlement, and to winter working when fewer demands were made on the farm labourer's time.

Lime kilns were located in sheltered and well-drained areas. Gullies and ditches around the kiln may have been for drainage purposes, with the stake-built structures to the east serving as temporary shelters for those tending the kiln. Post-medieval evidence for lime kilns in this area, which have often been commemorated in field names, would appear to indicate a long tradition of use (Chapter 3).

Structure G could be interpreted as a small agricultural structure, possibly used for winnowing or threshing crops. A crop-drying oven, 17182, in the north-eastern area of the dry ground suggests a shift of crop-drying activity to the north, away from its earlier locus in Area 2. Large quantities of waste material in deposits in Areas 2 and 3 represent all stages of crop-processing, and also include quantities of burnt clay and charcoal that may derive from the dismantling of crop-drying ovens. From this evidence, it would appear that crop processing remained a major activity throughout the medieval period.

Other structural remains from the early medieval period are more difficult to interpret. The curving Ditch 34 and fenceline may have screened metalworking activities, using water from the nearby well. There is some hammerscale and slag in nearby features, although metalworking evidence on the whole is sparse, and the crucible and smithing-hearth fragments are found at some distance. Given that any metalworking waste in previous periods is likely to have been re-worked into features, there was little to be gained from any analysis of its distribution. Metalworking is likely to have been a relatively small-scale, transient activity, which was undertaken sporadically for mending or manufacturing trade or agricultural implements, as the need arose. Enclosure F, and other more enigmatic structural evidence found to the east of Ditch 2, suggests a stock management function, and Enclosure F is of a similar form and size to the slightly earlier Enclosure D, to the north. The deposits of mixed animal bone in Area 2, discussed above in relation to tanning, indicate that carcass preparation continued to be practiced in this period, with evidence from the pits suggesting an increase in butchery waste at this time.

It is somewhat surprising, given that wool and the wool industry played such an important part in the region's economy, that there is no evidence for weaving or textile manufacture at Recreation Way, particularly as sheep are the predominant domestic species represented in assemblages from this period. There is some sparse evidence for occupations beyond humble subsistence activities, in the form of a gaming piece, and a facetted slate rod which may have been either a mason's tool or a reading stylus. The pottery assemblage is informative about trading links, which may be applicable to the whole settlement. In the Middle Saxon period, the dominance of Ipswich Wares indicates that a principal supply-route ran overland, either directly from Ipswich, or via the important regional centre at Brandon. The focus of later Saxon and early medieval supply subsequently switched to Thetford, with much of the pottery supplied from the town's own production, with other regional imports probably acquired through Thetford's market. The pottery also reflects direct trade links with Bury St Edmunds. Evidence for trade along the river routes to the Great Ouse and to the coast are less tangible, and without good assemblages from within the settlement core of Mildenhall, it is difficult to assess the extent to which the material from Recreation Way reflects the full range of trading connections that Mildenhall as a whole may have enjoyed.

In the immediate post-conquest period, Mildenhall may not have comprised a large nucleated settlement. Regional studies suggest that patterns of land use in the south and west of East Anglia were established in the Late Saxon period, and were characterised by hamlets scattered along valleys, augmented in some places by dispersed farms (Williamson 2005, 19). The emergence of common fields in the Late Saxon period in the north and west of East Anglia effectively fossilised the settlement pattern, and many medieval villages developed from these origins (Martin 2008, 217). However around Mildenhall common fields were only present on the 'hards' (i.e. non-fen locations), and the development of a village in its present location cannot be attributed to this factor. Breen (Chapter 3) argues that Mildenhall developed an urban core (later referred to as 'High Town'), in line with its increasing prosperity in the early medieval period. This increase in prosperity and population density is not reflected in any substantial way in the evidence from Recreation Way, which appears to have retained a characteristically marginal status throughout the early medieval period, somewhat similar to that of the Late Saxon period. The production of lime can be added to the number of activities suited to areas on the margins of settlement, which will have included crop processing, animal husbandry and iron-working on a small scale. A further addition to these activities, although not conclusively proven to have taken place in any of the excavated features, may be hemp processing, a foetid and polluting activity suited to riverside or fen-edge locations (Geary et al. 2005, 321), and ideally located downstream from domestic occupation. The wells at the north end of the site may reflect an eastward expansion of the urban core of Mildenhall during the 11th to 13th centuries. As the land became increasingly built-up, fences and walls may have impeded access to previous sources of water (such as the river, or communal wells). Moreover, activities such as tanning, hemp retting and a general increase in waste disposal, would have made the water supply provided by the river less potable than in earlier periods.

The indications from economic evidence are that those who discarded their waste material on the site, and who therefore presumably lived in close proximity, experienced a low standard of living throughout the medieval period, despite the expansion of Mildenhall, which by the mid-14th century had become the fourth largest town in Suffolk (Chapter 3). As an indicator of status, it is notable that the percentage of glazed-ware pottery at Recreation Way is comparable with rural, rather than urban sites, although the presence of some types of pottery suggests direct trade links with Bury St Edmunds which are not otherwise typical of other rural settlements in the area (Anderson, Chapter 4), but may reflect Mildenhall's status within the abbey's holdings as one of its wealthiest and most prized possessions. Faunal remains suggest improvements in animal husbandry from the Saxon period, but not in patterns of consumption. Sheep remained the mainstay of the pastoral economy, although cattle probably provided the larger source of animal protein. Some high-status foodstuffs, such as figs and venison were also recorded, but in very small quantities. The number of eel bones suggests that local resources were important, but there is a singular lack of evidence for the exploitation of wild birds or animals. The pike was an expensive fish, although occasional small specimens may represent an incidental catch from the netting of eels. The evidence at Recreation Way, until its decline in the late 14th century, bears comparison with the site at Broad Street, Ely (Cessford *et al.* 2006), a site that was marginal to a more densely-populated urban centre, albeit one that was larger and, on evidence, more prestigious than Mildenhall. The environmental evidence from Broad Street suggests that a similar range of resources were available. Eel was consumed here, but as at Recreation Way, there is little evidence for the exploitation of wild birds or animals. At Broad St, (ibid., 93), marine fish do not appear in the archaeological record until the 15th and 16th centuries, and then only rarely; at Recreation Way a single marine fish bone was identified. At Ely, the economic indicators from the Broad Street site can be compared with the excavation of areas more central to the town (Alexander 2003; Dickens and Whittacker forthcoming; Regan 2001), where different patterns of consumption reflect both higher status and access to a wider range of resources (Cessford *et al.* 2006, 92). If this comparison is valid, the evidence from Recreation Way does not reflect the general economic conditions in the heart of the settlement at Mildenhall, which may well have enjoyed a better standard of living, although not necessarily comparable with that of some of the larger and more prestigious urban centres of the region.

The decline in activity at Recreation Way is amply demonstrated by a sharp fall-off in the discard of pottery. Only 32 late medieval/post-medieval sherds were recovered from the site (to be compared with 542 medieval sherds), and these were principally derived from the small cluster of pits in the north-west of the site, and the backfilling of a well. If any other activity took place on the site in this period, it left no material remains, and was thus unlikely to be of the same character or intensity as in the preceding medieval period. The revision of field boundaries represented principally by Ditches 37 and 38 appears to have been a short-lived development of the 13th or 14th centuries, judging by the date of the pottery within the ditch fills. However, given the absence of later pottery, any cut features remaining open in the following centuries were more likely to have received residual pottery than contemporary material. This boundary is not amongst the pre-enclosure boundaries depicted on the 1812 map (Fig. 3.1a), or on Young's map of 1834 (Fig. 3.1b). A field boundary situated a few metres to the south, and first shown on the 1904 OS map, appears to be a later feature.

The fields were probably used for grazing, as the site displays no evidence of plough-furrows from this period, but it is possible that the 'stetch' ploughing method may have been employed, which produces low ridges that seldom survive as earthworks, and would have been unlikely to survive the levels of modern truncation evident at Recreation Way. Recent studies have concluded that 'stetch' ploughing was carried out widely across East Anglia in the post-medieval period, and probably during the medieval period too (Martin 2008, 33). It is notable that the range of activities attested on the site during preceding centuries, and which were broadly typical of those taking place on the periphery of the nearby settlement, cease in the 14th century. The historical sources suggest that Mildenhall was thriving at this time, with a rapid elevation in status from the eighth to the fourth largest town in Suffolk in the years between 1327 and 1377. When the fortunes of Mildenhall began to wane in the 15th century, the decline was swift, but a contraction of activity had already taken place at Recreation Way. The reasons for this early decline in activity at the site are probably complex, and without sufficient comparable evidence from elsewhere in Mildenhall, must remain a matter of speculation. The loss of properties adjacent to the north end of the site, in the town fire of the mid-16th century, would be consistent with the evident disuse of the well and the backfilled pits, but otherwise left no other discernible mark on the archaeological record.

V. Continuity and change
by Mary Alexander

The environment and topography
The local environment and topography exert a strong influence on the way in which a site is occupied, and on the uses to which it is put. Through examination of the environmental record, we can chart how the local environment and the use of the local environment changed, or remained the same, throughout the period of human use and occupation. The use of ecofacts (and artefacts) to examine change through time must be undertaken with caution, and in the knowledge that the later the feature, the more likelihood there is that it contains residual material which has been either accidentally or deliberately introduced. The evidence can tell us much about the environment, but each set of data has its limitations. Geoarchaeology can tell us much about the conditions under which deposits accumulated, although the information is limited to the specific location of the sample, and may not be representative of a wider area. Land snail and pollen assemblages provide evidence for local habitats, while seeds and charcoal are effective indicators of what has been selected from the wider

environment and brought on to the site for use and consumption.

The correlation between regional climatic or environmental changes and their impact at the local level is rarely a simple one. Where sufficient evidence is available, it would appear that, although the wider environment was affected by climatic trends, local and regional environments remained relatively stable, and the exploitation of these environments changed little throughout the period under study. Other than in Areas 2 and 3, the site remained dry, although water-tables rose in winter and occasionally severe winters may have led to floods. The earliest evidence from Area 3 is for a wide, low-energy channel, probably one of many braided channels of the River Lark, running close to the chalk edge, and cutting through sands and gravels thought to have derived from late glacial or early post-glacial outwash rivers. The channel was probably still open during the Late Mesolithic/Early Neolithic period, but by the Late Bronze Age it had silted up, and throughout the period under discussion a moist floodplain environment prevailed, with fluctuating levels of inundation from the river. Much of the molluscan evidence derives from a slow-moving body of well-vegetated water, and from this it must be assumed that the River Lark ran closer to the site in prehistory than it now does in its artificial channel. The conditions indicated here are consistent with the climatic record of the 1st millennium BC, when gradual deterioration resulted in generally wetter conditions and a rising water-table in the fens. The coincidence of these conditions with the first activity recorded at Recreation Way on the higher ground has already been discussed (see Chapter 6.1, above).

Pollen from the Late Bronze Age peat formation in Area 3 indicates a mix of pasture and arable land, with possible cereal cultivation nearby. A low percentage of pollen from woodland species is indicative of the beginnings of woodland clearance. Molluscan and pollen evidence suggest that a similar environment prevailed on the dry ground throughout the occupation of the site, when the immediate environment was open, and dominated by grassland used as pasture. The climate (although subject to minor fluctuations) was conducive to farming, and the environmental evidence reflects this degree of environmental stability, together with the continuing expansion of farmland through woodland clearance.

The economy
Comparison of the seed assemblages from the Late Bronze Age and Iron Age periods shows exploitation of the same variety of habitats (arable, hedgerow/woodland/scrub, marshland, pasture/disturbed and heathland). Barley and spelt wheat were the dominant crop species in the Late Bronze Age, and the proportion of emmer/spelt wheat relative to barley increases in the Iron Age assemblages. Percentage comparisons in weed species from the Iron Age suggest that, by this period, a large part of the surrounding landscape was under cultivation. The Iron Age charcoal evidence appears to support regional observations for continuing woodland clearance; here the use of scrub and hedgerow-type species may be linked to the comparative scarcity of slower-burning woodland species. Harvested crops appear to have been uprooted rather than scythed in the Iron Age, and hulled cereals were probably dried in small batches over a hearth.

Given the disparity in the size of the bone assemblages from the Bronze Age and the Iron Age periods, and the possibility that the Late Bronze Age pit at Recreation Way contains deposits which had been selected for deposition, any assessment of changes in animal husbandry between the two periods must be viewed with caution. In the animal bone assemblage from the Bronze Age pit, cattle outnumbered sheep, and there was evidence that these animals might have been managed for milk production, but this balance would appear to be atypical of the period (Higbee, Chapter 5.IV). From the more abundant Middle Iron Age assemblage, the emphasis is on the rearing of sheep primarily for meat, although artefacts for weaving were also found on the site. In keeping with the evidence from the earlier period, cattle kept for milk and traction were an important aspect of the pastoral regime.

From the more limited evidence available for the Late Iron Age, the economic basis of the settlement appears to have remained stable. Gradual changes in sheep husbandry indicate that wool production became a more important element of the economy. Spelt wheat dominated the crop assemblage, although emmer wheat, oats and barley were also grown. The Late Iron Age witnessed the introduction on the site of a purpose-built crop dryer, possibly used to separate chaff from cereal grain, or for malting. The increase in efficiency resulting from this type of feature is commonly regarded as a development of the Roman period, implying crop-processing on a more organised scale, and typically associated with changes in land ownership and the need to supply surplus to estate centres or to towns (Cobain, Chapter 5.VIII). In this instance, the location of the features cutting the backfill of the Late Iron Age ditch suggests changes in land-use which may have been linked to wider political and economic realignments a century or more before the Roman conquest.

Despite the contrasts in the character of the settlement remains during the Iron Age and Roman periods, there is much to suggest that farming and the local economy continued along the same lines, with small changes to the economic basis of the area introduced over long periods of time. The Roman farming community represented in the evidence from Recreation Way continued to have access to the same wide range of physiographic zones; the relative percentages of cultivated crop species were equivalent to those of the Iron Age, with spelt wheat and barley dominant, and a similar range of other plants, both cultivated and wild, were exploited for food and medicinal purposes. There may have been a number of reasons for a slight increase in the percentage of barley processing waste, given that this crop could be put to a variety of uses. One minor change from the Iron Age animal bone assemblages is that pig, normally considered to be indicative of higher-status Roman sites, is less frequently found than in preceding Iron Age periods. In other respects the assemblages are similar, with sheep being the most numerous of the farmed animals. Despite the apparently low status of the Roman-period settlement, there was less emphasis on the exploitation of wild fauna than in preceding periods, possibly reflecting the influence of Roman cultural norms, which were not, however, apparent in other dietary choices.

The general trend towards the use of free-threshing wheat and rye is reflected in the Recreation Way assemblages. Early populations may have been relatively transient, and have shifted around in the locality, and while settlement was definitely focussed elsewhere in the Early Saxon period, the general picture was probably of local continuity. Certainly the evidence for arable farming, and particularly the weed seeds associated with hulled wheat (grown in Roman times) in Early Saxon assemblages, has been suggested as providing evidence for the use of the same fields for the same purposes (Cobain, Chapter 5.VIII). By the Middle Saxon period, the quantity of cereal-processing waste at Recreation Way indicates that crop processing was being undertaken on a large scale, with a locus for crop-drying kilns situated at the south of the higher ground. The evidence for plants grown to counteract decreasing soil fertility, together with evidence for a decrease in woodland areas, are both indicators of intensive farming in the local landscape. Animal bone assemblages indicate that cattle farming was the most important element of the pastoral economy. This is the only period in the history of the site where sheep do not dominate the animal bone assemblages, and this situation is anomalous compared with other regional sites of the period. As an apparent manifestation of specialist production, this evidence might indicate control by an estate centre, wîc or emporia site (Higbee, Chapter 5.IV).

The changing character and significance of the site through time

The character and extent of the Bronze Age occupation is difficult to determine from the surviving evidence, other than in its very sparseness it appears typical of excavated evidence from this period. The primary purpose of large pit 20238 was for the extraction of water, and it can be surmised from the quantity of domestic waste in its backfill that this feature was located for the convenience of a nearby settlement. There is otherwise little to say about the period after the waterhole is backfilled, other than that the absence of Early Iron Age activity in those locations favoured by settlement both before and afterwards appears to reinforce a pattern observed for this region (Medlycott 2011, 29), and there is no obvious precursor to the earthworks constructed with such ambition and scale in the Middle Iron Age period.

The Iron Age is arguably the era of the site's greatest significance. Whether defensive or for show, the massive ditches elevated the site's importance, and it clearly played a prominent role in the maintenance of power or control for one element of the local community. The political impetus behind this construction has been discussed above (Chapter 6.I), but no firm conclusions can be reached. From a strategic point of view, the topography of the site is well used, with the floodplain to the south effectively serving as the fort's southern defence. Despite the monumentality of the enclosure ditches, other aspects of the use of the site remain obscure. The pottery assemblage has been discussed as a possible indicator of high status and ritual activity, but its occurrence at the Bridge House Dairies site shows that it is not specifically associated with the enclosed area (Brudenell, Chapter 4.VII). Structures, or the evidence for structures, are absent from the fort interior, which contained a large number of storage pits. However, these are not specific to the enclosure either, occuring beyond its boundaries and on the unenclosed Bridges Dairies site.

Although the western part of the site remained enclosed in the Late Iron Age (assuming Ditch 6 serves the

same purpose as the earlier ditches), there was a dearth of features within the enclosed area, and a scarcity of domestic waste. These may denote a later change of use to a purely agricultural function, such as grazing. The absence of storage pits in the Late Iron Age at Recreation Way is a feature noted from a number of contemporary sites. Some models of Late Iron Age social change have identified both the abandonment of hill-forts and the lack of storage pits as visible signs of the shift from forms of social control based on hill-forts and feast-giving, towards a means of enhancing social standing through trade and the exchange of prestige goods (van der Veen and Jones 2006). This suggestion was examined at Wandlebury in Cambridgeshire, although the possibility that these changes signified the onset of harsher conditions was also considered (Medlycott 2011, 23; Webley 2005). The construction of the corn-dryer at Recreation Way would appear to suggest that crop yields continued to be abundant. Other explanations could include above-ground granaries replacing grain storage pits (Campbell 2008), but these are not apparent at Recreation Way.

In some respects, the Roman evidence points to a radical change in the function of the site, and in its regional significance. Although the large Iron Age Ditches 1 and 6 were still present in the form of linear hollows, the period of Roman occupation did not appear to incorporate or adapt these existing features, and there was some evidence of deliberate infilling. As stated above (Chapter 6.II), the Late Iron Age defended settlement had been abandoned before, or shortly after, the Roman conquest and the hearth cut into the upper fills of Ditch 6 might suggest that a decline in use may have begun up to a century earlier. The Roman-period settlement at Recreation Way was both undefended and unremarkable.

The probable loss of evidence for structures in the preceding periods has been discussed above (Chapter 6.I), and in this period there is a comparable lack; the only possible structural evidence comprised a possible semicircle of postholes at the north end of the site; a humble structure built in the Iron Age tradition, and of a type now recognised as a common feature of Roman farmsteads. In this instance, this structure, and the paddocks, corn dryers and out-lying burials, all point to activity on the periphery of a farming community of relatively lowly status. A tenant farm belonging to a local estate would fit with the picture provided by the Roman evidence from this area of the fen edge (Chapter 6.II).

Although there was less intense use of the site in the Early Saxon period, the local evidence (discussed in Chapter 6.III) provides a general picture of an area that did not suffer decline or abandonment in the post-Roman period. Little can be said about the Early Saxon presence, other than the presence of pottery from this date suggests that the lands on the higher ground continued to be tended, although settlement was located elsewhere. The Roman paddocks on the floodplain were buried beneath alluvium as the water-table rose, and the generally wetter conditions experienced in the Early Saxon period may have been a contributing factor in settlement shift.

The evidence of the 8th/9th centuries, and of the period up to the Norman Conquest, again indicates land-use on the margins of the settlement, and this status is preserved into the post-conquest years. The continuity of activity at Recreation Way (preserving a marginal status through to the medieval period) suggests that the centre of

Mildenhall was fixed on the west side of Recreation Way in the Late Saxon period, or even earlier, and that the medieval town developed from this pre-conquest settlement. As discussed above, the impetus for this consolidation of settlement location cannot be linked to the creation of common fields at this time. The establishment of a church or the development of mills on the river may have been contributing factors, although this remains conjectural. An early 11th century charter (Chapter 3) of Edward the Confessor naming a pre-existing place-name of Mildenhale gives further credence to the pre-Norman establishment of settlement in this location.

The re-establishment of substantial ditched features, and a general increase in activity from the mid-Saxon into the early post-Conquest period, suggests a degree of enclosure and demarcation of space not seen since the Iron Age, and again, the function of these ditches is uncertain. The Middle Saxon Ditch 4 would be effective in corralling cattle, but could also serve in a defensive role, and might therefore have been a necessary precaution had the settlement specialised in any valuable commodities, as suggested for the faunal remains (Higbee, Chapter 5.IV). A dual role for the medieval ditches might also be envisaged, both as an effective defence, and possibly as an ambitious demarcation of an expanding town that never quite fulfilled its promise.

VI. Conclusion
by Mary Alexander

The investigations at Recreation Way provided a rare opportunity to investigate a relatively large area of past settlement and activity on the eastern fen edge. Other than the excavations at Bridge House Dairies (Woolhouse 2010) no other recent development in the locality had provided an opportunity to excavate a site of any size. Knowledge of past activity in the immediate area was based on chance finds and small-scale investigations, and of the site itself almost nothing was known. Although some evidence of past activity could be anticipated from the locality of the site, the range and significance of the evidence that was revealed was unexpected. Over large parts of the site, a deep sequence of archaeological deposits was excavated and as a consequence the site has provided a large body of evidence deriving from human activity spanning three millennia. The analysis of this evidence has provided much information on how the local landscape was utilised, how local resources were exploited, and about the changing patterns of settlement within the site itself. On a wider level many aspects of the evidence had much to offer to current research themes, both on a local and a regional level.

The discovery of Late Bronze Age activity at Recreation Way has made an important contribution to the study of settlement chronologies and settlement shift in the Bronze Age. The cessation of activity at West Row Fen and the appearance of activity at Recreation Way have been discussed (Chapter 6.I) and an important link made between the relative heights of the two settlement areas in relation to rising water-tables. The later Bronze Age activity at the site is a marker of fen edge occupation in this period; the presence of a waterhole suggests this type of feature is more common in the region than previously thought. The quantities of domestic waste found in the large Bronze Age pit cannot have been transported far from their source, but the settlement from whence they derive remains elusive. This would not appear to be unusual for this region, and in Chapter 6.I the discussion touches on the difficulty of defining sites of this period even where large areas have been investigated. Although the pit at Recreation Way can tell us little about the form or location of the nearby settlement, the large assemblage of pottery has proved to be intrinsically valuable in the study of later Bronze Age typologies in the region. In addition the corroboration provided by two radiocarbon dates enhances the contribution that this assemblage can make to a chronology for the Bronze Age period in the region (Medlycott 2011, 20).

This volume has also examined the Iron Age evidence in terms of social organisation, and settlement form and function. The nature of the occupation in the Middle and Late Iron Age is intriguing. The defensive or symbolic function of the massive ditched enclosure has been extensively discussed in Chapter 6.I, postulating a role in the defence of the Iceni territory and as a candidate for a later oppidum.

It is worth considering how different and possibly more simplistic our interpretation would be of the evidence at Recreation Way without knowledge of the undefended and unenclosed contemporary settlement at Bridge House Dairies. By considering both sites together we come to a much more nuanced interpretation of the society they represent. Both sites are considered to be part of the same settlement zone, within which some areas may hold a different status (the missing evidence for roundhouses at both is attributed to the lighter soils).

The status of Recreation Way is explored in the pottery assemblage, which has a 'surprisingly' large component of late La Tène-style decorated pottery. The number and variety of decorated pots outweighs the assemblages from other sites in the region, and, with a series of radiocarbon dates and the petrographic study conducted on some sherds from Recreation Way, the analysis has made a notable contribution to the study of decorative traditions in East Anglia. Although the significance of these pots is still not clear nor why they occur in such numbers at Recreation Way, on a wider scale, the analysis of the large and well-dated assemblage of Middle Iron Age pottery has contributed much to the chronological issues of Middle Iron Age pottery in the region (Medlycott 2011, 29).

The evidence from Recreation Way spans a considerable period of time and aspects of continuity and change are discussed in Chapter 6.V. One of the most interesting questions posed by the site sequence is why the prestigious and possibly defended Iron Age enclosure fell out of use. Chronologies of this period are difficult to tease out, but if the radiocarbon date for the hearth above Ditch 6 is taken at face value, the neglect of the ditched element of the settlement is not associated with the Roman conquest, but occurs much earlier. A great deal of effort was expended in the construction of this defensive, or symbolically defensive architecture in the Middle and Late Iron Age and various reasons have been suggested for why the ditches were no longer maintained. Environmental, political or social change may have played a part. Chapter 6.I touches on the volatile political situation in the century before the Roman conquest and it is possible that the population that controlled the river crossing at Recreation Way were subjugated at this time, or the geopolitical boundaries shifted and the site lost its defensive or symbolic status. The increasing importance of trade and the demise in the older forms of social control represented by the hill-fort are discussed in Chapter 6.V as a possible contributing factor.

The Roman evidence from the site has furthered our understanding of the character of the Roman occupation at Mildenhall, although the site is not considered to represent the core of settlement (Chapter 6.II). Many aspects of the evidence suggest a more humble site than its Iron Age predecessor, probably fitting into a regional farming regime based on a central estate and a series of small tenant farms. Evidence suggests Early Saxon use of the site was minimal, probably in response to worsening environmental conditions, and it did not include occupation. Physical remains from the Middle and later Saxon period are considerably more robust and provide a notable contribution to studies of settlement patterns in this region, particularly as the site represents the first certain location for settlement in an area where occupation was strongly indicated by chance finds and a number of cemeteries, but where no clear settlement remains have been previously identified. The site is rural, with stock enclosures, field boundaries and rubbish pits. Firm evidence for domestic structures did not survive, but this was a situation common to all periods of the site. Most of the excavated evidence can be comfortably ascribed to the prosaic activities of a simple rural existence, but there are some aspects, particularly of the animal bone deposition that suggest some features were a focus for unusual depositions. This aspect of Saxon settlements has been a topic of recent discussion and the site provides further material for debate (see Chapter 6.III). Another notable element of the Saxon remains is the pottery assemblage which, together with the medieval component is one of the largest in the area, and has allowed a better understanding of pottery production, trade routes and supply of pottery in the region.

The location of the large medieval boundary on the alignment of the paired Iron Age enclosure ditches would appear to be coincidental. In size, the medieval ditch is also comparable to these earlier ditches. However the significance that this ditch may have held in the past is now obscure, and a link with the town boundary remains tenuous (Chapter 6.IV). The evidence from both sides of the boundary suggested a range of activities that would have been equally suited to a purely rural location, or to an area on the periphery of settlement. As with earlier periods, there was no evidence for substantial buildings, although the base of a lime kiln was well preserved.

A robust analysis of the environmental remains provided opportunities to compare the economic basis of all major periods of occupation. This highlighted some changes, notably in the adoption of new forms of wheat, but only the animal assemblage from the medieval period suggested any form of specialisation. In general the analysis suggested a continuity of farming practices and an exploitation of local resources that remained steady throughout the history of the site.

Appendix 1: Human Bone Catalogue

Abbreviations:

11	=	Tooth present	a	=	Moderate periapical abscess
11	=	Tooth present, alveoli absent	*bcc*	=	Slight buccal cervical caries
-	=	Alveoli and tooth absent	bcc	=	Moderate buccal cervical caries
X	=	Tooth lost antemortem	dac	=	Moderate distal approximal caries
/	=	Tooth lost post-mortem	DCC	=	Considerable distal cervical caries
U	=	Unerupted tooth	drc	=	Moderate distal root caries
E	=	Erupting tooth	DAC	=	Considerable distal approximal caries
CA	=	Congenitally absent tooth	mac	=	Moderate approximal caries
R	=	Root only	MAC	=	Considerable approximal caries
cl	=	Slight calculus	oc	=	Moderate occlusal caries
cl	=	Moderate calculus	OC	=	Considerable occlusal caries
g	=	Moderate granuloma	C?	=	Considerable caries

Dental charts (FDI 1971)

Deciduous dentition:

Maxillae
Right   Left

55	54	53	52	51	61	62	63	64	65
85	84	83	82	81	71	72	73	74	75

Right   Left
Mandible

Permanent dentition:

Maxilllae
Right   Left

18	17	16	15	14	13	12	11	21	22	23	24	25	26	27	28
48	47	46	45	44	43	42	41	31	32	33	34	35	36	37	38

Right   Left
Mandible

Period 3

Skeleton no: 21386
[Cut]; (Fill): [20495]; (21920)
Completeness: 10%; the cranium, the mandible, atlas and the axis
Preservation: Excellent
Age: 26–35 years *(Early middle adult)*
Sex: Male (+1)
Stature: Indeterminable
Position: n/a
Orientation: n/a
Dental inventory:

cl	*cl*	*cl*		*cl*									*cl*	*cl*	*cl*
18	17	16	15	14	13	12	11	21	22	23	24	25	26	27	28
48	47	46	43	44	43	42	41	31	32	33	34	35	36	37	38
														oc	oc
cl	*cl*	*cl*	*cl*	*cl*	*cl*	*cl*	*cl*	*cl*	*cl*	*cl*	*cl*	*cl*	*cl*	*cl*	*cl*

Dental pathology: Caries (2/32), calculus (23/32), and slight dental attrition.
Skeletal pathology: Moderate porosity of the palatal processes of the maxillae (30×15 mm).
Metrical indices:
Cephalic: 64.39 *(Dolichocranic)*
Non-metric traits and anomalies: Bilateral lambdoid ossicles, unilateral parietal foramen present (right), unilateral coronal ossicle present (right), unilateral epipteric bone present (left), unilateral foramen of Huschke present (left), unilateral mastoid foramen exsutural (right), unilateral mastoid foramen absent (left), bilateral posterior condylar canal patent, precondylar tubercle present, unilateral accessory lesser palatine foramen present (right), and an unilateral supraorbital foramen complete (right).
Radiocarbon date: 2115 ± 30 BP; 204–49 cal. BC (2 sigma) (SUERC-48057)
Isotope values: $\delta\,^{13}C = -20.5$; $\delta\,^{13}N = 10.5$ (ibid.)

Period 4

Skeleton no: 22028
[Cut]; (Fill): [21979]; (22030)
Completeness: 75%; The squama of the occipital bone, the left parietal bone, the left arch of the axis, four cervical, four thoracic and four lumbar vertebrae, a sacral vertebra, five left and seven right ribs, the left scapula and clavicle, the distal left humerus, the right humerus, the left proximal ulna, the left distal radius, a metacarpal, the femora, and the proximal left tibia.
Preservation: Excellent
Age: 39–41 weeks *in utero (Neonate)*
Sex: Indeterminable
Stature: Indeterminable
Position: Supine
Orientation: E–W
Dental inventory: Not present
Skeletal pathology: Not present
Radiocarbon date: 2137 ± 30 BP; 211–86 cal. BC (2 sigma) (SUERC-48064)
Isotope values: $\delta\,^{13}C = -20.5$; $\delta\,^{13}N = 10.5$ (ibid.)

Period 5

Skeleton no: 17085
[Cut]; (Fill): [17048]; (17085)
Completeness: 10%; Fragments of the radii, the distal right ulna, the right ilium, and the diaphysis of the femora and tibiae.
Preservation: Good
Age: 31 weeks *in utero (Foetal)*
Sex: Indeterminable
Stature: Indeterminable
Position: Unknown
Orientation: Unknown
Dental inventory: Not present
Skeletal pathology: Not present

Skeleton no: 20808
[Cut]; (Fill): [20809]; (20807)
Completeness: 40%; The occipital bone, the parietal bones, the temporal bones, a malleus and incus of unknown side, the right zygomatic, the sphenoid, fragments of the right maxilla, the mandible, the left arch of the atlas and a cervical vertebra, four thoracic vertebrae, three lumbar vertebrae, five left and five right ribs, the left scapula, the ulnae, the radii, two metacarpals, seven proximal hand phalanges, three middle hand phalanges, the right pubis and ischium, the proximal femora and a metatarsal.
Preservation: Very good
Age: 36–38 weeks *in utero (Neonate)*
Sex: Indeterminable
Stature: Indeterminable
Position: n/a
Orientation: N–S
Dental inventory:

/	/	-	-	-	U	U	-	-	-
/	/	/	/	/	/	/	/	/	/

Skeletal pathology: Not present
Radiocarbon date: 1830 ± 30 BP; 119–253 cal. BC (2 sigma) (SUERC-48066)
Isotope values: $\delta\,^{13}C$ = –19.1; $\delta\,^{13}N$ = 12.0 (ibid.)

Skeleton no: 20812
[Cut]; (Fill): [20813]; (20811)
Completeness: 80%; The skull, five left and eight right ribs, the scapulae, the clavicles, the arm bones, four metacarpals and three phalanges from the left hand, three metacarpals and three phalanges from the right hand, the ilia, the ischia, the leg bones and most of both feet.
Preservation: Moderate/Good, some surface erosion.
Period: Roman (Period 3)
Age: 5–6 years (Young child)
Sex: Indeterminable
Stature: Indeterminable
Position: Crouched, on left side
Orientation: N–S
Dental inventory:
Deciduous dentition:

55	54	53	52	51	61	/	63	64	65
85	84	83	82	81	/	72	73	74	75

Permanent dentition:

-	U	16	U	U	U	U	U	U	U	U	U	U	26	U	-
U	U	46	U	U	U	U	U	U	U	U	U	U	36	U	U

Dental pathology: Not present
Skeletal pathology: Not present

Skeleton no: 21080
[Cut]; (Fill): [21094]; (21081)
Completeness: 85%; The squama of the occipital bone, the parietal bones, the temporal bones, the frontal bone, the right greater wing of the sphenoid, fragments of the maxillae, the zygoma, the body of the mandible, the fovea of the atlas, the axis–C6, T1–T3, L3–L5, fragments of the sacrum, five left and two right ribs, fragments of the scapulae, the clavicles, the arm bones, six carpals, the metacarpals and eleven phalanges from the left hand, four metacarpals and four phalanges from the right hand, fragments of the coxa, the leg bones, the calcanei, the tali, and the cuboid and fifth metatarsal from the left foot, and the cuboid, the metatarsals and two proximal phalanges from the right foot.
Preservation: Excellent
Period: Early medieval (Period 4)
Age: 26–35 years (Early middle adult)
Sex: Male (+1)
Stature: 170.86 ± 3.94 cm (Trotter and Gleser 1958); 168.32 ± 3.85 cm (Sjøvold 1990)
Position: Supine, the left arm extended and the right arm slightly flexed with the hand resting on the right hip.
Orientation: N–S
Dental inventory:

							OC		bcc	DCC						
										bcc						
-	-	-	-	-	13	12	11¹	21¹	-	23	24	-	-	-	-	
48	47	46	45	44	43	42¹	41¹	31¹	32¹	33	34	35	X	37	CA	
		MAC	dac				oc					dac				
		a	a				a									
cl	cl	cl	cl	cl	cl					cl						

¹ Very worn occlusal surfaces, probably extra-masticatory.

Dental pathology: Caries (7/20), calculus (7/20), chronic periapical abscesses (3/15), antemortem tooth loss (1/15), and moderate dental attrition.
Skeletal pathology: Porotic patches at the superior margins of the external meati on both temporal bones (left: 10×7 mm; right: 8×6 mm). Porotic lesions on the inferior surface of the base of the right greater wing of the sphenoid (13×10 mm), right side unknown due to fragmentation. Moderate vertebral osteophytosis on L4. Slight to moderate ossified ligamentum flavum on four thoracic vertebrae. Enthesophytic spur (10×4 mm) on the anterior-medial aspect of the distal diaphysis of the left humerus; the distal attachment for the *m. brachialis*. Marginal osteophytosis (3 mm) on the anterior-distal margin on the left lunate. Probable crush fracture of the left scaphoid, resulting in severe marginal osteophytic build-up of the anterior(?) margin and a large eburnated facet (12×7 mm) on the inferior surface, of unknown articulation. Marginal osteophytosis (2 mm) on the anterior-inferior labium of the lunate surface of the right coxae. Articular fracture of the talar articular surface of the right tibia, at the base of the malleolus process. Secondary moderate marginal osteophytosis (4 mm) and an eburnated surface on the anterior aspect of the articular surface of the malleolus process (11×10mm). Moderate osteophytosis (2–3 mm) of the posterior facet for the talus on the left calcaneus, and corresponding osteophytes (3 mm) on the posterior margin of the talus. Marginal osteophytosis is also noted on the anterior-medial extension of the tibial articulation of the left talus. All changes likely to be secondary to the tibial articular fracture.
Metrical indices:
Cephalic: 76.17 *(Mesocranic)*
Platymeric (left): 80.34 *(Platymeria)*
Platymeric (right): 80.61 *(Platymeria)*
Platycnemic (left): 75.27 *(Eurycnemia)*
Platycnemic (right): 75.01 *(Eurycnemia)*
Robusticity indices:
Femur (left): 13.37
Femur (right): 13.24
Non-metric traits and anomalies: Bilateral mastoid foramen absent, bilateral third trochanter and bilateral peroneal tubercle.
Radiocarbon date: 1856 ± 30 BP; cal. AD 81–234 (2 sigma) (SUERC-48059)
Isotope values: $\delta\,^{13}C$ = –19.7; $\delta\,^{13}N$ = 10.8 (ibid.)
Other: The bones from the right foot were found in silting deposit 20792.

Skeleton no: 21921

[Cut]; (Fill): [21922]; (21920)

Completeness: 75%; The occipital bone, the parietal bones, the temporal bones, the frontal bone, the zygoma, the nasal bones, fragments of the sphenoid, the anterior half of the left maxilla, T12, L4–L5, the sacrum, the coccyx, the distal humeri, the radii, the right ulna, the left second metacarpal, three proximal hand phalanges, the coxa, the femora, the left patella, the tibiae, the fibulae, the calcanei, the tali, the navicular bones, the left first and second cuneiform bones, the left cuboid, the left second and third metatarsal.

Preservation: Excellent

Age: = 46 years *(Older adult)*

Sex: Male (+2)

Stature: 171.90 cm (Trotter and Gleser 1958); 169.25 ± 3.85 cm (Sjøvold 1990)

Position: n/a

Orientation: S–N?

Dental inventory:

									g C ?		R	X	X	X	X	-
-	-	-	-	-	-	-	-	/	/							
-	-	-	-	-	-	-	-	-	-	-	-	-	-	-	-	-

Dental pathology: Caries (1/1), granuloma (1/7) and antemortem tooth loss (4/7).

Skeletal pathology: Blunt porosity on the suprameatal spines of both temporal bones (left: 8×5 mm; right: 7×5 mm). Considerable porosity on the palatal process of the left maxilla (27×13 mm). Intervertebral osteophytosis on the bodies of L4 and S1. Osteoid osteoma on the anterior surface of the mid-diaphysis (15×8 mm) and on the posterior surface of the distal diaphysis, just lateral of the linea aspera (8×4 mm) of the right femur. Plaque of striated periostitis on the interosseous surface of the mid-diaphysis (7×7 mm) of the left tibia and more extensively on the right tibia where dense striated periosteal new bone is present on the medial surface of the entire distal diaphysis (116×20 mm) and on the interosseous surface of the mid-diaphysis (115×20 mm) which also displayed some cortical thickening (42×19 mm). Dense sclerotic periostitis on the interosseous surface of the distal diaphysis of the left fibula (54×6 mm).

Metrical indices:

Cephalic: 78.01 *(Mesocranic)*

Platymeric (left): 82.57 *(Platymeria)*

Platymeric (right): 81.13 *(Platymeria)*

Platycnemic (left): 79.01 *(Eurycnemia)*

Platycnemic (right): 70.73 *(Eurycnemia)*

Robusticity indices:

Femur (left): 14.25

Non-metric traits and anomalies: Unilateral lambdoid ossicle present (left), unilateral parietal foramen present (right), unilateral epipteric bone present (right), unilateral ossicle at asterion (left), and a unilateral mastoid foramen exsutural (right).

Radiocarbon date: 1840 ± 30 BP; cal. AD 85–242 (2 sigma) (SUERC-48058)

Isotope values: $\delta\,^{13}C = -19.7$; $\delta\,^{13}N = 10.2$ (ibid.)

Skeleton no: 20979

[Cut]; (Fill): [20977]

Completeness: 20%; The anterior portion of the right maxilla, two thoracic and one lumbar vertebra, three left and three right ribs, the left humerus and ulna, the left femur and a fibula.

Preservation: Good

Period: Roman

Age: 37–38 weeks *in utero (Neonate)*

Sex: Indeterminable

Stature: Indeterminable

Position: Disarticulated

Orientation: Indeterminable

Dental inventory: Not present

Dental pathology: Not present

Skeletal pathology: Not present

Other: This skeleton was identified during post-excavation.

Period 6

Skeleton no: 2019

[Cut]; (Fill): [2021]; (2018)

Completeness: 75%; The occipital bone, the parietal bones, the temporal bones, a malleolus and the incus bones, the frontal bone, the sphenoid, the frontal process of the left maxilla, the left zygomatic, the body of the mandible, the atlas–C4, C7–L5, the ribs, a sternebra, the sacrum, the scapulae, the clavicles, the arm bones, the left third and fourth metacarpals, the right metacarpals, three proximal hand phalanges, the coxae, the femora, the patellae, the proximal tibiae and the proximal fibulae.

Preservation: Excellent

Age: 17–18 years *(Adolescent)*

Sex: Female (–2)

Stature: Indeterminable

Position: n/a

Orientation: S–N?

Dental inventory:

-	-	-	-	-	-	-	-	-	-	-	-	-	-	-	-
E	/	46	/	44	43	/	41	31	32	33	34	35	36	37¹	U
							cl	cl	cl		cl	cl			

¹ Foramen caecum

Dental pathology: Calculus (5/11) and slight dental attrition.

Skeletal pathology: Sacro-coccygeal synostosis. Healed osteomyelitis of the anterior surface of the mid-diaphysis of the right fourth metacarpal; resulting in a bony bridge axially across the anterior surface with a cloaca canal transverse across the bone. The margins of the lesions are smooth and indicative of healing of long standing. Unclear aetiology, possibly tuberculosis. Porotic patch on the anterior surface of the neck on both femora (8×13 mm).

Period 7

Skeleton no: 22070

[Cut]; (Fill): [21005]; (21003)

Completeness: 80%; The frontal bone, the nasal bones, the axis, C4–T9, T12–L4, the sacrum, the coccyx, the sternum, three left and eight right ribs, the scapulae, the arm bones, the metacarpals, four hand phalanges, the ilia, the right pubic bone, the femora, the left patella, the lower legs, the calcanei, the left first metatarsal and a proximal foot phalanx.

Preservation: Very good

Age: 12–14 years *(Adolescent)*

Sex: Indeterminable

Stature: Indeterminable

Position: Disarticulated

Orientation: n/a

Dental inventory: Not present

Skeletal pathology: Not present

Skeleton no: 22071

[Cut]; (Fill): [21005]; (21003)

Completeness: 10%; Parts of the left scapula, the proximal half of the left humerus, the coxae, and the proximal left femur.

Preservation: Very good

Age: 36–45 years *(Late middle adult)*

Sex: Male (+1)

Stature: Indeterminable

Position: Disarticulated

Orientation: n/a

Dental inventory: Not present

Skeletal pathology: Degenerative notch on the anterior aspect of the superior margin of the acetabulum of the left coxae (10×8 mm).

Metrical indices:

Platymeric (left): 76.16 *(Platymeria)*

Non-metric traits and anomalies: Third trochanter (left).

Skeleton no: 22072
[Cut]; (Fill): [21005]; (21003)
Completeness: 50%; The squama of the occipital bone, the parietal bones, the temporal bones, the base of the right greater wing of the sphenoid, the left maxilla, the left zygomatic, the mandible, the atlas–C4, C7, T3–L5, the sacrum, the left and the right ribs, fragments of the left scapula, the left distal humerus, the right humerus, the ulnae, the left radius, the coxa, and the proximal femora.
Preservation: Very good
Age: 26–35 years *(Early middle adult)*
Sex: Male (+1)
Stature: 171.59 ± 4.57 cm (Trotter and Gleser 1958); 168.60 ± 4.94 cm (Sjøvold 1990)
Position: Disarticulated
Orientation: n/a
Dental inventory:

Dental pathology: Caries (6/14), calculus (9/14), chronic periapical abscesses (3/20) and slight dental attrition.
Skeletal pathology: Slightly asymmetric sacrum, with the inferior portion in a slight anterior-lateral scoliosis, and slight to moderate ossified ligamentum flavum on T9–T11.
Metrical indices:
Platymeric (left): 76.06 *(Platymeria)*
Platymeric (right): 82.37 *(Platymeria)*
Robusticity indices:
Humerus (right): 22.26
Non-metric traits and anomalies: Unilateral mastoid foramen exsutural (left), unilateral mastoid foramen absent (right), hypotrochanteric fossa (right), bilateral third trochanter, atlas posterior bridge (left), and transverse foramen bipartite C4 (right).

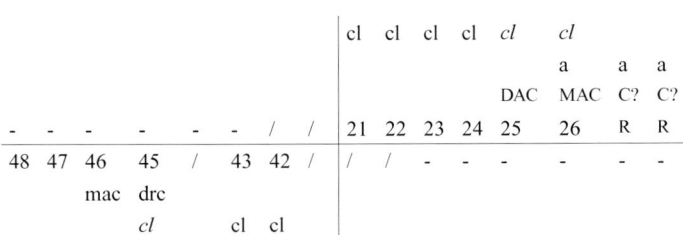

								cl	cl	cl	cl	*cl*	*cl*		
													a	a	a
											DAC	MAC	C?	C?
-	-	-	-	-	-	/	/	21	22	23	24	25	26	R	R
48	47	46	45	/	43	42	/	/	/	-	-	-	-	-	-
		mac	drc												
			cl		cl	cl									

Appendix 2: Table 5.11 The number and range of insects
(overleaf)

	Ecological codes	6 Saxon	7 Medieval — Area 2				7 Medieval — Area 3									Phytophage (plant feeding) associations (information from Koch 1989; 1992)
context number		**2086**	**2050**		**2051**		**3009**				**3016**				**3870**	
Sample number		2042	2035	2039	2036	2040	3001	3002	3005	3008	3010	3012	3014	3016	3043	
Sample weight kg		9	11	7.8	8	9	8.5	6.6	3.3	3.7	3.3	3.4	3.6	3.6	1.5	
Sample volume l		10	10	9	10	10	10	8	4	5	4	4.5	4	4	1.5	
HEMIPTERA																
Family, genus and spp. Indet.		1	1	1	-	-	2	-	1	-	-	-	-	-	1	
COLEOPTERA																
Carabidae																
Notiophilus biguttatus (F.)	ws	-	-	-	-	-	-	-	-	1	-	-	-	-	-	
Elaphrus spp.		-	-	-	-	-	-	-	-	-	-	-	-	-	-	
Loricera pilicornis (F.)		-	-	-	-	-	1	-	-	-	-	-	-	1	-	
Clivina fossor (L.)		-	-	-	1	-	1	-	-	-	-	-	-	-	-	
Dyschirius globosus (Hbst.)		1	-	-	1	2	-	1	-	-	1	-	-	2	-	
Trechus quadristriatus (Schrk)		-	-	-	-	-	-	-	-	-	1	-	-	-	-	
Bembidion doris (Panz.)		-	-	-	-	-	-	-	-	-	-	-	1	-	-	
B. gutula (F.)		1	-	-	-	-	1	-	-	-	-	-	-	-	-	
Bembidion spp.		2	1	3	1	2	1	1	2	1	-	-	-	1	2	
Harpalus spp.		-	-	-	1	1	-	-	-	1	-	-	-	-	-	
Bradycellus spp.		-	-	-	-	-	-	-	-	-	-	-	-	1	1	
Pterostichus strenuus (Panz.)		-	-	-	-	1	-	-	-	-	-	-	-	-	-	
Pterostichus diligens (Sturm)		-	-	-	-	1	-	2	1	1	-	-	-	-	1	
Pterostichus nigrita (Payk.)	ws	-	-	-	-	-	-	-	-	-	-	-	-	-	1	
P. anthracinus (Ill.)	ws	-	-	-	-	-	-	-	-	-	-	-	-	-	1	
Pterostichus gracilis (Dej.)	ws	-	-	-	1	-	-	-	-	-	-	-	1	-	-	
Pterostichus minor (Gyll.)	ws	1	-	-	-	-	1	-	1	-	-	-	-	-	-	
Pterostichus niger (Schall.)		-	-	1	-	1	-	-	-	-	-	-	1	-	-	
Pterostichus melanarius (Ill.)		1	-	-	-	1	-	-	-	-	-	-	-	-	-	
P. madidus (F.)		-	-	-	-	-	-	-	-	-	-	2	-	-	-	
Calathus fuscipes (Goeze)		-	-	-	-	-	1	-	-	1	-	-	-	-	-	
Agonum gracile (Gyll.)	ws	-	1	1	-	-	-	-	-	-	1	-	-	1	-	
Agonum sp.		-	-	2	-	-	-	-	-	-	-	-	-	1	-	
Amara spp.		1	-	-	-	-	-	-	-	-	1	-	-	-	1	
Odacantha melanura (L.)	ws	-	-	-	-	-	-	-	-	1	-	-	-	-	-	Usually on Phragmites australis (Cav.) Trin. ex Steud. (Common reed)
Haliplidae																
Haliplus spp.	a	-	-	1	-	-	3	-	-	-	-	-	1	1	-	
Dytiscidae																
Hyphydrus ovatus (L.)	a	-	-	-	-	-	-	-	-	-	-	1	1	-	-	
Coelambus impressopunctatus (Schall.)	a	-	-	1	-	-	-	-	-	-	-	-	-	-	-	
Hygrotus inaequalis (F.)	a	-	-	-	1	-	-	-	-	1	-	-	-	-	-	
Hydroporus scalesianus Steph.	a	-	-	-	-	-	-	-	-	1	-	-	-	-	-	
Hydroporus palustris (L.)	a	1	-	-	-	-	-	1	-	1	-	-	-	-	1	
Hydroporus spp.	a	-	-	-	-	-	-	1	-	-	-	1	1	-	-	
Porhydrus lineatus (F.)	a	-	-	-	-	2	1	1	-	-	-	-	1	-	-	
Colymbetes fuscus L.	a	-	-	-	-	-	1	-	-	-	-	-	-	-	-	
Noterus clavicornis (Geer)	a	1	-	-	-	1	6	1	-	1	-	-	1	2	1	
Noterus crassicornis (Müll.)	a	-	-	-	1	-	-	1	-	1	-	-	-	2	2	
Agabus spp	a	-	-	-	2	2	1	-	-	-	-	-	1	1	-	
Ilybius spp.	a	-	-	-	-	-	-	-	-	1	-	-	1	-	-	
Dytiscus spp.	a	-	-	-	-	-	-	-	-	-	-	-	-	1	-	
Gyrinidae																
Gyrinus spp.	a	1	-	-	-	1	2	-	1	-	-	-	1	-	1	
Hydraenidae																

166

Period		6 Saxon	Area 2			7 Medieval	Area 3		Phytophage (plant feeding) associations (information from Koch 1989; 1992)
context number	Ecological codes	2086	2050	2051	3009	3016		3870	
Hydraena testacea Curt.	a	-	-	-	-	-	-	1	
Hydraena britteni Joy	a	1	-	-	-	-	-	1	
Hydraena spp.	a	3	1	-	-	-	-	1	
Ochthebius minimus (F.)	a	3	1	3	2	1	-	2	
Ochthebius spp.	a	7	18	13	22	3	-	4	
Limnebius spp.	a	-	1	1	-	1	-	1	
Hydrochus brevis (Hbst.)	a	1	1	-	-	-	-	-	
Helophorus spp.	a	1	1	1	3	1	-	-	
Hydrophilidae									
Coelostoma orbiculare (F.)	a	-	2	2	3	3	-	1	
Sphaeridium ?lunatum F.	df	-	-	1	-	1	-	1	
Cercyon ustulatus (Preyssl.)	a	-	-	-	2	-	-	1	
Cercyon haemorrhoidalis (F.)	df	-	-	-	1	-	-	1	
Cercyon melanocephalus (L.)	df	-	-	-	1	-	-	-	
Cercyon unipunctatus (L.)	df	-	-	-	-	-	-	1	
Cercyon atricapillus (Marsh.)	df	-	-	-	1	1	-	-	
Cercyon analis (Payk.)	df	1	3	4	2	2	-	-	
Cercyon tristis (Ill.)	df	1	-	3	-	-	-	-	
Cercyon sternalis Shp.	ws	-	-	2	-	-	-	2	
Megasternum boletophagum (Marsh.)	ws	4+	3	5	-	1	-	-	
Cryptopleurum minutum (F.)	df	-	1	1	-	1	-	-	
Hydrobius fuscipes (L.)	a	-	1	-	2	-	-	1	
Laccobius spp.	a	-	1	2	1	-	-	2	
Helochares c.f. lividus (Forst.)	a	-	-	-	1	1	-	-	
Helochares spp.	a	-	1	1	-	-	-	-	
Cymbiodyta marginella (F.)	a	-	-	-	2	-	-	-	
Chaetarthria seminulum (Hbst.)	a	-	-	3	3	4	2	1	
Histeridae									
Onthophilus striatus (Forst.)	df	1	-	-	-	-	-	-	
Acritus nigricornis (Hoffm.)	df	-	1	-	1	1	-	-	
Gnathoncus nanus (scriba)	df	-	-	1	-	-	-	-	
Grammostethus marginatus (Er.)	df	1	-	1	1	-	-	-	
Hister spp.	df	-	1	-	1	1	-	-	
Atholus bimaculatus (L.)	df	-	1	1	-	-	-	-	
Silphidae									
Silpha spp.		-	-	1	-	-	-	-	
Catopidae									
Nemadus colonoides (Kr.)	1	-	-	1	1	-	-	-	associated with rot holes in trees and birds nests in woodland
Choleva sp.		-	-	-	1	-	-	-	
Clambidae									
Clambus spp.		-	-	1	1	1	-	-	
Scydmaenidae									
Scydmaenidae Gen. & spp. indet.		-	1	-	1	1	1	-	
Orthoperidae									
Corylophus cassidoides (Marsh.)		1	5	-	-	1	1	2	
Orthoperus spp.		-	-	3	-	-	-	1	
Ptiliidae									
Ptiliidae Genus & spp. indet.		-	-	1	-	1	-	2	
Staphylinidae									
Micropeplus staphylinoides (Marsh.)		-	-	1	-	-	-	-	
Proteinus spp.		-	-	-	-	-	-	-	

Period context number	Ecological codes	Area 2 — 6 Saxon 2086	Area 2 2050	Area 2 2051	Area 3 — 7 Medieval 3009	Area 3 3016	Area 3 3870	Phytophage (plant feeding) associations (information from Koch 1989; 1992)
Eusphalerum sp.		-	-	-	-	-	-	
Omalium riparium (Thoms.)		-	1	-	1	-	-	
Omalium rivulare (Payk.)		-	1	2	-	-	-	
Xylodromus concinnus (Marsh.)		1	2	2	-	-	-	
Olophrum spp.		2	-	2	-	-	1	
Lesteva heeri Fauv.	ws	-	3	10	2	2	4	
Lesteva longelytrata (Goeze)	ws	-	8	-	-	-	-	
Lesteva spp.	ws	7	-	-	6	-	-	
Coprophilus striatulus (F.)		-	-	-	-	-	1	
Trogophloeus bilineatus (Steph.)		-	-	-	-	-	-	
Trogophloeus spp.		1	1	1	1	-	-	
Oxytelus sculptus Grav.		-	1	3	2	-	-	
Oxytelus rugosus (F.)		2	5	6	2	2	2	
Oxytelus sculpturatus Grav.		-	-	1	2	1	1	
Oxytelus nitidulus Grav.	ws	5	2	3	-	-	1	
Platystethus arenarius (Fourc.)	df	2	3	5	-	-	-	
Platystethus cornutus (Grav.)	ws	1	3	1	-	1	-	
Platystethus nitens Sahlb.	ws	1	3	-	-	-	-	
Stenus spp.		7	8	8	6	2	5	
Paederus spp.		-	-	1	1	-	1	
Stilicus orbiculatus (Payk.)		1	-	3	1	-	1	
Lithocharis spp.		-	-	-	-	-	-	
Lathrobium spp.		-	-	1	1	1	2	
Leptacinus spp.	oa	-	-	3	-	-	-	
Gyrohypnus fracticornis (Müll.)		3	2	7	1	2	2	
Xantholinus spp.		2	1	2	1	1	2	
Neobisnius spp.		-	1	3	1	-	-	
Philonthus spp.		3	-	4	3	1	-	
Philonthus spp.		-	2	8	-	2	3	
Tachyporus spp.		1	2	2	1	1	1	
Bolitobius spp.		-	1	1	-	-	-	
Tachinus rufipes (Geer.)		1	-	3	1	1	1	
Tachinus spp.		1	-	2	-	-	-	
Aleocharinidae Genus & spp. Indet.		3	5	4	5	1	3	
Pselaphidae								
Rybaxis sp.		-	-	1	-	1	1	
Brachygluta spp.		-	1	1	-	-	-	
Cantharidae								
Cantharis sp.		-	-	1	-	-	-	
Elateridae								
Agriotes spp.	p	-	-	1	1	1	-	
Adelocera murina (L.)	p	-	-	1	-	-	-	
?Ctenicera cuprea (F.)	p	1	-	-	-	-	-	
Athous haemorrhoidalis (F.)	p	-	-	1	-	-	-	
Dascillidae								
Dascillus cervinus (L.)		1	-	-	-	-	-	
Helodidae								
Helodidae Gen. & spp. Indet.	a	-	1	5	5	2	3	
Dryopidae								
Dryops spp.	a	2	1	2	3	3	1	
Oulimnius spp.	a	1	-	1	1	-	-	

Period	Ecological codes	6 Saxon	Area 2			7 Medieval	Area 3		Phytophage (plant feeding) associations (information from Koch 1989; 1992)
context number		**2086**	**2050**	**2051**	**3009**		**3016**	**3870**	
Georissidae									
Georissus crenulatus (Rossi)	a	1	-	-	-	-	-	-	
Nitidulidae									
Brachypterus urticae (F.)	p	-	2	-	1	-	-	-	*Urtica dioica* L. (stinging nettle)
Meligethes spp.		-	1	9	1	-	-	1	
Cucujidae									
Monotoma spp.		-	-	1	-	-	-	-	
Cryptophagidae									
Cryptophagus spp.		-	3	3	1	-	-	-	
Atomaria spp.		-	5	1	1	-	2	1	
Phalacridae									
Phalacrus corruscus (Panz.)	ws	1	1	-	-	-	-	-	
Phalacrus caricis Sturm		-	1	-	1	-	-	-	
Phalacrus spp.	ws	-	1	-	-	-	-	-	
Lathridiidae									
Enicmus minutus (Group)		-	1	3	-	-	-	1	
Corticaria/corticarina spp.		2	1	1	-	-	-	1	
Colydiidae									
Aglenus brunneus (Gyll.)		-	-	1	-	-	-	-	
Coccinellidae									
Coccidula rufa (Hbst.)		-	-	-	1	-	-	-	
Thea vigintiduopunctata (L.)		-	-	-	1	-	-	-	
Lyctidae									
Lyctus linearis (Goeze)	1	-	1	1	-	-	-	-	
Anobiidae									
Anobium punctatum (Geer)	1	-	1	1	-	-	-	1	
Ptinus pectinicornis (L.)	1	-	-	-	1	-	-	-	
Ptinidae									
Ptinus ? fur (L.)		2	-	1	-	-	-	-	
Anthicidae									
Anthicus formicarius (Goeze)	df	-	-	2	-	-	-	-	
Mordellidae									
Anaspis spp.		-	-	1	-	-	-	-	
Scarabaeidae									
Georupes spp.	df	1	1	-	1	-	-	-	
Onthophagus joannae Goljan	df	1	1	-	-	-	-	-	
Onthophagus spp.	df	1	-	1	-	-	-	1	
Oxyomus silvestris (Scop.)		2	3	2	-	-	-	1	
Aphodius ?arenarius (Ol.)	df	1	-	-	1	-	-	-	
Aphodius contaminatus (Hbst.)	df	5	-	-	2	-	-	1	
Aphodius sphacelatus (Panz.) or *A. prodromus* (Brahm)	df	-	3	5	2	2	-	-	
Aphodius porcus (F.)	df	-	-	1	1	-	-	-	
Aphodius lapponum Gyll.	df	-	2	2	-	-	-	-	
Aphodius fimetarius (L.)	df	-	1	1	-	-	-	1	
Aphodius fasciatus (Ol.) / *A. putridus* Herbst	df	-	-	1	-	-	1	-	
Aphodius granarius (L.)	df	-	4	-	1	-	-	-	
Aphodius spp.	df	-	-	-	1	-	3	3	
Phyllopertha horticola (L.)	p	-	1	3	1	-	-	1	
Chyrsomelidae									
Donacia clavipes F	ws	4	2	4	13	2	4	5	*Schoenoplectus lactustris* (L.) Palla (Common club-rush)
Donacia marginata Hopp	ws	1	-	-	1	-	-	-	On *Sparganium ramosum* (Erect burr-reed)

Period / context number	Ecological codes	Area 2 — 6 Saxon 2086	Area 2 2050	Area 2 2051	7 Medieval 3009	7 Medieval 3016	Area 3 3870	Phytophage (plant feeding) associations (information from Koch 1989; 1992)
Donacia crassipes F.	ws	-	-	-	-	1	-	Nymphaea alba L. and Nuphar lutea (L.) (White and yellow water lily)
Donacia aquatica (L.)		-	-	-	-	1	-	on Glyceria spp. and Carex spp. (sweetgrass and sedges)
Donacia impressa Payk.	ws	-	-	-	-	1	-	Schoenoplectus lacustris (L.) Palla (Common club-rush)
Donacia simplex F.	ws	1	1	-	-	-	-	Range of water reeds and rushes
Donacia cinerea Hbst.	ws	1	2	1	1	6	1	Usually on Typhea spp. (Bulrush)
Plateumaris braccata (Scop.)	ws	-	-	2	1	1	-	Phragmites australis (Cav.) Trin. ex Steud. (water reed)
Plateumaris sericea (L.)	ws	1	4	1	-	-	-	Usually on Carex spp. (sedges)
Lema spp.	p	-	-	-	-	1	-	
Phaedon cochleariae (F.)	p	-	-	-	3	-	-	the 'mustard beetle': on a range of Cruciferae
Phaedon spp.	p	1	1	1	-	-	-	
Phyllodecta vulgatissima (L.)	1	-	-	-	-	-	-	usually on Salix spp. (willows)
Hydrothassa marginella (L.)	ws	-	-	-	4	-	1	Often Caltha palustris L. (Marsh marigold)
Prasocuris phellandrii (L.)	ws	-	-	-	4	-	1	On aquatic Apiacae (Umbellifers)
Phylloreta spp.		2	3	3	1	-	-	
Haltica spp.		-	-	-	2	-	-	
Chaetocnema concinna (Marsh.)		1	2	-	1	1	1	
Chaetocnema spp.		-	1	1	-	-	-	
Psylliodes sp.	p	1	-	3	-	-	-	
Bruchidae								
Bruchus spp.		-	-	1	-	-	-	
Scolytidae								
Phloeophthorus rhododactylus (Marsh.)	1	-	-	1	-	-	-	Often on Cytisus species (Brooms)
Platypodidae								
Platypus cylindrus (F.)	1	1	-	-	-	-	-	Normally under bark of Quercus and Fagus spp (oak and beech)
Curculionidae								
Apion aeneum (F.)	p	-	-	4	-	-	-	Common mallow (Malva sylvestris L.)
Apion urticarium (Hbst.)	p	1	1	1	-	-	-	Urtica dioica L. (stinging nettle)
Apion? craccae (L.)	p	-	-	1	-	-	-	Vicia species (various vetches)
Apion spp.	p	2	3	7	3	-	2	
Phyllobius sp.	p	-	-	6	1	-	1	
Barypeithes spp.		1	-	-	-	-	-	
Sitona suturalis Steph.		-	-	-	-	-	2	
Sitona flavescens (Marsh.)	p	-	-	-	2	1	2	Trifolium species (Clover)
Sitona cylindricollis (Fahrs.)	p	-	1	-	-	-	-	Melanotus spp. (melliots)
Sitona humeralis Steph.	p	-	-	-	-	-	-	Often on medicks (Medicago) and clover (Trifolium)
Sitona spp.		1	2	1	7	1	2	
Larinus planus (F.)	p	-	-	-	1	-	1	on Cirsium spp. (thistles)
Bagous spp.	ws	2	-	3	3	-	2	
Tanysphyrus lemnae (Payk.)	a	2	1	2	-	-	-	Lemna spp. (Duckweed)
Notaris acridulus (L.)	ws	-	-	1	1	-	-	Often on Glyceria maxima (Hartm.) Holmb. (reed sweet-grass) and other Glyceria species (sweet-grasses)
Thryogenes spp.	ws	-	-	1	-	-	-	
Curculio spp.	1	-	-	-	3	1	-	
Leiosoma deflexum (Panz.)	ws	1	1	-	1	-	-	Caltha palustris L. (Marsh marigold)
Alophus triguttatus (F.)		1	1	-	-	-	-	
Hypera spp.	p	-	1	-	-	-	-	Mainly Trifolium spp. (Clover)
Limnobaris spp.	ws	-	-	-	-	-	-	Juncaceae and Cyperaceae (rushes)
Eubrychius velutus (Beck)	a	1	-	2	-	-	-	Myriophyllum spp. (Water-milfoils)
Micrelus ericae (Gyll.)	m	-	-	1	1	1	1	On Calluna and Erica spp. (Heathers)
Ceutorhynchus contractus (Marsh.)	p	-	-	2	2	-	-	Usually associated with Resedaceae and Papaveraceae (mignonettes and poppies)
Ceutorhynchus quadridens (Panz.)	p	-	6	5	-	-	-	
Ceutorhynchus spp.	p	3	2	3	2	1	1	

170

Table 5.11 — The number and range of insects

Period		Ecological codes	6 Saxon	Area 2		7 Medieval		Area 3	Phytophage (plant feeding) associations (information from Koch 1989; 1992)
context number			2086	2050	2051	3009	3016	3870	
Cidnorhinus quadrimaculatus (L.)		p	1	-	1	1	-	1	*Urtica dioica* L. (stinging nettle)
Mecinus pyraster (Hbst.)		p	-	1	3	-	-	1	*Plantago lanceolata* L. (plantain)
Miarus campanulae(L.)		p	-	-	1	-	-	-	*Campanula* spp. (hairbells)
Gymnetron labile (Hbst.		p	-	1	1	-	-	-	*Plantago lanceolata* L. (plantain)
Gymnetron pascuorum (Gyll.)		p	-	1	2	1	-	-	*Plantago lanceolata* L. (plantain)
Gymnetron spp.		p	1	1	3	-	-	-	*Plantago lanceolata* L. (plantain)
Rhynchaenus sp.		l	-	-	-	-	1	-	
Rhamphus pulicarius (Hbst.)		l	-	-	-	-	-	1	*Salix* (Willow)
DIPTERA									
SUBORDER CYCLORRHAPHA									
Family, genus & spp. indet.			11	14	16	9	12	3	
Hippoboscidae									
Melophagus ovinus L.			-	2	-	-	-	-	

Ecological coding

a = aquatic water beetles, ws = water side taxa often associated with emergent vegetation, df = taxa often associated with dung, p = taxa associated with grassland and open areas, l = taxa associated with trees
m = taxa associated with moorland

Nomenclature for Coleoptera (beetles) follows that of Lucht (1987).
The host plants for the phytophage species of beetle that were recovered are predominantly derived from Koch (1989; 1992). Plant taxonomy follows that of Stace 2010.
In order to aid interpretation, where possible, taxa have been assigned to ecological groupings.
The Coleoptera ecological groupings follow a simplified version of the scheme suggested by Robinson (1981; 1983).
The occurrence of each of the ecological groupings is expressed as a percentage in Table 5.12, and is illustrated in Figures 8 and 9.

Table 5.11 The number and range of insects

171

Bibliography

Primary sources

Cambridge University Library
CUL Hengrave Hall MSS 1 (1)

Suffolk Record Office, Bury St Edmunds

Sale particulars
HD1180/57 July 1933 Mildenhall Manor Estate, Mildenhall. (Manor house and grounds, Nut Tree Farm, Holywell House Farm, Crow Ground Farm, smallholdings and accommodation land, building plots and cottages)

Bunbury Collection

Enclosure Records
E18/410/1 Copy of Enclosure Act Mildenhall and associated papers 1807
E18/410/2 Copy of Enclosure Award Mildenhall 1812

Deeds
E 18/420/9/13A Edmund Mildenholes Chantry 1549–1556

Calkhill Street
E18/452/12/5 Messuage and Croft in Calkhillstreet'1540
E18/452/13/5 2 Messuages in Calkhylstrete opposite the church 1478
E18/452/13/7 Messuage and ½ acre in Calkhill Street 1557
E18/452/14/5 Messuage, 3r croft and pondyard in Calkehyl Street 1532
E18/452/15/3 Messuage lately built 1552
E18/452/16/4 Land on which a burnt tenement stood Calken Street next to the chantry 1561
E18/452/18/3 Messuage in Calkynglane 1504
E18/452/18/4 Messuage and 3r croft and pondyard 1532
E18/452/20A/9 Pightle in Calkhill Lane 1583
E18/452/76/5 Pightle at Calkehill Lane 1581
E18/452/121/(1–2) 1472, (7) 1564 and (9) 1581 various properties

Limekilns
E18/452/16/5 Meadow formerly called Auncells now called Lyne Kells 1569
E18/452/14/14 Meadow called Auncells now called Lyme Kelles 1573

The Baille or Bayle
E18/452/16/1 deed 1455
E18/454/2 rental 1483
E18/400/1/3 rental 1501
E18/454/4 rental1539
E18/452/16/2 deed 1541
E18/452/6/6–7 deed 1572

Mills
E18/452/37 Mildenhall Mills 1613–1822
E18/452/45/7 Newly Built 4 watermills 1802

Manorial Records
E18/454/2 Rentals Manor of Twamhill 1440s –1510
E18/454/4 Rental Manor of Aspalls 1538–1552

Terriers and Surveys
E18/454/5-7 Field Books 1574
E18/454/14 Terrier of Sir Henry North's lands held of the Crown and Trinity College 1611

Artificial Collections
HD527/1 account repairs to Mill at Mildenhall 1544
HD1749/2/16 Deeds to various properties in Calkehill Street etc *c*.1581

Navigation
E2/17/1 Papers Relating to Lark & Ouse Navigation 1636–1841

Suffolk Quarter Sessions Records
Q/R1 30A Pre-Enclosure Map *c*. 1807
Q/RI 30B Enclosure Map 1812
Q/RI 24 Enclosure Award Mildenhall 1812

Mildenhall Rural District Council
EF505/1/81 Mildenhall Inclosure award and map 1812
EF505/1/82 Map of Mildenhall parish by W.H. Young 1834
1374/27 Reference to Map of Mildenhall parish by William Young 1834
EF505/1/83 Map of the eastern half of Mildenhall parish by David Haylock 1851 (not available for research)

Secondary sources

Aitkinson, E. and Aitkinson, M.D., 2002 — 'Sambucus nigra L.', *J. Ecology* 90, 895–923

Albarella, U., 2004 — 'Mammal and bird bones', in Wallis, H., *Excavations at Mill Lane, Thetford 1995*, E. Anglian Archaeol. 108, 88–99

Albarella, U., 2006 — 'Pig husbandry and pork consumption in medieval England', in Woolgar C.M., Serjeantson, D. and Waldron, T. (eds), *Food in Medieval England: Diet and Nutrition* (Oxford, Oxford University Press), 72–87

Albarella, A., Johnstone, C. and Vickers, K., 2008 — 'The development of animal husbandry from the Late Iron Age to the end of the Roman period: a case study from south-east Britain', *J. Archaeol. Sci.* 35, 1828–48

Albarella, U., Beech, M., Curl, J., Locker, A., Moreno García, M. and Mulville, J., 2009 — *Norwich Castle: excavations and historical survey, 1987–98 part III: a zooarchaeological study*, E. Anglian Archaeol. Occ. Paper 22

Alexander, M., 2003 — 'A medieval and post-medieval street frontage: investigations at Forehill, Ely', *Proc. Cambridge Antiq. Soc.* 92, 135–82

Allen, M.J., 1995a — 'Ditch and feature fills', in Cleal, R.M.J., Walker, K.E. and Montague, R., *Stonehenge in its landscape. Twentieth-century Excavations*, English Heritage Archaeol. Rep. 10, 4–6

Allen, M.J., 1995b — 'Land molluscs', in Wainwright, G. and Davies, S., *Balksbury Camp, Hampshire, Excavations 1973 and 1981*, English Heritage Archaeol. Rep. 4, 92–100

Allen, M.J., and Wyles, S., 1994 — 'The contemporary land use and landscape of the King Barrows as evidenced by the buried soils and molluscs', in Cleal, R, and Allen, M.J., 'Investigation of Tree-Damaged Barrows on King Barrow Ridge and Luxenborough Planation, Amesbury', *Wiltshire Archaeol. Natur. Hist. Mag.* 87, 76–81

Anderberg, A-L., 1994 — *Atlas of seeds: Part 4* (Uddevalla, Swedish Museum of Natural History)

Anderson, R., 2005 — 'An annotated list of the non-marine Mollusca of Britain and Ireland', *J.Conchology* 38(6), 607–637

Anderson, S., 2001 — *Castle Hill, Orford (ORF 032): the finds* (unpubl. report for Suffolk CC Archaeological Service)

Anderson, S., 2003 — *Consolidated Support, RAF Lakenheath (ERL116): the finds* (unpubl. report for Suffolk CC Archaeological Service)

Anderson, S., 2004 — 'The pottery', in Wallis, H., *Excavations at Mill Lane, Thetford*, E. Anglian Archaeol. 108, 67–86

Anderson, S., 2005   *Dentist, RAF Lakenheath (ERL101): the finds* (unpubl. report for Suffolk CC Archaeological Service)

Anderson, S., 2006   *Rectory, refectory and range: pottery from three moated sites in Norfolk and Suffolk* (paper presented at Medieval Pottery Research Group conference, Chester, 2006)

Anderson, S., 2011   *Days Road, Capel St Mary, Suffolk (CSM 030): post-Roman pottery* (unpubl. archive report for Cambridge Archaeological Unit)

Anderson, S., 2013a   *Clare Castle (CLA 079): summary pottery assessment* (unpubl. archive report for Suffolk CC Archaeological Service)

Anderson, S., 2013b   *New Museum Store, West Stow Country Park (WSW 076): post-Roman pottery* (unpubl. archive report for Suffolk CC Archaeological Service)

Anderson, S., 2016   'Medieval pottery', in Woolhouse, T., *Medieval Dispersed Settlement on the Mid Suffolk Clay at Cedars Park, Stowmarket*, E. Anglian Archaeol. 161, 64–85

Andrews, P., 1995   *Excavations at Redcastle Furze, Thetford, 1988–9*, E. Anglian Archaeol. 72

Anon., 1829   *A Topographical and Historical Description of the County of Suffolk* (Woodbridge)

Ashby, S., 2007   *Bone and Antler combs*, Finds Research Group AD 700–1700 datasheet 40

Ashdown, R. and Evans, C., 1981   'The animal bones', in Partridge, C., *Skeleton Green: a Late Iron Age and Romano-British site*, Britannia Monograph Ser. 2, 205–35

Ashwin, T., 1999   'Studying Iron Age Settlement in Norfolk', in Davies, J. and Williamson, T., *Land of the Iceni: the Iron Age in Northern East Anglia*, Studies in East Anglia History 4, (Centre of East Anglian Studies, University of East Anglia) 100–24

Ashwin, T. and Bates S., 2000   *Excavations on the Norwich Southern Bypass, 1989–91 Part 1: Excavations at Bixley, Caistor St Edmund, Trowse, Cringleford and Little Melton*, E. Anglian Archaeol. 91

Atkins, R. and Connor, A., 2010   *Farmers and Ironsmiths: Prehistoric, Roman and Anglo-Saxon Settlement beside Brandon Road, Thetford, Norfolk*, E. Anglian Archaeol. 134

Bailey, M., 1989   *A Marginal Economy: East Anglian Breckland in the Later Middle Ages*, Cambridge Studies in Medieval Life and Thought, fourth series: 12 (Cambridge, Cambridge University Press)

Bailey, M., 2007   *Medieval Suffolk: An Economic and Social History 1200–1500* (Woodbridge, Boydell Press)

Baker, P., 2014   'Subsistence and animal use', in Ashwin, T. and Tester, A., *A Roman Settlement in the Waveney Valley: Excavations at Scole, 1993–4*, E. Anglian Archaeol. 152, 392–97

Bales, E., 2004   *A Roman Maltings at Beck Row, Mildenhall, Suffolk*, E. Anglian Archaeol. Occ. Paper 20

Barnes, G. and Williamson, T., 2006   *Hedgerow History. Ecology, history and landscape character* (Oxford, Oxbow Books)

Barrett, J., 1978   'The EPRIA prehistoric pottery', in Hedges, J.D. and Buckley, D.G., 'Excavations at a Neolithic causewayed enclosure, Orsett, Essex, 1975', *Proc. Prehist. Soc.* 44, 268–88

Barrett, J., 1980   'The pottery of the later Bronze Age in lowland England', *Proc. Prehist. Soc.* 46, 297–319

Bass, W.M., 1995   *Human Osteology* (Columbia, Missouri Archaeological Society)

Bates, P.J. and Winham, R.P., 1985   'Loomweights', in Fasham, P.J., *The Prehistoric Settlement at Winnal Down, Winchester: Excavations of MARC3 Site R17 in 1976 and 1977*, Hampshire Field Club Monogr. 2 (Gloucester, Allan Sutton Publishing), 90

Bayley, J., 1985   'Chalk objects', in Fasham, P.J., *The Prehistoric Settlement at Winnal Down, Winchester: Excavations of MARC3 Site R17 in 1976 and 1977*, Hampshire Field Club Monogr. 2 (Gloucester, Allan Sutton Publishing), 80–81

Behre, K-E., 2008   'Collected seeds and fruits from herbs as prehistoric food', *Vegetation History and Archaeobotany* 17, 65–73

Bennett, K.D., Whittington, G. and Edwards, K.J., 1994   'Recent plant nomenclatural changes and pollen morphology in the British Isles', *Quaternary Newsletter* 73, 1–6

Berggren, G., 1981   *Atlas of seeds: Part 3* (Arlöv, Swedish Museum of Natural History)

Berry, A.C. and Berry, A.J., 1967   'Epigenetic variation in the human cranium', *J. Anatomy* 101, 361–79

BGS (British Geological Survey), 2014   'Geology of Britain Viewer'. Available: http://maps.bgs.ac.uk/geology viewer_google/googleviewer.html Accessed: 8 April 2014

Bishop, M.J., 1974   *The Mollusc of Wicken Fen with some additional records*, Cambridgeshire and Isle of Ely Naturalists Trust Annual Report 1974, 1–4

Blinkhorn, P., 2010   'Anglo-Saxon and later pottery', in Atkins, R. and Connor, A., *Farmers and Ironsmiths: Prehistoric, Roman and Anglo-Saxon Settlement beside Brandon Road, Thetford, Norfolk*, E. Anglian Archaeol. 134, 70–9

Blinkhorn, P., 2012   *The Ipswich Ware Project. Ceramics, Trade and Society in Middle Saxon England*, Medieval Pottery Research Group Occ. Paper 7

Boessneck, J., 1969   'Osteological differences between sheep (*Ovis aries*) and goat (*Capra hircus*)', in Brothwell, D. and Higgs, E.S., *Science in Archaeology* (London, Thames and Hudson), 331–58

Boessneck, J., von den Driesch, A., Meyer-Lempennau, U. and Weschler-von Ohlen, E., 1971   *Das Tierknochenfunde aus dem Oppidum von Manching*, Die Ausgrabungen in Manching 6

Bond, J.M. and O'Connor, T.P., 1999   *Bones from medieval deposits at 16–22 Coppergate and other sites in York* (London, Counc. Brit. Archaeol.)

Booth, P., Dodd, A., Robinson, M. and Smith, A., 2007   *The archaeology of the gravel terraces of the upper and middle Thames. The early historical period: AD 1–1000*, Thames Valley Landscapes Monograph 27 (Oxford, Oxford University School of Archaeology)

Bourdillon, J. and Coy, J., 1980   'The animal bones', in Holdsworth, P., *Excavations at Melbourne Street, Southampton, 1971–76*, Counc. Brit. Archaeol. Res. Rep. 33, 79–121

Breen A.M., 2008   *The Mildenhall Rentals 1501* (Suffolk Family History Society)

Brett, M., 2009 — *Land at Recreation Way, Mildenhall, Suffolk: Archaeological Evaluation* (unpubl. Cotswold Archaeology report 09203)

Brett, M. and Young, R., 2010 — *Land at Recreation Way, Mildenhall, Suffolk, Phase 1 (storage tank and associated services): Written Scheme of Investigation for an Archaeological Excavation* (unpubl. Cotswold Archaeology document)

Brickley, M. and McKinley, J. (eds), 2004 — *Guidelines to the standards for recording human remains*, Inst. Archaeol. Paper 7 (Reading, Institute for Archaeology)

Bridgland, D.R. and Lewis, S.G., 1991 — 'Introduction to the Pleistocene geology and drainage history of the Lark Valley', in Lewis, S.G., Whiteman, C.A. and Bridgland, D.R. (eds), *Central East Anglian and Fen Basin; Field Guide* (London, Quaternary Research Association), 37–44

Britnell, J.W., 2000 — 'Worked bone and antler ornaments', in Barrett, J.C., Freeman, P.W.M. and Woodward, A., *Cadbury Castle Somerset: the later prehistoric and early historic archaeology*, English Heritage Archaeol. Rep. 20, 202

Britton, K. and Huntley J., 2011 — 'New evidence for the consumption of barley at Romano-British military and civilian sites, from the analysis of cereal bran fragments in faecal material', *Vegetation History and Archaeobotany* 20, 41–52

Broadbent, B.H., Broadbent, B.M. and Golden, W.H., 1975 — *Bolton standards of dentofacial developmental growth* (St Louis, C.V. Mosby)

Bronk Ramsey, C., 2009 — 'Bayesian analysis of radiocarbon dates', *Radiocarbon* 51(1), 337–60

Brooks, S.T. and Suchey, J.M., 1990 — 'Skeletal age determination based on the os pubis: A comparison of the Ascádi-Nemeskéri and Suchey-Brooks methods', *Human Evolution* 5, 227–38

Brothwell, D., 1981 — *Digging up Bones* (New York, Cornell University Press)

Brown, A., 1994 — 'A Romano-British shell-tempered pottery and tile manufacturing site at Harrold, Bedfordshire', *Bedfordshire Archaeol. J.* 21, 19–107

Brown, N., 1991 — 'Middle Iron Age Decorated Pottery around the Thames Estuary', *Essex Archaeol. Hist.* 22, 165–66

Brown, N. and Murphy, P., 1997 — 'Neolithic and Bronze Age' in Glazebrook, J., *Research and Archaeology: a Framework for the Eastern Counties, 1. Resource assessment*, E. Anglian Archaeol. Occ. Paper 3, 12–22

Brudenell M., 2010 — 'Late Bronze Age pottery', in Tabor, J., *Land east of Day Roads, Capel St Mary, Suffolk. An Archaeological Excavation* (unpubl. Cambridge Archaeological Unit report 957)

Brudenell, M., 2011a — 'Late Bronze Age and Early Iron Age pottery in Norfolk – a review', in Davies, J. (ed.), *The Iron Age in Northern East Anglia: New Work in the Land of the Iceni*, Brit. Archaeol. Rep. Brit. Ser. 549, 11–24

Brudenell M., 2011b — 'Late Bronze Age pottery', in Evans, C. and Patten, R., 'An Inland Bronze Age: Excavations at Striplands Farm, West Longstanton', *Proc. Cambridge Antiq. Soc.* 100, 19–26

Brudenell, M., 2011c — 'Iron Age pottery', in Hogan, S., *Moreland Road, Ipswich. Post Excavation Assessment* (unpubl. Cambridge Archaeological Unit report 996)

Brudenell, M., 2012 — *Pots, Practice and Society: an investigation of pattern and variability in the Post-Deverel Rimbury ceramic tradition of East Anglia* (unpubl. DPhil thesis, Univ. York)

Brudenell, M., 2013 — 'The Later Prehistoric Pottery', in Atkins, R., *Iron Age to Roman Settlement at Low Park Corner, Chippenham, Cambridgeshire: Archaeological Excavation Report* (unpubl. Oxford Archaeology East Report 1275)

Brudenell, M., forthcoming — 'The Middle Iron Age pottery', in Evans, C. and Lucy, S., *Mucking, Essex: excavations by Margaret and Tom Jones (1965–78): the prehistoric and Roman landscape* (Cambridge, Cambridge Archaeological Unit)

Bryant, S., 2000 — 'The Iron Age', in Brown, N. and Glazebrook, J. (eds) *Research and Archaeology: a framework for the eastern counties 2. Research Agenda and Strategy*, E. Anglian Arachaeol. Occ. Pap. 3, 14–18

Brudenell, M. and Cooper, A., 2008 — 'Post-middenism: depositional histories on Later Bronze Age settlements at Broom, Bedfordshire', *Oxford J. Archaeology* 27(1), 15–36

Buckland, P.I. and Buckland, P.C., 2006 — *BugsCEP Coleopteran Ecology Package* (version: BUGSCEP 7.63 Downloaded March 2013) Available: http://www.bugscep.com

Buckland, P.C. and Perry, D.W., 1989 — 'Ectoparasites of sheep from Storaborg, Iceland and their interpretation: piss, parasites and people, a palaeoecological perspective', *Hikuin* 15, 37–46

Buikstra, J. and Ubelaker, D.H. (eds), 1994 — 'Standards for data collection from human skeletal remains, Arkansas', *Archaeological Survey Research Series* 44

Bulleid, A. and Gray H.S., 1911 — *Glastonbury Lake Village Volume I* (Glastonbury, Glastonbury Antiquarian Society)

Butler, C., 2005 — *Prehistoric Flintwork* (Stroud, Tempus)

Butot, L.J.M. and Neuteboom, W.H., 1958 — 'Overt Vertigo moulinsiana (Dupuy) en haar voorkomen in Nederland', *Basteria* 22, 52–63

CA (Cotswold Archaeology) 2007 — *Technical Manual 1: Fieldwork Recording Manual* (unpubl. Cotswold Archaeology guidance document)

CA (Cotswold Archaeology) 2003 — *Technical Manual 2: The taking of samples for paleoenvironmental and palaeoeconomic analysis from archaeological sites* (unpubl. Cotswold Archaeology guidance document)

CA (Cotswold Archaeology) 1995 — *Technical Manual 3: Treatment of Finds Immediately after Excavation* (unpubl. Cotswold Archaeology guidance document)

Campanacci, M., Ruggieri, P., Gasbarrini, A., Ferraro, A. and Campanacci, L., 1998 — 'Osteoid osteoma: Direct visual identification and intralesional excision of the nidus with minimal removal of bone', *J. Bone and Joint Surgery* 81-B, 814–20

Campbell, B.M.S., 2000 — *English seigniorial agriculture, 1250–1450* (Cambridge, Cambridge University Press)

Campbell, G., 1992 — 'Bronze Age Plant Remains', in Moore, J. and Jennings, D. *Reading Business Park: a Bronze Age Landscape*, Thames Valley Landscapes: The Kennet Valley, Volume 1 (Oxford, Oxford

Archaeological Unit/Oxford Committee for Archaeology), 103–10

Campbell, G., 2008 'Plant utilization in the countryside around Danebury: a Roman perspective', in Cunliffe, B. (ed) *The Danebury Environs Programme: a Wessex Landscape During the Roman Era. Volume 1: Overview* (Oxford, English Heritage and Oxford University School of Archaeology), 53–74

Campbell, G. and Straker, V., 2003 'Prehistoric crop husbandry and plant use in southern England: development and regionality', in Robson Brown, K.A., *Archaeological Sciences 1999: Proceedings of the Archaeological Sciences Conference, University of Bristol, 1999*, Brit. Archaeol. Rep. Internat. Ser. 1111, (Oxford, Archaeopress), 14–30

Cappers, R.T.J., Bekker, R.M. and Jans, J.E.A., 2006 'Digital seed atlas of the Netherlands. Groningen Archaeological Studies 4 (Eelde, Barkhuis)'. Available: <http://seeds.eldoc.ub.rug.nl/> Accessed: March 2014

Carruthers, W.J., 2007 'Charred plant remains', in Timby, J., Brown, R., Biddulph, E., Hardy, A. and Powell, A., *A slice of rural Essex. Archaeological discoveries from the A120 between Stansted Airport and Braintree*, Oxford Wessex Archaeology Monogr. 1

Carruthers, W., 2011 'Chapter 7: The charred, mineralised and waterlogged plant remains', in Mudd, A. and Webster, M., *Iron Age and middle Saxon settlements at West Fen Roads, Ely, Cambridgeshire. The consortium site*, Northampton Archaeology Monogr. 2, Brit. Archaeol. Rep. Brit. Ser. 538, 110–16

Cessford, C., Alexander, M. and Dickens, A., 2006 *Between Broad Street and the Great Ouse: waterfront archaeology in Ely*, E. Anglian Archaeol. 114

Chappell, H.G., Ainsworth, J.F., Cameron, R.A.D. and Redfern, M., 1971 'The effect of trampling on a chalk grassland ecosystem', *J. Applied Ecology* 8, 869–82

Clark, J., 1995 *Medieval Finds from Excavations in London 3: the medieval horse and its equipment c. 1150–1450* (London, The Stationery Office)

Coad, J.G. and Streeten, D.F., 1982 'Excavations at Castle Acre Castle, Norfolk, 1972–1977: Country House and Castle of the Norman Earls of Surrey', *Archaeol. J.* 139, 138–301

Cohen, A., and Serjeantson, D., 1996 *A manual for the identification of bird bones from archaeological sites* (London, Archetype Publications Ltd)

Coles, J.M., 1987 *Meare Village East: The excavations of A. Bulleid and H. St George Gray 1932–56*, Somerset Levels Papers 13

Cool, H.E.M., 2006 *Eating and Drinking in Roman Britain* (Cambridge, Cambridge University Press)

Coope, G.R., 2006 'Insect faunas associated with Paleolithic industries from five sites of pre-Anglian age in central England', *Quaternary Science Reviews* 25, 1738–54

Coope, G.R., 2010 'Coleopteran faunas as indicators of interglacial climates in central and southern England', *Quaternary Science Reviews* 29, 1507–14

Copinger, W.A., 1909 *The Manors of Suffolk* (Manchester, Taylor, Garnett, Evans & Co. Ltd)

Cox, S., 2010 *Land at Recreation Way, Mildenhall, Suffolk, Phase 2 (town centre car park): Written Scheme of Investigation for an Archaeological Excavation* (unpubl. Cotswold Archaeology document)

Crabtree, P., 1989 *West Stow, Anglo-Saxon Animal Husbandry*, E. Anglian Archaeol. 47

Crabtree, P., 1990 'Zooarchaeology and complex societies: some uses of faunal analysis for the study of trade, social status, and ethnicity', in Schiffer, M.B., *Archaeological methods and theory 2* (University of Arizona Press), 155–205

Crabtree, P., 1994 'Animal exploitation at East Anglian Villages', in Rackham, J., *Environment and economy in Anglo-Saxon England*, Counc. Brit. Archaeol. Res. Rep. 89, 40–54

Crabtree, P., 1996 'Production and consumption in an early complex society: animal use in Middle Saxon East Anglia', *World Archaeol.* 28(1), 58–75

Crabtree, P., 2012 *Middle Saxon Animal Husbandry in East Anglia*, E. Anglian Archaeol. 143

Craig, C.R., Knüsel, C.J. and Carr, G.C., 2005 'Fragmentation, mutilation and dismemberment: an interpretation of human remains on Iron Age sites', in Parker Pearson, M. and Thorpe, I.J.N. (eds), *Warfare, Violence and Slavery in Prehistory. Proceedings of a Prehistoric Society Conference at Sheffield University*, Brit. Archaeol. Rep. Internat. Ser. 1374 (Oxford, Archaeopress), 165–80

Cra'ster, M.D., 1969 'New Addenbrooke's Iron Age site, Long Road, Cambridge', *Proc. Cambridge Antiq. Soc.* 62, 21–8

Croft, P., 1979 'The mammalian bones from feature 1', in Partridge, C., 'Excavations at Puckeridge and Braughing 1975–9', Hertfordshire Archaeol. 7, 73–92

Cromwell T.K., 1818 *Excursions in the County of Suffolk* (London and Essex, Longman, Hurst, Rees, Orme and Brown)

Crummy, N., 1983 *Colchester Archaeological Report 2: The Roman small finds from excavations in Colchester 1971–9* (Colchester, Colchester Archaeological Trust)

Crummy, N., 2002 'From Self-Sufficiency to Commerce: Structural and Artifactual Evidence for Textile Manufacture in Eastern England in the pre-Conquest Period', in Koslin, D.G. and Snyder, J.E. (eds), *Encountering Medieval Textiles and Dress: Objects, Texts, Images* (New York), 25–43

Cunliffe, B., 1984 *Danebury an Iron Age hillfort in Hampshire: Volume 2 The excavations, 1969–78: the finds*, Counc. Brit. Archaeol. Res. Rep. 52 (London)

Cunliffe, B. and Poole, C., 1991 *Danebury an Iron Age hillfort in Hampshire: Volume 5 The excavations, 1979–88*, Counc. Brit. Archaeol. Res. Rep. 73

Cunliffe B., 2005 *Iron Age Communities in Britain* (4th edition, London, Routledge)

Cussans, J.E.M. and Philips, C., 2016 'The animal and bird bone', in Nicholson, K., *A Late Iron Age and Romano-British farmstead at Cedars Park, Stowmarket, Suffolk*, E. Anglian Archaeol. 160, 119–48

Dallas, C., 1984 'The pottery', in Rogerson, A. and Dallas, C., *Excavations in Thetford 1948–59 and 1973–80*, E. Anglian Archaeol. 22, 117–66

Davies, J.A., Gregory, T., Lawson, A., Rickett, R. and Rogerson, A., 1991 — *The Iron Age Forts of Norfolk*, E. Anglian Archaeol. 54

Davies, J. and Williamson, T. (eds), 1999 — *Land of the Iceni: the Iron Age in Northern East Anglia*, Studies in East Anglia History 4, Centre of East Anglian Studies University of East Anglia

Davies, P., 1999 — *Snails: archaeology and landscape change* (Oxford, Oxbow)

Davies, P., Gale, C.H. and Lees, M., 1996 — 'Quantitative studies of modern wet-ground molluscan faunas from Bossington, Hampshire', *J. Biogeogr.* 23, 371–7

Davies, P. and Grimes, C.J., 1999 — 'Small-scale variation of pasture molluscan faunas within a relic watermeadow system at Wylye, Wiltshire', *J. Biogeogr.* 26, 1057–63

Davis R.H.C., 1954 — 'The Kalendar of Abbot Samson of Bury St Edmunds and Related Documents', *Camden Third Series* 84

Davis, S.J.M., 2003 — 'Animal bone', in Evans, C., *Power and Island Communities: excavations at the Wardy Hill Ringwork, Coveney, Ely*, E. Anglian Archaeol. 103, 122–31

Dickens, A. and Whittacker, P., in prep. — *Palace and Kitchen: excavations at Ely King's School*

Dobney, K., Jacques, D. and Irving, B., 1996 — *Of butchery and breeds: report on the vertebrate remains from various sites in the city of Lincoln*, Lincoln Archaeology Studies 5

Dobney, K., Jacques, D., Barrett, J. and Johnstone, C., 2007 — *Farmers, Monks and Aristocrats: The Environmental Archaeology of Anglo-Saxon Flixborough, Excavations at Flixborough Volume 3* (Oxford, Oxbow Books)

Drury, P., 1993 — 'The later Saxon, medieval and post-medieval pottery', in Rodwell, W. and Rodwell, K., *Rivenhall: Investigations of a Villa, Church and Village, 1950–1977, Vol. 2*, Chelmsford Archaeol. Trust Rep. 4.2, Counc. Brit. Archaeol. Res. Rep. 80

Duff, A.G., 2012 — *Beetles of Britain and Ireland, Volume 1: Sphaeriusidae to Silphidae*, (Norfolk: A.G. Duff Publishing)

Dyer, C., 1994 — *Everyday Life in Medieval England*, reprinted 2000 (London, Hambledon)

Edmonds, M., 1995 — *Stone Tools and Society. Working Stone in Neolithic and Bronze Age Britain* (London: B.T. Batsford)

Egan, G. and Pritchard, F., 1991 — *Medieval Finds from Excavations in London: 3 Dress Accessories c. 1150–1450* (London, The Stationery Office)

Elsdon, S., 1975 — *Stamp and Roulette Decorated Pottery of the La Tène Period in Eastern England: a Study in Geometric Designs*, Brit. Archaeol. Rep. 10

Elsdon, S., 1992 — 'East Midlands Scored Ware', *Trans. Leicestershire Archaeol. Hist. Soc.* 66, 83–91

EH (English Heritage), 1991 — *Management of Archaeological Projects* 2

EH (English Heritage), 2006 — *MORPHE: The Management of Research Projects in the Historic Environment*

EH (English Heritage), 2011 — *Pre-industrial Lime Kilns*, English Heritage Introductions to Heritage Assets

Evans, C., 2000 — 'Iron Age forts and defences', in Kirby, T. and Oosthuizen, S. (eds), *An Atlas of Cambridgeshire and Huntingdonshire History* (Cambridge, Centre for Regional Studies)

Evans, C., 2013 — *Process and History: Prehistoric Communities at Colne Fen, Earith*, Cambridge Archaeological Unit Landscape Archives Series, The Archaeology of the Lower Ouse Valley Vol. 1

Evans, C. and Serjeantson, D., 1988 — 'The backwater economy of a fen-edge community in the Iron Age: the Upper Delphs, Haddenham', *Antiquity* 62, 360–70

Evans, J., 1991 — 'Some notes on the Horningsea Roman pottery', *Journal Roman Pottery Studies* 4, 33–43

Evans, J.G., 1972 — *Land Snails in Archaeology* (London, Seminar Press)

Evans, J.G., Davies, P., Mount, R. and Williams, D., 1992 — 'Mollusc taxocenes from Holocene overbank alluvium in southern central England', in Needham, S. and Macklin, M.G. (eds), *Alluvial Archaeology in Britain*, Oxbow Monograph 27 (Oxford), 65–74

Evison, V.I., 1994 — *An Anglo-Saxon Cemetery at Great Chesterford, Essex* York, Council for British Archaeology Report 91

FDI (Fédération Dentaire Internationale), 1971 — 'Two digit system of designating teeth', *International Dental J.* 21, 104–6

Fifield, P.W., 1988 — 'The faunal remains', in Potter, T.W. and Trow, S.D., 'Puckeridge-Braughing, Hertfordshire: the Ermine Street excavations 1971–2: the Late Iron Age and Roman settlement', *Hertfordshire Archaeol.* 10, 148–55

Finnegan, M., 1978 — 'Non-metric variation in the infracranial skeleton', *J. Anatomy* 125, 23–37

Foster, G.N. and Friday, L.E., 2011 — *Keys to Adults of the Water Beetles of Britain and Ireland (Part 1)*, Handbooks for the Identification of British Insects 4/05, (London: Royal Entomological Society of London)

Fox, C., 1923 — *The Archaeology of the Cambridge Region: a topographical study of the bronze, early iron, Roman and Anglo-Saxon ages, with an introductory note on the neolithic age,* (Cambridge: The University Press)

Fryer, V., 2004 — 'Charred plant macrofossils and other remains', in Bales, E., *A Roman Maltings at Beck Row, Mildenhall, Suffolk*, E. Anglian Archaeol. Occ. Paper 20, 49–54

Gale, R. and Cutler, D.F., 2000 — *Plants in Archaeology. Identification Manual of Artefacts of Plant Origin from Europe and the Mediterranean* (Otley, Westbury and the Royal Botanic Gardens Kew)

Gallet, Y., Genevey, A. and Le Goff, M., 2002 — 'Three millennia of directional variations of the Earth's magnetic field in Western Europe as revealed by archaeological artefacts', *J. Phys. Earth Planet. Interiors* 131, 81–9

Garrow, D., Lucy, S. and Gibson, D., 2006 — *Excavations at Kilverstone, Norfolk, 2000–02*, E. Anglian Archaeol. 113

GSA (Geological Society of America), 1995 — *Rock-color chart*, 8th print with revised text, (Boulder, Colorado; Geological Society of America)

Geary, B.R., 2010   *Palynological assessment of samples from Mildenhall, Suffolk* (Birmingham University unpubl. report)

Geary, B.R., Hall, A.R., Kenward, H., Bunting, M.J., Lillie, M.C. and Carrott, J., 2005   'Recent palaeoenvironmental evidence for the processing of hemp (*Cannabis sativa* L.) in Eastern England during the medieval period', *Med. Archaeol.* 49, 317–32

Geber, J. and Murphy, E., 2012   'Scurvy in the Great Irish Famine: Evidence of Vitamin C deficiency in a mid-19th century skeletal population', *American J. Physical Anthropology* 148, 512–24

Gingell, C., 1992   *The Marlborough Downs: a Later Bronze Age landscape and its origins*, Wiltshire Archaeol. Natural Hist. Soc. Monogr. 1

Goodall, I.H., 1980   *Ironwork in Medieval Britain: An Archaeological Study* (unpubl. DPhil thesis, University College, Cardiff)

Gransden, A., 1964   *The Chronicle of Bury St Edmunds 1212–1301* (London, Thomas Nelson & Sons Ltd)

Gransden, A., 2007   *A History of the Abbey of Bury St Edmunds 1182–1256*, Studies in the History of Medieval Religion 31

Grant, A., 1982   'The use of tooth wear as a guide to the age of domestic animals', in Wilson, B., Grigson, C. and Payne, S., *Ageing and Sexing Animal Bones from Archaeological Sites*, Brit. Archaeol. Rep. Brit. Ser. 109, 91–108

Grant, A., 1989   'Animals in Roman Britain', in Todd, M., *Research on Roman Britain: 1960–98*, Britannia Monograph Ser. 11, 135–46

Gray, H. St G., 1933   'Trial excavation at the so-called Danish Camp at Warham, near Wells, Norfolk', *Antiq. J.* 13, 399–413

Green, H.S., 1980   *The Flint Arrowheads of the British Isles: a detailed study of materials from England and Wales with comparanda from Scotland and Ireland, Part I*, Brit. Archaeol. Rep. Brit. Ser. 75(i)

Green, M.A., 2001   *Dying for the Gods: Human Sacrifice in Iron Age and Roman Europe* (Stroud, Tempus)

Greenfield, H.J., 2006   'Sexing fragmentary ungulate acetabulae', in Ruscillo, D., 'The table test: a simple technique for sexing canid humeri', in Ruscillo, D., *Recent advances in ageing and sexing animal bones. Proceedings of the 9th ICAZ Conference, Durham 2002*, (Oxford, Oxbow Books), 62–86

Gregory, T. and Rogerson, A., 1991   'Chapter 4: General Conclusions', in Davies, J.A., Gregory, T., Lawson, A., Rickett, R. and Rogerson, A., *The Iron Age Forts of Norfolk*, E. Anglian Archaeol. 54, 69–72

Gregory, T., 1986   'Warham Camp', in Gregory, T. and Gurney, D., *Excavations at Thornham, Warham, Wighton and Caistor, Norfolk*, E. Anglian Archaeol. 30

Grieg, J.R.A. and Hall, A.R., 1981   'New fossil evidence for the past cultivation and processing of hemp (*Cannabis sativa* L.) in Eastern England', *New Phytologist* 89, 503–10

Guido, M., 1978   *The Glass Beads of the Prehistoric and Roman Periods in Britain and Ireland* (London, Thames and Hudson)

Gurney, D., 1995   'Small towns and villages of Roman Norfolk', in Brown, A.E., (ed.) *Roman Small Towns in Eastern England and Beyond*, Oxbow Monograph 52, 53–67

Gurney, D., 2003   *Standards for Field Archaeology in the East of England*, E. Anglian Archaeol. Occ. Paper 14

Hagan, A., 2006   *Anglo-Saxon food and drink. Production, processing, distribution and consumption* (Norfolk, Anglo-Saxon Books)

Hall, A., 2008   *Environmental Archaeology Bibliography*, Archaeology Data Service [data-set], York: Archaeology Data Service [distributor] doi:10.5284/1000225 Accessed 12 January 2014, Available: http://archaeologydataservice.ac.uk/archives/view/eab_eh_2004/

Hall, A. and Kenward, H., 2003   'Can we identify biological indicator groups for craft, industry and other activities?' in P. Murphy, and P.E.J. Wiltshire (eds) *The Environmental Archaeology of Industry*, Symposia of the Association for Environmental Archaeology 20, (Oxford: Oxbow Books) 114–30

Hallam, S., 1961   'Wash Coast-line levels since Roman Times', *Antiquity* 35, 152–5

Halstead, P., 1985   'A study of mandibular teeth from Romano-British contexts at Maxey', in Pryor, F. and French, C., *Fenland Project No. 1: Archaeology and Environment in the Lower Welland Valley Vol. 1*, E. Anglian Archaeol. 27, 219–24

Halstead, P., Collins, P. and Isaakidou, V., 2002   'Sorting the sheep from the goats: morphological distinctions between the mandibles and mandibular teeth of adult *Ovis* and *Capra*', *J. Archaeol. Sci.* 29, 545–53

Hambleton, E., 1999   *Animal husbandry regimes in Iron Age Britain: A comparative study of faunal assemblages from British archaeological sites*, Brit. Archaeol. Rep. Brit. Ser. 282

Hamerow, H., 1991   'Settlement Mobility and the "Middle Saxon Shift": Rural Settlements and Settlement Patterns in Anglo-Saxon England', *Anglo-Saxon England* 20, 1–17

Hamerow, H., 1993   *Excavations at Mucking Volume 2: The Anglo-Saxon Settlement* (London, English Heritage/British Museum Press)

Hamerow, H., 2006   'Special deposits in Anglo-Saxon Settlements', *Medieval Archaeol.* 50, 1–30

Hansen, M., 1987   *The Hydrophilidae (Coleoptera) of Fennoscandia and Denmark*, Fauna Entomologyca Scandinavica 18, (Leiden: Scandinavian Science Press)

Harcourt, R.A., 1974   'The dog in prehistoric and early historic Britain', *J. Archaeol. Sci.* 1, 151–75

Harris, E., Harris, J. and James, N.D.G., 2003   *Oak. A British History* (Oxford, Oxbow Books)

Hart, C.R., 1966   *The Early Charters of Eastern England* (Leicester, Leicester University Press)

Hartley, B.R. and Dickinson, B.M., 2008   *Names on Terra Sigillata. An Index of Makers' stamps and signatures on Gallo-Roman Terra Sigillata (Samian Ware). Volume 1 (A to AXO)*, Bulletin of the Institute of Classical Studies Supplement

Hartley, B.R. and Perrin, J.R., 1999   'Mortaria from Excavations by E. Greenfield at Water Newton, Billing Brook and Chesterton 1956–58', in Perrin, J.R., 'Roman Pottery from excavations at and near to the Roman Small Town of Durobrivae, Water Newton, Cambridgeshire, 1956–58', *J. Roman Pottery Stud.* 8, 129–35

Havard, T. and Holt, R., 2010 — *Land at Recreation Way, Mildenhall, Suffolk Post-Excavation Assessment and Updated Project Design* (unpubl. Cotswold Archaeology report 12114)

Hervey, F., 1925 — *The Pinchbeck Register* (Brighton)

Higbee, L., 2009 — 'Mammal and bird bone', in Lucy, S., Tipper, J. and Dickens, A., *The Anglo-Saxon Settlement and Cemetery at Bloodmoor Hill, Carlton Colville, Suffolk*, East Anglian Archaeol. 131, 279–304

Higbee, L., 2013a — 'Mammal, bird and fish bone', in Evans, C., Brudenell, M., Patten, R. and Regan, R., *Process and history: prehistoric communities at Colne Fen, Earith, Cambridge Archaeol. Unit Landscape Archives: the archaeology of the Lower Ouse Valley, Volume I* (Cambridge, Cambridge Archaeol. Unit), 201–12

Higbee, L., 2013b — 'Mammal, bird and fish bone', in Evans, C., Appleby, G., Lucy, S. and Regan, R., *Romano-British communities at Colne Fen, Earith: an inland port and supply farm, Cambridge Archaeol. Unit Landscape Archives: the archaeology of the Lower Ouse Valley, Volume II* (Cambridge, Cambridge Archaeol. Unit), 116–34

Higbee, L., 2013c — *Animal bone from East Anton, Andover,* (unpublished report for AC Archaeology)

Higbee, L., forthcoming a — 'Animal bone', in Caruth, J., *Hartismere Anglo-Saxon settlement*, E. Anglian Archaeol.

Higbee, L., forthcoming b — 'Animal bone', in Dickens, A., *Cambridge, Grand Arcade*, E. Anglian Archaeol.

Hill, J.D., 1995 — 'Ritual and Rubbish in the Iron Age of Wessex: a study in the formation of a specific archaeological record' Brit. Archaeol. Rep. Brit. Ser. 242

Hill, J.D., 1999 — 'Settlement, Landscape and Regionality: Norfolk and Suffolk in the pre-Roman Iron Age of Britain and Beyond', in Davies, J. and Williamson, T., *Land of the Iceni: the Iron Age in Northern East Anglia*, Studies in East Anglia History 4, (Centre of East Anglian Studies, University of East Anglia), 185–207

Hill, J.D., 2002 — 'Just About the Potter's Wheel? Using, Making and Depositing Middle and Later Iron Age Pots in East Anglia', in Woodward, A. and Hill, J.D. (eds), *Prehistoric Britain: the ceramic basis* (Oxford, Oxbow), 143–60

Hill, J.D., and Braddock, P., 2006 — 'The Iron Age pottery', in Evans, C. and Hodder, I., *Marshland communities and cultural landscapes, The Haddenham Project Volume 2* (Cambridge, McDonald Institute for Archaeological Research), 152–94

Hill, J.D., and Horne, L., 2003 — 'Iron Age and Early Roman pottery', in Evans, C., *Power and Island Communities: Excavations at the Wardy Hill Ringwork, Coveney, Ely*, E. Anglian Archaeol. 103, 145–84

Hillman, G., 1981 — 'Reconstructing crop husbandry practices from charred remains of crops', in Mercer, R., *Farming Practice in British Prehistory* (Edinburgh, Edinburgh University Press), 123–62

Hobbs, R., 1996 — *British Iron Age coins in the British Museum* (London, British Museum Press)

Hobbs, R., 2016 — *The Mildenhall Treasure, Late Roman Silver Plate from East Anglia* (London, British Museum Press)

Hodges, H., 1976 — *Artifacts, An introduction to early materials and technology* (London, John Baker)

Hodgson, J.M., 1976 — *Soil Survey Field Handbook*, Soil Survey Technical Monograph 5

Hodson, R., 1962 — 'Some pottery from Eastbourne, the 'Marnians' and the pre-Roman Iron Age in southern England', *Proc. Prehist. Soc.* 28, 140–55

Holmes, J., 1993 — 'Animal bone', in Williams, R.J., *Pennyland and Hartigans: two Iron Age and Saxon sites in Milton Keynes*, Buckinghamshire Archaeol. Soc. Monogr. Ser. 4, 199–206

Holmes, M., 2007a — 'Animal and fish bone', in Timby, J., Brown, R., Hardy, A., Leech, S., Poole, C. and Webley, L., *Settlement on the Bedfordshire Claylands: archaeology along the A421 Great Barford Bypass*, Bedfordshire Archaeol. Monogr. 8, 329–63

Holmes, M., 2007b — 'Animal bone', in Webley, L., Timby, J. and Wilson, M., *Fairfield Park, Stotfold, Bedfordshire: Later Prehistoric settlement in the Eastern Chilterns*, Bedfordshire Archaeology Monogr. 7, 103–16

Howe, M.D., Mackreth, D.F. and Perrin, J.R., 1980 — *Roman Pottery from the Nene Valley: a Guide*, Peterborough City Mus. Occ. Paper 2

IfA 2008 — *Standard and Guidance for Archaeological Excavation* (Chartered) Institute of Field Archaeologists (Reading)

Iles, M., 2001 — 'Animal bone', in Chowne, P., Cleal, R.M., Fitzpatrick, A.P. and Andrews, P., *Excavations at Billingborough, Lincolnshire, 1975–8: a Bronze-Iron Age settlement and salt-working site*, E. Anglian Archaeol. 94, 79–86

Ingle, C.J., 1993 — 'The Quernstones from Hunsbury Hillfort, Northamptonshire', *Northamptonshire Archaeology* 25, 21–33

Inizan, M-L, Roche, H. and Tixier, J., 1992 — *Technology of Knapped Stone* (France, Meudon)

Ixer, R.A. and Lunt, S., 1991 — 'Petrography of certain Pre-Spanish pottery of Peru', in Middleton, A. and Freestone, I. (eds), *Recent Developments in Ceramic Petrology*, British Museum Occ. Paper 81, 137–64

Jackson, R., 1990 — *Camerton: The Late Iron Age and Early Roman Metalwork* (London, British Museum Publications)

Jacobi, R., 1978 — 'The Mesolithic of Sussex', in Drewett, P. (ed.), *Archaeology in Sussex to AD 1500*, Counc. Brit. Archaeol. Res. Rep. 29, 15–22

Jessop, L., 1986 — *Coleoptera: Scarabaeidae*, Handbooks for the Identification of British Insects 5/11, (London, Royal Entomological Society of London)

Johns, C., 1996 — *The Jewellery of Roman Britain* (London, University College London)

Jones, G.G., 1984 — 'Animal bones', in Rogerson, A. and Dallas, C., *Excavations at Thetford 1948–59 and 1973–80*, E. Anglian Archaeol. 22, 187–92

Jones, G.G., 1993 — 'Animal and bird bone', in Dallas, C., *Excavations in Thetford by B.K. Davison between 1964 and 1970*, E. Anglian Archaeol. 62, 176–91

Jones, R. and Serjeantson, D., 1983 — 'The animal bone from five sites at Ipswich', *Ancient Monuments Laboratory Report Old Series* 3951

178

Jones, R.T., Sly, J., Beech, M. and Parfitt, S., 1988
'The animal bones', in Martin, E., 'Burgh: the Iron Age and Roman enclosure, E. Anglian Archaeol. 40, microfiche A3–B6

Jope, M., 1991
'Other objects of copper alloy (mainly bronze)', in Cunliffe, B. and Poole, C., Danebury an Iron Age hillfort in Hampshire: Volume 5 The excavations, 1979–88, Counc. Brit. Archaeol. Res. Rep. 73, 328–33

Jordan, C., 2009
Land at Recreation Way, Mildenhall, Suffolk: Archaeological Desk-Based Assessment (unpubl. Cotswold Archaeology report 09128)

Kenward, H., 1987
Insect remains from Bridge Street Ipswich, Ancient Monuments Report New Series 195/87, (London: English Heritage)

Kenward, H. and Allison, E., 1994
'Insects' in Ayers B.S., Excavations at Fishergate, Norwich 1985, E. Anglian Archaeol. 68, 45–48

Kenward, H.K. and Hall, A.R., 1995
Biological Evidence from Anglo-Scandinavian Deposits at 16–22 Coppergate, The Archaeology of York 14/7, (London: Council for British Archaeology)

Kenward, H.K., Hall, A.R. and Jones, A.K.G., 1980
'A tested set of techniques for the extraction of plant and animal macrofossils from waterlogged archaeological deposits', Science and Archaeology 22, 3–15

Kerney, M.P., 1999
Atlas of the land and freshwater molluscs of Britain and Ireland (Colchester, Harley Books)

King, A., 1978
'A comparative survey of bone assemblages from Roman sites in Britain', Bulletin of the Institute of Archaeology 15, 207–32

King, A., 1984
'Animal bones and the dietary identity of military and civilian groups in Roman Britain, Germany and Gaul', in Blagg T.F.C. and King, A., Military and civilian in Roman Britain: cultural relationships in a frontier province, Brit. Archaeol. Rep. Brit. Ser. 136, 187–218

King, A., 1999
'Diet in the Roman world: a regional inter-site comparison of the mammal bones', J. Roman Archaeol. 12, 168–202

King, A., 2004
'Animal skeletal remains' in Blagg, T.F.C., Plouviez, J. and Tester, A., Excavations at a large Romano-British settlement at Hacheston, Suffolk in 1973–1974, E. Anglian Archaeol. 106, 188–95

King, J., 1996
'The animal bones', in Mackreth, D.F., Orton Hall Farm: a Roman and Early Anglo-Saxon farmstead, E. Anglian Archaeol. 76, 216–18

Kirby, J., 1735
The Suffolk Traveller (Ipswich and London)

Kirschvink, J.L., 1980
'The least-squares line and plane and the analysis of palaeomagnetic data', Geophysical J. Internat. 62, 699–718

Knight, D., 2002
'A Regional Ceramic Sequence: Pottery of the First Millennium BC between the Humber and the Nene', in Woodward, A. and Hill, J.D. (eds), Prehistoric Britain: the ceramic basis (Oxford, Oxbow), 119–42

Knocker, G.M., 1967
'Excavations at Red Castle, Thetford', Norfolk Archaeol. 34, 119–86

Knüsel, C., 2007
'Human Remains', in Van de Noort, R. and Collis J., 'Burial Rituals in the middle Iron Age', in Van de Noort, R., Chapman, H. and Collis, J.R., Sutton Common: the excavation of an Iron Age 'marsh-fort', Counc. Brit. Archaeol. Res. Rep. 154, 137–39

Koch, K., 1989
Die Kafer Mitteleuropas, Ökologie Band 2, (Krefeld, Goecke and Evers)

Koch, K., 1992
Die Kafer Mitteleuropas, Ökologie Band 3, (Krefeld, Goecke and Evers)

Kudo, S., Minuro, O. and Russel, W.J., 1983
'Ossification of thoracic ligamenta flava', American J. Roentgenology 141, 117–21

Labarge, M.W., 1965
A Baronial Household of the Thirteenth Century (London, Eyre and Spottiswoode)

Lamb, H.H., 1982
Climate, History and the Modern World (London, Methuen)

Langdon, C. and Scaife, R., 2009
'Pollen Analysis', in Daniel, P., Archaeological Excavations at Pode Hole Quarry. Bronze Age occupation on the Cambridgeshire Fen Edge, Brit. Archaeol. Rep. Brit. Ser. 484, 106–13

Lanos, Ph., 2004
'Bayesian inference of calibration curves: application to archaeomagnetism', in Buck, C. and Millard, A. (eds), Tools for Constructing Chronologies: Crossing Disciplinary Boundaries (London, Springer-Verlag), 43–82

Larsen, C.S., 2002
'Bioarchaeology: the lives and lifestyles of past people', J. Archaeological Research 10, 119–66

Last, J., 2004
'Prehistoric pottery', in Gibson, C., Lines in the Sand: Middle to Late Bronze Age settlement at Game Farm, Brandon, E. Anglian Archaeol. Occ. Paper 19, 36–41

Lawson, A.J., 1980
'A Late Bronze Age hoard from Beeston Regis, Norfolk', Antiquity 54, 217–19

Legge, A.J. and Dorrington, E., 1985
'Harlow Temple: the animal bones', in Clark, F.R. and Jones, I.K., The Romano-British Temple at Harlow, Essex (Gloucester, Alan Sutton), 122–33

Legge, A.J., Wiliams, J. and Williams, P., 2000
'Lambs to the slaughter: sacrifice at two Roman temples in southern England', in Rowley-Conwy, P., Animal Bones, Human Societies (Oxford, Oxbow Books), 152–57

Lethbridge, T.C., 1931
Recent Excavations on Anglo-Saxon Cemeteries in Cambridgeshire and Suffolk, Cambridge Antiquarian Society Quarto Series, New Series 3

Lewin, J., 2010
'Medieval and environmental impacts and feedbacks: the lowland floodplains of England and Wales', Geoarchaeology 25, Geoarchaeology Review Paper 3, 267–311

Lewis, J., Brown, F., Batt, A., Cooke, N., Barrett, J., Every, R., Mepham, L., Brown, K., Cramp, K., Lawson, A.J., Roe, F., Allen, S., Petts, D., McKinley, J., Carruthers, W., Challinor, D., Wiltshire, P., Robinson, M., Lewis, H. and Bates, M., 2006
Landscape evolution in the Middle Thames Valley: Heathrow Terminal 5 Excavations Volume 1, Perry Oaks, Framework Archaeology Monograph no.1, (Oxford and Salisbury, Framework)

Libois, R.M., Hallet-Libois, C. and Rosoux, R., 1987
Éléments pour l'identificationdes restes crâniens des poissons dulçaquicoles de Belgiquie et du Nord de la France 1 – Anguilliformes, Gastéiformes, Cyprinodontiformes et Perciformes, Fiches D'Ostéologie Animale Pour L'Archaéologie No. 3

Libois, R.M. and Hallet-Libois, C., 1988 — *Éléments pour l'identification des restes crâniens des poissons dulçaquicoles de Belgiquie et du Nord de la France 2 – Cypriniformes*, Fiches D'Ostéologie Animale Pour L'Archaéologie No. 4

Limbrey, S., 1975 — *Soil Science and Archaeology* (London, Seminar Press)

Lindroth, C.H., 1974 — *Coleoptera: Carabidae*, Handbooks for the Identification of British Insects 4/2, (London: Royal Entomological Society of London)

Livarda, A., 2010 — 'The environmental samples', in Woolhouse, T., *Bridge House Dairies, Worlington Road, Mildenhall, Suffolk, Archaeological investigation research archive report* (unpubl. Archaeological Solutions report 3569), 107–11

Liversidge, H.M., Herdeg, B., Rösing, F.W., 1998 — 'Dental age estimation of non-adult: a review of methods and principles', in Alt, K.W, Rösing, F.W. and Teschler-Nicola, M. (eds), *Dental anthropology, fundamentals, limits and prospects* (Vienna, Springer Verlag), 419–42

Lloyd, T.H., 2005 — *The English Wool Trade in the Middle Ages* (Cambridge, Cambridge University Press)

Locker, A., 2000 — 'Animal bone', in Lawson, A.J., *Potterne 1982–5: Animal husbandry in Later Prehistoric Wiltshire*, Wessex Archaeology Report 17, 101–17

Lott, D., 2009 — *The Staphylinidae*, Handbooks for the Identification of British Insects 12/5, (London: Royal Entomological Society)

Lovejoy, C.O., Meindl, R.S., Pryzbeck, T.R. and Mensforth, R.P., 1985 — 'Chronological metamorphosis of the auricular surface of the ilium: a new method for the determination of adult skeletal age at death', *American J. Physical Anthropology* 68, 15–28

Lucht, W.H., 1987 — *Die Käfer Mitteleuropas: Katalog*, (Krefeld: Goecke and Evers)

Lucy, S., 2000 — *The Anglo-Saxon Way of Death* (Stroud, Sutton Publishing)

Lucy, S. and Reynolds, A. (eds), 2002 — *Burial in Early Medieval England and Wales*, Society for Medieval Archaeology Monogr. 17 (London)

Lucy, S., Tipper, J. and Dickens, A., 2009 — *The Anglo-Saxon Settlement and Cemetery at Bloodmoor Hill, Carlton Colville, Suffolk*, E. Anglian Archaeol. 131

Luff, M., 2007 — *Coleoptera: Carabidae*, Handbooks for the Identification of British Insects 4/2, second edition, (London: Royal Entomological Society of London)

Luff, R., 1988 — 'The faunal remains', in Drury, P.J., *The mansion and other sites in the south-eastern sector of Caesaromagus*, Counc. Brit. Archaeol. Res. Rep. 66, Chelmsford Archaeol. Trust Rep. 3.1, 118–22

Luff, R., 1993 — *Animal bones from excavations at Colchester, 1971–85*, Colchester Archaeol. Rep. 12, (Colchester)

Mabey, R., 2007 — *Food for Free* (London, HarperCollins)

MacGregor, A., 1985 — *Bone Antler Ivory and Horn: the technology of skeletal materials since the Roman period* (Kent, Croom Helm Ltd)

Mackreth, D.F., 1996 — *Orton Hall Farm: a Roman and Early Anglo-Saxon Farmstead*, E. Anglian Archaeol. 76

Mackreth, D.F., 2011 — *Brooches in late Iron Age and Roman Britain* (Oxford, Oxbow)

Mainman, A.J. and Rogers, N.S.H., 2000 — *Craft, Industry and Everyday Life: Finds from Anglo-Scandinavian York* (York, York Archaeological Trust/Council for British Archaeology)

Manning, W.H., 1985 — *Catalogue of the Romano-British iron tools, fittings and weapons in the British Museum* (London, British Museum Publications)

Marshall, P., Tipper, J., Bayliss, A., McCormac, F.G., van der Plicht, J., Bronk Ramsey, C. and Beavan-Athfield, N., 2009 — 'Absolute dating', in Lucy, S., Tipper, J. and Dickens, A., *The Anglo-Saxon Settlement and Cemetery at Bloodmoor Hill, Carlton Colville, Suffolk*, E. Anglian Archaeol. 131, 322–9

Martin, E., 1979 — 'Suffolk Archaeological Unit Excavations 1978', *Proc. Suffolk Inst. Archaeol.* 34(3), 218–20

Martin, E., 1988 — *Burgh: The Iron Age and Roman Enclosure*, E. Anglian Archaeol. 40

Martin, E., 1989 — 'Commentary on the illustrated Iron Age pottery', in West, S., *West Stow, Suffolk: The Prehistoric and Romano-British Occupation*, E. Anglian Archaeol. 48, 65–8

Martin, E., 1993 — *Settlement on Hilltops: seven prehistoric sites in Suffolk*, E. Anglian Archaeol. 65

Martin, E., 1999 — 'Chapter 3. Suffolk in the Iron Age', in Davies, J. and Williamson T., 44–99

Martin, E., 2008 — 'The context of medieval farming and landholding in East Anglia, with a glossary of modern field-system descriptors' in Martin, E. and Satchell M., 2008, 11–37

Martin, E., 2008 — 'The origins of fields in East Anglia' in Martin, E. and Satchell M., 2008, 214–28

Martin, E. and Murphy, P., 1988 — 'West Row Fen, Suffolk: a Bronze Age fen-edge settlement site', *Antiquity* 62, 353–8

Martin, E. and Satchell, M., 2008 — *'Wheare most Inclosures be' East Anglian Fields: History, Morphology and Management*, E. Anglian Archaeol. 124

May, E., 1985 — 'Widerristhöhe und Langknochenmaße bei Pferd. Ein immer noch aktuelles Problem', *Zeitschrift für Säugertierkunde* 50, 368–82

Medlycott, M., 2011 — *Research and Archaeology Revisited: a revised framework for the East of England*, E. Anglian Archaeol. Occ. Paper 24

Mees, A.W., 1995 — *Modelsignierte Dekorationen auf südgallischer Terra Sigillata*, Forschungen und Berichte zur Vor- und Frühgeschichte in Baden-Württemberg 54

Meindl, R.S. and Lovejoy, C.O., 1985 — 'Ectocranial suture closure: a revised method for the determination of skeletal age at death based on lateral-anterior sutures', *American J. Physical Anthropology* 68, 57–66

Middleton-Stewart, J., 2011 — *Records of the Churchwardens of Mildenhall: Collections (1446–1454) and Accounts (1503–1553)*, Suffolk Records Society 54 (Woodbridge, Boydell Press)

Millett, M., 1995 — 'Strategies for Roman small towns', in Brown, A.E. (ed.), *Roman Small Towns in Eastern England and Beyond*, Oxbow Monogr. 52, 29–38

Mitich, L.W., 1997 — 'Intriguing world of weeds: Fumitory (*Fumaria officinalis* L.)', *Weed Technology* 11, 843–45

Møller-Christensen, V., 1958 — *Bogen om Æbenholt kloster* (Copenhagen, Dansk Videnskabs Forlag)

Monckton, A. and Grinter, P., 1997 — *Peterborough, Long Causeway (LCW 95): Plant macrofossils from medieval deposits from an archaeological excavation* (unpubl. University of Leicester Archaeological Services report)

Moore, P.D. and Webb, J.A., 1978 — *An illustrated guide to pollen analysis* (London, Hodder and Stoughton)

Moore, P.D., Webb, J.A. and Collinson, M.E., 1991 — *Pollen Analysis* (Oxford, Blackwell Scientific)

Morris, E., 1994 — 'Production and distribution of pottery and salt in Iron Age Britain, a review', *Proc. Prehist. Soc.* 60, 371–93

Morris, E., 1996 — 'Artefact production and exchange in the British Iron Age', in Champion T.C. and Collis J.R. (eds), *The Iron Age in Britain and Ireland: Recent Trends*. (Sheffield, J.R. Collis publications), 41–65

Morris, J., 2011 — *Investigating Animal Burials: ritual, mundane and beyond*, Brit. Archaeol. Rep. Brit. Ser. 535

Morris, J. and Jarvis, B., 2011 — 'What's so special? A reinterpretation of Anglo-Saxon 'special deposits', *Medieval Archaeol.* 55, 66–81

Morris, M.G., 2008 — *True Weevils (Part II). Coleoptera: Curculionidae, Ceutorhynchinae*, Handbooks for the Identification of British Insects 5/17c, (London: Royal Entomological Society)

Mortimer, R., Regan, R. and Lucy, S., 2005 — *The Saxon and Medieval Settlement at West Fen Road, Ely: the Ashwell Site*, E. Anglian Archaeol. 110

MPRG, 1998 — *A Guide to the Classification of Medieval Ceramic Forms Volume 2*, Medieval Pottery Res. Grp. Occ. Paper (London, Medieval Pottery Research Group)

Mudd, A., 2002 — *Excavations at Melford Meadows, Brettenham, 1994: Romano-British and Early Saxon Occupations*, E. Anglian Archaeol. 99

Murphy, P., 1995 — 'Part 5. Botanical evidence', in Wymer, J.J. and Brown, N.R., *Excavations at North Shoebury: settlement and economy in south-east Essex 1500BC–AD1500*, E. Anglian Archaeol. 75, 146–50

Murphy, P., 1997 — 'Environment and economy', in Bryant, S., 'Iron Age', in Glazebrook, J., *Research and Archaeology: a Framework for the Eastern counties, 1. Resource assessment*, E. Anglian Archaeol. Occ. Paper 3, 30–1

Murphy, P., Albarella, U., Germany, M. and Locker, A., 2000 — 'Production, imports and status: biological remains from a late Roman farm at Great Holts Farm, Boreham, Essex, UK', *Environmental Archaeology* 5, 35–48

Murphy, P., 1999 — 'Charred plant remains and molluscs', in Bedwin, O. and Bedwin, M., *A Roman malt house. Excavations at Stebbing Green, Essex*, E. Anglian Archaeol. Occ. Paper 6, 19–21

Murphy, P., 2003 — 'Plant macrofossils and molluscs', in Evans, C., *Power and Island Communities: excavations at the Wardy Hill Ringwork, Coveney, Ely*, E. Anglian Archaeol. 103, 84–112

Myres, J., 1977 — *A Corpus of Anglo-Saxon Pottery of the Pagan Period*, (Cambridge University Press)

Needham, S., 2007 — '800 BC, The Great Divide', in Haselgrove, C. and Pope, R. (eds), *The Earlier Iron Age in Britain and the Near Continent*, (Oxbow Books), 39–63

Needham, S. and Serjeantson, D., 1996 — 'Catalogue of worked bone and antler', in Needham, S. and Spence, T. *Runnymede Bridge Research Excavations, Volume 2: Refuse and disposal at Area 16 East Runnymede* (London, British Museum), 189–90

Neef, R., Cappers, R.T.J. and Bekker, R.M., 2012 — *Digital atlas of economic plants in archaeology, Groningen Archaeological Studies 17* (Elde, Barkhuis). Available: <http://depa.eldoc.ub.rug.nl.php> Accessed: March 2014

Newdick, J., 1979 — *The Complete Freshwater Fishes of the British Isles* (London, Adam and Charles Black)

Nilsson, A.N. and Holmen, M., 1995 — *The Aquatic Adephaga (Coleoptera) of Fennoscandia and Denmark II. Dytiscidae*, Fauna Entomologyca Scandinavica Vol. 35, (Leiden: E.J. Brill)

O'Connor, B., Foster, J. and Saunders, C., 2000 — 'Violence', in Barrett, J.C., Freeman, P.W.M. and Woodward, A., *Cadbury Castle Somerset: the later prehistoric and early historic archaeology*, English Heritage Archaeol. Rep. 20, 235–42

O'Connor, T.P., 1989 — *Bones from Anglo-Scandinavian Levels at 16–22 Coppergate*, The Archaeology of York 15 (3)

Ogden, A., 2008 — 'Advances in the palaeopathology of teeth and jaws', in Pinhasi, R. and Mays, S. (eds), *Advances in Human Palaeopathology* (Chichester, Wiley), 283–307

Ogilvie, A. and Farmer, G., 1997 — 'Documenting the medieval climate', in Hulme, M. and Barrow, E. (eds), *Climates of the British Isles* (London, Routledge), 112–33

Old-Maps, 2014 — Old-maps.co.uk Available: https://www.old-maps.co.uk/#/ Accessed: March 2014

Olsen, S.L., 1994 — 'Exploitation of mammals at the Early Bronze Age site of West Row Fen (Mildenhall 165), Suffolk England', *Annals Carnegie Museum* 63 (2), 115–53

Ortner, D., 2003 — *Identification of pathological conditions in human skeletal remains* (New York, Academic Press)

Parks, K., 2012 — *Iron Age and Roman arable practice in the east of England* (unpubl. DPhil thesis, Univ. Leicester)

Pavón-Carrasco, J., Rodríguez-González, J., Osete M.L. and Torta, M., 2011 — 'A Matlab tool for archaeomagnetic dating', *J. Archaeol. Sci.* 38, 408–19

Payne, S., 1973 — 'Kill-off patterns in sheep and goats: the mandibles from Asvan Kale', *Anatolian Studies* 23, 281–303

Payne, S., 1985 — 'Morphological distinction between the mandibular teeth of young sheep *Ovis* and goats *Capra*', *J. Archaeol. Sci.* 12, 139–47

Payne, S. and Bull, G., 1988 — 'Components of variation in measurements of pig bones and teeth, and the use of measurements to distinguish wild from domestic pig remains', *Archaeozoologia* 2, 27–65

PCRG (Prehistoric Ceramics Research Group), 2009 — *The Study of Later Prehistoric Pottery: General Policies and Guidelines for Analysis and Publication* (Oxford, Prehistoric Ceramics Research Group)

Peachey, A., 2010   'Pottery', in Woolhouse T., *Bridge House Dairies, Worlington Road, Mildenhall, Suffolk. Archaeological Investigation Research Archive Report* (unpubl. Archaeological Solutions report 3569)

Peglar, S.M., 1993   'The development of the cultural landscape around Diss Mere, Norfolk, UK, during the past 7000 years', *Review Palaeobotany Palynology* 76, 1–47

Pelling, R., 2011   'Charred plant remains from Creswell Field', in Hey, G., Booth, P. and Timby, J., *Yarnton: Iron Age and Romano-British settlement and landscape*, Thames Valley Landscapes Monogr. 35 (Oxford, Oxford University School of Archaeology), 523–34

Percival, S., 2012   'Prehistoric pottery', in Caruth J. and Goffin R., *Land South of Hartismere High School, Eye, Suffolk EYE 083. Post-excavation Assessment Report* (unpubl. Suffolk CC Archaeology Service report 2012/067)

Percival, S., 2013   'The Late Bronze Age pottery', in Heard, K., *Late Bronze Age settlement at Bloodmoor Hill, Carlton Colville, Suffolk CAC 042* (unpubl. Suffolk CC Archaeology Service report 2012/183)

Perrin, J.R., 1996   'The Roman Pottery', in Mackreth, D.F., *Orton Hall Farm: a Roman and Early Anglo-Saxon Farmstead*, E. Anglian Archaeol. 76, 114–90

PFAF (Plants for a future), 2014   *Linum usitatissimum* L. Available: http://www.pfaf.org/user/Plant.aspx?LatinName=Linum+usitatissimum Accessed: 6 May 2014

Poole, C., 1984   'Objects of baked clay', in Cunliffe, B., *Danebury: an Iron Age hillfort in Hampshire. Volume 2 The excavations 1969-78: the finds*, Counc. Brit. Archaeol. Res. Rep. 52, (London) 398–406

Potter, T. and Johns C., 1992   *Roman Britain* (London, British Museum Press)

Powell, A. and Clark, K.M., 2002   'Animal bones', in Mudd, A., *Excavations at Melford Meadows, Brettenham, 1994: Romano-British and Early Saxon occupations*, E. Anglian Archaeol. 99, 101–08

Prenda, J., Arenas, M.P., Freitas, D., Santo-Reis, M. and Collares-Pereira, M.J., 2002   'Bone length of Iberian freshwater fish, as a predictor of length and biomass of prey consumed by Piscivores', *Limnetica* 21(1–2), 15–24

Press, B., 2002   *Herbs of Britain and Ireland* (London, New Holland Publishers)

Prigg, H., 1874   'The tumuli of Warren Hill, Mildenhall', *Proc. Suffolk Inst. Archaeol. Hist.* 4, 287–99

Prummel, W. and Frisch, H-J., 1986   'A guide for the distinction of species, sex and body side in bones of sheep and goat', *J. Archaeol. Sci.* 13, 567–77

Pryor, F., 1996   'Sheep, stockyards and field systems: Bronze Age livestock populations in the Fenlands of eastern England', *Antiquity* 70, 313–24

Rackham, O., 2001   *Trees and Woodland in the British Landscape: the complete history of Britain's trees, woods and hedgerows* (London, Phoenix Press)

Radu, V., 2005   *Atlas for the identification of bony fish bones from archaeological sites*, Asociaţia Română de Arheologie Studii de Preistorie Supplementum 1/2005

Redfield, A., 1970   'A new aid to ageing immature skeletons: development of the occipital bone', *American J. Physical Anthropology* 33, 207–20

Regan, R., 2001   *Excavations south of the LadyChapel, Ely Cathedral, Cambridgeshire*, (unpubl. Cambridge Archaeological Unit report 419)

Reimer, P.J., Bard, E., Bayliss, A., Beck, J.W., Blackwell, P.G., Bronk Ramsey, C., Grootes, P.M., Guilderson, T.P., Haflidason, H., Hajdas, I., Hatt, C., Heaton, T.J., Hoffmann, D.L., Hogg, A.G., Hughen, K.A., Kaiser, K.F., Kromer, B., Manning, S.W., Niu, M., Reimer, R.W., Richards, D.A., Scott, E.M., Southon, J.R., Staff, R.A., Turney, C.S.M. and van der Plicht, J., 2013   'IntCal13 and Marine13 Radiocarbon Age Calibration Curves 0–50,000 Years cal BP', *Radiocarbon* 55 (4), 1869–87

Reynolds, A., 2002   'Burials, Boundaries and Charters in Anglo-Saxon England: a Reassessment', in Lucy, S. and Reynolds, A. (eds), *Burial in Early Medieval England and Wales* (Leeds, Maney), 171–94

Reynolds, A., 2009   *Anglo-Saxon Deviant Burial Customs* (King's Lynn, Oxford University Press)

Ricken, H. and Fischer, C. (eds), 1963   *Die Bilderschüsseln der römischen Töpfer von Rheinzabern: Textband mit Typenbildern zu Katalog VI der Ausgrabungen von Wilhelm Ludowici in Rheinzabern 1901–1914*, Materialen zur römisch-germanischen Keramik 7

Rixson, D., 2000   *The History of Meat Trading* (Nottingham, Nottingham University Press)

Roberts, C. and Cox, M., 2003   *Health and Disease in Britain: from prehistory to the present day* (Stroud, Sutton Publishing)

Robertson, D. and Smith, A.J., 2009   'The microbiology of the acute dental abscess', *J. Medical Microbiology* 58, 155–62

Robinson, M.A., 1979   'The biological evidence', in G. Lambrick and M.A. Robinson *Iron Age and Roman Riverside Settlements at Farmoor, Oxfordshire*, Counc. Brit. Archaeol. Res. Rep. 32, (London, Council for British Archaeology), 77–133

Robinson, M.A., 1981   'The use of ecological groupings of Coleoptera for comparing sites', in M. Jones and G. Dimbleby (eds), *The Environment of Man: The Iron Age to the Anglo-Saxon Period*, Brit. Archaeol. Rep. British Series 87, (Oxford, British Archaeological Reports), 251–86

Robinson, M.A., 1983   'Arable/pastoral ratios from insects?', in M. Jones (ed.) *Integrating the Subsistance Economy*, Brit. Archaeol. Rep. International Series 181, (Oxford, British Archaeological Reports), 19–47

Robinson, M., 1988   'Molluscan evidence for pasture and meadowland on the floodplain of the upper Thames basin', in Murphy, P. and French, C. (eds), *The exploitation of the Wetlands*, Brit. Archaeol. Rep. British Series 186, 101–12

Roe, F., 1996 — *Synthesis of Reports on Worked Stone* (unpubl. report for City of Lincoln Archaeological Unit)

Roe, F., 2008 — 'Worked stone', in Booth, P., Bingham, A-M. and Lawrence, S., *The Roman Roadside Settlement at Westhawk Farm, Ashford, Kent: excavations 1998–9*, (Oxford, Oxford Archaeology), 188–95

Rogerson, A., 1977 — *Excavations at Scole, 1973*, E. Anglian Archaeol. 5, 97–224

Rumble, A., (ed.) 1986 — *The Domesday Book: Suffolk*, (Chichester, Phillimore)

Ruscillo, D., 2006 — 'The table test: a simple technique for sexing canid humeri', in Ruscillo, D., *Recent advances in ageing and sexing animal bones. Proceedings of the 9th ICAZ Conference, Durham 2002*, (Oxford, Oxbow Books)

Salway, P., 1993 — *The Oxford Illustrated History of Roman Britain*, (London, Oxford University Press)

Scaife, R., 2014 — *Pollen assessment of palaeochannel 3617 and medieval peat 3016* (unpubl. AEA report AEA 161.4.01)

SCCAS (Suffolk County Council Archaeological Service), 2010a — *Brief and Specification for Excavation: Mildenhall Social Club and Car Park, Recreation Way, Mildenhall, Suffolk (F.2008/0268). Phase 1 (Storage Tank and Associated Services)* (unpubl. SCCAS document ref:/Recreation Way, Mildenhall 2010)

SCCAS (Suffolk County Council Archaeological Service), 2010b — *Brief and Specification for Excavation: Mildenhall Social Club and Car Park, Recreation Way, Mildenhall, Suffolk, (F/2008/0268). Phase 2 (Town Car Park)* (unpubl. SCCAS document ref:/Phase 2 Recreation Way, Mildenhall 2010)

Scheuer, J.L., Musgrave, J.H. and Evans, S.P., 1980 — 'The estimation of late fetal and perinatal age from limb bone length by linear and logarithmic regression', *Annals of Human Biology* 7, 257–65

Scheuer, J.L. and Black, S., 2000 — *Developmental Juvenile Osteology* (London, Academic Press)

Schoch, W., Heller, I., Schweingruber, F.H. and Kienast, F., 2004 — *Wood anatomy of Central European species*. Available: <http://www.woodanatomy/ch/. Accessed: March 2014

Schmid, E., 1972 — *Atlas of Animal Bones: for prehistorians, archaeologists and quaternary geologists* (London, Elsevier Publishing)

Schwartz, J.H., 1995 — *Skeletal Keys: an introduction to human skeletal morphology, development, and analysis* (New York, Oxford University Press)

Scull, C., 1992 — 'Before Sutton Hoo: structures of power and society in early East Anglia', in Carver, M.O.H. (ed.), *The Age of Sutton Hoo: the seventh century in north-western Europe* (Woodbridge, Boydell), 3–23

Sealey, P.R., 2007 — *A Late Iron Age Warrior Burial from Kelvedon, Essex*, E. Anglian Archaeol. 118

Sellwood, L., 1984 — 'Objects of bone and antler', in Cunliffe, B., *Danebury an Iron Age hillfort in Hampshire: Volume 2 The excavations, 1969–78: the finds* York, Counc. Brit. Archaeol. Res. Rep. 52, 371–95

Serjeantson, D., 1996 — 'The animal bone', in Needham, S. and Spence, T., *Refuse and disposal at Area 16 East Runnymede: Runnymede Bridge Research Excavations, Volume 2* (London, British Museum Press), 194–224

Serjeantson, D., 2006 — 'Animal remains', in Evans, C. and Hodder, I., *Marshland communities and cultural landscapes. The Haddenham project Volume 2*, Cambridge University McDonald Institute Monograph, 213–46

Serjeantson, D. and Woolgar, C.M., 2006 — 'Fish consumption in medieval England', in Woolgar, C.M., Serjeantson, D. and Waldron, T. (eds), *Food in Medieval England: Diet and Nutrition*, Medieval History and Archaeology Series (Oxford, Oxford University Press), 102–30

Shackley, M.L., 1976 — 'The Danebury project: an experiment in site sediment recording', in Davidson, D.A. and Shackley, M.L. (eds), *Geoarchaeology* (London, Duckworth), 9–21

Sjøvold, T., 1988 — 'Geschlechtsdiagnose am Skelett', in Knußman, R. (ed.), *Wesen und Methoden der Anthropologie. 1 Teil. Wissenschaftstheorie, Geschichte, morphologische Methoden* (Stuttgart, Fischer Verlag), 444–80

Sjøvold, T., 1990 — 'Estimation of stature from long bones utilizing the line of organic correlation', *Human Evolution* 5, 431–47

Smith D., 2011a — '[Romano-British] insect remains' in Jones, A. *Excavations at Little Paxton Quarry, Cambridgeshire, 1992–1998*, Birmingham Archaeol. Monogr. Series 10/ Brit. Archaeol. Rep. British Series 545, (Oxford, British Archaeological Reports), 265–77

Smith, D.N., 2011b — 'The insect remains from the trackway at Beccles, Norfolk', University of Birmingham Environmental Archaeology Services Report 193, (unpublished report for Birmingham ArchaeoEnvironmental)

Smith, D.N., 2012 — *Insects in the City: an archaeoentomological perspective*, Brit. Archaeol. Rep. British Series 561 (Oxford: Archaeopress)

Smith, D.N., Whitehouse, N., Bunting, M.J. and Chapman, H., 2010 — 'Can we characterise 'openness' in the Holocene palaeoenvironmental record? Analogue studies from Dunham Massey deer park and Epping Forest, England, *The Holocene* 20, 215–29

Smoothy, M.D., 1993 — 'The animal bone', in Havis, R., *Roman Braintree: excavations 1984–90*, Essex Archaeol. Hist. 24, 52–61

Sparks, B.W., 1961 — 'The ecological interpretation of quaternary non-marine Mollusca', *Proc. Linnaean Soc. London* 172, 71–80

Sparks, B.W. and West, R.G., 1959 — 'The palaeoecology of the interglacial deposits at Histon Road, Cambridge', *Eiszeitalter und Gegenwart* 10, 123–43

Spoerry, P., 2016 — *The Production and Distribution of Pottery in Cambridgeshire*, E. Anglian Archaeol. 159

Stace, C., 1992 — *New flora of the British Isles*, 1st edition, (Cambridge, Cambridge University Press)

Stace, C., 1997 — *New Flora of the British Isles*, 2nd edition, (Cambridge, Cambridge University Press)

Stace, C., 2010 — *New Flora of the British Isles*, (3rd edition), (Cambridge, Cambridge University Press)

Stallibrass, S., 1982 — 'Faunal remains', in Potter, T.W. and Potter, C.F.A., *Romano-British village at Grandford, March, Cambridgeshire*, British Museum Occ. Paper 35, 98–112

Stallibrass, S., 1996 'Animal bone', in Jackson, R.P. and Potter, T.W., *Excavations at Stonea, Cambridgeshire 1980–1985* (London, English Heritage), 587–611

STATS Limited, 2007 *Phase 1 and 2 Geotechnical and Geoenvironmental Report: Proposed Sainsbury's Store, Mildenhall* (STATS Limited unpubl. report 35937–001)

Stead, I.M., 1995 'The Metalwork', in Parfitt, K., *Iron Age burials from Mill Hill, Deal* (London, British Museum Press), 58–111

Stevens, C., 2011 'Crop husbandry as seen from the charred botanical samples from Yarnton', in Hey, G., Booth, P. and Timby, J., *Yarnton: Iron Age and Romano-British settlement and landscape*, Thames Valley Landscapes Monogr. 35 (Oxford, Oxford University School of Archaeology), 534–68

Stone, D.J., 2006 'The consumption of field crops in late medieval England', in Woolgar C.M., Serjeantson, D. and Waldron, T. (eds), *Food in Medieval England: Diet and Nutrition*, Medieval History and Archaeology Series (Oxford, Oxford University Press), 11–26

Suffolk Landscape 2014 Available: http://www.suffolklandscape.org.uk/ Accessed: March 2014

Sykes, N., 2006 'From cu and sceap to beffe and motton', in Woolgar C.M., Serjeantson, D. and Waldron, T. (eds), *Food in Medieval England: Diet and Nutrition*, Medieval History and Archaeology Series (Oxford, Oxford University Press), 56–71

Sykes, N.J., 2007 *The Norman Conquest: a zooarchaeological perspective*, Brit. Archaeol. Rep. Internat. Ser. 1656, (Oxford)

Symonds, R. and Wade, S., 1999 *Roman Pottery from Excavations in Colchester 1971–86*, (Colchester, Colchester Archaeological Trust)

Tester, A., Anderson, S., Riddler, I. and Carr, R.D., 2014 *Staunch Meadow, Brandon, Suffolk: a high status Middle Saxon settlement on the fen edge*, E. Anglian Archaeol. 151

Thomas, R. and Stallibrass, S., 2008 'For starters: production and supplying food to the army in the Roman north-west provinces', in Stallibrass, S. and Thomas, R., *Feeding the Roman Army: the Archaeology of Production and Supply in NW Europe* (Oxford, Oxbow Books), 1–17

Timson, J., 1966 '*Polygonum hydropiper* L.', *J. Ecology* 54, 815–21

Todd, T.W., 1921a 'Age changes in the pubic bone. I: the white male pubis', *American J. Physical Anthropology* 3, 285–334

Todd, T.W., 1921b 'Age changes in the pubic bone. III: the pubis of the white female', *American J. Physical Anthropology* 4, 1–70

Tomber, R. and Dore, J., 1998 *The National Roman Fabric Reference Collection: a handbook* (London, Museum of London Archaeology Service)

Tremlett, S., 2011 'Iron Age landscapes from the air: results from the Norfolk National Mapping Programme' in Davies, J. (ed.), 25–39

Trevelyan, G.M. (O.M), 1943 *Trinity College: An Historical Sketch* (Cambridge, Cambridge University Press)

Trotter M, and Gleser G.C., 1952 'Estimation of stature from long bones of American Whites and Negroes', *American J. Physical Anthropology* 10, 463–514

Trotter, M. and Gleser, G.C., 1958 'A re-evaluation of estimation of stature based on measurements of stature taken during life and of long bones after death', *American J. Physical Anthropology* 16, 79–123

Tuli, S.M., 2004 *Tuberculosis of the skeletal system: bones, joints, spine and bursal sheaths* (New Delhi, Jaypee Brothers Medical Publishers Ltd)

Van Arsdell, R.D., 1989 *Celtic coinage of Britain* (London, Spink)

Van de Noort, R. and Collis, J., 2007 'Burial rituals in the middle Iron Age', in Van de Noort, R., Chapman, H. and Collis, J.R., *Sutton Common: the excavation of an Iron Age 'marsh-fort'*, Counc. Brit. Archaeol. Res. Rep. 154, 182–4

Van de Noort, R., Chapman, H. and Collis, J.R., 2007 *Sutton Common: the excavation of an Iron Age 'marsh-fort'*, Counc. Brit. Archaeol. Res. Rep. 154

van der Veen, M., 1989 'Charred grain assemblages from Roman-period corn driers in Britain', *Archaeol. J.* 146, 302–19

van der Veen, M. and Jones, G., 2006 'A re-analysis of agricultural production and consumption: implications for understanding the British Iron Age', *Vegetation History and Archaeobotany* 15, 217–28

von den Driesch, A., 1976 *A Guide to the Measurement of Animal Bones from Archaeological Sites*, Peabody Museum Bulletin 1 (Cambridge Massachusetts, Harvard University)

von den Driesch, A. and Boessneck, J., 1974 'Kritische anmerkungen zur widerristhohenberechnung aus Langenmassen vor- und fruhgeschichtlicher Tierknochen', *Saugetierkundliche Mitteilungen* 22, 325–48

Wade, A.J., 2000 'Animal bone', in Lavender, N.J., 'Bronze Age and medieval sites at Springfield, Chelmsford: excavations near the A12 Boreham Interchange 1993', *Essex Archaeol. Hist.* 30, 19

Waller, M., 1994 *Fenland Project No. 9: Flandrian Environmental Change in Fenland*, E. Anglian Archaeol. 70

Webley, L. and Anderson, K., 2008 'Late Iron Age and Roman Pottery', in Evans, C. with Mackay, D. and Webley, L., *Borderlands. The Archaeology of the Addenbrooke's Environs, South Cambridge*, 63–75 (Cambridge, Cambridge Archaeological Unit)

Webley, L., 2005 'Evaluation Survey and Excavation at Wandlebury Ringwork, Cambridgeshire, 1994–97: Part II, The Iron Age Pottery', *Proc. Cambridge Antiq. Soc.* 94, 39–45

Webster, G., 1990 'A Late Celtic Sword-belt with a ring and button found at Coleford, Gloucestershire', *Britannia* 21, 294–5

West, S.E., 1963, 'The local pottery', in 'Excavations at Cox Lane (1958) and at the Town Defences, Shire Hall Lane, Ipswich (1959)', *Proc. Suffolk Inst. Archaeol.* 29(3), 246–72

West, S., 1985 *West Stow, the Anglo-Saxon Village, Suffolk*, E. Anglian Archaeol. 24

West, S., 1989 'The Iron Age Pottery', in West, S., *West Stow, Suffolk: the Prehistoric and Romano-British Occupation*, E. Anglian Archaeol. 48, 59–65

West, S., 1989 — *West Stow, Suffolk: the Prehistoric and Romano-British Occupation*, E. Anglian Archaeol. 48

Wheeler, E.A., Baas, P. and Gasson, P.E., 1989 — 'IAWA list of microscopic features for hardwood identification', *IAWA Bulletin ns* 10, 219–332

White W. 1874 — *Directory of Suffolk* 3rd edition (London 1874)

Williams, D.M., Gabrielsen, T.O. and Latack, J.T., 1982 — 'Ossification of the caudal attachments of the ligamentum flavum', *Radiology* 145, 693–7

Williams, J.T., 1963 — '*Chenopodium album* L.', *J. Ecology* 51, 711–25

Williams, R., 2004 — *Lime Kilns and Lime-Burning* (Shire Publications, second edition)

Williamson, T., 2005 — 'Explaining Regional Landscapes', in Harper-Bill, C. (ed.), *Medieval East Anglia* (Woodbridge, Boydell and Brewer), 11–32

Wilson, T., 1995 — 'Animal bones', in Andrews, P., *Excavations at Redcastle Furze, Thetford, 1988–9*, E. Anglian Archaeol. 72, 121–28

Wood, J.W., Milner, G.R., Harpending, H.C. and Weiss, K.M., 1992 — 'The osteological paradox: problems inferring prehistoric health from skeletal samples', *Current Anthropology* 33, 343–70

Woodward, A. and Hill, J.D., 2000 — 'The human bodies', in Barrett, J.C., Freeman, P.W.M. and Woodward, A. (eds), *Cadbury Castle, Somerset: the later prehistoric and early historic archaeology*, English Heritage Archaeol. Rep. 20, 109–111

Woolhouse, T., 2010 — *Bridge House Dairies, Worlington Road, Mildenhall, Suffolk: Archaeological Investigation Research Archive Report* (unpubl. Archaeological Solutions report 3569)

Wouters, W., Muylaert, L. and van Neer, W., 2007 — 'The distinction of isolated bones from plaice (*Pleuronectes platessa*), flounder (*Platichthys flesus*) and dab (*Limanda limanda*): a description of the diagnostic characters', *Archaeofauna* 16, 33–72

Wymer, J.J., Lewis, S.G. and Bridgland, D.R., 1991 — 'Warren Hill, Mildenhall, Suffolk (TL 744743)', in Lewis, S.G., Whiteman, C.A. and Bridgland, D.R. (eds), *Central East Anglian and Fen Basin; Field Guide* (London, Quaternary Research Association), 50–58

Yarrell, W., 1836 — *A History of British Fishes Vol. 1* (London, John van Voorst). Available: http://www.archive.org/stream/historyofbritish1836yarr Accessed: March 2014

Zohary, D., Hopf, M. and Weiss, E., 2013 — *Domestication of Plants in the Old World. The origin and spread of domesticated plants in south-west Asia, Europe, and the Mediterranean Basin* (Oxford, Oxford University Press)

Index

Illustrations are indicated by page numbers in *italics*. Places are in Suffolk unless indicated otherwise.

189

East Anglian Archaeology

is a serial publication sponsored by ALGAO EE and English Heritage. It is the main vehicle for publishing final reports on archaeological excavations and surveys in the region. For information about titles in the series, visit **http://eaareports.org.uk**. Reports can be obtained from: Oxbow Books, **https://www.oxbowbooks.com/oxbow/eaa** or directly from the organisation publishing a particular volume.

Reports available so far: